THE HUMANITARIAN RESPONSE INDEX 2008

Donor Accountability in Humanitarian Action

DARA

Development Assistance Research Associates

Madrid, Spain, September 2008

palgrave
macmillan

About DARA (Development Assistance
Research Associates)
DARA is an independent not-for-profit organisation
based in Madrid, Spain, committed to improving the
quality of humanitarian action and development aid
through evaluation and research. Through its work
DARA contributes to improving the effectiveness of
international aid and global efforts to reduce human
suffering, vulnerability, and poverty.

Headquarters
Felipe IV, 9 - 3° Izquierda
28014 Madrid – Spain
Tel.:   +34 91 531 03 72
Fax: +34 91 522 00 39

Brussels Office
Résidence Palace
Rue de la Loi, 155, Block C
4th and 6th floor 1040
Brussels – Belgium
Tel.:   +32 2 230 33 37
Fax: +32 2 280 20 36

Washington Office
1120 19th Street NW Ste. 322
Washington, DC 20036 – USA
Tel.:   +1 202 728 8681

Email: info@daraint.org
Web: www.daraint.org

First published 2009 by
PALGRAVE MACMILLAN
Houndmills, Basingstoke, Hampshire RG21 6XS and
175 Fifth Avenue, New York, N.Y. 10010
Companies and representatives throughout the world

PALGRAVE MACMILLAN is the global academic imprint of the
Palgrave Macmillan division of St. Martin's Press, LLC and of
Palgrave Macmillan Ltd. Macmillan® is a registered trademark
in the United States, United Kingdom and other countries.
Palgrave is a registered trademark in the European Union
and other countries.

ISBN-13: 978-0-230-22196-3
ISBN-10: 0-230-22196-3

This book is printed on paper suitable for recycling and made
from fully managed and sustained forest sources. Logging,
pulping and manufacturing processes are expected to conform
to the environmental regulations of the country of origin.

A catalogue record for this book is available from the
British Library.
A catalog record for this book is available from the Library
of Congress.

10 9 8 7 6 5 4 3 2 1
18 17 16 15 14 13 12 11 10 09

Printed and bound in Great Britain by
Hobbs the Printer Ltd, Totton, Hampshire

Contents

(Cont'd.)

Foreword

KOFI A. ANNAN

This year, the international community had to respond to a number of new disasters and complex emergencies, as well as continue to provide assistance to on-going humanitarian crises, which threaten the lives and livelihoods of millions of people.

The increasing incidence of natural disasters due to climate change and environmental stress underscores the need to scale-up comprehensive disaster risk reduction initiatives to support the most vulnerable. The rise in world food prices and global financial turmoil have also sharply increased the number of people living in hunger, putting at risk the considerable gains made over the past decade in reducing extreme poverty and achieving the Millennium Development Goals.

We can and must do better. We have the resources, the knowledge and the capabilities to do so. The world requires concerted action to help all those in need. The equal worth of every human life demands that the delivery of humanitarian aid be neutral, impartial, and based on needs – not driven by geopolitical interests, historical ties, domestic political agendas, or the attention of the world's media.

Last year, I had the privilege to launch the first Humanitarian Response Index (HRI), an innovative initiative to assess and rank OECD/DAC donor governments against their commitments to support good practices in humanitarian action. At the time, I spoke of my hopes that the Humanitarian Response Index, like the United Nations' Human Development Index, would stimulate dialogue amongst stakeholders and contribute to improving effectiveness, transparency and accountability in humanitarian action.

Have we moved forward since then?

The HRI has been successful in generating growing interest in and debate about the performance and accountability of donors in their efforts to save and improve the lives of people affected each year by disasters, and complex emergencies. The HRI helps to ensure that donor efforts are benchmarked and progress

is tracked, so that good practices become the norm, and not the exception. In doing so, it is a valuable tool for stakeholders of the humanitarian community to develop and improve.

This year's HRI is based on a rigorous analysis of data that tracks donor policies and funding practices, and draws on the views of more than a thousand key stakeholders about donor practice in 11 different crises across the globe. It reveals that there are still too many gaps between governments' commitments to the principles of Good Humanitarian Donorship (GHD) and actual practice on the ground.

For example, we can see from the HRI Crisis Reports that in conflict areas around the world, donor governments' military and security objectives too often take precedence over providing neutral and impartial humanitarian assistance and protection for civilians and non-combatants. Provision of safe humanitarian access is also a critical issue. In 2006 over 80 aid workers were killed across the globe. In 2007 humanitarian space has continued to come under attack in countries such as Afghanistan, Sudan and Somalia, resulting in more than 40 aid workers being killed in Afghanistan alone. This is simply unacceptable.

The HRI also reveals that we need to pay more attention to the question of linking emergency relief to longer-term human development strategies, and rooting disaster risk reduction strategies in local capacity development. The current global food crisis is a clear illustration of how crucial this long-term approach is. In the short-term, food aid must be increased to the most vulnerable, but to address the root causes of this hunger we need to think of building strategies that reinforce sustainable agriculture, fairer trade, and contingency planning for the effects of disasters and climate change on food production at the local and global levels.

Donors have a key role to play in finding solutions to these difficult challenges. That is, after all, the point of the Good Humanitarian Donorship Principles – to systematically apply recognised good practice in the decisions and actions of key players in the humanitarian system. By focusing on individual donors, the HRI promotes debate amongst policy makers and the public about the performance of their governments in the area of humanitarian action. It provides an opportunity to help improve the delivery of humanitarian action at all levels. The HRI contributes to a deeper understanding of how donors – individually and collectively – live up to the standards of good practice established in the Good Humanitarian Donorship Principles.

The HRI also draws attention to new and emerging issues that warrant further reflection and debate. How can we ensure that humanitarian aid is provided equitably, based on objective assessments of needs, and in accordance with humanitarian principles? And how can new donor countries – and a growing class of wealthy individuals – be encouraged to follow the lead of OECD-DAC countries by recognising and adopting good practices?

Improving the response and effectiveness of humanitarian action and of donor behaviour will not be easy or quick. Millions of people will continue to suffer the effects of disasters and violent conflicts in years to come, in part due to population increases, the impact of climate change and natural resource constraints. Humanitarian assistance will be required, not only for their very survival, but also for their long-term recovery.

As President of the *Global Humanitarian Forum* I am convinced that the HRI, as an independent and objective benchmarking exercise, will help us all to better understand the humanitarian system's strengths and weaknesses and significantly reinforce donors' commitment to good practice. The HRI helps guarantee that every dollar of humanitarian assistance is used to provide the right kind of aid, to the right people, at the right time. I am also convinced that over time, the HRI can help ensure that humanitarian assistance is used in ways that both help alleviate suffering and build a better tomorrow for those who are most in need. The millions of people affected by crises and emergencies deserve as much.

Acknowledgements

Producing the Humanitarian Response Index (HRI) is a monumental task. DARA would like to express its deep gratitude to the hundreds of people who actively supported and contributed to this year's HRI 2008.

First, sincere and genuine thanks to the many hundreds of representatives from humanitarian agencies working in the 11 different crisis countries visited by the HRI field teams. All of you generously made time in the midst of operations to answer our questions and respond to the Survey questionnaire. Many of you were instrumental in providing DARA with useful background information and logistical and administrative support. Your enthusiasm for the HRI initiative has motivated us to continue to improve and make it a useful tool for the humanitarian community. We hope that the HRI is as much your project, and that it reflects the challenges you face in your efforts to provide humanitarian assistance to those in need.

The HRI is constantly being improved, thanks to the valuable input and wise advice of the members of our Peer Review Committee. The individual members of the Committee are especially important, as each one offers broad experience of the humanitarian sector, fresh insights, and important perspectives. All have enriched our understanding of the issues and refined our approach. We would therefore like to mention the contributions of Jock Baker, Christian Bugnion, James Darcy, Veronique de Geoffroy, Claude Hilfiker, Eva von Oelreich, David Roodman, Ed Schenkenberg van Mierop, Manuel Sánchez-Montero, and Ricardo Solé-Arqués. Their support, encouragement, and constructive criticism have been key to ensuring that the HRI continues to evolve into a useful tool for policy debate and advocacy, to improve the quality and effectiveness of humanitarian action.

DARA also benefits from an Advisory Board whose members provide useful advice on how to ensure that the HRI is connected to the wider debate on humanitarian issues and global affairs. Without Jose Maria Figueres, the HRI would be entirely impossible. His unflagging enthusiasm and leadership has helped steer the entire project forward. Larry Minear's past work has been an inspiration to all of us working in the humanitarian sector. His contribution to this year's efforts and his endorsement of the HRI provided us with additional stimulus. Our heartfelt thanks, as well, to Iqbal Riza and Pierre Schori for their support, insight, and advice.

Dozens of staff members at the headquarters of humanitarian agencies have generously given not only helpful advice, but the key data used in constructing the Index. In particular, we would like to thank the staff of the IFRC, ICRC, UNICEF, UNHCR, UNDP, ISDR, UN/CMCS, OHCHR, UNRWA, and WFP for their valuable input. We would also like to thank all the representatives of the OECD/DAC donor agencies who provided data to DARA and who supported the HRI initiative. Without their support, we would not have been able to obtain the comprehensive set of data which enabled us to construct the Index.

While the entire staff of DARA has made an extraordinary effort to bring the HRI into being, there is a core group of people who deserve special mention for their work on the HRI 2008. Carlos Oliver was instrumental in managing the missions. With Ana Romero's help, he made sure that our teams were able to cover 11 humanitarian crises around the world. Riccardo Polastro's willingness to travel the distance for the HRI was greatly appreciated. Daniela Mamone's devotion to the project ensured that we were able to carry out HRI activities, manage the data, and function as a team. Without Nacho Wilhelmi's help in logistics, none of us would get from point A to point B. Daniela Ruegenberg provided outstanding research assistance in collecting and analysing much of the information that goes into the Index. Igor Hodson and Marybeth Redheffer have both played key roles in providing editorial support and research assistance in the preparation of the many texts for the HRI. Special thanks are due to

Philip Tamminga, who recently joined the HRI team to manage the project. Philip is spearheading efforts to consolidate the publication and help it to evolve as a practical tool for humanitarian policymakers and practitioners alike. Our sincere gratitude to all the members of the DARA teams who participated in field missions, or who contributed their labours in so many other of the critical tasks that make the HRI possible.

We would like to especially acknowledge the efforts of the principal editor of the HRI, Nancy Ackerman of AmadeaEditing, for her outstanding editing work, and to Hope Steele and Ha Nguyen for their painstaking efforts in getting the HRI ready for publication. Thanks to all of you for your patience and professionalism.

Finally, we would also like to extend our gratitude to Kofi Annan for his continued encouragement, support and great interest in the HRI.

Silvia Hidalgo, Director, DARA
Madrid, September 2008

Executive Summary

In 2007 the world continued to bear witness to the suffering of millions of people caught in humanitarian crises, ranging from earthquakes to decade old conflicts. Despite the considerable efforts and funds invested in humanitarian relief interventions, too many people did not receive the degree or form of assistance they so desperately needed. The Humanitarian Response Index (HRI) is a tool which aims to assess the performance of one crucial part in the humanitarian system: donor governments. As the principal providers of humanitarian assistance, donor governments have the power and responsibility to make the humanitarian system more effective and ensure that responses are aligned to needs, so that aid reaches the people who need it most. By measuring donor performance against the Principles and Good Practice of Humanitarian Donorship – a set of guiding principles established by the donors themselves – the Humanitarian Response Index aims to contribute to the debate on how to make humanitarian action more accountable and more effective.

Part One: The Humanitarian Response Index: Donor Accountability in Humanitarian Action

Chapter 1, "The Humanitarian Response Index 2008: Donor Accountability in Humanitarian Action," by **Silvia Hidalgo** and **Philip Tamminga** presents the background and methodology of the HRI, as well as the findings of this year's HRI.

The HRI ranks the performance of the 22 donor countries of the OECD Development Assistance Committee (DAC) plus the European Commission in funding and supporting humanitarian action. The aim of the HRI is to contribute to ongoing efforts to improve the accountability and quality of humanitarian aid and ensure that aid is used to assist those most in need in the most effective way possible. Built against the background of other international benchmarking and ranking tools, the HRI draws on 58 quantitative and qualita-

tive indicators which capture the essence of the Principles and Good Practice of Good Humanitarian Donorship, divided into five Pillars of good practice: Responding to needs; Supporting local capacity and recovery; Working with humanitarian partners; Promoting standards and enhancing implementation; and Promoting learning and accountability.

The chapter outlines the HRI process and methodology, as well as the principal humanitarian actors' response to the first HRI report in 2007 and subsequent changes and improvements made to this year's HRI. A Technical Appendix at the end of the chapter provides a detailed explanation of all of the indicators used to construct the HRI rankings and scores.

The chapter also provides an analysis of the results of this year's rankings, which show Sweden, Norway, and Denmark as the three top performing donors. The analysis first illustrates how well donors collectively perform within each Pillar, highlighting issues around donor practices that emerge from the eleven different crises studied as part of the HRI field research process, and then provides and overview of the performance of each individual donor. The chapter concludes with a presentation of the five areas where donors could work to make improve the quality, effectiveness and impact of their humanitarian assistance:

- Donor countries could do more to provide aid in an impartial, neutral and independent manner, not based on other objectives

- Donors should contribute to efforts to improve the quality and use of needs assessments to ensure that aid is in accordance to need

- Donors could do much more to harmonise and link relief efforts to early recovery and longer term development strategies

- Donors should invest more resources to strengthen the humanitarian system's capacity at all levels to ensure that the system is better prepared to respond to future crises

- Donors should assume more responsibility for ensuring implementation of international standards and good practice, and for improving accountability and performance.

Although these conclusions are not new – confirming much of what is already known in the humanitarian sector – the HRI offers a solid body of evidence to help understand the current state of affairs in donor practice, and highlights areas where donors and other humanitarian actors can work together to improve the quality, effectiveness and impact of humanitarian action.

Part Two: Perspectives on the HRI and current trends in humanitarian action

In each issue of the Humanitarian Response Index, we invite a number of specialists to provide their perspective on particular aspects of the humanitarian field. This year, the topics include a review of how well the HRI matches and validates the conclusions of other independent evaluations, with a specific focus on the United States as a donor, lessons learned in similar ranking exercises and the results can be used as policy and advocacy tools, the limitations in the use of needs assessments for funding and decision making, the imbalances underlying the relationship between donors, humanitarian actors and affected populations and the real difficulties of translating principles and policy statements on participation into effective mechanisms on the ground, and reflections on the challenges of implementing effective humanitarian action in the context of a "forgotten" crisis.

In Chapter 2, **Larry Minear** contributes his essay "the United states as Humanitarian Actor," to provide a balanced analysis that largely validates the "decidedly mixed review" of the United States in the HRI 2007. With considerable candour, backed up by careful research, he compares US practice in the field with the prevailing American self-image as a paragon of "generosity" and "compassion." He concludes that the five pillars that form the basis of the HRI's analysis are not only appropriate, but "broadly confirmed" by the independent studies by Minear and his colleagues (under the auspices of the Feinstein International Centre at Tufts University). Referring throughout to the 2006 OECD/DAC Peer Review (which also corroborates the problems flagged by HRI 2007), he discusses the deficiencies in the way

the United States carries out specific core principles of the GHD, focusing on the low marks received by the U.S. for alleviation of human suffering, impartiality, neutrality, and independence, and how these key features of the GHD have been compromised by security concerns and foreign policy objectives. He analyses the difficulty facing many countries (including the U.S.) in making the connection between relief and development, arguing that "getting [this] contextualisation right . . . is one of the four critical challenges facing humanitarian actors in the next decade," and that the current push to establish "coherence" between humanitarian and political/peacekeeping agendas often work to the disadvantage of humanitarian activities. Using field examples from many countries, Minear offers a helpful glimpse of efforts, successes, and failures US humanitarian enterprises in working with partners, building local capacity, implementing international guidelines, and promoting leadership and accountability. He concludes with some thoughts on how the HRI could be improved, and concludes that "accountability is too important to be left to donors, whether individually or severally... [a] workmanlike and forthright examination of the individual components of the system will surely help unleash missing synergies. The HRI is worth strengthening . . ."

In Chapter 3, "A Tale of Two Indices: the Commitment to Development Index as a Model for the Humanitarian Response Index," author **David Roodman** shares his views about the history of the earlier Commitment to Development Index (CDI) and the lessons it offers for the HRI, now in its second year. Roodman begins by reviewing the initial design of the CDI and the process by which its developers engaged target audiences, learning from both critics and detractors, gradually refining the instrument. He examines aspects of theory (or its absence), scaling and weighting, sensitivity analysis, and the trade-off between precision and transparency, and how each affects the design of an index, especially those aspects dealing with complexities of government policy, ethics, human psychology, political philosophy, and cultural interaction. By acknowledging with humility the debatable compromises involved in methodology and incomplete data, engaging with policymakers, welcoming commentary, dealing constructively with inevitable criticism, and partnering with organizations having credibility with target audiences, he encourages index makers to develop fruitful two-way relationships, so as to overcome the "inherently impolite" nature of an index, and gain broader acceptance of the goal of their work and message, namely, the improvement of humanitarian aid. For Roodman, "indexes are vehicles for interaction between people [who] expect from their interlocutors a blend of openness and strength of inner compass." After describing some of the reactions and critiques which greeted the CDI, both positive and negative, helpful and less so, he offers a number of "lessons" for other index makers, including the clear expression of goals and limitations, accessibility of the structure, and the ability to capitalize on change while achieving stability.

In Chapter 4, "Humanitarian Funding and Needs Assessments," author **John Cosgrave** discusses one of the thorniest challenges of humanitarian aid: how needs assessments are used (or not) for funding decisions, and looks at how humanitarian donorship has evolved since the enunciation of the core principles of the GHD in 2003. He examines recent developments in humanitarian funding, the extent to which needs are now being met, whether funding for different crises varies in proportion to needs, and how needs assessments can be improved. Basing his analysis on the findings of the Development Assistance Committee (DAC) of the OECD and the UN Financial Tracking System, he illustrates Official Development Assistance from 1990 to 2007, showing the value of development relief grants, official humanitarian aid as a percentage of all ODA, aid to Afghanistan and Iraq from 2000 to 2006, and concludes that the GHD appears to have little or no impact on support for Appeals up to 2007. Cosgrave then briefly analyses the effect of the Central Emergency Response Fund (CERF) and the impact of the media on humanitarian funding. Because the poor quality of needs assessments are a "recognized weakness of the humanitarian system," often referred to by donors as the cause of variable funding, Cosgrave looks to the four key aspects of the current humanitarian reform process as a hopeful prospect for improvement. Inadequate needs assessments cause delays in CERF applications and are fraught with methodological problems, often compromised by the contradiction between speed and quality. Illustrating his conceptual framework with a context knowledge tetrahedron, and concrete examples from the field, he offers specific recommendations for the improvement of needs assessments, including four kinds of knowledge: the disaster type and probable needs, the likely response to a disaster, its geographical extent, and the nature of the affected population and their capacities.

François Grünewald, in Chapter 5, entitled "New Approaches to Needs Assessment: Comprehensive and Rolling Diagnosis" adds to the analysis of the previous chapter and tackles many of the challenges involved in applying Principle 6 of the Good Humanitarian Donorship Initiative, the allocation of humanitarian funding *"in proportion to needs and on the basis of needs assessment."* He first discusses the weak links between needs identification and project design, pressure from media, politicians or domestic public opinion, high insecurity, and difficult choices among varying priorities and organizations, considering them central constraints for those who must make critical first decisions in the allocation of aid. The author then discusses in greater detail three major obstacles to good diagnosis: lack of comprehensiveness, lack of connection to funding requests, and evolving crisis conditions, before offering a number of concrete recommendations for "rolling diagnosis" and thinking "out of the box." Drawing on the work of his own colleagues and others researching the area of decision-making and analysis, Grünewald focuses on the need to improve the methods of gathering information, the importance of properly assessing the activities, capacities, and survival strategies of local actors, and on the characteristics of flexibility, humility, and an orientation to the social, as opposed to the hard, sciences, which enable those involved in diagnosis (as opposed to needs assessment) to deal more sensitively with rapidly changing conditions in the field. With reference to the GHD "principles for developing allocation frameworks," he offers an analytical matrix for engaging with local partners and suggests a new methodology for achieving more adequate participation and diagnosis.

Mary Anderson, in Chapter 6, entitled "The Giving-Receiving Relationship: Inherently Unequal?" shares the results of a unique undertaking in the humanitarian field: the Listening project. In order to test the perception of many humanitarian actors that the very act of giving to those in need creates an unequal relationship, the project, now in its third year, systematically and comprehensively interviews not only people on the receiving end of humanitarian aid, but also those participating in, or observing the chain of delivery. The results of the Listening Project are revealing and instructive. From the outset, Anderson says, people "recognize, welcome, and are grateful for" help received, and are impressed by the generosity and courage of those who "did not have to come" but who often take significant risks to do so. It is the "buts" which follow, which provide much food for thought for those engaged in the humanitarian enterprise. Anderson's paper focuses on how well humanitarians signal respect for the dignity and capabilities of communities in need, target delivery more effectively, enable fuller local ownership of projects and outcomes; in other words, treat people as equals in practice. Carefully distinguishing between acts of generosity and aid "programmes," and providing a rich array of eye-opening examples, she concludes that the inequality problem is a "product of conscious and intentional choices and approaches of providers." Some of these include predetermined or inappropriate donor agendas, an over-emphasis on speed of delivery, the lack of donor presence among aid recipients, and – despite the best intentions – exclusion of recipients of aid from the planning and delivery process. Anderson's conclusions underscore the contradictions between principles and policy statements such as the GHD and actual behaviour within the donor and humanitarian community.

In Chapter 7, "Tackling Ignorance and Neglect: Advocacy for a Broader Humanitarian Response in the Central African Republic," **Toby Lanzer** gives us an inside glimpse of how the crisis in the Central African Republic (CAR) was put on the humanitarian map, complementing this year's crisis report on that humanitarian crisis. How did it go from a country mostly unknown and ignored, characterised by Jan Egeland as "the world's most forgotten crisis," to more than tripling its total humanitarian funding in the space of a single year? Drawing on his previous experience with OCHA, Lanzer describes the processes which were put in motion during his tenure as Humanitarian Coordinator in the CAR to focus world attention on the development and humanitarian needs of this tiny African nation. He describes how France lobbied other countries, the BBC's visit in late 2005, and the engagement of UNICEF. By attracting prominent goodwill ambassadors, ensuring that information was widely available in English and in high-tech modalities such as Websites and blogs, drawing in major media, and tying the situation of CAR closely with neighbouring crises, CAR became more visible and better known to the aid community. Lanzer pays particular attention to the transition in humanitarian presence, from three wary UN agencies based in the capital, Bangui, making only 12 visits outside Bangui per month, to ten times that number, engaged in 145 missions per month, and from situation of suspicion and aggressiveness on the part of the government and population to one where NGOs were welcomed to all parts of the country. With increased presence came improved analysis, learning, participation, and the more effective use of aid, all of which, in a virtuous circle, attracted the involvement of greater numbers of humanitarian partners, and greatly increased funding. Lanzer concludes with a discussion of the methods and criteria used to select projects submitted

for funding to CAR's Coordinated Aid Programme set up in CAR. His reflections provide insights into the real challenges for donors to live up to the GHD principles and provide aid equitably to all countries in need, and serves as a good introduction to the crisis reports (including a report on CAR) which follow in Part Three.

Part Three: Crisis Reports

As part of the data collection for compiling the HRI rankings and scores, teams visited 11 different crisis locations to survey humanitarian actors and how they perceive donor actions in light of the GHD principles. Part Three offers overview analyses of crises in the following countries: Afghanistan, Bangladesh, Central African Republic, Chad, Colombia, the Democratic Republic of the Congo, Nicaragua, occupied Palestinian territories, Peru, Sri Lanka, and Sudan. Several countries (Colombia, Democratic Republic of Congo, Sudan) were included in the HRI 2007 report, allowing readers to see how the response to the crisis in each has evolved over the past year. Each report provides a brief outline of the crisis background and the humanitarian response, with particular emphasis on how donors contributed to the response, and an analysis of the successes and shortcomings of the international response. The countries visited provide a broad overview of how the GHD principles and related initiatives to improve humanitarian action, such as the UN reform process, are playing out in different situations ranging from disasters, conflicts, forgotten crises, and complex emergencies. As such, the crisis reports provide an excellent framework for putting the overall findings of the HRI in Part One and the issues raised by the authors in Part Two in context.

Part Four: Donor Profiles

Part four of this report offers an overview of donors' performance for each of the 22 countries ranked in the HRI 2008, as well as the European commission. Taken together, they provide a comprehensive overview of countries' humanitarian aid programmes, including how much aid is being given, how timely it is, to which emergencies, parts of the world, and to which sectors it is directed.

We also provide a list of the many acronyms used throughout the publication, a Glossary of frequently used terms, and an Appendix containing the full Survey which formed the basis for the qualitative measures in the Humanitarian Response Index.

1

PART ONE

The Humanitarian Response Index 2008

CHAPTER 1

The Humanitarian Response Index 2008:

Donor Accountability in Humanitarian Action

SILVIA HIDALGO and **PHILIP TAMMINGA**

Introduction[1]

Millions of people across the globe are affected by disasters, epidemics and conflicts each year. Disasters caused by natural phenomena affected 281 million people in 2007, equal to the population of France, the UK, Canada and Japan combined.[2] In addition, more than 45 million people are affected annually by war, the consequences of which are felt for years afterwards.[3] There is a humanitarian imperative to save lives, alleviate suffering, maintain human dignity, and assist those in need. However, despite considerable efforts and the best of intentions, the international humanitarian system is often unable to effectively meet all the needs of those affected by crises.

At a time of increasing threat of disasters related to climate change and the ever-present risk of outbreaks of armed conflicts, there is a need for more and, perhaps more significantly, more appropriate and effective humanitarian aid. Yet aid budgets are not growing in pace with needs, and efforts to reform the humanitarian system appear to be losing momentum. As the principal providers of funds for humanitarian assistance, donor governments have considerable influence and a particular responsibility to make the humanitarian system more effective so that aid reaches the people who need it most.

The Humanitarian Response Index (HRI), developed by DARA, annually assesses how well major donor countries are doing in helping people affected by humanitarian crises. The HRI ranks the performance of the 22 donor countries of the OECD Development Assistance Committee (DAC) plus the European Commission in funding and supporting humanitarian action. DARA created the HRI in the belief that it would complement other initiatives in a sector that needs increased capacity, quality and accountability, and new ways and means of measuring performance. The main aims of the HRI are to contribute to ongoing efforts to improve the quality of humanitarian aid and ensure that aid is used to help those most in need and in the most effective way possible.

Specifically, the HRI objectives are:

- To measure and benchmark the quality and effectiveness of donor governments' humanitarian assistance

- To contribute to greater transparency and accountability in donors' policies and practices

- To support a better contextual understanding of the policy and operational barriers that affect effective implementation of good donor practice

- To promote informed public debate and decision-making on humanitarian issues.

The HRI uses The Principles and Good Practice of Humanitarian Donorship (GHD), a set of 23 principles and guidelines agreed by OECD/DAC donors and the European Commission, as the framework by which to assess donors' performance. In this way, the HRI assesses how well donors are working towards the standards of good practice to which they have committed themselves.

The HRI process draws on extensive field research and data collection to construct a comprehensive picture of donor performance. The main outputs of the process include:

- The Index and donor rankings, which are built from over 55 qualitative and quantitative indicators that aim to capture the essence of the GHD *Principles*. The indicators are grouped into five key areas or Pillars of good practice, which are used to "score" governmental donors (see Boxes 1 and 2)

- The HRI Crisis Reports, which provide a more detailed analysis of each of the crises studied as part

Figure 1: HRI Process, methodology and outputs

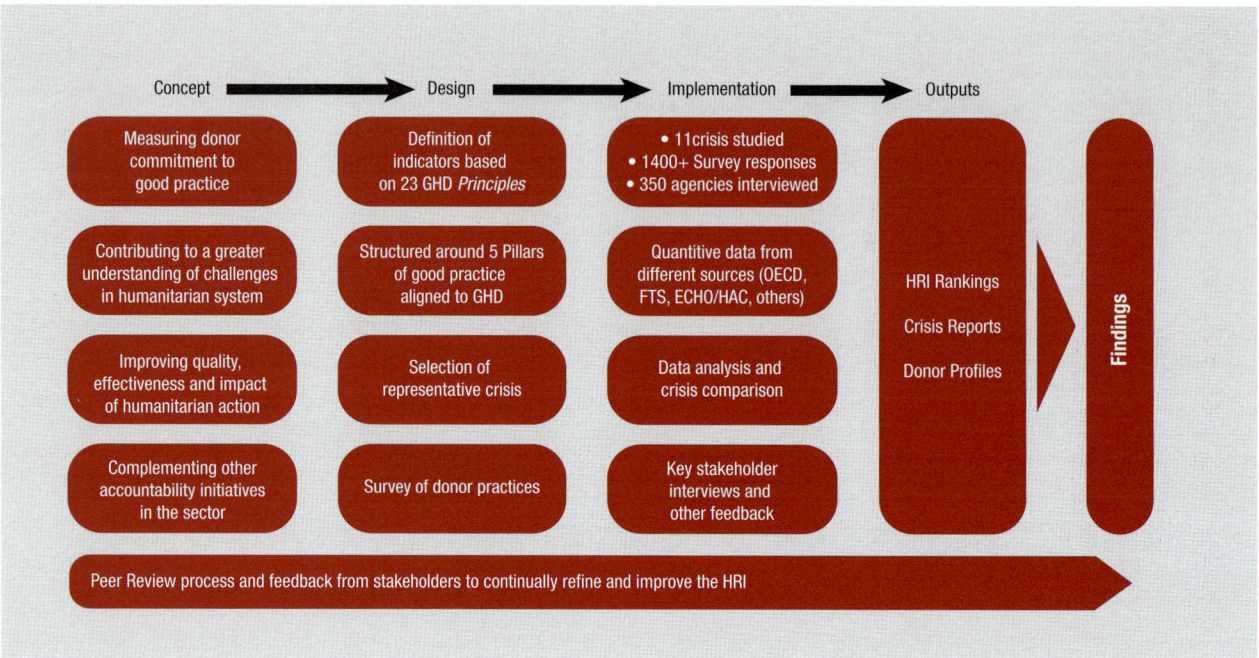

Concept → Design → Implementation → Outputs

Measuring donor commitment to good practice	Definition of indicators based on 23 GHD *Principles*	• 11crisis studied • 1400+ Survey responses • 350 agencies interviewed	
Contributing to a greater understanding of challenges in humanitarian system	Structured around 5 Pillars of good practice aligned to GHD	Quantitative data from different sources (OECD, FTS, ECHO/HAC, others)	HRI Rankings
Improving quality, effectiveness and impact of humanitarian action	Selection of representative crisis	Data analysis and crisis comparison	Crisis Reports Donor Profiles
Complementing other accountability initiatives in the sector	Survey of donor practices	Key stakeholder interviews and other feedback	Findings

Peer Review process and feedback from stakeholders to continually refine and improve the HRI

of the HRI process, with a focus on the response of donors and other parts of the humanitarian system to the crisis

- The Donor Profiles, which provide an overview of individual donor countries' humanitarian assistance.

The qualitative data for the HRI 2008 was generated from field research in 11 different crises around the world: Afghanistan, Bangladesh, the Central African Republic, Chad, Colombia, the Democratic Republic of the Congo, Nicaragua, the occupied Palestinian territories, Peru, Sri Lanka and Sudan. The process included interviews with more than 350 humanitarian organisations and donor agencies involved in the implementation of humanitarian programming, and more than 1,400 responses to a survey of donor practice. The quantitative data was compiled from a number of different sources, including the UN, ECHO/HAC, the World Bank, the IFRC and the ICRC. The HRI process also includes reviews of key policy documents and evaluations of humanitarian action.

The advantage of this triangulated approach is that it allows for a more complete view of donor performance. The use of an index helps to convey complex information about donor policy and practice in a relatively simple and easily understood format – a ranking – while allowing for a more detailed analysis of each of the individual indicators that make up the Index. Beyond the rankings, the HRI Crisis Reports allow for a nuanced picture of some of the key issues and challenges facing the humanitarian sector that may not be easily captured through the rankings and scores alone. At the same time, the donor rankings and profiles allow countries to track their own progress against their peers, and identify areas that may require further efforts for improvement.

Box 1: The five Pillars of the HRI and their relation to the GHD *Principles*

Pillar 1: Responding to needs
This Pillar assesses to what extent donor funding practices respect the fundamental humanitarian principles of impartiality, neutrality and independence and are aimed at saving lives, preventing and alleviating suffering, and restoring dignity. The indicators in this Pillar correspond to GHD Principles 2, 5, 6, and 11.

Pillar 2: Supporting local capacity and recovery
This Pillar assesses to what extent donor funds are provided to help build and support local capacity in disaster risk reduction, preparedness and response, as well as to support recovery and long-term development initiatives. The indicators in this Pillar correspond to GHD Principles 1, 7, 8 and 9.

Pillar 3: Working with humanitarian partners
This Pillar assesses how well donors support the work of agencies implementing humanitarian action response and their unique roles in the humanitarian system. The indicators in this Pillar correspond to GHD Principles 10, 12, 13, 14, and 18.

Pillar 4: Promoting standards and enhancing implementation
This Pillar assesses to what extent donors integrate internationally recognised standards and principles into their funding policies and practices, and ensure that these are applied. The indicators in this Pillar correspond to GHD Principles 3, 4, 16, 17, 19, and 20.

Pillar 5: Promoting learning and accountability
This Pillar assesses how well donors support initiatives to improve the quality, effectiveness and accountability of humanitarian action. The indicators in this Pillar correspond to GHD Principles 15, 21, 22, and 23.

Figure 2: HRI 2008 Donor Rankings by Pillar

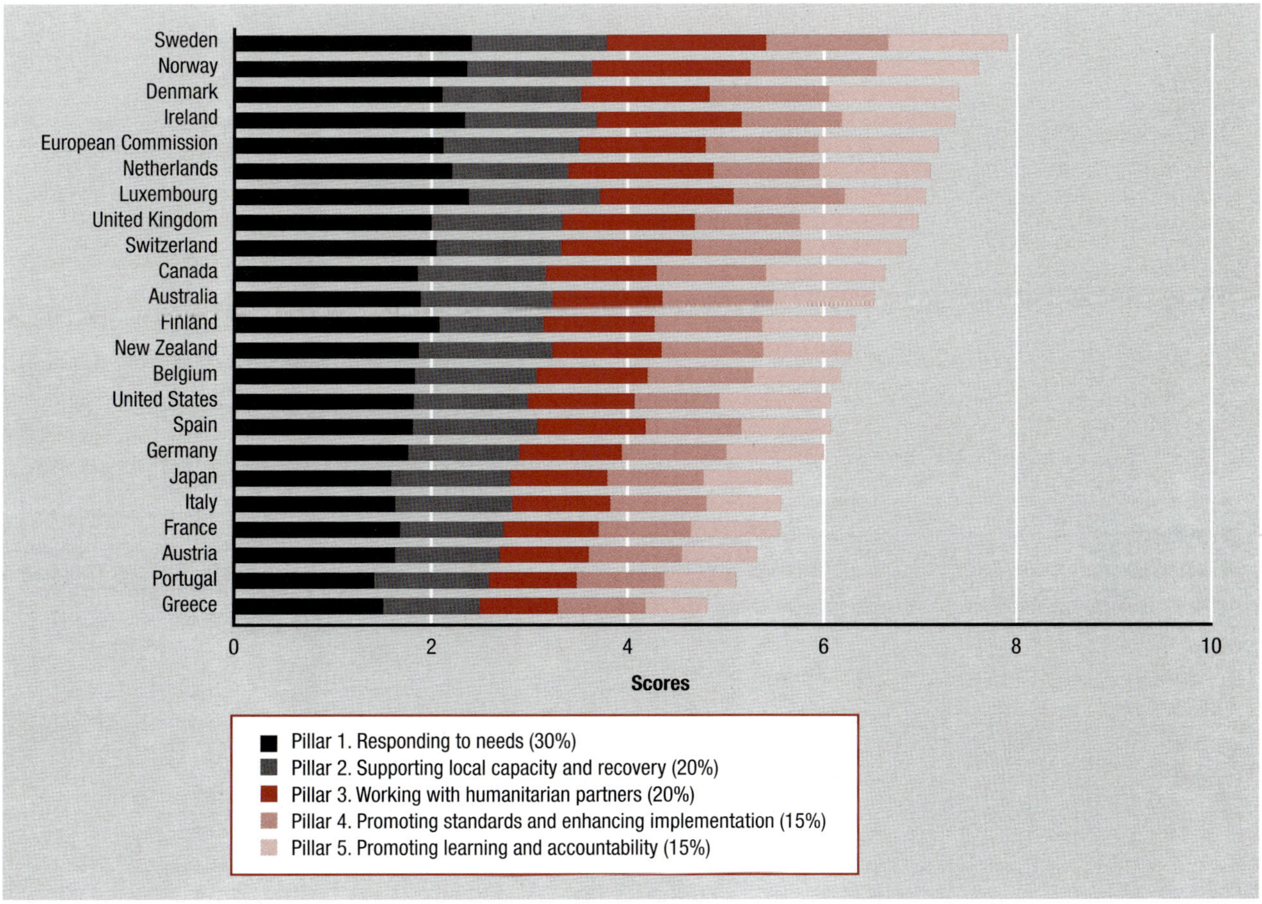

Legend:
- Pillar 1. Responding to needs (30%)
- Pillar 2. Supporting local capacity and recovery (20%)
- Pillar 3. Working with humanitarian partners (20%)
- Pillar 4. Promoting standards and enhancing implementation (15%)
- Pillar 5. Promoting learning and accountability (15%)

The HRI 2008 rankings (figure 2) show that donors individually and collectively could do more to ensure that their policies and practices reflect the orientations of the GHD *Principles*. There are great differences between donors, with some much closer to achieving the aspirations of the GHD, while others are lagging behind their peers. However, with all countries – even the top-ranked ones – there is room for improvement.

The overall findings from this year's HRI point to five key inter-related areas where the wealthy group of donor countries that comprise the OECD/DAC could focus their efforts, in conjunction with other actors, if they want to improve the quality, effectiveness and impact of humanitarian action:

1. **Wealthy countries could do more to strengthen their commitments to provide aid in an impartial, neutral and independent manner, not based on other priorities or objectives.** The findings from Pillar 1 indicate that donors are not always perceived as providing aid in an impartial, neutral and independent manner, nor where it is most needed. There are particular problems in politicised and protracted crises and complex emergencies, where too often other interests override humanitarian concerns.

2. **Wealthy countries should contribute to efforts to improve the quality and use of needs assessments to determine who needs assistance, where, and of what kind.** The findings under Pillar 1 also suggest that needs assessments, the principal instrument used by donors and operational humanitarian agencies to determine needs and allocate resources, can be improved and used more consistently in order to ensure that the right kind of aid reaches the right people at the right time.

3. **Wealthy countries could do more to support local capacity and link relief efforts to recovery and longer-term development strategies.** The findings from Pillar 2 suggest that it is still a challenge for the humanitarian system to adapt to local contexts, particularly in the area of engaging with local communities in programming, supporting and strengthening – not undermining – local capacity to respond, cope and recover from crises.

4. **Wealthy countries should systematically invest more resources into strengthening the humanitarian system's capacity at all levels.** The results from Pillar 3 show that there is a need to invest more efforts into ongoing UN humanitarian reform processes, and into capacity-building for all of the different operational partners in the humanitarian system to ensure that the system as a whole works better to meet current and future humanitarian needs.

5. **Wealthy countries should assume more responsibility for ensuring implementation of international standards and good practice, and for improving accountability and performance in humanitarian action.** In line with the findings from Pillars 4 and 5, donors could take a more active leadership role in promoting a shared understanding of good practice in humanitarian action. This includes strengthening their commitments to ensure that international principles and standards are being respected and applied, especially in the area of protection and assistance, and promoting greater accountability.

The following sections in this chapter explain these findings in greater detail, beginning with the background and context of the HRI, its methodology and limitations, the main changes for this year, and more analysis of the main findings by Pillars and individual donors. This chapter is complemented by thematic chapters on key issues facing the humanitarian sector contained in Part 2 of the publication, Crisis Reports analysing each of the 11 different crises studied for the HRI 2008 in Part 3, and profiles of individual donors in Part 4.

Background and context of the HRI

A large proportion of the US$8bn spent by the international community in humanitarian aid in 2007 depends on the funding of the OECD/DAC donors ranked by the HRI.[4] While considering international humanitarian response at large, the HRI focuses on the assistance provided by the 22 wealthy donor governments (along with the European Commission) that are part of the OECD/DAC countries. Humanitarian organisations have relied heavily on this form of funding; their engagement in specific crises and the aid programmes they provide depend overwhelmingly on donor government support.

Major failures of the humanitarian system during the genocide in Rwanda and other crises were the impetus for a series of initiatives to reform and improve the quality, performance, and accountability of the main actors engaged in humanitarian assistance. This included initiatives such as the formation of the Active Learning Network for Accountability and Performance (ALNAP), which brings together governments, the UN, the Red Cross Red Crescent Movement, NGOs, academia and evaluators to systematically share learning, evaluations and good practices in humanitarian action. There were also attempts to increase adherence to operational standards and codes of good practice, and improve accountability to affected populations, such as the Sphere Humanitarian Charter and Minimum Standards, and the Standard in Humanitarian Accountability and Quality Management developed by Humanitarian

Accountability Partnership - International.[5] Initiatives to reform the UN humanitarian system followed in 2005, spurred in part by the response to the crisis in Darfur, with the aim of improving coordination mechanisms and defining clearer responsibilities among operational agencies in critical areas.[6]

Several donor governments have in the past played key roles in promoting many of these reform initiatives. However, most of these initiatives focused on operational organisations' work on the ground, without looking at the unique role of donors within the system.[7] The Good Humanitarian Donorship initiative was a step in the right direction to correct this. In 2003, representatives of several donor agencies, many with long experience working on humanitarian issues, tried to systematically bring together lessons learned and good practices on how donor policies and decisions resulted in the success or failure of previous responses to disasters and conflicts – resulting in the GHD *Principles*.[8]

Box 2: Principles and good practice of humanitarian donorship

Endorsed by Australia, Austria, Belgium, Canada, Denmark, European Commission, Finland, France, Germany, Greece, Ireland, Italy, Japan, Luxembourg, New Zealand, Norway, Portugal, Spain, Sweden, Switzerland, the Netherlands, the United Kingdom and the United States.

Objectives and definition of humanitarian action

1. The objectives of humanitarian action are to save lives, alleviate suffering and maintain human dignity during and in the aftermath of man-made crises and natural disasters, as well as to prevent and strengthen preparedness for the occurrence of such situations.
2. Humanitarian action should be guided by the humanitarian principles of humanity, meaning the centrality of saving human lives and alleviating suffering wherever it is found; impartiality, meaning the implementation of actions solely on the basis of need, without discrimination between or within affected populations; neutrality, meaning that humanitarian action must not favour any side in an armed conflict or other dispute where such action is carried out; and independence, meaning the autonomy of humanitarian objectives from the political, economic, military or other objectives that any actor may hold with regard to areas where humanitarian action is being implemented.
3. Humanitarian action includes the protection of civilians and those no longer taking part in hostilities, and the provision of food, water and sanitation, shelter, health services and other items of assistance, undertaken for the benefit of affected people and to facilitate the return to normal lives and livelihoods.

General principles

4. Respect and promote the implementation of international humanitarian law, refugee law and human rights.
5. While reaffirming the primary responsibility of states for the victims of humanitarian emergencies within their own borders, strive to ensure flexible and timely funding, on the basis of the collective obligation of striving to meet humanitarian needs.
6. Allocate humanitarian funding in proportion to needs and on the basis of needs assessments.
7. Request implementing humanitarian organisations to ensure, to the greatest possible extent, adequate involvement of beneficiaries in the design, implementation, monitoring and evaluation of humanitarian response.
8. Strengthen the capacity of affected countries and local communities to prevent, prepare for, mitigate and respond to humanitarian crises, with the goal of ensuring that governments and local communities are better able to meet their responsibilities and co-ordinate effectively with humanitarian partners.
9. Provide humanitarian assistance in ways that are supportive of recovery and long-term development, striving to ensure support, where appropriate, to the maintenance and return

Box 2: Principles and good practice of humanitarian donorship continued

of sustainable livelihoods and transitions from humanitarian relief to recovery and development activities.

10. Support and promote the central and unique role of the United Nations in providing leadership and co-ordination of international humanitarian action, the special role of the International Committee of the Red Cross, and the vital role of the United Nations, the International Red Cross and Red Crescent Movement and non-governmental organisations in implementing humanitarian action.

Good practices in donor financing, management and accountability

(a) Funding

11. Strive to ensure that funding of humanitarian action in new crises does not adversely affect the meeting of needs in ongoing crises.

12. Recognising the necessity of dynamic and flexible response to changing needs in humanitarian crises, strive to ensure predictability and flexibility in funding to United Nations agencies, funds and programmes and to other key humanitarian organisations.

13. While stressing the importance of transparent and strategic priority-setting and financial planning by implementing organisations, explore the possibility of reducing, or enhancing the flexibility of, earmarking, and of introducing longer-term funding arrangements.

14. Contribute responsibly, and on the basis of burden-sharing, to United Nations Consolidated Inter-Agency Appeals and to International Red Cross and Red Crescent Movement appeals, and actively support the formulation of Common Humanitarian Action Plans (CHAP) as the primary instrument for strategic planning, prioritisation and co-ordination in complex emergencies.

(b) Promoting standards and enhancing implementation

15. Request that implementing humanitarian organisations fully adhere to good practice and are committed to promoting accountability, efficiency and effectiveness in implementing humanitarian action.

16. Promote the use of Inter-Agency Standing Committee guidelines and principles on humanitarian activities, the Guiding Principles on Internal Displacement and the 1994 Code of Conduct for the International Red Cross and Red Crescent Movement and Non-Governmental Organisations (NGOs) in Disaster Relief.

17. Maintain readiness to offer support to the implementation of humanitarian action, including the facilitation of safe humanitarian access.

18. Support mechanisms for contingency planning by humanitarian organisations, including, as appropriate, allocation of funding, to strengthen capacities for response.

19. Affirm the primary position of civilian organisations in implementing humanitarian action, particularly in areas affected by armed conflict. In situations where military capacity and assets are used to support the implementation of humanitarian action, ensure that such use is in conformity with international humanitarian law and humanitarian principles, and recognises the leading role of humanitarian organisations.

20. Support the implementation of the 1994 Guidelines on the Use of Military and Civil Defence Assets in Disaster Relief and the 2003 Guidelines on the Use of Military and Civil Defence Assets to Support United Nations Humanitarian Activities in Complex Emergencies.

(c) Learning and accountability

21. Support learning and accountability initiatives for the effective and efficient implementation of humanitarian action.

22. Encourage regular evaluations of international responses to humanitarian crises, including assessments of donor performance.

23. Ensure a high degree of accuracy, timeliness, and transparency in donor reporting on official humanitarian assistance spending, and encourage the development of standardised formats for such reporting.

The aim of the GHD initiative is to ensure that one critical component of the humanitarian system, namely donors, works in ways that strengthen rather than undermine efforts to save lives, alleviate suffering, and restore livelihoods. The GHD *Principles* reinforce the idea that donors have a role which complements the other parts of the humanitarian system, and that they have a special responsibility to ensure that their policies and decisions help uphold and promote impartial, neutral, independent and effective humanitarian action. The GHD works towards achieving efficient and principled humanitarian assistance based on a set of 23 *Principles* of good practice of humanitarian donorship.

The GHD *Principles* were adopted in 2005 by 22 members of the OECD/DAC and the European Commission. Since then, donors have developed a set of collective indicators and peer review processes as a means to track the overall progress of implementation. This approach is certainly valid, but it has its limitations. The major drawback of such an approach is that it does not provide the general public, humanitarian actors, or policy makers with easily accessible, transparent information about individual country performance. In fact, it may hide poor performers among the overall collective results – which is not conducive to making governments more transparent and accountable to their publics with regard to how humanitarian assistance is provided and how it can be improved. As noted in their article "Welcome to the Good Humanitarian Donorship club", Minear and Smillie suggest that the differences in the perceived level of donor commitment to the GHD *Principles* confirm "a need to monitor developments in this area and keep the pressure on governments to adopt national humanitarian policies and approaches consistent with the GHD framework."[9]

In addition, the internal focus of the collective processes could potentially isolate donors from wider debates about the quality and effectiveness of humanitarian assistance and its links to ongoing debates on development, security, and political concerns. Efforts to counter this, such as joint meetings between donors and the Inter-Agency Standing Committee held within the framework of the GHD initiative, are an encouraging sign of progress.

DARA itself has had direct experience in reviewing donor behaviour through its involvement with the Tsunami Evaluation Coalition (TEC) studies on funding

flows. The TEC studies revealed that many donors tried to act as "good" donors, but lacked guidance on what constituted good practice and a principled approach, despite the existence of the GHD initiative. Many donors felt pressured to make rapid funding disbursements in amounts well beyond actual needs. Others waited for comprehensive assessments before committing funding, but recognised the inadequacies in the quality of needs assessments and of overall coordination. The tsunami highlighted the difficulties of putting the GHD *Principles* into operation, and how easily a major emergency can undermine efforts to apply good practice.[10]

Following the TEC experience and other evaluations, DARA undertook a review of the existing accountability and evaluation mechanisms, and concluded that the sector would be well served by an independent, objective and impartial review of donor behaviour and performance. The HRI is intended to complement the collective indicators and peer review approach favoured by the OECD/DAC, as well as other initiatives.

After careful deliberation, DARA chose an index and ranking of donors as the means to present its findings on donor performance. Indices and international benchmarking efforts have a well established record for stimulating policy dialogue and providing incentives for changing institutional policy and practice. Over the past decade, more and more organisations have opted for the development of specific indices and scoring mechanisms with their associated rankings, such as the UNDP's *Human Development Index*, One World Trust's *Global Accountability Report* or the Center for Global Development's *Commitment to Development Index*.[11] The HRI was built against the background of this large body of work, with the aim of tracking the individual and collective progress of donors over time, and thereby providing a means to allow comparative analysis both between donors and progress at the individual level. There are, of course, limitations to the ranking approach, including the risk of over-simplifying what is inherently a complex issue – how to ensure that humanitarian assistance actually achieves its aim of preventing and alleviating human suffering.[12] Nevertheless, DARA believes that the benefits of an index and ranking approach, in combination with more detailed analysis of the response to different humanitarian crises, outweigh the disadvantages and allow for a more balanced perspective on donor performance.

Box 3: The expanding humanitarian club

The GHD *Principles* apply to the OECD/DAC countries. However, the HRI research confirms a growing trend of more and more non-traditional actors engaged in funding and implementing humanitarian assistance. Promoting and developing a shared understanding of good donor practices among this emerging group is a priority. DARA has begun to track some of these trends, and in future editions of the HRI will analyse in greater detail the implications for quality, performance and accountability in the sector.

Some of these new players include:

- *Decentralised donors:* Some countries such as Spain and Italy channel humanitarian assistance not only through the central government agency, but also through autonomous decentralised government agencies at the provincial level, without any specific oversight from the central agency and often with different working approaches and priorities. Many of these decentralised agencies are not aware of or have not signed up to the GHD *Principles*.

- *Multiple donor agencies within the same administration:* In other situations, a donor may have several different agencies providing humanitarian assistance, each with its own set of institutional priorities and procedures. For example, the United States channels assistance through USAID, OFDA, PRM and the State Department. Similarly, the European Commission has several directorates dealing with humanitarian issues, each with different budget lines and requirements. Add to this the use of military assets, and the picture becomes even more complex for operational actors working with multiple donor contacts.

- *The United Nations system as a donor:* Part of the UN humanitarian reform effort included the creation of new pooled funding mechanisms like the CERF to provide quick funding disbursements, mainly to UN agencies but also to support the work of other actors, such as NGOs. In some crisis contexts, the CERF has worked very well. However, many operational actors (including some UN agencies) have commented in the HRI field research that the funding approval process and reporting requirements are cumbersome, and that the UN too often follows its own agenda. Several operational agencies have suggested that the UN itself should be ranked against the GHD *Principles*.

- *New donors:* The donor club is no longer limited to the OECD/DAC. Many of the EU accession states are becoming more active in humanitarian action, and should in theory apply the GHD *Principles* to their working approaches. In several of the crises studied in the HRI 2008, non-traditional donors were among the top contributors of humanitarian assistance. For example, Saudi Arabia in Bangladesh and Venezuela in Nicaragua provided the bulk of assistance. The Crisis Reports also mention the growing influence of China and other emerging economies in Africa, and how private corporations, foundations and wealthy individuals are increasingly engaged in funding humanitarian assistance. The growing number of donors presents new challenges for coordination and alignment of humanitarian assistance, especially as much of this aid is not reported through FTS, and is provided directly to the government of the crisis-affected country, often with few conditions or requirements to follow good practice.

Response to the HRI 2007

The development of the first HRI in 2007 came after extensive consultations with the main stakeholders involved in humanitarian action – donors, UN agencies, the Red Cross Red Crescent Movement, and NGOs – which informed the design and methodology of the HRI. From the outset, DARA understood that the HRI would be an evolving tool, and that feedback and constructive criticism would enrich and improve the HRI over time, allowing it to earn its place as an independent and objective exercise that adds to efforts to improve the humanitarian system.

The launch of the 2007 HRI by former UN Secretary-General Kofi Annan and the subsequent efforts to share the first year's findings and gather feedback to improve the HRI were met with considerable interest within the donor and aid community and the wider public. The reaction from humanitarian organisations has been overwhelmingly positive. Most organisations have welcomed the initiative and its focus on donors as the missing piece in efforts to improve the accountability of the entire humanitarian system. DARA's interviews with hundreds of field staff directly engaged in operations have also been extremely positive, with many stating that the HRI's process and findings help to draw attention to the issues they face with donors in a way that does not compromise the inherent dependence of many agencies on donor funding – and the corresponding power imbalances that this can create. This feedback has confirmed DARA's assessment that a tool like the HRI will be of value to a vital set of stakeholders in the humanitarian system.

The donor community, on the other hand, has given the HRI mixed reviews. The fact that the HRI was conceived as an independent initiative, not sponsored by donors, was met with some surprise as most of the initiatives in the sector have relied heavily on donor funding and support. Nevertheless, individuals within donor agencies have expressed encouragement and have privately told DARA that the HRI serves to stimulate debate within their own agencies. In fact, some donor agencies have begun to use the information derived from the HRI indicators, and the HRI has perhaps indirectly contributed to the process of refining and improving the GHD collective indicators.

Other donor representatives, in particular the GHD focal points within donor agencies, have expressed a number of reservations about the HRI, voicing misgivings about the value of rankings and their potential to detract from the collaborative spirit within the GHD initiative. Some donors have also expressed some concerns about the methodology, such as the use of a survey that measures perceptions about donor performance. Other donors suggested that the GHD collective indicators were sufficient, and questioned whether the HRI might duplicate this work.

The HRI ranks individual donor performances against their peers, but this does not necessarily detract from the collaborative and consensual spirit behind the GHD. Rankings can be uncomfortable for the agencies under scrutiny, as they can cast light on various policy inconsistencies or deficiencies.[13] However, to argue against the HRI rankings would seem to be at odds with the kind of transparency and accountability that is now expected of governments, and every other part of the humanitarian system, of which both collective and individual performance assessments conducted through independent evaluation processes are an integral part.[14]

In fact, rankings have become an established part of the development and humanitarian assistance landscape. For example, the UNDP's *Human Development Index* ranks countries against a series of indicators, just as progress towards the Millennium Development Goals are tracked on a country-by-country basis. Similarly,

OCHA FTS publishes a ranking of top donors to humanitarian appeals. Donors themselves often communicate publicly that they are the "top global donor" compared to other countries, usually in terms of the absolute amount of funding, or that they are among the first to respond with assistance in a given emergency. In the wake of the response to the Indian Ocean tsunami, EU Commissioner Louis Michel declared that humanitarian donorship "should not be about a beauty contest", yet in private many donors will admit that "it is all about a beauty contest".[15]

In DARA's view countries should be judged on their performance as responsible donors, and on their progress in meeting the commitments that they have made. The HRI builds on a recognised set of principles of good practice that donors themselves have agreed to, and as such helps to hold donors accountable to their commitments, at the same time as raising awareness within the sector and wider public about how to best achieve the aims and objectives of humanitarian assistance. DARA is very grateful for all of the feedback it has received since the launch of the first HRI last year, and hopes not only that the methodological changes outlined below have gone some way to addressing the concerns raised, but also that this dialogue will continue, with the aim of contributing to improving the quality, effectiveness and impact of humanitarian action.

The HRI process and methodology

This section outlines the main points of the HRI process and methodology. A more detailed explanation of all the individual indicators, data sources and methodology can be found in the Technical Appendix at the end of this chapter.

The HRI methodology uses a combination of qualitative and quantitative data to generate 58 indicators which aim to capture the essence of the 23 *Principles* of good practice contained in the GHD. The GHD *Principles* are currently the only available reference for donor good practice, and have the additional advantage in that all OECD/DAC members and the European Commission have committed to implementing the *Principles*. In some cases, these indicators are a proxy of good practice as the GHD *Principles* themselves are at times not explicit, or can be interpreted differently as to what constitutes good practice. The indicators are then grouped into "Pillars" of good practice. Because some elements of humanitarian assistance are universally considered more important than others, the Pillars are weighted to reflect this.

The qualitative data comes from field research of a representative sample of different humanitarian crises around the world. The criteria used to select the crises included ensuring an adequate geographic coverage, the inclusion of both disasters and complex emergencies or conflicts, and high-profile versus "forgotten" crises. Consistent with these criteria, the crises chosen to assess donor behaviour for the HRI 2008 were: Afghanistan, Bangladesh, the Central African Republic, Chad, Colombia, the Democratic Republic of the Congo, Nicaragua, the occupied Palestinian territories, Peru, Sri Lanka and Sudan. Three of these, Colombia, the Democratic Republic of the Congo and Sudan, were covered in the HRI 2007 survey, thus ensuring a measure of continuity over the two-year period.

Field research was carried out during the period December 2007 to May 2008. DARA teams conducted a survey Questionnaire on Good Practice in Humanitarian Donorship with representatives of humanitarian organisations. Respondents were asked to provide their perception of the application of the GHD *Principles* by donors from whom they receive funding, using a 1-7 Likert scale. Teams attempted to cover all the agencies (UN, Red Cross Red Crescent, and national and international NGOs) engaged in the response, and in some cases interviewed up to 85 percent of the national and international agencies in the country. In total, representatives from more than 350 humanitarian organisations and donor agencies involved in the implementation of humanitarian pro-grammes were interviewed, and more than 1,400 responses to the survey were collected for the HRI 2008, providing a reasonable sample size for most donors. In some cases, there were not enough survey responses for five donors (Austria, Greece, Luxembourg, New Zealand and Portugal) to generate reliable analysis. To compensate for this, responses for these donors have been pooled with the responses from the HRI 2007 survey to ensure an adequate sample size, and checked carefully to ensure that this did not lead to a bias in the results. This is explained in more detail in the Technical Appendix at the end of the chapter. Table 1 provides a breakdown of the number of responses by donor and crises studied.

Table 1: HRI 2008: Distribution of survey responses by donor and by crisis surveyed

Donor	Number of responses
Australia	29
Austria*	30
Belgium	27
Canada	101
Denmark	43
European Commission	277
Finland	20
France	50
Germany	72
Greece*	23
Ireland	30
Italy	41
Japan	54
Luxembourg*	33
Netherlands	79
New Zealand*	30
Norway	80
Portugal*	26
Spain	102
Sweden	78
Switzerland	43
UK	95
USA	141
Total	**1504**

Crisis surveyed	Number of responses
Afghanistan	128
Bangladesh	155
Central African Republic	66
Chad	66
Colombia	92
Democratic Republic of the Congo	194
Nicaragua	65
Palestinian	211
Peru	99
Sri Lanka	175
Sudan	153
Total	**1404**

*Responses include 2007 survey sample.

The field research also draws on background documentation such as appeal documents, assessments, reviews and evaluations of the various crises. This was supplemented with open-ended interviews with donor representatives, local organisations and government authorities and, whenever possible and appropriate, people affected by the crisis. This information was used to validate and corroborate the survey responses, as well as provide a better understanding of the context of the crisis, and the behaviour of donors and other actors. It has been compiled into the Crisis Reports which are included in Part 3 of the HRI publication.

The substantial body of data generated through the field research is complemented by quantitative indicators constructed from data from a number of different sources, such as OCHA's Financial Tracking Service

Box 4: Distribution of qualitative and quantitative indicators by Pillar

Pillar 1: Responding to needs (30% of Index weight)

Qualitative indicators (HRI survey)

- Donor commitment to saving lives and maintaining dignity
- Impartiality of donor funding
- Neutrality of donor funding
- Independence of funding from political, military and other non-humanitarian objectives
- Funding in proportion to need
- Donor funding for needs assessments
- Speed of funding to new emergencies
- Funding to on-going crises
- Reallocation of funds from other crises
- Donor capacity for informed decision-making

Quantitative indicators

- Generosity of humanitarian funding
- Funding to crisis countries with historical ties and geographic proximity to donor
- Funding to forgotten emergencies and those with low media coverage
- Timely funding to complex emergencies through UN appeals
- Timely funding to sudden onset disasters and IFRC emergency appeals
- Sectoral distribution of funding through UN appeals
- Distribution of funding relative to ECHOs Crisis and Vulnerability Indices

Pillar 2: Supporting local capacity and recovery (20% of Index weight)

Qualitative indicators (HRI survey)

- Funding to strengthen disaster-preparedness mechanisms
- Funding to strengthen government capacity for disaster response and mitigation
- Funding to strengthen local capacity for disaster response and mitigation
- Funding to strengthen local resilience to cope with crises
- Involvement of beneficiaries in programme design and implementation
- Involvement of beneficiaries in monitoring and evaluation of the response
- Funding to ensure rapid recovery of sustainable livelihoods
- Funding aligned to support long-term recovery and development

Quantitative indicators

- Funding to strengthen local capacity for disaster response and mitigation
- Funding to international disaster mitigation mechanisms

Pillar 3: Working with humanitarian partners (20% of Index weight)

Qualitative indicators (HRI survey)

- Donor support to governments and local communities to achieve better coordination
- Donor support for effective coordination efforts
- Donor support for contingency planning and strengthening local response capacity
- Donor support for UN leadership and coordination role
- Donor promotion of the International Committee for the Red Cross
- Donor efforts to promote the role of NGOs and the Red Cross and Red Crescent Movement
- Predictable donor funding
- Reducing amount of earmarked funds
- Provision of flexible funding
- Provision of longer term funding arrangements
- Consistent donor support for implementation of humanitarian action

Quantitative indicators

- Funding for UN coordination mechanisms and common services
- Funding to CERF and pooled mechanisms
- Funding for UN Consolidated Inter-Agency appeals
- Funding for IFRC and ICRC appeals
- Funding for NGOs
- Amount of unearmarked funding

Pillar 4: Promoting standards and enhancing implementation (15% of Index weight)

Qualitative indicators (HRI survey)

- Donor respect and promotion of international humanitarian law
- Donor engagement in protection and assistance to civilians
- Donor respect and promotion of human rights
- Donor support to the needs of internally displaced persons
- Donor facilitation of safe humanitarian access
- Donor affirmation of the primary role of civilian organisations in humanitarian action

Quantitative indicators

- Implementation of international humanitarian law and funding to the ICRC as custodian of IHL
- Implementation of human rights law and funding to the OHCHR
- Implementation of refugee law and funding to the UNHCR

Pillar 5: Promoting learning and accountability (15% of Index weight)

Qualitative indicators (HRI survey)

- Donor commitment to accountability in humanitarian action
- Donor support to learning and accountability initiatives
- Donor encouragement of regular evaluations

Quantitative indicators

- Participation in and funding of main accountability initiatives
- Number of evaluations

(FTS), data published by the OECD/DAC on humanitarian development assistance, and information from UN agencies, the IFCR and ICRC. As with the qualitative indicators, some of the quantitative indicators are proxies for good practice, as the GHD *Principles* do not lend themselves easily to measurement in some cases, or because there is no reliable or readily available data source. Box 4 shows the qualitative and quantitative indicators and their distribution by Pillar.

Limitations of the HRI methodology

There are inevitably limitations inherent in the design of any index or measurement tool. DARA's approach has always been to openly recognise the shortcomings of the HRI, and to actively engage with donors, humanitarian actors and others to continuously improve the instrument. Some of the challenges faced by the HRI are the same as those facing the humanitarian system and, as such, difficult to compensate for in the design. For example, among the limitations of the HRI's current design is the difficulty of finding a common, universally-accepted definition of donor good practice. The GHD *Principles* are the closest to such a definition. However, the GHD *Principles* are dynamic and evolving and leave room for different interpretations of what in reality constitutes good practice, and there are likely to be other perspectives within the sector that are not captured by the GHD *Principles*. Despite ongoing efforts to reform the humanitarian system, donors still lack guidance on what constitutes good behaviour overall and in specific crises. The growing number of non-OECD/DAC donors, including governments, the private sector and individuals, is a case in point. How these actors view good practice is an issue that requires further analysis but is beyond the scope of the HRI in its current configuration.

Even among donors, there are diverse opinions about the appropriateness of some of the GHD *Principles*, or impediments to their full application due to the particular policy environment of the humanitarian crisis in question. There are differing views among donors, for example, on the value of channelling aid through bilateral or multilateral mechanisms. Some donor agencies have severe limitations on providing flexibility and non-earmarking in funding due to the particular legislative framework of the country. Similarly, there are differing approaches on how to calculate the value of in-kind humanitarian assistance or the use and appropriateness of military assets in the delivery of aid. These differences make it difficult for the HRI to

categorically define and benchmark good practice in absolute values.

Another difficulty, again common to any research comparing policy and practice, is how to convert the GHD *Principles* into specific, measurable indicators based on reliable data sources. More specifically, the HRI relies on quantitative data from sources that have their own weaknesses and limitations. OCHA's FTS, for example, was conceived as a central database to track humanitarian funding and allow for better analysis and decision making around coverage of needs, etc. Yet as OCHA itself recognises, the quality of the data suffers in that some donors and agencies do not submit information to the FTS in a timely manner – or at all, which is the case for many non-traditional and non-OECD donors or NGOs. Data from OECD/DAC databases is also often out-of-date and incomplete. There is a similar situation with, for example, IFRC appeals, which do not always record funding pledges provided directly through member Red Cross or Red Crescent societies. Furthermore, governments and NGOs in a crisis-affected country often have different approaches to capture and report aid flows. All these factors make it difficult to have a complete, comprehensive and reliable set of data for some of the indicators selected.[16] GHD Principle 23 commits donors to "ensure a high degree of accuracy, timeliness, and transparency in donor reporting on official humanitarian assistance spending, and encourage the development of standardised formats for such reports", yet far more has to be done in this regard.

The use of a survey tool to generate qualitative data presents its own set of difficulties, particularly around generating a representative sample and a sufficient response rate to ensure that survey results are valid and reliable. In fact, the HRI faced considerable problems in ensuring a minimum number of responses for some smaller donors, as explained above. Furthermore, it has proven a challenge to translate the GHD *Principles* into clearly formulated questions. At the field level, an operational challenge has been organising visits to crisis areas, which are sometimes hard to reach, and conducting surveys with humanitarian workers often in the middle of humanitarian operations. The timing of field missions may also affect the nature of the responses. For example, responses to the survey near the outset of a crisis may be very different to responses later on in the crisis due to changes in the level of engagement from donors. High staff turnover among agencies may also influence the responses, as the individual interviewed may not have a comprehensive overview of donor behaviour during the duration of the crisis.

Nevertheless, DARA is convinced of the value of systematically capturing the opinions of people directly engaged in the delivery of humanitarian action, as they have a relationship with donors, and can assess how well principles are being put into practice. These perspectives, properly captured and analysed, are essential for understanding how well donors are doing in following the GHD *Principles* in practice.

Main changes in the HRI 2008

DARA has regularly sought feedback on how to improve the HRI design and methodology. Stakeholders were engaged in numerous consultations following the release of the first edition of the HRI in November 2007, to present the HRI and collect input on how to improve it. A series of presentations and technical workshops were held to review the methodological underpinnings of the HRI, with the active participation of donors, members of the NGO community, UN agencies, the Red Cross Red Crescent Movement and leading experts. DARA also maintained direct contact with a number of individual donor representatives at a headquarters level and in the field who provided valuable feedback.

As a result of this process, DARA received suggestions for the improvement of specific formulations and definitions of the some two dozen quantitative data indicators which were developed as building blocks for HRI 2007, and have made other improvements to the HRI methodology, as outlined below. These include:

- Improving the survey design and increasing the number of crises surveyed from 8 to 11 countries, including some high-profile complex emergencies such as Afghanistan, in order to boost the number of survey responses and have a more comprehensive data set from different types of crises

- Revising and streamlining many of the quantitative indicators data, adding two new variables, and consolidating several others, for a more precise and reliable data set

- Improving the distribution of indicators to Pillars and renaming some of the Pillars and indicators to indicate more clearly what each measures

- Improving the means of presenting index scores by moving to a more intuitive 10 point scale (compared to the HRI 2007, which used a 7 point scale).

A more detailed explanation of the HRI 2008 methodology and the adjustments made since the first edition of the HRI can be found in the Technical Appendix at the end of this chapter.

Figure 3: HRI 2008: Correlation between quantitative and qualitative indicators

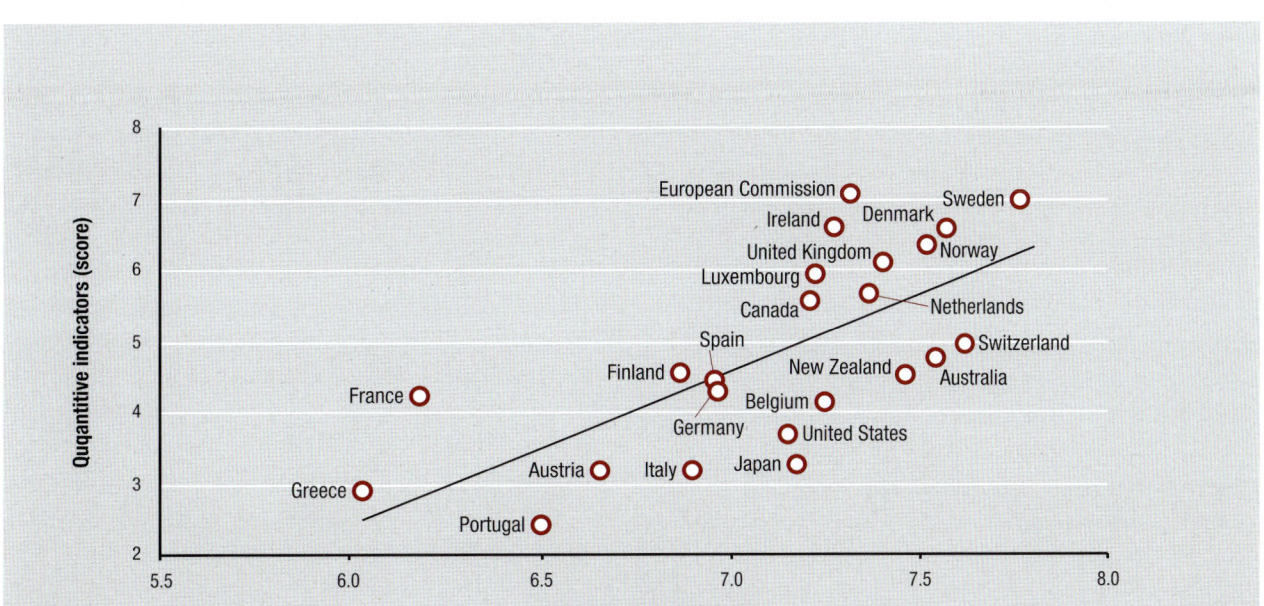

HRI 2008 main findings and analysis

Before examining the HRI 2008 results in more detail, it is important to place this year's exercise in context. The HRI 2008 is set against a backdrop of increased needs which are not covered by corresponding increases in aid budgets. Of note has been the dramatic increase in food and fuel prices, which according to some estimates has led to an additional 100 million people living in hunger, creating serious operational challenges for many humanitarian organisations.[17]

Within the humanitarian system, the ambitious plans for UN humanitarian reforms are proceeding at a sluggish pace, with significant challenges in implementing concepts such as the cluster approach, and strengthening the position of Humanitarian Coordinator. Meanwhile, the reform agenda has not necessarily been successful in including or relating to other parts of the system, such as the Red Cross Red Crescent and NGOs, and some suggest it is too UN-centric. Capacity continues to be a concern, both among operational actors and donor agencies. Many donors are facing serious resource limitations that challenge their ability to analyse and to contribute effectively to improving overall response efforts, much less to integrating and applying the GHD *Principles* to their own work.

The HRI 2008 findings must also be seen in light of the results of the HRI 2007. The pattern of the responses obtained in the 2008 survey broadly matches that gathered in the previous year's survey, as do the quantitative indicators. In addition, the findings from the Crisis Reports and surveys for the three crises that were repeated from 2007 show a high degree of correlation. This highlights the robust nature of the survey and quantitative data. (See figure 3.)

However, as explained above, several adjustments were made to improve the HRI. These included eliminating some indicators, adding some new ones, adjusting some to be more precise, and modifying the distribution of some indicators between the Pillars. While the basic structure and methodological framework of the HRI is similar enough between the two years, these adjustments mean that it is difficult to make direct comparisons for several reasons. First, the rankings are based on a comparison of each country relative to their peers in the group, not against any benchmark of "perfect" performance. Second, the Index aims to track progress over time, but as it is only two years old it is still too early to identify trends and patterns around specific countries. Similarly, many donors have recently undergone com-

prehensive reviews of their humanitarian assistance policies and funding commitments, but the impact of these changes will take time to register in the HRI. Therefore the ranking of a country relative to its position in 2007 is orientative, and not necessarily conclusive.

Table 2: HRI rankings 2007 and 2008

Donor	HRI 2008 Rank	HRI 2007 Rank
Sweden	1	1
Norway	2	2
Denmark	3	3
Ireland	4	6
European Commision	5	5
Netherlands	6	4
Luxembourg	7	12
United Kingdom	8	9
Switzerland	9	10
Canada	10	7
Australia	11	14
Finland	12	11
New Zealand	13	8
Belgium	14	15
United States	15	16
Spain	16	17
Germany	17	13
Japan	18	18
Italy	19	22
France	20	19
Austria	21	20
Portugal	22	21
Greece	23	23

This year's ranking (Table 2) shows that overall there are few differences in the rankings of the rated donor countries compared to 2007. Luxembourg shows the most change from 2007, moving up five places. This is partly due to the adjustment to the indicators on generosity and 'fair share', where in comparison to its GNI the country does well. Germany dropped four positions in the overall ranking, mainly due to its scores in Pillars 1 to 4 as compared to other countries. Australia also shows some movement since the 2007 ranking, principally due to improvements in the qualitatitive data from the survey, while Canada's lower ranking this year is partially explained by its scores in comparison to other countries in indicators such as funding for forgotten emergencies and crises with low media coverage, as well as its scores from survey data.

For the 2008 ranking, Sweden, Norway, Denmark, Ireland and the European Commission do well compared to their peers in their attempts to adhere to many of the principles contained in the GHD. These countries together occupied many of the top five slots in all five of the HRI's Pillars. The Netherlands, Luxembourg and the United Kingdom also ranked within the top third of the group. That said, all of these donors show gaps in their policies and practices, and a top ranking reflects that a donor has performed better than other donor countries in a given area, as opposed to what the donor can achieve and should aspire to.

Switzerland, Canada, Australia, Finland and New Zealand are part of the mid-range group of donors. These countries do relatively well in many of the Pillars, but in some areas do less well in relation to their peers. Others donors in this group include Belgium, the United States and Spain. The members of this group have room for improvement in various aspects of their humanitarian assistance policies and practices, and have some way to go before they can be ranked with the top donors.

Finally, there is a group of six countries, Japan, Italy, France, Austria, Portugal and Greece, which constitute the bottom of the Index, with scores that are consistently lower than the OECD/DAC average in each of the five Pillars of the HRI. These countries, for a variety of reasons that include the size of their humanitarian budgets, their experience and capacity, lag clearly behind the rest of their peers.

Because the rankings are based on a compilation of both the quantitative and qualitative data, the scores can disguise strengths and weaknesses in specific areas. In some cases, not all the negative or positive assessments by humanitarian agencies of individual donor behaviour are captured by the survey or the hard data. For example, while some donors came out well in the overall survey questionnaire results, in specific crisis contexts the results are mixed. Donors with a small number of survey responses overall are particularly problematic in that it is difficult to extract solid conclusions about their performance. The final proviso is that a relatively high score in any Pillar is not necessarily an indication of excellent performance, but rather, shows the ranking of a donor relative to its peers.

The following sections provide more detailed analysis of the HRI scores and quantitative and qualitative indicators, supported by evidence from the survey and the Crisis Reports. Table 3 provides a breakdown of the rankings and scores of donors by Pillar.

Table 3: HRI 2008 – Rankings and Scores by Pillars

	OVERALL RANKING		Responding to needs		Supporting local capacity and recovery		Working with humanitarian partners		Promoting standards and enhancing implementation		Promoting Learning and accountability	
Donor	Rank	Score	Rank	Score	Rank	Score	Rank	Score	Rank	Score	Rank	Score
Sweden	1	7.90	1	8.05	3	6.83	1	8.10	2	8.43	2	8.26
Norway	2	7.60	3	7.86	12	6.33	2	8.07	1	8.66	10	7.06
Denmark	3	7.39	7	7.02	1	7.06	8	6.57	3	8.10	1	8.94
Ireland	4	7.36	4	7.80	5	6.72	4	7.35	15	6.89	6	7.81
European Commission	5	7.18	6	7.07	2	6.90	9	6.45	4	7.64	3	8.25
Netherlands	6	7.10	5	7.38	16	5.91	3	7.38	10	7.22	7	7.65
Luxembourg	7	7.06	2	7.93	7	6.67	5	6.80	5	7.61	19	5.63
United Kingdom	8	6.98	10	6.66	8	6.66	6	6.77	12	7.15	5	8.14
Switzerland	9	6.86	9	6.85	10	6.35	7	6.66	7	7.43	9	7.28
Canada	10	6.62	13	6.21	9	6.48	12	5.63	8	7.41	4	8.17
Australia	11	6.51	11	6.30	6	6.69	13	5.58	6	7.52	11	6.92
Finland	12	6.32	8	6.93	21	5.29	10	5.67	9	7.23	13	6.41
New Zealand	13	6.28	12	6.24	4	6.78	14	5.55	14	6.90	16	6.05
Belgium	14	6.17	14	6.11	13	6.19	11	5.64	11	7.15	18	5.98
United States	15	6.08	15	6.08	17	5.81	16	5.46	23	5.73	8	7.61
Spain	16	6.07	16	6.04	11	6.34	15	5.50	18	6.48	14	6.12
Germany	17	5.99	17	5.87	19	5.63	17	5.26	13	7.06	12	6.65
Japan	18	5.66	21	5.29	14	6.04	19	4.93	16	6.53	17	5.99
Italy	19	5.56	20	5.44	15	5.94	18	5.01	17	6.53	21	5.07
France	20	5.55	18	5.59	22	5.23	20	4.84	20	6.29	15	6.08
Austria	21	5.32	19	5.44	20	5.31	21	4.55	19	6.32	20	5.10
Portugal	22	5.10	23	4.72	18	5.80	22	4.51	21	5.96	22	4.85
Greece	23	4.80	22	5.02	23	4.89	23	3.99	22	5.94	23	4.18

Pillar 1: Responding to needs

Responding to needs is the most heavily weighted Pillar in the HRI, corresponding to the core GHD *Principles* that the primary aims of humanitarian assistance should be to save lives, prevent and alleviate suffering, and restore dignity. The GHD *Principles* place a great deal of emphasis on donors providing humanitarian assistance in ways that are impartial, neutral, independent and focused exclusively on humanitarian objectives. The HRI findings show that many donors are still influenced by other factors when it comes to allocating humanitarian resources (see Table 4).

In this Pillar, two relatively small donors, Luxembourg and Ireland (ranked 2nd and 4th respectively), stood out for their performance, ranking in the top third of the group. They join Sweden (1st), Norway (3rd), the Netherlands (5th), the EC (6th), Denmark (7th) and Finland (8th). This group of donors best represents good efforts to align responses to need, generosity in the levels of funding committed, and ensuring that humanitarian assistance is impartial, neutral and independent. As such they are an example for others.

Three of the quantitative indicators evaluating the donors' global funding patterns give mixed results. As a group there is little correlation between donor humanitarian funding and the historical ties and geographic proximity of the recipient country suffering a humanitarian crisis – with the notable exceptions of Japan and Australia which, due to their regional funding policies, score far below the rest of their peers. However, in the indicators measuring funding to forgotten emergencies and those with low media coverage, and the sectoral distribution of funding through UN appeals, as a group donors score more poorly compared to other indicators, with a large variation between the top and bottom ranked donors. This would seem to indicate that there are numerous, and at times competing, reasons that drive donor funding beyond purely humanitarian concerns. Furthermore, it is important to note that of the quantitative indicators that make up this Pillar, the lowest results as a group are in the indicator on generosity of humanitarian assistance, although there is a considerable difference between the top and bottom donors. This perhaps reflects the apparent gap between global humanitarian needs and the resources available in the humanitarian system (see Box 5 for more on generosity).

In terms of the crises studied, the average survey score for all donors was typically higher in this Pillar for the response to disasters caused by natural phenomena in Nicaragua, Bangladesh and Peru. However, in conflicts and complex emergencies, scores were considerably lower, especially in the case of the occupied Palestinian territories and Chad.

In all crises, there was a drop in all responses when participants were asked if they felt that the donor's action was independent of political or economic objectives. This is particularly evident in protracted conflict situations, as revealed in the survey results and Crisis Reports for Colombia, the occupied Palestinian territories, Sri Lanka, Sudan and Afghanistan, where the intersection of political, security and economic interests too often clash with the humanitarian objectives of saving lives and preventing and alleviating suffering.

The figures and scores against the indicators are backed up by the analysis emerging from the field research and Crisis Reports. Even top-ranked donors at times demonstrate inconsistencies in their decisions to provide principled humanitarian aid where it is most needed, in proportion to needs.[18] In Afghanistan, despite acute needs and the ongoing conflict, many of the OECD/DAC countries – some directly engaged in the conflict are unwilling to qualify the situation as a humanitarian crisis, and channel funding mainly to nation-building and development programmes explicitly linked to existing Provincial Reconstruction Teams managed by their military. Similarly, the HRI field research in the occupied Palestinian territories shows that some donors were viewed as biased and that aid was not perceived as being necessarily directed in accordance to need.

As part of the survey, DARA also asked agencies if they had refused funding from any donors, and found that in all crises there were examples of this. The worst case was in Afghanistan, where humanitarian agencies had serious issues about OECD/DAC donors, many of whom are directly engaged in the conflict, mixing political and military objectives with humanitarian assistance. Similarly, but to a lesser extent, in Chad France was perceived as mixing political, military and humanitarian objectives.

Many aid agencies working in the occupied Palestinian territories and Colombia raised concerns about requirements imposed by some donors (particularly the United States and European Commission) to ensure that humanitarian assistance did not support groups classified as terrorist organisations. Several agencies interviewed often stated that this made it operationally impossible for them to work, and contravened humanitarian principles on impartiality, neutrality and independence. These issues are not new, but do reinforce the need for the international community to revisit the question of how to ensure humanitarian action meets its primary objectives of saving lives and alleviating suffering without compromising its basic principles.

A related issue emerging from the HRI findings is around needs assessments. One of the greatest weaknesses in the current humanitarian system is the absence of a homogenously recognised means of determining overall global needs – and criteria on how to distribute aid equitably among crises.[19] Good needs assessments are a critical tool for identifying what kind of assistance is needed, where and for whom. In theory, donors rely on needs assessments to make funding decisions, yet even the best assessments do not necessarily mean that appeals for assistance are funded adequately. Too many crises are still 'forgotten' and do not receive the attention or funding that they need, when they need it, compared to other crises.

It is also clear from the HRI findings that donors could do more to support operational actors to carry out needs assessments. Many of the humanitarian agencies interviewed stated that they themselves take on this responsibility, using their own resources. Too often this means trying to undertake a quick assessment in order to apply for funding, at the expense of a longer process engaging affected populations in identifying needs and designing appropriate and relevant interventions. As a result, there is typically a gap between donor commitments to meet immediate relief needs, and funding required to help people rebuild their lives after a disaster.

Similarly, donors consistently scored lower on survey questions about the reallocation of funds from different crises, and the perceived capacity of donors for informed decision-making. The scores around donor commitment to ongoing crises shows a significant gap between the responses to the protracted and highly politicised crises in Colombia and the occupied Palestinian territories and the scores from other crises. There are also mixed results in the quantitative indicators in this Pillar, which look at the appropriateness, timeliness and flexibility of funding. As a group, donors score poorly in the indicators for timely funding to complex emergencies with UN appeals, and lower still in timely funding to sudden onset disasters and IFRC emergency appeals.

Summary

The results from this Pillar suggest that despite the normative nature of the GHD *Principles*, donors as a whole are still perceived as not always respecting the principles of impartiality, neutrality and independence, nor providing funding based solely on humanitarian needs.

Box 5: Donor generosity relative to its GNI

Generosity is more than just giving money. The HRI 2008 includes a new indicator on the generosity of a country's humanitarian assistance in comparison to its Gross National Income (GNI). This indicator complements other indicators around the fair share of humanitarian assistance by giving credit to countries that shouldered a more generous share of the international burden of aid. Currently there is no accepted benchmark of how much a rich country should contribute to support humanitarian action, though the Millennium Development Goals call for a commitment to providing 0.7% of GDP for Official Development Assistance (ODA). There have been some suggestions of setting aside up to 10% of ODA funding for humanitarian assistance. Nevertheless, given the unpredictable nature of the number and magnitude of crises in any given year, some donors have put in place policies and mechanisms to ensure that funding is available to support ongoing crises without jeopardising funding for emerging crises. Generosity, however, is not the only issue – it is also about how the money is distributed and how it is used. Simply providing funding generously without any engagement with operational actors or the government of the crisis affected country as to how it will be spent, or monitoring and oversight on the quality of programming is a less than adequate approach. Finding a balance is a challenge for all donors.

Generosity of humanitarian assistance

Donor	Rank
Luxembourg	1
Norway	1
Sweden	3
Ireland	4
Netherlands	5
Denmark	6
Switzerland	7
Finland	8
Australia	9
New Zealand	10
United Kingdom	11
Canada	12
United States	13
Belgium	14
Spain	15
Germany	16
Greece	17
Italy	18
France	19
Japan	20
Austria	21
Portugal	22
European Community	N/A

Table 4: Pillar 1 Rankings

Qualitative indicators based on the Questionnaire on Good Humanitarian Donorship	Saving lives and maintaining dignity	Impartiality	Neutrality	Independence	Reallocation of funds from other crises	Funding needs assessments	Timely funding	Funding in proportion to need	Donor capacity for informed decision-making	Commitment to on-going crises
Donor										
Australia	11	9	13	14	2	1	1	6	5	13
Austria	19	15	10	15	22	21	12	21	N/A	20
Belgium	9	12	11	17	15	10	22	9	10	21
Canada	10	14	15	8	11	17	13	8	7	4
Denmark	13	1	2	12	9	3	9	5	14	10
European Commission	12	11	17	10	18	16	17	11	1	2
Finland	2	8	18	20	16	11	21	18	17	5
France	23	22	23	23	14	20	20	20	15	16
Germany	16	2	1	4	19	18	8	15	13	6
Greece	22	23	22	19	20	22	23	23	N/A	17
Ireland	4	5	5	2	4	4	7	2	18	1
Italy	20	20	19	18	21	19	18	16	12	12
Japan	15	16	8	11	10	12	15	13	6	14
Luxembourg	8	7	3	7	12	14	3	17	N/A	11
Netherlands	6	13	16	9	7	8	11	7	9	8
New Zealand	3	3	7	5	8	6	2	19	N/A	19
Norway	5	10	12	6	3	7	10	4	11	22
Portugal	21	21	9	21	23	23	19	22	N/A	23
Spain	14	17	20	13	17	15	16	12	16	14
Sweden	7	4	4	3	1	5	6	1	4	3
Switzerland	1	6	6	1	5	2	5	3	8	9
United Kingdom	18	18	14	16	6	9	14	10	3	7
United States	17	19	21	22	13	13	4	14	2	18

PILLAR 1: RESPONDING TO NEEDS

Quantitative Indicators	Funding to crisis countries with historical ties and geographical proximity	Funding to forgotten emergencies and those with low media coverage	Timely funding to complex emergencies with UN appeals	Timely funding to onset disasters and IFRC emergency appeals	Generosity of humanitarian assistance	Distribution of funding relative to ECHO's Crisis and Vulnerability Indices	Sectoral distribution of funding through UN appeals
Donor							
Australia	21	11	7	12	9	2	9
Austria	2	14	22	19	21	1	1
Belgium	13	1	20	18	14	3	4
Canada	10	15	11	8	11	4	17
Denmark	11	21	5	2	6	22	8
European Commission	20	10	16	16	N/A	6	7
Finland	5	7	13	4	8	9	12
France	12	1	15	11	19	10	10
Germany	17	13	19	13	16	13	6
Greece	6	20	10	22	17	14	18
Ireland	8	9	1	15	4	11	19
Italy	7	17	21	3	18	12	13
Japan	22	22	14	9	20	5	11
Luxembourg	3	3	8	20	1	18	20
Netherlands	15	12	6	6	5	16	5
New Zealand	16	18	17	5	12	15	15
Norway	9	8	4	21	1	19	16
Portugal	N/A	N/A	N/A	N/A	22	23	N/A
Spain	14	19	9	1	15	7	14
Sweden	1	6	1	10	3	20	21
Switzerland	4	4	18	14	7	21	22
United Kingdom	18	5	3	7	10	17	1
United States	19	16	12	17	13	8	1

Main Sources: OCHA FTS, OECD/DAC, the World Bank, IFRC, the Federal Reserve, ECHO, Alertnet

Addressing this is therefore an outstanding challenge for donors, in particular in conflicts and politicised complex emergencies. Failure to do so can both jeopardise the security and effectiveness of humanitarian action, and even lead to operational agencies rejecting certain donors' funds. The results also reflect the gap between available funds and global humanitarian needs, and the fact that, despite existing efforts, there remain many underfunded or forgotten crises and no shared understanding of global humanitarian needs. Lastly, if donors are to fully support GHD Principle 6 "allocate humanitarian funding in proportion to needs and on the basis of needs assessments" they could do more to fund and improve the quality of needs assessments, and promote a continual process of monitoring how needs evolve over the course of a crisis.

Pillar 2: Supporting local capacity and recovery

Pillar 2 *Supporting local capacity and long-term recovery* is based on the GHD *Principles* that recognise that an effective emergency response must meet immediate needs, while respecting and building local capacity to cope with crises, and laying the foundation for longer term recovery and development. The reasons are more than obvious: a crisis can push back years of development efforts, especially at the level of human and social capital. According to some estimates, every dollar invested in disaster risk reduction and preparedness is equivalent to a saving of roughly seven dollars in disaster response.[20] Similar estimates are made for conflict prevention.[21] At the community level, people need to have the information that helps them prepare for and respond to crises, and to quickly recover after a crisis. The HRI findings confirm that donors could improve in the area of supporting local capacity and linking relief to recovery and development, as well as in the area of supporting beneficiary involvement and participation in programming. (See Table 5).

Denmark takes top place in Pillar 2, followed by the European Commission and Sweden. New Zealand and Ireland also did well in this Pillar, ranking 4th and 5th respectively, demonstrating a particular niche in supporting work in this area, despite their size compared to larger donors. Australia (6th), Luxembourg (7th) and the United Kingdom (8th) also did reasonably well in comparison to their peers in supporting local disaster preparedness, and response capacity and recovery.

Nevertheless, donors in general did not receive high marks in the survey questions for this Pillar in each crisis. The survey responses are supported by the two quantitative indicators in the Pillar, which include

the second and third lowest average scores compared to the scores for other quantitative indicators in the Index. In general, the scores in this Pillar largely reflect many of the issues and concerns raised in the humanitarian sector over the past decade, demonstrating that this is still a problematic area for both donors and implementing agencies alike.[22]

The overall perception of donor support for issues around linking relief, recovery and development was lowest in Chad, followed by the Central African Republic and the Democratic Republic of the Congo. This is perhaps explained by the nature and complexities of the crises in these countries. Nevertheless, it is important to note the concerns of humanitarian agencies working in these crises that donors are not doing well to support longer-term recovery and development. The highest scores in this area were from Colombia, followed by Sri Lanka. This is interesting, considering that both countries are also facing protracted and politicised conflicts, but could possibly be explained by the relatively high response capacity of the state and local actors compared to other countries.

In general, survey responses were low on questions asking if the objectives of donors' humanitarian assistance were consistent with preventing or strengthening emergency preparedness. Similarly, the perception of humanitarian actors about strengthening local and government capacity for response and mitigation were also low, particularly in Chad, the Democratic Republic of the Congo and the Central African Republic. Sudan, Sri Lanka and Peru were also below average, while Bangladesh, Nicaragua and Colombia showed the highest scores in this area, probably reflecting the investment in capacity building and disaster management in these countries.

Another interesting area is the question regarding the participation of affected populations in the design, implementation, monitoring and evaluation of programming. Here scores for Afghanistan were the lowest, whereas Sri Lanka, Colombia, Chad and the Democratic Republic of the Congo were all above average, showing that despite the difficult challenges in implementation in these contexts, donors have done reasonably well in supporting mechanisms for participation. In the case of Sri Lanka, longer-term presence of donors and operational actors due to post-tsunami programming, and the corresponding relationships developed with local actors, may explain why the scores are higher here.

With regard to the issues around linking relief to recovery and development, the HRI findings point to

Table 5: Pillar 2 Rankings

Qualitative indicators based on the Questionnaire on Good Humanitarian Donorship	PILLAR 2: SUPPORTING LOCAL CAPACITY AND RECOVERY							
	Strengthening preparedness	Involvement of beneficiaries in design and implementation	Involvement of beneficiaries in monitoring and evaluation	Strengthening government capacity for and response mitigation	Strengthening local capacity for and response mitigation	Strengthening resilience to cope with crises	Aligned to long-term development aims	Ensuring rapid recovery of sustainable livelihoods
Donor								
Australia	12	8	9	10	9	3	10	4
Austria	20	21	19	17	5	20	23	21
Belgium	9	11	2	5	19	14	11	5
Canada	11	14	14	8	8	15	14	14
Denmark	17	3	5	6	1	8	1	3
European Commission	7	1	5	11	2	7	16	18
Finland	5	16	20	16	23	23	20	23
France	22	23	22	21	22	21	15	17
Germany	10	17	18	20	15	19	21	19
Greece	21	21	23	22	21	22	22	22
Ireland	18	4	9	23	17	4	13	20
Italy	19	19	13	3	7	13	9	13
Japan	3	20	17	13	14	16	5	11
Luxembourg	8	15	16	19	20	18	17	7
Netherlands	6	7	7	12	15	17	12	12
New Zealand	1	18	21	1	13	5	3	1
Norway	4	12	11	4	18	9	6	9
Portugal	23	2	4	18	10	10	18	14
Spain	16	9	15	15	3	2	7	8
Sweden	2	6	1	2	4	6	4	6
Switzerland	13	13	8	9	6	1	2	2
United Kingdom	14	5	3	7	11	12	8	10
United States	15	10	12	14	12	11	19	16

Quantitative Indicators	PILLAR 2: SUPPORTING LOCAL CAPACITY AND RECOVERY	
	Funding to strengthen local capacity	Funding to international disaster risk mitigation mechanisms
Donor		
Australia	7	4
Austria	20	19
Belgium	5	18
Canada	6	5
Denmark	15	1
European Commission	3	8
Finland	16	19
France	22	14
Germany	13	16
Greece	21	19
Ireland	1	13
Italy	23	11
Japan	19	9
Luxembourg	9	1
Netherlands	18	17
New Zealand	1	19
Norway	17	7
Portugal	8	19
Spain	10	10
Sweden	11	3
Switzerland	12	12
United Kingdom	4	6
United States	14	15

Main Sources: OCHA FTS, OECD/DAC, the World Bank, IFRC, UNDP, ICRC, ISDR, the Federal Reserve

the need for both the development cooperation and humanitarian action sectors to align approaches and ensure greater policy coherence. Humanitarian agencies face great difficulties in trying to balance meeting short-term needs with longer-term recovery and development, which are often exacerbated by donors' procedural and policy practices that can hamper such efforts. Many agencies interviewed mentioned complex funding proposal processes, requirements to spend funds quickly within unrealistic timeframes, and lack of long-term financing arrangements as complicating their already difficult remit.

In light of the Millennium Development Goals and the Paris Declaration, development cooperation is beginning to systematically review aid efficiency, effectiveness and harmonisation, and apply the lessons learned in policy and practice.[23] Although humanitarian assistance has traditionally been isolated from development cooperation at both strategic and operational levels both sectors could benefit from a rethink as to how the two could work together more closely.

An encouraging sign is that many donors have begun to frame their humanitarian action policies within a broader development context that includes conflict prevention, conflict management, conflict reduction, peace-building, and post-conflict rehabilitation and recovery programmes. In particular, in line with their commitments under the Hyogo Framework for Action (HFA), there is a desire to better integrate disaster risk reduction into humanitarian action and development assistance. Nevertheless, there is still a long road ahead before these policy changes are reflected in donor practice at the field level. In this regard, many humanitarian agencies are better sighted on the issues and have made more progress to integrate them into their operational work than donors have. However, these issues raise concerns over retaining the impartial, neutral and independent nature of humanitarian action.

Summary

The evidence in this Pillar reflects many of the well-known and longstanding challenges faced by the humanitarian system in supporting disaster preparedness and mitigation initiatives, linking with recovery and long-term development efforts, and ensuring appropriate beneficiary participation. However, it also indicates that funding and support for these initiatives vary considerably between donors and across crises. Furthermore, more than just increased funding is required if donors wish to effectively strengthen local capacity to prepare,

mitigate and respond to crises; efforts should address all levels from the community up, and international tools and mechanism should be adapted to the local context, including, for example, the challenges posed by weak and failed states. Similarly, to systematically promote GHD Principle 9, donors may need to further review the relationship between their humanitarian and development policies, for example aligning the first of these with initiatives such as the Paris Declaration and the MDGs, without losing sight of the need to maintain the aims, objectives and independence of humanitarian action.

Pillar 3: Working with humanitarian partners

The third Pillar *Working with humanitarian partners* assesses how well donors support the work of agencies implementing the humanitarian response. The GHD *Principles* explicitly recognise the distinct but complementary roles of the UN system, the International Red Cross Red Crescent Movement, and NGOs in humanitarian action. The GHD *Principles* suggest that each of these channels is legitimate and important for a balanced and complementary response, and that donors should support the work of these agencies.

The HRI findings in this Pillar point to the need to strengthen the overall capacity of the humanitarian system to respond to current and future needs. The HRI Crisis Reports show that the international humanitarian system is stretched to the limit and faces enormous difficulties in meeting the needs of the millions of people whose lives are disrupted by crises. The better donors in this Pillar include Sweden (1st), Norway (2nd), the Netherlands (3rd) and Ireland (4th), closely followed by Luxembourg (5th), the United Kingdom (6th) and Switzerland (7th), but in general, all donors could do more in this important area. (See Table 6).

To a certain extent, the scores in this Pillar reflect the quality of the relationship between donors and their partners. Interestingly, in all of the crises studied, there is a significant and consistent pattern of lower responses in the survey questions that pertain to this Pillar compared to all other Pillars, highlighting that this is an area where donors in general have significant room for improvement. The lowest scores were seen in Nicaragua, Peru, and Chad, with Afghanistan at the bottom of the list. The occupied Palestinian territories, Bangladesh, Colombia, the Democratic Republic of the Congo and the Central African Republic all scored close to the overall average, while Sri Lanka scored well above.

The survey results are backed up by the quantitative indicators for this Pillar which show the lowest scores by group average compared to quantitative indicators in the other four Pillars. While some donors scored significantly above the average in some of the indicators, most scores were consistently low, with the donor average in the indicator on funding UN coordination mechanisms and common services the lowest scored in the Index. The results also reflect the evident differences between individual donor policies and their preferred funding channels including, for example, very mixed levels of support for the CERF and other quick disbursement mechanisms. These are important issues to address, given the emphasis of the UN humanitarian reforms on using the cluster approach and the role of the Humanitarian Coordinator as a means to improve coordination. These mechanisms perhaps do not yet receive an adequate level of support from donors to allow them to function effectively.

The HRI survey results show that there are three main areas of concern for operational agencies: reducing earmarking; longer-term funding arrangements; and supporting contingency planning and strengthening response capacity. Donors in all crises generally received poor marks for each of these questions. This is supported by many of the comments made in interviews conducted by the HRI teams, where many organisations complained about the lack of flexibility in funding, and the complexity of often different funding procedures for different phases of the response. In particular, several organisations noted the unrealistic short-term timeframe imposed by many donors for expending funds. On the positive side, donors generally scored reasonably well on the issue of the predictability of funding.

In some cases, the organisations interviewed indicated that they had refused funding from donors because they considered it inappropriate and too earmarked (often in reference to in-kind assistance or to a non-priority sector), or directed to specific geographic or programme areas where the donor had an interest, rather than where needs were greatest or where the organisation had experience and operational capacity. Other reasons included a lack of flexibility, heavy, bureaucratic procedures and the associated administrative costs. Interestingly, many of these comments are directed towards donors that are perceived as having the most capacity for informed decision-making. While it may be difficult to show a direct correlation between donor capacities and the perception of how difficult or easy donor procedures are for operational actors, it is an area that would benefit from further analysis.

There is often a sense of urgency in implementing a rapid response to a crisis, with donors under pressure to disburse funds at the expense of a proper contextual analysis and the time to build relations with actors in the field. But funding is not always the only issue. The response to Hurricane Mitch 10 years ago and the more recent Indian Ocean tsunami demonstrate that, despite the massive volume of funding available, the humanitarian system continues to be ill-equipped to respond to major crises and to build on local capacity. Often there are issues around safe humanitarian access, or the simple logistical challenges and huge expenses involved in having a presence in the crisis area – areas where formulas on costs-per-beneficiary simply cannot be calculated. In situations of protracted conflicts and complex emergencies and failed states, local capacity is often extremely weak, which is an additional factor, as seen in many of the HRI Crisis Reports. This is an important point, as donors and the UN agencies like WFP rely heavily on national Red Cross Red Crescent societies, NGOs and local organisations to deliver assistance and implement programmes at the community level. Yet this part of the humanitarian system often receives the least attention and assistance to build its own sustainable capacity.

On the positive side, the findings from the HRI Crisis Report for Bangladesh confirm that a long-term investment in capacity building can pay huge dividends in terms of saving lives. However, the overall HRI 2008 findings demonstrate that in general donors are not doing well when it comes to making an investment in building response capacity. Wealthy countries have the opportunity and responsibility to invest in building the capacity of their partners and to support improvements in the humanitarian system, so that when the next crisis hits, the international humanitarian system is ready. This type of investment is needed at all levels.

Local and national government authorities also need support to build their response capacity. At a time when more and more major emergencies require international interventions, host governments and local authorities also need tools and training on how to integrate international response mechanisms into national response systems. Similarly, the international humanitarian system needs to build its capacity and understanding of how to adapt international response mechanisms to local conditions, respecting and building local capacity and supporting long-term recovery. Donors can help by ensuring the funding and programmes they support help to build this critical capacity. Several of the crises studied found this to be an issue.

Table 6: Pillar 3 Rankings

Qualitative indicators based on the Questionnaire on Good Humanitarian Donorship	PILLAR 3: WORKING WITH HUMANITARIAN PARTNERS										
	Helping governments and local communities achieve better coordination	Supporting effective coordination efforts	Promoting NGOs and the Red Cross Movement	Supporting UN leadership and coordination role	Promoting ICRC	Predictable funding	Reducing earmarking	Flexible funding	Longer-term funding arrangements	Consistent support for implementation of humanitarian action	Supporting contingency planning and strengthening response capacity
Donor											
Australia	4	5	15	3	1	12	6	9	11	4	12
Austria	8	17	16	N/A	N/A	19	21	23	21	18	17
Belgium	11	12	11	10	5	15	12	16	9	1	9
Canada	13	15	12	9	7	8	13	13	13	17	19
Denmark	10	8	2	7	4	11	8	6	4	3	1
European Commision	6	4	10	12	11	9	23	18	14	8	14
Finland	18	12	20	11	16	20	5	10	20	21	7
France	23	23	21	18	18	17	22	15	18	20	23
Germany	20	18	13	16	14	5	19	20	19	16	16
Greece	22	22	22	N/A	N/A	23	18	21	23	23	22
Ireland	21	19	8	15	12	14	20	2	10	6	2
Italy	5	9	17	13	15	21	11	19	17	19	20
Japan	14	11	19	5	8	10	16	17	16	11	15
Luxembourg	19	15	18	N/A	N/A	18	4	4	5	15	4
Netherlands	12	7	4	8	10	3	7	8	6	7	11
New Zealand	1	10	6	N/A	N/A	16	1	1	7	13	10
Norway	7	1	5	1	2	4	2	3	2	5	8
Portugal	16	21	23	N/A	N/A	22	10	22	22	22	21
Spain	17	20	14	17	17	7	13	12	3	14	18
Sweden	2	2	7	2	3	2	3	5	1	2	5
Switzerland	3	3	1	4	5	1	9	7	12	9	3
United Kingdom	9	6	3	6	9	6	15	11	8	12	13
United States	15	14	9	14	13	13	17	14	15	10	6

Quantitative Indicators	PILLAR 3: WORKING WITH HUMANITARIAN PARTNERS					
	Funding UN coordination mechanisms and common services	Funding to NGOs	Funding to CERF and other quick disbursement mechanisms	Unearmarked funding	Funding UN Consolidated Inter-Agency Appeals	Funding IFRC and ICRC Appeals
Donor						
Australia	8	19	13	18	13	13
Austria	22	17	10	10	19	16
Belgium	9	15	12	19	11	11
Canada	11	14	8	15	9	12
Denmark	5	9	7	10	6	8
European Commision	N/A	4	N/A	23	N/A	N/A
Finland	6	18	9	12	7	6
France	19	11	19	9	18	18
Germany	20	1	15	20	17	17
Greece	17	20	22	14	21	20
Ireland	1	6	1	6	1	7
Italy	15	16	16	13	20	19
Japan	21	22	21	22	14	21
Luxembourg	16	10	1	17	1	1
Netherlands	4	5	1	1	5	5
New Zealand	12	21	14	5	15	10
Norway	1	3	1	4	1	4
Portugal	18	23	17	1	22	22
Spain	13	13	10	11	16	15
Sweden	1	8	1	7	1	1
Switzerland	7	12	11	3	12	1
United Kingdom	10	1	1	8	8	9
United States	14	7	20	21	10	14

Main Sources: OCHA FTS, OECD/DAC,ICRC, IFRC, the Federal Reserve

At the international level, many efforts have gone into reforming the humanitarian system, but the conclusions of the HRI field research show mixed results in how those reforms are working in different crisis contexts. The GHD Principles recognise the critical role of the UN system, the Red Cross Red Crescent and NGOs in implementation of humanitarian action. But the donor community cannot rely on these vital actors without also supporting and investing in building the institutional capacity of these humanitarian partners. Donors can play a role in ensuring that the reform agenda of the humanitarian system is re-energised and accelerated, and that it moves beyond its current focus on the UN. This includes supporting coordination mechanisms, investing in contingency planning and providing long-term funding arrangements to allow all parts of the system to maintain a standing capacity to respond efficiently to multiple emergencies around the world. This theme appears frequently in many of the crises reports for this year's HRI.

The quality of the relationship and the level of trust between donors and operational actors are an important factor in ensuring an effective, coordinated response. Donors could benefit from strengthening their relationship with humanitarian partners on whom they can rely to implement parts of their humanitarian aid programmes when the need arises. One way donors could facilitate their partners' work would be by, for example, establishing framework agreements and easy access to contingency funds, and ensuring that the procedures that govern this relationship are flexible and not bureaucratic, especially when it comes to adapting quickly to changing needs.

The perceptions of operational agencies in the different crises studied also suggest that rich countries need to invest in strengthening their own capacity to make informed decisions based on good assessments of needs, good knowledge of the context, and a good understanding of what works well. Some donors have reduced their staff resources, which makes it more difficult to monitor and follow-up on the funding they provide to different operational agencies and crises, much less build and maintain a good relationship with partners. In order to improve the quality of humanitarian action, donors should consider how to invest in and expand their own capacity to better assess unfolding and continuing needs, and coordinate efforts. Otherwise, there is a risk that humanitarian assistance provided by donors will be misguided or will be used ineffectively and inefficiently. The focus of these efforts should be to boost donor capacity and expertise at both headquarter and field level without, however, supplanting or undermining the experience, roles and responsibilities of operational agencies or national organisations and authorities where it exists.

Summary

The results in this Pillar are among the lowest in the Index which suggest that there is significant scope for improvement in donors' relationships with their humanitarian partners. Donors rely on their implementing partners to ensure that the assistance they provide reaches those in need. Conversely, humanitarian agencies rely on donor funding to allow them to operate. As reflected in the GHD *Principles* this relationship needs to be balanced and equitable, and respectful of the principles that guide the work of partners, particularly those of neutral, impartial humanitarian action. If donors are to achieve the aims of the GHD *Principles* to improve the overall effectiveness of the delivery of humanitarian aid, they should consider the benefits of strategically investing in building the capacity of the different elements of the humanitarian system – and the costs if they do not. This investment is critical if the system is to respond adequately to the increasing demands on it, much less make the critical improvements needed to function efficiently and effectively. To support their humanitarian partners more effectively, donors could continue to streamline and harmonise their procedures and processes, provide longer-term, flexible funding arrangements, and support contingency planning and coordination mechanisms. Perhaps most importantly, donors could collectively invest in ensuring the success of the UN humanitarian reform process.

Pillar 4: Promoting principles and standards

The promotion and application of internationally recognised standards and principles is the fourth Pillar of the HRI. It is built around the GHD *Principles* that call on donors to integrate such standards into their policies and practices, and ensure that partners do likewise.

Here Norway (1st), Sweden (2nd) and Denmark (3rd) take the top three slots. The European Commission (4th), Luxembourg (5th), Australia (6th), Switzerland (7th) and Canada (8th) make it into the top third of the group. France, Portugal, Greece and the United States occupy the lowest ranks in this Pillar. (See Table 7).

The three quantitative indicators used in this Pillar measure the implementation of and support for interna-

Table 7: Pillar 4 Rankings

Qualitative indicators based on the Questionnaire on Good Humanitarian Donorship	PILLAR 4: PROMOTING STANDARDS AND ENHANCING IMPLEMENTATION					
Donor	Donor engagement in protection and assistance to civilians	Respecting or promoting human rights	Respecting or promoting international humanitarian law	Supporting needs of internally displaced persons	Facilitating safe humanitarian access	Affirming primary role of civilian organizations
Australia	17	15	7	1	1	10
Austria	22	21	N/A	N/A	19	21
Belgium	3	7	9	14	15	1
Canada	7	10	12	13	12	15
Denmark	4	2	4	16	8	5
European Commission	11	16	10	6	11	14
Finland	16	5	2	5	21	19
France	23	23	18	18	22	20
Germany	18	17	11	15	6	17
Greece	21	22	N/A	N/A	23	22
Ireland	20	14	15	9	16	16
Italy	10	20	16	10	18	12
Japan	9	11	5	2	17	2
Luxembourg	15	19	N/A	N/A	7	8
Netherlands	12	9	8	12	10	9
New Zealand	8	6	N/A	N/A	5	13
Norway	2	4	3	4	3	7
Portugal	14	7	N/A	N/A	4	23
Spain	19	12	17	17	20	4
Sweden	1	3	6	3	2	6
Switzerland	5	1	1	11	9	3
United Kingdom	13	13	14	8	14	11
United States	6	18	13	7	13	18

Quantitative Indicators	PILLAR 4: PROMOTING STANDARDS AND ENHANCING IMPLEMENTATION		
Donor	Implementing international humanitarian law	Implementating human rights law	Implementing refugee law
Australia	12	12	6
Austria	10	16	18
Belgium	9	16	10
Canada	7	5	8
Denmark	6	3	3
European Commission	N/A	N/A	N/A
Finland	5	19	7
France	17	8	17
Germany	13	9	13
Greece	14	13	22
Ireland	19	2	15
Italy	16	20	16
Japan	15	21	21
Luxembourg	3	7	5
Netherlands	18	11	4
New Zealand	11	18	9
Norway	1	1	1
Portugal	21	6	20
Spain	20	10	11
Sweden	1	4	2
Switzerland	4	15	14
United Kingdom	8	14	12
United States	22	22	19

Main Sources: OCHA FTS, OECD/DAC, the World Bank, EU, ICRC, OHCHR, UNHCR, the Federal Reserve

tional humanitarian law, human rights law and refugee law, including ratification of treaties and funding to the agencies entrusted with promoting the application of these international laws. Across the three indicators donors perform relatively homogenously, with the notable exceptions of Norway, which scores well, and the United States, which scores poorly. The average donor scores are lowest in the area of support for refugee law.

There is wide variance between the overall scores in this Pillar when looking at the 11 crises studied. The responses to the survey in Sri Lanka and Peru, at the top of the list, score well above the responses from other crises, followed by Sudan, Bangladesh and Chad. The responses in Colombia were just below the average, while the responses collected in the occupied Palestinian territories, Afghanistan, Nicaragua and the Central African Republic all have similar scores well below the average in this Pillar.

Some of this variance is due to the nature of the crisis studied. Surveys from conflict situations and complex emergencies show similar low scores for questions around protection and assistance to civilians, with similar low scores on questions on safe humanitarian access. This, in fact, is one of the most common concerns expressed by humanitarian agencies, where the perception is that donors can and should do much more to advocate and support these issues in crisis-affected countries, especially human rights, and international humanitarian law. Yet these are precisely the situations were several humanitarian agencies felt that many donors fail to apply the very international laws, principles and standards that they have themselves committed to.

One question that received generally positive responses in all of the crises studied was whether donors were perceived as affirming the primary role of civilian organisations. However, again there were differences in Afghanistan and Colombia, where the responses were lower than the overall average, and where comments from agencies reflect uneasiness about the confusion between military and political objectives, the use of private contractors, and the aims of humanitarian assistance.

Many donors consistently ranked low in promoting the use of quality standards and principles, as called for in the GHD Principles. Even donors that are perceived as doing reasonably well in promoting such principles and standards could do more to monitor and follow-up their application by the humanitarian partners. Many of the humanitarian agencies interviewed stated that they consistently attempt to apply such standards, not because this is an explicit requirement of donors, but because this is part of their own commitment to good practice.

Summary

The results reflect that there is considerable divergence in donor performance in different crises – with scope for greater efforts to be made in conflict situations, in which the very international laws and principles referred to in the corresponding GHD *Principles* are most likely to be violated. This is especially the case for providing more vigorous support for protection and assistance, and for donors to use their influence with host governments and other actors to ensure safe humanitarian access. As well as respecting and promoting international principles and guidelines themselves, if donors want to systematically make these an integral part of humanitarian actions they will require effective means to support their application by operational partners.

Pillar 5: Promoting learning and accountability

The fifth Pillar, learning and accountability, shows how well donors support initiatives to improve the quality and effectiveness of humanitarian action.

Denmark, Sweden, the European Commission, Canada and the United Kingdom are the top five donors in this Pillar, reflecting a strong commitment to promoting the use of evaluations to inform policy and programming, and support for accountability initiatives in the sector. Ireland (6th), the Netherlands (7th) and the United States (8th) also did well in this Pillar. (See Table 8).

In the quantitative indicators for the Pillar, donors as a group score relatively well in comparison to other Pillars, though there is still evident room for improvement. There is also significant variation between the highest and lowest scoring donors, in particular in the indicator evaluating participation in and funding for accountability initiatives.

Donors were perceived as doing reasonably well in all of the crises studied in this Pillar. Nicaragua and Bangladesh were the two crises with the top scores in this Pillar, followed by the Central African Republic, Sudan and Sri Lanka. Afghanistan also was above the average. The crises with below average scores were Colombia, Peru and the occupied Palestinian territories. The response for Chad was considerably lower than the average.

In terms of some of the specific questions asked in the survey, the perception of donor commitment to accountability in humanitarian action was reasonably high in all crises. However, there were a wide range of responses on whether donors encouraged regular evalu-

Table 8: Pillar 5 Rankings

PILLAR 5: PROMOTING LEARNING AND ACCOUNTABILITY			
Qualitative indicators based on the Questionnaire on Good Humanitarian Donorship	Commitment of accountability in humanitarian action	Supporting learning and accountability initiatives	Encouraging regular evaluations
Donor			
Australia	7	6	12
Austria	18	18	18
Belgium	4	14	5
Canada	15	12	8
Denmark	2	1	3
European Commission	9	10	2
Finland	1	16	20
France	23	22	23
Germany	14	15	21
Greece	22	23	22
Ireland	18	13	6
Italy	16	21	10
Japan	10	17	19
Luxembourg	17	9	11
Netherlands	12	7	7
New Zealand	11	2	15
Norway	13	8	13
Portugal	21	20	16
Spain	20	19	17
Sweden	6	4	4
Switzerland	5	3	14
United Kingdom	3	5	1
United States	8	11	9

PILLAR 5: PROMOTING LEARNING AND ACCOUNTABILITY		
Quantitative Indicators	Participating in and funding accountability initiatives	Number of evaluations
Donor		
Australia	10	14
Austria	21	18
Belgium	15	20
Canada	3	1
Denmark	1	3
European Commission	4	2
Finland	7	17
France	11	12
Germany	17	6
Greece	21	20
Ireland	1	9
Italy	19	20
Japan	18	13
Luxembourg	21	15
Netherlands	8	8
New Zealand	16	18
Norway	13	9
Portugal	20	20
Spain	14	15
Sweden	5	4
Switzerland	9	9
United Kingdom	6	5
United States	12	7

Main Sources: OCHA FTS, OECD/DAC, Accountability initiatives, the Federal reserve

ation. In this question, Bangladesh showed the highest scores, followed by the Democratic Republic of the Congo, and the Central African Republic. Chad and Sri Lanka were the crises with the lowest average scores.

This is an area where many donors and humanitarian agencies have a positive common interest. Evaluations of humanitarian action are becoming more and more a standard procedure for both parties, and there is evidence from many of the crises studies that some of the organisations dedicated to monitoring and promoting quality and accountability in the sector are actively present in the field in the midst of the crisis to promote better responses by operational actors. However, when looking at the issues emerging from the Crisis Reports, it is also clear that the utilisation of evaluations is low,[24] and systematically applying learning remains a challenge for the sector. What is also clear from the field research is that an area where donors rarely invest is in an assessment of the quality of their relationship with their partners, and an evaluation of their own performance. The HRI has helped to raise this issue as a valid question, and will continue to promote this as a line of research.

Furthermore, the comments from many of the humanitarian agencies interviewed as part of the HRI field research show that there is a perception that donors could do much more to apply and promote the same standards for transparency and accountability that are expected from their partners – particularly in politicised crises.

A broader dimension of accountability is the responsibility of donors to ensure that the overall humanitarian system works better to meet its objectives of saving lives and restoring dignity for people affected by disasters and crisis. In many respects, the HRI 2008 findings reflect the shortcomings in the international humanitarian response system, such as effective coordination and the uneven implementation of the clusters approach. Although an in-depth analysis of these problems is beyond this report, the subsequent chapters in the publication reviewing the 11 crises visited by HRI teams provide insights into these issues and other areas that require further debate.

Perhaps one of the most striking findings from the HRI process is the lack of awareness of the GHD initiative among humanitarian agencies. According to the HRI survey results, just over a third (34.5 percent) of representatives of humanitarian agencies interviewed knew about the GHD *Principles*, but another third (33 percent) of their colleagues had never even heard of the initiative (49 percent in Afghanistan, 41 percent in Chad and Bangladesh). Even in pilot implementation

countries, such as the Democratic Republic of the Congo, 25 percent of the agencies surveyed had no knowledge of the initiative. The very process of preparing the HRI has done much to disseminate the GHD *Principles*, but if the aim and intent of the GHD initiative is to encourage a wider understanding and application of Good Humanitarian Donorship Principles and Best Practice, it would seem that donors themselves have to do much more to disseminate the principles and ensure implementation at the field level.

Summary
The results suggest that donors on the whole do well in following GHD Principles 15, 21, 22 and 23, although there is considerable divergence between the highest and lowest ranked donors. This raises the possibility that accountability, learning and best practice is not prioritised equally within the donor group, and that those donors who could benefit most from this are at risk of being left behind. Collectively, donors could do much more to work towards a shared understanding among themselves about what is good donor practice and make more efforts to disseminate these messages further across the humanitarian system, including integrating new and non-traditional donors into the dialogue. In order to ensure that the spirit of the GHD is translated into tangible improvements in the implementation of humanitarian action, donors should do more to monitor the application of the outcomes of evaluations and learning exercises in their policies, procedures and partners, and strengthen their commitment to improving accountability towards populations affected by crises.

Individual donor rankings and scores

The following section provides an overview of the ranking and scores for each of the 23 donors included in the HRI. It is not intended as a full assessment of donor performance, but rather highlights areas in which donors scored well and those in which they did not. These overviews are based on the compilations of scores from the quantitative and qualitative indicators in the HRI. The overview also includes, when appropriate, a description of how the donor is perceived in different crises based on a comparison of the average survey question scores across the 11 crises.[25]

Australia

Australia is ranked 11th in the 2008 HRI. Australia ranked best compared to its peers in Pillars 2 and 4 – 6th in both – and worst – 13th – in Pillar 3. In breaking down the Index by individual indicator, Australia ranked among the top donors for funding needs assessments, timely funding, promoting the ICRC, supporting needs of internally displaced persons and facilitating safe humanitarian access. However, it ranked 21st in funding crisis countries with historical ties and geographical proximity, 19th in funding NGOs, 18th in unearmarked funding, 17th in donor engagement in protection of and assistance to civilians and 15th in respecting or promoting human rights. On the other hand, Australia is perceived as providing timely funding, confirmed by its high rankings for all three timeliness indicators in the Pillar. It is also judged to have ample donor capacity (5th). On the positive side, Australia's scores reflect its strong support for needs assessments and the timeliness of its funding procedures. Its regional funding policy however, appears contrary to the spirit of the GHD.

Austria

Austria is ranked 21st in the 2008 HRI. Austria's low overall position is due to its consistently low ranking across the Pillars: 19th in Pillars 1 and 4, 21st in Pillar 3 and 20th in the remainder. In terms of specific indicators, Austria was top ranked in sectoral distribution of funding through UN appeals and distribution of funding relative to ECHO's Crisis and Vulnerability Indices, second in funding crisis countries with historical ties and geographical proximity, fifth in strengthening local capacity for response and mitigation and 8th in helping governments and local communities achieve better coordination. It ranked last in alignment to long-term development aims and flexible funding, and second to last in reallocation of funds from other crises, timely funding to complex emergencies with UN appeals, and donor engagement in protection and assistance to civilians. Austria clearly has much room for improvement suggesting that it might benefit from a comprehensive review of its policy framework in light of the GHD *Principles*.

Belgium

Belgium is ranked 14th in the 2008 HRI. Belgium ranked 11th in both Pillar 3 and 4 and 18th in Pillar 5. Nevertheless, it ranked first in the indicator for funding to forgotten emergencies and those with low media coverage, as well as in its consistent support for implementation of humanitarian action and in affirming the primary role of civilian organisations. Furthermore, it ranked second in involvement of beneficiaries in monitoring and evaluation and third in distribution of funding relative to ECHO's Crisis and Vulnerability Indices. However, its worst indicator scores were second to last in timely funding, 21st in commitment to on-going crises, 20th in timely funding to complex emergencies within UN appeals and the number of evaluations, and 19th in strengthening local capacity for crisis response and mitigation.

Canada

Canada is ranked 10th in the 2008 HRI. It ranked 4th in Pillar 5 and 13th in Pillar 1, the most important component of the HRI. A breakdown by indicators shows that Canada ranked first in the number of evaluations, third in participation in main accountability initiatives, fourth in both commitment to on-going crises and in distribution of funding relative to ECHO's Crisis and Vulnerability Indices and fifth in implementing human rights law. It came in fourth for its commitment to ongoing crises and fifth for funding international disaster-risk mitigation mechanisms. Canada's worst scores were 19th in supporting contingency planning and strengthening response capacity, 17th in funding needs assessments, sectoral distribution of funding through UN appeals and consistent support for implementation of humanitarian action, and 15th in commitment to accountability in humanitarian action.

The perception of Canada's performance across the 11 humanitarian crises reviewed by the HRI is remarkably close to the average score of the other donors. Its best scores, just above the average, were in questions related to donor capacity for informed decision-making and support for the role of the ICRC. However, it is slightly below the average in a number of questions, most notably relating to the reallocation of funds from one crisis to the other and the funding of needs assessments, as well as on support to implementing agencies' contingency planning and response capacity. It also only ranked 14th for impartiality and 15th for neutrality.

Overall, Canada scores well in the areas of learning and evaluations, and for linking its humanitarian assistance to longer-term recovery and disaster-risk reduction. However, an area of weakness is supporting contingency planning and building response capacity. Given its reputation in the past as a champion for international principles, its low scores for neutrality and impartiality are unexpected.

Denmark

Denmark is ranked third in the 2008 HRI, with first place rankings in both Pillar 2 and 5, 7th place in Pillar 1 and 8th in Pillar 3. Denmark did well on timely funding to sudden onset disasters and IFRC emergency appeals, funding to international disaster risk mitigation mechanisms, and implementing human rights and refugee law, as well as promoting learning and accountability by participating in and funding accountability initiatives and by requesting a significant number of evaluations. However, it ranked quite low in the distribution of funding relative to ECHO's Crisis and Vulnerability Indices and in funding to forgotten emergencies and those with low media coverage.

Humanitarian agencies in the field positively perceived the performance of Denmark. Denmark scored slightly below the group average in questions relating to preventing or strengthening preparedness for emergencies, the perception of its capacity for informed decision-making, and its support for IDPs. By contrast, Denmark scored well on other questions relating to the international guiding principles such as the respect and support for human rights and international humanitarian and refugee law. It also did particularly well in questions relating to support for long-term development, as well as in its support for operational actors' contingency planning and response capacity.

European Commission

The European Commission is ranked 5th in the 2008 HRI. The EC ranks 2nd in Pillars 2 and 3rd in Pillar 5, but does less well in Pillars 1 (6th) and Pillar 3 (9th). By indicator, the European Commission ranked well in funding to strengthen local capacity, participating in and funding accountability initiatives, and both encouraging regular evaluations and the number of evaluations carried out. Perhaps unsurprisingly, the EC ranked last in unearmarked funding, as well as 20th in funding to crisis countries with historical ties and geographical proximity and 18th in reallocation of funds from other crises and ensuring rapid recovery of sustainable livelihoods. The EC achieves 16th place in alignment to long-term development goals.

Based on the survey results, the European Commission is perceived as doing well in working with local partners to reach vulnerable populations. It has a first place ranking in the HRI for involving beneficiaries in design and implementation, and in donor capacity for informed decision-making, in supporting effective coordination efforts (4), in monitoring and evaluation

(5), in strengthening local capacity for response and mitigation (2), and in strengthening resilience to cope with crises (7). The EC's lack of flexibility and bureaucratic character was also captured by the survey. For example, it receives the bottom ranks for reducing earmarking of funds (23) and for the flexibility of its funding (18). Another issue is the timeliness of funding, where the EC receives a 17th and 16th place ranking in all three of the indicators related to this.

Finland

Finland is ranked 12th in the 2008 HRI. Its best ranking was 8th in Pillar 1, a lowest ranking of 21st in Pillar 2. Finland ranked first in indicators for commitment to accountability in humanitarian action, second in both saving lives and maintaining dignity and respecting or promoting international humanitarian law, 4th in timely funding to sudden onset disasters and IFRC emergency appeals, and 5th in strengthening preparedness. However, Finland scored less well in issues relating to its work at the local community level. For example, it ranked last in strengthening local capacity for response and mitigation, strengthening community resilience to cope with crises and ensuring rapid recovery of sustainable livelihoods. Furthermore, it ranked 21st in both timely funding and consistent support for implementation of humanitarian action.

France

France is ranked 20th in the 2008 HRI. It ranked 15th in Pillar 5, 20th in Pillars 3 and 4 and second to last in Pillar 2. In its top rankings by indicators, France ranked first in funding to forgotten emergencies and those with low media coverage, 8th in implementing human rights law, 9th in unearmarked funding and 10th in distribution of funding relative to ECHO's Crisis and Vulnerability Indices and sectoral distribution of funding through UN appeals. The other side of the coin is that France ranked 22nd in funding to strengthen local capacity and 19th in generosity of humanitarian assistance.

Overall France is poorly perceived by operational actors in the field. It only scored above the average in questions relating to support to ongoing crises. It has poor scores across the board, but is especially perceived to be performing badly in the questions relating to the respect for the humanitarian principles of humanity, impartiality, neutrality and independence and the respect of human rights and international law, longer-term funding and also in involving beneficiaries in design and implementation. It is also perceived as not offering much support to either the role of the ICRC or the UN.

Germany

Germany is ranked 17th in the 2008 HRI. Its top ranking was 12th in Pillar 5. However, it ranked 17th in both Pillars 1 and 3, and 19th in Pillar 2. In terms of specific indicators, Germany ranked first in the neutrality and funding to NGOs indicators, as well as 6th in sectoral distribution of funding through UN appeals and number of evaluations. Germany's lowest rankings by indicator were 20th in funding to UN coordination mechanisms and common services and in unearmarked funding.

In the survey, Germany generally scored below the donor average in most questions, particularly in questions relating to flexible and long-term funding arrangements as well as in helping governments and local communities achieve better coordination. However, it scored above average in the issues relating to the respect for the humanitarian principles of humanity, impartiality, neutrality and independence – a clear advantage over many of its peers.

Greece

Greece is ranked last (23rd) in the 2008 HRI, reflected in its poor ranking in all Pillars: 22nd in Pillars 1 and 4, and 23 in the remaining Pillars. Greece's highest ranking by indicator was 6th in the funding to crisis countries with historical ties and geographical proximity and 10th in timely funding to complex emergencies within UN appeals. However, Greece ranked last (23rd) in the indicators for impartiality, involvement of beneficiaries in monitoring and evaluation, predictable funding, facilitating safe humanitarian access and supporting learning and accountability initiatives. There is, overall, little evidence the country is actively engaged in promoting and implementing the GHD *Principles* and there is considerable room for improvement of its humanitarian policy and practices.

Ireland

Ireland is ranked 4th in the 2008 HRI. In the rankings by Pillars, Ireland ranked 4th in Pillars 1 and 3, but did less well in Pillar 4 where it received a 15th place ranking. In terms of some of the specific indicators, Ireland ranks first for funding UN coordination activities and for funding UN appeals. Ireland is the top donor by size for funding to CERF and other pooled mechanisms. It also stands out for providing flexible funding through its 6th place in unearmarked funding and its 2nd for perceived flexibility. It has good scores on indicators for commit-ment to on-going crises and funding to strengthen local capacity and UN coordination mechanisms.

However, the perception of Ireland's performance by operational actors in the field in comparison to the other donors fluctuates considerably. For example, it is perceived as doing well in comparison with the donor average in the questions relating to the fundamental humanitarian principles of impartiality, neutrality and independence. However, it scores significantly below the average for the question relating to donor capacity to make informed decisions, as well as support for government disaster preparedness and risk reduction and support for better effective coordination.

Italy

Italy is ranked 19th in the 2008 HRI. Its top ranking by Pillar was 15th in Pillar 2 and 20th and 21st in Pillars 1 and 5. Italy ranked 3rd in the indicators for timely funding to sudden onset disasters and IFRC emergency appeals, as well as strengthening government capacity for response and mitigation. It ranked 5th in helping governments and local communities achieve better coordination and 7th in funding to crisis countries with historical ties and geographical proximity. On the other hand, it ranked last (23rd) in funding to strengthen local capacity, and 21st in reallocation of funds from other crises, timely funding to complex emergencies with UN appeals, predictable funding, and supporting learning and accountability initiatives.

The perception of Italy in the field is generally poor. It scored marginally above the donor average in only six questions, most notably in questions relating to funding for disaster-risk reduction and preparedness, and for support for coordination. By contrast, Italy was perceived as performing particularly poorly in comparison to other donors in questions relating to the reallocation of funds from one crisis to another, the funding of needs assessments, and the timeliness of funding. Similarly, Italy scored significantly below the average in relation to supporting operational actors' contingency funding and response capacity. Lastly, although Italy scored above average in the question relating to the encouragement of regular evaluations, it was perceived as performing noticeably below the average in supporting learning and accountability initiatives.

Japan

Japan is ranked 18th in the 2008 HRI. The country is ranked 14th in Pillar 2 and 16th in Pillar 4. However, Japan also ranked 21st in Pillar 1, the most important

Pillar in the Index. By indicator, Japan ranked 5th in distribution of funding relative to ECHO's Crisis and Vulnerability Indices and 9th in funding to international disaster-risk mitigation mechanisms and timely funding to onset disasters and IFRC emergency appeals. Japan, however, ranked 21st in implementing refugee law and penultimate (22nd) in funding NGOs, forgotten emergencies and crisis countries with historical ties, geographical proximity and low media coverage, as well as in reducing unearmarked funding.

How Japan is perceived by operational actors follows relatively closely the average perception of other donors. However, it does slightly better than average in relation to questions regarding the protection of civilians, and respect for human rights, international guidelines for internally displaced people and international humanitarian law. Japan is also perceived to perform better than average in supporting the role of the UN and the primary position of civilian organisations. However, it scores below average in supporting the inclusion of beneficiaries in all cycles of the programme as well as in supporting learning and accountability initiatives and encouraging regular evaluations.

Luxembourg

Luxembourg is ranked 7th in the 2008 HRI. This is a particularly good performance given its limited size. It highest ranking is in Pillar 1, where it placed 2nd. Its lowest ranking was 19th in Pillar 5. In the specific indicators, Luxembourg ranked first in generosity of humanitarian assistance, funding to international disaster-risk mitigation mechanisms, funding to CERF and other quick disbursement mechanisms, and funding UN Consolidated Inter-Agency Appeals and other appeals. It however ranked 21st in participation in main accountability initiatives, and 20th in strengthening local capacity for response and mitigation, as well as timely funding to sudden onset disasters and IFRC emergency appeals. It also ranked 19th in respecting or promoting human rights and 18th in distribution of funding relative to ECHO's Crisis and Vulnerability Indices.

The Netherlands

The Netherlands is ranked 6th in the 2008 HRI. The country ranked third in Pillar 3 and 5th in Pillar 1. However, it ranked 10th in Pillar 4 and 16th in Pillar 2. By indicator, the Netherlands ranked first in the unearmarked funding and funding to CERF and other quick disbursement mechanisms indicators, third in predictable funding, 4th in promoting NGOs and the

Red Cross Movement and implementing refugee law, and 5th in generosity of humanitarian assistance. In contrast, the Netherlands ranked 18th in funding to strengthen local capacity and implementing international humanitarian law, 17th in strengthening community resilience to cope with crises and funding to international disaster-risk mitigation mechanisms, and 16th in the indicator for neutrality.

Across the majority of survey questions the Netherlands scores marginally better than the donor average. It only drops below the average perception for donors on four questions: supporting government and community disaster preparedness and response capacity; supporting long-term recovery; and supporting ongoing crises.

New Zealand

New Zealand is ranked 13th in the 2008 HRI and, as a small donor, has done well at finding a niche for itself in the OECD/DAC group. Its highest ranking by Pillar is a 4th place position in Pillar 2 but it is 14th in Pillars 3 and 4 and 16th in Pillar 5. New Zealand ranked first in the indicator for funding to strengthen local capacity, ensuring rapid recovery of sustainable livelihoods, helping governments and local communities achieve better coordination, reducing earmarking and flexible funding. This contrasts with the overall negative trend in these areas. On the other hand, it ranked 21st in both involvement of beneficiaries in monitoring and evaluation and funding to NGOs, and 19th in funding in proportion to need, commitment to on-going crises, and funding to international disaster risk mitigation mechanisms.

Norway

Norway is ranked second in the 2008 HRI, with a first place ranking in Pillar 4, second in Pillar 3 and third in Pillar 1. However, Norway did less well with respect to Pillar 5, with a 10th place ranking, and Pillar 2, where the country is ranked 12th. In specific indicators, Norway ranked first in terms of generosity of humanitarian assistance, as well as for indicators on funding and supporting UN coordination mechanisms, and for implementing IHL and refugee law. A 2nd place ranking in multi-year funding is another positive area. Its weakest areas were in the indicators for commitment to ongoing crises, ranked 22nd, and a ranking of 21st in timely funding to sudden onset disasters and IFRC emergency appeals. Norway also did poorly in terms of funding to strengthen local capacity for disaster response and mitigation.

Norway is positively perceived by operational agencies in the field, scoring only just below the average in two questions relating to donor capacity for informed decision-making, and strengthening community disaster preparedness and response capacity. In particular, Norway is perceived as performing well in its support for the role of NGOs, the UN and the ICRC, as well as coordination efforts in the humanitarian system. However, the survey findings also point to a perception that Norway could do better in its efforts to adequately involve beneficiaries in programming and evaluations, as well as supporting local capacity.

Portugal

Portugal ranked penultimate (22nd) in the 2008 HRI. The country ranked 18th in Pillar 2, second to last (22nd) in Pillars 3 and 5, and last in Pillar 1. In terms of the Index's individual indicators, Portugal ranked first in unearmarked funding, second in involvement of beneficiaries in design and implementation, and 4th in involvement of beneficiaries in monitoring and evaluation and facilitating safe humanitarian access. However, it ranked last in distribution of funding relative to ECHO's Crisis and Vulnerability Indices, reallocating funds from other crises, strengthening disaster preparedness, funding to NGOs, and in affirming the primary role of civilian organisations. It also ranked second to last for generosity of humanitarian assistance. As the scores show, there is a considerable disparity between the GHD *Principles* and Portugal's actual humanitarian policies and practices.

Spain

Spain is ranked 16th in the 2008 HRI. Its top ranking is 11th in Pillar 2, which contrasts with 18th in Pillar 4. Spain ranked first in the indicator for timely funding to sudden onset disasters and IFRC emergency appeals, and 7th in distribution of funding relative to ECHO's Crisis and Vulnerability Indices. However, it ranked 20th in implementing international humanitarian law, and 19th for funding forgotten emergencies and those with low media coverage.

Compared to other donors, Spain has mixed results from the survey. It scored above average in particular in questions relating to support for community disaster preparedness and resilience. It also was perceived as doing well in ongoing and predictable funding to crises. However, in many other questions it scored below average, including questions relating to the reallocation of funding from one crisis to another, donor capacity to make informed decisions, support for the role of the UN and the ICRC, and questions regarding support for learning and accountability initiatives and encouraging regular evaluations. Spain has recently increased its levels of assistance and is more actively engaged with the humanitarian sector, although the results of this are not necessarily reflected in this year's HRI.

Sweden

Sweden is ranked first in this year's Index. Its good performance is evenly distributed across the Pillars, ranking first in Pillars 1 and 3, second in Pillars 4 and 5 and third in Pillar 2. Sweden occupies the top place in 12 of the 58 indicators used to construct the Index and one of the top five slots in almost three-quarters of all these. For example, the country ranked first in the indicators for funding UN, IFRC and ICRC appeals, as well as in supporting IHL and involving beneficiaries in monitoring and evaluation and multi-year funding. Sweden's lowest rankings were 21st in the indicator for sectoral distribution of funding through UN appeals and 20th in the indicator around distribution of funding relative to ECHO's Crisis and Vulnerabilty Indices.

Based on the average scores for survey responses from all the crises studied, Sweden is generally perceived as a good donor by humanitarian agencies in the field in comparison to its peers. Sweden scored above average in questions relating to respect for the fundamental principles of humanitarian action. It also did particularly well in questions relating to the reallocation of funding from one crisis to another, and in providing funds for needs assessments. It was also perceived as doing well in supporting coordination efforts. Sweden scored well above the average in responses to questions relating to long-term funding arrangements, an area in which other donors are generally perceived as doing poorly.

Switzerland

Switzerland is ranked 9th in the 2008 HRI. The country ranked 7th in Pillars 3 and 4 and 10th in Pillar 2. By individual indicator, Switzerland ranked first in the indicators for funding IFRC and ICRC appeals, respecting or promoting human rights and respecting or promoting international humanitarian law. However, it ranked 21st in distribution of funding relative to ECHO's Crisis and Vulnerabilty Indices, 22nd in sectoral distribution of funding through UN appeals, 18th in timely funding to complex emergencies with UN appeals, 15th in implementing human rights law and 14th in encouraging regular evaluations.

In the field, humanitarian agencies perceived Switzerland as a good donor. In fact, it scores below the donor average in only two questions, relating to involvement of beneficiaries in the design and implementation of programmes and long-term funding arrangements. Switzerland is perceived particularly well in terms of strengthening community resilience to cope with crises, aligning its humanitarian funding to long-term development aims and ensuring rapid recovery of sustainable livelihoods areas in which other donors on the whole perform badly. It also does well in another area in which donors as a group struggle, namely in supporting contingency planning and strengthening partner response capacity. Perhaps unsurprisingly, Switzerland's funding is perceived as being more independent from political, economic and military objectives than that of other donors. It is also strongly perceived as a country which respects and promotes human rights and international humanitarian and refugee law.

United Kingdom

The United Kingdom is ranked 8th in the 2008 HRI. The UK ranked 5th and 6th in Pillars 5 and 3 but only achieved 12th in Pillar 4 and 10th in Pillar 1. The UK scores in specific indicators include top rankings in sectoral distribution of funding through UN appeals, funding to CERF and other quick disbursement mechanisms, and funding to NGOs. It also ranked third in involvement of beneficiaries in monitoring and evaluation. However, it scored 18th in funding to crisis countries with historical ties and geographical proximity, 17th in distribution of funding relative to ECHO's Crisis and Vulnerabilty Indices, and 14th in implementing human rights law.

At the field level, the UK is on the whole perceived by operational agencies as a good donor. It rarely scores below the average, with the exception being questions relating to the independence of funding from political or economic (and depending on the crisis, military) objectives, the protection and assistance of civilians, indicators around the aims and objectives of humanitarian action, ongoing support to crises, and earmarked funding. On the other hand, it is perceived as having good capacity for informed decision-making, and as encouraging beneficiary participation in all elements of the project cycle. Furthermore, it scores well in supporting the role of NGOs, the UN and the ICRC – reflecting a good balance of its funding to multilateral funding mechanisms. It also does well in supporting learning and accountability initiatives, and in encouraging regular evaluations, reflecting its reputation for its engagement with issues of improving quality, performance and accountability in the sector.

United States

The United States is ranked 15th in the 2008 HRI. The country is ranked 8th in Pillar 5 but last (23rd) in Pillar 4. In terms of specific indicators it ranked first in sectoral distribution of funding through UN appeals, and 7th in both funding to NGOs and number of evaluations. However, the US ranked 21st in the indicators for unearmarked funding, and 22nd in implementing international humanitarian law and implementing human rights law.

The US ranks below average in the survey of agencies it funds in the field. In fact, only in eight questions did it score just above the average, with its best scores coming in questions relating to the provision of funds in a timely manner and support for operational actors' contingency planning. Significantly, it scored below average in questions relating to the neutrality, impartiality and independence of humanitarian aid. It was also perceived as performing below average in supporting long-term development and sustainable livelihoods. It remains to be seen to what extent the current review of the United States' development and humanitarian policy framework will reflect and reinforce the GHD *Principles*.

Conclusion

The HRI intends to provide, on an annual basis, an independent and objective analysis of donor performance set against their commitments to apply good practice in humanitarian donorship, as well as an assessment of the state of humanitarian action in different crises across the globe. In doing so the HRI helps to draw attention to how governments and humanitarian actors can improve their own performance and accountability.

After two years, the HRI is beginning to show areas where donors collectively can do more to uphold the GHD *Principles*, as well as specific areas where individual donors can improve in relation to their peers. The HRI 2008 findings show that there are great differences among donors, with the policies and practices of some donors more closely aligned to the GHD *Principles* than others. However, all countries – even the top ranked ones – have room for improvement. This is both a collective and individual responsibility. The HRI findings show that there is still too little consistency in the actions and behaviour of donors and the overall humanitarian system in different crisis situations. This underscores the need to work towards a more predictable, reliable and principled response to all crises. This is one of the underlying aims of the GHD *Principles*, which is, to a certain extent, shared by the UN humanitarian reform process and many of the quality and accountability initiatives of the sector. The HRI 2008 shows that this ideal is still far from reality.

There are five main conclusions that emerge from the 2008 HRI that suggest how wealthy donor countries can contribute to improving the quality, effectiveness and impact of humanitarian action.

First, wealthy countries could do more to strengthen their commitments to provide aid in an impartial, neutral and independent manner, not based on other priorities or objectives. The GHD *Principles* place a great deal of emphasis on donors respecting the fundamental principles and objectives of humanitarian action. The HRI 2008 findings for Pillar 1 show that donors are not always perceived as providing aid in an impartial, neutral and independent manner, nor where it is most needed. The findings show that too many donors are still biased and influenced by other factors when it comes to allocating resources, and too many crises around the world continue to be a showcase for poor practice, despite all of the lessons from the past. In many places humanitarian assistance continues to be compromised by wealthy countries' political, economic or security agendas, while elsewhere other crises are forgotten and neglected.

Second, wealthy countries should contribute to efforts to improve the quality and use of needs assessments to determine who needs assistance, where, and of what kind. The HRI 2008 findings under Pillar 1 also suggest that there are gaps in the area of needs assessments that should be addressed to ensure that humanitarian assistance is provided in accordance to needs. The findings show that there are disparities in the quality and consistent use of needs assessments. Needs assessments help to prioritise aid programmes and ensure that the right kind of assistance reaches the right people, at the right time. If humanitarian donorship is truly to be needs based, donors could contribute to improving global needs assessments tools with clear transparent criteria on how to allocate – or reallocate - resources at the global levels for a more equitable response between crises. Donors could also support

their humanitarian partners in funding and improving harmonised needs assessments at the country level and promoting a continual process of monitoring the evolving context and assessing how needs change, as well as making available the necessary flexible funding to adapt responses accordingly. Donors could therefore help promote a more nuanced position that balances the need for rapid assessments with the time needed to engage affected populations in identifying their evolving needs.

Third, wealthy countries could do much more to harmonise and link relief efforts to early recovery and longer term development strategies. The HRI 2008 findings from Pillar 2 confirm a perennial challenge in the humanitarian sector – how to better link relief to recovery and long-term development, and strengthen the resilience of populations affected by crises. Humanitarian agencies often struggle to find appropriate means to achieve a balance between meeting short-term needs and laying the foundation for recovery and development. The HRI findings show that some donor policies and procedures can accentuate the gap between relief, recovery and development, rather than facilitating more integrated and harmonised efforts. Similarly donor procedures can facilitate or impede efforts to effectively engage local communities in defining and implementing programmes that meet their needs.

In light of the renewed efforts to promote implementation of the Paris Declaration on aid harmonisation and efficiency and the Hyogo Framework for Action, as well as the fast-approaching target of meeting the Millennium Development Goals by 2015, this is an area where wealthy countries could do more to align their humanitarian policies with these initiatives. This is a complex issue with no easy solution, but it remains clear that new approaches and ways of thinking are needed.

Fourth, wealthy countries should invest more resources to strengthen the humanitarian system's capacity at all levels. The HRI findings under Pillar 3 indicate that in general donors could do much more to prioritise capacity building in the humanitarian system as an integral part of their assistance. Given the heavy strains on the humanitarian system, there is an urgent need to invest more in making sure that the system as a whole works better to meet current and future humanitarian needs. For example, donors can do more to fund and prioritise efforts to strengthen community-level and government capacity to reduce risks, and prepare for and respond to a crisis. At the same time, there is a deficit in donor support for strengthening the capacity of humanitarian organisations that make up the system. Without investing in areas such as contingency planning and standing operational capacity, the system will be hard-pressed to deal with the increasing demands placed on it. Donors need to approach this issue strategically, and consider the benefits of investing in building the capacity of the whole system – not just parts of it – and do so in a holistic way that encourages harmonisation and coordination among different levels. This might include increased support for the UN humanitarian reform process to ensure that it is strengthened and expanded to include other components of the humanitarian system – including means to integrate more closely with existing capacities at the national and local level. The risks and human costs of failing to invest in building this capacity could be catastrophic.

Fifth, wealthy countries should assume more responsibility for ensuring implementation of international standards and good practice, and for improving accountability and performance in humanitarian action. In line with the findings from Pillars 4 and 5, donors could take a more active leadership role in promoting a shared understanding of good practice in humanitarian action. The HRI findings show that there is inconsistent application of the international laws, principles and standards that guide and inform effective humanitarian action, especially those that attempt to ensure that people affected by crisis receive the support, protection and assistance they require. Collectively donors need to renew efforts to ensure these tools are used consistently, particularly in conflict situations, where such laws are often needed most, but most frequently ignored by some donors themselves.

The HRI findings highlight the crucial role that donors can play in helping the humanitarian system become more effective. Accountability is more than just how and where donor money is spent – it is about making the whole aid system work better. The international humanitarian system would benefit enormously if donors collectively worked with their partners towards building a shared understanding among all stakeholders of what is good donor practice, and how humanitarian agencies can be more accountable to the people affected by crises. At the same time, the findings show that donors could also work towards more systematic use of evaluations for learning, and monitor the applications of these lessons.

These conclusions are not new – most have been raised time and time again in many evaluations and reviews of the humanitarian system. In that sense, the HRI reinforces and confirms much of what is already known in the sector. What is perhaps unique is that the HRI findings are based on a research process that included studies of 11 different crises, extensive interviews with hundreds of representatives of humanitarian organisations and donor agencies, and a systematic analysis of specific indicators that gauge and measure good practices. The HRI therefore offers a solid body of evidence which helps to understand the current state of affairs in donor practice, and highlight areas where donors and other stakeholders in the humanitarian system can work together to improve the quality, effectiveness and impact of humanitarian action.

The GHD *Principles* remain a valuable aspirational tool to guide the action of donors. However, it remains a challenge to operationalise many of the *Principles*, while the language and concepts behind others seem outdated in the current context of the humanitarian sector. Governments would do well to continually review and update the GHD *Principles* so that they remain relevant in light of changes in the sector and continue to meet their original purpose – to improve donors' actions and behaviours. In this sense, the recent European Consensus on Humanitarian Aid offers an opportunity for donors to look for further alignment and coordination of their approaches to humanitarian assistance.[26] Donors should be recognised for their efforts to develop collective indicators, pilot the application of GHD Principles in countries like the Democratic Republic of the Congo and engage with other parts of the sector, like the IASC. These are all important and positive steps, and donors should be encouraged to continue to work in this direction as a means to build and complement individual and collective strengths.

For its part, DARA hopes that the HRI findings will contribute to a better understanding of the limitations and opportunities for improvement in the current humanitarian system, and how collective and individual donor action to improve that system can benefit the millions of people who depend on humanitarian action to safeguard their lives and dignity. DARA will continue to refine and improve the HRI in order to promote and facilitate a more informed debate on performance and accountability in humanitarian action.

Technical Appendix

The survey

Efforts were made to boost the overall sample size for the 2008 survey. This was done in two ways: by increasing the number of crisis countries visited from eight in 2007 to 11 in 2008, and by deepening and widening the coverage of the survey within each crisis country visited. These efforts were largely successful and sample sizes were increased for the majority of donors. Nevertheless, there were five countries for which it proved difficult to gather at least 20 responses; these were Austria, Greece, Luxembourg, New Zealand and Portugal. As noted in 2007, small donors with modest humanitarian assistance budgets will tend to operate through a correspondingly smaller number of implementing agencies, and in fewer crises than larger donors with a well-established record of humanitarian programmes. For these five countries we used a pooled sample of survey data which included responses to the 2007 and 2008 surveys. For all countries other than these five, survey responses in 2007 and 2008 were highly correlated, suggesting that perceptions about donor performance do not shift dramatically from year to year.[27] This indicates that using pooled data from two years to boost sample size for the five countries mentioned is unlikely to have introduced any systematic bias in the survey results. Despite the challenges faced with these small-sample countries, the 2008 survey had a total of 1,404 responses, representing a 37 percent increase over 2007. Efforts will continue to be made to increase sample sizes in future compilations of the HRI.

Changes to quantitative data indicators

A number of changes were made to the quantitative data indicators. The primary motivation here was to improve the specification, either because new data emerged which allowed for better definition or, in a few cases, because feedback received from donors or operational agencies permitted a more accurate or appropriate representation of the underlying variable. Furthermore, reflecting calls for some streamlining of this part of the HRI, the number of quantitative data indicators was reduced from 25 to 20, reflecting the elimination or consolidation of seven indicators from the HRI 2007 and the addition of two new ones this year. Our decision to streamline our approach has been

pragmatic: for instance, the indicator developed in 2007 to capture the predictability of donor funding was dropped this year, after further analysis persuaded us that, important as this principle is explaining why question 12.01 was included in the survey, both in 2007 and 2008 it was not being captured appropriately with that particular specification. Second, we dropped the indicator on funding in cash, as it did not provide a full picture of the overall split between cash and in-kind contributions, which is difficult to capture.

We also saw scope for some consolidation of the quantitative data indicators included in Pillar 3 (Working with humanitarian partners). Thus, whereas in 2007 we had "Funding to CERF" and "Funding quick disbursement mechanisms" as two separate measures, this year these have been consolidated into a single "Funding to CERF and pooled mechanisms" measure. Likewise, IFRC and ICRC funding appeals have been brought together under a single indicator "Funding IFRC and ICRC Appeals". A similar change was made in Pillar 5, through the consolidation into a single indicator that now aggregates participation and funding of the main donor accountability initiatives.

The two new indicators included this year are:

1. Generosity of humanitarian assistance: While some of the "fair share" indicators developed last year (still included this year) accomplished this to some extent, we thought it advisable to buttress this with the introduction of a more explicit measure that, beyond issues of quality in the delivery of humanitarian assistance, gives credit to countries which shouldered a more generous share of the international burden of aid.

2. Implementing refugee law: Pillar 4 has benefited from the inclusion of a new indicator which contains some explicit measures of the extent to which countries implement refugee law and fund the UNHCR, in its role as promoter and guardian of refugee law and the agenda for protection.

Finally, we complemented a number of indicators with additional information and data:

1. Donor funding of the 2008 WFP Special Appeal on food price rises was added to the indicator capturing funding to UN appeals. This special appeal was considered an important example of needs that arise during a calendar year, and the response by

donors illustrates their ability to respond adequately to sudden needs.

2. Donor funding to ICRC was added to the indicator measuring implementation of international humanitarian law. This was considered appropriate, as it is the prime organisation charged with implementing international humanitarian law.

3. In a similar vein, funding to OHCHR was added to the indicator measuring implementation of human rights, mainly due to its role as the principal body charged with overseeing implementation of human rights through its treaties, but also through its other functions. In addition, because of its importance for protecting and promoting human rights at the national and regional levels, new information supplied by OHCHR was added on the accreditation status and, thus, quality of national human rights institutions.

In addition to the above, changes were made to the specification of a number of quantitative data indicators with the aim of either streamlining and/or making the definition more transparent. For instance, adjustments were made to the indicator assessing funding to crisis countries with historical ties and/or located in the donor's geographical proximity. While this indicator continues to give credit to countries whose funding decisions are, on the whole, less swayed by whether the recipient country is geographically close or has historical ties to the donor, this year we introduced a "needs-based" adjustment which, other things being equal, gives more credit to donors whose funding allocations are more in line with CAP budgets for those emergencies. In the same spirit, last year's indicator on funding to emergencies relative to the degree of media coverage, the sector to which funding is allocated, or whether the emergency is classified as forgotten, has now been amended to include only the degree of media coverage and the status of the emergency as forgotten or not. The sectoral dimension is captured in a separate indicator, called "Sectoral distribution of funding through UN appeals" (G.6.02). A detailed list and definitions of the quantitative data indicators included in the HRI 2008 is presented in the following section.

Pillar 1: Responding to needs

Generosity of humanitarian assistance
This is a simple indicator that shows total humanitarian funding in relation to GNI. Credit is given to countries which shouldered a more generous share of the international burden of humanitarian aid. While some of the "fair share" indicators presented elsewhere in this table accomplished this to some extent, it was thought advisable to buttress this more explicitly with the introduction of a new measure.

Funding to crisis countries with historical ties and geographic proximity to donor
GHD Principle 2 calls for the implementation of humanitarian action that is humane, impartial, "solely on the basis of need" and independent from "political, economic, military or other objectives". Despite commitment to these humanitarian principles, international humanitarian financing is considered inequitable, and not reflective of comparative levels of need. Donors are often motivated to intervene for reasons such as historical links and/or geographic proximity that are unrelated to the above principles. In order to proxy the adherence to concepts of impartiality and independence, a mapping of 23 donors against over 120 recipient countries assesses whether the donor country enjoys strong historical links with the recipient country and whether it is geographically close. The more independent the distribution of total donor funding to recipient countries is from historical links or issues of geography, as reflected by the UN Consolidated Appeals Processes (CAPs), the higher the score attributed to the individual donor. There is no presumption, for example, that a donor country should not fund a former colony. Rather, the indicator assesses whether the preponderance of funding is allocated to countries having strong historical or geographic links to the donor, adjusting for total donor funding to emergencies, and allocating scores across donors in a way that gives higher credit to countries who are less swayed by such considerations.

Funding to forgotten emergencies and those with low media coverage
This indicator captures other dimensions of Principle 2: Since donor funding should fundamentally be guided by considerations of need, it will be important to reward donors whose humanitarian interventions are not biased against forgotten emergencies and are reasonably independent of extensive media coverage. The indicator

considers more than 120 emergencies in 2007 and classifies donor funding by the extent of media coverage each emergency receives, and by whether the emergency in question has been classified as "forgotten".[28]

Timely funding to complex emergencies through UN appeals

The timely delivery of resources in the event of a humanitarian crisis is strongly supported by the *Principles*. Indicator H5.01 calculates funds within an appeal committed or disbursed to complex emergencies in the first quarter after the appeal date as a percentage of total funds within the appeal committed or disbursed to those crises for 2007. It is taken as a proxy for the timely delivery of funds to such crises, based on the corresponding collective indicator.

Timely funding to sudden onset disasters and IFRC emergency appeals

Funds committed to individual sudden onset disasters and IFRC emergency appeals disbursed within the first month after the appeal date, as a percentage of total funds within an appeal committed to those crises up to six months after the disaster declaration. This Indicator is different from that of timely funding to complex emergencies through UN appeals only to the extent that the indicator applies to sudden onset disasters (as opposed to complex emergencies) up to six months after onset, and also captures funding through the IFRC.

Sectoral distribution of funding through UN appeals

Principle 6 calls on donors to "allocate humanitarian funding in proportion to needs and on the basis of needs assessments". This indicator is based on UN needs assessment methodology albeit imperfect to capture for each donor the deviations in the sectoral distribution of funds with respect to the global requirements for funding identified for emergencies by means of the CAPs. It measures sectoral distribution of funding committed to priority sectors (identified for emergencies by means of the CAPs), measured in relation to the normative benchmark established by revised requirements.

Distribution of donor funding relative to ECHO's 2007 Crisis and Vulnerability Indices

This indicator builds on ECHO's 2007 global needs and vulnerability assessment[29] which identifies the most vulnerable countries as those most in need of humanitarian assistance. The crisis and vulnerability indicators include human development and poverty, health of children,

malnutrition, mortality, access to health care, prevalence of HIV-AIDS, tuberculosis and malaria, the gender-specific human development and Gini Indices, and crisis indicators such as ongoing or recently resolved conflicts, recent natural disasters and the extent of population movements. This indicator maps donor funding to over 100 recipient countries according to the ECHO's Crisis and Vulnerability Index scores and rewards donors whose humanitarian assistance is allocated to the most needy and vulnerable countries, as identified by a total score of over four, summing up both indices. In 2007, this reflected those emergencies that together received some 80 percent of ECHO's humanitarian funds.

Pillar 2: Supporting local capacity and recovery

Funding to strengthen local capacity for disaster mitigation and response as a percentage of total Official Development Assistance (ODA)

Integrating relief and development is considered to be essential for ensuring that outcomes initiated during a humanitarian intervention are sustainable. It is clear that the returns to investment in humanitarian assistance will be higher where long-term development issues have been addressed in a comprehensive manner during the emergency phase. However, donors often lack mechanisms for funding recovery and reconstruction work. H8.01 captures a donor's commitment to local capacity building, by looking at funding of reconstruction relief and rehabilitation, on the one hand, and disaster prevention and preparedness, on the other, as percentage of total ODA.

Funding to international disaster mitigation mechanisms (UNDP Thematic Trust Fund for Crisis Prevention and Recovery, to the World Bank/ISDR Global Facility for Disaster Reduction and Recovery and to Disaster Preparedness-ECHO), as a percentage of total ODA

This indicator captures donor commitment to disaster risk reduction and crisis prevention, focusing on the biggest multilateral mechanisms available to fund recovery and reconstruction work. The indicator adds donor financing of the UNDP's Thematic Trust Fund for Crisis Prevention and Recovery (2006), the World Bank's Global Facility for Disaster Reduction and Recovery (2007), and in the case of the EC, to its designated Disaster Preparedness facility (DIPECHO), as a percentage of total ODA.[30]

Pillar 3: Working with humanitarian partners

Funding to UN coordination mechanisms and common services ("coordination and support services") as a percentage of requirements as a fair share

Principle 10 addresses aspects of the relationship between donors, the United Nations and the International Red Cross and Red Crescent Movement, and non-governmental organisations. Donors recognise the critical role played by these three actors in the delivery of humanitarian assistance and are, therefore, called upon to maintain a broadly balanced selection of partners between UN, NGO and the Red Cross Movement, based on their competence and capacity. Grounded in the collective indicators, indicator H10.01 recognises the leading role of the UN agencies in humanitarian action particularly in the light of the new cluster approach to sector coordination by capturing funding to the United Nations coordination mechanisms and common services during 2006–2007 as a share of total requirements, using a fair share criterion. This criterion takes into account the share of an individual donor's GDP in total OECD/DAC GDP in allocating scores across donors. Funding amounts are defined as those contributing to "coordination and support services" inside UN CAPs.

Funding to the Central Emergency Response Fund (CERF) and pooled mechanisms

Principle 12 is derived from donor concern for the need to develop good practices in donor financing and management of financial resources. Specifically, it addresses the issue of the desirability of ensuring flexibility in funding to United Nations agencies, so as to "ensure a more predictable and timely response to humanitarian emergencies, with the objectives of promoting early action and response to reduce loss of life".[31] Indicator H12.01 brings in two components, weighted equally. First, it takes funding to CERF as a percentage of total humanitarian assistance. It then adds donor funding to the main mechanisms other than CERF for committing funding under flexible terms. Unlike CERF, these mechanisms allow funds to be disbursed to key humanitarian organisations more widely than to only UN agencies, funds, and programmes, and enable the Humanitarian Coordinators to act independently and robustly in support of humanitarian objectives. The funds considered for this second component of the indicator are: the IFRC's Disaster Relief Emergency Fund, the Common Humanitarian Funds piloted in

Sudan and Democratic Republic of Congo in 2006, Emergency Response Funds in 2007 for the Central African Republic, DRC, Ethiopia, Indonesia, Iraq, occupied Palestinian territories, Somalia, Sudan and Zimbabwe. Scores are allocated based on a country's share of total GNI.

Funding to UN Consolidated Inter-Agency Appeals as fair share

Principle 14 encourages donors to respond to appeals of the United Nations and the Red Cross and Red Crescent Movement, giving them a leading role in responding to humanitarian emergencies. The UN Consolidated Inter-Agency Appeals Process (CAPs) identifies the funding needs of the crises they apply to. This indicator calculates donor funding to the 2006–2007 CAPs as a proportion of total needs. In estimating donor scores, we use a fair share concept, which takes into account the share of an individual donor's GDP in total OECD/DAC GDP, in keeping with the reference in Principle 14 to equitable burden-sharing considerations in determining the size of contributions. Given the humanitarian implications of much higher food prices during the past year, this indicator also includes, using a fair share measure, funding to a special appeal by the World Food Programme.

Funding to IFRC and ICRC appeals as percentage of needs met for these appeals as fair share

The International Red Cross and Red Crescent Movement consisting of the IFRC, the ICRC and Red Cross and Red Crescent National Societies have their own annual appeals process. This indicator captures the funds directed to IFRC appeals, both annual and emergency in 2007, and ICRC appeals as a share of total needs. As with the previous indicator, a fair share criterion is used in allocating scores to individual donors.

Funding for NGOs as percentage of humanitarian aid and restrictiveness of relationship

Acknowledging the important role NGOs play in delivering humanitarian aid, donor support and recognition of this key role is measured in this indicator by donor funding to NGOs in relation to total humanitarian assistance in 2006 and 2007. In addition, this indicator rewards those donors which can fund foreign NGOs, instead of being restricted to funding only NGOs of their own nationality.[32]

Percentage of unearmarked funds to agencies (OCHA, UNHCR, IFRC, ICRC, WFP) out of total humanitarian assistance to these agencies Principle 13 calls upon donors to "enhance the flexibility of earmarking, and of introducing longer term funding arrangements". This indicator gives credit to donors which provide a greater share of their humanitarian assistance in unearmarked form during the period 2006–2007.

Pillar 4: Promoting standards and enhancing implementation

Implementation of international humanitarian law and funding to ICRC Principle 4 calls for donors to "respect and promote the implementation of international humanitarian law, refugee law and human rights". This indicator captures three dimensions of implementation. First, from a total of 24 key international humanitarian law treaties,[33] it registers the total number of international instruments actually ratified, accepted, approved, or acceded to by individual donor countries. Second, implementation requires that states adopt domestic laws and regulations as well as spread knowledge of the relevant Conventions and Protocols as widely as possible; the indicator therefore gives additional credit to countries that have created national commissions aimed at ensuring effective application of International Humanitarian Law, as advocated by the ICRC.[34] Finally, the indicator includes total donor funding in relation to GNI of the ICRC, in its role as promoter and guardian of international humanitarian law.

Implementation of international human rights law and funding to the UN Office of the High Commissioner for Human Rights This indicator also captures three dimensions of implementation. First, it gives credit to donors in proportion to the number of principal legal instruments on human rights and accompanying protocols they have ratified, accepted, approved, or acceded to, including the International Convention on the Elimination of All Forms of Racial Discrimination, the International Covenant on Economic, Social and Cultural Rights, the International Covenant on Civil and Political Rights, the Optional Protocol to the International Covenant on Civil and Political Rights, the Convention on the Elimination of All Forms of Discrimination Against Women, the Optional Protocol to the Convention

on the Elimination of All Forms of Discrimination Against Women, the Convention Against Torture and Other Cruel, Inhuman or Degrading Treatment or Punishment, the Convention on the Rights of the Child, as well as the Council of Europe Human Rights Conventions and Protocols. Second, it gives credit to donors that have duly accredited national human rights institutions in proportion to their accreditation grades, determined by the OHCHR. A third dimension included is core funding (in relation to GNI) to the Office of the High Commissioner for Human Rights, as promoter and guardian of international human rights treaties.

Implementation of international refugee law and funding to the Office of the UN High Commissioner for Refugees This indicator encompasses three elements: first, whether the state in question is a party to the principal legal instruments of international refugee law, including the 1951 Refugee Convention, the 2000 Convention Against Transnational Organised Crime, the 1954 Convention Relating to the Status of Stateless Persons, and the 1961 Convention on the Reduction of Statelessness, as recommended by UNHCR's Plan of Action; second, the indicator gives credit to countries that accept persons as part of the Office of the United Nations High Commissioner for Refugees resettlement programme; finally, it also gives credit to countries reflecting levels of funding (in relation to GDP) to UNHCR, in its role as promoter and guardian of refugee law and the agenda for protection.

Pillar 5: Promoting learning and accountability

Participation in and funding of main accountability initiatives Principle 21 commits donors to "support learning and accountability initiatives for the effective and efficient implementation of humanitarian action". A number of initiatives exist, including the Sphere Project and the Humanitarian Accountability Project (HAP), aimed at defining standards for field level action. Others aim to improve the overall management (Quality COMPAS), or the human resources (People in Aid) of organisations.[35] ALNAP (Active Learning Network for Accountability and Performance in Humanitarian Action) has a unique role in promoting evaluation and learning from experience as a tool to improve overall performance of agencies and donors. The indicator seeks to capture both a) donor support for and commitment to these initiatives by capturing various dimensions of their participation, and b) funding assigned to ALNAP and HAP, as well as to those projects that support learning and accountability and are listed in OCHA FTS for the years 2006 and 2007.[36] The scores are calculated in relation to total humanitarian assistance funding. In the case of ALNAP, membership in, and attendance to biannual meetings are considered key factors in evaluating support. The indicator assigns different weights to each initiative, reflecting their relative importance in terms of impact on humanitarian action to date, with ALNAP and Sphere accounting for 70 percent of the total weight under item a) above.

Number of evaluations

Principle 22 encourages donors to make "regular evaluations of international responses to humanitarian crises, including assessments of donor performance". Evaluations assess humanitarian interventions according to defined criteria such as relevance, efficiency and impact, and are useful to assess lessons learned to enhance the effectiveness of future donor interventions. Donors can evaluate their own performance, commission evaluations of activities carried out by organisations funded by them, or engage with other agencies and donors in joint exercises. This indicator counts the number of publicly available individual evaluations carried out, or funded, by donors in the last four years (2004–2007). It also includes a measure of joint evaluations, given their broader scope. The indicator also takes into consideration the existence of evaluation guidelines, viewed as another means of promoting the practice of evaluations.

Notes

1   DARA would like to thank all the many people who have made contributions to the methodological framework, indicators and data analysis for the HRI 2008. Thanks is also due to Igor Hodson and Daniela Ruegenberg for editing and data analysis. DARA is especially grateful for the input and advice received by our Peer Review Committee members, who have also provided invaluable feedback to improve the chapter.

2   IFRC, 2008, p. 193.

3   DFID, 2006, p.2.

4   The figure according to OCHA is as high as 85% of overall humanitarian aid financing. (OCHA, 2008).

5   Many donors were behind efforts to improve quality and accountability in the sector, and provided support for initiatives such as ALNAP. However, of the more than 65 different initiatives identified in a recent inventory by ALNAP, the HRI is the only one that focuses on donor accountability and performance, and is one of the few that is not directly funded or supported by donors. (See the ALNAP website for more details: www.alnap.org).

6   Egeland, 2007.

7   For example, the UK and Sweden in particular were instrumental in developing the revised Central Emergency Revolving Fund (CERF) and pushing forward many of the UN humanitarian reforms approved in 2006.

8   See Schaar, 2007 for more details on the origins of the GHD.

9   Minear and Smillie, "Welcome to the Good Humanitarian Donorship club."

10   Flint and Goyder. 2006.

11   For more information see: http://hdr.undp.org/en/reports/; http://www.oneworldtrust.org; and http://www.cgdev.org/section/initiatives/_active/cdi

12   David Roodman's chapter in this year's HRI, "A Tale of Two Indices", compares the HRI to the Commitment to Development Index, and offers valuable advice on how to construct an index and communicate the results in ways that are accessible and understandable to a broad audience (Roodman, 2008.).

13   The chapter contributed by Mary B. Anderson in this year's HRI which describes how aid and aid agencies are perceived by beneficiaries - and how uncomfortable this can be for organisations, provides a parallel to the reaction to the HRI, and highlights why a neutral, independent process can be of great value (Anderson, 2008).

14   The chapter contributed by Larry Minear in the HRI 2008, reviews the methodology and findings from the HRI 2007 and concludes that the HRI's independent assessment of donors is useful and necessary and that the HRI's assessment is backed up by several other independent studies (Minear, 2008.)

15   EurActiv, 2005.

16   The proxy indicator currently used in the HRI to gauge need – at least in financial terms - is based on UN CAP and the Red Cross Red Crescent Movement appeals, without any judgment on the accuracy, validity or quality of those appeals. Unfortunately, this measure does not include many agencies (particularly local NGOs) that are not part of the CHAP process and therefore misses out an important dimension of the overall needs in any given crisis.

17   WFP, 2008.

18   For example, according to OCHA's FTS, Denmark provided a mere USD 51,046 in humanitarian aid in the CAR, considered the world's most neglected crisis. (OCHA, 2008).

19   See for example the chapters by John Cosgrave "Humanitarian Funding and Needs Assessment" and Francois Grunewald, "New Approaches to Needs Assessment: Comprehensive Rolling Diagnosis" for more analysis of the limitations of needs assessments (Cosgrave, 2008 and Grunewald, 2008.).

20   Simms and Reid. 2005.

21   Benn, 2006.

22   ALNAP has also published a number of reports on the issue (ALNAP, "Global Study")

23   OECD, 2005a.

24   See "The utilisation of evaluations" by Peta Sandison. (Sandison, 2006).

25   To ensure a more fair and accurate assessment of donors in crises, the analysis is only based on those donors with at least 30 responses to the survey. This means that donors with a lower number of responses are not included in this analysis, although as explained above, they have been included in the calculations of the overall index scores and rankings, using pooled data from the 2007 and 2008 surveys.

26   Council of the European Union, 2007.

27 The use of pooled data is a well established practice in statistical analysis. With particular reference to the estimation of indexes, the Commitment to Development Index, for instance, pools data over three annual periods, using a discount factor which attaches greatest weight to the most recent data set.

28 Forgotten crises were defined on the basis of the following sources: OCHA, 2008; Médecins Sans Frontières, 2007; ECHO, 2007b. The extent of media coverage was based on the media tracking methodology developed by Reuters/AlertNet, at http://www.alertnet.org/thefacts/chart/mediamonitoringmethodology.htm

19 ECHO, 2006.

30 This indicator will certainly not provide the complete picture of donors' disaster risk reduction efforts, because these are often channelled as bilateral aid or involve regional initiatives that are not adequately captured by our indicators. In addition, these initiatives are sometimes recorded or couched as environmental projects, for example on desertification, although they are usually disaster risk reduction projects. However, from 2009 on, the HRI will be able to rely on much more detailed information about individual country initiatives and funding in the DRR area, due to the large and comprehensive information-gathering exercise currently being undertaken under the auspices of ISDR. This will undoubtedly improve the assessment of Pillar 2 issues within the Index.

31 UN General Assembly, 2005.

32 These data were provided directly to DARA by donors during the HRI field visits

33 The principal legal instruments on international humanitarian law are listed in the European Union guidelines on promoting compliance with international humanitarian law (European Union, 2005).

34 See ICRC (1997) Advisory Service on International Humanitarian Law: 1) Implementing International Humanitarian Law: From Law to Action, and 2) National Committees for the Implementation of International Humanitarian Law.

35 For more information see: http://www.sphereproject.org/; http://www.hapinternational.org/; http://www.projetqualite.org/compas/outil/; and http://www.peopleinaid.org/.

36 Using search terms "Learning and accountability," and "evaluation," to identify relevant projects funded by donors.

References

Active Learning Network for Accountability and Performance in Humanitarian Action (ALNAP). Review of Humanitarian Action Series. http://www.alnap.org/publications/rha.htm

Active Learning Network for Accountability and Performance in Humanitarian Action (ALNAP). The Global Study on Participation and Consultation of Affected Populations in Humanitarian Action. At: http://www.alnap.org/

Anderson, Mary B. 2008, "The Giving-Receiving Relationship: Inherently Unequal?" Humanitarian Response Index 2008. Ed. DARA. Hampshire: Palgrave Macmillan. Chapter 6.

AusAID. 2001. Peace, Conflict and Development Policy. At: http://www.ausaid.gov.au/publications/pubout.cfm?ID=3617_162_5546_3187_691

———. 2002. Peace Conflict and Development Policy. June. At: http://www.ausaid.gov.au/publications/pdf/conflict_policy.pdf

———. 2005. Humanitarian Action Policy. January. At: http://www.ausaid.gov.au/publications/pdf/humanitarian_policy.pdf

———. 2006. Promoting Growth and Stability. A White Paper on the Australian Government's Overseas Aid Program. At: http://www.ausaid.gov.au/publications/pubout.cfm?Id=6184_6346_7334_4045_8043

van Beijnum, M. and L. van de Goor. 2006. The Netherlands and its Whole of Government Approach on Fragile States. Clingendael Institute: The Hague. August. At: http://www.clingendael.nl/publications/2006/20060800_cru_paper_sudan.pdf

Benn, Hilary. 2006. Humanitarian and conflict reform – an emergency service for the world. (Speech) Department for International Development. 23 January. At: http://www.dfid.gov.uk/news/files/Speeches/wp2006-speeches/humanitarian230106.asp

Canadian International Development Agency (CIDA). Humanitarian Assistance. At: http://www.acdi-cida.gc.ca/CIDAWEB/acdicida.nsf/En/JUD-1261545-RJU

Council of the European Union. 2007. A European Consensus on Humanitarian Aid: Working Together to Help People in Need. Brussels. 18 December. At: http://www.ieei.pt/files/A_European_Consensuson_Humanitarian_Aid.pdf

Danish Ministry of Foreign Affairs. 1998. Act on International Development Cooperation. Act No. 541. 10 July. At: http://www.um.dk/en/menu/DevelopmentPolicy/DanishDevelopmentPolicy/ActOnInternationalDevelopmentCooperation/

———. 2000. Denmark's Development Policy – Analysis – Partnership 2000. DANIDA. At: http://www.um.dk/Publikationer/Danida/English/DanishDevelopmentCooperation/DenmarksDevelopmentPolicyAnalysis/index.asp

———. 2002. Strategic Priorities in Danish Humanitarian Assistance. DANIDA. At: http://www.um.dk/Publikationer/Danida/English/MultilateralAssistance/StrategicPrioritiesDanishHumanitarianAssistance/strategy.pdf

———. 2004a. A Joint Evaluation: Humanitarian and Reconstruction Assistance to Afghanistan, 2001–2005. DANIDA. At: http://www.um.dk/NR/rdonlyres/F48036CB-D540-41D0-8AC3-AED57D551194/0/Afghanistan_summaryReport.pdf

———. 2004b. Humanitarian and Rehabilitation Assistance to Kosovo 1999–2003. Evaluation Report. DANIDA. At: http://www.um.dk/Publikationer/Danida/English/Evaluations/Kosovo2005/Kosovo.pdf

———. 2007. A World for All: Priorities of the Danish Government for Danish Development Assistance 2008-2012. DANIDA. At: http://www.um.dk/NR/rdonlyres/0290D748-D013-4365-95F3-A6CC92FD6E93/0/a_world_for_all.pdf

Cosgrave, John. 2008, "Humanitarian Funding and Needs Assessment" Humanitarian Response Index 2008. Ed. DARA. Hampshire: Palgrave Macmillan.

Department for International Development (DFID). 2006. Saving lives, relieving suffering, protecting dignity: DFID's Humanitarian Policy. London. June. At: http://www.dfid.gov.uk/Pubs/files/humanitarian-policy.pdf

Disaster Preparedness European Commission (DIPECHO). At: http://ec.europa.eu/echo/aid/dipecho_en.htm

Dutch Ministry of Foreign Affairs. 2006. Dutch Humanitarian Assistance: An Evaluation. IOB Evaluations No. 303. At: http://www.euforic.org/iob

———. 2008a. Humanitarian Aid Policy 2008. Humanitarian Aid Policy Rules. At: http://www.minbuza.nl/en/themes,humanitarian-aid/dutch-humanitarian-aid/Grant-policy-framework-for-humanitarian-aid-2005.html

———. 2008b. Order of the Minister for Development Cooperation. 27 March. No. DMV/HH-0058/08.

Egeland, Jan. 2007."Progress on the Front Lines." Humanitarian Response Index 2007. Ed. Silvia Hidalgo and Augusto López-Claros. Hampshire: Palgrave Macmillan.

EurActiv. 2005. "EU warns against tsunami aid 'beauty contest'." 6 January. At: http://www.euractiv.com/en/sustainability/eu-warns-tsunami-aid-beauty-contest/article-133776

European Commission Humanitarian (Aid) Office (ECHO). 2006. Global needs and vulnerability assessment. At: http://ec.europa.eu/echo/policies/needs_en.htm

———. 2007a. Crisis and Vulnerability Index. At: http://ec.europa.eu/echo/files/policies/strategy/fca2007.xls

———. 2007b. The Shadow of Forgotten Crises. Brussels. At: http://ec.europa.eu/echo/files/media/publications/forgotten_crises_2007_en.pdf

European Union. 2005. "European Union guidelines on promoting compliance with international humanitarian law (IHL)." Office Journal of the European Union. C 327/04). At: http://eur-lex.europa.eu/LexUriServ/LexUriServ.do?uri=OJ:C:2005:327:0004:0007:EN:PDF

Flint, Michael and Hugh Goyder. 2006. "Funding the tsunami response." Tsunami Evaluation Coalition (TEC). July At: http://www.tsunami-evaluation.org/NR/rdonlyres/BBA2659F-967C-4CAB-A08F-BEF67606C83F/0/funding_final_report.pdf

German Federal Foreign Office (FFO). 2006. Bericht der Bundesregierung über die deutsche humanitäre Hilfe im Ausland 2002 bis 2005. At: http://www.auswaertiges-amt.de/diplo/de/Aussenpolitik/Themen/HumanitaereHilfe/downloads/BerichtHH2002-2005.pdf

———. 2007a. Integrating Disaster Risk Reduction in European Humanitarian Assistance. Report commissioned by the Federal Foreign Office and the German Committee for Disaster Reduction. Humanitarian and Development Network. At: http://www.auswaertiges-amt.de/diplo/de/Aussenpolitik/Themen/HumanitaereHilfe/downloads/ReportOnIntegratingDisasterRiskReduction.pdf

———. 2007b. The Federal Government's Humanitarian Aid. At: http://www.auswaertiges-amt.de/diplo/en/Aussenpolitik/Themen/HumanitaereHilfe/Downloads/Humanit_C3_A4reHilfederBundesregierung2007.pdf

Grunewald, Francois. 2008. "New Approaches to Needs Assessment: Comprehensive Rolling Diagnosis." Humanitarian Response Index 2008. Ed. DARA. Hampshire: Palgrave Macmillan.

Hidalgo, S. and A. Lopez-Claros. 2008. The Humanitarian Response Index 2007. Hampshire: Palgrave Macmillan.

House of Commons International Development Committee. 2006. Humanitarian response to natural disasters. Seventh Report of Session 2005-2006. 24 October. At: http://www.publications.parliament.uk/pa/cm200506/cmselect/cmintdev/1188/1188i.pdf

International Committee of the Red Cross (ICRC). 1997. The ICRC Advisory Service on International Humanitarian Law. International Review of the Red Cross. No. 319 31 August. pp.456–457. At: http://www.icrc.org/web/eng/siteeng0.nsf/html/57JNRP

International Federation of Red Cross and Red Crescent Societies (IFRC). Disaster Relief Emergency Fund. At: http://www.ifrc.org/what/disasters/responding/drs/tools/dref.asp

———. 2008. World Disasters Report. At: http://www.ifrc.org/publicat/wdr2008/summaries.asp

Irish Aid. 2005. White Paper on Irish Aid. Government of Ireland. At: http://www.irishaid.gov.ie/whitepaper/

Japan International Cooperation Agency. 2007. Emergency Disaster Relief. At: http://www.jica.go.jp/english/schemes/emer.html

Médecins Sans Frontières. 2007. Top Ten Most Underreported Humanitarian Stories of 2007. At: http://www.msf.org/msfinternational/invoke.cfm?objectid=F77A3EAE-15C5-F00A-2512CE940378E72C&component=toolkit.report&method=full_html

Minear, Larry. 2008. "The United States as Humanitarian Actor." Humanitarian Response Index 2008. Ed. DARA. Hampshire: Palgrave Macmillan.

Minear, Larry and Ian Smillie. Undated. "Welcome to the Good Humanitarian Donorship club." Humanitarianism and War Project, Tufts University. At: http://www.odihpn.org/report.asp?id=2707

Norwegian Ministry of Foreign Affairs. 2008. Peer Review 2008: Memorandum. Oslo. April. At: http://www.norad.no

———. 2007. Norwegian policy on the prevention of humanitarian crises. Report No. 9 (2007–2008). Oslo. At: http://www.regjeringen.no/pages/2054072/PDFS/STM200720080009000EN_PDFS.pdf

Organisation for Economic Co-operation and Development (OECD). 2003. Ireland, Development Assistance Committee (DAC), Peer Review. Paris: OECD. At: http://www.oecd.org/dataoecd/25/43/21651179.pdf

———. 2004. Japan, Development Assistance Committee (DAC), Peer Review. Paris: OECD. At: http://www.oecd.org/dataoecd/43/63/32285814.pdf

———. 2005a. The Paris Declaration on Aid Effectiveness. 2 March. At: http://www.oecd.org/document/18/0,2340,en_2649_3236398_35401554_1_1_1,00.html

———. 2005b. Australia. Development Assistance Committee (DAC). Peer Review. Paris: OECD. At: http://www.oecd.org/dataoecd/10/39/34429866.pdf

———. 2005c. Norway. Development Assistance Committee (DAC). Peer Review. Paris: OECD. At: http://www.oecd.org/dataoecd/49/43/34622621.pdf

——— 2005d. Sweden. Development Assistance Committee (DAC). Peer Review. Paris: OECD. At: http://www.oecd.org/dataoecd/14/43/35268515.pdf

——— 2005e. Switzerland. Development Assistance Committee (DAC). Peer Review. Paris: OECD. At: http://www.oecd.org/dataoecd/9/59/35297586.pdf

———. 2006a. Germany. Development Assistance Committee (DAC). Peer Review. Paris: OECD. At: http://www.oecd.org/dataoecd/54/0/36058447.pdf

———. 2006b. Netherlands. Development Assistance Committee (DAC). Peer Review. Paris: OECD. At: http://www.oecd.org/dataoecd/49/38/37531015.pdf

———. 2006c. United Kingdom. Development Assistance Committee (DAC). Peer Review. Paris: OECD. At: http://www.oecd.org/dataoecd/54/57/37010997.pdf

———. 2006d. The United States. Development Assistance Committee (DAC). Peer Review. Paris: OECD. At: http://www.oecd.org/dataoecd/61/57/37885999.pdf

———. 2007a. European Community. Development Assistance Committee (DAC). Peer Review. Paris: OECD. At: http://www.oecd.org/dataoecd/57/6/38965119.pdf

———. 2007b. Canada. Development Assistance Committee (DAC). Peer Review. Paris: OECD. At: http://www.oecd.org/dataoecd/48/61/39515510.pdf

———. 2007c. Denmark. Development Assistance Committee (DAC). Peer Review. Paris: OECD. At: http://www.oecd.org/dataoecd/46/35/39166375.pdf

———. 2007d. Spain. Development Assistance Committee (DAC). Peer Review. Paris: OECD. At: http://www.oecd.org/dataoecd/21/14/39710206.pdf

———. 2008a. France. Development Assistance Committee (DAC). Peer Review. Paris: OECD. At: http://www.oecd.org/dataoecd/4/10/40814790.pdf

———. 2008b. Luxembourg. Development Assistance Committee (DAC). Peer Review. Paris: OECD. At: http://www.oecd.org/dataoecd/33/60/40912874.pdf

Office for the Coordination of Humanitarian Affairs (OCHA). 2008. Financial Tracking System. At: http://ocha.unog.ch/fts2/page-loader.aspx?page=home

Overseas Development Institute (ODI) Humanitarian Policy Group. 2006. Humanitarian Response to Natural Disasters: A briefing paper prepared by the Humanitarian Policy Group for the International Development Committee inquiry into Humanitarian Response to Natural Disasters. London. May. At: http://www.odi.org.uk/HPG/papers/ODIparliament_briefing_disasters.pdf

Reuters/AlertNet. Media monitoring – methodology. At: http://www.alertnet.org/thefacts/chart/mediamonitoringmethodology.htm

Roodman, David. 2008. "Tale of Two Indices: The Commitment to Development Index as a Model for the Humanitarian Response Index." Humanitarian Response Index 2008. Ed. DARA. Hampshire: Palgrave Macmillan.

Sandison, Peta. 2006. "The utilisation of evaluations." ALNAP Review of Humanitarian Action in 2005. December. At: http://www.alnap.org/publications/RHA2005/rha05_Ch3.pdf

Schaar, Johan. 2007. "The Birth of Good Humanitarian Donorship" Humanitarian Response Index 2007. Ed. Silvia Hidalgo. Hampshire: Palgrave Macmillan.

Simms, Andrew and Hannah Reid. 2005. Up in Smoke: Africa. Working Group on Climate Change and Development. New Economics, Foundation. London. July. At: http://www.iied.org/pubs/pdfs/9560IIED.pdf

Spanish Ministry of Foreign Affairs. 2005. The Master Plan for Spanish Cooperation 2005–2008. At: http://www.aecid.es/03coop/6public_docs/2seci/2doc_coop_esp/ftp/Plan_Director_Ing.pdf

———. 2007. Humanitarian Action Strategy Paper. Spanish Development Cooperation. At: http://www.maec.es/SiteCollectionDocuments/Cooperaci%C3%B3n%20espa%C3%B1ola/Publicaciones/DES%20AH%20Resumen%20ing.pdf

Stoddard, Abby, Dirk Salomons, Katherine Haver, and Adele Harmer. 2006. Common Funds for Humanitarian Action in Sudan and the Democratic Republic of Congo: Monitoring and Evaluation Study. New York: Center for International Cooperation. December. At: http://www.cic.nyu.edu/internationalsecurity/docs/H_Common%20Funds%20Monitoring%20and%20Evaluation%20Report%20December%202006.DOC

Swedish International Development Cooperation Agency. 2005. Reducing the risk of disasters: SIDA's effort to reduce poor people's vulnerability to hazards. June. At: http://www.sida.se/sida/jsp/sida.jsp?d=118&a=17204&language=en_US

———. 2006. Guidelines: General grants for minor humanitarian projects. October. At: http://www.sida.se/sida/jsp/sida.jsp?d=118&a=25797&language=en_US

———. 2007. Guidelines: SIDA grants to non-governmental organisations for humanitarian projects. February. At: http://www.sida.se/sida/jsp/sida.jsp?d=118&a=25432&language=en_US

Swedish Ministry of Foreign Affairs. 2004a. The Government's Humanitarian Aid Policy. Comm. 2004/05:52. 16 December. At: http://www.regeringen.se/content/1/c6/09/36/93/5755b712.pdf

———. 2004b. Government guidelines for SIDA's work with humanitarian assistance. UD2004/60685/GS.

———. 2007a. The New Development Cooperation Policy. Budget Bill 2008: Fact sheet on the Swedish Government's Budget Bill for 2008. 20 September. At: http://www.regeringen.se/content/1/c6/09/23/99/9b36aee7.pdf

———. 2007b. Strategy for Multilateral Development Cooperation. 30 March.

Swiss Agency for Development and Cooperation. 2002. Solidarity Alive, Humanitarian Aid. At: http://www.regeringen.se/content/1/c6/08/38/43/4a7cef2b.pdf

Swiss Federal Department of Foreign Affairs. 2005. Solidarity Alive: Humanitarian Aid Strategy 2005. Bern. At: http://www.deza.admin.ch/ressources/resource_en_23576.pdf

———. 2007. Humanitare Hilfe des Bundes, Strategie 2010. Bern. March. At: http://www.deza.admin.ch/ressources/resource_de_153478.pdf

——— Bureau for Crisis Prevention and Recovery (BCPR). 2006. 2006 Annual Report: Crisis Prevention and Recovery: Thematic Trust Fund. At: http://www.undp.org/cpr/documents/whats_new/cpr_ttf_2006.pdf

United Nations General Assembly. 2005. "Strengthening of the coordination of emergency humanitarian assistance of the United Nations." Resolution A/RES/60/124. 15. At: http://www.unicef.org/emerg/files/Res_60_124.pdf

United Nations International Secretariat for Disaster Reduction (ISDR). 2007. Disaster Risk Reduction, 2007 Global Review. ISDR/GP/2007/3. At: http://www.preventionweb.net/english/documents/global-review-2007/Global-Review-2007.pdf

Watanabe, M. 2003. Japan's humanitarian assistance. ODI Humanitarian Practice Network. At: http://www.odihpn.org/report.asp?id=2617

Willitts-King, Barnaby. 2004. "Germany's Twelve Basic Rules of Humanitarian Assistance Abroad." Box 3 in Good Humanitarian Donorship and the European Union: A study of good practice and recent initiatives. Final report. Development Cooperation Ireland. 15 September. p.12. At: http://www.goodhumanitariandonorship.org/EU_GHD_study_final_report.pdf

World Bank. 2007. Global Facility for Disaster Reduction and Recovery. At: http://gfdrr.org/index.cfm?Page=home&ItemID=200

World Food Programme (WFP). 2008. WFP Crisis Page – High Food Prices. At: http://www.wfp.org/english/?ModuleID=137&Key=2853

2

PART TWO

Perspectives on the HRI and Needs Assessment

CHAPTER 2

The United States as Humanitarian Actor

LARRY MINEAR, Feinstein International Center, Tufts University (retired)

The performance of the United States as a humanitarian actor received decidedly mixed reviews in DARA's Humanitarian Response Index (HRI) 2007. Overall, the United States was ranked 16th among the 23 members of the Organisation for Economic Co-operation and Development (OECD).[1] These rankings range from a high of 2 for promoting learning and accountability to a low of 23 for implementing international guiding principles. The U.S. places 16th in responding to humanitarian needs, 13th in working with humanitarian partners, and 10th in integrating relief and development. According to the quantitative or "hard data" indicators, the U.S. ranks an even less flattering 20th.

The HRI assessment challenges the view of the United States, deeply embedded in the American psyche and regularly reinforced in the rhetoric of public officials, as the world's pre-eminent humanitarian actor, the paragon of global compassion. A recent example of this self-image is a statement by President George W. Bush, announcing an initiative requesting Congress to provide an additional US$770 million for food aid and food security to assist countries experiencing food shortages and run-away food prices. "The American people are generous people and they're compassionate people," he said at a press conference on 1 May 2008; "to whom much is given, [and] much is expected."[2]

The self-image of the United States as a generous and compassionate nation is well grounded in American history. It has roots in relief efforts in Europe by Herbert Hoover during and after World War I, the Marshall Plan following World War II, and more than half a century of high-profile American food and other aid to the victims of natural disasters and armed conflicts. The stark contrast between US behaviour as assessed by the Humanitarian Response Index and Americans' self-image suggests either faulty metrics or delusions of humanitarian grandeur.

The Index assesses the performance of governments using indicators that have also figured prominently in

research with which I have been associated in recent years. The research was conducted by the Humanitarianism and War Project, which I co-founded in 1991 and co-directed until my retirement in mid-2006, and by its successor efforts at Tufts University. Our work provides something of a commentary on the findings of the HRI exercise. This commentary may be useful even though our research does not rank performance by individual governments and even though some of our individual country studies predate the time period reviewed by the HRI.

My conclusion is that the five pillars against which the HRI assesses government performance are appropriate and that the HRI's assessment is broadly confirmed by our own independent studies. Both judgments reflect an emerging consensus that humanitarian action should no longer be viewed as a series of disparate emergency relief interventions by individual states, a metric in which the United States often excels. Gone are the days when "the quality of aid was thought to be less important than the nobility of intentions."[3] Humanitarian action is instead coming to be viewed as an agreed framework of principles and rights, of responsibilities, and accountabilities within which aid programmes are mounted. From this more systemic vantage point, US performance leaves much to be desired.

The HRI and US performance

The upswing in the scale and profile of humanitarian action in the post-Cold War era has been well documented and needs no recapitulation here.[4] The past decade has witnessed, on the one hand, incremental growth in the levels of humanitarian activities and, on the other, growing concern across the international community about the conduct and effectiveness of global humanitarian action. Surveying the disheveled state of the enterprise in April 2003 in a study that found its way into the Good Humanitarian Donorship

(GHD) discussions, Ian Smillie and I identified four key elements: "Humanitarianism is not the main driver of donor behaviour in financing humanitarian work; the donor humanitarian policy framework is inconsistent and contradictory; in its application, the whole of the humanitarian endeavor is less than the sum of its parts; and the humanitarian enterprise is marked by a climate of mistrust and lack of transparency."[5]

Frustration at the confusion pervading the humanitarian sector led governments in June 2003 to launch the GHD initiative, which provided both a framework of core principles and a forum for reviewing and monitoring their implementation.[6] Taking GHD principles as an agreed upon behavioural framework, the non-governmental group Development Assistance Research Associates (DARA) identified five "pillars" of performance to serve as the core of an independent Humanitarian Response Index. In order to measure performance by each of the 23 OECD members (22 states and the European Commission) in each of these five areas, DARA employs 57 indicators, 32 "soft" or qualitative data from visits to countries experiencing major crises, and 25 reflecting "hard" or quantitative data.

The HRI is necessarily a complex instrument which, in the short time since its development and initial application in 2007, has provoked considerable controversy. Some governments have questioned its approach, some its conclusions. Some have challenged the professional *bona fides* of DARA, some the very idea that governments can or should be held accountable individually for their stewardship of humanitarian obligations and resources. This chapter accepts the HRI categories for the purposes of discussion, saving questions about the instrument as whole and particular benchmarks for its concluding section.

The chapter refers throughout to a peer review of US government performance carried out by the OECD/DAC in 2006.[7] That review basically confirms the problems flagged in the HRI assessment but places them within what it views as the continuing role of the United States as "a leader in international development cooperation because of the size of its economy, its ability to influence global action and its presence within the international donor community.[8]

Pillar I: Responding to humanitarian needs

The Humanitarian Response Index finds serious deficiencies in the present fidelity of the United States to core humanitarian principles. Of the 23 OECD members whose performance is reviewed, the United States

is ranked 18th in terms of the alleviation of suffering, 21st in its respect for impartiality, 21st as regards neutrality, and 23rd with respect to independence. To what extent does field-based data derived from our research confirm this severe indictment of the American stewardship of the fundamentals of the humanitarian project and practice?

Our most recent research, *Humanitarian Agenda 2015: Final Report. The State of the Humanitarian Enterprise,*[9] involved more than 2000 interviews in 12 countries. Our final report confirmed a serious crisis of humanitarianism in the post 9/11 world. "International action aimed at assisting and protecting the most vulnerable is, for the most part, inextricably linked to a northern security agenda," we concluded. "Humanitarian action occupies a crucial but increasingly precarious position at the intersection of a) international political/security agendas and b) the coping strategies of people affected by crisis and conflict. It is instrumentalized and torn between principle and pragmatism as perhaps never before, particularly in high-profile crises."[10] An earlier study, *The Charity of Nations: Humanitarian Action in a Calculating World,* provides a detailed review and analysis of the impact of American political agendas on its conduct of humanitarian activities.[11]

The penetration of aid decisions by security concerns is confirmed by the 2006 OECD/DAC peer review of United States government performance. While its comments are framed in terms of US development cooperation policy, they apply equally to humanitarian matters. "Historically," the review concludes, "the US has justified its development assistance policies in terms of both recipient country needs and its own foreign policy objectives. The events of 11 September 2001 and the 'War on Terror' which grew from them have provided the starting point for a renewed American interest in development co-operation."[12]

The United States is not the only government whose security agenda infiltrates humanitarian activities characterised by human need, neutrality, impartiality, and independence. However, as the sole surviving superpower in the post-Cold War era, that hegemon exercises a dominant global role, privileging its own national security, defined largely in political and military terms, and minimizing the contribution of effective humanitarian and human security efforts.[13] A further review might also document the negative impact of the US approach on the performance of other states.

The penetration of humanitarian action by American political agendas is not limited to the post-9/11 period.

During the Cold War, US officials provided what they called "humanitarian" aid to the Nicaraguan Contras and to other insurgencies seeking to topple communist regimes in such places as Afghanistan, Angola, and Cambodia.[14] Other major powers with less established traditions of humanitarian assistance also aided selected regimes around the world to further their own political agendas." To be sure, there were exceptions to US politicisation of humanitarian action. One was the decision by President Ronald Reagan in 1984 to provide emergency food assistance to people in Mengistu's Ethiopia on the grounds that "A hungry child knows no politics." Yet such allocations have been the exception rather than the rule.[15] The tendency to nest humanitarian principles within the broader rubric of US national security has contributed to the more general tendency to approach the core concept of humanitarianism in terms that are "self-defined and self-referential."[16]

The post-9/11 era is the latest chapter in a well-established US saga in which humanitarian action is ever the bridesmaid but rarely the bride. This latest permutation involves deep tensions between human need and humanitarian response, on the one hand, and terrorism and anti-terrorist agendas on the other. The pattern that emerges is troubling but not surprising. "While humanitarianism in an age of terrorism may enjoy a higher profile than in earlier eras, its newfound visibility is a mixed blessing. Although augmented attention to the human condition in unstable areas was a welcome development, we noted a fundamental contradiction between an anti-terrorism that divides the world into good guys and bad guys and a humanitarianism that refuses to draw invidious distinctions among people whose governments espouse hostile political or military philosophies."[17]

A recent example confirms the recurring lack of respect by US officials for the essentials of humanitarian action. In the wake of Hurricane Katrina in August 2005, the United States received offers of aid in cash and kind valued at US$1 billion from some 100 countries and international organisations. The offers ranged from US$500 million in crude oil and cash from Kuwait to US$25,000 from Sri Lanka, itself still recovering from the 2004 tsunami. Bangladesh, itself no stranger to hurricanes, offered technical assistance and US$1 million in cash, Cuba 1,100 doctors, Venezuela food, potable water and eye care, and Canada 1,000 relief personnel and four naval and Coast Guard vessels.[18] The outpouring of international support and solidarity was focused on the Gulf coast and New Orleans in particular.

Multiple offers of assistance placed the Bush administration in an awkward position. The president initially rejected the more political offers, including one of oil from Iran – an "Axis of Evil" nation – saying that the United States could take care of itself. Yet the administration ended by requesting 500,000 meals ready-to-eat from the European Union and air transport from NATO. Its wariness in accepting emergency aid suggested that, with the tables turned and the United States on the recipient end, the self-styled paragon of humanitarian virtue viewed offers of assistance essentially as an object of suspicion rather than an act of solidarity. "It was as if the world's generosity were an affront."[19]

The HRI uses other indicators than the core principles of humanitarian action to assess donor performance in responding to human needs. The hard data it compiles ranks the U.S. 1st in the distribution of funding relative to historical ties and geographic proximity: that is, US aid allocations were relatively independent of regional favouritism. The United States ranks 2nd in allocations of funding, according to ECHO's Global Needs Assessment, and 6th in its provision of funds for priority sectors in given crises. Yet if considerations of impartiality and proportionality are not altogether lacking in US country and sectoral allocations, they do not offset poor performance by the United States in the critical areas of neutrality and independence. The importance of core principles is reflected by the fact that Pillar 1 receives the largest weight among the five pillars (30 percent) in calculating each nation's composite score.

Pillar II: Integrating relief and development

The HRI gives the United States higher marks for integrating relief and development, a category in which the U.S. places 10th among the 23 members of the OECD group. This ranking reflects strong performance in consulting with beneficiaries and supporting rapid recovery of sustainable livelihoods (in each of these indicators it places 2nd), strengthening preparedness (4th), strengthening resilience to cope with crises, encouraging better coordination with humanitarian partners, and supporting long-term development aims, placing 7th in each of these indicators. The U.S. placed 14th in strengthening local capacity to deal with crises.

Our research confirms the importance of these various facets of humanitarian action and itself finds US performance mixed. On the positive side is creation by the United States Agency for International Development (USAID) of an innovative Office of Transition Initiatives

(OTI), founded in 1994 as a separate office in its Bureau of Humanitarian Response, to design and implement "overt political programs in crisis-prone countries in transition from war to peace."[20] In Haiti, OTI efforts concentrated on reintegrating members of the armed forces as an investment in restarting the national economy, strengthening democratic institutions, and enhancing security. Training was provided to some 4,867 demobilised soldiers. Yet of these, a USAID evaluation later found, only 304 found employment. A total of 1,790 men were trained as auto-mechanics, far in excess of available job slots, while the 602 who learned computer skills also had difficulty finding employment. In short, the result of OTI's promising Haiti initiative "confirms the triumph of short-term thinking, short-term mandates, and short-term funding over entrenched long-term problems and needs."[21]

In reviewing local capacity building efforts, the role of the US government surfaces particularly in the cases of Bosnia and Mozambique. In Bosnia, USAID gave an American NGO, the International Rescue Committee, an umbrella grant designed "to strengthen local, community-oriented NGOs with training and technical assistance as well as project assistance.[22] Another innovative initiative, the creation of a Bosnian NGO Foundation which was designed to provide training, advocacy, and continuing support to local NGOs after the emergency was over, failed to receive USAID funding. Its requests were turned down as well by the EU, the UK and other bilateral donors, the World Bank, and several foundations on the grounds that it sought funding that would continue after the donors themselves had left.[23]

A review of efforts to rebuild the health sector in Mozambique as the civil war was winding down in the early 1990s notes the involvement of Finland, Switzerland, Norway, Canada, Ireland, Denmark, and the United States, as well as of the EU and the World Bank. Donors adopted a wide variety of approaches. Some underwrote NGOs in the interest of quick and tangible results; others sought to reinvigorate the Mozambican ministry of health with an eye to the longer term challenge of helping to establish the capacity of the state. The many NGOs involved, both international and local, themselves espoused differing approaches to building government capacity and supporting civil society. We gave high marks to the approach taken by Finland, but did not reach a judgment about the effectiveness of the US approach itself.[24]

A study commissioned by USAID examined the extent to which, since the inception of American foreign aid, USAID and its predecessor agencies have given priority attention to supporting the livelihoods of people affected by major crises, beyond the provision of emergency relief.[25] While the nomenclature for what is now called "supporting livelihoods" has changed over the years since the initial US intervention in Cuba (1898–1902), we document considerable activity by the government over the years in looking beyond relief efforts and seeking to integrate relief and development, even though we stopped short of evaluating the effectiveness of US efforts in this area.

The United States is not alone in experiencing difficulties in strengthening local capacity. Our study of capacity-building confirmed the importance of the benchmarks identified in the HRI instrument while underscoring the finding that the results of the sum total of all donor activities in the area of local capacity-building remained distressingly small. "Good intentions notwithstanding," we concluded, "outsiders appear to have great difficulty working effectively with local organizations … during humanitarian emergencies. When they do, the relationship is more often one of patronage than partnership."[26]

Our research suggests several factors that would reinforce the HRI assessment of the United States in integrating relief and development. One is its practice of supporting the work of NGOs, many of which are operational in crisis settings well in advance of, and continuing well in the aftermath of, a given emergency. (The U.S. places 8th among OECD actors with regard to promoting the role of NGOs and 1st in funding them, according to the respective soft and hard data provided under Pillar III.) Another is the profile of USAID itself as a major actor on the international development scene. At the same time, the performance of the United States in this area cannot have been helped by the heavy attrition of USAID staff in recent years – the agency is currently seeking to restore some of the slots that had been eliminated – or by the burgeoning role of private contractors and the Department of Defense. The OECD/DAC peer review confirms that "the continued redirection of Official Development Assistance away from USAID… carries risks, both because it is the most experienced [US] government provider of aid and because it contains much of its development expertise."[27]

While the HRI examines the important interconnections between relief and development, it fails to situate humanitarian activities in relation to political and military frameworks. Getting that contextualisation right, however, is arguably one of the four critical challenges faced by the humanitarian enterprise during the next decade. Our country case study-based data finds that the current drive among donors – the OECD/DAC discussions being but one instance – to establish "coherence" between humanitarian and political/peacekeeping agendas more often than not works to the disadvantage of humanitarian interests and activities.[28] From our perspective, the failure to contextualise humanitarian action in relation to those wider frameworks represents a weakness of the OECD/DAC guidelines themselves. In fact, the OECD/DAC peer review urges the United States "to pursue approaches that best unite development, defence, diplomatic, and humanitarian communities in fragile states."[29] A few years ago in correspondence with the Active Learning Network for Accountability and Performance in Humanitarian Action (ALNAP), I urged that such approaches be clarified in the interest of protecting humanitarian activities from instrumentalisation within such frameworks, multilateral and bilateral alike.[30]

Pillar III: Working with humanitarian partners

The HRI ranks the United States 13th among the 23 OECD members in working with humanitarian partners. The United States does best in supporting donor preparedness in implementing humanitarian action (3rd), facilitating humanitarian access (6th), promoting NGO roles, supporting contingency planning and capacity building efforts (8th in each), and providing predictable funding (10th). In the other four benchmarks, the United States places in the lower half of OECD members: in longer-term funding arrangements (12th), supporting effective coordination efforts (13th), flexible funding (14th), and reducing earmarking (17th). As with Pillar II, these criteria tend to be more programmatic and operational than the more policy-oriented benchmarks of Pillar I.

Here, too, the research data is mixed. In the first Gulf War, troops in the US-led Operation Provide Comfort established mutually beneficial relationships with non-governmental and UN organisations. The troops took the lead in assisting and protecting Iraqi Kurds who had fled into the mountains along Iraq's border with Turkey in March 1991, at the same time providing civilian aid organisations with regular briefings, as well as telecommunications, transport, and protective cover. The "basic discipline and organisation injected by the military into a fluid situation," we concluded, provided "a firm point of reference" for emergency efforts and facilitated a smooth and prompt transition to UN and NGO management of humanitarian activities.[31]

In a number of crisis settings, the United States has funded efforts to coordinate the work of NGOs. In Kigali, for the Rwanda relief operation, this took the form of providing a liaison to primarily American private relief groups; in Zagreb, for activities in the former Yugoslavia, the function had a wider international focus. In a variety of locations, USAID's Disaster Assistance Relief Teams (DARTs), dispatched quickly into emergencies to assess needs and formulate response strategies, typically sought out NGO, UN, and Red Cross agencies on the ground and took their capacities into account in their recommendations regarding procedures and costs.

The cultivation of humanitarian partnerships by the US government had more mixed outcomes in global War on Terror settings. Our findings in Afghanistan with respect to the variations in relationships between individual OECD governments and NGOs broadly coincided with those of the HRI. The Dutch, who ranked 1st in the HRI's hard-data indicator regarding the provision of unearmarked funds, made clear to our researchers that "they were not interested in "flag-flying." By contrast, the Japanese, 17th among the OECD group for that benchmark, were "very much interested in seeing our flag." In 22nd place, the Americans, who as of 2004 had contributed fully 80 percent of all humanitarian resources to post-9/11 Iraq, were "not known for their modest and self-effacing ways." One EC official, speaking off the record, said that "The European Community is the worst flag-flyer around." The EC placed 23rd in the flagging order.[32]

Provincial Reconstruction Teams (PRTs), an American innovation in Afghanistan later transplanted to Iraq, created major problems for NGOs and UN organisations alike. Military officials viewed PRTs as positive, representing, in the words of one, "the first time in years that the US military has had money and supplies to provide humanitarian relief on the ground." "What's going on here," countered one NGO official, is a distortion of humanitarian affairs that "could redefine humanitarian work globally."[33] Indigenous as well as American NGOs had great difficulty collaborating with the US government, both in Kabul and in US-sponsored PRT locations around the country. US security protocols made it difficult for NGOs, particularly indigenous ones, even to obtain physical access to US officials.

In Iraq, NGOs experienced shrinking operational space and reduced security as a result of what their coordinating committee described as "the increased use of humanitarian aid as a political tool including labeling entire military campaigns as humanitarian missions, the provision of assistance through for-profit groups (private contractors), adulteration of the concept of civil society to become equal to sub-contractor, [and] co-option of the community approach by certain elements within the armed forces."[34] NGOs took particular exception to what they saw as "abuse of the term 'humanitarianism.'" "In declaring NGOs to be a 'force multiplier' and 'an important part of our combat team,' Secretary of State Colin Powell stripped NGOs of their independent and neutral character and implied that NGO motivations were indistinguishable from those of the Coalition."[35] United Nations organisations and personnel faced a similar quandary.[36] As in Afghanistan, indigenous NGOs found relationships with US officials even more problematic than did private American groups. Overall, US collaboration with humanitarian agencies has been demonstrably less successful in high-profile emergencies, where political objectives tend to drive allocations and programming, and more successful in crises in which the United States has had fewer perceived political stakes.

In Colombia, where there was a plethora of humanitarian organisations, indigenous and international, private and governmental, serious tensions developed not only between the US authorities and the representatives of other donor governments but also between USAID officials and American and indigenous NGOs. US government insistence that those American groups receiving US aid guarantee that their activities not benefit any of the armed groups complicated the functioning of aid agencies. This was the case even though just prior to 9/11, the United States had placed paramilitaries linked to the government – along with anti-government FARC insurgents – on its list of terrorist organisations. Meanwhile, the prohibition by Colombian authorities against dealings with the armed non-state actors put the state on a collision course with humanitarian and human rights organisations.[37] On one occasion, when the Colombian president himself accused the International Committee of the Red Cross (ICRC) and several NGOs by name of being supporters of the "terrorists," the United States lodged a behind-the-scenes protest. For the most part, however, the US role as Colombia's Number One patron and its view of the conflict as an element in a wider global war against terrorism undercut US relationships with potential humanitarian partners.

We found recurring examples of how the earmarking of funds inhibited responsiveness to needs as they presented themselves (the United States is ranked 22nd on this indicator). Although the United States has been the largest single contributor to the ICRC's work, the ICRC, in Iraq and elsewhere, has had to exercise particular vigilance to protect its operational autonomy and delimit the terms of its collaboration with Washington. Hard data compiled by the HRI ranks the United States 14th in the funding of ICRC appeals, 18th in the funding of IFRC appeals and 19th in the Red Cross Movement, 14th in the funding of UN coordination mechanisms and common services, and 16th among funders of the UN's Central Emergency Response Fund (CERF).

The OECD/DAC Peer Review underscores a number of the problem areas in Pillar III identified by the HRI. Among the OECD/DAC recommendations offered are greater predictability in US aid levels, "working more with other donors," more consultation and collaboration with "informed partners outside government," and "approaches to local ownership that are results-based (rather than being tied only to US procurement) and that do not include congressional earmarks."[38]

Pillar IV: Implementing international guiding principles

The United States ranks 23rd among the OECD group in implementing international guiding principles. It places 9th with respect to engagement in risk mitigation, 13th in enhancing security, 17th in protecting human rights, and 18th in affirming the primary role in humanitarian activities of civilian organisations. In terms of the hard data compiled by the HRI to measure implementation of international humanitarian and human rights law, the United States brings up the rear. Supplementing the qualitative data marshaled from country visits, the HRI's hard data weakens the overall rating of the United States in this important pillar.

A recurrent finding of our research has been the lack of firm US commitment to the international legal framework for humanitarian action and to multilateral institutions. The United States has been an unenthusiastic supporter of many humanitarian, human rights, and refugee laws and international codes of conduct such as the Convention on the Rights of the Child and the International Code of Marketing Breastmilk Substitutes.[39] (Its continuing opposition to the Kyoto Protocol demonstrates a similar stance in the environmental sphere.) The United States is not a signatory to the two Additional Protocols of 1977 to the Geneva Conventions of 1949, which address conduct in the kinds of international and non-international armed conflicts that have come to characterise modern warfare.

At a more operational and programmatic level, the US preference for bilateral over multilateral channels for its humanitarian and other assistance is well documented. That preference is also reflected in the hard data compiled for Pillar 3, where the United States is ranked first in its funding of NGOs – most of them presumably American – but 13th in underwriting the UN's CERF, and 14th in its support of UN coordination mechanisms and common services. Few analysts would quarrel with the HRI's observation that the United States "does not operate naturally as a multilateralist," although some see this as a more major shortcoming than others.[40]

The lack of importance attached by US administrations of both political parties to international law is reflected in the conduct of American troops on the frontlines of the global War on Terror in Afghanistan and Iraq. Based on interviews primarily of members of the US National Guard, our 2007 study found that soldiers were "not particularly conversant with the details of military ethics," even though confronted on a day-to-day basis with formidable ethical choices. While aware of the operative US rules of engagement, those interviewed mention "only on rare occasions their legal obligations to function within the framework of the Geneva Conventions and Protocols."[41]

A 2006 survey by the US Army in Iraq reported that one third of those interviewed believed that torture should be allowed if it helped gather important information about insurgents. Fewer than half held that "non-combatants should be treated with dignity and respect," while about ten percent acknowledged having mistreated civilians in Iraq.[42] One sergeant in the Florida National Guard noted that "By Geneva Convention standards, you were not supposed to conduct missions near hospitals, mosques, schools, or residential areas." He went on to acknowledge, however, that "We broke every rule there was." The leader of his platoon, he said, was well aware that depriving detained prisoners of sleep for 48-hour periods failed to "meet Red Cross or Geneva Convention standards" but did not challenge the practice for fear of aggravating his commanding officer.[43]

But the data contain more positive views of international law as well. Some interviewees underscore the importance of behaving according to recognised international standards. They view the abuses committed by US troops, intelligence operatives, and contractors at Abu Ghraib as complicating their own missions and

compromising their own safety. Some were "particularly irate that such behavior, carried out in the protected confines of detention centers, increased the vulnerability of units that were considerably more exposed." A number reported that the military included discussions of international rules of warfare in their pre-deployment training and that, later on, in an effort to control the damages associate with the publicised abuses, the military had provided some soldiers with crash courses in Geneva Convention law.

Some of those interviewed drew a direct link between "no holds barred" behaviour by troops on the battlefield and the cavalier attitude of US political leaders. "The wider context for the ethical confusion conveyed by soldiers," we indicated, "arguably mirrors efforts by the President, the Vice President, and senior Pentagon officials to redefine and relax the country's established international obligations, both of individual soldiers and of the US legal system as a whole." We suggested "a connection between the views of administration officials who regard the Geneva Conventions and Protocols as 'quaint' and the actions of soldiers who felt no particular obligation to function within internationally agreed parameters."[44]

Whatever the particulars of day-to-day conduct on the frontlines, one result of the administration's framing and pursuit of the Global War in Terror is that the United States has lost much of its traditional identification around the world with humane and humanitarian values. "Since the shock of 9/11," concludes Joseph S. Nye, Jr., "the United States has been exporting fear and anger, rather than our more traditional values of hope and optimism. Abu Ghraib and Guantanamo have become more powerful global icons of America than the Statue of Liberty."[45] Humanitarian initiatives by the US government have arguably been undercut by the fallout.

From a variety of settings, however, emerges a recurring lack of US commitment to respect the essentially civilian nature of humanitarian action. (Principle 19 of the Good Humanitarian Donorship initiative affirms "the primary position of civilian organisations in implementing humanitarian action, particularly in areas affected by armed conflict.") In the case of Kosovo, NATO military contingents, as well as bilateral troops from the United States and the United Kingdom, made an indispensable contribution to the protection and assistance of Kosovar refugees in Macedonia and Albania as well as of civilians in Kosovo itself. British troops stepped into the breach, in the absence of humanitarian agencies, to build refugee camps for Kosovars fleeing across the border into Macedonia in 1999. Their initiative, undertaken at the request of the UN High Commissioner for Refugees, was the kind of "last resort" use of the military provided for in the Oslo guidelines, and reflected GHD principles.

Yet the Kosovo conflict also saw a blurring of the essential civilian nature of humanitarian action as a result of NATO descriptions of its "humanitarian war" and NATO's framework of civilian-military coordination (CIMIC). NATO defined CIMIC as "A military operation, the primary intention and effect of which is to support a civilian authority, population, international or non-governmental organisation, the effect of which is to assist in the pursuit of a military objective."[46] US aircraft on the tarmac at the Tirana airport, part of NATO's Albania Force (AFOR), were described as having a "humanitarian" mission but also included US Apache helicopters in the event that an eventual ground assault was needed.

The United States and its NATO partners also blurred distinctions between humanitarian and military action. While the US military made a good-faith effort to assist aid agencies in the Kosovo crisis, a number of the agencies found such assistance problematic. "If I had known then what I know now about the difficulties of dealing with the US military," commented one NGO official, "I would have said 'no' in the first place."[47] In a broader sense, US humanitarian action in the Kosovo crisis was characterised by a "preference shown by governments for military over humanitarian actors and for bilateral over multilateral institutions."[48]

In other settings as well – for example, Pakistan, Iraq, and Afghanistan – US and allied forces undertook major civic action efforts designed to assist and protect local civilian populations and to win and cement their loyalties. "Hearts and minds" activities by military personnel in such varied settings have had both positive and negative results. In the case of the devastating earthquake in northern Pakistan in October 2005, the US military played a valuable role in speeding relief to those affected. The strategic importance of Pakistan to the United States in its Global War on Terror lent urgency to the effort, which resulted in what the *Wall Street Journal* called "one of America's most significant hearts-and-minds successes so far in the Muslim world."[49] The Pakistan military also received high marks for its role in the relief effort, although local perceptions became more negative as the reconstruction process languished.

Interviews confirm that most US troops in Afghanistan and Iraq view civic action work (some call it affectionately "hugs and drugs") in strongly positive terms. "Combat is only one facet of the military, a necessary evil we must sometimes wage against evil people," remarked one National Guardsman from Utah. Hearts and minds activities, he went on to say, were "the height of my deployment." The Pentagon itself publicises such activities by US "boots on the ground" around the world as "a force for good." At the same time, the selection by the military of local communities for such activities according to "where they stand on the insurgency" drew such populations more deeply into the conflict. There was also an evident disconnect between the priorities of local communities and the civic action work driven by the security needs of outside military forces. "In short," we concluded, "the ambiguities of hearts and minds activities are far more of a serious issue than realized by many of the troops, or by their publicists."[50]

One of the distinguishing features of the post-Cold War era has been an increased role by the military in the humanitarian sector. This was particularly evident in the contribution of international military forces to the response to the genocide in Rwanda. Our study examined the activities of troops provided within the multilateral framework of the UN Assistance Mission for Rwanda (UNAMIR) as well as those operating bilaterally. The 3,000 US troops committed to the US Operation Support Hope in 1994 achieved their basic objectives of halting deaths due to disease and starvation and lending support to aid organisations. "There were serious problems, however, in planning, operational strategies, cost and cost-effectiveness, and broader US policy. The US initiative was launched without adequate consultation with UN and NGO officials on the ground, other military contingents, and the Zairean and Rwandan authorities. Responding only in late July to a humanitarian crisis that had erupted in April, Operation Support Hope also adopted certain questionable operational strategies and proved a costly investment when more cost-effective and preventive approaches might have been found."[51] US maneuvers in the UN Security Council before and during the genocide delayed international as well as US responses to the unfolding tragedy. The United States failed to enhance the security and protect the human rights of Rwandans prior to or during the genocide, although it was an essential participant in the broader international effort to protect refugees and internally displaced Rwandans later on.

Once again, the OECD/DAC peer review underscores items flagged in the HRI. Noting that the percentage of US overseas development assistance (ODA) channeled multilaterally has dwindled from 26 percent to 8 percent in recent years, the review "encourages the US to review its role in multilateral financing" and "to play a stronger role in financing the multilateral system." (State Department officials caution that OECD/DAC definitions of multilateral assistance consider that *any* assistance provided with conditions or earmarks to multilateral organisations are counted as bilateral.)[52] With respect to the interface of aid activities and the military, the OECD/DAC peer review requests the United States and other governments to maintain policies based on "development experience and good practice." Noting "the rapidly growing Official Development Assistance role of the Department of Defense," the peer review observes that "while deploying military forces to support humanitarian operations in sudden major crises, it is critical to protect the independence and impartiality of humanitarian and development action."[53]

In sum, the HRI conclusions about US performance in implementing international guiding principles are amply confirmed from other quarters. The United States tends to view international humanitarian and legal frameworks as largely voluntary and optional, quite capable of being finessed in light of the "exceptional" circumstances. Uneven and often token investment in the multilateral system tends to reinforce the U.S. as a go-it-alone player. As the international community moves toward an understanding of humanitarian action not as a series of isolated events but as a "regime" with a legal framework and binding obligations, the United States risks becoming increasingly isolated in this regard.

Pillar V: Promoting leadership and accountability

The HRI ranks the United States second among the 23 OECD actors, surpassed only by the European Community, in promoting leadership and accountability. The individual benchmarks that figure in this ranking include supporting accountability in humanitarian action (here the United States ranks 1st), encouraging regular evaluations (4th) and supporting specific learning and accountability initiatives (10th). The overall US position is reinforced by hard data indicators related to the number of evaluations (2nd), support to main accountability initiatives (7th), and the funding of other accountability initiatives (16th). The HRI terms US performance in Pillar V "stellar."[54]

Our research confirms the supportive role played by the US government in ALNAP, both in the quality of personnel representing the United States at ALNAP's biennial meetings over the years and in the financial underwriting provided. (Tufts University is itself an ALNAP member.) USAID was present at the creation of the Sphere Project, a major substantive contributor to its standards in several sectors, and its largest governmental funder. My impression is that the United States has been less engaged in and supportive of the Humanitarian Accountability Partnership, and even less so of People in Aid and Quality COMPASS, although I have had less exposure to these undertakings myself.

In the 1970s and 1980s, I had occasion to review USAID programme evaluations with an eye to formulating recommendations for NGO advocacy with the US Congress for improved US government policies and programmes. I was impressed with the rigour and candour of USAID's in-house and commissioned studies – for example, of the impact of food assistance for rural road construction on community life in West Africa – and with the fact that USAID findings and recommendations were made available to the public. (The self-critical evaluation by USAID of training for demobilised soldiers in Haiti has already been cited.) At the end of the day, however, many of the "lessons identified" in USAID evaluations have not become "lessons learned" and incorporated into agency practice.[55]

US food assistance programmes over the years offer a case in point as regards both American leadership and American resistance to change. The United States has been not only the originator of the concept of food assistance, but also the largest single food aid supplier, and also the largest contributor to the United Nations World Food Programme. At the same time, the United States has resisted improvements to food aid programmes, such as the purchase of food commodities in developing countries themselves, and the shipment of food on non-US flag carriers. (The OECD/DAC peer review urges that USAID officials "work to muster Congressional support for locally sourced commodities and consider cash-based alternatives."[56]) While projections of economists differ, it is quite likely that the impact of current US subsidies that encourage the production of ethanol from agricultural crops will have contributed more to higher food prices for the world's poor than American food assistance programmes (themselves reduced by higher food prices) will have been able to offset.

Instances of outright humanitarian obfuscation by the United States must also be acknowledged. A case in point is the role of the U.S. in the international effort to ban landmines. The human costs of landmines had emerged as a major humanitarian issue in the 1990s, reflecting the residue of their indiscriminate use during the Cold War and their proliferation in post-Cold War conflicts. Successful action to draft and ratify a treaty banning landmines – the formal process began with a meeting in Ottawa in October 1996 and culminated in agreement on the text of a treaty in September 1997 – represented creative strategizing and action by four sets of actors: the International Campaign to Ban Landmines (ICBL), a transnational NGO coalition; the International Red Cross; several United Nations organisations; and a coalition of sympathetic governments.

"The treaty was a striking achievement," we concluded, "not least because it was resisted by the most powerful state in the international system. The case is a rare instance where the United States was opposed on a matter of security policy by a number of its weaker allies and lost the battle."[57] Governments normally allied with the U.S. remained unpersuaded by American insistence on exemptions to cover its military needs (e.g., anti-tank systems and Korea) and were alienated by the "heavy-handed tactics" used by the United States in its efforts weaken the treaty. Stung by the rebuff represented by the overwhelming adoption of the treaty, the U.S. announced its own initiative a month later "to eliminate the threat posed by land mines to civilians everywhere on the face of the earth by the end of the next decade." US Secretary of State Madeleine K. Albright and US Secretary of Defense William Cohen announced with great fanfare the appointment of a Special Representative of the President and Secretary of State for Global Humanitarian Demining and a doubling of US funding for "humanitarian demining," for which it was already the lead donor. "We also respect the Ottawa process and want to continue working with it [sic]," said Secretary Albright, "although our nation's unique responsibilities for international security have not permitted us to sign the treaty negotiated at Oslo."[58] While the US initiative may itself have had some positive effects, the humanitarian benefits of the treaty the Americans opposed were indisputably far more wide-ranging.

As a whole, US performance in this pillar may be both under-appreciated and over-valued by the HRI. On the one hand, the indicators employed may fail to capture some of the intangible leadership brought by the United States to the humanitarian sector. Perhaps also minimised is the sheer magnitude of US humanitarian action, an aspect that receives more attention in observations by the OECD/DAC regarding the United States' "unparalleled operational and technical capacity to respond to major crises."[59] In contrast to our own research, the Index may also fail to identify the aforementioned "drag effect" exercised by US officials on other donors as well as the slippage in the government's management of US humanitarian interests. In recent years, USAID and its humanitarian focal point, the Office of Foreign Disaster Assistance (OFDA), have lost considerable ground both within the councils of US government decision-making and vis-à-vis the Department of Defense. Rapid personnel turnover at the leadership level has also undercut the expertise of USAID and its bureaucratic standing. A similar erosion of interest and energy has been evident on Capitol Hill. Fortunately, there remain many civil servants within USAID and the State and Agriculture Departments and many on Capitol Hill who are fully committed to faithful and creative stewardship of American humanitarian traditions and resources.

Reflections on the Index

The findings of the initial application of the HRI to the performance of donor governments are broadly confirmed by research with which I have been associated. At the same time, changes will doubtless be needed in the future to refine the benchmarks and fine tune their application. That has been the process as well with other such instruments – counterparts in the areas of development, the physical quality of life, transparency, and failed states come to mind – which, with each successive iteration, have gained in accuracy and credibility.

As the HRI is examined and refined, a number of issues may bear further study.

First, *the pillars and their proportional weighting.* The performance of each government is ranked on the basis of a composite score in which the pillars receive various percentages: 30 percent (Pillar I), 20 percent (Pillar II), 20 percent (Pillar III), 15 percent (Pillar IV), and 15 percent (Pillar V). One improvement might be to weight these five categories equally, reflecting the relative importance of each. Another would be to consolidate Pillars II and III, which have a more operational emphasis and which, taken together, would afford a larger critical mass of data. Some of the individual indicators (and the disproportionate impact of particularly low scores on some of them) will also merit review. Should analysts, like the proverbial university professor, discard several of the low scores as unreflective or overall performance?

Second, *the countries selected for visits.* The seven countries chosen for field visits in 2007 included some – for example, the DRC, the Sudan, and Colombia – which have severely challenged the resourcefulness of the international community. Yet major emergencies such as Afghanistan and Iraq, which have consumed disproportionate shares of humanitarian assistance flows globally and from particular nations, are conspicuous by their absence in the 2007 selections. Their inclusion would doubtless have a significant impact on performance assessments. Unless countries are selected each year that are broadly representative of the range of humanitarian challenges faced at a particular time, the relative performance of governments from one year to the next will be difficult to assess.

Third, *coherence*. The most difficult challenge for humanitarian actors working in internal armed conflicts is that of contextualizing assistance and protection activities in relation to the prevailing political and military frameworks. As noted above, this is a broader challenge than simply that of integrating relief and development (Pillar I), and it is not picked up adequately in either the HRI pillars or the OECD/DAC guidelines. Pressure for a "whole of government" approach, in which humanitarian activities become part and parcel of wider frameworks, often compromises their essential independence. The different configurations chosen – we describe the options as involving the integration, insulation, or independence of humanitarian and human rights activities in relation to political and peacekeeping frameworks – have a major bearing on the success of aid efforts.

Fourth, *the donor club*. The ranking of humanitarian performance of the 23 OECD/DAC actors reinforces the impression that humanitarian action is largely a Western and/or Northern impulse, activity, and project. Experience confirms, however, that in crises themselves, much of the action is local in nature, with indigenous traditions and agencies playing a key role. The HRI's focus on official development assistance also understates the importance of other flows, including military aid, commercial transactions, and private remittances. The instrument, as presently constructed, also focuses on governments, to the exclusion of the other actors who make up the humanitarian enterprise. The distinctions between donors and recipients also perpetuate the kinds of divisions between "us" and "them" which humanitarian action at its best manages to overcome.

The HRI thus risks confirming the provincialism of humanitarian action as traditionally understood. Our latest examination of the issue of universality in the humanitarian enterprise highlights "the recurrent need to democratize the humanitarian mission. At the global level, this means reaching out to other traditions of helping, such as those that infuse Islam, for example, and

exploring questions about how the northern/western oligopoly in humanitarianism might be opened up and restructured."[60] Moreover, while donor government policies have a direct bearing on the success of humanitarian initiatives, the key roles played by other actors and implementing agencies also need to be acknowledged.

Finally, *the assessment process*. The United States and several other donors question the utility of the DARA undertaking, arguing that performance assessment is better left to the peer review process within the OECD's Development Assistance Committee. The appropriateness of assessing the performance of individual donors rather than "the donor community" has also come under fire. Yet accountability is too important to be left to donors, whether individually or severally. If the Good Humanitarian Donorship was born of the conviction that the whole of humanitarian action is lamentably less than the sum of its parts, a workmanlike and forthright examination of the individual components of the system will surely help unleash missing synergies. The HRI is worth strengthening rather than jettisoning.

Towards a humanitarian regime

The core concept of humanitarianism is stunning in its simplicity: providing people *in extremis* with the necessary assistance and protection. In reality, however, humanitarian action is bewilderingly complex. "Like other 'isms' … humanitarianism propounds lofty goals which serve to hide deep contradictions, conflicting alignments and power plays, manipulations and instrumentalizations, personality cults, struggles over resources, and sometimes, shady financial transactions."[61] The bad news – that the United States, a leader of traditional humanitarian action, is no longer in the vanguard – is offset by the good news that humanitarianism itself is on the way to becoming more systematic. The new humanitarianism is less reflexive and more reflective, less Western and more global, less autocratic and more mutual, less one-size-fits-all and more context-specific, less national security-driven and more human security-oriented, less atomistic and more regime-like.

Specialists in political theory and international organisations define an international regime as a set of "implicit or explicit principles, norms, rules, and decision-making procedures around which actors' expectations converge in a given area of international relations."[62] In recent years, the international community has devised and refined regimes in such areas as nuclear non-proliferation, counter-terrorism, human rights, climate change, and anti-personnel landmines. A new "international atrocities regime" now even has its own acronym, IAR.

"The most significant effect of regimes," comments one specialist, "stems from their ability to define and impose categories for state actors."[63] In some areas, regimes have been promoted by the key state actors involved. That was the case in the US role in creating the Bretton Woods financial institutions, the World Bank and the International Monetary Fund, following World War II. The United States played a similar formative role in the creation of the UN World Food Programme. A hegemon such as the United States may realise a benefit from burden-sharing with other states. Yet when regimes become established, they may extract a certain accountability from states, hegemonic or otherwise.

The humanitarian regime that has evolved during the post-Cold War era has clarified the obligations of two sets of governmental actors: host governments experiencing crises and other governments in a position to assist them. In UN General Assembly Resolution 46/182 of December 1991, governments affirm the basic obligations of sovereign host governments to meet the basic human needs and protect the basic human rights of their civilian populations. The resolution also specifies, however, that when host governments fail to act, governments may intervene to assist and protect vulnerable populations. Their obligation to do so has been further refined in more recent affirmations of the global "responsibility to protect." As explained by UN Secretary-General Ban Ki-moon, that responsibility involves "the inherent obligation of every State to protect its populations from genocide, war crimes, ethnic cleansing and crimes against humanity." The international community, he says, must "take collective action through the United Nations to protect populations from such serious crimes and violations when States manifestly fail to do so."[64]

If the freedom of sovereign host governments to treat or mistreat their civilians without fear of outside intervention has been narrowed, so, too, has the autonomy of outside governments to mount humanitarian activities in whatever ways they see fit. In exercising their humanitarian responsibilities to civilian populations *in extremis,* donor governments are themselves now increasingly obliged to follow certain norms and rules. Although the evolution of the humanitarian regime is not sufficiently advanced so as to "exert influence in world politics that is practically independent of state

sovereignty," the freedom once enjoyed by the world's humanitarian hegemon has substantially eroded.

The United States cannot have it both ways. It cannot claim to be the leader of global forces for good, on the one hand, and then fail to take due responsibility for the evident shortcomings in the world's humanitarian efforts. Looking to the future, it has two choices: it may continue its past traditions of responding to individual crises as they arise, mounting major relief interventions sometimes alone, sometimes in concert with other donors; or it may situate its activities firmly within the emerging global humanitarian regime, where its own profile may be less identifiable but where humanitarian challenges are more fully shared. Rather than fighting what has the makings of an ultimately unsuccessful rearguard action to preserve its assumed humanitarian hegemony, the United States should nurture a new breed of leadership that would reflect the expressed values of the American people and the legitimate expectations of the wider world.

Notes

1   There were 22 OECD countries evaluated (excluding the Czech Republic); the 23rd actor is the European Community.

2   White House Press Secretary, 2008.

3   Steven Hansch, 2008.

4   See, for example, Weiss and Minear, eds., 1993. Of particular relevance is the chapter by Fred C. Cuny, "Humanitarian Assistance in the Post-Cold War Era," pp. 151–170.

5   Smillie and Minear, 2003, adapted from Section 2, Key Findings, paras. 2.1, 2.2, 2.3, and 2.4.

6   The setting for the development and adoption of the GHD initiative is described in Schaar, 2008, pp. 37–44.

7   Facilitated by the OECD/DAC Secretariat, the OECD/DAC peer review process involves examination of an individual government's performance by officials from two other OECD/DAC members. Their findings are then discussed by the Development Assistance Committee as a whole, with OECD/DAC members – including the government reviewed – given an opportunity to comment. Each written review thus conveys broad consensus among OECD/DAC members regarding a given government's performance.

8   OECD Development Co-operation Directorate, 2006, p. 10.

9   Donini et al., 2007.

10 Ibid., p. 3. The countries examined were Afghanistan, northern Uganda, Sudan, Burundi, Liberia, Colombia, the Occupied Palestinian Territory, Iraq, Sri Lanka, DRC, Pakistan, and Nepal. A related case study examined the impact of the global War on Terror on members of the US National Guard serving in Afghanistan and Iraq.

11 Smillie and Minear, 2004. See in particular Chapter 6, "Foreign Policy Imperatives".

12 OECD/DAC, op. cit., p. 10.

13 An earlier report, based on country studies in Afghanistan, Kosovo, and Sierra Leone, concluded that the understanding of security itself differed significantly among three major sets of actors: American and other military personnel engaged in peace support operations, international assistance agencies, and local communities. See Donini et al., 2005.

14 See Minear and Weiss, 1993, pp. 20–21.

15 For a more extended discussion, see Minear, 2000, p. 37 and 1988–89, pp. 76–93.

16 The term is used by Antonio Donini in his paper "The Far Side: The Meta-function of Humanitarianism in a Globalized World," (2008). While Donini does not apply the term specifically to the United States, the U.S., to one degree or another under this administration or that, has often been associated with efforts to blur the concept or finesse humanitarianism's core elements.

17 Donini et al, 2007, p. 14. This statement, summarizing the 12 country studies in *Humanitarian Agenda 2015,* builds in particular on reviews of Colombia, Afghanistan, and Iraq.

18 Minear, 2005.

19 Ghosh, 2008.

20 Smillie, 1998, p. 9.

21 Ibid., p. 11.

22 Smillie and Todorovic, 2001, p. 28.

23 Ibid., p. 43.

24 Lubkemann, 2001.

25 Lautze and Stites, 2003.

26 Smillie, ed., 2001, p. 1.

27 OECD/DAC, 2006, p. 12.

28 Minear, 2006, pp. 17–23.

29 OECD/DAC, 2006, p. 10.

30 Correspondence between the author and John Mitchell and Tony Beck of ALNAP [undated].

31 Minear et al, 1992, pp. 36–37.

32 Smillie and Minear, 2004, p. 99.

33 Ibid., p. 103.

34 Statement by the NGO Coordination Committee in Iraq (NCCI), 5 August 2004, quoted in Rodriguez, 2007, p. 115.

35 Rodriguez, op. cit., p. 115.

36 For a detailed review of the problems that UN relief efforts faced in delimiting their association with the occupying forces, see Hansen, 2007. See also Hansen's earlier Iraq reports, available on the Feinstein International Center (FIC) website.

37 Minear, 2006, p. 28.

38 OECD/DAC, 2006, p. 14.

39 The legal framework for humanitarian action is addressed in hree Tufts studies in particular: see O'Neil, *A Humanitarian Practitioner's Guide to International Human Rights Law* (1999); Frohardt and Minear, *Protecting Human Rights: The Challenge to Humanitarian Organizations,* (2000); Kenny, *When Needs are Rights: An Overview of UN Efforts to Integrate Human Rights in Humanitarian Action* (2000).

40 Altinger et al., 2007, p. 29. US officials have also pointed out that some offices of the US government, including the State Department's Bureau for Population, Refugees, and Migration, provide resources primarily through multilateral organisations.

41 Minear, 2007, p. 35.

42 Carey (2007) quoted in Minear, 2007, p. 35.

43 The soldier in question was Sgt. Camilio Mejia who, following an initial tour of duty in Iraq, refused to return and became an outspoken critic of US policy and practice. Minear, 2007, pp. 36 and 20.

44 Ibid., p. 36.

45 Nye, 2008, p. 84.

46 Minear, et al., 2000, p. 64.

47 Ibid., pp. 25–26.

48 Ibid., p. 40.

49 Stephens (2005) quoted in Wilder, 2007, p. 45.

50 For the discussion of hearts and minds activities, see Minear, 2007, pp. 43 and 46.

51 Minear and Guillot, 1996, pp. 124–125.

52 We flagged this issue several years ago with respect to the annual reviews of aid flows prepared by Development Initiatives, which uses the OECD/DAC definitions. State Department officials also point out that some offices within the US executive branch, for example, the Bureau of Population, Refugees, and Migration, channel as much as 75–80 percent of their resources through multilateral agencies.

53 OECD/DAC, 2006, p. 14.

54 Altinger et al., p. 28.

55 The Peer Review also identifies the need for "strengthening the monitoring and evaluation of partner work, in particular through promoting the views of beneficiaries at all stages of the project cycle, and in expanding the use of Good Humanitarian Donorship indicators in internal reporting frameworks, including at field level."

56 OECD/DAC, 2006, p. 15.

57 Hubert, 2000, p. xi.

58 Press Briefing on Land Mine Policy, October 31, 1997, Washington, D.C.

59 OECD/DAC, 2006, p. 15.

60 Donini et al., 2007, p. 12.

61 Donini, 2008, p. 1.

62 Krasner, ed. 1982, p. 1.

63 Sasikumar, 2005.

64 "Responsibility to protect a 'profound moral imperative in today's world,' says Secretary-General in Message to Global Center Opening, 14 February 2008.

References

Altinger, Laura, Silvia Hidalgo, and Augusto López-Claros. 2007. "The Humanitarian Response Index 2007." In Hidalgo and Lopez-Claros, eds. 2007. *The Humanitarian Response Index 2007: Measuring Commitment to Best Practice.*

Carey, Benedict. 2007. "Stress on Troops Adds to U.S. Hurdles in Iraq." *New York Times.* 6 May.

Cuny, Fred C. 1993. "Humanitarian Assistance in the Post-Cold War Era." FRONTLINE/Online. July. At: http://pbs.gen.in/wgbh/pages/front-line/shows/cuny/laptop/coldwar.html

Donini, Antonio. 2008. "The Far Side: The Meta-function of Humanitarianism in a Globalized World." Paper presented at the annual meeting of the International Studies Association, San Francisco. March.

Donini, Antonio, Larry Minear, Ian Smillie, Ted van Baarda, and Anthony C. Welch. 2005. *Mapping the Security Environment: Understanding the Perceptions of Local Communities, Peace Support Operations, and Assistance Agencies.* Medford, MA: FIC.

Donini, Antonio, Larissa Fast, Greg Hansen, Simon Harris, Larry Minear, Tasneem Mowjee, and Andrew Wilder. 2007. *Humanitarian Agenda 2015: Final Report. The State of the Humanitarian Enterprise.* Medford, MA: Feinstein International Center.

Frohardt, Mark, Diane Paul, and Larry Minear. 2000. "Protecting Human Rights: The Challenge to Humanitarian Organizations." Occasional Paper 35. Providence RI: Watson Institute.

Ghosh, Amitav. 2008. "Death Comes Ashore." *New York Times,* 10 May, A27.

Hansch, Steven. 2008. Humanitarian Response Index Briefing. Washington, D.C. 21 May.

Hansen, Greg. 2007. "Taking Sides or Savings Lives: Existential Choices for the Humanitarian Enterprise in Iraq." 30 June. At: http://www.reliefweb.int/rw/rwb.nsf/db900sid/SJHG-74Q429?OpenDocument

Hidalgo, Silvia, and Augusto López-Claros, eds. 2007. *The Humanitarian Response Index 2007: Measuring Commitment to Best Practice.* Hampshire and New York: Palgrave Macmillan.

Hubert, Don. 2000. "The Landmine Ban: A Case Study in Humanitarian Advocacy." Providence, RI: Watson Institute.

Kenny, Karen. 2000. "When Needs are Rights: An Overview of UN Efforts to Integrate Human Rights in Humanitarian Action." Occasional Paper 38. Providence, RI: Watson Institute.

Krasner, Stephen, ed. 1982. *International Regimes.* Ithaca, NY: Cornell University Press.

Lautze, Sue and Elizabeth Stites. 2003. "More than Seeds and Tools: An Overview of OFDA Livelihood Interventions 1964–2002." Medford, MA: FIC, March.

Lubkemann, Stephen C. 2001. "Rebuilding Local Capacities in Mozambique: The National Health System and Civil Society." In Ian Smillie, ed., *Patronage or Partnership.* pp. 77–106.

Minear, Larry. 1988–89. "The Forgotten Human Agenda." *Foreign Policy* 73. Winter 1988–89. pp. 76–93.

———. 2000. *The Humanitarian Enterprise: Dilemmas and Discoveries.* Bloomfield, CT: Kumarian Press.

———. 2005. "Katrina turns tables on U.S. aid." Reuters Alertnet. 13 September.

———. 2006. *Humanitarian Agenda 2015: Colombia Country Study.* July. [Medford: FIC]

———. 2007. *The U.S. Citizen-Soldier and the Global War on Terror: The National Guard Experience.* Medford, MA: FIC.

Minear, Larry, U.P.B. Chelliah, Jeff Crisp, John Mackinlay, and Thomas G. Weiss. 1992. "United Nations Coordination of the International Humanitarian Response to the Gulf Crisis 1990–1992." Providence, RI: Watson Institute.

Minear, Larry and Thomas G. Weiss. 1993. *Humanitarian Action in Times of War: A Handbook for Practitioners.* Boulder, CO and London: Lynne Rienner Publishers.

Minear, Larry and Philippe Guillot. 1996. *Soldiers to the Rescue: Humanitarian Lessons from Rwanda.* Paris: OECD.

Minear, Larry, Ted van Baarda and Mark Sommers. 2000. "NATO and Humanitarian Action in the Kosovo Crisis." Occasional Paper 36. Providence RI: Watson Institute.

Minear, Larry and Hazel Smith. 2007. *Humanitarian Diplomacy: Practitioners and Their Craft.* Tokyo, New York, and Paris: United Nations University Press.

Nye, Joseph A. Jr. 20008. "Toward a Liberal Realist Foreign Policy: A Memo for the Next President." *Harvard Magazine.* March-April.

O'Neil, William G. 1999. *A Humanitarian Practitioner's Guide to International Human Rights Law.* Occasional Paper 34. Providence RI: Watson Institute.

OECD Development Co-operation Directorate. 2006. *Peer Review: Main Findings.* Paris: OECD.

Rodriguez, Claudia. 2007. "The Legitimacy of Humanitarian Action in Iraq." In Larry Minear and Hazel Smith, *Humanitarian diplomacy.*

Sasikumar, Karthika. 2005. "Regimes at Work: A Comprehensive Analysis of the International Non-Proliferation and Counter-terrorism Regimes." Paper presented at the annual conference of the International Studies Association. 5 May.

Schaar, Johan. 2008. "The Birth of the Good Humanitarian Donorship Initiative." In Hidalgo and Lopez-Claros, *The Humanitarian Response Index 2007.*

Smillie, Ian. 1998 "Relief and Development: The Struggle for Synergy." Occasional Paper 33. Providence, RI: Watson Institute.

———, ed. 2001. *Patronage or Partnership: Local Capacity Building in Humanitarian Crises.* Bloomfield, CT: Kumarian Press and International Development Research Center.

Smillie, Ian and Goran Todorovic. 2001. "Reconstructing Bosnia, Constructing Civil Society: Disjuncture and Convergence," in Ian Smillie, ed., *Patronage or Partnership.*

Smillie, Ian and Larry Minear. 2003. *The Quality of Money: Donor Behavior in Humanitarian Financing.* Medford, MA: Feinstein International Center. Tufts University.

———. 2004. *The Charity of Nations: Humanitarian Action in a Calculating World.* Bloomfield, CT: Kumarian Press.

Stephens, Bret. 2005. "Chinook Diplomacy: The U.S. military wins hearts and minds in Pakistan." *The Wall Street Journal Online.* 22 December.

Weiss, Thomas G. and Larry Minear, eds. 1993. *Humanitarianism Across Borders: Sustaining Civilians in Times of War.* Boulder, CO: Lynne Rienner Publishers.

White House Press Secretary. 2008. "President Bush Discusses Food Aid." Office of the White House Press Secretary. 1 May.

Wilder, Andrew. 2007. "Perceptions of the Pakistan Earthquake Response: Pakistan Country Study." In Donini et al., *Humanitarian Agenda 2015.*

CHAPTER 3

A Tale of Two Indices:

The Commitment to Development Index as a Model for the Humanitarian Response Index

DAVID ROODMAN, Center for Global Development

Introduction

Indexes, which distill large amounts of information into a few numbers, have steadily gained popularity among policy advocates and researchers in recent decades. Indexes help make abstract ideas seem more concrete. They attract attention because the human mind is drawn to conflict and competition, which indexes exploit by rating and ranking. Moreover, modern information technology has made it much easier to collect and process large data sets.

By producing the Corruption Perceptions Index, for example, Transparency International helped raise corruption from a vague background concern among development experts to a major focus, and spurred progress on an international treaty, the Anti-Bribery Convention, to combat it. The UN Development Programme's Human Development Index, by factoring in literacy and longevity, gave popular credence to the idea that economic development is about more than income. Indexes today number in the hundreds, covering everything from education policies of European Union members, to the fragility of nation states, to business-friendly policies in Vietnamese provinces.

A more subtle strength of index projects is that the act of measurement can bestow authority on those who measure – though they must still earn it through good index design. All public policy decisions require choices between alternatives. These alternatives are almost always hard to compare because of lack of information about likely effects and ethical difficulties, such as how to weigh the short-term versus the long-term (discount rates). While armchair policy analysts can enjoy the luxury of dodging the toughest choices, indexers, like policymakers, must take them head on. And while their formulas will always be debatable, choosing among alternatives is inherent in public policy, not just index making.

And the insight they gain by persevering can give them something to contribute to policy discussions that can too easily founder in abstractions.

Each index has a unique character, shaped by its subject matter, the quality and structure of available data, the budget, and the target audience. Indexes are also shaped by their creators' larger strategies for social change. Indeed, every rating system is both an algorithm and a *project* that should include a two-way exchange of ideas with target audiences. Thus, what determines the success of an index project is both the design of the index, and the ways in which those managing it engage with their audiences, through consultation and outreach. An index project is more than an index.

This chapter reviews the history of the Commitment to Development Index (CDI), and draws lessons for the Humanitarian Response Index project. Like the HRI, the CDI is not only a policy-relevant index but a policy-measuring one, and takes the rich-country donor government as its unit of analysis. It also focuses on the actions of rich countries as they affect poor countries and aims to reach officials governing those actions both directly and via the press. Although the two indexes differ in important ways – the CDI's terrain is far broader, going beyond humanitarian aid to all aid, and beyond aid to many other policies – the similarities are, nevertheless, strong enough to make the CDI's experience relevant for the younger HRI. If that experience is any guide, the HRI will experience initial challenges to acceptance and evolve significantly in its early years. But through dialogue with its audiences, it will eventually achieve stability in its design and earn its place in the world of humanitarian donorship.

The Commitment to Development Index

The CDI, like the Center for Global Development (CGD) which produces it, focuses on how rich-country governments affect developing countries. It rates and ranks 21 rich countries on how much their policies in seven areas help or hurt poorer countries – not just foreign aid, which gets the most attention in this context, but also policies relating to trade, migration, investment, the environment, military affairs, and technology.[1] The CDI asks such questions as: How open are countries' borders to goods and workers from poorer countries? How supportive are developing country governments of healthy investment? How active and constructive are they in international security affairs such as peacekeeping? Do their policies impede the flow of new ideas across borders?

The CDI has one component for each major policy area covered. In its first release in 2003, there were six: aid, trade, investment, migration, environment, and peacekeeping. In the second edition, the peacekeeping component was broadened and renamed "security," and a component on technology added. The subject population for the index is the membership of the Development Assistance Committee, the official donor club, sans Luxembourg, because it is so small. Each of the 21 countries receives a score in each of the seven areas, and overall scores are simple averages of component scores. The index aims to measure not the absolute impact of individual rich countries, but the degree to which they are realizing their potential to help. In other words, it controls for size. Thus small countries such as Denmark and the Netherlands can score well despite modest aggregate impact. (See Figure 1.)

The Center for Global Development (CGD) has revised and updated the CDI annually. The design changed significantly in the second and third cycles, but has been more stable since then. As with many indexes, its purpose is not only to measure, but to use ranking to draw attention to issues, educate the public and policymakers, stimulate thinking and debate, and serve as a flagship for an institution.

As indexes go, the CDI is ambitious. It strives to measure the quality of a huge range of policies with respect to a broad and poorly defined outcome: development in poorer countries, despite major gaps in data and limited understanding of how various policies actually affect development. This gives the CDI an edgy and paradoxical character. On the one hand, what it sets out to do is arguably impossible. On the other, the CGD believes that it is worth doing for the sake of public education. And, given that it is to be built, it must be built in a way that is intellectually defensible, since the CGD wants to be respected as a research institution. The challenge in designing the CDI, then, was to do something that is analytically impossible in a way that is analytically credible. The same can be said for almost any index of policy.

Lessons from the CDI

Index-making can be hard to do well. How hard depends in part on the concept to be crystallized. Tricky issues that arise include: clear definition of the concept to measure, the relative weight various components deserve, trade-offs between complexity and realism, and the tension between improving the index over time, maintaining comparability with past results, and more. The more difficult these questions are to resolve, the more they become *political* issues, as the choices made by the index devisers arouse criticism from people who respond out of a mixture of discomfort and genuine disagreement. While this section reviews issues encountered in the construction of the CDI, all pertain to the HRI as well.

Lack of a theoretical model

There is no overall model for the development process and the role of rich-country policies within it. In the case of the CDI, no overarching theory describes how aid, trade, environmental, and other policies affect development in various parts of the world, which of them matter most, or how they interact. As a result, for example, the top-level structure of the CDI – the simple averaging of seven component scores – is atheoretical.

The HRI shares this problem. Its domain is much narrower and easier to analyze. And donors have agreed to a set of principles of good humanitarian donorship. Perhaps as a result, the HRI designers felt confident enough not to "equal-weight" the five main components of their index. For example, they seem reasonably confident that basic patterns in donor responses to humanitarian needs (Pillar 1) are more important than internal mechanisms for learning (Pillar 5), giving the first twice the weight of the second. Still, they could not credibly claim that even this weighted averaging precisely captures the way that the five aspects of humanitarian response represented by their five components interact. For example, the aspects must often interact multiplica-

Figure 1. Commitment to Development Index 2007

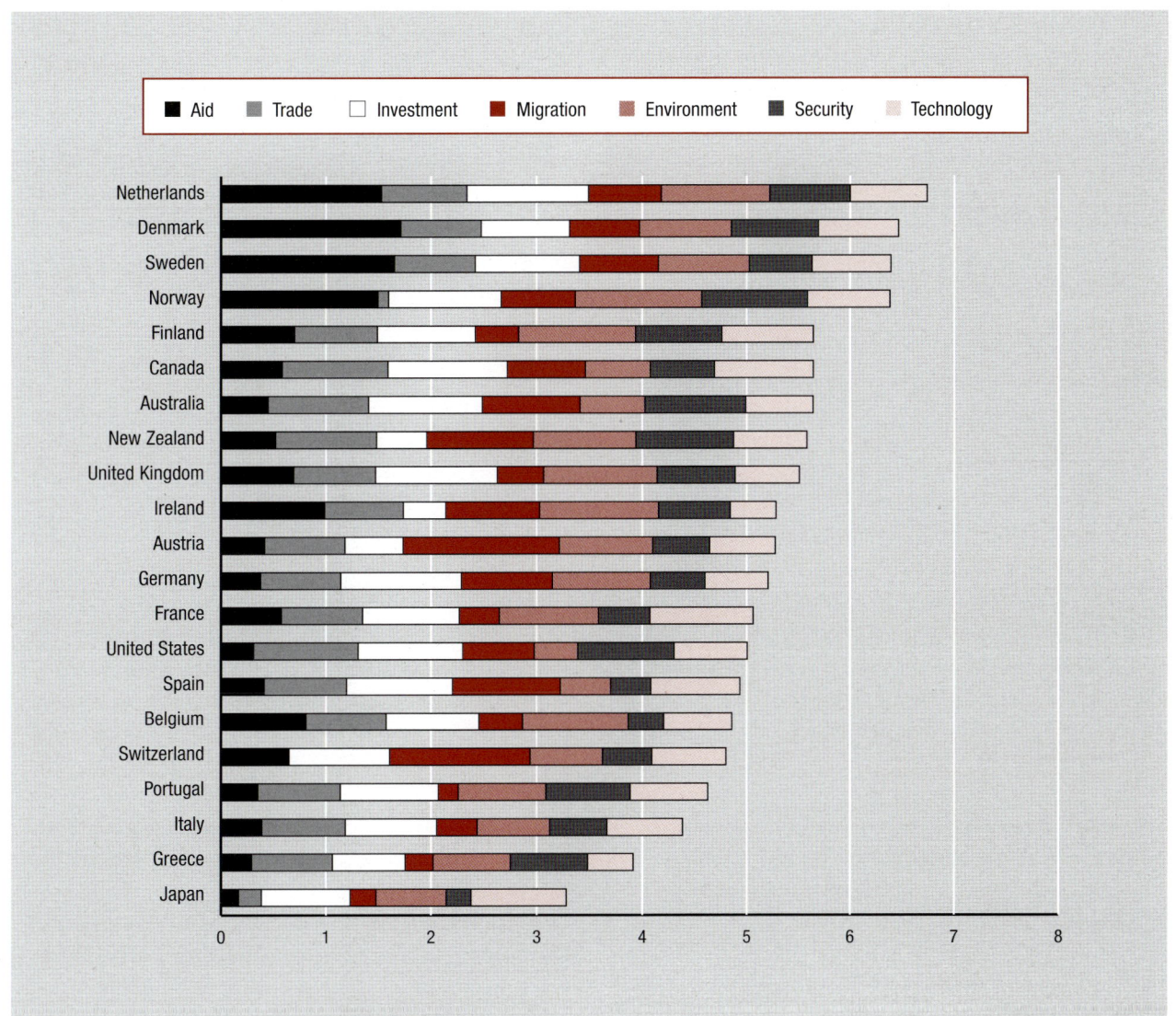

tively, not just additively, or must vary in importance depending on the context, and so on.

The problem here is not just technical, that is, not something that could ever be solved by gathering more information about the impact of donors' aid policies or humanitarian responses. Our ignorance will always be pervasive. What fills this vacuum for most people is political philosophy, deep ideas about how the world works and how governments can effectively intervene. One person suggested that the CDI reward every dollar of US defense spending because, it was argued, the United States is the sole hegemon, the guarantor of global stability and protector of democracy. Another has

submitted that every dollar of US defense spending should be penalized. The Center for Global Development, seeking to live up to the "center" in its name, has sometimes responded to such fundamental disputes by seeking common ground. Thus, the CDI security component takes no stand on defense spending generally, and, notably, it is neutral on the invasion of Iraq, in the sense that this is neither rewarded nor penalized. (But this lack of reward does not look neutral to most fervent supporters and opponents of the invasion.) Of course, every design choice in an index implies a stand, each one no doubt with its dissenters; and the decision to take these stands must reflect to some extent the biases of the designers. No choice can make the philosophical disagreements go away.

The more expansive an index, the more likely it is to cross such ideological fault lines. An index of bureaucratic efficiency, for example, may be straightforward conceptually. Not so the definition of good conduct for a rich country on the world stage.

Scaling and weighting

A substantial set of issues surrounds how to scale and weight scores on various indicators and composites thereof. A principle that shapes the CDI is that in the face of ignorance about the "true" parameters – not to mention the functional form of the development "production function" – it is best to be transparent and minimally arbitrary to avoid seeming biased.

With regard to "normalization" of scores – putting them on a standard scale – one early question was how to present the results. Should they be numbers? Or letter grades like those used in American universities? Should countries be grouped, or strictly ordered? The CGD chose to present numerical scores and to create a full ranking, because doing otherwise would have added another level of inherently arbitrary processing. Also, grouping would have dulled the provocative effect of ranking.

There remained the question of how to normalize readings on various indicators onto a common scale in order to combine them. In general, there are four axioms it would be nice for any normalization system to satisfy:

1. Normalized scores should fall in an intuitive range such as 0–10;

2. They should have the same average, say 5, so that, for example, 6 reliably means "above average";

3. They should have the same standard deviation, so that 2 points above the average always means the 98th percentile, as an example;

4. Zero should map to 0, so that a country that gives no aid cannot earn an aid score of 3 or –2.

On indicators of "bads" such as trade barriers, axiom 4 would analogously require that a complete absence of the thing scored corresponds to an intuitive maximum such as 10. If one also requires for simplicity that normalizations are linear, meaning that each 1-point increase in a raw score causes the same amount of change in its

normalized version, then one has two degrees of freedom per indicator. For example, the decision regarding which raw scores map to 0 and 10 nails down the whole scoring system. Two degrees of freedom are not enough to ensure that all four axioms are satisfied.

As a result, index designers usually must decide which axioms matter most. The CGD favored axioms 1 and 4 in the first edition, then switched to 2 and 4, with a few exceptions. Specifically, most indicators are now normalized by first dividing by the average for all scored countries, then multiplying by 5. For "bad" indicators such as pollution, where a lower number is good, normalized scores are then subtracted from 10. This guarantees that average performers get scores of 5 (axiom 2), and that 0 maps to 0 for "good" indicators and to 10 for "bad" ones (axiom 4). Since countries that are average on a "good" indicator get a 5, those that are twice the average get a 10, and those even better score above 10. Similarly, a country twice as bad as average on a "bad" indicator gets a 0, and one even worse gets a negative score. Thus the intuitive 0–10 scale (axiom 1) is sometimes violated, which can confuse audiences. The benefit comes from eliminating confusing situations such as that of Switzerland in the first CDI. Because all scores were then forced into the 0–10 range (axiom 1), Switzerland scored higher on trade than aid (4.0 versus 3.3) but was actually below average on trade and above average on aid.

Almost none of the CDI indicators are normalized relative to some ideal score. It is rare in the policy world for consensus to coalesce around a target performance level that is intellectually credible. It has been suggested, for instance, that the CDI measure of aid quantity be scaled against the ideal of 0.7 percent of GDP, a rate of giving embodied in several official international documents. But that number is arbitrary, and an index that took it on board would be signaling that it prioritizes political correctness over serious policy analysis.[2] There are exceptions. All "Annex I" industrial countries except Croatia, Kazakhstan, and the United States have signed the Kyoto Protocol on climate change. The ideal value of 1 on a binary indicator of ratification status is clearly defensible on serious policy grounds.[3]

Intimately related to the scaling issues are those of weighting. Indeed, changing the normalization of an indicator – as in the switch between years 1 and 2 in the CDI – is equivalent to changing the weight on that indicator to the extent that it affects the dispersion of normalized scores. Nevertheless, scaling and weighting are distinct notions in the minds of most readers and raise separate issues. Readers may pass over questions of scaling with little comment, but then strongly question choices of weight.

The first design question around weights is whether or not to equal-weight. The answer depends in part on how confident the designers are that one component is more important than another. The CDI migration component gives 65 percent weight to indicators of openness to immigration and only 20 percent to one of countries' assistance to refugees and asylum seekers. The scholars at the Migration Policy Institute, who wrote the background paper, believed that openness of the labor market helps developing countries much more than acceptance of their refugees and asylum seekers. The HRI gives more weight to bottom-line measures of the quality of humanitarian response than to intermediate goals of learning and accountability.

The top level of the CDI, in contrast, takes the unweighted average of the seven component scores. That has brought criticism. Robert Picciotto, the former director of the World Bank's Independent Evaluation Group, wrote cleverly, "To be approximately right is better than to be precisely wrong."[4] However, there has been no consensus among those opposed to equal-weighting the CDI on the right weights. Some have favored aid and trade, others want extra weight for migration since total earnings gains for émigrés dwarfs aggregate aid and trade flows, while others point to the tremendous importance of climate change and technological innovation, and so on. This argues for the minimally arbitrary choice of simple averaging in the CDI.

The important thing for index designers is to recognize the trade-off in deviating from equal weighting. First, deviating from equal weights invites more criticism of the weights chosen. Many will understand equal weighting for what it is: an expression of agnosticism. Unequal weights are held to a higher standard. Second is the presentational cost. Most people feel they understand simple averages. Fewer could explain what a weighted average is. Nevertheless, if the designers of an index believe that unequal weights would greatly improve the meaningfulness of an index, these costs can be worth paying.

Whatever the weights chosen, most people understand that the "correct" ones are unknowable. Yet few understand that the very idea of "correct weighting" is hardly well defined itself. To see this, let us think more carefully about the idea of "equal weighting." Consider: changes to the CDI's scaling system between 2003 and 2004 changed the spreads (standard deviations) of scores on various components, thus their effective weights. Yet

the CDI was a simple average of component scores both years. So which year truly gave equal weight to the seven policy areas? Both – and neither. Or ponder this example: suppose one wanted to develop an index of how big a person is, factoring in both weight and height. Suppose weight is measured in kilograms and height in meters. What *weights* – forgive the pun – should be put on these two factors? A simple average – though some might call it "equal weighting" – would, in fact, confer dominance on weight in kilograms since the numbers would be bigger there, ranging in the hundreds while height ranged mostly between 1 and 2. Measuring height in millimeters instead would flip the comparison. But if not these "equal weights," then what? In the end, there is no canonical formula for the right weights.

On reflection, equal weighting is a chimerical notion. Phrasing in terms of policy indexes, what one *could* ask is that *any two measured policy changes that have an equal effect on the outcome of interest, such as coping with and preventing humanitarian disasters, have an equal effect on the index*. The emphasis here is not on grand questions of whether foreign aid, say, is more important than foreign trade, but on how specific policy changes in those domains compare on well defined outcomes. When it comes to comparing policy domains as a whole – which is what indexes often appear to do at their top levels – there is no such thing as truly equal weighting.

The argument can be extended to "unequally weighted" indexes such as the HRI. The meaning of weights such as 20 percent and 10 percent on the various components is ultimately unclear. In particular, they are not saying that a 20 percent-weighted component is exactly twice as important as a 10 percent-weighted one. This should be an additional source of humility for the designers of the index, as well as for its critics.

Sensitivity analysis

Sensitivity analysis should be a matter of course when developing composite indexes in a research context. But in a communications context, in a sound bite world, it can undermine the credibility of an index. And the CDI and HRI are, above all, communications tools. Moreover, in indexes that combine so much information, one should take as given that results depend significantly on assumptions, including assumptions that go quite deep into political philosophy. Accepting this, sensitivity analysis may not be very enlightening. Finally, there can be hundreds of parameters to test, so that ana-

The Humanitarian Response Index 2008

lyzing the importance of all of them would quickly overwhelm a limited budget and human cognition.

For these reasons, the CDI designers have not analyzed the sensitivity of the index to a great extent. Put simply, it would not greatly advance the goals of the project. Two experiments with changing the weights tend to buttress this choice. The first is an exploration of the effects of systematically varying the top-level weights. As reported in the overall CDI technical paper,[5] 63 non-standard versions of the CDI were generated: first with the weight on aid raised to 2, then 3, and so on up to 10, while weights on the other components were held at 1, then the same for trade, and then for the other components.[6] The correlations between the official overall 2007 CDI scores and the modified ones were then calculated. For all the components, ten-fold overweighting yields a score correlation of 0.48–0.86 with the original. Whether this constitutes robustness remains in the eye of the beholder and ultimately does not seem to speak to the CDI's mission of bringing certain messages to the public.

In the second experiment, Shyamal Chowdhury and Lyn Squire surveyed development experts in the global North and South to elicit their preferred weights for the CDI's major components.[7] In their results, average preferred weights on several are statistically different from equal weighting. However, the differences are not great, and the correlation between the standard CDI and the re-weighted one is 0.992.

For the HRI, a striking sensitivity test is the scatter plot of hard data indicator versus survey-based results. In effect, this shows what would happen if either group of indicators were zero-weighted. The correlation proves to be strong, meaning that sensitivity to weighting between these two groups is low, and adds to the credibility of both sets of measures.

The "black box problem"

Another common issue in policy indexes is the tradeoff between precision and transparency. The CDI is sometimes cast as a counterpart of the Human Development Index (HDI). But the two are quite different. The HDI measures an outcome, development, with a small collection of intuitive indicators such as GDP per capita and life expectancy. This makes the HDI simple. Like the Humanitarian Response Index, the CDI measures government policies and actions, which are complex and diverse in themselves and have equally complex and diverse relationships with development outcomes around the world. As mentioned above, the CDI

evolved substantially in response to comments during its first three editions; many of these comments pointed out things the CDI excluded or important distinctions it did not make. Thus there is an inherent tendency toward complexity in policy indexes.

Moreover, conceptual rigor sometimes argues for formulas that are simple in concept but complex in practice. For example, the CDI's foreign aid component assesses both quantity and quality of aid. The initial design draft done by William Easterly ranked donors on aid/GDP and a few quality indicators, and then took an average of the ranks. This was easy to understand, but contrary to sensible theory, since quantity and quality ought to interact multiplicatively, not additively. Otherwise, a donor that gave a penny of high-quality aid could outrank one that gave $10 billion in medium-quality aid. The current aid component design works quite differently. Each quantum of aid that a donor gives a country is discounted for quality factors such as the apparent appropriateness of the recipient for aid (a "selectivity" weight based on poverty and governance quality); then the discounted quanta are summed for each donor. Although the result is an aid component that is more conceptually sound, it is also opaque, as it involves thousands of calculations in a custom database.

There are ways to minimize the black box problem. One is to keep the top-level structure of the index, which receives the vast majority of the attention, simple. Another is to make available to the reader plain-language summaries of what the components reward and penalize, as well as country reports that summarize the sources of each nation's performance. Last, is to fully document the calculations, in technical papers, public spreadsheets and databases. In the experience of the CGD, these steps allow the index promulgator to limit, though certainly not eliminate, the trade-off between precision and transparency.

The tensions in public learning

CDI design has been a public learning exercise. Each edition has provoked commentary that influenced the subsequent one – a two-way relationship that is to be welcomed. After three design cycles, the pace of change slowed markedly, though it has never stopped. Nevertheless, major year-to-year methodological changes posed a transitional communications challenge because changes in measurement dwarfed changes in what is measured. Between the first and second editions, seven countries saw their ranks change by more than 11, out of 21. Some asked how the index could be taken seriously as a policy metric if readings jumped that much from year to year. (Most of these critics also pointed to what they saw as additional design problems, which led to more methodological changes!)

A complex policy index that froze in year one could be seen as arrogant, thus intellectually suspect. And it would appear unresponsive to the community it is trying to reach. Inasmuch as an index is embedded in a larger project of construction engagement with this audience, complete inflexibility can be counterproductive. On the other hand, an index that does not appear to converge over time shows a lack of intellectual moorings. Indexes are vehicles for interaction between people, and thoughtful people expect from their interlocutors a blend of openness and strength of inner compass.

So the healthy development of an index can include significant changes in the first few years, as was the case for the CDI. One way of minimizing the cost of methodological disruption is to back-calculate each iteration of the methodology to earlier years to allow meaningful comparisons over time, something the CDI project has done since its third edition. As for communications strategy, index promoters can put their best feet forward, explaining their pride in the improvements that have been made. In the case of the CDI, the CGD felt that the benefits of public learning – building a more credible index and demonstrating openness to feedback from key audiences – outweighed the costs, provided that the index methodology stabilized in due course.

Indexing as outreach

Policy indexes such as the CDI and the HRI aim to bring certain facts and ideas to new audiences. So a full understanding of the strengths and prospects of an index must be based on a view of the index not just as a set of procedures for gathering and combining data, but also as part of a larger project of engagement with audiences.

Indexes are inherently impolite. They are meant to draw attention to their creators, or at least what the creators have to say. They do so at the cost of simplifying complex issues. And they "name and shame." Accepting this reality, it becomes valuable for people running index projects to do what they can through diplomacy to soften any ire and maximize the positive impact. This can be especially helpful for an index whose key audience is fairly sharply defined, as in the case of the HRI, which needs most of all to reach administrators of humanitarian aid.

So an effective index *project* will tend to develop along a path with both a cyclical rhythm and longer-term trajectory. The release of each edition, perhaps especially through exposure in the media, will force those graded to pay attention. For the CDI, one important channel has been from newspapers to members of parliament to top high-level development cooperation officials. Those subjected to this potentially uncomfortable splash of accountability may, understandably, challenge the methodology of the index. Those challenges are also an opportunity – an opening for conversation between those graded and those grading that can help the index-makers learn, and lead to broader acceptance of their work, and, more importantly, their messages.

Critics will challenge an index – especially if it is new – on several grounds. They will question its methodology. They will question the indexing approach itself, pointing out the false appearance of precision. There will also be questions about the authority of the makers of the index to pass judgment on others. Who funds them? Whom did they consult? The more astute challengers will interconnect questions of method and authority by pointing out underlying assumptions, such as about the proper role of the state in solving public problems. These arguably tag the index makers as coming from a particular point of view – left- or right-wing, European or American, Eastern or Western, Northern or Southern – and may undermine their credibility.

The foundations of any response to criticism, it should be said, are a conceptually solid design and the clear independence of its designers. Some problematic indexes have withered under criticism once released. Beyond this, within the realm of outreach, index projects have taken several kinds of steps to head off and respond to such criticisms, and to exploit the openings for dialog:

- *Partnering with organizations that are credible with target audiences.* The Asia Foundation, for example, partners with the Vietnam Chamber of Commerce and Industry (VCCI), a state-led umbrella organization for the private sector, in producing the Vietnam Provincial Competitiveness Index. It compares provincial governments on how supportive a business environment they create. Within Vietnam, the index is associated almost exclusively with the VCCI, and that has given the index credibility all the way up to the Prime Minister.

- *Meeting, listening, and learning.* Conversations with the policymakers whose policies are scored can take place in many ways. As much as possible, the discussion should be two-way, with the indexers viewing it as a source of ideas for how to improve their product. Listening also tends to diffuse the emotional component of attacks on the index. One formal example is the CDI Consortium, which CGD organized in 2005 to bring together representatives from bilateral donor agencies. The Consortium includes 11 of the 21 countries rated, meets annually to advise CGD on the CDI project, and partially funds it.

- *Persisting.* There is a natural progression from objection to acceptance. An index that survives the stronger initial round criticism has a good shot at usefulness long term. Once the initial antibodies dissipate, there is greater hope for moving debate toward the important questions: not just how to measure policy, but how to improve it.

All this discussion about the tensions that indexes can create should not overshadow the fact that many people accept indexes easily enough, understanding that they are, above all, exercises in strategic communications, carried out by people who know they do not have all the answers, and care most about getting others to ask the right questions.

The ranking device has worked well for the CGD. The CDI has been cited in the *Economist,* the *New York Times,* the *Washington Post,* the *Los Angeles Times,* the *Financial Times,* and many other newspapers worldwide via major wire services. NHK television, BBC World Service, Voice of America, and other broadcast services have also covered it. University professors are teaching from the CDI, probably what the CGD is best known for. So it is serving its intended purpose of introducing people to the institution, its mission, and its work.

The most engaged audience has been officials at bilateral aid agencies. They are the people most responsible for thinking about how their governments' policies affect developing countries. The Dutch and Finnish governments, as part of their efforts to frame development policy as being about more than foreign aid, have adopted the CDI as an official metric of development policy performance. The Australian government commissioned two high-quality papers critiquing the CDI in its first year.[8] The CDI has influenced development policy white papers in Australia, Canada, Finland, and

Norway. And aid agencies officials from many of the CDI countries have provided written or oral comments informally, or have asked questions as they report to their ministers on their country's CDI performance.

One of the strongest responses has come from Japan, a country that once took pride in being the world's largest donor (the U.S., France, Germany, and the U.K. have since surpassed it). Japan finishes firmly in last place on the CDI, because of its tight barriers to workers and goods from developing countries, minimal contributions to peacekeeping, and an aid program that is actually modest for the country's size. In general, Japan is rightly proud of its economic accomplishments over the last 60 years, and of having made them in a distinctive Japanese way. Yet along with the pride comes, somewhat paradoxically, a sensitivity to how the rest of the world views their country. For many Japanese, who see their country as leading the economic expansion in Asia, and as a moral exemplar with its peace constitution, the CDI seems implausible. Hence, the strong Japanese reaction. But even most Japanese recognize that Japan is more closed than the other 20 rated countries. And a core belief embedded in the CDI is that openness in rich countries is good for poorer ones. Certainly, the ability to export to the big US market helped Japan develop rapidly.

In direct response to the CDI, the director-general of the Economic Cooperation Bureau of Japan's Ministry of Foreign Affairs wrote an opinion piece in 2003 in the *Asahi Shimbun,* a leading Japanese newspaper, out of fear of the "misunderstandings that may result from the publication of the ranking worked out by a well known think tank in an authoritative political journal."[9] It has been a hot topic in an email discussion group involving a thousand or more Japanese aid officials around the globe. In my experience, many Japanese have been quite critical of the CDI, but nearly always polite and constructive in discussing it. The Ministry has argued that, rather than creating an incentive for improvement, the CDI is undermining support in Japan for foreign aid by casting the country as a hopeless failure. The job of the Ministry and its career foreign servants is, of course, to defend current government policy. People in other parts of the government have told me they think the CDI has been beneficial by stimulating discussions about the quality of Japan's aid, and providing a wake-up call about the costs of Japan's insularity. Here, in a nutshell, we see the spectrum of responses an index can generate.

Lessons

The challenges and successes of the Commitment to Development Index offer lessons for the HRI and other index projects.

Clarity of concept and purpose is essential

It is important from the start to understand the concept being measured and the ultimate goals of the index project. In the case of the CDI, goals include spurring research and policy reform and building the reputation of a new institution, specifically a reputation for blending serious analysis with practical creativity. These goals influence the details of the index design and should be communicated to the audience. If goals beyond measurement itself are made clear, this helps people to take the project in the right spirit and not to hold the index to the standard of perfection. While remaining aware of the index's defects, one should publicly criticize it as a measurement tool only enough to demonstrate humility, and then explain that it is a means to greater ends. An index that pretends to be more than it is loses credibility.

Big, simple ideas get attention

Transparency International's Corruption Perceptions Index and the UN Development Programme's Human Development Index are examples of indexes that not only embody big, easily grasped ideas (corruption, human development as more than money income), but have promoted those ideas in the public consciousness worldwide. They demonstrate that grand indexes can have real impact. Of course, it may be entirely appropriate for a given index project to focus on a narrower idea, such as technology use in business or investment in primary education in Latin America, and aim at a narrower audience.

Top-level accessibility is invaluable for a complex index

A reader who can easily understand the idea and overall structure of an index will feel oriented and more prepared to buy into the whole construct. Most readers will not explore beyond the top level of structure. It is also important for plausibility to summarize in plain language the details that the reader cannot see. This strategy allows for an index that reflects at its roots the complexities of policy, while catering to the busy lay reader.

Public learning need not be fatal

CDI designers made substantial improvements in the second and third editions. This understandably engendered criticism because a few countries jumped up or down in the ranking. But public learning had several benefits. Any change adds interest, and the worst enemy of a communications strategy is boredom. Change can actually add credibility by signaling that the designers do not claim to hold a monopoly on the truth, thus that the ultimate purpose of the index is to provoke and educate, not measure. Finally, it makes for a better index in the long run. Excellence is normally achieved through continual feedback and learning. It is important, however, to guard against misleading inter-temporal comparisons when the methodology is changing substantially. It is probably also best to stabilize the design after a few years.

An attack on an index is a victory if one purpose of the index is to raise awareness

When most people turn to the question of how rich countries affect poorer ones, they think of foreign aid. The Center for Global Development aimed to change that idea, in part through the CDI, by showing people that trade, migration, and other policies matter at least as much, and need reform. We therefore consider most criticism of the CDI to be a sign of success, since it means that people are talking about things we believe deserve more attention. That is better than being ignored.

Conclusion

The Humanitarian Response Index, now one year old, has not been ignored. As its creators would, no doubt, be the first to admit, debatable compromises are embedded in its methodology, and the underlying data are incomplete. But the history of one index, the CDI, offers much hope that, over time, its acceptance will only grow, that attention will shift from whether the weights are right to how to improve humanitarian aid, and that the index itself will be a new force prodding reform that will benefit the planet's most deserving people.

Notes

1   Birdsall and Roodman, 2003; Roodman, 2007.

2   On the history of the 0.7 percent target, see Clemens and Moss, 2005.

3   United Nations Framework Convention on Climate Change, Kyoto Protocol: Status of Ratification, available at: http://unfccc.int/files/essential_background/kyoto_protocol/application/pdf/kpstats.pdf

4   Picciotto, 2003.

5   Roodman, 2007.

6   My colleague Michael Clemens suggested these tests.

7   Chowdhury and Squire, 2006.

8   McGillivray, 2003; Castles, 2004.

9   Furuta, 2003.

References

Birdsall, Nancy and David Roodman. 2003. "The Commitment to Development Index: A Scorecard of Rich-Country Policies." Washington, D.C.: Center for Global Development. April.

Castles, Ian. 2004. "Evaluation of Donor Performance Monitoring Initiatives." AusAID. February.

Chowdhury, Shyamal and Lyn Squire. 2006. "Setting Weights for Aggregate Indices: An Application to the Commitment to Development Index and Human Development Index." *Journal of Development Studies* 42(5):761–71.

Clemens, Michael and Todd Moss. 2005 "Ghost of 0.7%: Origins and Relevance of the International Aid Target." Working Paper 68. Washington, D.C.: Center for Global Development.

Furuta, Hajime. 2003. "ODA Report Unfairly Portrays Japan's Efforts." *Asahi Shimbun,* 8 September.

McGillivray, Mark. 2003. "Commitment to Development Index: A Critical Appraisal." AusAID. November.

Picciotto, Robert. 2003. "Giving Weight to the CGD Rankings: A Comment on the Commitment to Development Index." Global Policy Project. Available at: http://www.globalpolicyproject.org/indexComment.html

Roodman, David. 2007. "The Commitment to Development Index: 2007 Edition." Washington, D.C.: Center for Global Development. October.

United Nations Framework Convention on Climate Change, Kyoto Protocol: Status of Ratification. Bonn. Available at: http://unfccc.int/files/essential_background/kyoto_protocol/application/pdf/kpstats.pdf

CHAPTER 4

Humanitarian Funding and Needs Assessment

JOHN COSGRAVE, Independent Consultant

Humanitarian action is intended to prevent death and suffering. One of the most fundamental principles of such action is that it should be proportionate to humanitarian need. This principle is enshrined in documents such as the Code of Conduct for humanitarian action,[1] which states that assistance should be on the basis of need alone, neutral, impartial, and independent, and not be influenced by race, creed, or any other factor. These core concepts form the basis of the Good Humanitarian Donorship *Principles,* as agreed to in 2003.

This paper looks at how humanitarian donorship has developed since 2003 and attempts to answer four questions:

- How has humanitarian funding developed in the recent past?

- Given these changes, to what extent are humanitarian needs now being met?

- Does humanitarian funding for different crises vary in proportion to need?

- If poor needs assessments are a problem, how can we improve their quality to better match funding in proportion to need?

The approach to each of these four questions will be based on analysis of data from the Development Assistance Committee (DAC) of the OECD and the UN Office for the Coordination of Humanitarian Affairs (OCHA) Financial Tracking Service (FTS), and a review of recent evaluations and publications in the sector.

How has official humanitarian funding changed since 2003?

Before looking at humanitarian funding, it is useful to look at the way in which all official development assistance has been changing.[2]

Figure 1 shows the value of Official Development Assistance (ODA) from 1990 to 2007 in constant dollar terms. After a trough in the late 1990s, ODA, including debt relief, rose to a new peak in 2005, with the Gleneagles meeting and the Make Poverty History campaign. Overall ODA has fallen sharply since 2005, but that is because so much aid was allocated as debt relief[3] in that year.

As shown in Figure 2, official humanitarian assistance was experiencing positive growth in 2003 when the GHD *Principles* were agreed. It peaked in 2005, principally due to the exceptionally large aid flows resulting from the December 2004 Indian Ocean tsunami, and the October 2005 Pakistan earthquake. Since then, it has fallen somewhat. Measured in constant dollar terms, from year to year, humanitarian aid fell by 8 percent in 2006 and by 12 percent in 2007. As a proportion of all other ODA (excluding debt relief), official humanitarian aid has averaged 7.3 percent during 2000–2007, up from an average of 5.2 percent for the period 1990–1999 (Figure 2).

This rise reflected, in part, increased humanitarian aid for Afghanistan (strongest in 2002) and Iraq (in 2003). Afghanistan and Iraq accounted for 30 percent of all humanitarian aid flows to identified recipient countries in 2003 (Figure 3). Authors such as Darcy and Hoffman[4] have suggested that the high priority given to Afghanistan and Iraq by donors was influenced by political rather than humanitarian concerns.

Has humanitarian aid – acknowledged to be inadequate at the Stockholm meeting of 2003 – increased to meet real humanitarian needs?

Humanitarian aid from official sources has been falling since the 2005 peak. Measured in constant dollar terms from year to year, humanitarian aid fell by 8 percent in 2006 and by 12 percent in 2007. What is worse, official humanitarian aid has been falling as a proportion of all ODA. In 2007, official humanitarian aid represented the same proportion (7.7 percent) of other ODA,

Figure 1. Official Development Assistance: All donors 1990 to 2007, showing the value of debt relief grants

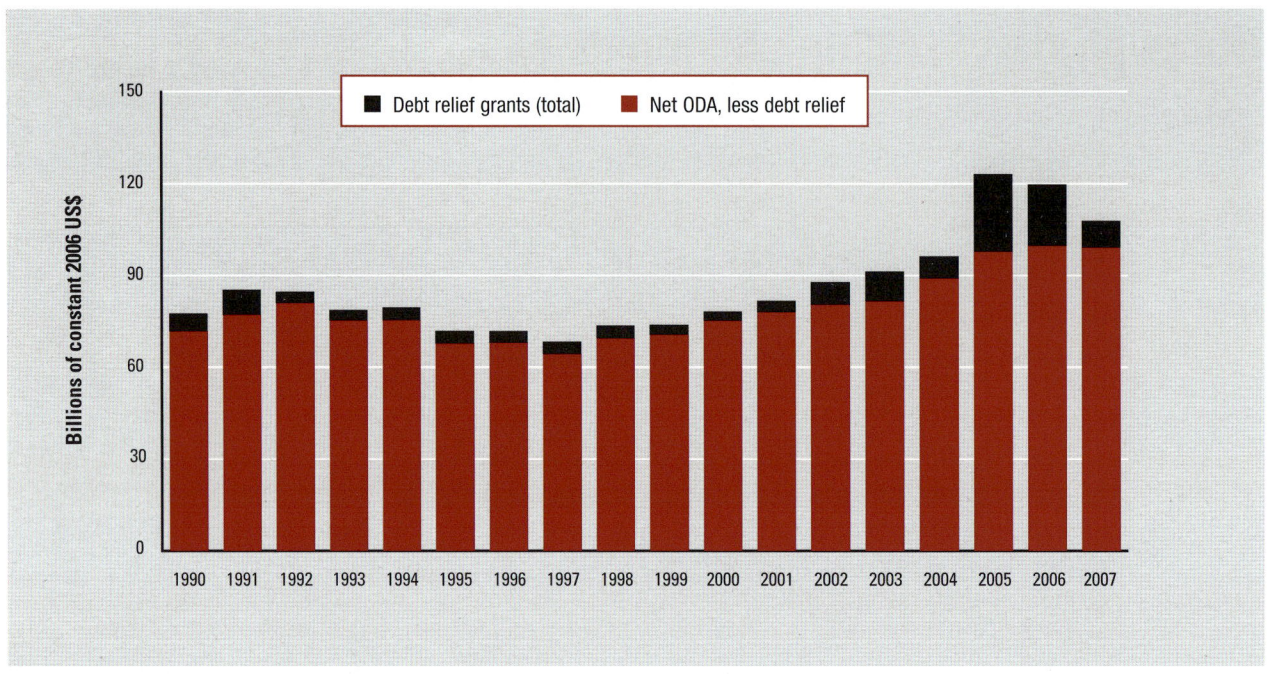

Source: OECD/DAC Table 1, 2 May 2008. 2007 data are preliminary.

Figure 2. Official Humanitarian Aid 1990–2007 in constant US$, as a percentage of all other ODA (excluding debt relief)

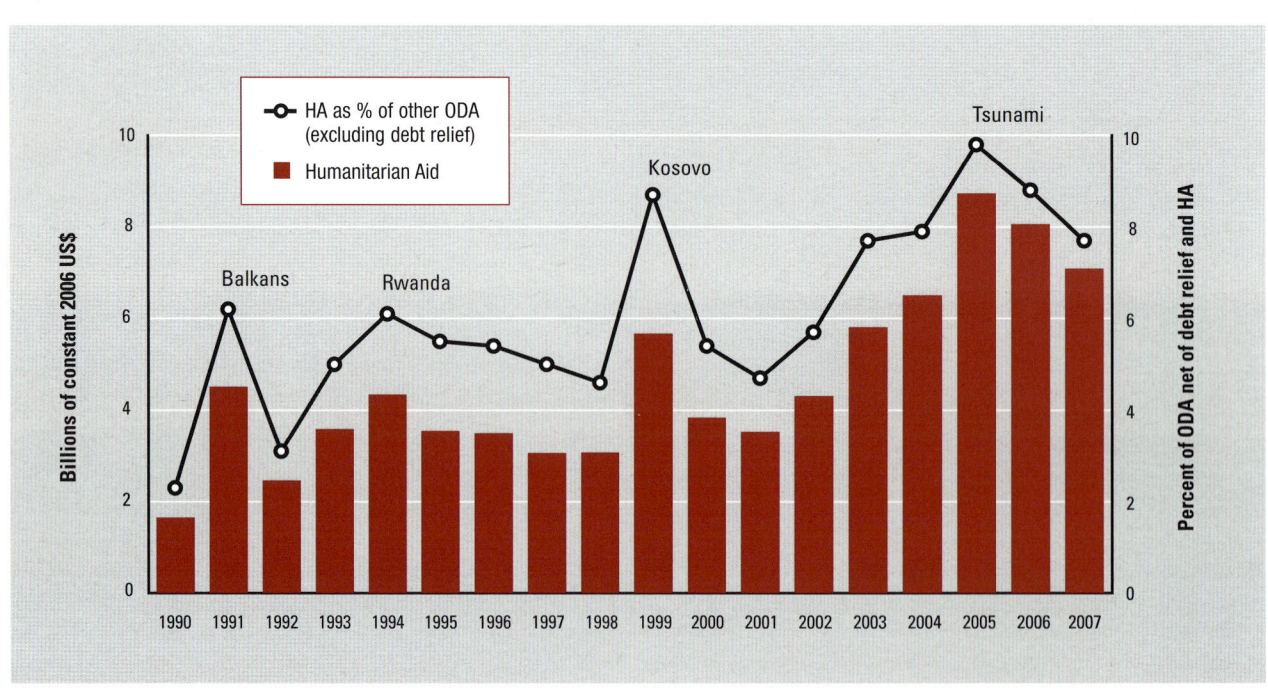

Source: OECD/DAC Table 1, 2 May 2008. 2007 data are preliminary.

Figure 3. Humanitarian Aid to Afghanistan and Iraq, 2000–2006

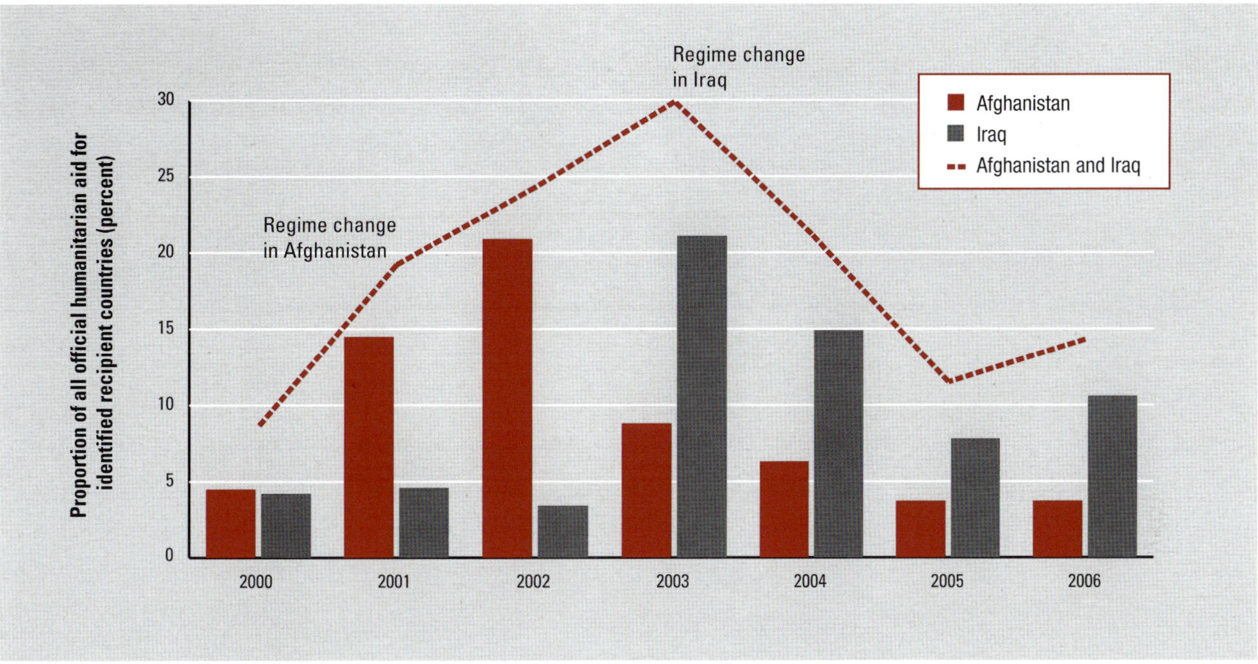

Note: Two-thirds of humanitarian aid was for identified recipient countries during this period.
Source: OECD/DAC, 2008b, Table 2a.

(less debt relief) that it did in 2003. Considering only OECD donors – the group from which the Good Humanitarian Donors are drawn – the proportion of other ODA (less debt relief) fell from 7.8 percent in 2003 to 7.3 percent in 2007.

In economics, the definition of a recession is two quarters with negative growth. Since a year is probably a better period to measure something as inherently variable as humanitarian aid, it is probably fair, after two years with negative growth in humanitarian funding, to say that the official humanitarian sector is in recession until the next large humanitarian crisis.[5]

Are needs being met?

Measuring needs

There is no infallible indicator of the level of humanitarian needs. One proxy in use is the humanitarian Consolidated Appeal issued by the United Nations – although these are widely acknowledged not to be a perfect measure of need.[6] However, they do represent a consensus among the UN agencies about the level of need and can be a useful yardstick against which to assess donor allocations.

While support for Appeals varied from a low of 55 percent (2001) to a high of 76 percent (2003), support over the nine years has been 68 percent on average.[7] Over the nine years, the worst supported Appeal (in March 2007 for the floods in Zambia) raised only 12.4 percent of the requested amount, while the best supported Appeal (2006 for Lebanon) raised 123.1 percent of the requested amount. Analysis of the standard deviations of the distribution of the level of support reveals no discernable pattern.

The commitment to Good Humanitarian Donorship in 2003 seems to have had no impact on support for UN Appeals up to 2007. Figure 4 shows there has been no difference in the overall level or the variability of support either before or after 2003. Official humanitarian aid increased slightly in 2004 and then soared in 2005,[8] due to the impact of the December 2004 Indian Ocean tsunami and the October 2005 Pakistan earthquake.

The evidence of Figure 4 would suggest that assistance is not proportionate to need, if UN Appeals represent even a rough approximation of needs.

Figure 4. Support for UN Flash Appeals (new emergencies) and Consolidated Appeals (ongoing crises) 1999–2007

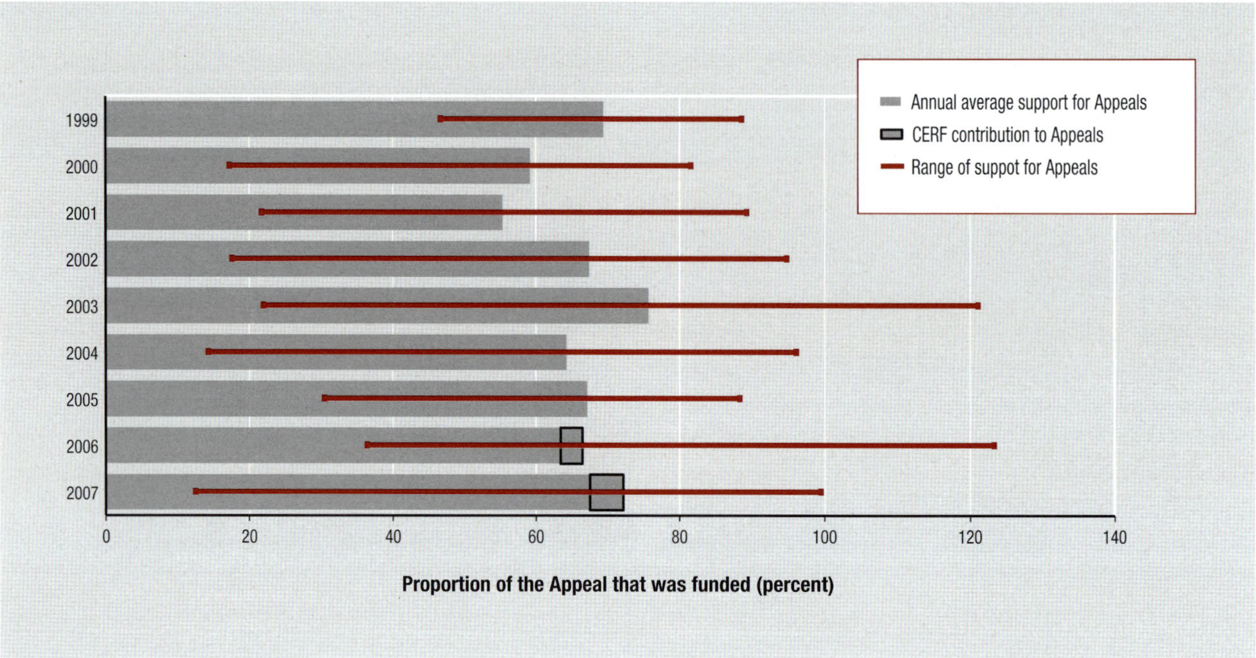

Legend:
- Annual average support for Appeals
- CERF contribution to Appeals
- Range of suppot for Appeals

Proportion of the Appeal that was funded (percent)

Notes: Thick bars show average support. Thin lines show range of funding. Funding from CERF in 2006 and 2007 shown by small boxes.
Sources: OCHA, 2008a and 2008d.

The impact of CERF

One innovation since 2003 has been the introduction of the Central Emergency Response Fund (CERF). This replaced the Central Emergency Revolving Fund on 9 March 2006 with a new facility that added up to US$450 million of grants to what had previously been a US$50 million revolving loan fund.[9] In 2007, the first full year of operation for the new CERF, it provided 6.5 percent of all funding for UN Flash and Consolidated Appeals.[10]

CERF is fully coherent with the Good Humanitarian Donorship Initiative. It provides a large pool of unearmarked funds for humanitarian response for both new emergencies and for the underfunded ones. It attracted US$299 million from donors in 2006 and US$385 million in 2007.[11] Contributions and pledges for 2008 already totalled US$431 million by the end of May, giving a cumulative total of US$1,115 million.[12]

CERF is remarkable in that it attracts funding – admittedly small contributions – from aid *recipients* as well as from the major donors. Some countries are both contributors and recipients of CERF funds (Haiti, Indonesia, Lebanon, and Pakistan). The number of contributing nations has grown from 52 in 2006 to 78 in

2008.[13] However, over 70 percent of the funding was provided by only five donor countries.[14]

CERF can provide two types of grants: a) for new emergencies, and b) for under-funded emergencies. Since its launch in March 2006 to 20 July 2008, CERF had provided US$585 million (66 percent of disbursements) for sudden onset emergencies and US$302 million (34 percent of disbursements) for under-funded emergencies.[15]

The growth of CERF means that it is a significant recipient of official humanitarian funding. It accounted for more that 5 percent of all official humanitarian funding in 2007 and this percentage will probably be higher in 2008.

CERF is of particular importance to UN Appeals. Even in 2006, when it had been in operation for just under 10 months, CERF contributed 4.6 percent of all funding to UN Consolidated Appeals.[16] This rose to 6.5 percent in 2007.[17] The additive effect of CERF can be seen in Figure 4. CERF can be quite an important source of funding for individual appeals. Of the total funds for the Flash Appeal for the Mozambique floods, 42 percent were provided by CERF.[18] The Interim Review of CERF's first year of operation noted that since its introduction, the median level of support for Flash Appeals had increased from 20 to 30 percent at the one-month mark.[19]

However, even though CERF represents a major improvement in humanitarian funding for the United Nations, it is still plagued by a number of problems. The first of these is delay. Delays in CERF money reaching affected populations have several causes: the time taken to prepare the request and review the application; to disburse CERF funds; and to disburse funds to NGOs and local implementing partners. CERF requests must be agreed upon by the UN Country Team before being submitted. This same requirement slowed CERF funding after the Pakistan[20] and Mozambique floods.[21]

The delay caused by review was a significant problem in the early days of the CERF, but is now said to have improved.[22] Oxfam research showed serious delays both at HQ level and in the field in the first year of operation.[23]

Actual disbursement is often slowed by UN financial rules.[24] The CERF Secretariat sits in OCHA, itself bound by the financial rules of the UN Secretariat.

Finally, there is the issue of onward disbursement to NGOs, in cases where these have indirect access to the funds. Although Oxfam noted in March 2007 that the CERF Secretariat was experimenting with innovative funding mechanisms, the International Council of Voluntary Agencies (ICVA) noted seven months later that *"there continue to be delays in CERF money reaching NGOs – and again, particularly national and local NGOs."*[25]

The speed of onward disbursement compounds another problem with CERF, the lack of direct NGO access to the funds. The need to access funds through UN agencies and the International Organization for Migration (IOM) means that NGOs must go through those agencies' bureaucratic processes for Project Partnership Agreements, all of which takes time. The lack of direct NGO access was a precondition for General Assembly agreement on CERF.

Thus, while CERF has been a positive development, these delays mean that it is not normally a ready source of funds in the initial period of the response to a crisis, when the life-saving potential is greatest.

The impact of the media

Bernard Kouchner is credited with saying that where there is no media, there is no emergency. This was a reference to the impact of the media on funding. There is no link between the level of humanitarian need and media interest in the story.[26] However, where there is

an interesting story, media attention and funding often both increase.

It may be that the level of support for different Appeals is a reflection of the media interest, the so-called "CNN effect,"[27] where television coverage of events drives government policy. However, the impact of the media on official aid is disputed. One study found that media coverage only influences official funding for emergencies, where there is no overriding strategic interest, and where strategic interest exists, it determines the level of funding.[28]

The CARMA media analysis group looked at the press coverage in Western media for six humanitarian disasters: Hurricane Katrina, Darfur, the 2003 Bam earthquake (Appeal in 2004), the December 2004 tsunami (Appeal in 2005), 2005 Hurricane Stanley, and the 2005 South Asia earthquake.[29]

Although a comparison of the level of press coverage for these six crises with the related UN Consolidated and Flash Appeals suggests at first glance that there is a positive relationship between media coverage and official donations, the disaster with the *lowest* level of media coverage, Hurricane Stanley, had the second highest level of official donor support for the UN Appeal for Guatemala (Figure 5).

Sectoral funding

Figure 6 shows that support by sector was variable in 2006 and 2007 relative to sectoral need, as identified through funding requested in the Consolidated Appeals Process (CAP) for specific sectors.[30] Mine action was the worst supported sector in 2006, but the best supported in 2007. While food managed to get good support in both years, vital humanitarian sectors such as health, water and sanitation, and shelter showed low levels of support.

Donors often respond to complaints about the variability of funding by referring, justifiably, to the variable quality of funding requests and to the lack of underlying needs assessments of good quality. Some aspects of the current humanitarian reform process should improve the quality of such funding requests and needs assessments. The UN Humanitarian Reform initiative consists of the following four pillars:[31]

1. The cluster approach, to improve coordination (within and between sectors, at global and field levels) by creating partnerships between and among all humanitarian actors working together towards commonly agreed objectives;

Figure 5. Relationship between support of UN Appeals and press coverage in four disasters

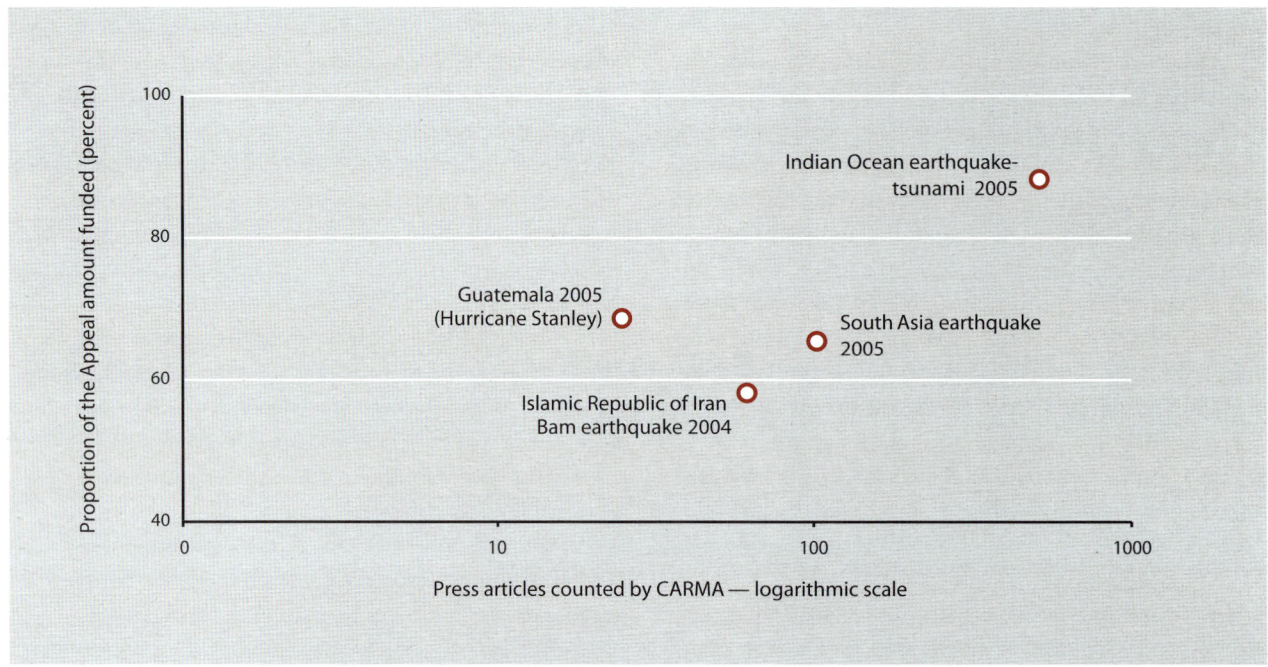

Sources: OCHA FTS, 2008a and CARMA, 2006.

Figure 6. Donor support by sector for UN Appeals, 2006 and 2007

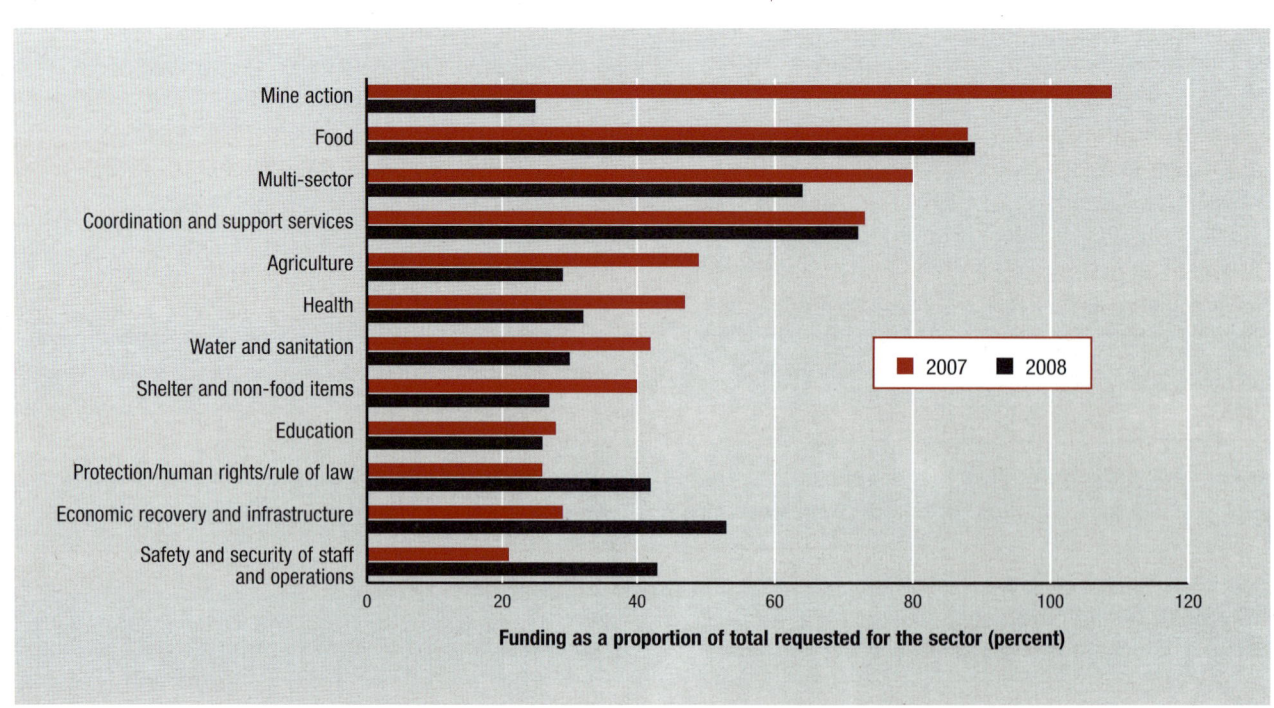

Source: OCHA FTS, 12 April 2008.
Note: Data understate overall donor support and exclude 8 percent of the total funding for unspecified sectors in 2007.

2. Better quality humanitarian leadership, through better trained Humanitarian Coordinators;[32]

3. The Central Emergency Response Fund (CERF);

4. Building partnership, by involving all humanitarian actors, not only UN agencies.

Better quality leadership, broader partnership, and the cluster approach should improve the quality of funding requests by bringing more experience to the table, reducing the number and size of inappropriate requests, and ensuring that requests are better grounded in the actual situation in the field. It is possible to test whether these reforms have had an impact by looking at the level of donor support for Appeals in 2007.

Of particular interest is whether using the cluster approach leads to better donor support for sudden-onset emergencies. Using the cluster approach when Flash Appeals are being prepared should result in more discussion and a better quality Appeal. Flash Appeals from countries using the cluster approach[33] received a higher level of support in 2007 (58.9 percent of all Appeals funded) than Flash Appeals from countries not using the cluster approach (55 percent of all Appeals funded).[34]

Speed vs. quality: The fundamental assessment contradiction

Poor quality needs assessments are a recognised weakness of the humanitarian system. This has continued with the introduction of CERF, with Oxfam noting that needs assessments were one of the sources of delay in CERF funding applications,[35] and the CERF Interim Review observing that there is a "methodological problem" in the implementation of needs assessments for CERF applications,[36] and that CERF applications "lack comprehensive needs assessment information."[37]

One of the contradictions of needs assessments in large sudden-onset emergencies is that, while a comprehensive needs assessment would increase their understating of the situation and help them to better target aid, donors may be under pressure to commit funds as quickly as possible, before any comprehensive assessment can be done.

This means that low-quality initial assessments often have a disproportionate impact on donor funding. The unlinking of decisions and assessment leads to the situation where "in many of the most serious humanitarian situations, there was a lack of crucial information available to decision-makers, and the kinds of needs assessments required to generate this are conducted only sporadically."[38]

Instead, donors rely on the media for information. For example, the Tsunami Evaluation Coalition (TEC) study on needs assessments found that "the mass media seems to have been the prime if not only influential source of information on needs for individual or institutional decision-makers outside the affected countries."[39] Some disaster response guidelines formally acknowledge the role of information from the media in making assessments.[40] The media can also play a role in disseminating assessment information, as happened in Thailand with the United Nations Disaster Assessment and Coordination (UNDAC) team after the tsunami.[41]

Agencies face a similar trade-off between the quality of needs assessments and the potential for saving lives. The better the quality of the assessment, the better it reflects real needs, the more effective will be the assistance. However, in sudden-onset humanitarian crises, the greatest needs occur at the beginning of the crisis, and faster assistance is most effective in reducing death and suffering. This results in a basic conflict between speed and effectiveness: with time, the potential life-saving effect of any intervention decreases, while the potential quality of the need assessment increases. Every needs assessment is a compromise between speed and effectiveness.

Improving needs assessments

The lack of adequate needs assessments is a recurring issue in humanitarian response. Many studies have pointed to insufficient needs assessments.[42] The 2006 *Review of Humanitarian Action* by the Active Learning Network for Accountability and Performance (ALNAP) referred to needs assessments as "the fundamental flaw of the humanitarian system."[43] Two years earlier, in its critique of weak needs assessments, the ALNAP *Review* made the point that needs assessment is not the same as needs understanding.[44]

Many humanitarian operations are launched in advance of assessments. Experienced humanitarian response managers draw on their experience to identify what the needs are likely to be (Box 1). The following section considers how experienced managers can do this and the risks involved in this approach.

Box 1. Fast action in Tanzania

In late 1993, over 250,000 Burundi refugees sought sanctuary in western Tanzania. The majority returned within six weeks, but several thousand remained. The number in western Tanzania fluctuated in 1994 as fresh incidents in Burundi forced people to flee at different times.

In one of the large influxes in 1994, a group of refugees arrived at a mission station in the morning. The missionaries immediately began to give out food and blankets to those arriving so that they could keep warm during the night. By noon, they had exhausted their supply of blankets.

Most of the first refugees to arrive were young, single, healthy adults who had made the best speed in the long trek from Burundi. In the afternoon families began to arrive, together with the sick and elderly. But there were no blankets for them, as they had all been given out to the first arrivals, some of whom then sold them to the later arrivals.

In this case of the Burundi refugees, the missionaries might have foreseen at the outset that the first arrivals were not going to be the people most in need. The typical scenario was for fighting (or rumours of fighting) to cause whole villages to flee. People arrived with relatively little portable property with them and might have had to surrender some or all of this to opportunistic criminals as they crossed the border. In 1993, Tanzanian villagers gave ready support to the first refugees. By 1994, the villagers had relatively little to give. Support was available in UNHCR-supported refugee camps run by different NGOs in conjunction with the government. The numbers of refugees fluctuated wildly from dozens to thousands. All of this was well known in 1994 and should have helped the missionaries to make a more accurate assessment.

The four dimensions of any humanitarian emergency are: a) the nature of the disaster, b) its extent, c) the nature and capacities of the affected population, and d) the likely response to it. These dimensions can be represented as a context knowledge tetrahedron (Figure 7).

The solution proposed here is that assessments be built, to the extent possible, on knowledge that is available *before* the disaster. This implies preparatory work by agency headquarters on the context of different disaster types, and by humanitarian managers in different countries on the nature and capacities of populations affected by potential disasters. While the likely extent of the disaster is largely unknown – although agencies can plan for this by using different scenarios – the likely response to the disaster may be partially known.

Knowledge of the pattern of needs associated with the disaster type

First, managers can use their knowledge of the disaster type to predict probable needs. Different disaster types create different needs.[45] For example, earthquakes in countries with weak or weakly enforced building codes, or where public sector corruption is common,[46] can be expected to generate many fatalities and trauma injuries.

However, the ratio of deaths to injuries can vary very widely.[47] More severe events have higher ratios of dead to injured. For example, after the tsunami, the UN Emergency Response Coordinator estimated that there were probably four people injured for every fatality in Indonesia. The actual figure turned out to be six deaths for every person seriously injured,[48] or about 4 percent of the numbers predicted. The figure of four injured per death was found only in India, where the tsunami waves were much lower. The initial overestimate of the number of injured had a practical consequence: an oversupply of field hospitals in Indonesia.[49]

It is not clear that senior managers always understand the risks of different disaster types. The tsunami saw warnings of a large-scale "second wave" of deaths. The head of the World Health Organisation's Health Action in Crisis, predicted that as many again could die from disease as died in the tsunami,[50] but scaled back his estimate the following day, warning that there was "a pretty good chance that as many as 50,000 could die of disease."[51] After three months, WHO reported that there had been no outbreaks of disease.[52] It is now well documented that disease does not inevitably follow disaster.[53]

Epidemics of disease are very rare after geophysical disasters (earthquakes, volcanic eruptions, and landslides) where there is no large-scale displacement. A recent review of 600 such disasters found only three cases where epidemics followed the disaster.[54] Floods generally lead to displacement and the need to provide camps. Trauma injuries are low, but diarrhoeal disease may be higher.

Figure 7. The emergency context tetrahedron

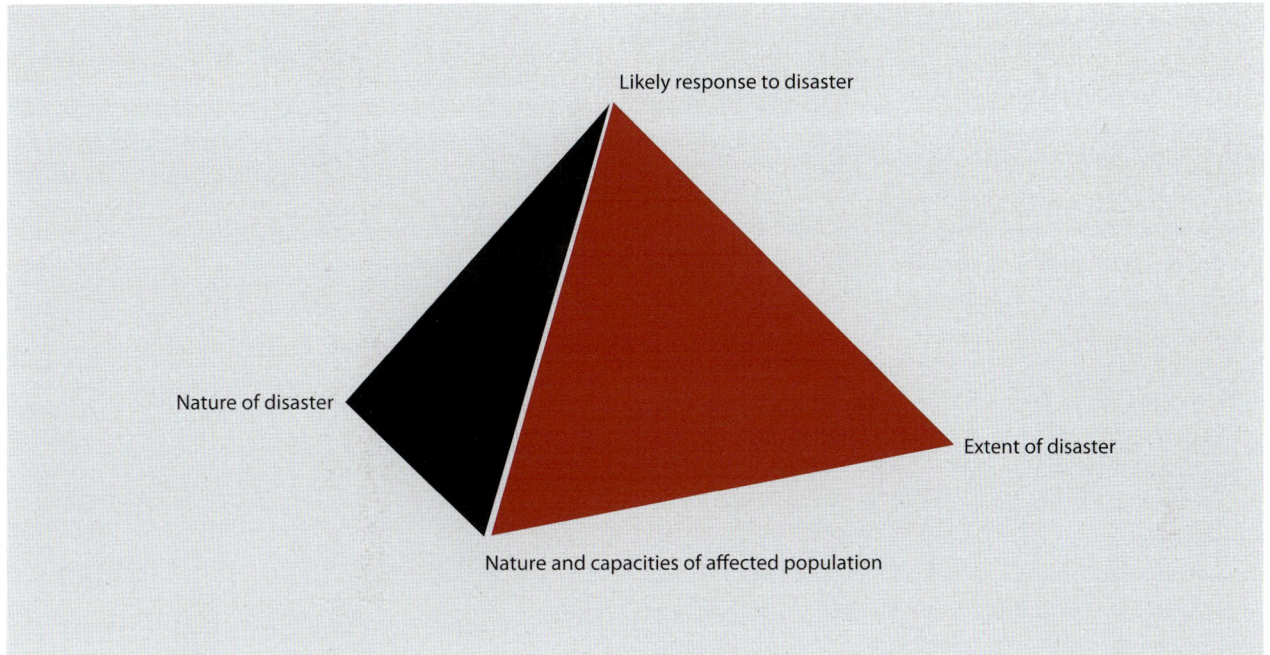

If agencies had paid closer attention to what we already know about disasters, they could have conserved on resources in the tsunami response. Similar close attention to the nature of other disasters can contribute to appropriate interventions prior to a detailed assessment. After the Pakistan earthquake, UNHCR immediately dispatched tents to the affected area without an assessment, so that some lucky families spent only one night without shelter.[55]

Thus, the first step in estimating needs in a disaster response is learning about the typical patterns of need associated with different types of disasters.

Knowledge of the likely response to disaster

When needs are met quickly by government or by existing agencies, the need is lessened for other agencies to act. For example, India has an extensive disaster response capacity and can usually deal with most disasters internally.

After the 2004 tsunami, the role for NGOs in India was reduced, as the government was able to act more quickly.[56] One complication is that the likely response will vary with the level of funding. For example, those affected by flooding in Bangladesh in 2004 received only US$3 of international assistance per person, as compared to US$7,100 per person received by those affected by the 2004 tsunami.[57]

Agencies already take the likely response into account when deciding to respond to disasters. Few agencies would mobilise an international team for large scale flooding in India, but they might do so for a country with a less developed response capacity.

The nature of the affected population and their capacities

The most important determinant of the likely need of the population is based on an understanding of the population. The needs of the population depend in part on their resources and practices and on how the affected population is organised. Rich communities that have significant resources may have less need of assistance. Communities that are well organised with strong social structures which survive a disaster are better able to deal with it than communities with weak social structures. The strong social networks in Jogjakarta (Indonesia) and the practice of *gotong royong* (communal labour exchange) meant that these populations had fewer relief needs and experienced speedier recovery.[58]

Ignorance of local culture is a persistent problem in disaster response. After the Kosovo crisis, the refugees in Macedonia were supplied with bottled water and portable toilets, complete with toilet paper. However, the Kosovo refugees preferred to use water rather than paper for personal hygiene. So they took the water bottles into the toilet, and then threw them into the toilet after use, with the result that the portable toilets filled quickly, causing major problems for the sludge-suction trucks which emptied the portable toilets.

A similar problem arose when the Kosovo refugees used disposable nappies (diapers) for infants. Since no provision for disposing of the used nappies had been made, people threw them into the portable toilets as well.

Considerable effort went into building refugee camps in Albania. But because they had the resources to pay for their own food and accommodation, the refugees preferred to stay with private families, despite the fact that this was not a sustainable solution to their problems.[59]

The Kosovo crisis highlighted the importance of remittance income, which covered the accommodation costs of many families. Officially recorded remittance flows in 2004 were already twice the value of all ODA – possibly three times if informal flows were included.[60] Officially recorded remittance flows to developing countries were estimated at US$240 billion in 2007.[61] Remittance flows should be seen as an important resource for a disaster-affected population, as they represent livelihood sources, some of which are not affected by the disaster.[62]

Insufficient knowledge about the affected population and their capacities is one of the major factors in poor humanitarian response and is compounded by the apparent unwillingness of many humanitarian actors to *ask beneficiaries what they need* instead of making their own assumptions.

The geographical or other extent of the disaster

The extent of a disaster is usually the great unknown. At the start of the response – when access is difficult and the geographical extent and numbers of people affected are unknown – considerable effort may be expended to ascertain these facts. This was one of the reasons why it took so long to establish the final death toll from the tsunami in Indonesia.

Another challenge is identifying the worst-affected areas, key to the prioritisation of the aid effort. This can sometimes be established quickly or may take considerable time. Once again, knowledge of both disaster type and community capacity can help to identify areas of greatest need more quickly.

Conclusion

Humanitarian funding has been falling since 2005, in the absence of any new large scale humanitarian disasters. This makes it all the more critical that what funds are available be aligned more closely to needs.

If UN Consolidated and Flash Appeals are taken as a gross indicator of humanitarian need, and support for these Appeals as an indicator of overall official support, then humanitarian needs are clearly not being met. While, on average, they attract funding of more than two-thirds of the requested amount, there is a wide variation between different Appeals. The cases of Afghanistan and Iraq suggest that official funding for humanitarian action is influenced by a wide array of forces, not only humanitarian concerns. Various studies have found a positive relationship between the level of media coverage and the official funding of a crisis, suggesting that factors other than need may be influencing funding choices, a view reinforced by the variability in funding by sector between different years relative to sector needs as identified within the Appeals.

The low quality of needs assessments and the project proposals arising from them is sometimes given as a reason for the variability of funding. In theory, Flash Appeals prepared under the cluster system should be more inclusive and of better quality than those prepared with narrower involvement of the humanitarian community. There is some weak evidence that Flash Appeals which are prepared under the cluster system are slightly better at attracting donor funding than other Appeals.

CERF is assuming a significant role in humanitarian funding, accounting for 6.5 percent of all support for UN Flash and Consolidated Appeals in 2007 and providing over half the funds for some Appeals. However, as was discussed earlier, CERF is also plagued by needs assessment problems. All of this suggests that better quality needs assessments are a prerequisite for meeting the basic humanitarian principle of proportionality.

However, needs assessment takes times, creating a conflict not only with the political requirement for donors to act quickly after a high-profile emergency, but also with the humanitarian need for agencies to act quickly to save lives. The greatest potential for saving lives is at the very beginning of a sudden-onset disaster. Thus, there is a basic trade-off between the need for speed of action, speed of funding, and the quality of assessments.

In the face of these persistent problems, how can the humanitarian community improve the quality of assessments, and the quality of the funding requests based on given assessments? One approach is to look at a radically different way of doing needs assessments, that is, by building on prior knowledge, rather than starting as if nothing were known.

The four dimensions of any humanitarian emergency include the nature of the disaster, its extent, capacities of the affected population, and the likely response to it. Experience of previous disasters can tell us what problems the disaster is likely to cause. The nature and capacities of the affected population can be known beforehand. Knowledge of previous disasters and of the nature and capacities of the affected population give us a good indication of the likely response to the disaster. This means that of all of the dimensions only the extent of the disaster cannot be known beforehand.

By addressing post-disaster assessment needs *before* a disaster occurs, agencies can overcome the conflict between the need to act quickly and the need for high quality assessments. Only when we have high quality assessments that establish real needs can we advocate for funding that is proportionate to those needs.

Notes

1. Steering Committee for Humanitarian Response (SCHR) and International Federation of Red Cross and Red Crescent Societies (IFRC), 1994.

2. Readers interested in this topic are advised to consult the Development Initiatives reports on funding, which are more comprehensive than the discussion here. However, the latest report (Development Initiatives, 2008) does not include the OECD funding figures for 2007.

3. Even though no money changes hands, debt relief is counted in the aid totals, as it has a cost for taxpayers in donor countries in the form of foregone debt repayments.

4. Darcy and Hofmann, 2003, pp. 48–52.

5. Readers interested in learning more about changing aid volumes, and particularly aid flows from other than official sources, should consult the Global Humanitarian Assistance reports from Development Initiatives (2008).

6. Vaux (2006, p. 78) noted that *"UN Appeals are often used by donors as the basis for aid allocations but bear little relationship to need."*

7. OCHA FTS, 2008a, 2008d.

8. OECD/DAC, 2008a.

9. CERF Secretariat, 2008e, p. 1.

10. OCHA FTS, 2008c.

11. CERF Secretariat, 2007, 2008b.

12. CERF Secretariat, 2008c.

13. CERF Secretariat, 2008b, 2008c. This number may increase further before the end of the year. Seven additional countries made pledges between 7 April and 17 July 2007.

14. The UK, the Netherlands, Sweden, Norway, and Canada were the top five funders of the CERF. Ireland and Spain have consistently been the sixth and seventh largest donors.

15. CERF Secretariat, 2008a.

16. OCHA FTS, 2008b.

17. OCHA FTS, 2008c.

18. The CERF provided US$12.2 million for rapid response projects in Mozambique in 2007 (CERF Secretariat, 2008d) equivalent to the 46 percent of funding for the Mozambique Floods Appeal out of US$26.6 million for the Appeal (OCHA FTS, 2008d). However, one CERF-funded WFP project (emergency response to the effects of drought, floods and cyclone in southern and central Mozambique) was not regarded as part of the Floods Appeal funding (CERF Secretariat, 2008d and OCHA FTS, 2008g). When this project is excluded the CERF funding for the Mozambique Floods Appeal drops to US$11.2 million, or 42 percent of the funding for the Appeal (OCHA FTS, 2008g).

19. As the difference is greater than CERF's contribution – as a percentage of both Flash and Consolidated Appeals – it may be that some of this difference is due to other factors.

20. Young et al., 2007, p. 16.

21. Cosgrave et al., 2007, p. 38.

22. Faure and Glaser, 2007, p. 48.

23. Oxfam International, 2007, p. 2.

24. Goss Gilroy Inc., 2007, p. 34.

25. ICVA, 2007, p. 1.

26   CARMA, 2006.

27   Belknap, 2001.

28   Olsen et al., 2003.

29   CARMA, 2006.

30   OCHA FTS, 2008e, 2008f.

31   OCHA, 2007. Originally the humanitarian reform had only three pillars (see Loupforest, 2006). The fourth pillar, building partnerships, was added later, presumably in response to NGO criticisms of the UN focus of the humanitarian reforms process.

32   However, the International Council of Voluntary Agencies (ICVA) notes that the UN appears to have moved away from appointing trained Humanitarian Coordinators, and reverted to appointing largely untrained Resident Coordinators as Humanitarian Coordinators. This practice undermines the objectives sought in the second pillar of humanitarian reform. The Resident Coordinator's priorities are broader than the humanitarian agenda. This continuing role of the joint Resident Coordination/Resident Coordinator may explain why some eight out of ten project submissions to the CERF are more likely to be rejected by the CERF Secretariat than by the Resident Coordinator/Humanitarian Coordinator (see Faure and Glaser, 2007, p. 47).

33   OCHA, 2008.

34   OCHA FTS, 2008d.

35   Oxfam, 2007, p. 9.

36   Faure and Glaser, 2007, p. 31.

37   Ibid, p. 33.

38   Darcy and Hofmann, 2003, p. 6.

39   de Ville de Goyet and Morinière, 2006, p. 11.

40   Navy Warfare Development Command, 2005, p. 5 of Ch.3.

41   OCHA, 2005, pp. 6 and 11.

42   As highlighted by the IDP synthesis study in Borton et al., 2005, p. 138.

43   Vaux, op. cit., p. 77.

44   ALNAP, 2004, p. 18.

45   The papers from ALNAP and ProVention on lessons learned from previous disasters provide information on the needs likely to arise in disaster types, such as floods (Alam, 2008), earthquakes (Cosgrave, 2008), or slow-onset food crises (Hedlund, 2008).

46   A recent study of 344 earthquakes found that public sector corruption is positively related to earthquake deaths (Escaleras et al., 2007).

47   Alexander, 1985.

48   Telford et al., 2006, p. 36.

49   WHO, 2005a.

50   WHO, 2004.

51   PBS OnlineNewsHour, 2004.

52   WHO, 2005b, p. 5.

53   Toole, 1997, p. 79.

54   Floret et al., 2006, p. 543.

55   Cosgrave and Nam, 2007, p. 20.

56   Bhattacharjee et al., 2005, p. 41.

57   Telford et al., 2006, p. 21.

58   Manfield, 2007, p. 4; Wilson et al., 2007, pp. 5–7.

59   Suhrke et al., 2000, p. 81

60   World Bank, 2006, pp. 85 and 88.

61   Ratha et al., 2007, p. 1.

62   However, this was not the case in Pakistan, where family members who had been sending money returned home to assist their families.

References

Alam, K. 2008. *Flood disasters: Learning from previous relief and recovery operations.* London: Active Learning Network for Accountability and Performance in Humanitarian Action (ALNAP). At: http://www.alnap.org/publications/pdfs/ALNAP-ProVention_flood_lessons.pdf

Alexander, D. 1985. "Death and injury in earthquakes." *Disasters* 9(1):57–60.

Active Learning Network on Accountability and Performance in Humanitarian Action (ALNAP). 2004. Review of Humanitarian Action in 2003: Field Level Learning. London.. At: http://www.odi.org.uk/ALNAP/publications/rha.htm

Belknap, Margaret H. 2001. "The CNN Effect: Strategic Enabler or Operational Risk?" Pennsylvania: US Army War College. At: http://www.iwar.org.uk/psyops/resources/cnn-effect/Belknap_M_H_01.pdf

Bhattacharjee, Abhijit Vivek Rawal, Charlie Fautin, Judy-Leigh Moore, Sylvester Kalonge, and Vivien Margaret Walden. 2005. "Multi-Agency Evaluation of Tsunami Response: India and Sri Lanka." 20 July. CARE International, Oxfam GB, and World Vision International. At: http://www.careinternational.org.uk/2989/emergencies/multiagency-evaluation-of-tsunami-response-india-and-sri-lanka.html

Borton, John, Margie Buchanan-Smith, and Ralf Otto. 2005. Support to Internally Displaced Persons: Learning from Evaluations. Synthesis Report of a Joint Evaluation Programme. Stockholm: Swedish International Development Agency. At: http://www.sida.se/sida/jsp/sida.jsp?d=118&a=3435&language=en_US

CARMA. 2006. *CARMA Report on Western Media Coverage of Humanitarian Disasters. January.* At: http://www.carma.com/research/CARMA%20Media%20Analysis%20-%20Western%20Media%20Coverage%20of%20Humanitarian%20Disasters.pdf

CERF Secretariat. 2007 (31 December). *CERF Pledges and Contributions: Donors 2007.* At: http://ochaonline.un.org/cerf/Donors/Donors2007/tabid/1817/Default.aspx

———. 2008a (20 July). "CERF funds by window since its launch on 9 March 2006." At: http://ochaonline.un.org/Default.aspx?tabid=1805

———. 2008b (4 February). *CERF Pledges and Contributions: Donors 2006.* At: http://ochaonline.un.org/cerf/CERF2006/Donors2006/tabid/1818/Default.aspx

———. 2008c (17 July). *CERF Pledges and Contributions: Donors 2008.* At: http://ochaonline.un.org/cerfhtml/PC_2008_170708.pdf

———. 2008d (20 July). *Countries receiving CERF funds 2007: Project Detail Mozambique.* Dynamic link at: http://ochaonline.un.org/Default.aspx?tabid=1801

———. 2008e. *CERF Factsheet.* 21 January. At: http://ochaonline.un.org/OchaLinkClick.aspx?link=ocha&docId=1085496

Cosgrave, John, Célia Gonçalves, Daryl Martyris, Riccardo Polastro, and Muchimba Sikumba-Dils. 2007. "Inter-agency real-time evaluation of the response to the February 2007 floods and cyclone in Mozambique." May. Geneva: Inter-Agency Standing Committee. http://ochaonline.un.org/ToolsServices/EvaluationandStudies/ESSReports/tabid/1325/Default.aspx

Cosgrave, John and Sara Nam. 2007. *Evaluation of DG ECHO's Actions in Response to the Pakistan Earthquake of 2005.* Brussels: ECHO.

Cosgrave, John. 2008. "Responding to earthquakes 2008: Learning from earthquake relief and recovery operations." London and Geneva: ALNAP and ProVention. At: http://www.alnap.org/publications/pdfs/ALNAPLessonsEarthquakes.pdf

Darcy, James and Charles-Antoine. Hofmann. 2003. "According to need? Needs assessment and decision-making in the humanitarian sector." September. Humanitarian Policy Group Report No. 15. London: Overseas Development Institute. At: http://www.odi.org.uk/HPG/papers/hpgreport15.pdf

Development Initiatives. 2008. *Global Humanitarian Assistance 2007/2008.* London: Development Initiatives. At: http://www.globalhumanitarianassistance.org/pdfdownloads/GHA%202007.pdf

Escaleras, Monica, Nejat Anbarci, and Charles A. Register. 2007. "Public sector corruption and major earthquakes: A potentially deadly interaction." *Public Choice* 132(1):209–30.

Faure, Sheila Dohoo. and Max Glaser. 2007. *Central Emergency Response Fund: Interim Review. Final Report.* 19 September. New York: OCHA. At: http://ochaonline.un.org/OchaLinkClick.aspx?link=ocha&docId=1073098

Floret, Nathalie., Jean-François Viel, Frédéric Mauny, Bruno Hoen, and Renaud Piarroux. 2006. "Negligible Risk for Epidemics after Geophysical Disasters." Electronic Version. *Emerging Infectious Diseases* 14: 543–548. At: http://www.cdc.gov/ncidod/eid/vol12no04/pdfs/05-1569.pdf

Good Humanitarian Donorship. 2003. *Principles and Good Practice of Humanitarian Donorship.* At: http://www.reliefweb.int/ghd/a%2023%20Principles%20EN-GHD19.10.04%20RED.doc

Goss Gilroy Inc. 2007. *Central Emergency Response Fund: Review of First Year of Operations: Final Report.* 14 June. Ottawa: Canadian International Development Agency. Humanitarian Assistance and Peace and Security Division. At: http://ochaonline.un.org/OchaLinkClick.aspx?link=ocha&docId=1040006

Hedlund, Kerren. 2008. "Slow-onset disasters: Drought and food and livelihoods insecurity: Learning from previous relief and recovery responses." London and Geneva: ALNAP and ProVention. At: http://www.alnap.org/publications/pdfs/ALNAP-ProVention_lessons_on_slow-onset_disasters.pdf

International Council of Voluntary Agencies (ICVA). 2007. "ICVA Executive Committee Statement with regards to the Humanitarian Reform Process on the occasion of the 136th ICVA Executive Committee Meeting Geneva, 25–26 October 2007." Geneva: ICVA. At: www.icva.ch/doc00002607.doc

Loupforest, Christelle. 2006. "The Three Pillars of Humanitarian Reform." The UN-Business Focal Point. July. At: http://www.enewsbuilder.net/focalpoint/e_article000614343.cfm?x=b11,0,w

Manfield, Peter. 2007. "Early Recovery from Java Earthquake 2006/7." August. Jakarta: UN Humanitarian Coordinator/Resident Coordinator's Office.

Navy Warfare Development Command. 2005. "Humanitarian Assistance/Disaster Relief (HA/DR) Operations Planning: TACMEMO 3-07.6-05." August. Newport: Office of the Chief of Naval Operations. At: http://www.au.af.mil/au/awc/awcgate/navy/tm_3-07-6-05_navy_ha&dr_ops_plng.pdf

Office for the Coordination of Humanitarian Affairs (OCHA). 2005. *UNDAC Mission Report: Indian Ocean Tsunami: Thailand 28 December 2004 to 12 January 2005.* Bangkok. At: http://www.un.or.th/pdf/assessments/UNDAC-Mission_Report_Thailand-21_01_2005.pdf

———. 2007. *The Four Pillars of Humanitarian Reform.* New York: September. At: http://www.terzomondo.org/library/essentials/The_humanitarian_reform-Four_Pillars.pdf

———. 2008. *Cluster Approach Roll-out.* At: http://www.humanitarianreform.org/humanitarianreform/Default.aspx?tabid=310

——— FTS. 2008a. *Appeals and Funding: Trends Analysis.* At: http://ocha.unog.ch/fts2/index.asp?action=1&var=appeal_title&dir=asc

——— FTS. 2008b. *Consolidated and Flash Appeals 2006. Summary of Pledges and Contributions by Donor.* 12 April. At: http://ocha.unog.ch/fts/reports/daily/ocha_6_2006.XLS

——— FTS. 2008c. *Consolidated and Flash Appeals 2007: Summary of Pledges and Contributions by Donor.* At: http://ocha.unog.ch/fts/reports/daily/ocha_6_2007.XLS

——— FTS. 2008d. *Consolidated and Flash Appeals 2007: Summary of Requirements and Pledges/Contributions by affected country/region.* At: http://ocha.unog.ch/fts/reports/daily/ocha_21_2007.XLS

——— FTS. 2008e. *Consolidated and Flash Appeals 2006: Global requirements and funding per sector.* At: http://ocha.unog.ch/fts/reports/daily/ocha_R30_Y2006.XLS

——— FTS. 2008f. *Consolidated and Flash Appeals 2007: Global requirements and funding per sector.* At: http://ocha.unog.ch/fts/reports/daily/ocha_R30_Y2007.XLS

——— FTS. 2008g. *Flash Appeal: Mozambique Floods and Cyclone Flash Appeal 2007: Table G: Total Funding per Donor (to projects listed in the Appeal) (carry over not included): Report as of 20 July 2008: (Appeal launched on 12 March 2007).* At: http://ocha.unog.ch/fts/reports/PDF/OCHA_R5_A760.PDF

——— FTS. 2008h. *Flash Appeal: Mozambique Floods and Cyclone Flash Appeal 2007: Table F: List of commitments/contributions and pledges to projects listed in the Appeal as of 20 July 2008.* Geneva: OCHA Financial Tracking System. At: http://ocha.unog.ch/fts/reports/PDF/OCHA_R2_A760.PDF

Olsen, Gorm Rye, Nils Carstensen, and Kristian Høyen. 2003. "Humanitarian crises: Testing the 'CNN effect.'" *Forced Migration Review* 1(16):39–41. At: http://ics.leeds.ac.uk/papers/pmt/exhibits/819/olson.pdf

Organisation for Economic Co-operation and Development-Development Assistance Committee. (OECD/DAC). 2008a. *DAC Table 1: ODA by Donor: OECD.Stat Extracts online database.* At: http://stats.oecd.org/wbos/default.aspx

———. 2008b. DAC Table 2a: *ODA by Recipients by Country: OECD. Stat Extracts online database.* At: http://stats.oecd.org/wbos/default.aspx

Oxfam International. 2007. *The UN Central Emergency Response Fund one year on.* Oxford. 9 March At: http://www.oxfam.de/download/cerf_one_year_on.pdf

PBS Online News Hour. 2004. "Health Risks: Interview with Dr. David Nabarro." 29 December. At: http://www.pbs.org/newshour/bb/asia/july-dec04/health_12-29.html

Ratha, Dilip, Sanket Mohapatra, K. M. Vijayalakshmi, and Zhimei Xu. 2007. "Remittance Trends 2007." 29 November. Washington: World Bank, Development Prospects Group, Migration and Remittances Team. At: http://siteresources.worldbank.org/EXTDECPROSPECTS/Resources/476882-1157133580628/BriefingNote3.pdf

Steering Committee for Humanitarian Response (SCHR) and International
    Federation of Red Cross and Red Crescent Societies (IFRC). 1994.
    *Code of Conduct for the International Red Cross and Red Crescent
    Movement and Non-Governmental Organizations (NGOs) in Disaster
    Relief.* Geneva. Disaster Policy Department, International Federation
    of Red Cross and Red Crescent Societies. At: http://www.icrc.org/
    Web/eng/siteeng0.nsf/html/p1067

Suhrke, Astri, Michael Barutciski, Peta Sandison and Rick Garlock. 2000.
    "The Kosovo refugee crisis: An independent evaluation of UNHCR's
    emergency preparedness and response." Refugee Survey Quarterly.
    19. pp. 203-221. Geneva: UNHCR.

Telford, John, John Cosgrave, and Rachel Houghton. 2006. *Joint
    Evaluation of the international response to the Indian Ocean tsuna-
    mi: Synthesis Report.* July. London: Tsunami Evaluation Coalition.
    At: http://www.tsunami-evaluation.org/NR/rdonlyres/2E8A3262-
    0320-4656-BC81-EE0B46B54CAA/0/SynthRep.pdf

Toole, M. 1997. "Communicable Diseases and Disease Control." In Eric.
    K. Noji, ed. *The public health consequences of disasters.* New York:
    Oxford University Press. pp. 79–100.

Vaux, Tony. 2006. "Proportion and distortion in humanitarian assistance."
    In J. Mitchell, ed. *ALNAP* Review of Humanitarian Action: Evaluation
    utilisation. London: ALNAP. pp. 35–88. At: http://www.odi.org.uk/
    ALNAP/publications/RHA2005/rha05_Ch2.pdf

de Ville de Goyet, Dr. Claude and Lezlie C. Morinière. 2006. *The role of
    needs assessment in the tsunami response.* London: Tsunami
    Evaluation Coalition. At: http://www.tsunami-evaluation.org/NR/
    rdonlyres/8A8A61A4-4533-4CCA-A3E9-F2EE094AB9F7/
    0/needs_assessment_final_report.pdf

World Health Organization. 2004. "Highlight of press conference on South
    Asia disaster." 28 December. Geneva.

———. 2005a. *Inter-Agency Rapid Health Assessment: End of Mission
    Report, from the Offshore Platform–USS Abraham Lincoln.* 13-19
    January. At: http://www.who.int/hac/crises/international/
    asia_tsunami/final_report/en/print.html

———. 2005b. *WHO's Response to the Tsunami: A Summary.* Geneva.
    At: http://www.searo.who.int/LinkFiles/Reports_Tsunami_and_
    after-summary.pdf

Wilson, Pauline, Donal Reilly, Ryan. Russell, Malaika. Wright, Astri. Arini,
    Desideria Cempaka, Eri Diastami, Listya Narulita, Maria Angela
    Anindita, YB Johan Dwi Bowo Santosa, Yos Handani, and Yustina
    Tri Wahyuningsih. 2007. *Joint Evaluation of Their Responses to
    the Yogyakarta Earthquake.* Jakarta: CARE, Catholic Relief
    Services, Save the Children and World Vision Indonesia. At:
    http://www.ecbproject.org/publications/ECB2/Yogyakarta%20Earth
    quake%20Multi-Agency%20Evaluation%20Indonesia%20-%20Full
    %20report.pdf

World Bank. 2006. *Global economic prospects 2006: Economic
    Implications of Remittances and Migration 2006.* Washington, DC.
    At: http://www-wds.worldbank.org/external/default/WDSContent
    Server/IW3P/IB/2005/11/14/000112742_20051114174928/
    additional/841401968_200510327112047.pdf

Young, Sir Nicolas, Dr. Saba Gul Khattak, Kaiser Bengali, and Lucia Elmi.
    2007. *IASC Inter-Agency Real Time Evaluation of the Pakistan Floods/
    Cyclone Yemyin: Final version.* 31 October. New York: OCHA for the
    Inter-Agency Standing Committee. At: http://ochaonline.un.org/
    ToolsServices/EvaluationandStudies/ESSReports/tabid/1325/
    Default.aspx

CHAPTER 5

New Approaches to Needs Assessment:
Comprehensive and Rolling Diagnosis

FRANÇOIS GRÜNEWALD, President, Groupe URD[1]

For every complex problem, there is a simple solution;
but it is often a bad one.

– Montesquieu

Theory is when we understand a phenomenon, even if nothing works.
Practice is when things work, and we don't necessarily understand why.
Theory and practice is when nothing works, and we do not understand why.

– Fernando Marcellino, Former Dean,
Huambo Agricultural University,
assassinated by Sawimbi troups

Introduction

In a world of scarcity, resource management always entails difficult choices, according to priorities established in accordance with particular criteria. The allocation of funds for humanitarian action is no exception to this dilemma. In many instances, the tough laws of media and political pressure frequently govern fund allocations. The result is a world divided into well financed "media sexy" humanitarian operations and forgotten crises, sectors attracting rich resources (most often food aid), and those crises pushed to the side (for example, support for survival strategies). It is only recently that donors have paid more deliberate attention to other parameters, especially to prioritising when confronted with a large number of crises at once. Fund allocation between crises – or within a given crisis between sectors and agencies – remains a perilous exercise. The magic "needs-based prioritisation," which would ease such difficult decisions, is something akin to the pursuit of the Holy Grail in the donor community.

One of the first such initiatives, known as the Department for International Development (DFID) Benchmarking Initiative,[2] did not succeed. However, it is considered a pioneering effort among those of several other agencies, such as the UN Office for the Coordination of Humanitarian Assistance (OCHA),[3] the United States Agency for International Development (USAID),[4] and the Overseas Development Institute

(ODI)[5] which have made this a high priority of the aid agenda. It is in this context that the founders of the 2003 Good Humanitarian Donorship Initiative (GHD) developed Principle 6: *"Allocate humanitarian funding in proportion to needs and on the basis of needs assessment."*[6]

Yet, most recent research observations continue to indicate that operationalising Principle 6 remains very difficult. Too often, there are very weak links between needs identification and project design, and great difficulty in effectively making funding allocations "according to needs," as decisions are still made under pressure from politicians or domestic public opinion, without the capacity for aid delivery in the field, and with limited access to the affected populations due to high insecurity.

But these critical choices also have to be made at the crisis level: Which needs take priority? Food? Water? Health? Shelter? The level of resources mobilised will depend very much on what is considered the priority. Choices are also dependant on other factors, such as domestic policies regarding in-kind or cash contributions, which areas are more easily funded, and which agencies are to be supported – for example, a UN agency through the Consolidated Appeals Process (CAP), or a domestic NGO with a powerful home constituency.

What is wrong with this situation? Are there some unavoidable constraints which cannot be easily overcome, and if so, why? Why are the good will and strong commitment of donors so difficult to put into practice?

The present paper will try to elaborate three aspects of this question: the first section will discuss, on the basis of a few examples, some of the key lessons learned in the field about the difficulty achieving the proper vision of humanitarian action and how we make the choice to respond to certain needs as opposed to others. We will discuss the continuing prominence of the media and public pressure and the fact that donors are, in the final analysis, extensions of political entities, with political "masters." Next, we will identify and explore in greater detail some of the technical and methodological issues, including weaknesses in diagnosis. Three major obstacles to good diagnosis will be discussed: a) lack of comprehensiveness; b) lack of connection to funding requests; and c) diagnoses that are out of date because of changes in the crisis situation and related humanitarian needs.

We conclude by making proposals and asking questions about how we can do better collectively as a complex system comprising different entities with varied mandates, comparative advantages, and strategies. Many of these issues were raised at a joint conference in 1999, organised by Groupe URD and the French NGO Coordination SUD, called "Forgotten crises, protracted crises, humanitarian challenges, European stakes." Have we made progress since then?

Lessons from recent experience

The December 2004 tsunami triggered a massive and extremely generous response from all over the world – what some journalists called "wave two" or the "aid wave."[7] On the basis of images, rather than on field assessments, agencies and resources came from all over the world to assist the affected populations. Then "wave three" flooded the region: evaluators and journalists looking either for the lessons to be learned, or worse, for the juicy stories of wrong doing, or of aid mismanagement. Not only were issues of relevance, effectiveness, efficiency, and impact already high on the agenda by March 2005, but also questions about coordination, the role of national and local institutions, and the transition from relief to development. Despite the specificity of the crisis, a sense of *déjà vu* soon developed, as the strengths and weaknesses of the relief community became apparent, raising a methodological question: even when financial resources are unlimited, what are the factors limiting the quality of the five key phases of the project management cycle (PMC): diagnosis, design, implementation, monitoring, and evaluation?

The situation in Chad illustrates another related issue: the limited capacity of the aid industry to think out of the box. Over the past few years, the aid sector has demonstrated the capacity to develop highly sophisticated ready-made emergency response techniques, yet shown relatively poor ability to adjust these on-the-shelf approaches to different and often changing environments. With few exceptions, the humanitarian sector seems to use the same blueprint, regardless of the context. Moreover, despite frequent claims that participation is paramount and that the voices of the affected popula-

tions must be listened to, a top-down, technical-expert approach is still more the rule than the exception and preconceived notions take precedence over locally conceived solutions.

It is interesting to note that evaluations quickly identified some of the critical bottlenecks causing these difficulties:

- low quality of initial diagnosis

- poor correspondence between the technical appraisal and socio-cultural and political realities

- inability of the humanitarian industry to adjust to changing situations and needs

When a crisis reaches their radar screens, many agencies rush to the field to carry out a "needs assessment" and immediately write a project proposal, to be presented as rapidly as possible to the donors, since competition for the funds is often fierce. Agencies are also prone to image-making and attracting media attention. Comprehensive descriptions of complex realities do not sell newspapers, much less raise funds. Thus, aid actors tend to focus on visible symptoms rather that on the more subtle issues, resulting in less insightful and lower quality analyses. Complexity is not media-friendly, and not easily understood by the decision-makers who have to hastily allocate large amounts of money in order to satisfy their political masters.

In short, four key elements seem to be ignored:

a) From needs assessment to comprehensive diagnosis. A needs assessment by itself is not sufficient for designing an appropriate response. A comprehensive diagnosis implies also good situation analysis, proper capacity appraisal – a point identified by the Tsunami Evaluation Coalition (TEC) – and a fine-tuned constraints assessment. Many flaws in the response could be avoided if the sector called it "diagnosis" rather than "needs assessment." Of course, the diversity of the crisis type (speed of onset, magnitude, urgency of the required intervention) implies that the methodology has to be adjusted. Rapid-onset disasters require a different approach from protracted crises.

Weak diagnoses make for inappropriate responses, as in the following:

- Many agencies launch programmes on the basis of insufficient information about the specific nature and scale of needs and their context;

- Activities undertaken by local institutions are often underestimated;

- Existing survival strategies of local actors are either ignored or not considered, either as a means to reduce acute needs, or to meet needs in dangerous operational contexts;

- Rapidly changing estimates of disaster impact and of the number of casualties create difficulties when there is a call for rapid scaling up, or an acute need to target and prioritise the response.

b) Linking needs assessment with programme design. A weak link between assessment and design betrays a problem with the process itself. In a normal decision-making process, there are four phases:

1. Diagnosis (problem identification)

2. Identification of possible options (option identification)

3. Risk assessment

4. Choice of one or another operational analysis (SWOT8, cost/benefit, do–no–harm, risk assessment, etc.).

In the humanitarian sector, there is most often no diagnosis at all. Evaluators encounter many difficulties when confronted with the need to assess the relevance of a programme or project, as relevance defines the adaptation of an intervention and a set of characters, including needs, constraints, risks, etc. There is rarely a presentation of different options, consequently, even more rarely a presentation of the rationale behind the choices made. It is unfortunate – although not surprising – that, in view of the limited range of options from exploratory missions and the ensuing decision-making process, a simple solution is often chosen, one that is usually perceived to be more acceptable to donors, and thus more likely to be financed. Compliance with standards often becomes more important than responding to the complex combination of needs and survival strategies, or the diverse expressions of the capacities and constraints.

Risk assessment is also poor in many cases, rarely incorporating multi-scenario planning. One scenario

may be chosen, but not made explicit, and the rest is put in the last column, called "hypotheses and critical assumptions" of the logical framework.

Lip-service only is paid to the oft-cited do–no–harm principle, and very seldom is there a possible-harm analysis in the diagnosis – and if there, only vaguely incorporated into programme design. Even if there is a proper diagnosis, the final product is often designed in such a way as to meet donor requirements and expectations.

c) Involvement of affected populations and local institutions in initial appraisal and consecutive programme design. Despite the rhetoric, participatory approaches are still rarely applied in the field and when they are, it is often only instrumental. Projects such as the Global Study on Participation,[9] the Listening Project,[10] and others have demonstrated that the aid system and its funding mechanisms provide little opportunity or incentive – despite good intentions – for strong engagement with affected populations and their civil society institutions. Principle 7 of the GHD which asks donors to "request implementing humanitarian organisations to ensure, to the greatest possible extent, adequate involvement of beneficiaries in the design, implementation, monitoring and evaluation of humanitarian response" is still infrequently practiced. At the assessment stage, it is either not applied, or used as a means for extracting information. And rarely is such information gathering transformed into practical aid. For this reason, affected populations and their local institutions have become understandably skeptical about the aid community as a whole and its desire to truly engage with them.

d) Building flexibility into the operational framework design. In crisis situations, turbulence and rapid change are the norm. The ability to adapt to these changing circumstances and needs is vital if programmes are to remain relevant. Like shooting at a moving target, it requires three simultaneous skills: first, the capacity and will to carry out "rolling diagnosis;" second, the acceptance by donors of programming flexibility; and third, some "arm twisting" in dealing with cumbersome administrative procedures. Speedy adaption to rapidly changing environments demands vision and proactivity, which should be part of every diagnostician's toolbox. The kind of multi-scenario planning used by the large corporations when confronted with a constantly changing economic and political environment makes excellent sense in the humanitarian aid sector, as it combines in-depth situation analysis, proper identification of stakeholders and their roles, and a sense of history and time perspective.

Such thinking outside the box seems to be absent in the humanitarian industry, preoccupied as it is with doing "good" rather than doing right!

How can we improve methods?

In their search for mechanisms to facilitate needs-based resource allocations between and within crises, and between sectors and agencies, donor agencies involved in the GHD formulated a set of criteria for developing frameworks for the allocation of funds (Box 1).

It is important to examine this set of criteria not only because they reflect the keen desire of the founders of the GHD to advance humanitarian thinking, but because of the challenges involved in putting them into practice.

Box 1. GHD Guiding principles for developing allocation frameworks

Objective – frameworks for allocation should rely to some extent on objectively verifiable data such as mortality rates.

Transparent – frameworks should elaborate the methodology behind the allocation in terms of assumptions, underlying data sources, and the rationale for the decisions taken.

Systematic – frameworks should be configured such that different individuals analysing the same situation should come to broadly similar allocation decisions.

Practical/workable – frameworks should involve a level of effort that is realistic to expect decision makers, and those who support them, to actually implement them.

Robust but not rigid – providing guidance but not constraining professional judgement.

Strategic – providing an integrated, high level picture of the situation that can be used to compare different crises.

Source: Good Humanitarian Donorship, 2007b.

Diagnosis in relation to the nature and dynamics of crises

The discourse on methods and diagnosis must take into consideration diverse crisis dynamics, sector specificities, and the abilities and mandates of different organisations.

Rapid-onset natural disasters (earthquakes, tsunamis, hurricanes, etc.). The initial response to such events – in the first few hours and days – follows a set format and aims at the immediate saving of lives: fire brigades, civil protection, search-and-rescue, etc. Yet, a minimum of diagnosis is both possible and extremely useful. There is great added value in getting context-related information, the latest satellite images, recent maps – much of it available on the Web and via satellite connexions. Needs in these situations are in a constant state of flux. After the immediate collection of the dead, mourning, and the delivery of first aid, affected populations immediately focus on reconstruction, economic survival, and preparation for their crucial next steps. These factors must be rapidly integrated into the diagnosis.

Slow-onset natural disasters (droughts, progressive floods, etc.). In these situations, diagnoses should be based less on typical humanitarian criteria and indicators, and more on information arising from development projects and early warning systems. This would allow for a more systematic approach to mitigation options and to the early support of *positive* survival strategies – as opposed to *negative* ones, which are often the last options, but which have a negative impact on the environment and on the social fabric.

Complex political emergencies. These situations usually leave time for fine-tuning the diagnosis, but insecurity remains a key constraint. The concept of "complex political emergency" emerged in the mid-1990s, when it became clear that a series of factors had to be taken into account in a holistic diagnosis. Because these crises are of long duration, having complex historical causes, and many stakeholders, they demand an open analysis of many factors, and an understanding of war economy and its "entrepreneurs," and of sustainable local survival strategies.

Methodological challenges: The dictatorship of numbers

Visibility and political motivations are often critical push factors for mobilisation and for the allocation of resources to one crisis as opposed to another. These considerations often mean that humanitarian actors make only opportunistic use of diagnosis: the easier the access to the crisis location, the more data can be collected; the more data available, the more likely it is that the crisis will be at the top of the aid agenda. This bias is well known to epidemiologists and specialists of statistical analysis. Attention is more difficult to attract where information is scarce, diagnosis incomplete, and scientific data collection difficult. However, a weak or even absent diagnosis is not a good enough reason to eliminate a crisis from consideration by the aid community. Compare Chechnya and the 2004 tsunami.

Thus, one must take extreme care when using numbers and statistics, so that the proverbial "dictatorship of numbers" does not overwhelm common sense. Medicine and public health lie at the heart of humanitarian activities and development. It is not surprising, then, that the specific approaches and methods of these disciplines tend to weigh heavily in framing the methodological ideology of the humanitarian aid industry. Such social sciences as ethnology, anthropology, political science, micro-economy, and coping mechanisms are rarely utilised, despite their high potential in shedding light on our reading of situations.

For some analysts, it is a self-fulfilling prophecy that in order to obtain resources, there have to be morbidity and mortality rates below the emergency threshold. Even if the crisis is obvious, most donors tend to wait for the high malnutrition rates to be provided by Action Contre la Faim (ACF), Save the Children Fund (SCF) or Médecins Sans Frontières (MSF). These numbers may look scientific, but sometimes hide methodological bias. Moreover, data collection quality is often below the optimum, and data may be computerised without benefit of checking to ensure that the appropriate mathematical model is being applied. For example, the calculation of ratios is often based on denominators having a known 20 to 30 percent margin of error. This is especially the case for demographic data, for we most often do not know how many people live in a given place, or died during a crisis. Extrapolation is often done without sufficient methodological caution. The reports of these organisations tend to display attractive and colourful figures which are often mere artifact, in which form takes precedence over content.

In emergencies, time is of the essence, whereas sophisticated epidemiological studies require time-consuming, painstaking work. So, we must sometimes accept that aid stakeholders (donors and agencies) have to make tough decisions on the basis of insufficient information. But perhaps it is equally important to accept that it is better to be 80 percent right *on time*

than 100 percent right *too late* – bearing in mind Chamber's principles of optimal ignorance.[11] Crisis situations rarely offer the kind of stable context in which one can indulge in carefully randomised replication of scientific protocols, access good witnesses, or carry out double-blind studies – all fundamental to evidence-based methodologies.

Concentration on indicators such as mortality and malnutrition, which can be studied scientifically but which are late indicators, prevents early intervention. Although they are increasing in use, early warning indicators – which measure only risks and trends – are rarely taken into account by humanitarian actors.

The weak link: Institutional analysis of existing stakeholders

Many evaluations have stressed that one of the many weaknesses of humanitarian intervention, especially in natural disasters, is insufficient engagement with either state or non-governmental institutions in the countries where disasters have occurred. There are many reasons for this, but one is the absence of methods to assess these national actors, their capabilities and limitations, and the advantages and risks of working with or through them.

Groupe URD has been developing tools and frameworks for analysing this aspect of humanitarian work, based on five concepts:

- Understanding the history of the institution;

- Identifying the individuals who created and nurtured it, and their motives;

- Observing and analysing their achievements;

- Analysing its governance, administration, and financial picture;

- Considering how participation can be utilised in different phases of a project.

Table 1 is a proposed framework for applying this analytical method to collaboration with local and national organisations.

Comparing crises and allocating resources: Who gets them and who does not?

It is not only warring parties and the furies of nature that wield the axe. Donors also control the way they allocate resources – a fact they are keenly aware of. Therefore, much energy is expended trying to find a model to classify crises according to severity and to allo-

Table 1. Analytical matrix for collaboration with local partner organisations

Analytical level	Criteria	Remarks
Structural indicators	Status, size of organisation, date of creation, internal organisation, and reporting chains (executive board, governance structure, etc.).	Institutions with a proven local record should be given priority; institutions with affiliations to organisations in Europe or North America should not necessarily be seen as better deliverers of aid than indigenous NGOs.
Civil society	Reality of the non-profit nature of the structure, modalities of decision-making, transparency and democracy in the management, legitimacy of the board.	
Operational capacity/ability to deliver	Experience in the domains targeted by programmes; capacity to carry out diagnosis, execute programmes correctly and in participatory manner, and capacity to utilise resources and deliver on commitments.	Behind many partnership agreements, there may be many sub-contracts, diluting responsibility and reducing effectiveness; transparency and supporting capacity are essential to success of joint endeavours.
Management	Human resource capacity and good financial management; ability to prepare project documents, reports, etc.	Requests from local civil society organisations which, though relatively weak can demonstrate strong anchorage in their society should not be penalised; rather, the collaborative effort should include a strong capacity development component.
Financial independence	Capacity to mobilise funds from different sources (donors, civil society, constituency) and generate cash flow.	
Socio-political astuteness	Intelligent socio-political analysis and its use in positioning the institution in the local political context; capacity of partner organisation to understand and apply humanitarian principles, to be conflict-sensitive, to navigate in complex and sensitive circumstances.	It is not always easy to know who's who and to identify the games of different stakeholders; involvement in the institutional landscape requires excellent negotiating skills.
Risk management	Capacity to identify risks and manage them.	The capacity to anticipate and deal with risks requires the ability to work in turbulent times and areas, sensitivity, pragmatism and a proactive approach.

cate resources according to needs in such a way that the inevitable choices can be objectivised. But does such mathematical precision actually exist?

The parameters of these hard choices are numerous. Efforts such as the DFID Benchmarking Initiative, the Integrated Food Security and Humanitarian Phase Classification (IPC),[12] the SMART project,[13] and the ECHO Vulnerability and Crisis Index[14] illustrate the search for answers that will enable decision-makers to be less dependent on the CNN effect. This has serious implications for humanitarian action and involvement. By way of illustrating the huge methodological chal-

lenges involved, if one were to use the current IPC model, it is likely that neither the war in Bosnia, nor Kosovo, nor Chechnya would have been rated crises that warranted attention.

Conclusion

The road to better humanitarian aid is strewn with many obstacles. If we use a quality assurance approach, as proposed in Quality COMPAS,[15] and identify the critical points to be managed in order to improve programmes, diagnosis takes first priority. It is the basis of programme design, resource allocation, and action. To properly undertake this task and the ensuing process of regular updating (rolling diagnosis) in rapidly changing situations, there is a need for a specific methodology and a paradigm shift.

Lack of money is only one aspect contributing to poor quality diagnosis. More resources allocated to improving the quality of diagnosis are needed and donors can facilitate this by including a clause specifying the amount to be used for diagnosis. The current effort of ECHO in pooling resources to support joint independent assessments in Chad, South Sudan, and the Sahel region are laudable. However, funding may not be the most significant constraint. The others are in our heads, our behaviour, and in our books.

One of them is the need for a changed methodology, with a stronger focus on early, rather than late, indicators. If we wait for mortality rates and anthropometric nutritional indicators to tell us when we have reached "emergency threshold," we have already lost all the options for damage control and disaster mitigation. Donor reactivity in that direction, as demonstrated during the 2005–2006 drought in the Horn of Africa, varies widely, but globally is low.

Another touches the debate on crisis comparison. Is the absence of a model the critical point on the road to an objective crisis rating and related resource allocations? In rapid-onset disasters, we will not have the data on time to intervene. In protracted, complex emergencies, data are only available from the accessible zones, and even then weakly credible, due to methodological flaws. Are common sense and experience still useful values in the face of evidence-based ideology in areas where evidence is often window-dressing and institutional PR?

Participation can make a huge difference in the quality, appropriateness, and sustainability of humanitarian action. Principle 7 was rightly enshrined in the GHD. But it should be viewed neither as a quick fix nor a cheap solution. It requires humility – not always the outstanding characteristic of humanitarian actors – time, and specialised human resources, all of which are rarely available. The participation route also implies that aid agencies, donors, and local authorities are ready to open Pandora's box. If agencies and donors are genuine in their wish to engage with populations, they must be ready to go beyond standardised approaches and best-practice guidelines, to adjust to turbulent and changing conditions. Principle 5 of the GHD, which calls for flex-

ibility, points us in that direction. But participatory approaches call for another kind of staffing – people more oriented to the social, than to the hard, sciences – and to other time frames, since interaction requires time. In order to comply with donors' frequent requests for multiple reports, aid workers spend more time at their computers than in the field, engaging with populations and improving diagnosis. At the very least, an orderly reporting process to meet a coordinated funding approach from donors would go a long way towards improving the quality of diagnosis and facilitating participation, in accord with GHD Principle 23.

Are they ready? Are we ready?

Notes

1 URD stands for Urgence, réhabilitation, développement.

2 DFID, 2005.

3 OCHA, 2007.

4 SMART, 2007.

5 Darcy, 2003.

6 Good Humanitarian Donorship, 2007a.

7 Werly, 2005.

8 Acronym for "Strengths, weaknesses, opportunities, and threats."

9 Groupe URD, 2002.

10 CDA Collaborative Learning Projects, 2007.

11 Chambers, 1992.

12 World Food Programme, 2007.

13 SMART, 2007.

14 ECHO, 2008.

15 Groupe URD, 2006.

References

Bradt D. 2008; Evidence-Based Decision Making Leadership Opportunities for Donors: A Report for the Evidence-based Workgroup of the Good Humanitarian Donor Initiative; Technical Support Group; OFDA/USAID.

CDA Collaborative Learning Projects. 2007. The Listening Project. At: www.cdainc.com

Chambers, R. 1992. "Rapid but relaxed and participatory rural appraisal: Towards applications in health and nutrition." Discussion paper 331. Brighton: University of Sussex. Institute of Development Studies.

Darcy, James. 2003. "According to need? Needs assessment and decision-making in the humanitarian sector. A public meeting at the ODI to launch HPG Report 15." Overseas Development Institute.

Department for International Development. 2005. DFID Benchmarking Initiative. At: http://www.icva.ch/doc00001488.html

European Commission Humanitarian Aid department. (ECHO). 2008. *Vulnerability and Crisis Index.* At: http://ec.europa.eu/echo/files/policies/strategy/gna2008.pdf

Good Humanitarian Donorship. 2007a. *23 Principles and Good Practices of Humanitarian Donorship.* At: http://www.goodhumanitariandonorship.org/

———. 2007b. "Strengthening needs-based allocation: next steps for GHD donors." At: http://www.goodhumanitariandonorship.org/Better%20needs-based%20allocation%20note%2031%20July%20revised%20final.doc

Groupe URD. 2002. "Global Study on participation by Affected Populations in Humanitarian Action." With ALNAP. At: http://www.globalstudyparticipation.org/

———. 2006. Quality COMPAS. At: http://www.compasqualite.org/en/index/index.php

Office of the Coordinator of Humanitarian Aid (OCHA). 2007. *Needs Analysis Framework: Strengthening the analysis and presentation of humanitarian needs in the CAP.* IASC CAP Sub-working group. At: http://ochaonline.un.org/cap2005/webpage.asp?Page=1567

Office for International Development (ODI). 2003. *According to need? Needs assessment and decision-making in the humanitarian sector.* HPG Report 15. Humanitarian Policy Group. September. At: http://www.odi.org.uk/HPG/papers/hpgreport15.pdf

Standardized Monitoring and Assessment of Relief and Transitions. (SMART). 2007. At: http://www.smartindicators.org/

Werly, Richard. 2005. "Tsunami. La vérité humanitaire. Alternatives internationales. At: http://alternatives-internationales.fr/l-humanitaire-en-catastrophe-s—-revue—humanitaire-_fr_art_289_28525.html

World Food Programme. 2006. Integrated Food Security and Humanitarian Phase Classification. Technical Series. At: http://www.methodfinder.com/wfpatlas/userimages/file3.pdf

CHAPTER 6

The Giving-Receiving Relationship:

Inherently Unequal?

MARY B. ANDERSON, Executive Director, Collaborative Learning Projects, CDA

Introduction

The humanitarian assistance community struggles with what we perceive to be an inherently unequal relationship between givers and receivers of help. We *intend* to treat people with dignity and respect in order to signal our equality. However, at some basic level, many humanitarian actors believe that the reality of their plenty alongside the reality of others' needs establishes such a fundamental human dichotomy that inequality is inevitable. Given this perception, humanitarian assistance workers are seeking better approaches, in order to redress what they see as the inherent inequality between giver and receiver.

Some of these approaches are conceptual, based on what kind of relationships humanitarians would like to establish with recipients of assistance. Others are practical, having to do with programming techniques and modalities. Working *with,* rather than *for,* ensuring accountability to communities as well as to donors, and "involving beneficiaries in the design, implementation, monitoring and evaluation of humanitarian response"[1] have all become common parlance among humanitarian actors as they attempt to address inequality between givers and receivers.

But one might ask: Do people within communities that receive aid also perceive an inherent and inevitable inequality? Do they, too, struggle to find ways to ameliorate or redress it? Or is it possible that the very expectation of inequality on the part of aid providers shapes and causes unequal relations which are neither inevitable nor inherent?

These are the questions that this paper will explore. We first look at how international humanitarian agencies think about the inequality dilemma and some of the steps they take to address it. Next, we turn to the voices and ideas of the people who live in recipient societies, collected through a systematic and compre-

hensive Listening Project which is described more fully below. We compare how recipients feel about inequality and its causes with the approaches of the aid providers. We conclude with a discussion of the implications of our findings for international assistance and how what we have learned could inform approaches that affirm, rather than undermine, essential human equality.

The struggle of international humanitarian actors with inherent inequality

International humanitarian actors are concerned by the unequal status they enjoy relative to the people they seek to help. They have goods that others need. They have options that others do not have. They are usually safe and well fed when others are not. They can choose whether or not to respond to a crisis, whereas those who are struck by crisis have no choice. They can choose to leave (evacuate) if conditions become too difficult. Local people cannot leave or, if they do, face the uncertainty of being displaced persons or refugees. Humanitarians who are committed to saving lives and alleviating suffering start with many advantages relative to those whose lives are at risk and who are suffering. These advantages make many humanitarians uncomfortable, even as they form the basis for the humanitarian action.

One manifestation of this discomfort is the ongoing discussion among humanitarian workers of which terminology to use when referring to the people they help. Humanitarians rejected *victims* – although the media and some NGO fundraisers still find it apt when exciting public reactions to crises – because it was seen to reinforce the divide between helper and helpless. Some humanitarians use the term *beneficiaries* to make explicit their commitment to improving the lives of the people they assist.[2] Others prefer *recipients* as a simple and modest descriptor of the people to whom they deliver services, letting the people who receive them be the judges of whether or not they benefit from these services. Recently, a number of NGOs have adopted business language, calling the people they serve *clients,* in order to affirm their right to assess what is offered in the same way that buyers of products evaluate and choose among optional market offerings.

The words chosen carry messages, intended to avoid being paternalistic or patronizing. Humanitarians want to signal respect and establish positive relationships through language, even as they – the holders of things that people in crisis need – deliver these things to needy people.

The search for proper terminology is paralleled by a search for appropriate ways to work with communities in need. *Participatory processes* and *partnerships* have become *de rigueur* in aid delivery. It is common for humanitarian NGOs to claim that they involve recipient communities in all aspects of programming. Increasingly, international agencies partner with local NGOs or hire local staff in order to show their respect for local culture, ideas, and capacities. By ceding decision-making and evaluation roles to people on the receiving side of the equation, humanitarians mean to signal and to actualize equality.

Humanitarians' choice of language and their efforts to involve local communities in all stages of programming are driven by pragmatic, as well as ideological, motives. Language choices and programming strategies are expected to both honor and reinforce the dignity of people who have suffered a calamity and to improve the effectiveness of programming by ensuring better understanding of local needs and more accurate targeting of assistance. These choices are expected to go some way toward redressing the inherent inequality in the relationships between givers and receivers.

The Listening Project

Before turning to our discussion of how people in recipient societies of humanitarian efforts see this problem, we should first describe the source of the ideas that form the basis for this discussion.

One way to get answers to the questions this paper addresses is to ask the people who live in the societies where humanitarians ply their trade. Over the past two years, the Listening Project (LP) of CDA Collaborative Learning Projects[3] has been asking such questions of a wide range of people who live in countries where vari-

ous types of international assistance has been offered. The Listening Project (LP) has engaged many international and local NGOs in visiting communities and talking with people about how they, the local observers, feel about the processes and impact of international efforts to help in their societies. What have they observed? How do they judge the cumulative effects of aid processes? How do they *feel* about this assistance?

Through open-ended conversations, listening teams have heard, recorded, and reported the analyses, ideas, insights, and judgments of a broad range of people. Included are people who have directly received assistance, others who have been a part of the chain of assistance delivery (as, for example, by working with an international or local NGO), or people who occupy positions from which to observe the processes of aid, such as, for example, a business person in a town struck by the tsunami or a government official who sees international actors in his/her area. Across 13 countries where teams have listened to date,[4] where many different types of assistance have been provided, we have heard remarkable consistency and commonality of insights and judgments.[5] Even the areas of broad disagreement found in any one country are also found in most other countries. Where people have questions, their counterparts in other countries have the same questions. Where they have certainties, these too are mirrored elsewhere.

This paper will report the broad (and preliminary[6]) findings of what people are saying about how it feels to be on the receiving side of aid. Specifically, we will look at how they see the issue of inequality between givers and receivers. We will look at what they say, both about the messages of assistance delivery, and about the programming approaches of the humanitarian actors.

How well are humanitarians doing?

How well do humanitarians signal respect for the dignity and capabilities of communities in need? How well do they ensure better targeting of delivery and fuller local ownership of outcomes? How well do they help people who need and want help? How well are they doing at overcoming inequality, at treating the people they help as equals?

What people in recipient societies say about humanitarian assistance

The explicit message of assistance...

People consistently express their deep appreciation for the broad and intended message of international humanitarian assistance. "We did not expect anyone to help us. When these people arrived, we were amazed." "They did not have to come here and they came." "You saved our lives. Without your help, we would be dead by now."[7]

People tell us that the generosity and risk-taking of humanitarian action is impressive. They recognize it, welcome it, and are grateful for it.

Interestingly, in thousands of Listening Project conversations, we have not heard anyone worry about the terminology humanitarians use to describe the – beneficiaries, recipients, or clients of assistance! People understand and accept the impulse to help people in need as a natural impulse. Perhaps because today's aid recipients feel that, if they were in a position to help others who suffered from a calamity, they would do so, they do not interpret the act of giving as an indication of inequality.

It is worth noting that in some societies where international aid actors arrive, the traditions of giving represent strikingly different relations from those assumed by Western aid providers. For example, in Buddhist societies, the giver of alms to monks is the supplicant, asking for the privilege of giving to someone who is seen as more holy. The essential difference in such circumstances from those of crisis is, of course, that monks (and other ascetics) voluntarily adopt poverty, whereas crisis survivors – yet another term chosen to signal respec – do not. Nonetheless, an assumption of superiority of giver to receiver may not always be accurate.

Listening Project conversations show that there is broad and basic human identity with acts of generosity. Many people who receive assistance see this generosity as affirming, rather than belittling.

This is the good news. There is also bad news.

The implicit messages of assistance and how it is provided

The translation of the idea of generosity into pro-grammes, however, is *not* affirming, according to many of the voices heard through the LP. The processes and structures by which assistance is delivered soon erode the affirming message of humanitarianism. The same people who express appreciation for life-saving help also describe how the programming processes leave them disappointed, discouraged, disempowered, and resentful. Most conversations have begun with expressions of appreciation, but move quickly to negative analysis. People say, "You saved our lives, but…." or "International help is good, but…" The "buts" they go on to discuss are both explicit and instructive.

According to many people living in societies on the receiving end of assistance, inequality between aid provider and aid receiver is *not* inherent. It is a product of conscious and intentional choices and approaches of providers. What begins as an affirming generosity becomes a system of externally-driven delivery of things and services to people who are, over time, weakened not only by the crisis they have experienced but also by the assistance they receive.[8] What many see as having represented a relationship of humane equality becomes a systematic reinforcement of inequality as a result of policies and practices of the humanitarian assistance actors.

Below we outline four categories of explicit, instructive critique that the Listening Project has heard again and again, in place after place where humanitarian assistance has been offered.

Pre-packaged programming/donor agendas

People resent aid packages that are pre-determined and inappropriate. They say:

"NGOs are inflexible in the types of assistance (they provide)…it is top-driven and is simply channeled down to us."[9]

"Some international NGOs come with their own agendas and are driven and influenced by the priorities set by their donors."[10]

One Listening Team summarized what they had heard. "There are common complaints that NGOs take a blanket approach and arrive with pre-planned pro-grams…"[11] Another concluded, "NGOs are often bound by rigid proposal submission deadlines set by donors and this hinders their ability to consult communities."[12]

Even people who live in very remote areas are remarkably savvy about international forces and how these play out in the aid they do, or do not, receive. Many complain about how "the donor agenda" sets the terms for decisions and outcomes that occur in their towns and villages, without regard for the real situations in those locations.

Zimbabwe provided an interesting example of this. Many people there talked about how the international community's disapproval of Zimbabwe's governance has meant that all assistance comes as emergency rather than development aid. As a result, they say, they receive no help that is focused on longer-term, systemic issues that badly need to be addressed. Further, they report that the international focus on HIV/AIDS has so proscribed the targeting of many aid efforts that they go exclusively to those affected by HIV/AIDS.

The grandparents of four orphaned grandchildren said, "We don't understand the beneficiary selection process … .Yesterday, an NGO distributed blankets but only our HIV+ granddaughter got one. What about her siblings, they are orphans too!"[13]

Another person asked, "Did donors think that only children living with HIV/AIDS would eat the donated food when others in the family are also hungry?"[14]

Similarly, in Kosovo, people describe the negative and inappropriate impact of "the donor agenda." They note how the shift in funding focus from helping Kosovar Albanians just after the NATO bombing to supporting the return of Kosovar Serbs (to achieve the international objective of a multi-ethnic society) increased inter-group animosity. They resent the imposition of others' standards on their crisis.

One person said, "…we went to talk to [an international] agency. We asked them to help poor families that were not displaced but we were told that this was not possible. We said, 'Well what do we have to do to get assistance, leave Kosovo and come back again?'"[15]

People in Kosovo also talked about their reactions to the international targeting of multi-ethnic communities, often to the neglect of mono-ethnic ones.

One person said, "To get aid, not only does your community have to have many ethnic groups, they have to have problems with each other too!"[16]

In another community, people explained that they had received a school, a health clinic, and an electrical grid in their village: "We got all this aid because the village was 'multi-ethnic.' The NGOs were fulfilling their own conditions. We heard this on TV."[17]

These comments are common. In many places people describe the negative consequences of the labeling that goes with external ideas about who should get assistance. When external donors decide that IDPs are "most needy," others who may have suffered equally have no access to help. When contributions are raised to serve "tsunami victims," people who are homeless because of fighting do not qualify for support. Hearing this from many local people, a number of whom have themselves been recipients of assistance, challenges the humanitarian system's commitment to provide aid "solely on the basis of need."[18]

What we are hearing is that beneficiary criteria established by humanitarian actors often do not match the circumstances where assistance is delivered. When what appears to be the greatest need from outside is not the appropriate circumstantial criterion, people on the recipient end of aid are disturbed not only by the inappropriateness of delivery and its inefficiencies but also by the disrespect that such determinations from outside communicate.

LP has heard no one in a recipient country worry about whether they are called a *beneficiary* or a *client*. We have heard many people express their anger at the arrogance of outsiders who predetermine need in categories that they feel are biased and inappropriate in their society, or apply programming approaches developed in quite different societies. Some used the word "insulted" to describe how they felt when NGOs brought pre-packaged assistance.

Resentment is increased when people are urged to "participate" in programme planning and design, but they soon see that choices and decisions have already been made – outside. The power they are asked to exercise and the options that are open to them are prescribed and proscribed by aid donors and headquarters miles from their realities. When pre-determined limits or approaches are driven by geo-political considerations unrelated to people's real needs and/or ideas, external dominance of internal efficacy is even stronger.

Speed

Humanitarians often say that the necessity of working rapidly to meet dire need does not allow time for interacting with and developing the participation of local communities. Many people in recipient societies also recognize that some things need to be done quickly to save lives. Some say that "the best thing" about NGOs is that they can act more quickly than governments.

However, with broad consistency, people who have suffered crises told the Listening Project that the emphasis on speed has multiple negative consequences. A focus on speed, they say, overrides attention to learning about local realities that would allow providers to do good programming. Without such knowledge, many say, outsiders make numerous mistakes that cannot be compensated for by speediness. Some note that crises are brief ("three months") and that humanitarian agencies regularly provide assistance for some time beyond this. They say:

"Calm down and visit and get to know the people. Don't run in with your own agenda."[19]

"People come from the outside and do not spend time to get to know the community and the area. They see what is on the surface and they only see problems."[20]

"In the rush to get things done, too often the intended beneficiaries and potential local partners are left out of the discussions, and thus money gets wasted."[21]

"They do not spend enough time to select the right beneficiaries and rely too much on the…leaders to choose beneficiaries."[22]

Criticisms of speed came up, primarily, in LP conversations with people who had suffered rapid and extensive emergencies. These remarks were related to humanitarian assistance, not to development assistance. This finding has surprised some humanitarians who equate efficiency with the response speed of international aid. When we hear from survivors a reasonably argued plea to slow down and take time before delivering or acting, our notions about timeliness – and about our definition of efficiency – are challenged.

We hear people resenting the disrespect for their ideas, abilities, and concerns that they see coming from hurried work. They see mistakes being made which could have been prevented with just a little more time spent in getting to know local realities. They say that, when internationals think that speed matters most, they are "arrogant" and "bossy." They see the single-minded focus on speed as a programming choice that reinforces external dominance over internal concerns and circumstances and, that also produces waste and misdirection.

Presence

Closely linked to the criticisms of speed are communities' comments about the physical absence of donors and international staff. Many people tell us that they want to see more of international aid providers, they want more direct contact. They want to talk to and with international humanitarians.

"Aid workers should live with us, see how we are living."[23]

"Writing down notes on a piece of paper can be lost, but coming here and staying with us for a week can imprint our experiences on your heart."[24]

"They arrive; they help us; they leave. And we never hear from them again. So, what did we do wrong?"[25]

"NGOs always come and ask, but only from the headman…You should get your information directly from us. Sub-district office people babysit people in the village. I understand that your staff needs to talk to district people, but they are not our parents. We can make decisions for ourselves."[26]

People have several reasons for wanting more international presence. First, they want the respect that direct contact implies and reinforces. They want to be *known* by the people who come to work with them in crisis. They often do not want more *things;* what they want are colleagues to engage with them in problem-solving. As the Bolivia Listening teams found, "What most of the people we talked with wanted far more of was continuity, meaning some level of continued contact with assistance agencies, not necessarily in the form of additional funding."[27]

Second, many feel that internationals are fairer than local political leaders who historically are enmeshed in systems of patronage. When internationals follow through on allocations of goods, the right people are more apt to get them. In many countries, people point out that local staff, who might want to be impartial, are nonetheless part of the local systems, and cannot operate outside of these norms.

Third, many people are incredulous that donors and international agencies would "give so much money" and not come back to see what happened.

"The donors just come and then leave. Wouldn't it be good to find out whether the project was working or not?"[28]

"People were frustrated that donors were so far removed from the assistance process, seemed unfamiliar with specific projects, and did not bother to come to communities to see how their money was being spent and whether or not it matched the needs of the intended beneficiaries."[29]

Finally, people want closer contact with international agencies who work with them in order to be able to hold those agencies more directly accountable for outcomes. The Zimbabwe Listening team wrote, "Communities would like to see international NGOs visit more often and establish more of a local presence. When they have problems, communities do not know who to turn to for support…For the most part, communities do not know how to initiate contact with NGOs or reach them to share ongoing concerns about a project underway."[30]

Presence matters to local people as one aspect of relationship. How can humanitarians hope to communicate equality and respect from a distance? Closeness and repeated interactions are an essential aspect of colleague-ship and exchange among equals. People in recipient societies recognize this. When we remove ourselves from local circumstances either because we are "too busy" or because the circumstances are "too dangerous," we create the inequality that we seek to overcome.

Participatory and partnering processes

The fourth category in which we hear many local people comment on the programmatic inequality they experience in humanitarian assistance is precisely the area that humanitarian actors rely on to correct the inequality of the relationship – namely, the participatory processes and partnership approaches that are now widely touted and used.

Overwhelmingly, people on the recipient end of assistance also laud participation. When they have it, they appreciate it. When they do not have it, they criticize its absence. In many LP conversations, people described effective participatory processes. What worked in one circumstances, however, did not always work in others. That is, local circumstances – which can only be known when we are sufficiently present in communities and when we take the time required to know them – determine what kind of participation is right. Common to all descriptions of "good participation," however, were the links that people made to the outcomes humanitarians seek – greater local ownership of efforts, better targeting of assistance to those who really need it and who will benefit from it, greater connection to longer-term progress. It seems abundantly clear that getting participation right is important for humanitarian, as well as development, assistance.

However, people resent being asked to participate in decision-making when they observe that their ideas and opinions carry very little weight in determining what happens. They say:

"Participatory planning is just a phrase. Money and time are limited from the donor side and an agenda has already been set long before agencies go into communities."[31]

"It seems as if NGOs need to empty their warehouses."[32]

The Listening Team in Bolivia captured the content of many of the conversations when they wrote:

"We…heard a lot about the disappointment, frustration and even humiliation that people felt when NGOs refused to treat them in [a participatory] manner and opted for a more vertical, authoritarian, top-down approach. There were comments about NGOs promising or feigning a participatory approach but in fact acting in a fashion that was quite different. This included NGOs relying too much on local leaders (sometimes a single leader) who themselves did not consult widely and openly and who dealt with others in an authoritarian manner."[33]

The Zimbabwe Team's report said "The evidence from all our conversations suggests that most recipient communities are not being significantly engaged in aid programming and decision-making."[34]

In Bosnia, the team reported that "A few people said that international agencies claim to be partners with their beneficiaries or local organizations, but then behave as the owners/bosses. One local NGO representative talked about walking out of a presentation by an international organization; she found it so arrogantly and condescendingly presented that she could not bear to stay."[35]

People want to and are ready to participate and be partners. But most say that the NGO approaches fall short of what they want. People describe meetings set up by NGOs for community participation, noting that these are often held at times that are inconvenient for many working people (because NGO staff must be back in their compounds before dark). Or meetings are dominated by people who know how to speak out, while others are excluded from real discussion. Many note that consultation with community "leaders" does not mean that anyone else in a community is involved in decisions. Some people say that NGO participatory processes are too time-consuming and partial. One Listening team noted that "Participating in select activities provides…little knowledge of the consequences and effects of…action and…little exposure to decision-making."[36]

In other places, people told of what they hoped would be positive opportunities for participation turning sour. For example, in Aceh, people described their involvement in writing project proposals on behalf of their communities to receive assistance. NGOs had invited these proposals to encourage community participation in programme design. However, what most people did not understand was that only a fraction of the proposals would actually receive funding. Therefore, from the beginning, unbeknown to the "participants," more proposals would be turned down than would be funded. A possibly valid participatory method went awry because of inadequate communication.

We discussed earlier the frustration and resentment people feel when they are encouraged to participate in planning and decisions, only to find out later that most things were decided by people outside the area. External agendas and pre-packaged assistance modalities consistently undermine claims to participation and belittle people's inputs.

Participatory processes can affirm respect and mutuality between aid provider and aid receiver. False or badly executed processes can communicate disrespect and exacerbate feelings of external dominance over internal concerns.

Implications for the future

From the four themes cited above — external agendas, too much concern with speed, lack of physical presence and failed participatory and partnership arrangements — it is clear that recipients of humanitarian assistance want more than handouts. Stressing their own insights and ideas, people want aid that involves contact, they want to interact with people whom they know to have useful skills and experience but they want to do it in ways that acknowledge their own knowledge and strengths as well. This kind of interaction would, it seems, affirm essential human equality. When it is missing, people feel belittled, used, and disrespected.

Good Humanitarian Donorship Principle 7 reads: *Request implementing humanitarian organizations to ensure, to the greatest possible extent, adequate involvement of beneficiaries in the design, implementation, monitoring and evaluation of humanitarian response.*

This is a weak principle. Why does it "request" rather than require that implementing organizations involve beneficiaries? Why does it introduce the possibility that it may not always be "possible" to involve them? How much involvement is "adequate" for affirmation of dignity and equality? How much is "adequate" for effective and efficient programming?

People on the receiving end of international humanitarian assistance see as essential their involvement from the beginning to the end of any assistance programme. They would involve themselves in appraisals and assessments, in discussions and decisions about operations and implementation, in close observation and monitoring of immediate and ongoing, expected and unexpected, impacts and, ultimately, in evaluating how well any effort has succeeded in saving lives, alleviating suffering and doing so in ways that respect and affirm the people who are helped.

All four areas of the critique offered above challenge the humanitarian assistance community. Where in the GHD Initiative do we hear the voices that are reflected here? If we want to be truly attentive to the thinking of those whom we intend to help, we will

need to rethink some of our basic premises and operational approaches.

For example, as government donors and international NGOs move increasingly toward coordination and coherence in order to assure policy and programmatic consistency, people in recipient societies tell of their resentment of international agendas as these play out in their societies. They seek variation in assistance, variation that takes into account *their* circumstances as these differ from those of other crises. They want assistance that is responsive to them and what *they* feel they need to address.

This does not mean that humanitarians must forget all that has been learned. On the contrary, people want the perspectives and experience that international actors bring. But, they want these to be balanced by a genuine respect for local realities and people's own priorities and needs. Finding the right mix for respecting local variations and continuing to apply lessons learned in previous settings is a challenge for international humanitarian assistance.

As humanitarian agencies look increasingly to business to develop systems for the most efficient delivery of emergency supplies, people are telling humanitarians to slow down and take time to know them before sending things. They are saying that rapidity too often makes delivery, even delivery of needed goods, go wrong. Speed, they say, is the wrong criterion for success.

Again, as noted, local people know that some things need to be done quickly. They appreciate the fact that international agencies have less red-tape than local bureaucracies. Finding the balance between sufficient speed to address urgent needs and sufficient time to talk with, listen to, and engage with people to ensure that assistance honors their realities is, again, a direct challenge for the way international humanitarian assistance is currently provided.

As individuals donate to agencies that report the lowest overhead relative to delivery of supplies, people receiving assistance tell us that, rather than more goods, they want more presence, which adds to overheads. As government donors and aid agencies reduce travel budgets and limit their international staff in crisis settings, people are asking for more direct contact and more personal interaction. People are telling us that absence signals distance and distance does not create a respectful relationship. At the same time, people appreciate increasing reliance by international agencies on local capacities as demonstrated by working with local partner organizations and hiring local people as staff. "It will be a challenge for humanitarian agencies to be present in many local situations in ways that build relationships and gather real information about local circumstances and, at the same time, work with local individuals and agencies to reinforce their capacities."

As agencies attempt to establish good partnerships with local agencies and participatory methods that engage local communities, we nonetheless hear from many people that these approaches, at least as they are often now implemented, are perceived as fake and insincere. In each setting where Listening teams have talked with people from small villages to governmental offices, they have heard fascinating and sensible ideas for better ways for aid agencies to determine needs, target deliveries, organize community involvement and manage their funds. People have creative and wise ideas about how things might be done in their own communities for real and lasting improvements. They do not know, and do not claim to know, everything they need to know to improve their lives. They welcome external ideas and material assistance. But they also know that the basis for genuine change that will substantially improve their lives and life prospects is not demeaning handouts but, instead, a full and engaging face-to-face relationship with others who care and who are willing to come to them, work with (not for) them, and add what they know to what is locally known to solve immediate and longer term problems.

Conclusion

We began this paper reflecting on the struggle of many dedicated humanitarians to address and overcome what they often see as an inevitable and inherent inequality between themselves and those they hope to help. From what we have heard through listening, however, it would seem that there is no inevitable and inherent inequality. Rather, it is systems and approaches that we create which perpetuate the lack of collegiality and respect that underpin equal relationships. The alternative is a real possibility. If we can find ways to listen to what we are told by people who live in the societies where we deliver humanitarian assistance, and hear what they tell us, we will have the opportunity to save lives and alleviate suffering without guilt about inequality., In fact, our ways of working will reinforce and affirm an essential equality where everyone contributes to the solutions to overwhelming problems.

Notes

1 Quoted from Principle 7 from the *Principles and Good Practice of Humanitarian Donorship* endorsed in Stockholm, 17 June 2003.

2 The dictionary definition of "benefits" is "something that has a good effect or promotes well-being." "Beneficiary": The person who is helped by some action or process. Recipient of a process that is intended to make a person's life better in some way, recipient of something that has a good effect or promotes well-being.

3 CDA Collaborative Learning Projects is a non-profit organization based on Cambridge, Massachusetts, formerly known as Collaborative for Development Actions. The Director of CDA'S Listening Project is Dayna Brown.

4 Aceh (Indonesia), Angola, Bolivia, Bosnia and Herzegovina, Cambodia, Ecuador, Ethiopia, Kenya, Kosovo, Sri Lanka, Thailand, US Gulf Coast, and Zimbabwe.

5 See www.cdainc.com for more detail on the Listening Project.

6 The Listening Project will visit a total of at least 20 countries by the end of 2009 and will, in addition, conduct a series of feedback workshops in multiple locations to invite reflection and further analysis on the findings from the listening teams' visits.

7 Examples of comments frequently heard by the Listening Project teams.

8 This finding is not new. One project in which I was deeply involved in the 1980s produced a book that traces the processes by which well-intentioned assistance undermines and weakens recipient societies. The book also traces the alternative, providing experience of how emergency assistance can in fact leave societies stronger and more resistant to subsequent crises. See Anderson and Woodrow, 1998.

9 Zimbabwe Listening Project Report, p.18.

10 Thailand Listening Project Report, p.37.

11 Zimbabwe Listening Project Report, p.20.

12 Ethiopia Listening Project Report, p.19.

13 Zimbabwe Listening Project Report, p.12.

14 Zimbabwe Listening Project Report, p.13.

15 Kosovo Listening Project Report, p.19.

16 Kosovo Listening Project Report, p.20.

17 Kosovo Listening Project Report, p.20.

18 As noted in the humanitarian principles of many agencies and endorsed in the Good Humanitarian Donorship *Principles* as well.

19 Thai Burma Border Notes, p.64.

20 Thailand Listening Project Report, p.35.

21 Conclusion drawn by a Listening team in Bosnia, Bosnia Listening Project Report, p.12.

22 Team comments in the Ethiopia Listening Project Report, p.13.

23 Ethiopia Listening Project Report, p.15.

24 Aceh Listening Project Report, p.14.

25 Bolivia Listening Project Report, p.5.

26 Thailand Listening Project Report, p.21.

27 Bolivia Listening Project Report, p.5.

28 Zimbabwe Listening Project Report, p.20.

29 Kosovo Listening Project Report, p.17.

30 Zimbabwe Listening Project Report, p.19.

31 Sri Lanka Listening Project Notes, p.23.

32 Aceh Listening Project Report, p.3.

33 Bolivia Listening Project Report, p.19.

34 Zimbabwe Listening Project Report, p.20.

35 Bosnia Listening Project Report, p.9.

36 Thailand Listening Project Report, p.5.

References

Aceh Listening Project Report. At: http://www.cdainc.com/cdawww/pdf/casestudy/lp_aceh_field_visit_report_english_Pdf.pdf

Anderson and Woodrow. 1998. *Rising from the Ashes: Development Strategies in Times of Disaster.* Boulder, CO: Lynne Rienner Publishers.

Bolivia Listening Project Report. At: http://www.cdainc.com/cdawww/pdf/casestudy/lp_bolivia_field_visit_report_english_Pdf_1.pdf

Bosnia Listening Project Report. At: http://www.cdainc.com/cdawww/pdf/casestudy/lp_bosnia_field_visit_report_english_Pdf_1.pdf

CDA Collaborative Learning Projects. The Listening Project. At: www.cdainc.com

Ethiopia Listening Project Report. At: http://www.cdainc.com/cdawww/pdf/casestudy/lp_ethiopia_field_visit_report_english_Pdf.pdf

Good Humanitarian Donorship. *Principles and Good Practice of Humanitarian Donorship.* At: http://www.reliefweb.int/ghd/a%2023%20Principles%20EN-GHD19.10.04%20RED.doc

Kosovo Listening Project Report. Forthcoming at: www.cdainc.com

Sri Lanka Listening Project Notes. Forthcoming at: www.cdainc.com

Thai Burma Border Notes. Forthcoming at: www.cdainc.com

Thailand Listening Project Report. At: http://www.cdainc.com/cdawww/pdf/casestudy/lp_thailand_field_visit_report_english_Pdf.pdf

Zimbabwe Listening Project Report. At: http://www.cdainc.com/cdawww/pdf/casestudy/lp_zimbabwe_field_visit_report_public_Pdf.pdf

CHAPTER 7

Tackling Ignorance and Neglect:
Advocacy for a Broader Humanitarian Response in the Central African Republic

TOBY LANZER, Humanitarian Coordinator, Central African Republic

In 2005, I knew nothing about the Central African Republic (CAR), except that the former Emergency Relief Coordinator, Jan Egeland, referred to the situation in the country as the "world's most forgotten crisis." Three years later, in mid-2008, it is far from forgotten, with NGOs, the International Committee of the Red Cross (ICRC) and UN agencies geared up and engaged to meet the needs of some 1 million people across the country.

How did things change for CAR and what were the factors behind the change? To what extent was the change under the control of key players? What can be learned from the experience and applied in similar cases? This chapter aims to address these questions, based on my experience as a policymaker before arriving in CAR in mid-2006, and as a practitioner there from June 2006 to June 2008. While it will address these issues by focussing more on humanitarian work than on development cooperation, the conclusions reached appear to be equally valid for the latter.[1]

Larger in area than France, with a population half the size of London, CAR is still unknown to many, but its lack of fame is no indicator of the gravity of the humanitarian needs and crippling poverty of its population. One of Africa's poorest countries, CAR, by 2003, had lived through years of *coups d'etat,* mutinies, and rebellions, all of which took a heavy toll on its people. With its health centres looted, schools abandoned or destroyed, and roads and infrastructure virtually non-existent, there were compelling humanitarian reasons for the international community to pay attention to the country's plight. Nonetheless, the country and the suffering of its people continued to pass unnoticed. In the heart of Africa lay a country of which few people had heard and in which fewer still, including aid agencies, saw reason to engage.

Before working in CAR I spent three years with the Office for the Coordination of Humanitarian Affairs (OCHA) managing the Consolidated Appeals Process, or CAP as it is more commonly known. CAP is a tool that helps aid agencies work together to analyse the political context and its humanitarian consequences, agree about the priority needs of the population, draw up a plan to meet them, and advocate for funding. In 2003, the UN in Bangui, capital of CAR, decided to prepare a Flash Appeal, followed later in the year with a CAP for 2004. The decision was spurred by the expectation at UN headquarters that their teams in the field would address needs in a coordinated manner, and that their colleagues in the field would be equally willing to cooperate. Despite these good intentions, CAR's first three joint Appeals (from 2003 to 2005) were disappointing, raising only US$16.2 million of the required US$44.6 million, or only 36.3 percent. And while the team in CAR made their best effort to shine a light on the human suffering in CAR, the very limited presence of aid agencies outside Bangui made gathering information and communicating it to the outside world difficult.

Factors behind the change

In early 2005, the UN deemed CAR one of the ten least reported stories in the world. What measures were taken, and by whom, to focus world attention on the development and humanitarian needs of CAR's 4 million people? Several steps and issues contributed to making CAR more visible, and to the increased attention and aid extended to the country.

First, France, the donor most closely engaged in CAR, took the decision in 2005 to lobby other donors to work in the country. France facilitated a meeting in Paris in July 2005, at which needs in CAR were discussed and donor countries were called on to provide support for the country's recovery and development. At the meeting, CAR was referred to as a country in a "post-conflict" condition, perhaps because the security situation had stabilised since the March 2003 *coup d'état* and elections had been conducted successfully in May 2005. France also played an active role in the UN Security Council and within the Bretton Woods institutions, calling on countries to support re-engagement in CAR. Having such a major donor as France as champion was significant and paved the way for those who were working to place CAR on the humanitarian radar.

Second, three key players within the United Nations began to focus on "forgotten" or "neglected" countries. David Nabarro, head of the World Health Organisation's Health Action in Crises, visited CAR with a BBC film crew in late 2005. The resulting video showed the terrible effects of a destroyed health-care system on the population. Around the same time, the head of UNICEF's emergency operation, Dan Toole, who had himself been a Peace Corps volunteer in CAR some twenty years earlier, decided that the UN agency for children needed to gear up its programmes in the country. UNICEF asked the chair of its Executive Committee to visit Bangui and his findings told a harrowing tale of neglect, not only by donors, but by the UN system itself. Simultaneously, the UN's chief advocate for such situations of conflict and mass suffering, Jan Egeland, became engaged, and spent much energy in 2005 and 2006 calling on aid agencies and donors to pay attention to the plight of the people of CAR.

Accessible information is needed if people are to become aware of a situation. Before arriving in CAR, I was surprised at how difficult it was to obtain information about the country in any language other than French. The absence of information about CAR in other languages struck me as a serious obstacle to non-French speakers – whether journalists, aid agencies, or donors – wishing to find out about the country. Accordingly, one of my top priorities upon arrival in Bangui was to become better informed and then work to get the word out, in English. By January 2007, a weekly newsletter was being issued, a blog and web site were up and running, an intranet was established so that humanitarian and development practitioners could exchange and classify information by region or sector, and Google Earth was used to map key issues. These Web-based tools made information instantly available to potential users inside and outside CAR.

A fourth way to gain attention for CAR was to get goodwill ambassadors or high-level officials to visit the country and speak about it. The actress Mia Farrow travelled to CAR in February 2007, became its advocate, and did much to put the country on the map, especially for the some 30,000 people who visit her blog daily. The UN Under-Secretary-General for Humanitarian Affairs, John Holmes, decided to include CAR as part of his first visit overseas after taking office in March 2007 and brought the work in CAR to the attention of the UN Security Council and UN agencies. The fact that his visit included a corps of press officers from the *BBC, The New York Times,* and other major media did much to boost the country's visibility. I then followed up by visiting various donor capitals to give briefings on CAR to consolidate these high-level contacts.

Finally, three other factors, unconnected with the actions of UN or donor governments played an important role. The lack of breaking emergencies throughout 2006 meant that journalists and others who follow the situation in poor countries were keen for news that might attract attention. With eyes that were already very much focussed on Darfur – which shares a long border with much of CAR's northeast – this hunger was satisfied in October 2006 when a new rebel group, known as the Union of Democratic Forces for Unity (UFDR),[2] burst onto the scene and occupied four towns in northeastern CAR. It is not known to what extent UFDR was linked to events in Sudan and how, if at all, the troubles in Darfur were spilling into CAR. However, these questions helped tie CAR to key events in which the majority of policymakers and practitioners in donor capitals were vitally interested. In addition, the events in the northeast came shortly after clashes between rebels and government forces in the northwest had already displaced some 200,000 people.

In sum, by the first quarter of 2007, CAR was far more visible and better known by aid practitioners, and this trend continued throughout the year and into 2008. Some of the factors which brought this about lay within the control of the aid community, and others – such as the geo-political realities of Darfur or of the UFDR militants – well beyond it. But by building on the advocacy begun by France and prominent figures, such as Jan Egeland, the team on the ground in Bangui was able to capitalize on growing interest and muster financial support for the humanitarian response which targeted 1 million people who had been directly affected by the conflict in the northwest and northeast.

To what extent did key players control the change?

Having managed to put CAR on the radar screen, the challenge for its champions was to explain events in the country, to convince donors that there was an effective plan in place to respond to people's needs, and to show that there could be a realistic and feasible response to the suffering.

Coming to grips with the situation outside Bangui was a daunting task. In mid-2006, the UN had some 400 staff members in CAR, 385 of whom were based in the capital – apparently assuming that working outside Bangui was too dangerous. Indeed, the UN had decided that almost all of the country outside Bangui was "security phase IV" and that any UN staff movements outside the capital (except to a small area southwest of Bangui) should take place under armed escort. On average, the UN conducted 12 missions per month outside Bangui, and had no presence outside the capital except in three towns. Only three organisations worked outside Bangui: an Italian non-governmental organisation (Coopi), *Médecins Sans Frontières,* and the International Committee of the Red Cross. Their work in the field showed that being there was possible. In order to understand what was happening in CAR's north, there was clearly a need for a strong group of aid agencies to be present in key areas. Therefore, I contacted the Inter-Agency Standing Committee (IASC) – the foremost mechanism for inter-agency coordination of humanitarian assistance involving key UN and non-UN humanitarian partners – and requested that they discuss CAR. This discussion took place in July 2006 and resulted in the decision to deploy an IASC team of professionals from NGO and UN agency headquarters in October 2006 to assess the situation. What emerged was the firm recommendation to IASC members – in particular the NGO consortia – to engage in CAR. The government gave clear signals that UN agencies and NGOs were welcome anywhere in the country, even in areas under rebel control.

Needless to say, the work would cost money, and the assumption was that money would be hard to come by for this "neglected crisis." It would have been easy to conclude that without money nothing could be done. CERF was a relatively new tool when I arrived in Bangui, so discussions ensued with OCHA headquarters about accessing funds, either through the rapid response or the underfunded window for UN implementing agencies. And, in order to foster close relations between UN agencies and NGOs, UN agencies were encouraged to accept CERF money and pass it on to NGOs. Thus, CERF was enormously helpful in kick-starting the operation in CAR, and provided seven organisations with US$5.7 million in 2006.

With the same objective of getting more money more quickly to help NGOs and UN agencies establish a presence in CAR, especially outside the capital, it was decided that the CAP for 2007 should include a small fund, called an Emergency Response Fund (ERF). In addition to covering start-up costs, the fund was created to finance projects addressing the consequences of breaking emergencies, such as refugee arrivals from Darfur. At the outset of 2007, the target for the ERF was a modest US$1 million, with which we hoped to assist a handful of NGOs to establish a presence in CAR. By mid-2007, however, the fund was drawing attention and money: Ireland, the Netherlands, Norway, Sweden, and the United Kingdom contributed US$5.7 million, enabling 12 NGOs to come to CAR. (As of May 2008, there were representatives of the aid community present in 20 locations *outside* Bangui.) Towards the end of 2007, donors were discussing the merits of pooled funds – already being used in the Democratic Republic of the Congo and Sudan. By February 2008, this discussion bore fruit as the donors decided – partly on the basis of their positive experiences with ERFs – that CAR and Ethiopia would be the next to have pooled funds. In other words, CAR's Emergency Response Fund paved the way for what is hoped will be still larger and broader donor engagement.

As aid agencies were deployed in the northwest and northeast of the country, our analysis of the political situation and likely scenarios became sharper. We were able to deepen our understanding of the consequences of insecurity on people's lives, and fine-tune the humanitarian response to enable more appropriate aid. For example, whereas we initially thought that internally displaced people (IDPs) would need continuous injections of food aid, we quickly learned that if they had access to land, they could manage on their own if supported with seeds and tools and supplemented by some food aid during the planting and lean seasons. Such an approach was not only more in line with real needs, but also cost effective. And donors, when informed of our approach, warmed to our efforts – and our transparency – and provided adequate support for food security projects. As awareness of and trust in our work grew, so did the number of donors who provided money to NGOs, ICRC, or UN agencies working in the field. Figure 1 shows the number of donors providing at least $500,000

Figure 1. Number of donors providing US$500,000 annually to aid agencies in CAR, 2005–2007

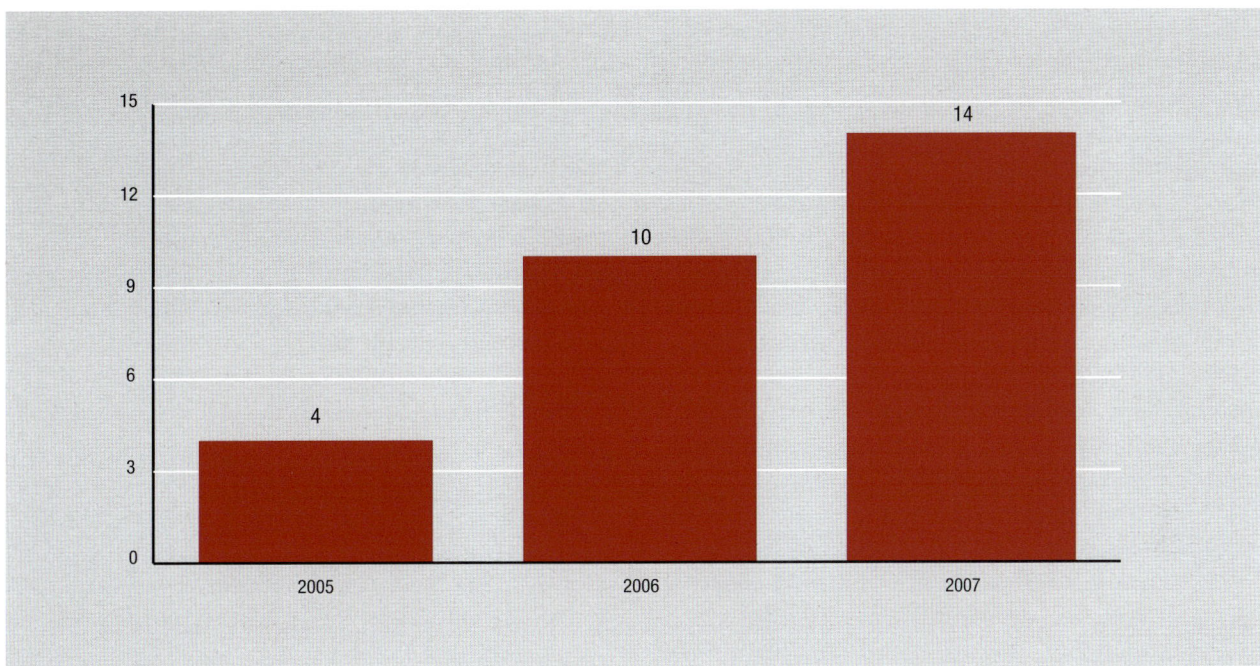

in humanitarian financing to aid agencies in CAR, annually, from 2005 to 2007.

What this table does not show is which donors came to support aid programmes in CAR. Beginning in 2006, we benefited from the reliable support of countries such as Sweden, as well as managing to attract Ireland, a donor which really had none of the so-called easy or obvious reasons for providing aid to a country like CAR. A frank assessment of the situation, transparent communications, and a "can-do" attitude, seemed to be paying off, convincing donors of the most important reason to support our aid programme, namely, that hundreds of thousands of people are in need of help.

Before 2006, aid workers may have thought that they were mired in a cycle of "no money; therefore we cannot work; therefore, no results; therefore, no money coming in." Yet, by mid-2006, this changed to: "We are working and getting results; therefore, there is more money coming in." As aid agency presence expanded and more information was shared among them, a new challenge arose: organizing, analyzing, and sharing information. Here, the UN took a series of straightforward measures: it hired a small team of information specialists to put together a blog, an Internet site known as HDPT

(Humanitarian and Development Partnership Team), and an intranet. The latter served aid agencies as a shared drive where information could be sorted by region or sector. We also used some new technologies, such as Google Earth, which allowed us to map issues and track our work in the field, virtually in real time. As we developed these tools, we worked closely with NGOs and UN agencies to get their views about which tools were needed, how they should be developed, and how they might be synchronized with the work of the key organizations in the field.

By the first quarter of 2008, aid agencies had carried out some 200 different assessments in the northwest and northeast of the country. A mass of information existed, but much of it was disconnected or difficult to process. There was no database or baseline to speak of, and the government's ability to monitor the situation – for example, via disease surveillance systems – was very weak. HDPT members agreed to use the Needs Analysis Framework (NAF) – a tool developed by the IASC in 2005 – to pool assessment data and construct an overall view of needs in CAR. The idea was that, once elaborated, the NAF could be referred to and updated periodically, say every four months, in order to allow a second stage of analysis: trends. Making statements about the situation and consequent needs of a population today is one thing; but the ability to compare today's situation with that of months or years ago and show how the situation has evolved, takes the analysis – and therefore planning and response – to a much higher level.

The much-discussed cluster system, which began in CAR in August 2007, was directly related to the need to become more organized and improve the quality of analysis, so that we could improve humanitarian action. To my surprise, the cluster system was welcomed by NGOs and UN agencies in CAR as an opportunity, at the sector level, to share information, analyze, plan, implement, and monitor together. Participation in the cluster system was widespread, although some clusters have performed better than others. Success can hinge on leadership, and two groups in particular, food security and logistics, benefited from professionals who took the system seriously and had a collaborative approach to working with NGOs. Both clusters managed to gain the respect and participation of the main organizations and foster a sense of ownership and added value. At no stage were the meetings of these two clusters mere get-togethers. Agendas were clearly mapped out, with specific objectives, points for discussion, and outputs. Meetings, never longer than one hour, were followed up with clear notes that were written up within 48 hours of each session and shared for comments. As a result, people took part, comfortable in knowing what was expected and what the meetings would achieve. We are now working to replicate these positive experiences across the cluster system, pushing UN headquarters to ensure that their teams in the field receive the support, training, and staff they need to carry out their responsibilities as cluster leads.

As mentioned earlier, the CAP is a tool for aid agencies to work together in analysing the political context and its humanitarian consequences, agree on needs, draw up a plan to address them, and lobby for funding. The first step in the process of elaborating the CAP is usually a workshop and CAR was no exception. I decided to participate personally from start to finish and communicated my hope to country representatives of NGOs, the ICRC, and UN agencies that they would do likewise. The aim was not to have all organisations at the workshop, but rather, to have the main organisations and, in particular, their decision-makers. By having agency representatives in the room to discuss issues, and agree on what was happening and how we should act as

a consequence, we were able to use time effectively and foster a sense of partnership. Of course, some organisations, such as ICRC, are careful of such efforts to bring together the aid community, but we made it clear at each step that joint analysis and coordinated planning would in no way diminish or infringe on the independence of organisations.

Setting priorities was a key issue in discussions regarding the CAP, which in CAR we called Coordinated Aid Programme – as opposed to the more common Consolidated Appeals Process. After thorough discussion, aid agencies working in CAR managed to agree on the following six criteria by which we analysed projects submitted as part of the CAP; each project was to

- take place in a region directly affected by violence

- occur in a priority sector

- require quick funding, for example, because of a planting season deadline

- help the overall aid operation

- be gender sensitive

- build local capacity

To be included in the CAP, projects had to meet at least three of these criteria and those that did not were either revised or not included. The aim of these efforts was to avoid falling into the trap of listing endless needs, without taking the tough decisions on what the priorities should be. The purpose was to produce a strategic document showing donors the pragmatic approach to humanitarian action of aid agencies working in CAR. Donors have called on NGOs and UN agencies to prioritise and at the 2008 CAP inauguration, chaired by the UN Secretary-General on 23 January, they had high praise for its ground-breaking success in prioritisation. Now six months later (June 2008), it is fair to ask to what extent donors have funded priority projects. Figure 2 shows the preliminary results in answer to this question, one which we are monitoring closely with donors, in the hope that immediate and high priorities are met before others.

In a comparison of the CAR appeals of 2003 to 2008, it is striking to note that the 2007 and 2008 programmes show a clear assessment of the political and security situation and a realistic approach to how agencies can address the humanitarian consequences. There is

Figure 2. Donor funding of priority projects

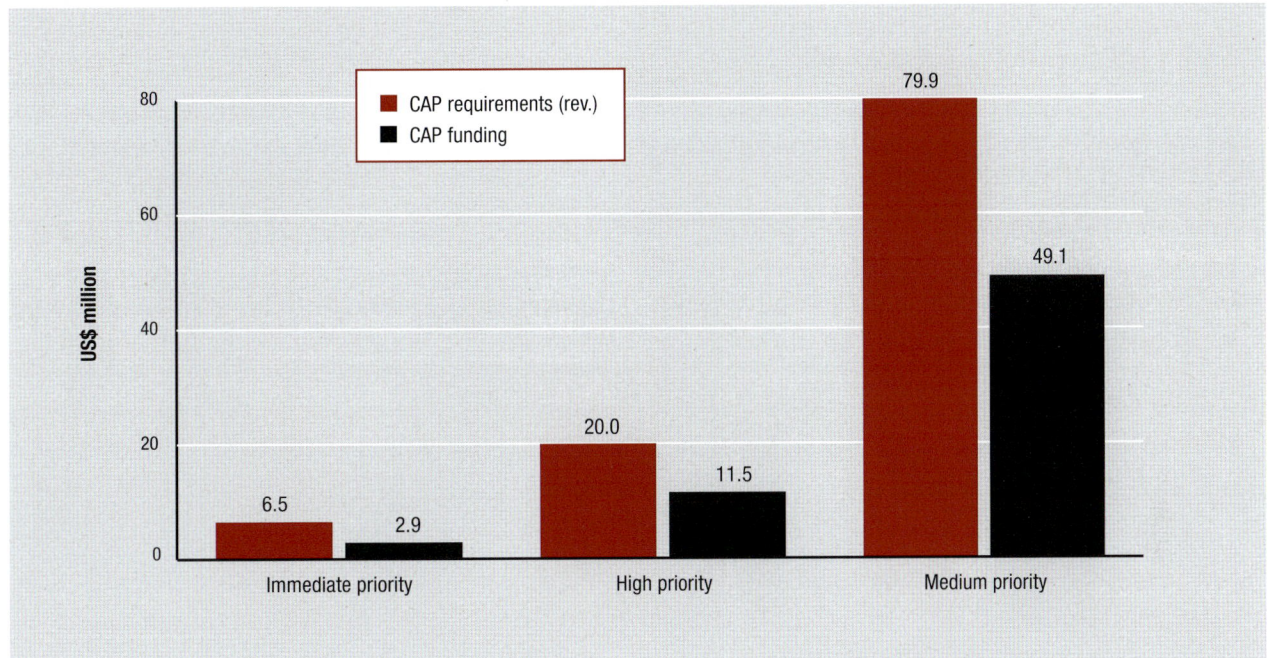

an emphasis on analysis and working together. The language employed is straightforward and clear. It was important, as well, to acknowledge mistakes, faults, and weaknesses. We were sure that, in doing so, donors would realize that we were not only being honest – donors clearly want partners they can trust – but that we were also doing our best to stay in touch with the evolving realities on the ground. Other issues which made the CAR CAPs of 2007 and 2008 more "appealing" were a series of annexes which highlighted the role of NGOs in the aid operation, provided readers important population data, and showed how the humanitarian operation was linked to overall aims for poverty reduction and development.

One weakness which NGOs and UN agencies recognized was that our monitoring and evaluation was inadequate. While by mid-2008 our ability to analyze trends had improved, we were still unable to state clearly, either at the level of clusters or overall, how the situation of the population affected by violence had changed and why. While this failing might be in the nature of social science, we can and must do better. The NAF, described earlier, is a tool we are counting on to remedy this shortcoming. By repeating the exercise regularly, we

expect to be able to see more explicitly how needs have changed and, we hope, be in a position to attribute this to humanitarian response (or other factors) and recalibrate our work accordingly.

In a context such as that of CAR, needs for humanitarian action, recovery, and development can overwhelm the practitioners on the ground. It is often stated in Bangui that "every day feels like the first day." The extent to which needs are met – in other words, discussions of proportionality of response – has yet to be addressed, perhaps because much of our focus during the past two years has been on getting things up and running, as Figure 3 illustrates. In 2006, total humanitarian funding reaching CAR almost exceeded the total of the preceding three years put together; the 2006 total of $25.8 million more than tripled in 2007.[3]

The total of humanitarian financing for 2008 is again expected to climb, showing that donor awareness of CAR and response to need here continues to grow. Their support has led to a major increase in agency presence throughout the country and puts us in a stronger position to gauge overall need and the proportion of it that we are addressing. For example, the number of UN missions outside Bangui has climbed more

Figure 3. Humanitarian funding to CAR by year, 2003 to 2007

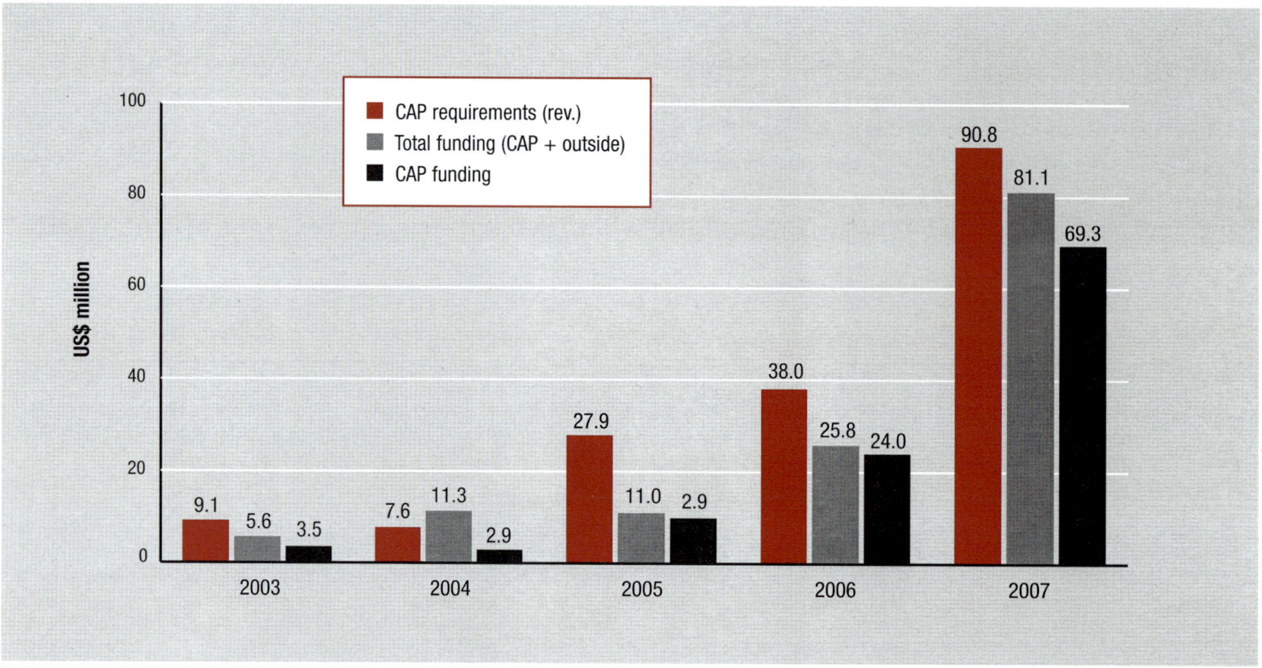

Legend:
- CAP requirements (rev.)
- Total funding (CAP + outside)
- CAP funding

Y-axis: US$ million

2003: 9.1, 5.6, 3.5
2004: 7.6, 11.3, 2.9
2005: 27.9, 11.0, 2.9
2006: 38.0, 25.8, 24.0
2007: 90.8, 81.1, 69.3

than tenfold from 12 per month to 145 per month. The UN now has eight sub-offices, up from only three outside Bangui in mid-2006. We can say with confidence now that the CAPs have been well funded since 2006. One proof of our success in gaining visibility for the country – and concomitant funding for a more robust humanitarian response – is that projects in CAR are no longer eligible for the CERF "underfunded" window.

Conclusion

A central lesson from the CAR experience is that aid programmes can exist and find support, even in a country that is unknown, that has much less strategic interest than any of its neighbours, and that has few historic or economic ties with donors. The conventional wisdom, viz. that only White House interest or the CNN factor results in increased aid flows, does not hold in the case of CAR and need not be the case in similar situations. The international system has significant amounts of money for all sorts of aid programmes and some of these funds can be made available for countries such as CAR. Of course, naysayers can question whether it is the right type of money, for the right types of

programmes, but in a country that is so poor, that has so few partners, and where one quarter of the population is in desperate need of humanitarian assistance, almost any available funding can be put to good use. The trick is to get the money. And for this, our experience shows that a combination of concerted advocacy, high-quality information tools, and professionalism can make a significant difference. Indeed, many of the factors used to draw attention to CAR were under the direct control of NGOs, UN agencies, or the Humanitarian Coordinator.

Donors, whoever they are and whether acting directly or indirectly, face a simple challenge: find credible partners with meaningful programmes so that donor budgets can be spent. No donor – whether a foundation, a multi-lateral instrument such as the Global Fund, or a bilateral country – wants to finish its budgetary cycle with money left in the accounts. And donors want to join a winning team and support programmes that work. Yet another way to "market" CAR: the size of the country and its population suggests that working in any sector or region of the country should be possible. Results are attainable. The situation is manageable. In other words, what we offered donors in CAR was a possible success story which could potentially be used as an example to be replicated elsewhere.

A third lesson from CAR is the fact that aid is welcome. This makes a huge difference to aid agencies and donors. While there are difficulties in reaching CAR, establishing a presence, and moving around the country once there, the obstacles are smaller than in many other countries. Members of the population and the civil service are welcoming, friendly, and helpful. And, the aggression that is often associated with life and work in big cities such as Kinshasa or New York is nowhere to be found in provincial Bangui. Feeling welcome and being able to work constructively might seem low on aid agency priority lists, but for those in the field working in situations where violence is present and where we are dealing with the day-to-day suffering of populations at risk, knowing that as providers of protection and assistance we are not only safe, but welcome, is an attraction that no one in CAR or elsewhere dismisses lightly.

Notes

1   This article was written while serving as UN Humanitarian Coordinator, Resident Coordinator for Development Cooperation, and UNDP Resident Representative.

2   Transl. from the French *Union des Forces Démocratiques et du Rassemblement*.

3   From 2003 to 2005, projects in the CAP captured 58 percent of humanitarian financing reaching CAR. In 2006 and 2007, that proportion was 87 percent. This showed the centrality of the tool in helping to ensure a coordinated and strategic humanitarian response.

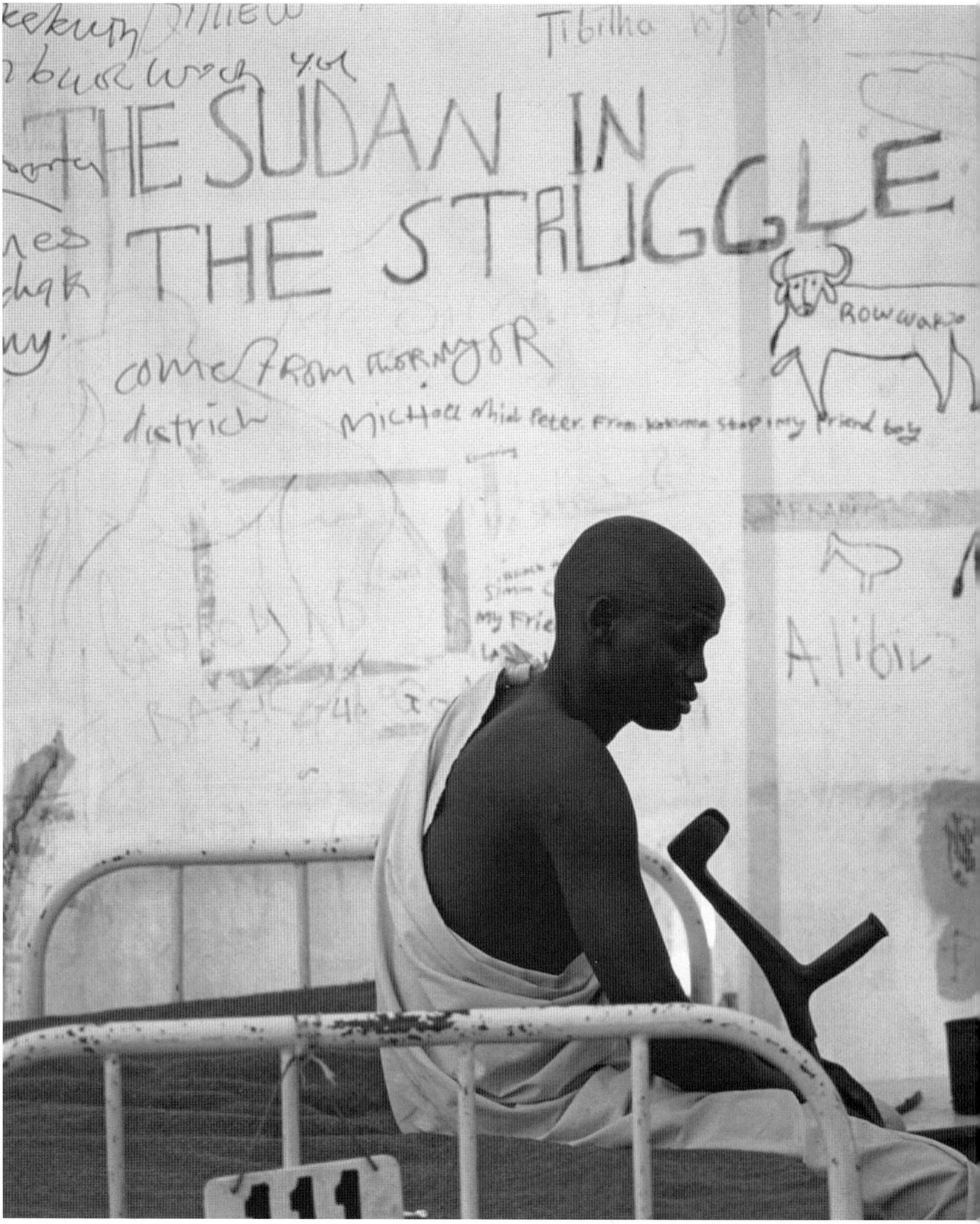
THE SUDAN IN
THE STRUGGLE
come from
district
111

3

PART THREE

Crisis Reports

Introduction

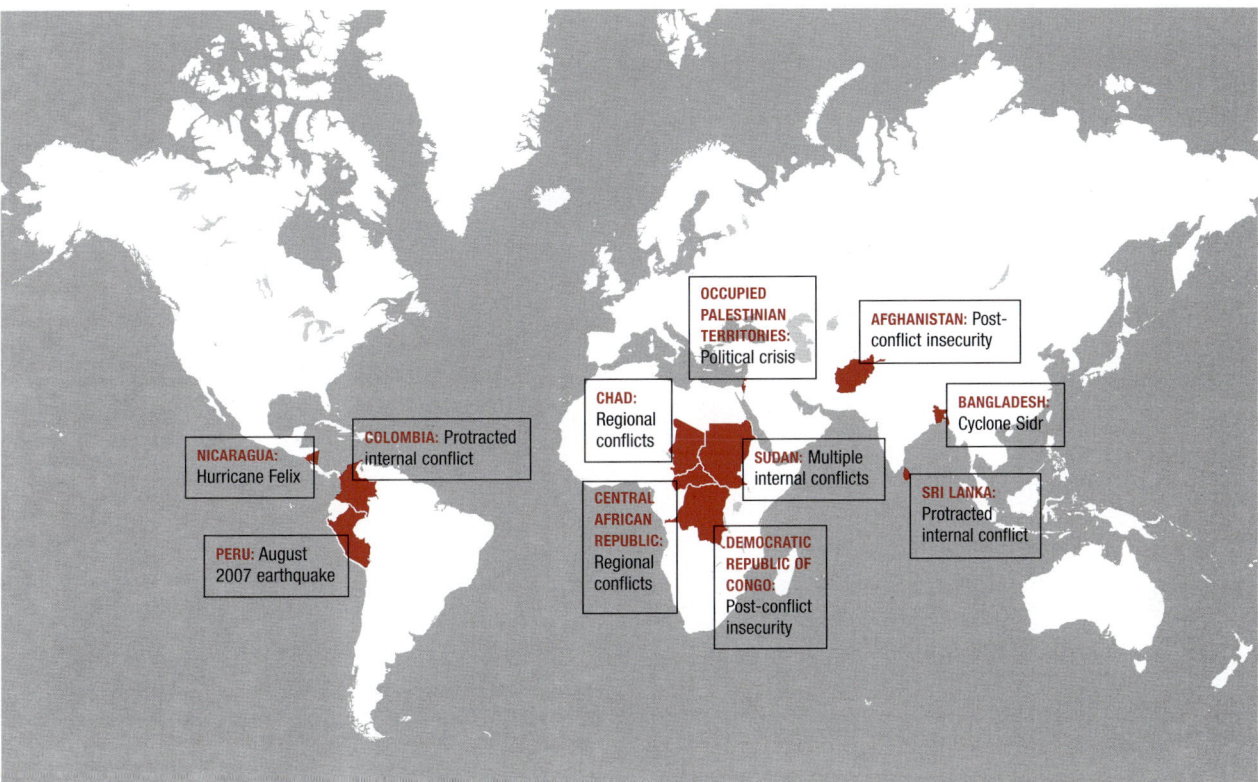

A large part of the Humanitarian Response Index (HRI) is based on visits to different humanitarian crises to assess donor performance in the field in light of the Good Humanitarian Donorship (GHD) *Principles.* The field missions illustrate the specific constraints and challenges humanitarian actors face in providing effective relief in each crisis, as well as shared features which may help to identify where improvements are needed in the global humanitarian system.

This year, the HRI included reports of missions to 11 different crises around the world: Afghanistan, Bangladesh, the Central African Republic, Chad, Colombia, the Democratic Republic of the Congo, Nicaragua, the occupied Palestinian territories, Peru,

Sri Lanka, and Sudan. These countries were selected to reflect the diversity of crises in 2007, including sudden-onset disasters, internal and regional conflicts, protracted crises, and forgotten and complex emergencies. At the same time, the crises represent a range of other factors that influence the humanitarian response, such as media coverage and political interest, levels of funding, and crises in failed and strong states. Three countries: Colombia, the Democratic Republic of the Congo, and Sudan, were included in the HRI 2007, providing an opportunity to track how the response has evolved.

While each report analyses a specific crisis and its response during 2007, a number of common issues emerge. For example, sudden-onset disasters, such as

Bangladesh, Nicaragua, and Peru, show that local capacity and disaster preparedness – both mentioned in the GHD *Principles* – are critical in determining an effective response. In these cases, many of the GHD *Principles* can be seen in donor practice, although there are significant differences between countries.

Similarly, in conflict and post-conflict situations, as in the remaining countries, the concerns for the effective application of the GHD *Principles* of neutrality and impartiality, as well as the protection of humanitarian space, are raised again and again. The crisis report on Afghanistan also clearly reveals that where donor governments have multiple agendas – including security, state-building, and long-term development – humanitarian assistance appears to suffer. The protection of civilians, one of the key points in the GHD, is also noted as weak and inadequate in most of these contexts.

In situations of complex emergencies, where a number of factors combine to dramatically increase the vulnerability of the population, donor behaviour is often found wanting. Here, the challenge is to provide integrated responses based on needs and the promotion of human rights. In this regard, the application of the GHD Principle on linking humanitarian action, recovery, and long-term development is a complex and often unmet challenge.

The crisis reports also illustrate how the UN humanitarian reform process is put into practice, including the challenge of adapting the cluster approach in contexts where both the state and local capacity is reasonably high or almost completely non-existent. The use of new funding mechanisms, such as the Central Emergency Response Fund (CERF) and Pooled Funds, also emerges from several reports as an issue that requires further attention, with mixed results depending on the context.

Finally, many of the reports reveal the increasing number of nontraditional donors contributing to responses to emergencies across the globe. Promoting good practice and following recognised principles among this group of actors is a crucial area for further analysis.

These are all issues that future editions of the HRI will examine in greater detail. The primary aim of the HRI is to contribute by these analyses to a richer understanding of these complex issues, with a view to promoting the continued improvement of humanitarian action.

Afghanistan

AT A GLANCE

Country data *(2006 figures, unless otherwise noted)*

- 2007 Human Development Index: NA
- Population (2005): 25.1 million
- GNI per capita (Atlas method, current US$): NA
- Population living on less than US$2 a day (1990–2004): NA
- Life expectancy (2005, in years): 42.9
- Infant mortality rate (2005): 165 per 1,000 live births
- Under five infant mortality rate (2005): 257 per 1,000
- Population with sustainable access to improved water source (2004): 39 percent
- Adult literacy rate (over 15yrs of age) (1995–2005): 28 percent
- Primary education completion rate (2005): 38 percent
- Gender-related development index (2005): NA
- Official development assistance (ODA): US$3 billion
- 2007 Corruption Perception Index: ranked 172nd out of 179 countries

Sources: Transparency International, 2007; UNDP, 2007a and 2007b; World Bank, 2008.

The crisis

- 6.6 million Afghanis do not receive the minimum food requirement; 400,000 are seriously affected by natural disasters each year; 15,000 die of tuberculosis each year and one woman dies every half hour from pregnancy complications;
- Security deteriorated significantly in 2007, in the south and east of the country; more than 8,000 conflict-related fatalities; more than 500 security incidents;
- Two million primary school children (60 percent) are out of school (1.3 million are girls);
- 2007 floods affected over 10,000 families; heavy snowfalls killed over 800 and decimated livestock;
- Over 132,000 IDPs; 2.9 million registered Afghan refugees, many have lived as refugees for nearly two decades;
- 5 million returned to Afghanistan between 2002 and 2008, far beyond the country's absorption capacity.

Sources: WFP; UN Mission in Afghanistan; IDMC.

The humanitarian response

- There is no CAP for Afghanistan. Most donor funding is channelled bilaterally towards development or reconstruction interventions.
- National Solidarity Programme, recognised by the World Bank as the most effective national programme, lacks donor support with a cash deficit of US$197.33 million, representing an 87 percent shortfall.
- As of May 2008, Afghanistan ranked third among CERF funding recipients, with over US$51 million received since 2006.
- 16 DAC donors contributed humanitarian funds in 2007. Germany (US$32.2 million), ECHO (US$27.3 million), Norway (US$21.8 million), the Netherlands (US$19.2 million), and Canada (US$18.4 million) provided some 75 percent of the over US$152 million given.

Sources: OCHA; CERF Secretariat, Action Aid and ELBAG.

Afghanistan
A Security-Driven Agenda

MARTA MARAÑÓN, Deputy Director, DARA and Lucía Fernández, Evaluation and Research Coordinator, DARA

Introduction[1]

The Islamic Republic of Afghanistan is infamous for the actions of the past Taliban regime, the training camps of Al-Qaida, and the continuing war being waged by international forces to try to bring stability to the country. However, Afghanistan is less well known for the 6.6 million people who do not receive the minimum food requirement, for the 400,000 people each year seriously affected by natural disasters, the 15,000 who die of tuberculosis each year, and the women who die from complications during pregnancy every half hour.[2] There is a persistent humanitarian crisis, fuelled by the continuing conflict and lack of law and order, widespread poverty, and exacerbated by recurring natural hazards including earthquakes, droughts, heavy snow falls, and

floods, and, most recently, by the increase in the price of food. In addition, with 3 million refugees, Afghans make up the second largest population of refugees in the world, despite the return of 4.8 million since 2002[3] and over 132,000 displaced within the country.[4] Nevertheless, the humanitarian crisis in Afghanistan plays second fiddle to the objectives of security, counterterrorism, counter-narcotics and nation-building.

In fact, the nature and motives of the NATO-led invasion, of the subsequent state-building and post-conflict reconstruction efforts, and even of the continuing conflict, make it very difficult to analyse humanitarian efforts in Afghanistan. The complex situation illustrates the interface between political and military objectives and humanitarian action, as well as the ambiguous boundaries between humanitarian and development needs. As reflected in numerous studies and reports, as well as in the interviews by the Humanitarian Response Index team, respect for the fundamental humanitarian principles donors placed at the heart of the Good Humanitarian Donorship (GHD) *Principles* in 2003 have been severely tested in Afghanistan. Within this scenario, donors are failing to act as a coherent community, and to live up to GHD commitments.

The crisis: Humanitarian needs in the context of poor human development

Protracted conflict and a fragile state – non-existent in large areas of the country – have left a deep mark on the course of development in Afghanistan. The ousting of the Taliban regime in 2001 gave way to new conflicts, including not only the insurgency against the government, the International Security Assistance Force (ISAF) and the US operation, but also internal power struggles intertwined with criminal activities related to the narcotics trade. Nation-building is proving arduous and the new highly centralised presidential system is "inappropriate for a state emerging from decades of a civil war that had been stoked by regional, linguistic, ethnic, and sectarian grievances and disputes."[5] Therefore, in conjunction with high vulnerability to natural hazards, from a humanitarian point of view, Afghanistan represents a classic example of a complex emergency.

Security deteriorated significantly in 2007, in particular in the south and east of the country, with more than 8,000 conflict-related fatalities and more than 500 security incidents – improvised explosive devices, suicide attacks, roadside bombs, assassinations, and abductions – reported monthly. As a result, at least 1,500 civilians were killed and a large number internally displaced.[6] In fact, according to Amnesty International, "violations of international humanitarian and human rights law were committed with impunity by all parties, including Afghan and international forces and insurgent groups."[7] Law and order is also poorly enforced in large areas of the country, creating a growing threat to civilians and humanitarian actors alike.

Decades of war and the continuing conflict have created considerable interlinking, and at times indistinguishable, development and humanitarian needs. Afghanistan is one of the poorest countries in the world, ranked 174 out of 178 in the 2007 Human Development Index.[8] Despite some progress, such as

through the Basic Package of Health Care Services (BPHS), the lack of basic services, in particular education and health care, have deteriorated even further due to the worsening of security. As a result, estimated basic indicators are appalling. Life expectancy is barely above 43 years, and the literacy rate is 23 percent (32 percent for men, 13 percent for women). Only 31 percent of households have access to safe drinking water and 80 percent do not have electricity.[9] The Famine Early Warning System estimated that 20 percent of households were food insecure.[10] By June 2008, the United Nations Mission in Afghanistan (UNAMA) estimated that 45 percent of the population were food insecure or borderline.[11] Two million primary school-aged children (60 percent) are out of school, of whom an estimated 1.3 million are girls.[12] According to Oxfam, more than half of the schools are closed due to the violence in the provinces of Helmand, Kandahaar, Uruzgan and Zabul, while in Helmand alone 21 health centres could not function.[13] Women and girls face particular discrimination and difficulties: besides having one of the highest maternal mortality rates in the world (1,600 per 100,000 live births), 21 percent of women of reproductive age are malnourished, and 48 percent are anaemic.[14] According to Afghanistan's Ministry of Work, Social Affairs, Martyred, and Disabled, there are an estimated 2 million disabled persons, of whom 25 percent result from the conflict.[15] In 2007, 138 people were killed and 429 injured by landmines and explosive remnants of war, approximately half of whom were children.[16]

In 2007 there were still 3 million registered Afghan refugees, 2.1 million in Pakistan and 915,000 in Iran. [17] Most of these have lived as refugees for nearly two decades. However, 4.8 million people returned to Afghanistan between 2002 and 2008, a number far beyond the war-torn country's absorption capacity.[18] This includes the voluntary and assisted repatriation of 365,410 in 2007 and the forced repatriation of many others.[19] Pakistan and Iran have started large scale repatriation and deportations, with Pakistan planning to close four refugee camps with more than 150,000 Afghans in 2008.[20] More than 363,000 unregistered Afghans have been forced to return from Iran since April 2007; by contrast, only 7,054 registered refugees returned home voluntarily.[21] UNHCR estimates that an additional 540,000 people will return in 2008 and 2009.[22]

There are genuine concerns over the coercive nature of many of the returns,[23] and about the fact that the country lacks the capacity to integrate the large number of returnees. Likewise, humanitarian actors lack the capacity to address the immediate needs of the returnees. For example, more than 46 percent lacked adequate housing upon their return and 28 percent have no sustainable livelihood.[24] Landlessness and land disputes, as well as a lack of health and education services, the continuing conflict and high vulnerability to natural hazards were further problems faced by the returning population. UNHCR provided assisted returnees with US$100 to cover immediate needs; 10,000 families (approximately 68,000 people) also benefited from additional assistance for shelter.[25] In 2007, there were almost 132,246 registered internally displaced persons (IDPs), mainly Pashtuns and Kuchis displaced in the south and west due to drought and instability.[26] The plight of IDPs and returning refugees illustrates the blurred nature of the distinction between development and humanitarian needs.

Beyond the impact of the conflict, Afghanistan is also prone to recurring natural disasters. Heavy snowfalls in winter in the north, floods in spring, and drought in summer regularly cause fatalities and severe damage to livelihoods. For example, in 2007, flooding affected over 10,000 families,[27] while heavy snowfalls left over 800 dead – a figure close to the civilian fatalities caused by the conflict – and decimated livestock. The eastern provinces of Badghis, Farah, Ghor, and Herat were the hardest hit and the UN concluded that, "the 2007/08 winter emergency demonstrated that national disaster preparedness and response capacity need significant strengthening."[28]

The international response: Security first

The response to humanitarian needs in Afghanistan is hard to assess. The context of significant underdevelopment and the denial of a humanitarian crisis due the government and international supporters' emphasis on security and state capacity-building leave the field unclear in terms of defining roles and responsibilities. Aid to Afghanistan is subsumed under this rubric of post-conflict reconstruction and state-building, despite the continuation of the conflict. In fact, the international intervention in Afghanistan is by no means limited to the humanitarian sector. Rather, the international community continues to respond to security concerns originally triggered by the September 11 terrorist attacks and the links between Al-Qaida and the Taliban. As such, the international response is characterised by multiple overarching layers of military and civil structures and actors, with various decision-making and coordination mechanisms, as well as political agendas.

Most aid agencies in Afghanistan work on longterm development interventions in what could be defined as a context of reconstruction. The government of Afghanistan and the countries intervening militarily in the country – the same countries which happen to be the major humanitarian donors – deny that the situation in the country qualifies as a humanitarian crisis.[29] Therefore, the system-wide funding and coordination mechanisms that the international community has developed to improve the delivery of humanitarian aid are surprisingly absent in Afghanistan. For example, there is no UN Consolidated Appeals Process (CAP) for Afghanistan, and it was not until 2007 that UNAMA established a Humanitarian Affairs Unit and a Humanitarian Country Team. Instead, most official donor funding is channelled towards development or reconstruction interventions, most notably through bilateral channels in support of the Afghanistan Compact[30] and the Afghanistan National Development Strategy (ANDS).[31] However, according to interviews, for various reasons including corruption, this "money doesn't arrive in the field"[32] and in fact by 2007, the majority of the benchmarks set by the Compact had not been achieved. The slow progress with reconstruction raises concerns as to whether immediate humanitarian needs are being met.

Donor funding is also channelled to private contractors working directly for ISAF Provincial Reconstruction Teams (PRTs). These mechanisms threaten to undermine Principle 10 of the GHD *Principles* – namely the support for the unique role of the UN, the Red Cross and Red Crescent Movement, and NGOs in providing humanitarian assistance – as well as blurring the distinction between civilian and military providers of humanitarian assistance. PRTs are civil-military structures set up to provide a secure environment for development programmes. They are led by troop contributing nations, with their military components under the command of the ISAF. Because of the variety of countries involved in PRTs, this translates into varied priorities, working methods, and structures for each Afghan province, creating concerns among humanitarian actors that needs are not addressed equally across different provinces.[33] Again, this appears to jeopardize the key humanitarian principles enshrined in the GHD: that aid be impartial, neutral, independent, and in accordance with need.

Different ISAF countries have different approaches and priorities. In fact, some argue that European countries emphasize a political approach focussed on peacekeeping and nation-building, while the U.S. favours military solutions and adopts the lens of the War on Terror. This may, in part, explain the continuation of the conflict seven years after the invasion. Overall, the security-focussed approach has relegated meeting humanitarian needs and funding to second place. In fact, already in 2001, Médecins Sans Frontières noted, "of . . . greater concern is the mixing of humanitarian aid with military objectives. If the military are involved in delivering humanitarian assistance, it can be regarded by their opponents as an act of war: aid and aid workers can be legitimately targeted, and so denied to people in need." [34] The situation thus described has not changed substantially, raising the question whether lessons are being learned or ignored.

Furthermore, "being nation-led, they [PRTs] are often driven more by available funding or the political interests of the nation involved" rather than development or humanitarian considerations.[35] Priority is given to high, rapid-impact projects of reconstruction aimed at "winning hearts and minds," while other urgent needs are neglected. In addition, individual PRTs are not always in line with national structures and objectives. In fact, implementing aid programmes through PRTs seems to undermine the National Solidarity Programme (NSP), which has been recognised as the most effective national programme by the World Bank.[36] The NSP suffers a cash deficit of US$197.33 million, representing an 87 percent shortfall, highlighting the lack of donor support.

Despite this emphasis on security, the conflict rages on in the south and east, resulting in more civilian deaths, increased displacement, and shrinking humanitarian space. According to UNICEF, "during 2007, approximately 40–50 percent of the districts in the country were not accessible to UN missions for extended periods due to insecurity and movement restrictions."[37] This also affected access to many particularly vulnerable IDPs and returnees. Access is also reduced because humanitarian actors (both international and national staff) are no longer seen as neutral and are increasingly attacked. More than 40 World Food Programme convoys were attacked in 2007, and over 130 attacks were carried out against humanitarian agencies, with 40 aid workers killed and 89 abducted.[38] This particularly affected UN agencies because of their support for the ISAF mandate. In fact, some NGOs attempt to remain independent by not accepting funds from donors engaged in military operations. A further consequence of the increasing violence is that many organisations withdrew from the south of the country. This reflects the fact that the conflict arises in very concrete locations and does not affect the majority of the population. According to the UN, "70 percent of [conflict-related] security incidents occurred in 10 percent (40) of Afghanistan districts, home to 6 percent of the population," mainly in the south and east.[39]

Humanitarian funding: Scarce funds, scattered data

The lack of a UN Consolidated Appeal Process for Afghanistan signals the low profile of humanitarian concerns within the UN leadership in the country. This means that donors need to rely on individual appeals either by agencies or their own sources in the field (mostly military) to make funding decisions for humanitarian action. An analysis of humanitarian funding in Afghanistan is therefore limited by the lack of data on needs, and can only rely on information available through the Office for the Coordination of Humanitarian Assistance Financial Tracking Service (OCHA FTS). Since providing information to the FTS is voluntary, the data presented below could be incomplete.[40]

Out of the 23 OECD/DAC donors, 16 contributed humanitarian funds in 2007. Germany (US$32.2 million), the EC/ECHO (US$27.3 million), Norway (US$21.8 million), the Netherlands (US$19.2 million), and Canada (US$18.4 million) were the largest donors, together providing some 75 percent of the over US$152 million given. An important source of funds for humanitarian action in Afghanistan was the UN Central Emergency Response Fund (CERF). As of May 2008, Afghanistan ranked third among CERF funding recipients, with over US$51 million received since 2006.[41]

As for agencies, in 2007 most humanitarian funding was channelled through the UN system (41 percent), followed by 37 percent to NGO agencies, 13 percent directly to the government and 9 percent to the Red Cross and Red Crescent Movement. The largest recipient agencies were UNHCR, followed by WFP, the HALO Trust, Germany's GTZ, and the ICRC. In fact, the ICRC operation in Afghanistan is its fourth largest in the world after Sudan, Iraq, and the Palestinian Territories,[42] with a 2007 expenditure of over €30 million or US$41.3 million.[43]

Although CERF funds are not directly available to NGOs, the HRI 2008 mission found particularly striking the fact that many organisations were not even aware that so much money had been made available to UN agencies through this mechanism. This lack of knowledge is perhaps a sign that CERF is being used in Afghanistan not as a source of quick funding in emergencies, but to cover regular ongoing operations of the UN family, as preliminary conclusions of the ongoing evaluation of the CERF show. This seems to contradict the main purposes behind the launch of the CERF within the global humanitarian reform process, namely to fund rapid onset emergencies and to serve underfunded emergencies

Donor funding is also channelled through the Afghanistan Emergency Trust Fund (AETF).[44] The fund supports the Office of the Deputy Special Representative of the Secretary General to UNAMA through two memoranda of understanding: the first provides grants to NGOs working to address rehabilitation needs; the second is for humanitarian and development activities. Donations to this fund are not accounted for in OCHA FTS.

Of great concern to humanitarian agencies was varying donor practice according to geographic area and troop presence, linked to the PRT system. UN agencies and NGOs alike repeatedly raised the problem of the link between troop placement and availability of funding. For example, Canada, with most troops in the Kandahar province, was mentioned as trying to pressure agencies to work in the same area. In fact, with the exception of the USAID – which has a presence throughout the country – Sweden, the European Commission, and Norway, donors have mainly directed aid to the areas where their troops are deployed. There is a concern, therefore, that aid is not administered independently, nor necessarily according to need, as areas where the insurgency is more active, or where poppy cultivation is high, receive more aid than the rest.[45] As a result "peaceful provinces are not getting enough."[46] Furthermore, some agencies, including those affiliated with the UN, have rejected funds because these are too often earmarked to areas where they lack capacity.

Implementing agencies also rejected donor funds for humanitarian activities because of their connection to military structures and objectives. "We do not take funds from PRTs" was a frequent statement heard during HRI 2008 interviews. Some implementing agencies suggested that, in fact, ostensibly humanitarian interventions by PRTs focused on local military commanders and were primarily aimed at "winning hearts and minds," rather than addressing needs.

Implementing agencies also noted that funds, in particular from EC/ECHO, often took a long time to be disbursed and that sustained, long-term funding was

a problem. This is a significant deficit, given that the country faces recurring natural disasters every year. Connected to this, it was highlighted that, whereas the government was frequently and closely consulted and its future capacity to respond to a humanitarian crisis supported, this was not the case with the communities themselves, particularly in rural areas beyond Kabul. It is not surprising, therefore, that funds linking relief and development were also inadequate.

Many organisations interviewed complained that humanitarian funds were too often directed to government ministries, although the majority of programmes are ultimately implemented by NGOs. Since the government is seen to be party to the conflict, some organisations refused this funding, thinking that it would compromise the neutrality of their operations. By giving money directly to the government and avoiding direct NGO funding, donors, instead of supporting the special role of NGOs, as declared in the GHD *Principles,* are curtailing NGO capacity to access resources.

The European Policy Centre argues that, "individual donor members have failed to act as a coherent donor group."[47] Similarly, the UN Secretary General in March 2008 recognised that "more efforts . . . are needed to improve the impact and coordination of aid and to ensure that international assistance is driven by demand rather than by supply and is prioritized according to Afghan needs."[48]

The humanitarian system: Weak capacity and coordination

Due to the dominance of security, antiterrorism and reconstruction agendas, the humanitarian architecture keeps a low profile in Afghanistan. In fact, the resources and efforts devoted to humanitarian affairs within the UN integrated mission are scarce, if not minimal. To the dismay of humanitarian actors, there is no OCHA office in the country, its presence being limited to low profile personnel and diluted within UNAMA.

In the absence of OCHA, the Humanitarian Affairs Unit (HAU) coordinates humanitarian activities within UNAMA and is funded by Norway. However, this was only established in 2007. Furthermore, the HAU has 20 Humanitarian Affairs and Civil-Military Coordination Officers, clearly not enough to cover the complexities of a large and poorly communicated country faced with recurring natural disasters, conflict, and displacement. The discreet profile given to HAU so far is reflected in the considerable difficulties it faces in covering the operating costs of personnel. The appointment of a new UN Special Representative in March 2008 seems to present an opportunity to revamp the humanitarian profile of the integrated UN mission.

Again, for security reasons and changing context, humanitarian organisations have significantly reduced their presence since 2002, although the current level is still estimated to be around ten times what it was when the Taliban regime was in power.[49] However, expatriate personnel are often neither experienced nor skilled in humanitarian action, which makes them less vocal in raising issues and demanding compliance with international humanitarian standards. On the other hand, local organisations are not prepared to fill the void.

Although some basic coordination mechanisms exist in various sectors, implementing agencies assert that coordination of humanitarian action is poor. International NGOs are pushing for the introduction of the cluster system, which they believe will help to share information, assign specific roles and responsibilities, and, hopefully, result in more effective coordination. However, major UN agencies such as UNHCR, UNICEF, and the Red Cross and Red Crescent Movement are wary of introducing the cluster approach in Afghanistan, alleging that they lack the resources to make this work properly.

The lack of effective coordination and leadership makes it very difficult to gauge the scale of humanitarian needs. However, the January 2008 Joint Appeal for US$81.32 million launched by WFP, WHO, and UNICEF to cover the humanitarian consequences of the rise in food prices may be a sign of future improved coordination.

Conclusion

The Afghani people have suffered the consequences of almost three decades of war, compounded by the hardships of living in one of the poorest countries in the world, and exposure to many natural hazards. However, because of the deteriorating security situation, related to the fragility of the state, only a few humanitarian organisations remain. Security is often poor across the country, affecting safe access to the most vulnerable, not only to deliver aid but also simply to assess their needs. However, humanitarian needs remain high for the most vulnerable: returning refugees, IDP's, women, children, disabled persons, and communities affected by the con-

flict in the south and east and by natural disasters. Yet humanitarian needs are not sufficiently funded and humanitarian NGOs have difficulties in accessing funds that guarantee their neutrality and independence.

The international community's engagement in Afghanistan is clearly dominated by security, counter-terrorism, counter-narcotics and state-building concerns, and not by humanitarian needs. All funding is, in fact, donor-driven and is primarily directed towards reconstruction programmes, to "winning hearts and minds" and to strengthening the capacity of the government. Although the widespread poverty and the lack of services highlights the difficulty in distinguishing between development and humanitarian needs, the limited progress in improving the lives of ordinary Afghans – even seven years after the invasion – is worrying. The recent Joint Appeal by WFP, WHO, and UNICEF to respond to food price increases further illustrates the fine line between emergency and underdevelopment.

The objectives of the international community and the structures and mechanisms employed have caused confusion between military and humanitarian undertakings and have reduced humanitarian space and impact. With some exceptions, aid is generally geographically earmarked, tied to donor country troop deployment, and channelled through the PRTs. For many, this has jeopardised both the fundamental humanitarian principles of impartiality, neutrality, and independence found in Principle 2 of the GHD, and in turn the appropriateness and effectiveness of delivering humanitarian assistance. The targeting of aid agencies and the deaths of 40 aid workers in 2007 was tragic evidence of this. In contrast, much of the normal architecture for the delivery of humanitarian aid, such as a CAP or a strong OCHA presence, is largely absent. This raises the question of the effectiveness of the UN humanitarian reform agenda, and other initiatives such as the GHD, in the context of Afghanistan.

Much can be done to improve the humanitarian expertise in the country, including donor presence and UN leadership. A press statement in June 2008 by a number of international aid agencies, while lamenting the past deficiencies of the UN mission regarding humanitarian affairs, welcomed the visit to Kabul by the UN Under-Secretary-General for Humanitarian Affairs, Sir John Holmes.[50] There is hope, therefore, that the situation will improve and that the Afghan people will receive the attention they so desperately require and deserve.

Notes

1   The HRI team, composed of Farhad Antezar, Annette Courteix, Lucía Fernández and Marta Marañón visited Afghanistan in March 2008. The opinions expressed here are those of the authors and do not necessarily reflect those of DARA.

2   World Food Programme (WFP), 2008.

3   UNAMA, 2008.

4   IDMC, 2008.

5   International Crisis Group, 2008, p. 4.

6   UN General Assembly Security Council, 2008, p. 4.

7   Amnesty International Report, 2008.

8   UNDP, 2007.

9   Ibid.

10 USAID FEWS NET, 2007, p. 3.

11 UNAMA, 2008.

12 UNICEF, op. cit. p. 2.

13 Oxfam, 2008.

14 UNICEF, op. cit. p. 3.

15 US Bureau of Democracy, Human Rights and, Labor, 2007.

16 UN General Assembly Security Council, op. cit., p. 7.

17 UNHCR, 2007b, p. 260.

18 UNAMA, 2008.

19 UN General Assembly Security Council, op. cit., p. 12.

20 UNICEF, 2007op. cit. p. 2.

21 UN General Assembly Security Council, op. cit., p. 4.

22 UNHCR. 2007b, p. 260.

23 IRIN Asia, 2008.

24 UNHCR, 2007b.

25 Habibi and Hunte. 2006, p. 19.

26 CIA World Factbook, 2008.

27 UNICEF, op. cit., p. 2.

28 UN General Assembly Security Council, op. cit., p. 12

29 HRI field interview.

30 The 2006 Afghanistan Compact is a political agreement between the government, the UN, and donors, providing a five year framework for cooperation. It is implemented under the mandate of the Joint Coordination and Monitoring Board (JCMB), with representatives from 21 bodies of the international community.

31 The Afghanistan National Development Strategy (ANDS) was approved in April 2008. An Interim ANDS (IANDS) had been in place since 2006, laying out the government's priorities on security, governance, rule of law and human rights, and economic and social development.

32 HRI field interview.

33 HRI field interview.

34 Ford, 2001.

35 Oxfam, op. cit., p. 9.

36 ActionAid and and ELBAG, 2007, p. 43.

37 UNICEF, op. cit., p. 1.

38 UN General Assembly Security Council UN, op. cit., p. 5.

39 Ibid. p. 5.

40 All FTS data on this report was retrieved on February 7, 2008.

41 CERF Secretariat, 2007.

42 ICRC, 2007.

43 ICRC, 2008, p. 67.

44 The Afghanistan Emergency Trust Fund was established by the UN Secretary General in 1988 to manage funds in the period following the withdrawal of the Soviet military forces, and was formerly administered by OCHA.

45 Waldman. 2008, p. 29.

46 HRI field interview.

47 Korski, 2008, P. 5.

48 General Assembly Security Council, op. cit., p. 2.

49 Karim, 2006, p. 10.

50 United Nations, 2008, p. 4.

References

ActionAid Afghanistan and Economic Literacy and Budget Accountability for Governance (ELBAG). 2007. *Gaps in Aid Accountability: A Study of NSP Finances.* At: http://www.actionaid.org/assets/pdf/FEB%20ELBAG%20report.pdf

Amnesty International Report 2008. *The State of the World's Human Rights. Afghanistan.* At: http://thereport.amnesty.org/eng/regions/asia-pacific/afghanistan

Center for Policy and Human Development (CPHD). 2007. *Afghanistan Human Development Report 2007. Bridging Modernity and Tradition: Rule of Law and the Search for Justice.* Afghanistan Human Development Report 2007. At: http://hdr.undp.org/en/reports/nationalreports/asiathepacific/afghanistan/nhdr2007.pdf

Central Intelligence Agency (CIA). 2008. *World Factbook,* 2008, Afghanistan. 15 July. At: https://www.cia.gov/library/publications/the-world-factbook/geos/af.html

CERF Secretariat. 2007. *Countries receiving CERF funds since its launch on 9 March 2006.* At: http://ochaonline.un.org/cerf/CERFFigures/CountriesreceivingCERFfunds/tabid/1799/Default.aspx

The Economist. 2008. "Afghanistan's tribal complexity: In the dark. Far more than two sides to the conflict." 31 January.

Ford, Nathan. 2001. "Afghanistan-humanitarian aid and military intervention don't mix." Médecins Sans Frontières. 7 November.

Habibi, Gulbadan and Pamela Hunte. 2006. "Afghan Returnees from NWFP, Pakistan, to Nangarhar Province." April. At: http://www.unhcr.org/cgi-bin/texis/vtx/home/opendoc.pdf?tbl=SUBSITES&id=446066e72

International Committee of the Red Cross. 2008. *Annual Report 2007.* May. At: http://www.icrc.org/Web/Eng/siteeng0.nsf/htmlall/section_annual_report_2007

International Crisis Group. 2008. "Afghanistan: The need for international resolve." Asia Report No. 145. 6 February.

International Displacement Monitoring Centre (IDMC). 2006. "132,000 IDPs in September 2006, with thousands newly displaced by October 2006." At: http://www.internal-displacement.org/idmc/website/countries.nsf/(httpEnvelopes)/CD02D8752990FAF3802570B800 5A6F58?OpenDocument#sources

IRIN Asia. 2008. "Afghanistan-Iran: Iran says it will deport over one million Afghans." 4 March. At: http://www.irinnews.org/Report.aspx? ReportId=77107

Karim, Farahnaz. 2006. "Humanitarian action in the new security environment: Policy and operational implications in Afghanistan." Background Paper. Humanitarian Policy Group. September. At: http://www.odi.org.uk/HPG/papers/BGP_InsecurityAfghanistan.pdf

Korski, Daniel. 2008. *Afghanistan: Europe's Forgotten War.* European Council on Foreign Relations. 21 January. At: http://ecfr.3cdn.net/fcdc73b8da7af85936_q8m6b5o4j.pdf

Office for the Coordination of Humanitarian Assistance (OCHA). 2008. Financial Tracking Service.

Oxfam. 2008. "Afghanistan: Development and Humanitarian Priorities." January. At: http://www.oxfam.org.uk/resources/policy/ conflict_disasters/downloads/afghanistan_priorities.pdf

ReliefWeb. 2008. "Aid agencies welcome UN attention to the humanitarian crisis in Afghanistan." 1 July.

UNICEF. 2007. *Afghanistan Donor Update.* 25 July. At: http://www.unicef.org/infobycountry/files/Afghanistan_final_DU_25Ju l07.pdf p. 2.

———. 2008. *Humanitarian Action Update, Afghanistan.* 17 January. At: http://www.unicef.org/infobycountry/files/Afghanistan_HAU_ 17jan08.pdf

United Nations Mission in Afghanistan (UNAMA). 2008. *Humanitarian Factsheet.* 29 June. At: http://www.unama-afg.org/docs/_UN-Docs/_fact_sheets/2008/08June29-Humanitarian-fact-sheet-English.pdf

United Nations General Assembly Security Council. 2008. "The situation in Afghanistan and its implications for international peace and security." Report of the Secretary-General, A/62/722 S/2008/159. 6 March. At: http://www.unama-afg.org/docs/_UN-Docs/_repots-SG/2008/08march06-SG-report-SC-situation-in-afghanistan.pdf

United Nations Development Programme (UNDP). 2007. *Human Development Index. Afghanistan Human Development Report 2007.* New York. At: http://hdrstats.undp.org/countries/data_sheets/ cty_ds_AFG.html

United Nations High Commissioner for Refugees (UNHCR). 2007a. "Afghanistan – Still Major Challenges Ahead." October. At: http://www.unhcr.org/cgi-bin/texis/vtx/afghan?page=intro

———. 2007b. *Global Appeal 2008–2009: Afghanistan.* 1 December. At: http://www.unhcr.org/home/PUBL/474ac8e00.pdf

United States Agency for International Development (USAID). 2007. "Afghanistan Food Security Conditions and Causes. A special report by the Famine Early Warning Systems Network (FEWS NET)." At: http://www.reliefweb.int/rw/RWFiles2007.nsf/FilesByRWDocUnidFile name/RMOI-7B53N7-full_report.pdf/$File/full_report.pdf

United States Bureau of Democracy, Human Rights and, Labor. 2007. *2007 Country Reports, Afghanistan.* Department of State. 11 March. At: http://www.state.gov/g/drl/rls/hrrpt/2006/78868.htm

Waldman, Matt. 2008. "Falling Short. Aid Effectiveness in Afghanistan." Agency Coordinating Body for Afghan Relief (ACBAR). March. At: http://www.acbar.org/ACBAR%20Publications/ACBAR%20Aid%20 Effectiveness%20(25%20Mar%2008).pdf

World Food Programme. 2008. "Where We Work—Afghanistan: Food Security: Overview. At: http://www.wfp.org/country_brief/ indexcountry.asp?country=004

Bangladesh

AT A GLANCE

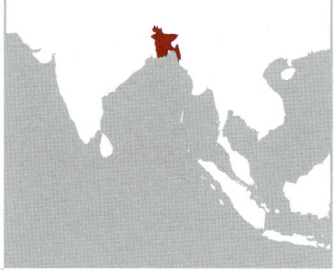

Country data *(2006 figures, unless otherwise noted)*

- 2007 Human Development Index: ranked 140th of 177 countries
- Population: 155.99 million
- GNI per capita (Atlas method, current US$): US$450
- Population living on less than US$2 a day (1990–2005): 84 percent
- Life expectancy: 64 years
- Infant mortality rate (2005): 54 per 1,000 live births
- Under-five infant mortality rate (2005): 73 per 1,000
- Population undernourished (2002–2004): 30 percent
- Population with sustainable access to improved water source (2004): 74 percent
- Primary education completion rate: 38 percent
- Gender-related development index (2005): ranked 120th of 177 countries
- Official development assistance (ODA): US$1.223 billion
- 2007 Corruption Perception Index: ranked 162nd out of 179 countries

Sources: Transparency International, 2007; UNDP, 2007a and 2007b; World Bank, 2008.

The crisis

- After two major floods, super-cyclone Sidr battered the country on 15 November 2007;
- Over 9 million people affected; 3,400 died; as of December 2007, 871 people still missing;
- 550,000 houses destroyed; 1 million more damaged; 300,000 families without shelter;
- 3 million without safe water, risking diarrhoeal disease and associated illnesses;
- Economic damage estimated at over US$2.3 billion; over 200,000 families lost source of income;
- Hundreds of schools, hospitals and other public facilities damaged or destroyed.

Sources: Government of Bangladesh Ministry of Food and Disaster Management.

The humanitarian response

- No UN Appeal launched, although major donors formed a Local Consultative Group, with a sub-group assigned to coordinate donor activities;
- Over US$426 million pledged to meet immediate needs;
- Non-traditional donors contributed significantly; OECD/DAC funded only 30 percent of total; highest contribution US$130 million from individual in Saudi Arabia; Saudi government gave nearly US$103 million. Kuwait, China, Iran, India, Libya, and Turkey ranked among top 20 donors.

Sources: Government of Bangladesh and OCHA FTS.

Bangladesh
Prepared for New Disasters?

PHILIP TAMMINGA, HRI Project Manager, DARA

© Abir Abdullah/epa/Corbis

Introduction[1]

Bangladesh, one of the world's most disaster-prone countries, has faced dozens of major disasters over its short history as a nation. Located on the Bay of Bengal, Bangladesh is particularly susceptible to seasonal cyclones, acting as a funnel for heavy precipitation from the Indian Ocean and creating extreme weather events. The country sits on the flood plain of several major rivers which drain from the mountainous regions of the Himalayas, making seasonal flooding another hazard often coinciding with the cyclone season.

The frequency of disasters has generated in Bangladesh a unique, indigenous capacity to prevent and respond to humanitarian crises. The international humanitarian system and donors have a long-standing engagement with the country, supporting not only frequent disaster response operations, but also longer-term disaster preparedness and development programmes. The Category 4 super-cyclone Sidr which battered the country on 15 November 2007 highlighted how local capacity, excellent relations with donors and humanitarian agencies, and an investment in disaster preparedness paid dividends by reducing deaths and injuries from the disaster – an excellent example for other disaster-prone countries.

The effective response to Cyclone Sidr demonstrated how existing in-country capacity can be balanced with international disaster response instruments, such as the cluster approach, and adapted to the country context. Overall, there is ample evidence that many key concepts of the Good Humanitarian Donorship (GHD) *Principles* are being applied, not necessarily through explicit awareness of the *Principles,* but as a result of an accumulation of experience and good practice.

However, the response also underlined shortcomings in the humanitarian system. Bangladesh has a high risk of experiencing a catastrophic humanitarian crisis in the future, due to factors of location, environmental degradation, global climate change, new threats such as avian-human influenza, and chronic poverty. This vulnerability raises serious concerns not only about the country's ability to sustain and increase its existing preparedness and response capacity, but also about how the international humanitarian response system may be adapted and integrated to best support Bangladesh to prevent, mitigate, and respond effectively to future human suffering.

Causes and impact of the crisis: Effects of multiple disasters

Cyclone Sidr followed two major floods in July and August 2007, which affected over 8 million people, mainly in the north and central regions of the country, causing over 1,100 deaths and major losses of crops and livestock. The country was also grappling with severe food shortages, rising fuel prices, spiralling inflation, and a serious outbreak of avian influenza. Cyclone Sidr exacerbated the existing precarious situation faced by millions of people in the country.

Damage from Sidr was mainly concentrated in the southern region, although districts in the centre and north were also affected. Winds of over 240 km/h uprooted trees and cut off communications and transportation to some of the most affected areas. Tidal waves of up to five metres caused extensive flooding and damaged embankments which protected people living along extensive rivers and waterways.

According to government figures, the cyclone affected over 9 million people and caused some 3,400 deaths. As of December 2007, there were still 871 people missing.[2] Over 550,000 houses were destroyed, and 1 million damaged, leaving more than 300,000 families without shelter. Contamination of ponds and tube wells was extensive, leaving 3 million people without access to safe water and increasing the risks of diarrhoeal disease and associated illnesses.

Economic damage is estimated at over US$2.3 billion, with agriculture, fisheries, and small-scale cottage industries most affected. Over 100,000 livestock and 2.5 million poultry were killed, severely compromising livelihoods and coping mechanisms. Over 200,000 families lost their source of income. Hundreds of schools, hospitals, and other public facilities were damaged or destroyed.[3] Prior to Cyclone Sidr, Bangladesh – ranking 140th on the Human Development Index – was on track to meet the Millennium Development Goals, but the storm jeopardised these advances.

The international donor response: The value of strong relationships at country level

In January 2007, clashes among supporters of the main political parties and deep-rooted corruption among political institutions and elites led the military to install a caretaker government shortly before scheduled elections.[4] This government maintained most functions, especially those related to disaster preparedness and response. Bangladesh is unusual in that it has established a permanent government coordinating body, the Disaster Management Bureau (DMB), as part of the Ministry of Food and Disaster Management (supported by the UNDP, DFID, and the EC), an important factor in explaining the relatively effective response to Sidr.

The government and the UN carried out joint rapid assessment missions within 48 hours, with environmental, agricultural, and livelihood needs assessments taking place shortly thereafter. Individual UN agencies, international, and national NGOs also conducted their own needs assessments focused on particular areas of intervention, or on specific geographic areas. Based on its needs assessments, the government prioritised relief efforts in the Bagerhat, Barguna, Patuakhali, and Pirojpur districts. This decision, while reasonable, caused concern among some agencies that other districts with less damage were being overlooked in relief and recovery efforts.

Despite the scope of the cyclone's damage, the caretaker government did not launch a formal international UN Appeal, but instead used its relations with the donor community already present in country to communicate its needs and request support. An earlier UN Appeal following the 2007 floods did not have good coverage, and there is some speculation that the government was reluctant to be seen as requiring assistance, or that a poor donor response would be interpreted as a lack of confidence in the government.

Interestingly, in Bangladesh the major OEDC/DAC donors present in the country have formed a Local Consultative Group (LCD), with a specific sub-group, the Disasters and Emergency Response (DER) group, to help coordinate donor activities during a crisis. This group was activated for Cyclone Sidr and was in constant contact with government authorities from the beginning of the crisis. Existing donor presence and working relationships with the government were enormously useful in allowing donors to quickly understand the situation, assess needs, and make funding decisions without going through appeal and approval procedures. Direct contact with donors was effective, resulting in pledges of over US$426 million for immediate needs, and, by all accounts, rapid disbursement of funds.[5]

The success of this approach calls into question the effectiveness and efficiency of the international UN Appeal mechanism in situations such as Bangladesh, where the government was able to directly articulate its needs to donors. It also suggests that a good understanding and sustained relationships among donors, governments, and implementing agencies may be a more effective means of mobilising resources than traditional Appeals. In this case at least, the GHD *Principles* calling for donors to support Appeal mechanisms were not particularly relevant, and donors may need to rethink their appropriateness and consider alternative funding mechanisms.

In terms of overall funding commitments, a significant number of non-traditional donors contributed to the response, with OECD/DAC funding constituting only 30 percent of the total. The highest contributor – an anonymous individual from Saudi Arabia – pledged over US$130 million, followed closely by the Saudi Arabian government, which pledged nearly US$103 million. Kuwait, China, Iran, India, Libya, and Turkey also rank among the top 20 donors, along with the NGO Islamic Relief. In many cases, these non-traditional donors contributed directly to the government, without carrying out their own assessments or imposing other preconditions.

With such a high proportion of non-traditional donors, there is a risk that some donors may not be aware of, or consider relevant, many of the mechanisms in the humanitarian system designed to promote quality, effectiveness, and accountability – including the GHD *Principles*. There is an additional risk that by not placing any conditions on aid, governments may be tempted to disregard the good practices and principles for humanitarian action, as expressed in the GHD. Thankfully, this did not appear to be the case in Bangladesh for Cyclone Sidr. Nevertheless, in order to avoid repeating mistakes of the past, the donor community, humanitarian agencies, and governments will have to work together to raise awareness and acceptance of these mechanisms, in particular of GHD *Principles* 1, 4 and 5.

Since the UN system has a long-standing presence in the country, with several agencies carrying out development and capacity-building programmes, agencies were able to reallocate personnel and resources when Cyclone Sidr struck. Approximately US$7 million was allocated from existing programmes and funds, and nearly US$20 million of Central Emergency Response Fund (CERF) was provided to various UN agencies. In comparison with other disasters, the CERF gave rapid approval and disbursed funds quickly, allowing UN agencies to quickly scale up response actions. However, some agencies with limited operational capacity had difficulty absorbing the rapid injection of funds and in spending the allocated funds in a timely, efficient manner.

The overall figures provided through the government and the UN system do not, however, reflect the full extent of funding, as other organisations launched appeals to support their immediate relief work. The International Federation of the Red Cross and Red Crescent Societies (IFRC), with a presence in the country for decades, launched a US$22.2 million Appeal for Sidr, 67 percent of which was covered, and reminded donors that previous Appeals for flood relief and recovery (funded at 66 percent) also required urgent support.[6] Other agencies, such as World Vision, Save the Children Alliance, and CARE mobilised funds internally or launched their own appeals. Most implementing agencies interviewed felt that donors allocated and disbursed funds in a timely, flexible manner, in accord with the GHD *Principles*. DFID, the European Commission Humanitarian (Aid) Office (EC/ECHO) and the United States Agency for International Development (USAID) were consistently mentioned as good examples of donors applying these principles. Because the country was moving out of the emergency phase and into the early recovery phase at the time of the HRI field mission, it was difficult to gather data on how much funding was committed to long-term recovery and rehabilitation. When the government – with significant technical support from the UN Resident Coordinator's Office – published its early recovery action plan in February, less than 30 percent of the nearly US$450 million funding required to carry out early recovery interventions had been received, with huge gaps in the areas of shelter, agriculture, livelihoods, and water, sanitation, and hygiene.[7]

Many agencies and organisations interviewed stated that they were in the laborious process of preparing proposals to donors for medium and long-term recovery activities, but could not be certain whether funding might be available or committed. The short time frame and level of detailed analysis required for proposals created problems for NGOs, who also found it difficult to navigate the various procedures required by donors for applications for relief versus long-term recovery. Indeed, even larger actors, such as UN agencies and the IFRC found this challenging. Preparing these proposals while simultaneously carrying out relief operations represents a significant investment in time and resources for implementing agencies – particularly smaller, local NGOs – with few, if any, guarantees of receiving funding. This illustrates the difficulty for agencies to plan recovery interventions effectively and ensure continuity and integration with their relief operations. It underscores the difference between the commitments expressed in the GHD *Principles* on supporting relief, rehabilitation, and development, and actual funding practices.

Implementation of the humanitarian response: Stretching local capacity to its limits

The initial response to Sidr was generally positive, albeit with the usual difficulties with capacity, inter-agency coordination, and information sharing seen in any large-scale disaster. According to most agencies consulted, the government's response was rapid and effective especially when compared to its reaction to the floods earlier in the year – when it was criticised for being slow to acknowledge the floods as a major emergency.

The Disaster Management Bureau monitored the cyclone's path, and issued regular situation reports prior to landfall. Improvements in weather satellite imagery and storm projections meant that, in contrast to previous disasters, there was sufficient advance warning to alert and evacuate the population to cyclone shelters, to pre-position relief stocks, and mobilise resources. The military, already widely deployed for a voter registration process, was diverted to support immediate relief efforts, support local authorities, and coordinate efforts. A special operations centre was set up in the severely affected Barisal district, with disaster management committees established at the Upazila and Union level.[8] These critically important measures would not have been possible

without the long-term support and investment by donors and the government in disaster preparedness and response capacity, in line with GHD Principle 8.

Bangladesh is also unique in the number of local NGOs engaged in disaster response activities. Many are involved in microcredit, in which Bangladesh has been a pioneer and world leader. Others have direct experience in disaster response, or, out of necessity, have included food distribution as an extension to their other programmes. This vast community-level network was mobilised quickly to support early evacuation, needs assessments, and relief operations. Many NGOs continue to work in recovery. There are allegations, however, that some local NGOs assisted existing beneficiaries of programmes, rather than acting impartially and according to need.[9]

GHD Principle 10 in action is well illustrated by the fact that donors supported a variety of different agencies in the response. Many UN agencies working in Bangladesh were able to reallocate staff and resources to support the response. UNICEF and the World Food Programme (WFP) were engaged in relief operations, with other agencies providing technical support and assistance in other areas. The IFRC and major international NGOs (CARE, Save the Children Alliance, World Vision, and Oxfam), with their established working relations with local partners and government authorities, were also present in the country at the time of Cyclone Sidr.

Because the cyclone followed on the heels of the severe floods, relief operations were still ongoing when it struck, with operational capacity on the ground and stocks of food, medicine, and other items that could be quickly redeployed. Nevertheless, the arrival of Sidr, so soon after the floods, severely stretched the resources of overburdened actors, in particular, organisations such as the Bangladesh Red Crescent and local NGOs.

Political parties have traditionally mobilised their networks and resources to provide relief and assistance, often as a means of currying favour with potential supporters. In the case of Sidr, the government restricted and discouraged these parties from engaging in relief activities. As a result, several agencies reported fewer cases of corruption, as compared to previous disasters. It is difficult to know whether to attribute reduced corruption to the actions of the caretaker government, the presence of the military, the absence of traditional political parties in relief activities, or to better oversight by donors and agencies already present and experienced in the country.[10]

Coordination and clusters: A unique approach

In the case of Sidr, the UN Office for the Coordination of Humanitarian Affairs (OCHA) was not the lead player in the international response, although it did provide limited technical assistance in the early stages. Instead, the UN Resident Coordinator's Office (RCO) provided central coordination of UN agencies and strongly supported the government's leading role in organising and coordinating relief efforts. This was a conscious decision, based on the view that there was sufficient government, NGO, and UN capacity to address immediate needs. There was also a legitimate concern that mobilising the full OCHA response apparatus could weaken existing local capacity and undermine the reasonably good working relationships between the UN and the government, a situation seen too often in other crises.[11]

The decision to place responsibility for coordination in the RCO had its drawbacks. Despite experience in disaster management, the government's capacity to lead and direct overall operations, though far greater than that of other countries, was limited, particularly at the district level. While some UN agencies, especially UNICEF and WFP, had highly competent people and experience, others were not as well prepared to take on disaster relief operations and provide support to the government above and beyond their existing programming. Familiarity with standard protocols, terminology, and inter-agency coordination in a large-scale disaster was sometimes lacking among both government and UN personnel. Finally, there were questions concerning the capacity of the RCO to handle a major emergency and its relationship to OCHA. Some suggested that the RCO needed greater technical capacity to make it a viable alternative to OCHA in such a situation.

The cluster approach, a fundamental element of UN humanitarian system reforms, was adapted by Bangladesh to the local context, but with mixed results. Six clusters were initially set up to provide coordination in the areas of food, health, water, sanitation and hygiene (WASH), emergency shelter, logistics, and early recovery. The relevant government ministry took the lead in coordination, with technical support provided by the international agency cluster lead. While attempting to meet international quality standards and methodologies, it was a challenge for many organisations participating in the clusters to respect the government's desire to lead and set priorities. Cluster groups debated definitions, working approaches, and roles, revealing the considerable work remaining to make the cluster – however sound a technical concept – a useful coordinating tool in practice. For example, there was no consensus within the shelter and early recovery clusters about the most appropriate approach to their use, nor how to make the link with other issues, such as livelihoods. This may have hampered rapid, practical, and lasting solutions to immediate needs, due, in part, to some actors' lack of familiarity and experience with key cluster concepts, and the challenge of modifying a tool that may be better suited to failed states, than to Bangladesh, where some response capacity already exists. The experience of Bangladesh shows that the cluster approach can work, but that the humanitarian system must better guide cluster lead agencies in adapting the cluster mechanism to local conditions.

As mentioned earlier, the country was entering the phase of early recovery and long-term rehabilitation at the time of the HRI field mission. Accordingly, in February 2008, clusters were reconstituted into seven "transitional working groups" (food, shelter, health, WASH, education, livelihoods, and agriculture), responsible for both development and implementation of recovery activities in each sector. This was an attempt to ensure good sectoral coordination and information sharing. But from the perspective of many respondents, the groups seemed unwieldy, with too much overlap to be effective.[12]

Similar criticism was heard regarding coordination meetings convened by the government. Many NGO actors (and UN agencies) suggested that they lacked sufficient detailed information to plan relief and recovery efforts, and that too much time was spent in these meetings, with little productive outcome. Many INGOs, working with local partners, developed their own informal coordination mechanisms for planning and coordinating joint actions at the field level. These provided a valuable mechanism for sharing information, and advocating collectively to the UN and government to respond to issues they were facing at the field level.[13]

Gaps in the response and recovery efforts: Linking relief, recovery, and development

As mentioned above, there are significant shortfalls in the funding pledged for activities in the early recovery plan, particularly for shelter and livelihoods. Without guaranteed funding and a comprehensive strategy, millions of people affected by the cyclone will continue to be at risk, particularly as the country moves into the next monsoon season. Agencies such as Oxfam have issued repeated warnings about the severity of this issue, and called on the government and the international community to take immediate action to address it.[14] The generous and rapid response of donors for initial relief operations contrasts sharply with the rather slow response to establishing predictable and long-term funding arrangements for agencies engaged in long-term recovery programmes, as called for in the GHD *Principles*. Similarly, the comparatively generous funding for food security highlights the need to ensure that donors allocate flexible and unearmarked funding to cover *all* needs and priorities, also a key element of the GHD *Principles*.

However, these are not the only areas of concern. During the HRI field mission, other gaps in the response and recovery efforts became apparent, including lack of standardisation of relief goods (both food and non-food items) and biases in their distribution to affected populations, creating unnecessary conflicts within and among affected communities. Similarly, the participation of vulnerable groups in the design and implementation of interventions seemed weak. Many organizations claimed to incorporate participation mechanisms as part of their normal procedures, but stated that most donors did not make it an explicit prerequisite for funding. In some cases, organisations felt unfairly criticised by donors for responding too slowly to the crisis, and felt that donors did not appreciate the time required to meet quality standards and ensure adequate engagement and participation with affected groups. This is surprising, given that the GHD *Principles* call for donors to promote beneficiary participation and the use of quality standards, such as SPHERE, in interventions.

Other examples of gaps in the response are in so-called "cross-cutting" issues. For example, while some actors are becoming more aware of the need for psychological support for affected populations, support for such interventions was extremely limited. Some respondents claimed that governments and donors tended to think that the people of Bangladesh are already so familiar with natural disasters that they did not require such assistance.[15] Similarly, integrating HIV/AIDS prevention and education measures into interventions, as called for in Inter-Agency Standing Committee (IASC) guidelines, was strangely absent.[16] Gender issues were also sidetracked in the immediate response. Several agencies reported the lack of culturally appropriate approaches in many relief distributions to feminine hygiene, to the design of emergency shelters, and the general lack of awareness of gender-based violence in the post-disaster environment.[17]

Although such issues appear repeatedly in disaster situations, it is disturbing – in light of the increasing recognition of their importance and the availability of specific guidelines to support their implementation – to note how little attention they received by either donors or the government,. In the case of Bangladesh, at least, there seems to be an assumption – based, in part, on the high degree of trust between the different players – that agencies will take the initiative to follow such standards, without systematic monitoring or follow-up from donors. A more likely explanation, based on field interviews, is that country-level representatives of donors and, in some cases, agency staff, were either unfamiliar with, or did not prioritise these guidelines and standards. Given the heavy responsibilities of local NGOs in implementing response activities and the predominance of non-traditional donors in Bangladesh, much more work must be done to mainstream these issues and for donors to actively contribute to such efforts.

To its credit, the caretaker government of Bangladesh recognised many of these challenges, and attempted to address them in the early recovery plan. For example, the shelter component includes proposals for an integrated community-led approach to building and managing new multi-function cyclone shelters, locating them closer to the community, and including provisions to protect livestock. The plan also recognises that while the existing shelters and other preparedness measures may have been sufficient for this emergency, significant efforts at the community level are needed to update and sustain them, if the country is to avoid major losses in future disasters.

Related is the issue of disaster risk reduction. Cyclone Sidr demonstrated the importance of disaster risk reduction and preparedness measures, and the need to pay closer attention to the question of climate change. Again, to its credit, the government has included provisions for disaster risk reduction in the early recovery plan, but the budget assigned to this – US$1.6 million out of a total US$442 million – is miniscule, and the plan lacks clear links to ongoing risk reduction and development efforts.

A UNDP programme for Capacity Building for Disaster Management, supported by DFID, was in its initial stages when Sidr struck, and will continue once relief operations wind down. The World Bank and other institutional donors are also committed to financing longer-term disaster risk reduction and climate change programmes in the country, and some donors are arranging for debt relief and loan repayment deferrals. But there is a risk that such measures may not be linked effectively to ongoing recovery activities, or that they will come too late to help the country prepare for the next major disaster. Donors must ensure timely, long-term support and a coherent and integrated approach to linking relief and development, as called for in the GHD *Principles*.[18]

Finally, one issue recognised in the GHD *Principles* which seems to have escaped the attention of the government, donors, and nearly all of the humanitarian actors in Bangladesh is that of institutional contingency planning. The country was fortunate that Cyclone Sidr did not occur at the same time as the floods, and that existing capacity was sufficient to meet immediate needs. The potential for a catastrophic disaster *combining* cyclones, floods, food shortages, and, for example, an outbreak of avian-human influenza is highly probable in a country like Bangladesh. But there is little evidence that there are contingency plans in place to prepare for less catastrophic emergencies, let alone such a worst-case scenario.

Indeed, given the heavy reliance on NGOs and international agencies to complement the government's response capacity and implement activities at the community level, it was worrisome to hear comments from so many humanitarian actors about the apparent lack of donor interest and support for building and sustaining capacity in contingency planning. Most disaster preparedness efforts are aimed at communities and government institutions, with little attention paid to the need to strengthen other parts of the response system. The prevailing attitude seems to be that local and international NGOs will somehow fill any response gaps, with no acknowledgement of the huge investment and resources required by NGOs to build and sustain a standing response capacity in this area. Equally troubling was the fact that that few humanitarian actors seemed to recognise this as a weakness.

How will local NGOs and other humanitarian agencies, already stretched to the limit, be able to cope with and respond effectively to multiple emergencies in the future? How can institutional capacity-building and contingency planning by both government and NGOs be strengthened and linked with existing community-based disaster preparedness measures? Finally, how can the international humanitarian response system better integrate and support local response capacities in future emergencies? These questions require immediate attention, and challenge donors to play a supportive role.

Conclusion

The response of Bangladesh to Cyclone Sidr offers a unique lesson in promoting and utilising local capacity to good effect, and shows how experience in disaster preparedness and good relations among donors, humanitarian actors, and government minimised the impact of the cyclone. However, it exposed limitations and gaps in capacity and coordination, and highlighted weaknesses in the ability of the humanitarian system to respond to frequent and multiple emergencies and to integrate the relief response with long-term recovery work. Sustained efforts are needed to restore livelihoods, provide long-term, cyclone-safe shelters, and undertake comprehensive disaster risk reduction measures, including contingency planning and comprehensive strategies to deal with climate change.

The response to Sidr demonstrated that many GHD *Principles* are being put into practice in Bangladesh. For the most part, the government, donors, and agencies acted in a neutral, impartial manner, according to need. At least initially, funding was timely and flexible. Respect for the different but complementary roles of different actors – government, UN, Red Cross Red Crescent, and NGOs – was key to the success of the response. The main weaknesses in applying the GHD *Principles* lay in minimal linking of relief to longer-term recovery, and insufficient long-term funding arrangements. More attention must be paid to the use of standards, and to supporting mechanisms for contingency planning.

Bangladesh offers an interesting case study in balancing respect for, and promoting, local capacity, and integrating the international humanitarian system into the response to a major disaster. While not overstating actual capacity, the government and local NGOs have a reasonable level of experience and capacity, as compared with crises elsewhere. Their long history of, and investment in, disaster preparedness must now be sustained and expanded to meet the demands of increasingly frequent and even more destructive natural disasters. The international humanitarian system, including donors, must learn how to engage and support that local capacity, without overwhelming it with externally-defined systems and solutions. This will enable them to respond effectively, in partnership with local actors, to future humanitarian crises.

Notes

1   The HRI team, composed of Valentina Ferrara, Daniela Ruegenberg, and Philip Tamminga visited Bangladesh in February 2008. The opinions expressed here are those of the author and do not necessarily reflect those of DARA.

2   These figures may have under-reported the reality, in part to preserve the public image of the country's caretaker government.

3   Figures originate in the Ministry of Food and Disaster Management, Government of Bangladesh.

4   Bangladesh has consistently ranked at the bottom of Transparency International's Corruption Perception Index. There are high expectations that the caretaker government will address the issue of political corruption, but also a degree of scepticism about how deep reform will go. See for example Rahman (2008) for a critical view of the ability of the caretaker government to institute comprehensive reforms.

5   Data on donor response are from the Government of Bangladesh, Financial Tracking System (FTS) and other sources.

6   For more details on the most recent Appeals for Bangladesh, see www.ifrc.org/where/country/cn6.asp?countryid=27

7   Government of Bangladesh, 2008.

8   Administrative units in Bangladesh.

9   HRI field interviews. See also the Transparency International Bangladesh assessment of NGOs in disaster relief at: http://www.ti-bangladesh.org

10 HRI field interviews.

11 HRI field interviews.

12 HRI field interviews.

13 HRI field interviews.

14 See for example the Oxfam reports at: www.oxfam.org/en/policy/briefingnotes/bn_bangladesh_cyclone_sidr_080214

15 HRI field interviews.

16 For background on the country response to HIV/AIDS in Bangladesh see: www.unaids.org/en/CountryResponses/Countries/bangladesh.asp and for the IASC guidelines see: www.humanitarianinfo.org/iasc/_tools

17 Several NGOs and local media raised this issue. See the special International Women's Day edition of *The Daily Star Weekend Magazine* (2008) which highlights the persistence of gender-based violence and the lack of representation of women in political decision-making bodies in Bangladesh.

18 See for example the UNPD and World Bank websites for more information on longer-term programmes: http://www.un-bd.org/ and http://web.worldbank.org/WBSITE/EXTERNAL/COUNTRIES/SOUTHASIAEXT/0,,contentMDK:21589647~menuPK:2246552~pagePK:2865106~piPK:2865128~theSitePK:223547,00.html

References

Akram, Shahzada M., Mahmud Tanvir, and Iftekharuzzaman. 2007. "Integrity in Humanitarian Assistance: Issues and Benchmarks." Dhaka: Transparency International. 18 December.

Costa, Thomas and Walter Eberlei. 2007. "European Community Aid to Bangladesh." Background paper. CIDSE and Caritas Europe. January. At: http://www.cidse.org/docs/200703201810542840.pdf

Daily Star Weekend Magazine. 2008. Special International Women's Day edition. 7 March. At: http://www.thedailystar.net/magazine/2008/03/01/index.htm

Government of Bangladesh. *Situation Reports.* Disaster Management Bureau. At: http://www.mofdm.gov.bd/

———. 2008. *Cyclone Sidr Early Recovery Action Plan.* Dhaka. February.

International Federation of the Red Cross and Red Crescent Societies. Cyclone Sidr Appeal and Operations Updates. At: www.ifrc.org/where/country/cn6.asp?countryid=27

Khalil, Tasneem. 2008. "Surviving Torture in Bangladesh." *International Herald Tribune.* 3 March.

Muslim Aid Bangladesh Field Office. 2008. Sidr Special Bulletin. Dhaka. January.

Office for the Coordination of Humanitarian Affairs. Financial Tracking Service. At http://www.reliefweb.int/FTS/

Oxfam. 2008. "After the cyclone: Lessons from a disaster." 15 February. At: http://www.oxfam.org/en/policy/briefingnotes/bn_bangladesh_cyclone_sidr_080214

Rahman, Anisur. 2008. "Missing the Opportunity to Free the Royal Bengal Tiger." *Daily Star Forum* 2(4). March.

Relief International. 2007. Cyclone Sidr Rapid Livelihood Needs Assessments. Dhaka. December.

Transparency International Bangladesh. 2006. "Problems of Governance in the NGO Sector: The Way Out." Dhaka.

———. 2007. *"Corruption Perception Index."* 26 February. Dhaka. At: http://www.ti-bangladesh.org

UNDP. Background documents and Sidr reports. At: http://www.un-bd.org/ and http://www.lcgbangladesh.org/derweb/cyclone/index.php

UNICEF. Cyclone Sidr Appeal and Updates. At: http://www.unicef.org/infobycountry/bangladesh_40555.html

WHO. Sidr Health Situation Reports. At: http://www.searo.who.int/en/Section1257/Section2263/Section2341/Section2402.htm

World Bank. Cyclone Sidr reports. At: http://web.worldbank.org/WBSITE/EXTERNAL/COUNTRIES/SOUTHASIAEXT/0,,contentMDK:21589647~menuPK:2246552~pagePK:2865106~piPK:2865128~theSitePK:223547,00.html

World Vision. 2008. Cyclone Sidr Fact Sheet. Dhaka. February.

Central African Republic

AT A GLANCE

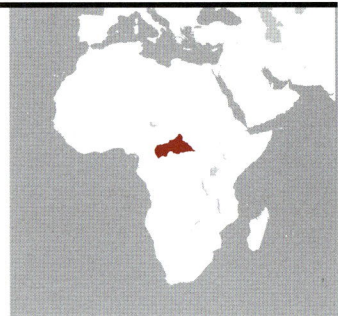

Country data (2006 figures, unless otherwise noted)

- 2007 Human Development Index: ranked 171st of 177 countries
- Population: 4.26 million
- GNI per capita (Atlas method, current US$): US$350
- Population living on less than US$2 a day (1990–2005): 84 percent
- Life expectancy (in years): 44
- Infant mortality rate: 115 per 1,000 live births
- Under five infant mortality rate: 175 per 1,000
- Population undernourished (2002–04): 44 percent
- Population with sustainable access to improved water source: 75 percent*
- Adult literacy rate (over 15yrs of age) (1995–2005): 48.6 percent
- Primary education completion rate (2005): 24 percent
- Gender-related development index (2005): ranked 152nd of 177 countries
- Official development assistance (ODA): US$134 million
- 2007 Corruption Perception Index: ranked 162nd out of 179 countries (TI)

* 26 percent only have access to safe drinking water
Sources: Transparency International, 2007; UNDP, 2007a and 2007b; World Bank, 2008.

The crisis

- New rebel groups attacked large towns to expand control; government troops burned over 100 villages in rebel strongholds, killing hundreds;
- Displaced in the north tripled to 280,000; total of 305,000 across the country, including 20,000 in Cameroon, 50,000 in Chad, and an estimated 210,000 internally displaced;
- 30 percent of children under five in conflict areas suffer chronic malnutrition;
- About one million people affected by widespread insecurity and in need of humanitarian aid;
- Most recent ceasefire signed on 9 May 2008; too early to know if it will lead to real change.

Sources: UNICEF, Human Rights Watch, WFP, UNDP, OCHA.

The humanitarian response

- Despite neglect of crisis, funding and international involvement more than tripled in 2007;
- Humanitarian funding minimal in 2006 (US$25.8 million); 2007 CAP requested US$49.5 million (health sector appealed for one-quarter of funds; FTS reports 2007 funding totalled US$81.1 million;
- ERF received US$5.7 million in 2007 (from Ireland, Norway, Sweden, United Kingdom, Netherlands); 83 percent of 2007 ERF funding channelled through NGOs;
- CERF main source of funding, encouraging organisations to establish presence in the CAR; in 2007, 35 offices established in the country, compared to seven in 2006;
- 2008 CAP requested US$92.6 million (double amount of 2007), to address equivalent level of need;
- Donors agreed in 2008 to establish a pooled fund for CAR;
- Humanitarian response conditioned by lack of awareness of crisis, and logistical and access problems;
- Top five donors: U.S. (US$18.4 million), EC/ECHO (US$10.4 million); UN CERF (US$7 million), Sweden (US$6.8 million); Ireland (US$5.5 million).

Sources: OCHA, UNDP.

Central African Republic
Adversity in a Silent Crisis

SILVIA HIDALGO, Director, DARA

Introduction[1]

The crisis in the Central African Republic (CAR) is practically unknown. In contrast to forgotten emergencies, it has never been in the limelight or received real attention. After more than three decades of misrule, the country remains trapped in a vicious circle of violence and insecurity, increasing poverty, aid dependency, and state failure. The CAR is regarded as a failed or even a "ghost" state with virtually no institutional capacity.[2] State presence outside of the capital is either weak or non-existent. A substantial part of the country is controlled by rebels or at the mercy of bandits. There are urgent humanitarian needs among the population, with new crises emerging regularly and life expectancy falling at a rate of six months every year, mainly due

to lack of adequate sanitation, and the high level of HIV/AIDS and preventable diseases. The UN Human Development Index ranks CAR as the sixth least developed country in the world. Furthermore, in a country of 4 million, over 300,000 people have been displaced, many of whom have fled to hideouts in the bush, where basic means of subsistence are often absent. In all, at least one million persons in the country are in need of humanitarian aid.[3]

The humanitarian response in the CAR has been unique. Despite its neglected crisis status, funding and involvement of international actors more than trebled in 2007. The response was also unusual, with the Central Emergency Response Fund (CERF) acting as a main source of funding, encouraging organizations to establish a presence in CAR.

The crisis: A state of insecurity

A succession of mutinies and rebellions has produced a permanent crisis in which the government has lost its monopoly on violence. Since President Bozizé, backed by Chad, took power in 2003 – the fourth *coup d'état* since the country's independence – his fragile government has been engaged in a low-level war with various rebel groups.[4]

The humanitarian situation deteriorated in 2005 as a result of the insurgency in the north and the brutality of armed gangs, rebels, and government forces. New rebel groups emerged in 2005, attacking major towns and increasing the area under their control. The military responded by attacking rebel strongholds and burning more than 100 villages. Government troops, who often view the local population as rebel sympathizers, have carried out hundreds of illegal killings and burned thousands of homes in the north.[5] There is, in fact, a perpetual state of insecurity, as law and order in the north has collapsed. Gangs of bandits in the north-west, known as *zaraguinas,* spread terror, cause massive displacement (approximately 100,000 people) and kidnap both children and adults for ransom. According to different sources, the bandits come mainly from Chad and, to a lesser extent, Niger. Ethnic rivalry, previously insignificant, is a new element in the conflict which has arisen from political misrule along ethnic lines. The latest ceasefire was signed on 9 May 2008. But it is still too early to know whether the truce will lead to peace and improve people's living conditions.

The result of this political turmoil and security void is a complex humanitarian crisis. Civilian protection and life-saving aid remain the most urgent humanitarian challenges in a situation where the dynamics of displacement are location specific and complex. Although there is a general lack of data on the extent of the crisis and its impact, approximately a quarter of the population, an estimated one million people, is affected by widespread and deteriorating insecurity.

Given the level of insecurity and human rights abuses, particularly in the north – many of which go unreported – the priority is the protection of the civilian population, demanding a stronger international protection presence. For example, in March 2007, 70 percent of houses in Birao – the main town of the Vakaga region near Sudan's Darfur region – were torched, and the town's schools and hospital looted and destroyed. Prior to the recent fighting with the Union of Democratic Forces for Unity (UFDR) rebel group, some 14,000 people lived in Birao. The UN estimated that no more than 600 people remained in the town, the vast majority having fled into the bush. Overall, the number of displaced in the north has tripled to 280,000, reaching a total of 305,000 across the entire country. This includes 20,000 Central Africans who have sought refuge in Cameroon, 50,000 in Chad, and an estimated 210,000 internally displaced.

Those displaced by abuse or attacks by bandits, rebels, and government troops often live in makeshift dwellings in the woods in pitiful conditions, often in desperate need of shelter, food, health care, clothing, blankets, and drinking water. In fact, the UN estimated that in 2007, 74 percent of the population did not have access to safe drinking water.[6] The limited availability of clean water and medical care leads to the prevalence of diseases such as malaria, meningitis, and typhoid.

Those affected by the violence subsist mainly on cassava and wild roots. The conflict disrupts farming and commerce, exacerbating food insecurity. In 2006 an estimated 17,150 children died due to lack of vaccination, proper nutrition, or safe drinking water, while 30 percent of children under five in conflict areas suffer from chronic malnutrition.[7]

Thus, the violence and displacement take place against a backdrop of poverty, underdevelopment, and a lack of services. In fact, over 70 percent of households live below the poverty line and access to basic education and health care is limited and worsening. Life expectancy is declining and (depending on sources) has dropped to 37 or 39 years of age.[8] According to UNICEF, the incidence of HIV/AIDS is above 15 percent and rising. There are already 140,000 HIV/AIDS orphans in the country. At the time of the Humanitarian Response Index mission, a doctor had been recently kidnapped by *zaraguinas* and medical personnel were on strike as a result of insecurity.

The humanitarian response: Why is the crisis neglected?

The crisis in CAR has in the past received limited attention from donors and agencies alike. In 2006, there was minimum humanitarian funding of only US$25.8 million. Aside from Médecins Sans Frontières (MSF) and the International Committee of the Red Cross (ICRC), humanitarian agencies were for the most part absent. In fact, MSF included CAR in its "'Top Ten' Most Underreported Humanitarian Stories" in 2007;[9] the UN High Commissioner for Refugees, António Guterres, has called it "the most neglected crisis in the world;" UNICEF named it "Africa's most forgotten nation;"[10] similarly, Alertnet Factiva ranks CAR as one of the least reported crises.

The crisis in CAR is less visible because of the country's relatively small population and the small number of people who are affected, scattered throughout the north, Chad, Cameroon, and Sudan. As a result, the population in need is dispersed, less visible, and harder to reach than people accommodated in camps. The international neglect can also be explained by the proximity and magnitude of other major crises, such as those in the Democratic Republic of the Congo, and, more recently, in Chad and Darfur. Ironically, however, the presence of Sudanese refugees in the border region of Vakaga has attracted attention to CAR.

CAR lacks a champion on the international scene, such as the UK for Zimbabwe, the United States for Liberia, or Belgium for the DRC. France, the former colonial power, has a long list of more populated and troubled former colonies in which it has greater vested interests. Complicating matters, reports on the CAR are generally in French and are less accessible to the wider stakeholder community. In fact, their translation as of 2006 into English has been a key factor in raising awareness of the crisis. Lastly, the country itself is landlocked and physically isolated from the rest of the world.

Thus, the humanitarian response in CAR has been conditioned by lack of awareness of the crisis, limited international involvement, and logistical and access problems. The response has been partial and incomplete, as a result of insufficient funding and limited agency presence. Despite recognising the existence of needs in CAR, certain international NGOs, such as Oxfam and CARE, have been unable to establish operations in the country because of their limited capacity to effectively and efficiently reach the disparately located population in need, and because of the high costs associated with programme implementation and aid delivery.[11] It is in such contexts as that of CAR, with high-cost, chronic emergencies, that NGOs face significant problems in both conceiving viable programmes and addressing humanitarian needs.

The level of need and lack of development in the country poses further challenges in terms of defining areas, common standards, and criteria for intervention.

For example, agencies involved in water and sanitation activities admitted that, at times, they simply did not know where to begin.[12]

Determining need: Limited coverage and capacity vs. pervasive need

In addition to funding difficulties, there are important practical and logistical barriers to the implementation of effective, timely, and appropriate humanitarian relief in CAR. Given the context of widespread poverty and the dearth of services, compounded by the limited previous presence of humanitarian agencies, relief workers claim they have difficulty knowing where to begin. Because looting and displacement have disrupted agricultural production – now desperately low – food is a key sector in need, despite the country's agricultural potential. Houses and fields have been burned, and animals and assets often stolen.

In other areas, it is estimated that bush schools are required for 75,000 displaced children. Access to safe water was even more problematic because of displacement and insecurity; in fact, across the entire country, only 26 percent of the population has access to safe drinking water.[13] One clear success, however, has been increased protection by the presence of international actors in the country. Thanks to enhanced advocacy and the impact of reports by Human Rights Watch in advance of the September 2007 donor's conference, suffering and abuse no longer escape the attention of the international community. Overall, the protection cluster was considered by many observers "deficient but improving."[14]

However, just reaching survivors of the crisis is complex and expensive. The Central African Republic is landlocked, with poor infrastructure. Its principal river is only navigable six to seven months of the year and during the rainy season the north-east region of the country is difficult to access. As the UN Humanitarian Coordinator explained, "it is difficult to get stuff into the country. It is almost impossible to buy things in the country and it is very hard to move things from one part of the country to another. And costs are rising. At one stage, in 2006, there was only one truck available for the north-west of the country."[15] At the time of the HRI mission, there was no cement in the country and, as a result, organizations were experiencing great difficulty in carrying out water and sanitation programmes. Advocacy work is also difficult because most communities are isolated and the majority of families do not have even a radio.

As mentioned earlier, aid delivery is complicated by the fact that the displaced are not accommodated in camps, but are scattered throughout the north and are difficult to find and reach. In the words of the UN Humanitarian Coordinator, "you can distribute aid to three people and then have to drive 50 minutes to reach five more people."[16] As a result, beneficiaries often end up receiving only one form of assistance, which makes for a less than comprehensive response. For example, in some areas people were receiving exclusively food aid and lacked the most basic non-food items, such as shelter, access to basic health services, and primary education, while in others, food aid was absent, but sanitation services were provided. On the positive side, the absence of IDP camps in a conflict setting avoids other problems, such as increased dependency and the undermining of the capacity and way of life of the survivors. Similarly, the HRI mission found that in the areas where IDPs were accommodated near settlements, there was no resentment on the part of the local population, many of whom often tried to assist the displaced.

In this difficult context, agencies whose resources are already overstretched have trouble responding to new episodes of displacement, and there are many areas where needs are not met due to a lack of presence, capacity and resources. While the cluster approach plays an important role in defining priorities within different sectors, needs assessments are few and far between in CAR. Most assessments are done quickly and do not provide a comprehensive analysis – although donors generally respond to assessments despite their flaws.[17]

One such flaw is the lack of involvement of beneficiaries in defining their needs and the most appropriate response. Those interviewed stressed that beneficiary involvement at an early stage would be more likely to guarantee that the right aid was provided, but that it would *not* guarantee that those most in need would receive assistance. In fact, the concept of beneficiary participation in needs assessments was considered inappropriate and not applicable in the context of CAR.

Therefore, tools such as the Good Enough Guide[18] and the SPHERE Standards[19] were not appropriate reference points for many agencies in CAR.

Donor response: Scaling up the international response

The international response to CAR has been limited and not proportionate to existing needs. In a country largely unknown to the world with only 4 million inhabitants, aid agencies claim it is difficult to obtain funding for either development or humanitarian aid activities. However, the funding for 2007 was equal to that received for the four preceding years. For 2007, NGOs and UN agencies participating in the UN Consolidated Appeals Process (CAP) requested US$49.5 million to carry out 59 projects, with the health sector appealing for the largest amount – over one quarter of the funds. In fact, according to the UN Office for the Coordination of Humanitarian Assistance Financial Tracking System (OCHA FTS), total humanitarian aid for CAR in 2007 amounted to US$81.1 million, compared to US$25.8 million the previous year. In 2007, the largest sources of funds were: the United States, with US$18.4 million (22.6 percent of total funding); ECHO with US$10.4 million (12.8 percent); the UN Central Emergency Response Fund (CERF), with US$7 million (8.6 percent); Sweden with US$6.8 million (8.3 percent); and Ireland with US$5.5 million (6.8 percent).[20] The 2008 CAP appealed for US$92.6 million, nearly twice the amount of the preceding year, to address what is considered to be an equivalent level of need.

In fact, although funding was very low in 2006, UN agencies and NGOs received more money than in the previous three years combined. 2007, therefore, marked a sea-change in the level of the humanitarian response in CAR, representing a significant leap in a developing trend. Significantly, in 2007, following an increase in funding and awareness of the crisis in CAR in the international community, 35 offices of humanitarian actors were established in the country, compared to only seven one year earlier.

The critical role played by organisations such as MSF and the ICRC, both of which engage in advocacy for both international attention and funding and are not frightened by beneficiary cost and resource-capacity issues, cannot be underestimated. As in many other crises, and as highlighted in the February 2008 Montreux VIII Retreat, there is a need for "strong well-trained, competent leadership of the humanitarian system at the country level."[21]

These changes in the humanitarian response to CAR raise a number of questions about how much this neglect results from insufficient donor funding, insufficient demand by agencies, or the lack of a concentrated significant number of beneficiaries. Low-level needs and piecemeal interventions do not help to generate the establishment of NGO country programmes or funding interventions. In turn, the limited engagement by humanitarian actors and a lack of donor presence in the field fails to generate a significant response. Therefore, although donors have been criticised for their lack of funding, just how much demand, or, more importantly, humanitarian response capacity, has actually existed? MSF, a main advocate and provider of humanitarian aid in CAR, has not been a source of demand, as it shies away from government funding in order to preserve its independence. Major NGOs such as Oxfam, CARE, and World Vision are not present in CAR, while the UN only scaled up its presence in 2006. Donor engagement in CAR has been mainly the product of increased UN leadership, although NGOs generally still provide the bulk of front-line humanitarian assistance.

There are four types of bilateral humanitarian aid donors in the CAR: (i) the largest donors, which visit the field to discuss programmes, such as the United States, the European Commission, and Sweden; (ii) the committed donors which fund at a distance, such as Ireland, Japan, the Netherlands, Canada, and Finland; (iii) the absent donors who have yet to register CAR on their radar screen; and (iv) France.

The donors most engaged in programming discussions in the field were the United States, EC/ECHO, France, and Sweden. In this respect the US Office of Foreign Disaster Assistance (OFDA), the European Commission's Directorate General for Humanitarian Aid (ECHO), and the UK Department for International Development (DFID) – despite its limited funding in CAR – are considered to have the highest technical expertise. However, the OFDA guidelines were perceived as more technical and burdensome. ECHO was considered slow in processing proposals, weak in supporting coordination – as they have no presence in the clusters – and late in providing funding to CAR. Nevertheless, ECHO is seen as the donor that most insists on adherence to good practice. At the time of the HRI mission, it was announced that ECHO would establish a permanent presence in the capital Bangui. In contrast, the US covered CAR with personnel based in the Democratic Republic of the Congo. Finally, Sweden was regarded as the donor that cared the most about beneficiary involvement (GHD Principle 6), and Ireland as the donor that most supported protection and proved most predictable and timely in its funding.[22]

Given the general neglect of this crisis, it is hardly surprising that some donors do not contribute funds to CAR, or that they provide very limited amounts. In this respect, Denmark was especially singled out, with mention also of the UK and, to some extent, Norway.[23] China, however, has a visible presence – as it does in other parts of Africa – although its aid is limited to the development sector.

France, and to a less extent the US, are regarded as donors that have political and economic interests in CAR, while other donors were seen to be either completely or largely impartial.[24] In view of its lead presence and role in the European Union Force (EUFOR),[25] France is also regarded as having military interests and allied to a specific side in the political conflict. The presence of France plays a key role in ensuring some level of access both within and into CAR, because of its troop presence at the airports of Kaga Bandoro and Birao. France has also indirectly contributed to increased security and access to certain areas in the north, with the main rebel group accepting French presence in December 2007. Paradoxically, France was said by implementing agencies to be poor in respecting human rights, and specific mention was made of the killing of civilians by a French helicopter in December 2006 in N'dele. In contrast, France has publicly advocated in favour of human rights. President Sarkozy met with Human Rights Watch and pressured the CAR government to control their military and presidential guard. Finally, although France funds major UN agencies such as the World Food Programme (WFP), it is perceived as being partial to funding of French organizations.

The fact that other countries have no diplomatic representation in CAR has increased the perceived influence of France, which also permanently holds the EU representation responsibilities in CAR, because there are no other EU ambassadors. The overall volume of French aid to CAR amounted to €75 million between 2003 and 2006 – actually, €95 million, if support for the Economic and Monetary Community of the Central African States (CEMAC) peacekeeping force is included – and while these sums are modest in absolute terms, they are significant for CAR.[26] According to OCHA FTS data for 2007, France has contributed US$4.3 million to CAR in humanitarian aid.

Increasing response: Good practice within the limits of current humanitarian aid reform

The array of challenges facing humanitarian actors in CAR has meant that the response is in many ways unique. There is close collaboration among aid implementing agencies and many instances of good practice. Ensuring partnerships between UN agencies and NGOs requires constant effort, sustained by the work of both OCHA and the Humanitarian Coordinator. The Humanitarian and Development Partnership Team (HDPT), managed by OCHA, brings together all humanitarian and development organizations as a new form of the Inter-Agency Standing Committee (IASC) country working group. The HDPT website was set up to explain the humanitarian and development crisis in CAR to a wider audience and as a means of encouraging debate and information exchange.[27] Coordination has also been strengthened by the establishment of clusters and the Emergency Response Fund (ERF). But since coverage is low, clusters do not function beyond Bangui.

The use of the CERF has also been innovative as, in addition to helping kick start operations, it has been used strategically to create a demand and expand the coverage of UN agencies and operations into the field and into areas affected by insecurity.[28] However, this use of CERF funds may not be the most efficient, since funds must be channelled through UN agencies, incurring high administrative and transaction costs. This illustrates the rigidities of the CERF funding mechanism, despite this being part of the UN reform initiative. In 2007, the ERF was introduced to help NGOs establish offices and to respond to breaking emergencies, with the clusters used to decide which projects should be funded. In 2007, ERF received US$5.7 million and was funded by Ireland, Norway, Sweden, the UK, and the Netherlands. NGOs received 83 percent of ERF funding in 2007. By the end of that year, ERF was empty, except for US$150,000, kept in reserve and eventually used to respond to a meningitis outbreak in Kaga Bandoro in January 2008. For 2008, US$5.6 million has been pledged by Ireland, Sweden, and the United Kingdom. Donors have also agreed to establish a pooled fund in 2008, reflecting the trust they have in the current system, and because it is an attractive funding mechanism for those without an embassy or presence in the country. France, in contrast, prefers to fund through direct mechanisms, giving greater visibility to its funding.

The Coordinated Aid Programme (CAP)[29] for CAR was established not only as an appeal process, but as a tool to plan, implement, coordinate, and monitor HPDT activities.[30] The CAP was a collective effort with all heads of UN agencies, NGOs, and the ICRC participating for three days in its design. Lack of prioritisation within Consolidated Appeals Processes has been a major problem in the past, as they offer donors limited guidance on where funds are most needed. For the CAR CAP, six criteria were used to prioritise projects: relevance to key needs and strategic priorities, location, timing, the extent to which a project supports humanitarian action, gender, and capacity-building. However, as needs assessments and response capacity are still not up to par compared with other crises with a stronger international presence, the CAP is not regarded by certain agencies as providing clear direction on how to respond to needs throughout the year. There are also incomplete needs assessments and clear differences in agency capacity. Furthermore, coverage is still incomplete, with the population scattered and new episodes of violence creating new needs. Nevertheless, monitoring the funding of the 2008 CAP should prove of interest to determine how donors react to prioritisation, and if prioritised projects are immediately funded.

Finally, there has been stronger leadership by the Humanitarian Coordinator, along with a call for greater transparency. This, together with the need for increased prioritisation and needs-based approaches, has facilitated a different way of working. UN documentation out of Bangui openly recognises the existing shortcomings and lessons learned, key to future improvement.

While 2007 for many implementing agencies was seen as a start-up year, the objective for 2008 is to consolidate, build on progress, and maintain the presence established, in order to stand by people struck by crisis and meet their priority needs.

Conclusion

Limited international presence to date has not created many opportunities for evaluating the humanitarian response in the Central African Republic. However, both the response, and the lack of it, deserve the humanitarian community's attention.

Despite its natural resources, life expectancy is below 43 years in CAR and the country's statistics are among the worst on the planet, with frequent epidemics – even gangrene – causing many preventable deaths. Years of unstable government has left the economy and services such as health care in shambles. How is it possible that both a country and a crisis have been largely ignored by the UN, donors, and many NGOs alike? Whose role is it to draw attention to the plight of survivors of the crisis in CAR? Does the system enable donors to be present in such places as CAR, when even NGOs such as Oxfam, CARE, or World Vision face resource and capacity constraints in establishing operations?

Since logistics are the number one challenge, costs are high and interventions are difficult. Paradoxically, while aid agencies claim it is difficult to obtain funding from donors, CAPs have been relatively well funded. Therefore, the situation in CAR also highlights the gaps between existing needs, CAPs, and capacity. How can the CAP for 2006 have been so much lower than that of 2007, despite similar or even higher levels of need? Why were only a handful of agencies present in 2006? How can donors ensure that there is an appropriate humanitarian response in crises such as CAR is experiencing? On the other hand, given the scale of pressing needs elsewhere – such as the Democratic Republic of the Congo – to what extent is the growing response to the crisis in CAR driven by its visibility as a country-based CAP and response? Lessons must be learned from this predicament. An analysis of the causes, consequences, and response should be drawn from the crisis in CAR, in order to improve future humanitarian performance.

The May 2008, the peace deal signed between the CAR government and the main rebel groups brought increased hope for the future, but it has not ended the present humanitarian crisis. Indeed, donors and implementing agencies must not close their offices nor divert their attention, but instead must continue to search for more appropriate and effective ways to help those in desperate need in a neglected country and a failed state.

The Humanitarian Response Index 2008

Notes

1   The HRI team, composed of Silvia Hidalgo, Carlos Oliver, and Soledad Posada, visited the Central African Republic in March 2008. The HRI team expresses its gratitude to all those interviewed in CAR. The opinions expressed here are those of the author and do not necessarily reflect those of DARA.

2   International Crisis Group, 2007.

3   OCHA, 2006.

4   President Bozizé was later elected in May 2005 in largely free and fair elections.

5   Human Rights Watch, 2007.

6   OCHA, 2007.

7   OCHA, 2006.

8   World Food Programme, 2006 and World Bank, 2007.

9   MSF, 2007.

10 UNICEF, 2007.

11 HRI field and headquarters interviews, March 2008.

12 HRI field interview, March 2008.

13 OCHA, 2007.

14 HRI field interview, March 2008.

15 HRI field interview, March 2008.

16 HRI field interview, March 2008.

17 This was emphasized in relation to the assessment done by the World Food Programme (WFP) and the UN Food and Agriculture Organization (FAO) which, despite its limited nature, prompted a funding response on the part of donors.

18 See OXFAM, 2007.

19 SPHERE Project, 2004.

20 All figures from OCHA Financial Tracking System, dated June 30 2008.

21 International Council of Voluntary Agencies, 2008.

22 HRI field interview, March 2008.

23 HRI field interview, March 2008.

24 HRI field interview, March 2008.

25 Under a UN Security Council resolution, the 3,700-strong EUFOR is charged with protecting refugee camps, while the smaller UN Mission in the Central African Republic (MINURCAT) focuses on training police and advising authorities on human rights and security threats. EUFOR Chad/Central African Republic will remain in Chad and CAR until March 2009.

26 International Crisis Group, 2007.

27 HDPT Central African Republic, 2008.

28 The CERF was the second most important mechanism for donor funding in CAR in 2007.

29 While CAP officially stands for Consolidated Appeal or Consolidated Appeals Process, in CAR the equivalent is referred to as the Coordinated Aid Programme.

30 The 2008 CAP includes three strategic priorities: enhancing the protection of those affected by the conflict, particularly in the north; providing life-saving assistance; supporting improvement of the link between relief and recovery activities.

References

Amnesty International. 2007. "Central African Republic: Civilians in peril in the wild north." 19 September. AFR 19/003/2007.

HDPT Central African Republic. 2008. "News Bulletin 69." (14–21 July). Blog at: http://hdptcar.net/

Human Rights Watch. 2007. "State of Anarchy: Rebellion and Abuses against Civilians." 14 September. Volume 19, No.14(A).

———. 2008. "Central African Republic: Chadian Army Attacks, Burns Border Villages." 19 March.

International Council of Voluntary Agencies. 2008. *Montreux VIII, Retreat on the Consolidated Appeal Process and Humanitarian Financial Mechanisms.* Convenors' Conclusions. 21–22 February. Unpublished.

International Crisis Group. 2007. "République Centrafricaine: Anatomie d'un État fantôme.» 13 December.

Médecins Sans Frontières. 2007. "MSF Releases Tenth Annual 'Top Ten' most Underreported Humanitarian Stories 2007." At: http://www.msf.org/msfinternation-al/invoke.cfm?objectid=F77D789B-15C5-F00A-25E9EE3D5D3ED448&component=toolkit.pressrelease&method=full_html

Office for the Coordination of Humanitarian Affairs (OCHA). 2006. *Consolidated Appeals Process (CAP): Appeal 2007 for Central African Republic.* 30 November.

———. 2007. *Consolidated Appeals Process (CAP): Appeal 2008 for Central African Republic.* 10 December.

OXFAM. 2007. *Impact Measurement and Accountability in Emergencies: The Good Enough Guide.* Oxford: OXFAM Publishing.

SPHERE Project. 2004 (rev.) *SPHERE Humanitarian Charter and Minimum Standards in Disaster Response.* Geneva. At: http://www.sphereproject.org/content/view/27/84/lang,English/

UN News Service. 2008. "Armed bandits force tens of thousands of Central Africans to flee homes." 23 May.

UNICEF. 2007. *Humanitarian Action Report 2007.* At: http://www.unicef.org/har07/index_37588.htm

World Bank. 2007. *Central African Republic at a Glance.* At: http://devdata.worldbank.org/AAG/caf_aag.pdf.

World Food Programme. 2006. *Projected 2007 Needs for WFP Projects and Operations. Central African Republic.* At: http://www.wfp.org/appeals/Projected_needs/documents/by_countries/140.pdf

Chad

AT A GLANCE

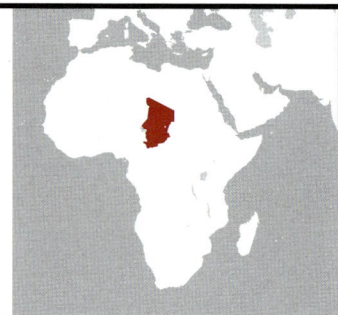

Country data *(2006 figures, unless otherwise noted)*

- 2007 Human Development Index: ranked 170th of 177 countries
- Population: 10.47
- GNI per capita (Atlas method, current US$): US$450
- Population living on less than US$2 a day (1990–2004): NA
- Life expectancy (in years): 51
- Infant mortality rate: 124 per 1,000 live births
- Under five infant mortality rate: 209 per 1,000
- Population undernourished (2002–2004): 35 percent
- Population with sustainable access to improved water source (2004): 42 percent
- Adult literacy rate (over 15 yrs of age) (1995–2005): 25.7 percent
- Primary education completion rate: 31 percent
- Gender-related development index (2005): ranked 151st of 177 countries
- Official development assistance (ODA): US$284 million
- 2007 Corruption Perception Index: ranked 172nd out of 179 countries

Sources: Transparency International (TI); 2007; UNDP, 2007a and 2007b; World Bank, 2008.

The crisis

- 2002–2003 initial wave of refugees arriving in south and east Chad faced high mortality and malnutrition; over 250,000 refugees in eastern Chad and 50,000 in the south; 180,000 IDPs across east and south-east; an additional 50,000 Chadian refugees in Sudan and 12,000 in Cameroon;
- Refugees comprise around 22 percent of the population in impoverished east; host population's access to water, health services, and education inadequate; refugee presence and relief operations caused higher commodity prices, somewhat counterbalanced by increased employment opportunities;
- Increasing militarisation of communities and ongoing military recruitment in IDP sites added to overall deterioration of security;
- New waves of refugees arrived in 2008, including at least 12,000 in eastern Chad, resulting from instability after failed coup in N'Djamena;
- Global Acute Malnutrition rate of the refugee population decreased from 36–39 percent in 2004 to 9 percent in the east in 2006.

Sources: Inter Agency Health Evaluation; UNICEF; Human Rights Watch.

The humanitarian response

- The initial 2007 CAP requested US$170 million, followed by appeal for additional US$102 million; 99 percent of Appeal funded, with 84 percent from DAC donors;
- Additional funding provided outside the CAP, especially through ICRC, for total of US$308 million in 2007;
- With US$81 million funding in 2007, UNHCR contracts implementing agencies; received funds from 22 donors (19 DAC, CERF, South Africa, and Vatican); contributions directed mainly to east Chad;
- US largest donor, providing over US$133 million, US$80 million for food aid; ECHO gave US$39.8 million; UK, Germany, and Ireland each provided less than 3.5 percent of total humanitarian funds.

Source: OCHA.

Chad
Internal Power Struggles and Regional Humanitarian Crisis

RICARDO SOLÉ-ARQUÉS, Independent Consultant, Development and Humanitarian Aid

Introduction[1]

The Republic of Chad, twice the size of France, with 10 million inhabitants, is among the poorest countries in the world, ranking 170th out of 177 countries in the Human Development Index.[2] Like other countries in the Sahel, it is affected by a chronic, multidimensional, structural conflict, characterized by political instability, the collapse of traditional conflict-resolution mechanisms, the emergence of armed groups, and trans-border involvement of neighbouring conflicts, with many of the hallmarks of a complex emergency.

Regional and localised conflicts have triggered significant humanitarian consequences since 2003, when large numbers of people fleeing the internal conflicts in Sudan's Darfur region and in the Central African

Republic (CAR) sought refuge in Chad. Since then, the humanitarian crisis has worsened, particularly in 2006 and 2007, when a large number of internally displaced persons (IDPs) joined the already large number of refugees in Chad. Despite the difficulties created by the new humanitarian needs of the displaced and continuing problems of humanitarian access due to insecurity and logistical challenges, donors have been generous. Nevertheless, the humanitarian response has been patchy, with shortcomings in coordination and inadequate linking of relief with development efforts.

The nature of the crisis: From an internal political problem to a regional humanitarian emergency

After becoming independent from France in 1960, Chad suffered a series of civil wars and successive coups, partly reflecting competition between ethnic groups and divisions between north and south. Libya eventually invaded, but was expelled when Hissein Habré came to power, with support from France and the African Union Organisation. More than 40,000 people disappeared or were reported killed under Hissein Habré's dictatorial regime between 1982 and 1990.[3] With the support of France, Habré was deposed by the current President and former General, Idris Déby, and multi-party politics and a new constitution were introduced. Since then, President Déby has won three elections, all apparently flawed, and has resisted a number of attempts to overthrow him by force.

Since 2003, the country has been engulfed in a conflict with regional ramifications, driven not only by long-standing competition between the predominantly Arab north and the sub-Saharan African south, between nomadic herders and sedentary farmers, and between Anglophone or Francophone post-colonial models, but also between regional influences of Western (the United States and France) and emerging powers (China and Iran).[4]

The competition for water and access to grazing land between nomadic herders and sedentary farmers has shaped social and economic relations and has been a traditional cause of conflict. Furthermore, oil resources have been exploited commercially since 2003. Oil revenues are likely to add another layer of complexity to the conflict, rather than contributing to socio-economic development. The so called "resource curse," where natural resources drive conflict and corruption, seems applicable to Chad.[5]

The instability of the situation is enhanced by the weak legitimacy of the Chadian government and the democratic immaturity of the country. This context fosters opposition groups based on clan and ethnicity, who resort to violence rather than seeking democratic alternatives. The conflict is exacerbated by the state's lack of effective control of large areas of the country, especially in the east and the south-east. In these areas, numerous armed groups not only fight each other, but attack the local civilian population. The resulting insecurity and climate of impunity allows for widespread violations of international humanitarian law (IHL) and human rights, as well as seriously impinging on the delivery of humanitarian aid.

The Darfur crisis, the political situation in the Central African Republic (CAR) and instability in Chad are all closely interlinked, increasingly so since 2002. The 2002 coup in CAR triggered the first wave of refugees to Chad. Since then, the trans-border nature and movement of armed groups continue to fuel insecurity in northern CAR, while in eastern Chad the situation deteriorated after the first influx of refugees from Darfur in 2003. In fact, the Sudan and Chad governments accuse each other of supporting opposition groups and armed militias in the other country. Reflecting this, the attack on Chad's capital N'Djamena in February 2008 was carried out by rebels based in, and supplied from, Darfur. The ensuing government repression resulted in the destruction of hundreds of homes in N'Djamena and the flight of 18,000 refugees to Cameroon.[6] The subsequent rebel retreat triggered clashes between Chadian factions in Darfur and a new wave of refugees (at least 12,000) to eastern Chad.

Following the regional escalation of the crisis, the 2007 UN Security Council, in its Resolution 1778, recommended the establishment of a multidimensional force, located in both Chad and CAR "to address the humanitarian situation in the two countries and to stem the spill-over from Sudan's Darfur conflict."[7] This led to the establishment of the United Nations Mission in the Central African Republic (MINURCAT), with 300 police and 50 military liaison officers, and the European Force (EUFOR), a 4,000-strong (predominantly French) European military and police force, mandated to protect civilians and humanitarian operations. These missions face issues of coordination and a confusion of mandates, in particular given French support to the Chadian government, which could jeopardise the mission's neutrality. Similarly, EUFOR's logo – the European flag – is the same as that of ECHO-funded NGO projects. Finally, in the opinion of many observers, MINURCAT and EUFOR forces are poorly equipped and not mandated to deal with the banditry and lightly armed rebel groups in their assigned areas, rendering the military presence ineffective in protecting civilians and humanitarian staff.

The humanitarian impact of the crisis:
High vulnerability, scarce resources and breaches of protection – protracted crisis vs. acute IDP emergency

The initial wave of refugees arriving in 2002 in the south of Chad, and in 2003 in the east, faced a critical situation, with high mortality and malnutrition rates. Currently, more than 250,000 refugees live in eastern Chad and 50,000 in the south, with around 180,000 IDPs across the east and south-east. There are an additional 50,000 Chadian refugees in Sudan and 12,000 in Cameroon.

In 2007, the refugees in the east (principally from Darfur) were gathered in 12 camps, while those in the south, hosted in four sites, were primarily from the Central African Republic. New arrivals are normally placed in existing sites, in some cases stretching the available capacity. However, in terms of humanitarian standards and delivery of basic services, the situation in the camps was judged to be acceptable. In general, this was also the case for the IDP sites, although these faced a more volatile situation, including occasional raids by armed groups.

Until 2006, the crisis was seen primarily as spillover from the Darfur conflict, and the response was predominantly oriented towards the refugees. The distant possibility of the refugees' return set the conditions for a protracted crisis. Therefore, the humanitarian response was focussed on a stable caseload (number of refugees) with specific needs, as well as on support to local communities and early recovery strategies. However, the situation changed when rebels directly threatened the capital and the Chadian government in April 2006, and government forces retreated from large areas in the east. This created a power vacuum in the region which led to factional and inter-ethnic violence and incursions from Darfur-based armed groups, triggering the displacement of more than 140,000 people between late 2006 and mid 2007. The increasing militarisation of communities and ongoing military recruitment in IDP sites – including of children – has added to the overall deterioration of the security situation. New waves of refugees arrived in 2008, including at least 12,000 in eastern Chad, as a consequence of the instability created after the failed coup in N'Djamena.[8]

In terms of the number of refugees, the spillover of the CAR crisis into the south of Chad has been less significant than the one in Darfur to the east, and the challenges not as complex, strategically, logistically or financially. Greater ethnic homogeneity, the absence of

significant numbers of displaced people, as well as a better security situation and access to land, explain the better outlook in the south. Moreover, access to the sites in the south has always been easier for humanitarian actors. But even in the south, an additional 8,000 refugees from CAR joined the existing 40,000 in 2008, further destabilising the situation. And despite decreasing aid dependency and improved livelihood prospects, the roots of the conflict and the lack of security in northern CAR remain unchanged.

Chad is already a poor country and the east in particular faces extreme poverty and scarcity of resources. For this reason, the impact of the refugees and displaced on local resources cannot be ignored. Refugees already represent around 22 percent of the population in the east. In fact, access to health services, education, and water and sanitation are often better in the refugee camps than in the surrounding local communities. The level of Global Acute Malnutrition (GAM) in the refugee population decreased from 36–39 percent[9] in 2004 to 9 percent in the east in 2006.[10] In contrast, the GAM in the host population has been estimated at 36–39 percent. The presence of refugees and relief operations has also resulted in a rise in commodity prices, although this is partially compensated for by an increase in employment opportunities. Tensions between host communities and the refugees have been reported, but seem to have subsided after the proactive policy of humanitarian agencies of assisting host communities through aid programmes.[11]

Insecurity is widespread in eastern Chad, affecting access to the affected population and the delivery of humanitarian aid. Aid agencies and relief workers have been and still are the subject of attacks and robberies; tragically, for example, Pascal Marlinge, head of mission of the Save the Children Fund, was killed only two days after the HRI team interviewed him in Abeche.

Some reports suggest that specific communities receive less humanitarian assistance because their political alignment and ethnicity make access to them more risky, so that they are sometimes deliberately ignored by the Chadian authorities.[12] However, it is commonly accepted that a certain level of protection can be granted inside the refugee sites, although this entails a considerable investment by aid agencies. The situation *outside* the camps is judged precarious.

Logistical difficulties created further complications, as road transport in the country is limited to six months a year. The rainy season, from May/June to October, renders the roads impassable throughout the country, and limits the movements of both humanitarian actors and warring factions alike. For the latter, these months are used for rearming and building up new alliances, while humanitarians must store up enough supplies before the rains begin.

The donor response to the crisis: Unmatched generosity

The response to the request for humanitarian funds for Chad has been quite generous. In 2006, 80 percent of the required US$193 million for the UN Consolidated Appeal Process (CAP) was collected, in addition to the US$31 million contributed outside the Appeal.[13] The new situation in 2006–2007 increased needs – mainly the result of additional numbers of IDPs. These were addressed through supplementary CAPs in 2007 in February, April, and July, requesting an additional US$102 million, beyond the initial US$170 million. This multi-appeal process was not always clear, as sector breakdown was not consistent from one document to the other and duplications occurred – although these were eventually corrected. Nevertheless, 99 percent of the CAP was funded in 2007, with 84 percent of the funds coming from OECD/DAC donors.[14] Additional significant funding was provided outside the UN Appeal[15] to the Red Cross Red Crescent Movement, especially the ICRC, as had occurred in previous years. Overall, 19 OECD/DAC donors provided humanitarian funds in 2007: the US, EC/ECHO, the UK, the Netherlands, Japan, Canada, Germany, Sweden, France, Finland, Norway, Ireland, Switzerland, Italy, Denmark, Spain, Luxembourg, Belgium, and Austria.[16] In total, over US$308 million of humanitarian aid was provided in 2007.

The allocation of aid per beneficiary in Chad is the second highest in the world. With CAP requirements of around US$377 per beneficiary, this is slightly less than the CAP requirements for the Democratic Republic of the Congo (US$393), but higher than those for Sudan (US$221).[17] High per capita allocations in Chad are probably related to the logistics involved in the delivery of humanitarian aid, the extra costs associated with the poor security, and the relatively small case load.

The US was by far the largest donor in 2007, providing more than US$133 million (43.3 percent of total humanitarian funding), of which more than US$80 million was for food aid. The US adopted a regional approach, linking the response to the crisis in Chad financially and operationally to the response to the

Darfur conflict. However, these funds are not reflected in the figure reported for Chad in the Financial Tracking Service (FTS). For the fiscal year 2007/2008, the U.S. contributed US$1.196 billion to Sudan and eastern Chad.[18] The lion's share of these funds (US$853 million) went for food aid, but logistical support for aid operations, such as air services and telecommunications, was also funded. It should also be noted that US funding was explicitly earmarked for IDPs and refugees from the CAR. Additional investments related to Quick Impact Projects and poverty reduction interventions in targeted communities are also not accounted for by the FTS. The United States has regional strategic interests which go beyond humanitarian action, most notably because the Sahel has been described as a breeding ground for radical Islamism.

In 2007, EC/ECHO provided US$39.8 million (12.9 percent of total humanitarian aid), of which US$9.4 million was spent for food aid, with UNHCR receiving US$8.1 million and US$800,000 for eastern and southern Chad, respectively. The next largest donors were the UK, Germany and Ireland, each contributing less than 3.5 percent of the total humanitarian funds.

France's contribution to humanitarian aid in 2007 was modest (US$5.5 million to the CAP), of which US$1.8 million was for food aid and US$1.5 million for UNHCR, including assistance to IDPs. France also earmarked an additional US$1.1 million for bilateral aid to the government of Chad to provide assistance to IDPs and purchase commodities, in line with GHD Principle 8, which calls for donors to support local capacity to respond to crises.

In 2008, France committed €10 million to the Stabilisation Programme, intended to support the return of displaced people. However, this programme has raised concerns among the humanitarian community, as it risks encouraging IDPs to return before security conditions are stable. French officials, however, assured the HRI mission of their firm commitment to respect for The Guiding Principles on Internal Displacement,[19] as called for in the GHD *Principles*.

As the former colonial power, France has significant influence in Chad, as well as strategic interests in the region. In fact, its backing for the current government has been explicit throughout the crisis, including bilateral aid and technical assistance, as well as military and logistic support. France is also the EU diplomatic representative to the government in N'Djamena. France also pushed for the deployment of MINURCAT and EUFOR and is the principal financial and troop contributor to EUFOR. During the HRI mission, implementing agencies raised concerns over the role of France, and whether its vested interests compromise the extent to which it honours the GHD *Principles*. However, many agencies believed that the principles of impartiality, neutrality and independence were largely being respected.

Implementation of the humanitarian response: Multi-sector assistance and pending cluster coordination

The response to the crisis by humanitarian agencies has been determined by the logistic difficulties involved, insecurity in the east, agency access to funds, and weak coordination mechanisms.

Since the start of the crisis in 2003, the main player in the humanitarian response has been UNHCR, which received US$81 million in 2007 from 22 donors (19 OECD/DAC plus CERF, South Africa, and the Vatican). The UN agency is responsible for camp management and protection, and has provided aid both directly, and as a contractor of implementing agencies. The financial contributions were focused mainly on eastern Chad (US$45.8 million), while southern Chad received US$2.9 million, with a further US$8.4 million for IDPs. Additionally, an unspecified US$12.5 million was allocated, allowing UNHCR to direct them according to need. The World Food Programme – the largest operation in terms of funds and logistics – received US$139 million in 2007. Other UN agencies, such as UNICEF (US$15 million) and WHO (US$2.7 million) also had specific areas of intervention alongside NGO partners. Reflecting the difference in refugee numbers and the level of need, as well as larger logistical difficulties, more funds are directed towards the east than to the south of the country. Access to arable land and better livelihood conditions also help explain the lower allocation of resources to the south.

Donor support to multi-sector needs and food aid illustrates how they perceive the crisis and its response. The donor response may reflect the approach of the UNHCR, which is based on integrated multi-sector interventions, including protection. This contrasts with the cluster approach, where an agency is designated as the lead for a specific sector, with the presumed aim of improving quality and accountability for programming in that sector. The lack of consistency in sector breakdown among the different Appeals is also probably a contributing factor in keeping donors away from funding by sector. Multi-sector funding accounted for US$90.1 million (33 percent of total funding), while food aid accounted for US$128.4 million (47 percent), and coordination and support services for US$19 million (6.9 percent), leaving only 13 percent for the remaining sectors.

Clearly underfunded were education (12 percent of requirements), protection (38 percent), and economic recovery (33 percent).[20] However, these apparently underfunded sectors are addressed, in principle, through UNCHR's multi-sector funding. Although multi-sector funding tends to give more flexibility to the implementing agency, many NGOs interviewed complained that it also allows UNHCR to act as subcontractor of programmes to NGOs. There is a need for a better balance between the necessary flexibility of allocation of funds and the intended accountability to donors and to beneficiaries.

While UNHCR was quick to request funds and respond to the new needs in 2007, OCHA was the agency that took the lead in responding to the needs of the increasing number of displaced. It is generally agreed that the needs of IDPs have been addressed to a lesser extent than those of refugees, mainly due to the logistical and operational difficulties in reaching them. The situation of the displaced is more fluid and they are more exposed to episodes of violence, harassment by different armed groups, and are also targeted for attacks and retaliation following clashes among different factions. In fact, violence against civilians and the spread of terror are often used as military tactics. Many of these armed groups are not averse to accepting state support when it suits them, and this situation exposes IDPs to increased vulnerability in terms of violations of international humanitarian law.

The increase in OCHA's funding provided the opportunity to create new dynamics for coordination, to extend their field presence, and introduce the cluster approach to improve coordination and accountability. However, coordination seems to be a pending concern in the response in Chad. It became evident during the HRI mission that the coordination and leadership roles of OCHA and other UN agencies are far from optimal. There was also weak coordination among the sectors, contravening the spirit of the UN humanitarian reform agenda, which aims to improve accountability and leadership in sector response through the cluster approach. During 2007, the Inter-Agency Standing Committee country team requested the development of the cluster approach, and OCHA tried to promote cluster leadership and coordination with a new sector configuration. However, this appears to have been only partially applied, and then only to IDP-oriented programmes. A lack of leadership in some sectors, and resistance to change in existing mechanisms probably explains the slow implementation of the cluster approach. OCHA's attempt to introduce the cluster system from mid-2007 is still not consolidated, despite the reasonable level of funding obtained for OCHA's activities (US$4.1 million, or 71 percent of the revised requirements). This is the result not only of the weaknesses inherent in the cluster approach itself, but also of the difficulties in the pre-existing situation in the field. As a result, the modus operandi of UNHCR, with its uncontested leverage regarding coordination issues, has become even more important in defining the approach in Chad.

Furthermore, since most donors are not present in the country, coordination seems to consist of internal negotiation between the UN and NGOs, resulting in little real involvement by donors – other than ECHO – in coordination matters. Geographically, coordination also seems to suffer some shortcomings. The main hub for humanitarian aid is the eastern town of Abeche, where most agencies working in that region maintain a presence. However, it has been reported that communication with headquarters in N'Djamena is poor, and it appears that the same situation applies in the south.[21]

Despite the revised CAP and the increase in funding requirements, not all agencies were able to increase their operations and prevailing insecurity prevented both adequate needs assessments and the implementation of the response. NGOs are basically subcontracted by UNHCR or other UN agencies, but in some cases have their own relative weight as actors in the crisis. This is especially true of Oxfam, Care, International Medical Corps (IMC), Première Urgence (PU) and Cooperazione Internazionale (COOPI), all of which manage significant funds within and outside the CAP process. It is also worth noting the significant presence of the ICRC; according to data from OCHA FTS, the ICRC receives around US$15 million outside the UN CAP, and their reported expenditure in Chad come to US$24 million.[22]

As explained above, the main challenges facing the humanitarian operation in Chad are insecurity and logistics, with frequent carjackings, vandalism of NGOs offices, and occasional aggression towards humanitarian workers.[23] Most humanitarian actors expressed frustration at the prevailing insecurity, although the deployment of EUFOR may change this in future.[24] The heightened vulnerability of the displaced and the difficulties in granting basic protection inside the camps are also important causes of concern for the humanitarian community.[25]

New refugees began arriving in 2008 – around 12,000 to the eastern Chad from Darfur, and 8,000 to the south from the CAR – adding to the challenges of managing the existing caseload, including the need to adapt strategies to a protracted post-emergency situation that demands interventions in host communities and careful attention to sustainability and early recovery. However, these concerns must be balanced with more focused relief to vulnerable new arrivals, who suffer from high rates of malnutrition. In fact, in order to prevent tensions – and even for ethical reasons[26] – support to the host community has become part of the necessary response.

Nevertheless, linking relief and development is a considerable challenge in Chad. The capacity of local structures to absorb external aid for development programmes is very limited. State institutions, in particular in the east, are weak or non-existent and local capacity is very low. Therefore, the situation requires a primary focus on restoring and promoting livelihoods and early recovery programmes. This will go far to easing the structural drivers of the conflict and consolidate stable development in Chad, irrespective of other contextual determinants of the conflict. But in order to create the preconditions for peace, the international community must also adopt strategies addressing the factors driving the regional conflict.

Conclusion

The conflict in Chad constitutes a complex emergency involving refugees from neighbouring countries, a large number of IDPs, and refugee flows to Sudan and Cameroon. The conflict is closely interlinked with the crisis in Darfur, and armed groups and militias from both sides of the border are involved in the other country's conflict, contributing to the continuing flow of refugees. Structural, historic, political, and other regional conflicts all contribute to the volatile situation. It has yet to be seen if the benefits from oil exploitation are translated into better living standards for the general population, or if these fuel further conflict.

Insecurity and breaches of international humanitarian law, including attacks on humanitarian workers are common. These factors, along with difficulties of access, seriously constrain the humanitarian response. In particular, displaced and refugees closer to the Sudan border experience high levels of insecurity, and humanitarian access is very limited there. Security Council resolution 1778, and the deployment of EUFOR and MINUCAT could help to address the situation. However, these missions face complex problems before they can carry out their mandate. The interaction of the humanitarian community with a military force mandated to improve security and to facilitate the delivery of humanitarian aid will require careful implementation and mutual understanding between two very different cultures. Respect for GHD *Principles* 19 and 20 on military-civilian relationships will be key.

The single most significant evolution of the conflict in 2007 has been the unfolding of the IDP crisis, with more than 140,000 people forced from their homes from late-2006 into mid-2007. These events transformed the aid effort from a response to a protracted crisis with a stable caseload of refugees, to one facing a volatile and acute situation needing a more flexible and immediate response. The displaced constitute the most vulnerable group, due to their exposure to factional violence and forced recruitment, as well as the difficulties in access often faced by aid workers.

The international humanitarian response in 2007 was financially generous, covering 99 percent of the total requirements of the CAP, and providing additional funding to the ICRC and other implementing agencies. In fact, the response has provided acceptable standards of support to refugees and IDPs – at times, even better conditions and services than those available to the local population. Donors have favoured a multi-sector approach when allocating funds, but sector coordination and accountability through the UN cluster approach have so far been weakly implemented.

Overall, the situation in Chad requires an increased focus on restoring and promoting livelihoods and early recovery programmes, as a way to easing the structural causes of the conflict. The urgent need is for the donor community to develop a strategic approach, including the provision of relief, with the ultimate aim of creating the conditions for the consolidation of peace, not just in Chad but in neighbouring countries as well.

The Humanitarian Response Index 2008

Notes

1 The HRI team, composed of Ana Romero, Ricardo Solé-Arqués, and Kim Wuyts, visited Chad in April 2008. The opinions expressed here are those of the author and do not necessarily reflect those of DARA.

2 UNDP, 2008.

3 Hissein Habré is currently awaiting trial by an international court of justice in Senegal.

4 Hugon, 2008; and, ISIS, 2007.

5 Pegg, 2006.

6 Human Rights Watch, 2008.

7 United Nations Security Council, 2007.

8 Human Rights Watch, 2008.

9 Tomczyk et al., 2005.

10 Markus et al., 2006.

11 Ibid.

12 Human Rights Watch, 2008.

13 Most of the funds allocated outside the UN Appeal were destined for the Red Cross Red Crescent Movement, as well as to some agencies of interest to particular donors (e.g., Concern and Caritas), and some bilateral funding.

14 Non-DAC donors in 2007 were effectively private contributions (1.3 percent), and minimal contributions were forthcoming from Turkey, South Africa, and Cuba (0.1 percent from each). Carry-over funds, UN unearmarked allocations, and CERF together accounted for 10 percent of the total non-DAC funding.

15 Total funding provided outside the CAP amounted to US$34.9 million.

16 All figures taken from the Office for the Coordination of Humanitarian Affairs Financial Tracking Service (OCHA FTS) as of May 2008.

17 OCHA, 2007.

18 United States Agency for International Development (USAID), 2008.

19 See http://www.reliefweb.int/ocha_ol/pub/idp_gp/idp.html

20 OCHA FTS as of May 2008.

21 Norwegian Refugee Council, 2007.

22 ICRC, 2008.

23 Human Rights Watch, 2007; United Nations Secretary General, 2007.

24 HRI field interview, April 2008.

25 Human Rights Watch, 2007.

26 Notably in Chad but also elsewhere, agencies frequently face the ethical dilemma of providing better standards of living to refugee population than those available to the surrounding host population, arousing potential conflict. In response, sometimes substandard aid is provided to refugees in order to avoid inequities with host communities, while in other cases, aid is also directed to host communities. This is one of the unsolved problems of humanitarian interventions.

References

Hugon, Philippe. 2008. «Le conflit du Tchad de février 2008. Un obstacle nouveau à la résolution du conflit du Darfour?» *IRIS*. 12 February.

Human Rights Watch. 2007. "'They came to kill us': Militia Attacks and Ethnic Targeting of Civilians in Eastern Chad." State of Anarchy: Rebellion and Abuses against Civilians. September. At: http://hrw.org/reports/2007/car0907/index.htm

———. 2008. "Chad, Thousands Left Homeless by Forced Eviction." Human Rights News. 3 April. At: http://www.hrw.org/english/docs/2008/04/02/chad18416.htm

International Committee for the Red Cross. 2008. ICRC Annual Report: Chad. At: http://www.icrc.org/Web/Eng/siteeng0.nsf/htmlall/7EUD66/$FILE/icrc_ar_07_chad.pdf?OpenElement

ISIS. 2007, European security review, number 35, October 5, 2007.

Markus, Michael, Nigel Pearson, and Adoum Daliam. 2006. *Inter Agency Health Evaluation. Humanitarian Oasis in a Parched health sector: Refugees and Host Populations in Eastern and Southern Chad.* February. UNHCR.

Norwegian Refugee Council. 2007. "Internally displaced in Chad, trapped between civil conflict and Sudan's Darfur conflict." July.

Office for the Coordination of Humanitarian Affairs (OCHA). 2008. Financial Tracking Service (OCHA FTS).

———. Undated. Guiding Principles on Internal Displacement. At: http://www.reliefweb.int/ocha_ol/pub/idp_gp/idp.html

———. 2007. *Humanitarian Appeal.* At: http://ochadms.unog.ch/quickplace/cap/main.nsf/h_Index/CAP_2007_Humanitarian_Appeal/$FILE/CAP_2007_Humanitarian_Appeal_SCREEN.pdf?OpenElement

Pegg, S. 2006. "Can policy intervention beat the resource curse? Evidence from the Chad–Cameroon pipeline project." *African Affairs* 105:1–25.

Tomczyk, Basia, Eileen Dunne, Michelle Chang, Leisel Talley, and Curtis Blanton. 2004. "Emergency nutrition and mortality surveys conducted among Sudanese and Chadian villagers, North Eastern Chad." International Emergency and Refugee Health Branch and the Center for Disease Control. June.

United Nations Development Programme (UNDP). 2008. *Human Development Report 2007/2008. Fighting climate change: Human solidarity in a divided world.* New York.

United Nations Secretary General. 2007. *Report of the Secretary-General on the United Nations Mission in the Central African Republic and Chad.* S/2007/739. 17 December. At: http://daccessdds.un.org/doc/UNDOC/GEN/N07/642/58/PDF/N0764258.pdf?OpenElement

United Nations Security Council. 2007. *Resolution 1778 (2007).* 25 September. At: http://daccessdds.un.org/doc/UNDOC/GEN/N07/516/15/PDF/N0751615.pdf?OpenElement

United States Agency for International Development (USAID). 2008. *Sudan: Complex Emergency Situation Report #6.* (FY 2008). At: http://www.reliefweb.int/rw/rwb.nsf/db900sid/MUMA-7EH4CE?OpenDocument&rc=1&cc=tcd

Colombia

AT A GLANCE

Country data *(2006 figures, unless otherwise noted)*

- 2007 Human Development Index: ranked 75th of 177 countries
- Population: 45.56 million
- GNI per capita (Atlas method, current US$): US$3,120
- Population living on less than US$2 a day (1990–2005): 17.8 percent
- Life expectancy (in years): 73
- Infant mortality rate: 17 per 1,000 live births
- Under five infant mortality rate: 21 per 1,000
- Population undernourished (2002-04): 13 percent
- Population with sustainable access to improved water source (2004): 93 percent
- Adult literacy rate (over 15 yrs of age, 1995–2005): 92.8 percent
- Gender-related development index (2005): ranked 65th of 177 countries
- Official development assistance (ODA): US$988 million
- 2007 Corruption Perception Index: ranked 68th out of 179 countries

Sources: Transparency International (TI); 2007; UNDP, 2007a and 2007b; World Bank, 2008.

The crisis

- Despite efforts to demobilise paramilitary groups, 1,070 military incidents were registered in 2007, an increase of more than 30 percent from the previous year; rise of "new armed groups;"
- Second largest number of IDPs in the world, second only to Sudan; OCHA estimates over 270,496 persons newly displaced in 2007; CODHES estimates 305,966 displaced in 2007, compared to 221,638 in 2006;
- Acción Social registered 100,000 displaced for assistance; CODHES claims only 40 to 60 percent of displaced received official recognition or consequently state aid;
- 250,000 Colombian refugees in Ecuador, 200,000 in Venezuela, 17,000 in Brazil, 13,500 in Panama, 6,000 in Costa Rica;
- 54.2 percent of displaced expelled from rural areas; 69.2 percent do not wish or have been unable to return while 76.4 percent wish to remain where they live now;
- 28 of the country's 32 departments suffered floods in May and December 2007, affecting 1,500,000.

Sources: OCHA; CODHES; Acción Social.

The humanitarian response

- There is no CAP for Colombia;
- US is the main donor: US$750.5 million in bilateral assistance in 2007, of which US$145.7 million dedicated to economic and social needs, the remainder (US$604.7 million), destined for military and police assistance;
- OCHA reports 14 other donors contributed US$48.4 million in 2007; EC second largest donor (US$14.6 million); Norway (US$7.6 million); Netherlands (US$6.9 million); Germany (US$5.2 million).
- CERF contributed US$4 million in 2007 in flood assistance.

Sources: OCHA FTS; Just the Facts.

Colombia
The Displaced and the Forgotten

FERNANDO ESPADA, Communications Director, DARA

Introduction[1]

"My grandmother was born during the *Thousand Days War,* my mother during *The Violence.* When I was born, at the beginning of the 1960s, the guerrilla army was in the process of rearming itself. Not even the oldest people in Colombia know what it means to live in peace. There have always been killings of peasants, displacement, and war. In Colombia, violence has always been a way of life. Changing this reality is very difficult."[2] The person who said this, a Colombian working for an international NGO, was neither a pessimist, nor an exception among the humanitarian actors working in the worst and longest humanitarian crisis in Latin America. The crisis in Colombia is a complex conflict, in which improvements, if any, are very slow.

Indeed, since the HRI field visit to Colombia in 2007, little has changed.[3] The government remains unwilling to acknowledge that there is a humanitarian crisis in the country, and in the absence of a clear articulation of the crisis, donors seem more and more reticent to fund humanitarian activities, creating huge obstacles for humanitarian agencies who are trying to respond to the needs of millions of people.

If anything, one change has been an oversimplification of the conflict in the media, which undermines the work of humanitarian agencies trying to raise awareness of the crisis. Judging by international (and national) media coverage, one would think that the conflict is simply a battle between the Fuerzas Armadas Revolucionarias de Colombia (FARC) guerrillas and the state, a battle which has forced the terrorists to the brink of military defeat. The impression is also given that, trapped in the middle are approximately 3,000 kidnapped people, awaiting liberation by the Army or through *humanitarian arrangements* (exchanges often negotiated through the ICRC), which their families vocally demand. In other words, Colombia is made to look like the typical story of heroes and villains.

What is hidden behind the news reports is the largely untold story of a humanitarian crisis of massive proportions, a story of millions of people displaced by the conflict, torn from their lands, and languishing in poverty awaiting assistance. With the media focussed on kidnappings and the diplomatic disputes between Colombia, Venezuela, and Ecuador, very few media outlets have mentioned the key fact that makes the

Colombian humanitarian crisis one of the most tragic in the world: over 4 million people have been forced from their homes between 1985 and 2007.[4] The majority of these have not yet returned.

The very nature and scale of the crisis, as well as the corresponding humanitarian response, are controversial and paradoxical. Colombia is not a failed state. It is, without doubt, a state with very serious, as yet unresolved, problems, but which, nevertheless, has considerable institutional, political, economic, police, and military capabilities. Colombia is an established democracy with a strong economy. Notwithstanding these realities, the FARC is the largest and oldest functioning guerrilla group in Latin America. And although Colombia has the second largest number of internally displaced people in the world, second only to Sudan, not only is there no UN Consolidated Appeals Process (CAP) for Colombia, but international humanitarian aid is relatively limited.[5] Untangling the political and complex elements of the crisis, while maintaining the focus on the humanitarian needs of the population, is difficult but necessary.

The conflict: Impact of the Democratic Security doctrine

The conflict in Colombia can be traced back several decades and has undergone numerous changes, including various peace processes and the development of a lucrative war economy based on the illegal drug trade. Today, the principal actors are the state, the leftist guerrilla group FARC, and the Ejercito de Liberación Nacional (ELN), as well as *new armed groups,* which have not engaged in the recent, state-sponsored demobilisation process.[6]

Since coming to power in 2002, President Álvaro Uribe has promoted the doctrine of *Democratic Security,* "the real possibility for any citizen to enjoy, peacefully and without disruptions, his or her right to life, to dignity, to physical and spiritual freedom."[7] More specifically, the objectives of *Democratic Security* are:

- consolidation of state control of Colombian territory;
- protection of the population;
- elimination of illegal drug trafficking in Colombia;
- maintenance of a military deterrent capacity;
- protection of land, sea and river borders;
- efficient and transparent reporting of security issues.[8]

Uribe's approach is closely linked to that the of the of the United States and its support for Plan Colombia, which

aims to eradicate cocaine production, eliminate the guerrilla strongholds, and consolidate the central government, while simultaneously promoting economic liberalisation and the free trade agreement between the two countries. This strong security and economic emphasis has coloured the evolution of the humanitarian crisis in the past five years.

The principal characteristic of the Uribe presidency has been to emphasise the positive at the expense of acknowledging that there is a serious humanitarian crisis. In fact, some analysts suggest that Uribe's policies use the civilian population as a means to achieve security aims. By "involving the civilian population, particularly IDPs, in the confrontation, the state denies the principle of distinction [between military and civilian actors] and in fact reaches the level of obligatory cooperation, as there is no alternative behaviour other than supporting government policy against the terrorists. In this way, meeting the needs of the population is not the objective of the state but the means through which to impose itself on its adversaries [...] the processes of return for the displaced population are just one more strategy in the *Democratic Security* policy."[9]

While there has been a continuous decrease in the number of armed incidents since the election of President Uribe and, in turn, a weakening of the FARC, the government reports that, despite efforts to demobilise paramilitary groups, 1,070 military incidents were registered in 2007, an increase of more than 30 percent from the previous year.[10] In fact, there is evidence of the emergence of so-called *new armed groups* with "the same structures, the same composition and the same motivations as the former *paramilitary groups.*"[11] Although there is no conclusive figure, the Organization of American States believes the number of these groups is on the increase.[12]

Legislation passed in 2005, called The Justice and Peace Law and Decree 128,[13] was supposed to work towards national truth and reconciliation and to provide compensation to the victims of paramilitary violence. But two years after the law came into force, the reality is that the first 3,000 ex-paramilitaries charged have not faced serious penalties, and the victims have received virtually no compensation (on average about US$3.75 each), and less than 6 percent have seen their cases dealt with by the Public Prosecutor's Office. At this rate, said one critical jurist, "it will take 2,157 years to complete the 'Justice and Peace' judicial process" for all of the victims to have their cases heard by the justice system and receive compensation."[14]

Similarly, although there has been progress in recent years regarding respect for human rights and international humanitarian law, as recognised by UNHCR, according to data from the CINEP, the Colombian state is itself responsible for more than half of the violations of human rights, compared to one-third by the paramilitary groups and 10 percent by FARC.[15] Nearly 1,000 extrajudicial killings of civilians by the army were documented between 2002 and 2007, representing a 65 percent increase over the previous period.

Apart from recent military gains, the period of *Democratic Security* has resulted in more than half the total number of internal displacements registered since 1999. Once again, the reality is that military operations against guerrilla groups, in particular in the south-east of the country, have not been accompanied by the necessary assistance to the affected population.

Nevertheless, according to several sources, the government is determined to implement a public relations campaign to present Colombia to the world as a prosperous country that is safe for foreign investment.[16] This image does not fit with the fact that it is the country with the second highest number of internally displaced people, the highest number of victims due to anti-personnel mines, the apparent impunity for armed groups, and frequent unfavourable reports regarding human rights.

The humanitarian crisis: Civilian displacement as a tactic of war

As reported in the 2007 HRI report on Colombia, the interaction between the security objectives of the government and the interests (often economic) of the guerrillas, paramilitary groups, and drug cartels, have led to the forced displacement of thousands of people each year and the expropriation and theft of their land and possessions. The fluid nature of the conflict means that displacements continue at an alarming pace. OCHA estimates that over 270,496 persons were newly displaced in 2007, adding to the already staggering number of 4 million IDPs in a country with only 45.5 million people.

The figures are even higher according to the Colombian NGO CODHES,[17] which estimates that there were 305,966 people displaced in 2007 compared to 221,638 in 2006, confirming a rising trend over the past three years. In 14 departments of the country, the numbers of displaced people exceeded 10,000, and in two of them, Nariño and Antioquia, the figures are clos-

er to 30,000.[18] Nariño, the department with the highest number of displaced people, has almost all the fundamental elements of the conflict: massive deployment by the Army, the presence of paramilitary and guerrilla groups, coca cultivation, fumigations, and drug and weapon smuggling. Furthermore, Nariño has a high percentage of the most vulnerable indigenous and Afro-Colombian populations, and very high levels of poverty and social marginalisation.

The areas where displacement occurs illustrate the land appropriation and population control strategies employed by the armed actors. Common strategies in the conflict include the control of territory where coca is cultivated – either for exploitation or eradication – the fight for control of drug transportation routes, and the use of landmines by the guerrillas to control the advance of the Army or the confinement of the population as a military strategy. Once again, civilians become one more strategic factor and target in the fighting: 54.2 percent of those displaced were expelled from rural areas – where they were the land owners, tenants, or simply waged labourers – of whom 23.7 percent came from village areas and 22 percent from municipal capitals; 69.2 percent do not wish or have been unable to return, due to the persistence of the difficulties which forced them to leave.[19]

According to CODHES, displacements in 2007 were characterised by "the intensification of the recruitment of youth, even *en masse,* by armed groups;" "thousands of families of peasants, settlers, indigenous people, and Afro-Colombian communities facing a situation where the guerrillas, paramilitary, and drug-traffickers impose the cultivation of coca and poppies on their land, which, in turn, are an objective of eradication within the framework of military operations;" "the use of anti-personnel mines, particularly by guerrilla groups;" and the "false identification of civilians as terrorists or part of the guerrillas."[20] The strategy of confining the civilian population utilised by all the armed actors, together with threats and targeted assassinations of social, trade union, and displaced community leaders, should be added to the above factors.

The movement of the combat frontline from the centre of the country to its borders, in particular towards the south, has caused the flight of several hundred thousand Colombians to neighbouring countries over the past decade. At present, and according to figures from UNHCR, there are some 250,000 Colombian refugees in Ecuador, 200,000 in Venezuela, 17,000 in Brazil, 13,500 in Panama, and 6,000 in Costa Rica. Of the neighbouring countries, Ecuador has proven to be the most active in addressing the humanitarian needs of Colombian refugees. In 2007, the Government of Rafael Correa announced *Plan Ecuador,* "a response for peace, equality and development to the militarist, violent Plan Colombia," with which it intends to meet the needs of refugees and of the Ecuadorian population in the north of the country. On the other hand, UNHCR, with three offices in Ecuador, claimed that of the more than two-thirds of Colombian refugees living below the poverty line, only 10 percent have access to decent housing and one-third are working.

Clearly, one of the key issues in the Colombian situation, as in any other armed conflict, is the protection of the civilian population (Principle 3 of the GHD). However, neither the advance and seizure of territory by the Army, nor the available resources and capacity of the government agencies seem to effectively guarantee this protection. In fact, the two main governmental initiatives for protection: the Threatened Person Protection programme and the Communities at Risk programme are clearly insufficient to address the problems. And none of the humanitarian actors interviewed highlighted any international donor engagement or concern with this critical issue.

The displaced are threatened not only by insecurity, but by the risks of volcanic eruptions, earthquakes, floods, and landslides, all of which severely test not only the endurance of the affected population, but the response of the Colombian authorities and the national and international non-governmental humanitarian actors. Of the country's 32 departments, 28 suffered floods in May and December 2007, affecting 1,500,000 Colombians. The northern region of La Mojana was most damaged, with a total of 160,000 people affected. In response to the May floods and landslides, the UN Central Emergency Response Fund (CERF) provided approximately US$2.3 million in humanitarian aid and the EC US$1.4 million. CERF provided a further US$1.8 million in December.

Government response: The letter of the law vs. its implementation

The National Assistance System

The Colombian government is the main provider of humanitarian assistance, with a budget for the 2007–2010 period of US$2.2 million. Acción Social (Social Action) is the main state agency for assisting the dis-

placed population and for coordinating the National System for Comprehensive Attention to the Displaced Population. In spite of the relatively abundant funds at their disposal for assisting the displaced, Acción Social is still far from meeting its mission to offer "comprehensive assistance and lasting solutions for the displaced population, with a humanitarian approach based on dignity and the restitution of the rights of displaced families and seeking their social and economic integration in their places of origin or in those where they have been relocated."[21] In 2007, Acción Social had registered a little over 100,000 displaced persons (roughly one-third of the total) for assistance. According to CODHES, that number represents less than one-third of the number of newly displaced people in need. In fact, CODHES has claimed that only between 40 to 60 percent of displaced people received official recognition and, therefore, the state aid to which they are entitled.

The low level of those registered and the numbers excluded from Acción Social's registration process are significant, owing to the fact that field presence of Acción Social is dependant on the actions of the Army. Many of the displaced – in particular indigenous people and those in Afro-Colombian communities – cannot, or dare not, register, and many others lose their official state support as soon as they receive any other form of subsidy. Almost 70 percent of those displaced live in the outskirts of large cities and in medium-size towns, where they establish themselves among the poorest of the population, putting pressure on resources and increasing social tensions. The incidence of displacement is higher among women and girls, who frequently suffer sexual abuse or exploitation.

During his visit to Colombia in 2007, the United Nations High Commissioner for Refugees, António Guterres, praised the country's unique legislation, which explicitly recognises the rights of displaced persons. This *legal* peculiarity contrasts with the situation of other countries with high numbers of displaced people. However good the legislation may be on paper, its application in practice is uneven and problematic, as noted in a 2004 ruling by the Colombian Constitutional Court. The ruling, covering over 100 individual claims of violation of the basic rights of thousands of displaced people, states that: "the displaced are an extremely vulnerable sector of the population, due to the lack of appropriate and effective protection by the authorities. Repeated violations of their rights occur on a prolonged and massive scale, attributable to both the armed conflict and to the structure of the policy for assisting displaced people, while the resources of the latter, like its institutional capacity, are insufficient, and in violation of the existing regulations."[22] The court demanded that the government ensure the protection of the displaced, guarantee sufficient resources to meet their needs, and enforce full compliance by authorities of all policies and legislation.

The Colombian government, consistent with its tendency to deny the reality of the humanitarian crisis and its own responsibilities, has produced more than 20,000 pages of documentation, in an effort to overturn the court's ruling. However, an examination of this documentation by the Revision Chamber of the Constitutional Court left no doubt that, "the basic constitutional rights of the forcibly displaced population continue to be ignored in a systematic and massive manner, (and) … national and territorial entities responsible … must take urgent and immediate corrective measures to guarantee advances in order to overcome this unconstitutional state of affairs."[23]

As a result of the ruling, the government created the National Plan for Comprehensive Attention to the Displaced Population (2005),[24] and committed US$3.3 million (1 percent of GDP) to assist displaced people between 2006 and 2010. According to UNHCR, "the Colombian state has taken on its primary obligation to assist and protect the population that is victim of the violence."[25] But the agency goes on to conclude that, in spite of these institutional efforts, "the results are not yet felt by either the displaced population or by those working in support of this population as a general improvement in well-being nor in achieving lasting solutions."[26] In the words of a local NGO, "there is a gap between the central government and the local authorities, which are overburdened with work and whose civil servants, in many cases, are under-qualified and lack motivation."[27] Several other agencies in interviews with the HRI team highlighted persistent corruption and a lack of capacity as the other reasons behind the lack of progress in this area.

The international humanitarian response: Supply and demand

The United States is the main international actor in Colombia – although the most controversial, given its support for Plan Colombia. Bilateral assistance from the United States to Colombia reached US$750.5 million in 2007. Of this, only US$145.7 million was dedicated to the rather vague area of economic and social assistance,

theoretically including support for humanitarian needs, and requiring respect for human rights. The remaining funds, US$604.7 million, were destined for military and police assistance – a clear indication of the priorities of the donor.[28]

Aside from the United States, with its unique approach to aid in Colombia, 14 other donor countries contributed US$48.4 million in humanitarian aid to the Colombian crisis in 2007, according to OCHA FTS. The European Commission was the main donor with US$14.6 million (35.7 percent of total humanitarian aid), followed by Norway with US$7.6 million (18.5 percent), the Netherlands with US$6.9 million (16.8 percent), and Germany with US$5.2 million (12.6 percent).

CERF contributed US$6.3 million to Colombia in 2007, with US$4 million for assistance to those affected by floods, mainly in the region of La Mojana, and the remainder earmarked for assisting the displaced populations in Chocó and Nariño.

The complexity of the conflict in Colombia and the presence of a strong state have combined to create an international response largely determined by non-humanitarian factors. According to many of the agencies and organisations interviewed, there is wide recognition that although the Uribe government has, indeed, taken the lead role in providing aid, and "has proven it has the financial resources to assist the displaced," the general view is that the government agencies responsible for assistance are "overwhelmed and under-qualified," and "only interested in concealing the conflict and its consequences."[29] Some suggested that, in fact, the crisis is "overfunded" and "has great external support and a very low level of requirements," suggesting that this is perhaps because "no donor dares to criticise Uribe. Not because they trust him, but because they are afraid of (Hugo) Chávez (President of Venezuela) and wish to clip his wings."[30] Nevertheless, according to the same sources, the government "wishes to conceal the humanitarian crisis,"[31] and in order to do so, it must either get the humanitarian actors out of the country in the medium term, or, at the very least, control their activities.

There is no UN Consolidated Appeal Process for Colombia, partly due to the opposition of the Colombian government to any indication of the existence of a humanitarian crisis.[32] Nevertheless, OCHA has had an office in Colombia since 2003, to which three field offices and three satellite offices were later added. Their humanitarian coordination mission, mainly via the Inter-Agency Standing Committee (IASC), is conditioned directly by the Colombian government's attitude of denying and concealing the humanitarian crisis. This is a situation that inevitably affects most of the humanitarian actors in the country, among which are UNHCR, UNICEF, and UNIFEM, and some 40 international NGOs, the ICRC, and several national Red Cross societies.

It is in this highly politicised context that donors find themselves making decisions about how to allocate funds for the crisis. On the one hand, the state has demonstrated that it has a degree of response capacity and resources, but refuses to acknowledge the extent of the crisis; on the other, humanitarian agencies find it difficult to attract attention to the real extent of humanitarian needs, and face serious obstacles in their work. In some cases, donors have focused on longer-term development assistance, which tends to favour the consolidation the state and macro-economic issues at the expense of humanitarian assistance. Several donors are now considering directly financing the Colombian state via budgetary support, creating a scenario of "greater political influence of donors, but less independence for humanitarian actors."[33]

There is also evidence of donor fatigue, as donor and humanitarian agencies are finding it difficult to justify a continued presence and funding in a middle-income country, one which apparently has sufficient capacity and resources to meet the needs of its population. The fatigue is exacerbated by the political pressure exerted by Uribe government on the United Nations and donor countries, and the slow pace of change.[34]

Overall, the neutrality and impartiality of the humanitarian response, as enshrined in Principle 2 of Good Humanitarian Donorship, appears to be seriously compromised in Colombia. Despite a few grey areas in which there is movement in the international response, the majority of the humanitarian actors interviewed question the real reasons for decisions taken by donor countries, particularly the United States, with regard to their presence in Colombia.

Conclusion

The magnitude and characteristics of the humanitarian crisis in Colombia should be sufficient reason for the international community to give priority to the humanitarian response. The reality is different, both in terms of the amount of funds contributed and the media coverage of the country. The bulk of reports by different actors and the information collected by the HRI in

the field (in both 2007 and in 2008) suggest that the Colombian crisis is being deliberately concealed from the eyes of the world, in part to satisfy the government's own domestic priorities, and to present the image of a strong, competent state.

There is no doubt that Colombia shows laudable signs of being capable of progress, and this is reflected in the impressive figures regarding economic growth. However, it is even more important to consider the future of millions of Colombians who each year die, are forced to leave their homes, live under threat, are deprived of the most basic rights, or are used as weapons of war by all armed actors, without exception.

Perhaps the key to the future international response regarding the humanitarian crisis in Colombia lies in this statement by a local worker of an international NGO: "A lot is rotten, but no one says anything. There is a great deal of international support, but very few demands are made of the government. The partners should be more critical."[35] The Colombian state has proven that it has the financial resources to meet the needs of the displaced population, but there is still a long way to go before it proves its real commitment to assist the most vulnerable populations and ensures the effective protection of human rights. Donor countries can play a constructive role in supporting the government, but at the same time, must demand better support for the millions of people affected by the crisis.

Notes

1   The HRI team, composed of Fernando Espada, Marybeth Redheffer, and Nacho Wilhelmi, visited Colombia in April 2008. The opinions expressed here are those of the author and do not necessarily reflect those of DARA.

2   HRI field interview.

3   Hidalgo, 2008.

4   Consultoría para los Derechos Humanos y el Desplazamiento (CODHES), 2007.

5   Internal Displacement Monitoring Centre and Norwegian Refugee Council, 2008.

6   International Crisis Group, 2006, 2007a, and 2007b.

7   Uribe, 2002.

8   Republic of Colombia, Office of the President, 2003.

9   Piedad Caicedo et al., 2006.

10 OCHA, 2008.

11 HRI field interview.

12 Organisation of American States, 2006.

13 Amnesty International, 2008.

14   Center for International Policy, 2008.

15   Centro de Investigación y Educación Popular (CINEP), 2008.

16   The signing of the Free Trade Treaty with the United States, postponed by the American Congress from April 2008, is one of the first priorities of the Uribe Government.

17   Consultoría para los Derechos Humanos y el Desplazamiento [Consultancy for Human Rights and Displacement].

18   CODHES, 2008a.

19   CODHES, 2008b.

20   Ibid.

21   Acción Social, 2008.

22   La Sala Tercera de Revisión de la Corte Constitucional, 2004

23   Sala Tercera…, 2006.

24   República de Colombia. 2005.

25   UNHCR, 2007.

26   Ibid.

27   HRI field interview.

28   Just the Facts, 2008.

29   HRI field interview.

30   Ibid.

31   Ibid.

32   Hidalgo, 2008.

33   HRI field interview.

34   Ibid.

35   Ibid.

References

Acción Social. 2008. "Apoyo Integral a la Población Desplazada." At: http://www.accionsocial.gov.co/contenido/contenido.aspx?catID=295&conID=205

Amnesty International. 2008. "Justice and Peace Law and Decree 128." At: http://www.amnestyusa.org/Colombia/Justice_and_Peace_Law_and_Decree_128/page.do?id=1101862&n1=3&n2=30&n3=885

Center for International Policy. 2008. "The justice and peace process is going badly." 17 April. At: http://www.cipcol.org/?p=584

Centro de Investigación y Educación Popular (CINEP). 2008. "Intensity of armed conflict in Colombia." 2008. At: http://www.cipcol.org/files/2008_CINEP.pdf

Consultoría para los Derechos Humanos y el Desplazamiento (CODHES). 2007. "Information Bulletin, Nº 72." 30 November.

———. 2008a. Departamentos de llegada, años 2006–2007. 13 February.

———. 2008b. "Ahora por los desplazados." Bogota. 5 February.

Hidalgo, Silvia. 2008. "Colombia: A Crisis Concealed." In Hidalgo, S. and A. Lopez-Claros, eds. Humanitarian Response Index 2007: Measuring Commitment to Best Practice. Hampshire: Palgrave Macmillan.

Internal Displacement Monitoring Centre and Norwegian Refugee Council. 2008. Internal Displacement: Global Overview of Trends and Developments in 2007. April. At: http://www.internal-displacement.org/8025708F004BE3B1/(httpInfoFiles)/BD8316FAB5984142C125742E0033180B/$file/IDMC_Internal_Displacement_Global_Overview_2007.pdf

International Crisis Group. 2006. Tougher Challenges Ahead for Colombia's Uribe. Latin America Briefing No. 11. 20 October.

———. 2007a. Colombia's New Armed Groups. Latin America Report No. 20. 10 May;

———. 2007b. Colombia: Moving Forward with the ELN? Latin America Briefing No. 16. 11 October.

Just the Facts. 2008. "A civilian's guide to US defense and security assistance to Latin America and the Caribbean." US Aid to Colombia. All Programs, 2004–2009. At: http://justf.org/Country?country=Colombia

Office for the Coordination of Humanitarian Affairs (OCHA). Financial Tracking Service.

———. 2008. Infogramas Situación Humanitaria 2007. At: http://www.reliefweb.int/rw/RWFiles2007.nsf/FilesByRWDocUnidFilename/ASAZ-7CLC8P-informe_completo.pdf/$File/informe_completo.pdf

Organization of American States. 2006. Sixth quarterly report of the Secretary General for the Permanent Council on the peace process support mission in Colombia. March 2006. At: http://www.oas.org/speeches/speech.asp?sCodigo=06-0030

Piedad Caicedo, Luz, Daniel Manrique et al. 2006. Desplazamiento y Retorno Nº 1. Balance de una política. Evaluación de la política de retorno del gobierno de Álvaro Uribe. ILSA, Bogotá, 2006.

Republic of Colombia, Office of the President. 2003. Defence and Democratic Security Policy, 2003. At: www.mindefensa.gov.co/dayTemplates/images/seguridad_democratica.pdf

República de Colombia, Ministerio del Interior y de Justicia. 2005. Plan Nacional para la atención Integral a la Población Desplazada por la Violencia. At: http://www.accionsocial.gov.co/documentos/Desplazados.pdf

La Sala Tercera de Revisión de la Corte Constitucional. 2004. Sentencia Nº T-025 de 2004. At: http://www.acnur.org/biblioteca/pdf/2501.pdf

———. 2006. AUTO Nº 218 de 2006. At: http://www.mininteriorjusticia.gov.co/ADMINFILES/AUTO%20218%20DE%20AGOSTO%2011%20DE%202006.PDF

United Nations High Commissioner for Refugees (UNHCR). 2007. Introducción, concusiones y recomendaciones del balance de la política pública de atención integral a la población desplazada por la violencia 2004–2006. At: www.acnur.org/biblioteca/pdf/4901.pdf

Uribe, Álvaro. 2002. "Individual Safety and Freedom in Colombia." Bogotá. 20 November. At: http://web.presidencia.gov.co/discursos/discursos2002/noviembre/libertades.htm

Democratic Republic of the Congo

AT A GLANCE

Country data (2006 figures, unless otherwise noted)

- 2007 Human Development Index: ranked 168th of 179 countries
- Population: 60.64 million
- GNI per capita (Atlas method, current US$): US$130
- Population living on less than US$2 a day (1990–2004): NA
- Life expectancy: 46 years
- Infant mortality rate: 129 per 1,000 live births
- Under-five infant mortality rate: 205 per 1,000
- Population undernourished (2002–2004): 74 percent
- Population with sustainable access to improved water source (2004): 46 percent
- Primary education completion rate: NA
- Gender-related development index (2005): ranked 147th of 177 countries
- Official development assistance (ODA): US$2.056 billion
- 2007 Corruption Perception Index: ranked 168th out of 179 countries

Sources: Transparency International (TI). 2007; UNDP, 2007a and 2007b; World Bank, 2008.

The crisis

- 2007 saw relative stability, despite continuing violence in eastern region;
- 5.4 million people killed since 1998; 45,000 die monthly; 1,500 daily from malnutrition, epidemics, and conflict-related incidents;
- 2007 maternal mortality ratio from 1,289 to 3,000 deaths per 100,000 live births; over 300,000 children under five died from malnutrition;
- Cholera and Ebola killed hundreds in 2007; HIV/AIDS prevalence rate from 1.7 to 7.6 percent, 20 percent higher in conflict-affected areas;
- 80 percent of population live on less than US$1/day; under-employment at 81.7 percent; 11 percent of all deaths attributed to malnutrition;
- 1,480,000 displaced people returned home since conflict end; 760,000 in 2007;
- But in North Kivu, 436,000 displaced between December 2006 and February 2008; by end-2007, over 1.3 million displaced, half forced to flee in the last six months of 2007.

Sources: International Rescue Committee, 2008; OCHA, 2008a and 2008b; UNICEF, 2007; IRIN, 2007; OECD, 2008.

The humanitarian response

- Donors provided US$500 million in humanitarian aid in 2007;
- 2007 CAP received US$456 million (66% of US$686 million requested;
- Largest 2007 donors were U.S. (US$120 million,24 percent); EC/ECHO (US$69.7 million, 13.9 percent); and UK (US$66 million, 13.2 percent);
- In 2007, France tripled its contribution to US$7.8 million (1.6 percent of total); Germany and Japan, reduced their contributions; Belgium, Canada, Ireland, Luxemburg, the Netherlands, Norway, Spain, Sweden, and UK gave US$117.8 million to Pooled Fund (an increase of 27 percent over the 2006 budget); CERF contributed US$52.5 million (10 percent).

Sources: OCHA FTS, 2007

Democratic Republic of the Congo
The Giant with Feet of Clay

GILLES GASSER, Independent Consultant on Development and Humanitarian Aid

© Lynsey Addario/Corbis

Introduction[1]

After decades of spiralling conflict, rampant anarchy, and the collapse of the state, 2007 was a year of relative stability in the Democratic Republic of the Congo (DRC). Key political events took place in 2006 and 2007: the presidential and parliamentary elections, the formation of a new coalition government, and an institutional transition. Despite the violence, allegations of fraud, and suspicions of conspiracy surrounding this political process, Congolese institutions seem to be on a new track.

These positive developments have been welcomed – albeit with excessive euphoria and optimism – by donors and the international community, who are hoping that the sick giant of Africa is about to renounce years of violence and work towards peace and sustainable socio-economic development.

Despite these promising indicators, the scenario in the field and daily reality remains troubling. The country continues to be stuck in a disastrous humanitarian crisis. In the eastern provinces, the peace process is undermined by disputes between government forces and warlords over land and the control of lucrative mine resources. A persistent climate of insecurity is ravaging communities, where belligerents harass civilians, spread terror, and violate the most basic human rights. Despite the presence of the world's largest peacekeeping contingent, the UN Mission in the Democratic Republic of the Congo (MONUC), forced civilian displacement and increased vulnerability are the norm in many communities.

With the improvement of the security situation in some regions, aid did reach previously inaccessible people, contributing to the perception of increased humanitarian needs. Food security, access to potable water, and basic health are often absent. Another challenge to the path to stability and recovery is the strengthening of DRC socio-political institutions. The state apparatus is still not functioning – corruption reigns with impunity – and social services have collapsed.

The humanitarian response to the DRC crisis has increased substantially since 2005, the first year of reform of the humanitarian system. In 2007, donor support remained high, but the crisis was still underfunded. Additionally, humanitarian actors criticised the insufficient donor commitment to Good Humanitarian Donorship (GHD) *Principles* of humanity, impartiality, and needs-based response.

Causes of the crisis: Aftermath of Africa's first world war

DRC remains a country in crisis, the victim of its extraordinary natural resource wealth. For decades, none of the huge profits extracted from the Congolese soil have benefited the local population.

Since its independence in 1960, the history of the DRC has been characterised by corruption and civil war. The descent into the abyss began with Colonel Joseph Désiré Mobutu. After the 1965 military coup, he renamed the country Zaire and turned it into a base for operations against Soviet-backed Angola. But he also made Zaire synonymous with corruption and repression. The end of the Cold War and US backing accelerated the country's decline. In 1997, neighbouring Rwanda invaded to chase extremist Hutu militias. The anti-Mobutu rebels, led by Laurent Kabila, took advantage of the chaotic situation to drive Mobutu from power and renamed the country the Democratic Republic of the Congo. But the country's troubles continued. In 1998, a clash between Kabila and his former allies, Rwanda and Uganda, turned the country into a vast battleground – the first African World War.[2]

In 1999, belligerents signed the Lusaka Agreement to end the war. Despite the deployment of MONUC, countless violations persisted. In 2001, Kabila was killed and his 29 year old son, Joseph, took power. In 2002, a peace agreement was signed in Sun City, South Africa, nominally ending the war, maintaining Joseph Kabila as President, and setting up an interim administration, including members of the rebel groups. One of the key elements of the agreement was the demilitarisation of the country and the withdrawal of foreign forces. In 2005, the country held its first multi-party elections in 46 years. Joseph Kabila was elected President and his party won the most seats in the National Assembly. A coalition government headed by his former rival Antoine Gizenga was formed.

Unfortunately, in the eastern provinces of North and South Kivu, the situation remained chaotic and civilians continued to be victims of terrible exactions. On 23 January 2008, 40 groups participated in the Goma conference and signed an agreement calling for a ceasefire, the disarmament and demobilisation of combatants, and addressing humanitarian and human rights issues. The agreement has been widely welcomed but its concrete implementation in the field remains slow and uncertain.

In the rest of the country, state authority is weak, particularly in opposition-dominated provinces. Kinshasa, where Kabila controls key state institutions, is characterised by political repression and marginalisation of the opposition. The DRC is no longer considered a collapsed state, but rather a failed state, weak, corrupted, unable, and sometimes unwilling, to care for its people. The peace process is far from complete.

Humanitarian impact of the crisis

The signing of the Goma Agreement coincided with release by the International Rescue Committee (IRC) of its most recent report on *Mortality in the Democratic Republic of Congo.*[3] Based on the results of the five previous IRC studies,[4] the report estimates that 5.4 million people have died since 1998, and that 45,000 continue to die every month – 1,500 *daily* – from malnutrition, epidemics, and conflict-related incidents. IRC President George Rupp said that the loss of life in the DRC is equivalent to the entire population of Denmark, or the state of Colorado, dying within a decade. The crude mortality rate from 2004 remains unchanged (2.2 deaths per 1,000 people per month[5]), indicating that despite the peace agreement and political transition, the Congolese population remains in humanitarian crisis. Security did improve in many provinces, but remains critical in both Kivu and Ituri. In these regions, redeployment of MONUC is requested by many NGOs. During the elections, peacekeepers were sent all over the country to supervise the voting process. Humanitarian actors lamented the fact that troops were still deployed in stable provinces months after the elections, when their presence in both Kivu and Ituri was most needed to mitigate, if not prevent, the wave of violence that overtook these provinces in 2007. The persistent violence and the acute social crisis have had a terrible impact on the civilian population, mainly on women and children, who have been victims of terrifying aggression, murder, systematic rape, forced recruitment, and use of children as soldiers. In the province of North Kivu alone, 436,000 people were displaced between December 2006 and February 2008.[6] Countrywide, at the end of 2007 there were still more than 1.3 million displaced persons, more than half of whom were forced to abandon their homes in the last six months of 2007.[7]

Overall, the mortality rate in the DRC is one of the highest in the world. Most deaths are attributed to preventable or curable diseases, such as malaria, diarrhoea, measles, and meningitis, or to malnutrition. A United Nations Children's Fund (UNICEF) report indicates that in 2007, the maternal mortality ratio was 1,289 deaths per 100,000 live births, and rises to 3,000 deaths per 100,000 in conflict-affected areas.[8] UNICEF estimates that 10 percent of children are underweight at birth. Over half of the 620,000 deaths of children under five are attributed to malnutrition and micronutrient deficiencies.[9] The same sources reported that 20 percent of these deaths could be prevented through appropriate infant feeding. Multiple indicators show that there is a re-emergence of disease epidemics which had supposedly been eradicated. In 2007, cholera killed hundreds and 187 died of Ebola.[10] Also contributing to the high mortality rate is HIV/AIDS, rampant in the DRC. The Joint United Nations Programme on HIV/AIDS (UNAIDS) explains that the prevalence rate varies from 1.7 percent to 7.6 percent, depending on the region.[11] In conflict areas where women and children are victims of sexual violence, prevalence increases to 20 percent.

Years of conflict have destroyed the DRC's agricultural potential. It is a painful fact that in a country with a climate and soil favourable to the cultivation of a wide range of tropical and Mediterranean crops, and with the potential to feed all of Africa, 11 percent of all deaths in the DRC can be attributed to malnutrition.[12] In rural areas, the lack of money and the inability to obtain agriculture inputs, combined with insecurity, poor access to potable water, and absence of transport are undermining the recovery and the well-being of the civilian population.

The situation in the urban areas is also grim. Hundreds of thousands of people live in overcrowded conditions in dismally unhealthy shantytowns, without electricity, safe drinking water, or sanitation, their single daily concern being to find food. In the poorest suburbs of Kinshasa, no one seems to know what an NGO is or what the Red Cross flag means. This disturbing panorama has to be understood in the context of a failed state, with a disintegrated administration, disorganised services, generalised corruption,[13] and economic derailment. In 2007, the country was 168th out of 177 countries in the UNDP Human Development Index,[14] down one place from the previous year, when the DRC ranked 167th.[15] Despite the transition process and the multiple political and economic agreements, the DRC remains far below minimum international humanitarian standards. Subsistence mechanisms are very limited, with 80 percent of the population living on US$1 per day,[16] an underemployment rate of 81.7 percent,[17] and the Congolese economy considered one of the least competitive on the African continent.[18]

The humanitarian response

According to the Office for the Coordination of Humanitarian Affairs (OCHA) Financial Tracking System (FTS),[19] donors provided US$500 million to support humanitarian aid programmes in the DRC. Of this, the UN Consolidated Appeal for the 2007 Humanitarian Action Plan for the DRC received US$456 million, 66 percent of the US$686 million requested. Donor backing for humanitarian assistance programmes has increased constantly since the 2006 Humanitarian Action Plan (HAP) and the encouraging developments in the country. Long considered a "forgotten crisis," the DRC is now receiving greater attention from the donor community. This attitude can be attributed to several factors, including the promising political transition, the NGO campaign for greater donor attention, reinforcement of MONUC's mandate, improved security conditions allowing humanitarian actors to access beneficiaries, and the fact that the DRC was the pilot country for implementation of the GHD initiative.

FTS reports the largest donors of total humanitarian aid to the DRC in 2007 were: the US with US$120 million (24 percent of total humanitarian funding); the European Commission, US$69.7 million (13.9 percent); and, the UK, US$66 million (13.2 percent). It should be emphasised that France, criticised for its small commitments in 2006, almost tripled its contribution to US$7.8 million, a sum which still represented only 1.6 percent of the total donor contribution. By contrast, Germany and Japan, also taken to task for their insufficient commitments, *reduced* their contributions in 2007.

The UN Central Emergency Response Fund (CERF), a key mechanism in UN humanitarian reform, was the fourth largest source of funds in the DRC in 2007, contributing US$52.5 million (10 percent of all humanitarian funding).

Another key instrument in the implementation of humanitarian aid in the DRC is the Pooled Fund (PF), comprising 23 percent of the total amount contributed. The Pooled Fund is a common fund provided by various donors, managed by the Humanitarian Coordinator through OCHA (funds attribution) and UNDP (financial management, administration, and monitoring). In 2007, donor contributions to the PF amounted to US$117.8 million (from Belgium, Canada, Ireland, Luxemburg, the Netherlands, Norway, Spain, Sweden, and the United Kingdom), an increase of 27 percent over the 2006 budget. The UK was the most generous donor to the PF with US$58.6 million, representing 49.74 percent of the total PF budget and 93.8 percent of the overall contribution of the UK to the DRC HAP 2007 Appeal. The policy of the UK Department for International Development (DFID) of prioritising funds to the PF is worrisome to some humanitarian agencies who deplore the systematic channelling of funds through the UN system. The contributions of two other main donors to the PF, the Netherlands and Sweden, does not exceed 60 percent of their whole contribution to aid programmes in DRC, which NGOs consider more balanced.

The two main objectives of the humanitarian aid strategy have been to respond to the emergency and support the return process. The 2008 Humanitarian Action Plan focuses on the provinces to which almost 1,480,000 internally displaced people (IDPs) have returned since the end of the conflict, 760,000 of them in 2007.[20] In many cases, the displaced live with host families who take them in for several months, until they are able to return of their own accord to their villages. When the return is organised, UNICEF and NGOs provide the returnees with kits (for both individuals and communities) consisting of plastic sheeting, blankets, and other non-food items, but the kits are not much help in dealing with such major difficulties as land disputes and civilian protection. However, the UN High Commissioner for Refugees (UNHCR) is attempting to put in place essential administrative mechanisms for land redistribution, so that the return can be sustained.

These carefully delineated objectives were conceived at the cluster level and put in place in 2006. In the DRC, ten clusters have already been established at the national and local levels. OCHA (in charge of the overall coordination) encourages NGOs to participate. Clusters are seen as a positive element for assessment, coordination, and prioritisation of needs. But some are also criticised for being slow and non-participatory. A study by the Center on International Cooperation (CIC)[21] stressed that NGOs such as Médecins Sans Frontières (MSF) consider that the cluster approach sometimes "blurr[ed] the lines between humanitarian action and the political/military agenda," particularly in the cluster where MONUC replaced OCHA.

In 2007, the clusters that received most funding were food security (US$142.5 million), health (US$41.8 million) and logistics (US$45 million).[22] Several nutritional surveys conducted throughout the year showed that all the areas visited faced a food crisis. This situation was particularly worrisome in western provinces and in Kinshasa. This important gap has been identified by the 2008 HAP. Thus, subsistence mechanisms and government capacity to respond to the need will be analysed countrywide in the future. Areas affected by chronic poverty, and which comply with the previously mentioned criteria, could be included in the humanitarian map. This approach will have a significant impact on the redefinition of needs and on the geographical redeployment of NGOs.

Since the DRC elections, 17 donors, UN agencies, and the World Bank produced a Country Assistance Framework (CAF) linked to the Poverty Reduction Strategy Paper (PRSP). International development partners pledged US$4 billion in support of development in DRC, notably the implementation of its PRSP over the next 3 years (2008–2010). This means that the DRC will receive US$1.3 billion per year from bilateral and multilateral donors. Unfortunately, there is no clear planning and financing link between humanitarian programmes and development priorities.

Overall, in 2007, the humanitarian community achieved important objectives in the DRC. One critical element was the well-developed coordination structure supported by experienced humanitarian actors. Coordination also benefited from the competence of the OCHA team and firm leadership by the Humanitarian Coordinator. However, there is still a need to assess the impact of pilot initiatives in the DRC and to measure whether new funding mechanisms allow humanitarian actors to assist the population at risk in a more appropriate and timely manner.

Implementation of the response: Impact of the reform mechanism

Since 2005–2006, significant effort and resources have been allocated to reform the humanitarian process in the DRC. The purpose of the reforms was to deliver more adequate, flexible, and timely humanitarian financing, to ensure the standardisation of need assessments and of the broader scope of the sectors (cluster approach), and to reinforce the role of the Humanitarian Coordinator. Nevertheless, it remains unclear if these reforms have had a significant impact on beneficiaries.

The objectives of the Pooled Fund (PF), mentioned earlier, are to allocate funds to priority humanitarian needs, and improve response and coordination mechanisms. In 2007, the total PF (US$117.8 million) was equivalent to the second largest bilateral humanitarian donor to the DRC, second only to the United States.

The PF initiative, in line with the GHD *Principles,* has altered the humanitarian funding landscape in the DRC. But voices from the field are concerned about some of its dysfunctions. One of the main NGO concerns is that funds are channelled through the UN system, which allocated 5 percent of the total budget to cover administrative costs. NGOs see these as misdirected funds which they would prefer to dedicate to their programmes, as they would if they were receiving direct bilateral grants from donors. But the PF can also be seen as a convenient channel for donors to reduce their transaction costs and increase proportionally their volume of aid. NGOs also consider that slow UNDP management delayed disbursement of funds, increased administrative burdens, and delayed the implementation of aid programmes.

Excessive UN control of the process also arouses criticism, leading NGOs to request greater transparency and more participation in the decision-making process. Moreover, the PF is also seen as being excessively focused on short-term solutions, and therefore, limiting the impact of aid on beneficiaries. The three-month duration of most programmes is too short to be effective in the DRC, which requires longer-term commitments. One INGO complained that vulnerable Congolese are suffering from short-term donor priorities, giving the example of being able to easily access PF or CERF money for a three-month cholera response in Goma, but not being able to get funding for a substantial public health programme to address the real situation facing the population after the collapse of state health services.

They point out that cholera is now an annual occurrence in Goma.[23]

Multilateral financing mechanisms directly managed by the UN system also challenge NGO independence, and consequently NGO capacity to efficiently implement aid programmes. Many NGOs question the added value of such a system and underline the operational risks of functioning within a UN-dependent system. This can be a particularly critical point in a country like the DRC, where the Humanitarian Coordinator, the most powerful individual in the humanitarian community, is operating within the framework of an integrated UN mission with a strong political and military mandate.

Clearly, more manageable tools would appear to be the cluster approach and the Provincial Inter-Agency Committees (CPIA) – additional mechanisms of UN humanitarian reform – whose objectives are to raise standards, define provincial strategies, and ensure greater coordination and partnership in all 10 sectors. Cluster groups, at national and provincial levels, are useful tools to identify gaps, finance projects on the basis of needs and ensure the quality of technical aspects of selected projects in accordance with international standards (e.g., Sphere Standards, WHO guidelines, etc.). Thus, it seems that the system has been integrated and accepted by the majority of humanitarian actors, even though there are complaints about the administrative burdens imposed by the system and resistance to the central role of the United Nations.

It is probably too early to measure the impact of the United Nations reform in the DRC. Did the new instruments improve humanitarian actors work? Was aid more flexible, adequate, and timely? Have more lives been saved? For actors in the field, it is difficult to give categorical answers. However, there is one point on which all agree: instruments such as the PF, CERF, or the cluster approach have great potential and should be improved.

Donors and Good Humanitarian Donorship

In 2004, the DRC was selected as a pilot country for the GHD. Donors have developed their own coordination tools and discuss core principles, financial decisions, and prioritise programmes based on the guidelines of the Humanitarian Action Plan and have expressed strong support for all the recent initiatives taken to strengthen coordination of the humanitarian system. Nevertheless, the increasing importance of UN funding mechanisms is sometimes creating confusion in the

NGO community concerning the role and competence of some donors and of the Humanitarian Coordinator. One major donor interviewed in the field during the HRI mission admitted that the UN machinery is increasingly acting like a donor, generating a "competitive factor." The same donor admitted that the relationship between the Humanitarian Coordinator and donors lost its initial fluidity and transparency.

Nevertheless, humanitarian priorities in DRC are widely acknowledged. Protection remains a priority. Implementing agencies would like to see greater donor involvement in this fundamental element of Principles 3, 4 and 16 of the GHD. During the electoral process, the international community was present on the diplomatic and financial fronts. However, since the new government took power, key agencies blame both diplomats and donors for being too discreet about human rights violations. Agencies feel that there is a lack of coherence among the donors with regard to reform of the army, good governance, and support for the judicial system. After the elections, important economic development contracts were signed between the DRC government and international donors, but Human Rights Watch reports that very few of these donors expressed concern about current human rights violations or conditioned their aid on better protection for civilians.[24]

Another priority in the DRC is to support programmes for the return and reintegration of the displaced and refugees. OCHA estimates that 2008 will be marked by the return of 79,000 refugees and many of the 1.3 million displaced throughout the country. Areas of return are often isolated and difficult to access, due to the deterioration or absence of roads. Years of conflict have destroyed schools, and health and social centres. There are no jobs; agricultural activities remain precarious; social tensions are high. This troubling scenario calls for implementation of a long-term programme to fill the gap between humanitarian aid and development projects (Principle 9 of the GHD). On these issues, humanitarian agencies are critical of donors – an old debate to which they do not offer ready solutions. The development strategies of major donors are totally unknown to humanitarian actors and development agencies in the field. NGOs confessed that donors lose credibility with local actors because of slow implementation of their programmes. This is particularly true in the health sector, where the extreme slowness of the EC's Fond européen pour le développement (FED) programmes is so evident, that in Goma, the 9th FED is ironically called the 9th *Faible* ("weak"). However, it

should be pointed out that the greatest difficulty donors encountered is the absence of national and local counterparts. Thus, the humanitarian situation will greatly improve through the restoration of the Congolese state and its institutions.

The chronic problems in DRC could plunge a province into a humanitarian emergency in a matter of weeks. In the absence of an integrated long-term approach, the DRC is susceptible to a vicious cycle in which the assisted population risks suffering another crisis after humanitarian organisations withdraw. To bridge this gap, NGOs confess that they have to reshape their programmes in such a way that donors will still consider them emergency-oriented, although, in reality, they deal with development issues. Some donors are conscious of this problem and try to employ a more flexible definition of humanitarian needs in provinces where security improves. For implementing partners, this situation calls for more direct funding to NGOs.

A fundamental GHD Principle insists that funding decisions be based on a solid needs assessment. Since pilot projects have been implemented in the DRC, progress has been made in using common needs assessments. OCHA has supported inter-agency planning and multi-sector needs assessments in developing regional humanitarian action plans. The larger question is whether the available funding is proportionate to the needs identified. Donor support increased for the DRC since the GHD pilot project began, but so did their requests to use available funds more effectively. This mix of resource-based and needs-based planning permitted a larger and more rational coverage of humanitarian needs. Nevertheless, the implementation of these new tools does not guarantee coverage of identified needs. Major UN actors and NGOs often use the host family situation as an example. In the eastern part of the country, 70 percent of the displaced are living with host families. In most cases, the arrival of the IDPs doubled the size of the families, while house size and access to food and water remained unchanged. In many cases, the resources of host families were quickly exhausted, resulting in the general impoverishment of communities in areas affected by displacement.

Regarding neutrality, independence, and impartiality, implementing partners are critical of donor performance. "No war no work" is a formula used by some donors which is roundly criticised by NGOs. The eastern part of the DRC is the target of the vast majority of donor aid. The western part of the country has been virtually forgotten, despite the fact that some provinces *without* armed conflict registered the highest mortality and mal-nutrition rates. There is a general understanding that donors have given priority to solving the situation in the east in order to stabilise the country. However, many NGOs consider that any other country displaying the same vulnerability indicators as western DRC would be considered a priority emergency.

The very specific context of humanitarian interven-tion within an integrated mission, in which MONUC is a key player, should be kept in mind. Agencies explained that UN management of the Pooled Fund affects the neutrality and independence of programmes. Interviewees typically commented that donors improved in effective-ness and efficiency. The field expertise of donors such as ECHO or DFID is greatly appreciated. In the case of DFID, however, many NGOs warned that if the donor agency continues its policy of channelling the majority of its funds to the PF, it could lose identity and influence.

Finally, it should be emphasised that the survey team found humanitarian actors to be better informed about the GHD *Principles* than they were last year. Nevertheless, most still do not understand exactly what is expected from them and ask how the outcomes of the GHD initiative can be measured. Both donors and humanitarian organisations recognise that saving lives and alleviating suffering (Principle 1) is an objective that deserves total dedication and engagement. Yet, three years after the implementation of the pilot in the DRC, there is still a need to demonstrate how upholding the GHD *Principles* will meet this objective.

Conclusion

"Every day without major clashes is a victory for the peace process in DRC," explained a top UN representa-tive.[25] This statement eloquently expresses not only the hope for the country's recovery, but also its fragility. The encouraging picture emerging from the transition can-not eclipse the desperate situation in the eastern part of the country where civilians are victims of daily human rights violations and forced displacement.

Today, the main challenge is to convert hope and promise into reality. The international community's engagement remains essential to reaching this objective, but it must be more critical of how domestic as well as foreign belligerents fulfil their commitment to the peace process, to human rights, and to good governance. Although donor involvement in the east remains a pri-ority, humanitarian actors insist on the need to see donors more involved in the western part of the country. The same agencies are also concerned that more donors will channel their funds through the PF system. Moreover, the same NGOs fear that such a model could weaken their independence, and undermine their relations with donors. Clearly, the DRC needs not only humanitarian aid, but also a massive infusion of technical and long-term assistance.

Finally, the GHD remains a potential tool to rein-force the partnership between donors and implementing NGOs, representing a code of conduct for donors and encouraging coherent donor behaviour in response to humanitarian needs. The question remains whether Good Humanitarian Donorship is improving the lives of millions of Congolese and how this can be measured.

Notes

1 The HRI team, composed of Aldara Collet, Gilles Gasser, Carlos Oliver, Soledad Posada, and Kim Wuyts visited the Democratic Republic of the Congo in February 2008. The opinions expressed here are those of the author and do not necessarily reflect those of DARA.

2 The Kinshasa alliance included Zimbabwe, Angola, Chad, and Namibia. The Rwanda alliance included Rwanda, Uganda, and Burundi.

3 International Rescue Committee, 2008.

4 Since 2000, the IRC conducted five mortality surveys. The first conducted between 2000 and 2004, estimated that 3.9 million people had died since 1998, making DRC the world's deadliest humanitarian catastrophe since World War II.

5 This rate is twice the African average and almost twice the 1.3 per 1000 per month reported by UNICEF for the DRC in 1997, the year before the war began.

6 Office for the Coordination of Humanitarian Affairs (OCHA), 2008a.

7 OCHA 2008b.

8 UNICEF, 2007.

9 Ibid.

10 OCHA, 2008b, p. 6.

11 *IRIN,* 2007.

12 Ibid.

13 In the 2007 *Corruption Perceptions Index,* Transparency International ranked the DRC 156th out of 163 countries (Transparency International, 2007, p. 330).

14 UNDP, 2007, p. 232.

15 UNDP, 2006, p. 294.

16 UNICEF, 2007.

17 OECD, 2008, p. 255.

18 Conclusion of the *Africa Competitiveness Report, 2007,* released 13 June 2007 at the World Economical Forum on Africa.

19 OCHA, FTS, 2007.

20 OCHA, 2008b, p. 42.

21 Center on International Cooperation, 2006, p. 20.

22 OCHA, 2008b, p. 15.

23 Refugee Studies Centre, 2007, p. 31.

24 Human Rights Watch, 2007, pp. 75–76.

25 HRI field interview.

References

Center on International Cooperation. 2006. "Evaluation of the Pooled Fund in the Democratic Republic of the Congo: Component Report for the Study, Monitoring, and Evaluation of Common Funds for Humanitarian Action." CIC. New York University. 7 November.

Human Rights Watch. 2007. Renewed Crisis in North Kivu. October. At: http://hrw.org/reports/2007/drc1007/drc1007webwcover.pdf

International Rescue Committee. 2008. *Mortality in the Democratic Republic of Congo: An Ongoing crisis.* At: http://www.theirc.org/resources/2007/2006-7_congomortalitysurvey.pdf

IRIN. 2007. Democratic Republic of Congo (DRC) Humanitarian Country Profile. February. *Irin Humanitarian News and Analysis.* At: http://www.irinnews.org/country.aspx?CountryCode=CD&RegionCode=GL

Office for the Coordination of Humanitarian Affairs (OCHA). Financial Tracking Service. Geneva.

———. 2007. Humanitarian Action Plan 2007: Democratic Republic of the Congo. At: http://ochadms.unog.ch/quickplace/cap/main.nsf/h_Index/2007_DRC_ActionPlan_ENG/$FILE/2007_DRC_ActionPlan_ENG_SCREEN.pdf?OpenElement

———. 2008a. DR Congo: OCHA North Kivu Humanitarian Situation Update, 2–8 February. At: http://www.reliefweb.int/rw/RWB.NSF/db900SID/SHES-7BMRHV?OpenDocument

———. 2008b. République Démocratique du Congo: Plan d'action humanitaire 2008. At: http://ochadms.unog.ch/quickplace/cap/main.nsf/h_Index/2008_DRC_ActionPlan_FR/$FILE/2008_DRC_ActionPlan_FR_SCREEN.pdf?OpenElement

Organisation for Economic Co-operation and Development (OECD). 2008. African Economic Outlook: Democratic Republic of Congo. At: http://www.oecd.org/dataoecd/13/39/40577125.pdf

Refugee Studies Centre. 2007. *Humanitarian Reform, Fulfilling Its Promise? Forced Migration Review* 29. University of Oxford. December.

Transparency International. 2007. *Corruption Perceptions Index.* Berlin.

UNICEF. 2007. Humanitarian Action Report. At: http://www.unicef.org/har07/index_37592.htm

United Nations Development Program (UNDP). 2006. Human Development Report 2006: Beyond Scarcity: Power, Poverty and the Global Water Crisis. At: http://hdr.undp.org/en/media/hdr06-complete.pdf

———. 2007. Human Development Report: Fighting Climate Change: Human Solidarity in a Divided World. At: http://hdr.undp.org/en/media/hdr_20072008_en_complete.pdf

World Economic Forum. 2007. *Africa Competitiveness Report, 2007.* Geneva.

Nicaragua

AT A GLANCE

Country data *(2006 figures, unless otherwise noted)*

- 2007 Human Development Index: ranked 110th of 177 countries
- Population: 5.53 million
- GNI per capita (Atlas method, current US$): US$930
- Population living on less than US$2 a day (1990–2005): 79.9 percent
- Life expectancy (in years): 72
- Infant mortality rate: 29 per 1,000 live births
- Under five infant mortality rate: 36 per 1,000
- Population undernourished (2002–2004): 27 percent
- Population with sustainable access to improved water source (2004): 79 percent
- Adult literacy rate (over 15 yrs of age) (1995–2005): 76.7 percent
- Primary education completion rate: 73 percent
- Gender-related development index (2005): ranked 98th of 177 countries
- Official development assistance (ODA): US$733 million
- 2007 Corruption Perception Index: ranked 123rd out of 179 countries

Sources: Transparency International (TI). 2007; UNDP, 2007a and 2007b; World Bank, 2008.

The crisis

- Nicaragua is one of the world's most disaster-prone countries; in past decade, over 1.35 million people have been displaced or affected by disasters; over 3,500 killed; and between US$1.5 and US$3 billion in damage sustained;
- Hurricane Felix struck 4 September 2007, principally affecting the Región Autónoma del Atlántico Norte (RAAN), the North Atlantic Autonomous Region;
- 60 percent the RAAN's population lives below the poverty line, higher than the national average;
- Felix affected 34,000 households (approximately 200,000 persons), caused 235 deaths, destroyed 10,000 houses, and tore roofs from additional 9,000 homes and buildings;
- Over 86,000 hectares of land damaged; more than 6,000 livestock killed; monthly food aid requirements calculated at US$3.52 million.

Sources: World Bank, 2008a; Government of Nicaragua, 2007.

The humanitarian response

- The Nicaraguan government estimated recovery needs at US$400 million US$292 million requested through UN; UN Flash Appeal requested almost US$40 million;
- Largest humanitarian donors: EC/ECHO (US$8.2 million, 26.8 percent of total); U.S. (US$7 million, 22.7 percent); Sweden (US$1.5 million, 4.9 percent); CERF provided US$5 million (16.2 percent); unearmarked funds from other UN agencies (US$2.7 million, 8.7 percent);
- US$7.5 million more provided in response to heavy rains following hurricane: 55.8 percent from Canada; 22.1 percent from Switzerland; 17.5 percent from EC/ECHO;
- Venezuelan in-kind support and cash aid surpassed US$18 million.

Sources: Government of Nicaragua, 2007; OCHA FTS.

Nicaragua
Living in the Eye of the Storm

SILVIA HIDALGO, Director, DARA

Introduction[1]

Nicaragua has a long and painful history of sudden-onset disasters precipitated by natural phenomena[2] which have devastated lives, particularly those of the poor and most vulnerable, and suffocated the country's economic and human development. Poverty is widespread, with 46 percent of the population living below the poverty line. Only Haiti is poorer in Latin America. According to the World Bank, Nicaragua is one of the world's most disaster-prone countries, having suffered a major disaster every two years for the last century. In the past decade alone, over 1.35 million people have been displaced or affected by disasters; over 3,500 have lost their lives, and between US$1.5 and US$3 billion of economic damage has been sustained.[3]

Just as many humanitarian and regional actors were preparing initiatives to mark the 10th anniversary of the catastrophe caused by Hurricane Mitch, Nicaragua was once again struck by a hurricane. This time, Hurricane Felix affected principally the most marginalised and neglected Miskito people of the country's most vulnerable north-east Atlantic coast region.

The crisis: Felix and the marginalised North Atlantic region

Hurricane Felix struck on 4 September 2007. Ranked as a Category-5 hurricane on the Saffir-Simpson scale, Felix principally affected the *Región Autónoma del Atlántico Norte* (RAAN), the North Atlantic

Autonomous Region. This low-lying area is home to thousands of Miskito Indians, who depend on canoes to navigate shallow rivers and lakes to reach higher ground. Before making landfall, Felix had devastated the Cayos Miskitos, a fishing area crucial to the local economy. After battering the coastal communities, the hurricane headed inland in a south-westerly direction, across a sparsely populated area, leaving a trail of destruction some 60 km wide.

The RAAN is the largest and poorest region of Nicaragua, 60 percent of whose 308,000 inhabitants live below the poverty line – a much higher proportion than the national average. They are ethnically distinct from the rest of the population and enjoy a significant degree of political autonomy. Most of the rural communities affected by Hurricane Felix were home to Miskito Indians.

According to official estimates, Hurricane Felix directly affected close to 34,000 households (approximately 200,000 persons), and caused 235 deaths, with a further 133 persons still missing as of November 2007. Over 10,000 houses were completely destroyed by the hurricane, which tore the roofs from an additional 9,000 homes. Over US$4 million was required to cover temporary shelter requirements, under a plan presented by the government through UNDP. Over 273,000 corrugated zinc roofs were needed, at an average cost of US$15 each. Hundreds of public buildings and utilities, including schools, clinics, and water sources, were also damaged or destroyed.

In addition, monthly food aid requirements were calculated at US$3.52 million, in part because the hurricane disrupted the harvesting of several key crops.[4] Over 86,000 hectares of land were damaged and over 6,000 livestock killed.[5] However, the World Food Programme (WFP) did not receive sufficient funding to cover all food needs for the 200,000 beneficiaries estimated by the government. In practice, WFP focussed on covering 60 percent of the food aid requirements of 88,400 people. Small-scale fishing, officially the primary source of income for coastal communities, was also seriously disrupted due to the displacement of the fishermen, the loss of equipment, and the extensive destruction of marine areas.

While in most areas there were no possibilities to evacuate the population prior to the storm, after Felix was over, 12,700 people were evacuated to 72 camps, 65 of which were located in the regional capital Puerto Cabezas. However, the city was without electrical power and communications, and the airport runway and many roads were unusable, making it impossible for the first planes carrying humanitarian aid to land.

By the end of October, the Nicaraguan government estimated humanitarian and recovery needs at US$400 million. Although Hurricane Felix was a relatively small-scale catastrophe in terms of the number of victims and destruction caused, it must be seen in the context of disasters which are recurrent and which disproportionately affect the most vulnerable. It is in such situations that the concept of donor engagement to prevent and prepare for disaster has special meaning. In the wake of Hurricane Mitch, Nicaragua had embarked on a process of strengthening its capacity to deal with repeated disasters. In this respect, the country's efforts benefited from the aid related to post-Mitch recovery operations and more recent international assistance strategies. Nevertheless, preparations to respond to Felix were flawed.

The humanitarian response: An uneven relief effort

The effectiveness of the humanitarian response was uneven, and depended greatly on both the location and accessibility of communities and the presence and capacity of local organisations and actors. Crucially important was the fact that many international organisations were either not on the ground or lacked sufficient capacity, because the storm was initially expected to have the greatest impact on neighbouring Honduras.

The head of the Sistema Nacional para la Prevención, Mitigación y Atención de Desastres (SINAPRED), the national body for disaster prevention and response, quickly recognised the challenge posed by the extensive humanitarian needs, aggravated by the heavy rains which followed Felix. Nevertheless, even the initial basic needs concerning food and shelter were, according to SINAPRED, underestimated. The response action plan was subsequently estimated at US$400 million, of which US$292 million was requested through the United Nations by President Ortega.[6] The UN Flash Appeal, issued 10 days after the hurricane, requested almost US$40 million.

The initial response was hampered because many international and regional teams were prepositioned in Honduras, where the hurricane was expected to hit. For example, the International Federation of the Red Cross (IFRC) had no teams in Nicaragua. Therefore, where local organisations and NGOs were not present, coverage was very poor. Moreover, as in other disasters, there were disheartening examples of avoidable failures in the delivery of aid; in one such instance, water trucks were sent to distant communities, but were forced to return because there were no containers in which to store the water. Nevertheless, while there were many complaints reported in the national and local press, many external observers described the initial response as acceptable.[7]

The disaster response was managed by SINAPRED, with efforts by OCHA to enhance coordination and introduce sectoral clusters which would provide for greater transparency in aid prioritisation. However, the international humanitarian community is still uncertain regarding the applicability of international coordination systems, such as the cluster approach, in countries where the national government takes the lead during a humanitarian crisis.

Despite the national and international response, beneficiaries were often poorly informed about recovery plans and aid activities, and consequently had little ownership of the programmes implemented. For example, three months after the storm, community leaders in Sandy Bay were unsure whether they would receive aid. In hard-to-access areas, where communities carried out recovery activities with their own means, local appeals for expertise on how to apply disaster risk reduction standards in the rehabilitation of housing and public buildings often went unheeded.

Needs assessments did not clearly differentiate between pre-existing conditions, life-threatening situations, and beneficiary priorities. At the household level, they were patchy and limited, making targeting the most vulnerable within communities difficult. This was exacerbated by the fact that in the local culture, people were accustomed to sharing resources irrespective of differences in living conditions or means. Therefore allocating aid on a per-household basis meant that relief did not necessarily reach those most in need. In other instances, some in-kind assistance was distributed based on the criterion of whether a family member had been lost in the storm, hence, not according to a specific assessment of needs.[8]

Several factors came into play in the preparedness, relief, and recovery operation. As in other scenarios, the magnitude of the disaster was determined not only by the hurricane's intensity, but by the pattern of vulnerability of the people living in the area. The effectiveness of interventions was also conditioned by factors specific to the context and circumstances. Overall, four issues stand out:

Imperfect early warning and preparedness

Since the hurricane was initially expected to make landfall in Honduras, villagers in the RAAN received insufficient warning from officials. More significantly, many international emergency teams were not deployed in Nicaragua, but were in fact dispatched to Honduras. These failures were due not only to the shortcomings of the computer models used to predict the storm, but also to the fact that Felix developed strength in record time. US meteorologists claimed that Felix "strengthened more rapidly than any other storm on record, anywhere in the world."[9] Furthermore, although local authorities in the region did visit communities to warn them of the imminent storm and alerted many fishermen, there was an institutional fear of "crying wolf," stemming from their experience of the contrast between the alarm raised in the RAAN in 2005 regarding hurricane Beta and the limited damage which actually resulted.

While the RAAN is considered disaster prone and has benefited from earlier disaster preparedness and prevention efforts – implemented mainly by the Dutch Red Cross, *Gruppo Voluntario Civile,* and Oxfam through *Acción Médica Cristiana* – local people were not sufficiently disaster aware. Sunshine and good weather was deceptive, leading the population to believe that there was no imminent danger. The affected communities claimed that they first learned of the danger and believed the warnings when they saw the names of their towns and villages on television news. Many claimed that, despite warnings, many emergency decisions were not taken, for example, to close schools.

An isolated and culturally distinct region

While all concerned in the response were, in theory, clear that the area's cultural and linguistic differences required locally owned interventions, this was not always the case. Many existing national resources on disaster preparedness and response were less relevant to the specific cultural and geographic context and had to be translated or adapted. There were clear differences with respect to other areas of Nicaragua, as many community leaders, while proficient in Spanish, had never heard of climate change or been affected by a disaster. Therefore, although national and regional protocols and means for intervention existed, the high level of political autonomy, the remoteness of the region, and the lack of prior experience in disaster management in the RAAN all affected the response.

Institutional decentralisation often made it unclear at what level responsibilities lay. In practice, the Governor of the RAAN lacked the necessary capacity to manage the response and required support. Even when the international community tries to respect local capacity and promote locally owned responses, it is often difficult to know which level of authority should be supported, especially in view of the region's autonomy and decentralisation. It is unclear, therefore, what exactly "local" means.

Politicization in Nicaragua

Unsurprisingly given its history, Nicaragua remains politically polarised, despite recent right-left party coalitions. While humanitarian action is meant to be impartial, independent and neutral, disasters, particularly sudden ones, provide opportunities for political grandstanding and clientelism. For example, considerable visibility was given to the humanitarian support provided by Hugo Chavez's Venezuela, because of his government's close relationship with that of Nicaragua's President, Daniel Ortega. The government also argued that it had no funds with which to respond to either existing or new needs, given the constraints of its budget, debt repayment requirements, and the conditionality imposed by the International Monetary Fund, World Bank, and many traditional donors.

The new coalition government led by President Ortega promised in its electoral campaign to prioritise the RAAN, and the region's voters duly helped elect the Sandinista candidate. However, in the wake of hurricane Felix, there was considerable disgruntlement amongst many inhabitants of the RAAN, who regretted having voted for President Ortega, and making the accusation that "those who had wanted to become rich in positions of power now wanted to become millionaires and benefit from the disaster."[10] There were many claims that aid was misappropriated: for example, that local officials responsible for World Bank and other recovery projects recommended candidates to staff the projects in exchange for a quarter of their salaries.

Costly coverage and expensive logistics

Lack of means of transport and fuel made it difficult for the population to evacuate and for implementing agencies to reach affected communities. As many communities were far from Puerto Cabezas and only accessible by boat, logistics presented a real challenge and aid was concentrated in areas which were accessible by road, even though these were not the most affected by the storm. For example, communities in the badly damaged area of Sandy Bay, which lost 99 percent of its homes when hit by the eye of the storm,[11] received little assistance. Three months after the storm, many households there had only received one distribution of food aid. To make matters worse, prices of essential goods in the RAAN, already high by Nicaraguan standards, increased after Hurricane Felix, contributing to a decreased standard of living.

The international donor response: Scarcity of actors … but Venezuela

According to OCHA's Financial Tracking Service (FTS), the largest humanitarian aid donors for the response to Hurricane Felix were: the European Commission (ECHO), which committed US$8.2 million (26.8 percent of total funding); the US, with US$7 million (22.7 percent); and Sweden with US$1.5 million (4.9 percent). Other multilateral funding sources included the UN Central Emergency Response Fund (CERF), which provided US$5 million (16.2 percent), and unearmarked funds from other UN agencies amounting to US$2.7 million (8.7 percent), with the rest from other sources. A further US$7.5 million was contributed in response to the heavy rains which followed Hurricane Felix, 55.8 percent of which came from Canada, 22.1 percent from Switzerland and 17.5 percent from EC/ECHO.

Donors are principally involved in the provision of development aid through budgetary support to Nicaragua. However, the current government's relationship with traditional donors is strained and budget support is regarded as providing less leverage for promoting donor policies, including effective disaster risk reduction.

The European Commission, through ECHO, was the main donor, and although it was initially unclear whether it would, in fact, fund the emergency response, information from the field and the regional delegation in Managua prompted the Commission to act. A primary emergency decision for €1 million helped fund *Télécom Sans Frontières* to provide critical communication services, and the World Food Programme (WFP) and CARE to engage in water and sanitation activities. A later €5 million disbursement covered more comprehensive programming for communities that were harder to reach and incorporated an element of disaster risk reduction.

While in previous large disasters some members of the international donor community have advocated "turning disaster into opportunity" or "building back better," certain donors, especially those that focus on relief activities such as ECHO, put limits on the type of recovery assistance they provide. For example, at times the parameters of the primary emergency funding for water and sanitation did not allow for continuous monitoring and renewed assessment, which would have contributed to better understanding of the unfolding context and therefore aid appropriateness. Furthermore, communication with beneficiary communities is essential, so that assistance can be adjusted to meet their changing needs and the resulting response strategies can be shaped by the priorities and concerns of the survivors. These concerns – and the shift from relief to recovery – should be captured in a follow-up needs assessment. In this sense, ECHO, in the key sector of basic water supply, was viewed as inflexible, because it did not allow agencies to improve pre-existing water supply systems. This decision was regarded as being out of touch with local realities, the cultural context, and the government's desire to ensure that the response to the disaster led to real development.[12]

The United States provided mainly emergency relief supplies and air support. The US military airlifted aid out of Puerto Cabezas to hard hit areas as part of its Humanitarian Assistance Program, which works with countries in the region to improve disaster relief responses. Approximately US$1.5 million was spent for airlifts, while the US Office of Foreign Disaster Assistance (OFDA) provided small grants to NGOs.

Sweden, the third largest bilateral humanitarian donor for Felix, has traditionally been Nicaragua's most important provider of Overseas Development Assistance. While the two countries have strong ties and a good working relationship, in August 2007, barely a week before Hurricane Felix struck, Sweden announced that it would be limiting its aid to 37 countries, and that it was phasing out aid to Nicaragua within four years. This unilateral Swedish decision came as a surprise,[13] prompting Swedish diplomats in Managua to privately convey their dismay at the decision. The impact of Sweden's phased withdrawal will affect, above all, the transition to recovery and the incorporation of pro-poor growth policies which would positively contribute to the development of Nicaragua in general, and of RAAN, in particular.

The funds provided by CERF, along with the funds from other UN agencies, were crucial in the response, as a quick source of funding for the immediate response. They played a far more important role than, for instance, the Red Cross and Red Crescent Movement. The World Bank also assumed key responsibilities for implementing an emergency recovery project focusing on rehabilitation of housing, agriculture, and the fisheries. Several donors, including the European Commission, the United States, Switzerland, and Spain supported disaster risk reduction activities.

As in other sudden-onset disasters related to natural phenomena, private funding was critical. In fact, the Nicaraguan public immediately provided in-kind and cash support, through a national telethon in which donations were channelled through the Nicaraguan Red Cross. Many small, mainly religious, organisations travelled to the area to implement rehabilitation activities – primarily in the areas that were easier to reach, such as Krukira. International private donors such as the Bill and Melinda Gates Foundation also provided funding.

As for nontraditional donors, Venezuela was the most significant. Not only did Venezuelan brigades participate in search-and-rescue operations, but, according to the Nicaraguan government, seven months into the response, Venezuelan cash and in-kind support – in the form of food aid, housing material, medicines, fuel, etc. – surpassed US$18 million. In contrast to other donors, which tend to be cautious in their commitments, the Venezuelan Ambassador declared that Nicaragua could, "count on this aid, this cooperation not ceasing and continuing systematically."[14] However, the in-kind support was less adaptable to existing needs. Differences in criteria caused programming delays and stalled distribution and rehabilitation activities. For example, donations of roofing materials were provided for schools and public buildings, while some families were still without any shelter. Unfortunately, none of Venezuela's assistance is reported in the OCHA Financial Tracking Service, highlighting the deficiencies in monitoring humanitarian aid.

Conclusion

Hurricane Felix was not a large disaster in terms either of its impact or the level of funding directed towards the response. Yet, an analysis of the response to disasters such as Hurricane Felix provides an opportunity to assess disaster risk reduction efforts and how they can influence and improve emergency humanitarian responses. Such an assessment should include all dimensions of local capacity and how prior support has strengthened the local response. While it is recognised throughout the humanitarian sector that there is a need to respect and promote local capacity, the international community all too often equates the term *local,* as seen in Nicaragua, with the national level. Hurricane Felix illustrates the importance of distinguishing and prioritising needs and capacity building more locally, especially in contexts such as the RAAN, where decentralisation is, and must be, a reality, and where communities are isolated. International aid should aim to recognise, identify, use, and strengthen local capacity. It is important for agencies to seek to build and capitalise on existing local networks, and to strengthen existing coping strategies and support systems. A number of organisations and institutions have confirmed that they have learned this lesson from their response to Felix.[15] With little surge capacity in the area affected, the ability of the humanitarian community to respond to needs depended on the quality of truly local staff and organisations.

As witnessed in the aftermath of hurricane Felix, assessment, monitoring, and accountability requirements adopted by donors and agencies often rule out assistance in hard-to-reach areas. In combination with logistical constraints, beneficiary-cost calculations – factoring in efficiency and capacity considerations – often contradict GHD Principle 6, which gives priority to reaching those most in need, using a needs-based approach. In situations such as these, both the response and requirements should adapt to situational challenges on the ground.

Furthermore, strategies that are flexible enough to adapt to different phases and interventions will be the most effective way to reach vulnerable people with the right aid. Humanitarian action and development aid are separate types of assistance, for many well justified reasons. The timely rehabilitation of communities suffering from sudden-onset disasters requires flexibility and speed. Experience however shows that recovery is essentially a development issue. In the delicate transition from relief to recovery, repeated needs assessments should be carried out to prioritise communities' needs, adapt the response to an evolving context, and to long-term livelihood strategies. In a disaster-prone area like the RAAN, responses must mainstream disaster risk reduction, giving full consideration to social and cultural realities.

Finally, instruments such as the Financial Tracking Service must be upgraded to reflect the new role played by non-traditional donors, and to facilitate accurate reporting. The fact that Venezuelan aid is recorded in narrative reports on ReliefWeb, but not included in the FTS, highlights the need for greater coherence.

Notes

1. The HRI team, composed of Aldara Collet, Gilles Gasser, and Ana Romero, visited Nicaragua in November 2008. This report is based on the findings of the HRI mission and the field visits and interviews carried out by Silvia Hidalgo and Soledad Posada in Nicaragua in October–November 2007. The opinions expressed here are those of the author and do not necessarily reflect those of DARA.

2. Humanitarian disasters are often the result of the combination of natural phenomena, such as earthquakes or hurricanes, with "unnatural" factors, such as high levels of poverty.

3. World Bank, 2008a.

4. Government of Nicaragua, 2007.

5. World Bank, 2008b.

6. Government of Nicaragua, 2007.

7. HRI field interview.

8. SINAPRED, 2008.

9. Drye, 2007.

10. HRI field interview.

11. UNICEF, 2007.

12. HRI field interview.

13. Schulz, 2007.

14. Ibid.

15. HRI field interview.

References

Drye, Willie. 2007. "Hurricane Felix Forecasts Mostly Failed, Experts Say." National Geographic News. 5 September.

Government of Nicaragua. 2007. "De la Emergencia Humana y la Destrucción a la Recuperación y el desarrollo." [From humanitarian emergency and destruction to recovery and development]. Meeting of the National Emergency Advisory Council with representatives of the international community to consult about th estate of emergency. 23 October.

Office for the Coordination of Humanitarian Assistance. *Financial Tracking Service.*

Schulz, Nils-Sjard. 2007. "Nicaragua: a rude awakening for the Paris Declaration." FRIDE. November. At: http://www.fride.org/publication/285/nicaragua-a-rude-awakening-for-the-paris-declaration

SINAPRED. 2008. "Nicaragua: El hermano pueblo de Venezuela continua ayudando a los damnificados por el Huracán Félix." [Nicaragua: Venezuelans continue to aid the victims of Hurrican Felix] At: http://www.reliefweb.int/rw/rwb.nsf/db900sid/LSGZ-7C9EBX?OpenDocument

UNICEF. 2007. "Hurricane Felix: Nicaragua bears the brunt and Honduras endures heavy rains." 5 September. At: http://www.unicef.org/infobycountry/nicaragua_40782.html

World Bank. 2008a. "Nicaragua Hurricane Felix Emergency Recovery Project." Report No.: AB3659. At: http://www-wds.worldbank.org/servlet/WDSContentServer/IW3P/IB/2008/02/20//000076092_20080220134603/Rendered/INDEX/PID0Appraisal0Stage0HFERC0Feb02002008.txt

———. 2008b. "Project Paper on a Proposed Credit in the Amount of SDR 10.7 million (US$17 million) to the Republic of Nicaragua for a Hurricane Felix Emergency Recovery Project." Report No: 42266-NI. At: http://www-wds.worldbank.org/external/default/WDSContentServer/WDSP/IB/2008/02/27/000333037_20080227232558/Rendered/INDEX/422660PJPR0P101ly10IDA1R20081003011.txt

Occupied Palestinian Territories

AT A GLANCE

Country data *(2006 figures, unless otherwise noted)*

- 2007 Human Development Index: ranked 106th of 177 countries
- Population: 3.77 million
- GNI per capita (Atlas method, current US$) (2005): US$1,230
- Population living on less than US$2 a day (1990–2004): NA
- Life expectancy (in years): 73
- Infant mortality rate: 20 per 1,000 live births
- Under five infant mortality rate: 22 per 1,000
- Population undernourished (2002–2004): 16 percent
- Population with sustainable access to improved water source (2004): 92 percent
- Adult literacy rate (over 15yrs of age): 92 percent
- Primary education completion rate: 89 percent
- Gender-related development index (2005): NA
- Official development assistance (ODA): US$1.449 billion
- 2007 Corruption Perception Index: NA

Sources: Transparency International, 2007; UNDP, 2007a and 2007b; World Bank, 2008.

The crisis

- In 2007, for the first time, the number of deaths and wounded due to inter-Palestinian factional violence – mainly between Fatah and Hamas – surpassed casualties from the conflict with Israel;
- Violations of international humanitarian law and human rights carried out by all sides with impunity;
- In 2007, 34 percent of Palestinians were food insecure; 80 percent of the population in Gaza was dependent on food aid, and most Palestinian families spent 70 percent of income on food;
- 57 percent of the population in the West Bank and Gaza were classified as poor, living on less than US$2.1 per day (increasing to 70 percent in Gaza alone);
- Following the Palestinian Legislative Council elections, Israel's withholding of clearance revenues, and the international community's aid boycotted, the Palestinian Authority forecast that US$1.62 billion is needed in donor assistance to bridge the fiscal gap.

Sources: OCHA, 2008; WFP/FAO, 2007; PCBS, 2007.

The humanitarian response

- In 2007, the UN Consolidated Appeal Process (CAP) for the Occupied Palestinian Territories requested US$426 million, the world's third largest crisis in terms of total CAP requirements (after Sudan, US$1.22 billion and DRC, US$687 million) and US$221 per beneficiary (after DRC, US$391, and Chad US$311);
- The Temporary International Mechanism (TIM) was introduced in 2007 and provided US$890 million in aid to three main mechanisms and sectors: the Emergency Support Services Program (health, education and social services); the Interim Emergency Relief Contribution (energy utilities); and direct financial and relief assistance to vulnerable populations;
- The largest humanitarian donors in 2007 were: EC/ECHO (US$77.9 million), the US (US$75.9 million), and Norway (US$31 million);
- At the December, 2007, Paris conference, donors pledged US$7.710 million over 3 years, US$1.667 million for budgetary support and US$1.258 million for humanitarian aid.

Sources: OCHA, 2008; OCHA FTS.

Occupied Palestinian Territories
A Political Crisis with Humanitarian Consequences

RICARDO SOLÉ-ARQUÉS, Independent Consultant, Development and Humanitarian Aid

Introduction[1]

The survey for the Humanitarian Response Index 2008 in the occupied Palestinian territories (oPt) focuses on donors' responses to humanitarian needs.[2] A thorough analysis of the conflict is not intended here, but donors' response and behaviour cannot be understood without reference to the highly political and complex nature of the conflict. Having its roots in the Middle East decolonisation process and subsequently overlaid with Cold War dynamics, the context of the conflict between Israel and the Palestinians living in the West Bank (WB) and the Gaza Strip has evolved along with global changes, interlinking global agendas with the local conflict.

Both the political complexities of the conflict and its duration have affected the evolution of Israeli and Palestinian societies. On the Palestinian side, the rise of Islamic and Westernized elites and the adoption of autocratic practices will have a permanent impact on the way the crisis will play out in the future. Furthermore, collective perceptions in Israel and their corresponding political consequences will likely be affected by the current emphasis on the War on Terror, nuclear threats, and the re-shaping of the balance of power in the region.

A significant contextual development of 2007 in the occupied Palestinian territories was the factional and inter-Palestinian violence emanating from the power struggle after the electoral victory of the Islamic Resistance Movement (Hamas) in January 2006. As a consequence, in 2007, for the first time, the number of deaths and wounded that resulted from inter-Palestinian violence surpassed casualties caused by the conflict with Israel.[3] The collapse of the economy and rampant poverty are bringing the situation of the Palestinians close to the brink of a humanitarian disaster. In addition, the geopolitical split and economic gap between the West Bank and Gaza has deepened.

Restricted movement and fragmented territory have become prevalent in the occupied Palestinian territories and the ambiguity of international diplomacy has failed to be a restraining influence. The politicisation of aid has exacerbated the already precarious socioeconomic situation of Palestinians at large.

Determinants of the humanitarian crisis

From a humanitarian perspective, the Israeli-Palestinian conflict has deteriorated since the start of the second *intifada* in September 2000. Further aggravating the situation has been the donor countries' blockade of bilateral and institutional aid as a result of the January 2006 elections that brought Hamas to power.[4]

However, it has been stated in many instances that the Palestinian conflict does not constitute a humanitarian emergency. This assessment has been generally accepted because baseline indicators of the socioeconomic situation, mortality, and malnutrition have been stable and traditionally above those of neighbouring countries of comparable socioeconomic level, such as Jordan, Syria, and Egypt. The direct or indirect access to the trade and labour markets of Israel and to the technology of the Western world have provided better opportunities for the inhabitants of the occupied Palestinian territories, as well as a reserve of coping mechanisms. But it is also generally agreed that the situation – particularly regarding the impoverishment of the population and the dependency on humanitarian and relief aid – has been deteriorating. The exhaustion of coping mechanisms is difficult to measure, but should it occur, it will likely lead to serious humanitarian consequences. Thus, the crisis in the occupied Palestinian territories can be defined as a political crisis with eventual humanitarian consequences.

The causes of humanitarian deterioration are described in United Nations' Office for the Coordination of Humanitarian Affairs (OCHA) and World Bank documents;[5] they include the lack of protection of civilians and continuing violence; closure, movement restrictions, and lack of access; geo-political and institutional fragmentation; settlement expansion; and the fiscal crisis of the Palestinian Authority. The result of all these factors is distressing: increased food insecurity, diminished socioeconomic conditions, deteriorated quality of education and health care, threats to agricultural livelihoods, impaired access to water and sanitation, and civilians at risk and in need of protection.

The gravest consequence of this situation is the progressive and intense impoverishment of the population in the WB and Gaza. Moreover, the international community has become part of the problem by imposing a boycott on the Palestinian Authority (PA) throughout 2006 and 2007, thereby exacerbating the fiscal crisis, leading to the suspension of salaries and aggravating the economic situation. Increasing poverty is a vulnerability factor that is likely to have humanitarian repercussions. In 2007, 34 percent of Palestinians were food insecure,[6] 80 percent of the population in Gaza were already dependent on food aid, and 57 percent of the population in the WB and Gaza were classified as poor, living on less than US$2.1 per day (70 percent of the population in Gaza).[7] And Palestinian families now devote 70 percent of their resources to the purchase of food items.[8]

Issues of protection are particularly relevant in this crisis. Violations of International Humanitarian Law (IHL) by all sides are reported frequently, with many civilian casualties and human rights abuses.[9] In spite of all these breaches of IHL, the security forces and armed actors on both sides are accused of acting with impunity. Respondents to the HRI survey reported widespread concern over issues of protection. Many of the respondents expressed their perception that donors are neglecting their obligations or avoiding involvement in protection activities. They also highlighted the general weakness of donor involvement in raising these issues; the ambiguity of the diplomatic position towards Israel is one of the salient elements of the crisis.

Another major disappointment respondents expressed was the weak commitment of donors to facilitate access for humanitarian workers or goods. This passive attitude is particularly evident during military operations, or when security concerns lead to a closure or blockade.

Nevertheless, the important operation of International Committee of the Red Cross (ICRC), focused on protection issues, is among the largest in the world and is supported generously by donors. The ICRC has a specific mandate for protection, but also carries out relief activities in the territories. The main concerns the ICRC raised about the consequences of the conflict in terms of its humanitarian impact are associated with protection issues caused by the more stringent restrictions of movement, settlement expansion and settler violence, military operations, house demolitions, land confiscation, and the West Bank separation barrier. Ensuring that Palestinian farmers are able to access their land located on the Israeli side of the barrier was of particular concern for the ICRC.[10]

Economic outlook

Due to the combination of decreased GDP and high population growth,[11] Palestinian economy receded after the second *intifada,* with per capita income declining from US$1,612 in 1999 to US$1,129 in 2006, the most recent year for which data were available.[12]

According the World Bank, the most critical factor for the Palestinian economy is its composition, which does not bode well for future growth and prosperity. GDP is largely driven by government and private consumption from remittances and aid instead of being investment-led, thereby severely undermining the economy's productive capacity. Public investment has all but dried up because remittances and aid are directed in large part to covering wages and operating costs.

The fiscal position has worsened considerably since 2006, following the Palestinian Legislative Council elections, as Israel withheld clearance revenues and the international community boycotted aid. The deficit has spiralled, greatly increasing aid dependence. The PA forecasts needs of US$1.62 billion in donor assistance in order to bridge the fiscal gap, of which a staggering 94 percent will be directed to recurrent expenditures instead of development programs.

The private sector has practically collapsed both from the lack of investment and confidence and from the unpredictability of border crossings and checkpoints, which have contributed to bottlenecks in importing goods and curtailed exports. The PA has acted as a last resort employer because employment opportunities in Israel for Palestinians have petered out. Public-sector employment has grown by 60 percent from 1999 to 2006.

Determinants for the poor economic outlook are many and imply the need for PA reforms and more capital investment. Efforts to address weaknesses in Palestinian governance, such as imposing law and order or reforming the executive and judiciary, have been stunted by factional fighting and the paralysis of the Palestinian Legislative Council. The World Bank also identifies other factors related to the conflict as being connected to the poor economic performance: settlement growth, movement and access restrictions that have fragmented the economy into disconnected cantons, the annexation of wells and fertile land, and the bottleneck for trade created in the West Bank and Gaza.[13]

Gaza, in particular, has been hit harder by closures and the economic crisis. The current closure policy imposed after Hamas' takeover of the Strip risks endangering Gaza's private sector–led and export-driven economy. Industrial production has largely collapsed. The economy in Gaza is already entirely dependent on public-sector salaries and external aid. A critical factor is the gap created in the distinction between the socioeconomic situation in Gaza and in the West Bank, where the situation is not as dire although the increase in poverty is significant there as well.

Donors' response

Since the Oslo Accords in 1993, donors have been navigating the process of consolidating a Palestinian entity. External aid has been provided with one basic conditionality: the linking of development- oriented initiatives with overarching political objectives. This conditionality was based on three main factors: the security of Israel, support for the peace process, and economic liberalisation.[14]

Development aid, relief, and related conditionality

Donors' adherence to the Good Humanitarian Donorship (GHD) *Principles* of impartiality and neutrality has been questioned by respondents to the HRI survey, as all donors have adopted political positions. It is true that a significant number of donors have contoured the political conditionality by developing alternative mechanisms, and ultimately by increasing the allocations to humanitarian aid (HA).

The shift from institutional, development, and bilateral funding towards HA funding to civil society and non-government organisations (NGOs) has not been based on needs but instead on political circumstances. On account of the political context, donors have shifted between emergency and development aid; this is the subject of frequent complaints from NGOs. The peak of emergency aid through NGOs occurred in 2006, and was still significant in 2007.

Huge external financial injections into the occupied Palestinian territories have not resulted in real diplomatic engagement.[15] For example, the donors' failure to put sufficient pressure on the parties to the conflict to facilitate a productive negotiation process has, among other things, done little to stop the extension of settlements or the restrictions on access and movement that have helped to debilitate the Palestinian economy and society.[16]

During 2006–2007, after Hamas' success in the legislative elections, donors suspended bilateral and budgetary support and intensified aid conditionality, even affecting relief aid in many cases. The extent to which this measure affected humanitarian aid has not been properly evaluated. From the survey, we could infer that this conditionality has affected NGOs more than the Red Cross/Red Crescent (RC) Societies and UN agencies.

Furthermore, according to HRI Survey respondents, some donors have clearly requested that implementing partners agree on political conditionalities in order to qualify to receive the funds. Partners had to sign different types of disclaimers, waivers, or certificates committing themselves to not provide assistance or to not have operational relations with affiliated Hamas members when using donors' funding.[17] This has created discomfort; some agencies have refused funding permanently, while others that did so initially later reached informal agreements with donors to allow partners to be more flexible. UN agencies have enjoyed higher levels of tolerance when implementing programmes clearly involving technical departments of the PA run by Hamas. And in some cases, different agencies of the same donor country apply varying levels of conditionality and flexibility. The ICRC's mandate for independence seems to spare the organisation of the international community's, and specifically, donors' political conditionality. In addition, the ICRC seems to have attained multiyear or long-term funding arrangements in some cases, adding to its flexibility and independence.[18]

The situation came to a turning point after US-sponsored negotiations culminated in the Annapolis summit (November 2007), considered to be a resumption of the peace process. The PA's president appointed an Emergency Government, accepted as legitimate by the international community.[19] Basic conditionality was again fulfilled and donors consequently shifted their positions at a conference in Paris on December 17, 2007, where they pledged US$7.710 million for a period of three years, of which US$1.667 million was for budgetary support and US$1.258 million for humanitarian aid.

Funding, mechanisms to respond to the crisis

After the landslide success of Hamas in the legislative elections in January 2006 and the ensuing boycott, it became clear to the international community that alternative mechanisms should be found in order to minimise the consequences of the boycott on the general population.

The total figure of donor support in 2006 and 2007, in spite of the blockade, was probably higher than the average of previous years.[20] Furthermore, it is difficult to capture in official figures the funds channelled by Arab constituencies, official or private, to respond to the crisis, and even more difficult to capture the funds directed to support Hamas in Gaza. External support has skyrocketed in the occupied Palestinian territories as a result of the political position of the international community (IC), while the general socioeconomic situation has suffered a more severe deterioration than ever seen before.

The following are mechanisms the international community employed to mitigate the effects of the boycott.[21]

The temporary international mechanism (TIM)

Intended to minimise the drying up of institutional funding and to ensure the functioning of basic services, this mechanism was designed and put in place rather rapidly. Established in June 2006 and extended until the end of 2007, when the Paris donor conference resumed bilateral support to the PA in Ramallah, TIM managed to channel approximately US$890 million through three main mechanisms: the Emergency Support Services Program (ESSP), which finances the PA's health, education, and social services; the Interim Emergency Relief Contribution, supporting the energy utilities in the West Bank and Gaza; and direct financial and relief assistance to vulnerable populations.

The mobilisation of humanitarian aid

Since the start of the second *intifada,* donors shifted significant amounts of funding from previously planned development aid to humanitarian aid and enhancing multilateral support.[22] The boycott of 2006 and 2007 increased this trend.

Table 1 shows the amounts mobilised by donors since 2003, the total amount requested through the successive UN Consolidated Appeal Processes (CAPs), the

Table 1: Evolution of donors' commitments to humanitarian aid in the occupied Palestinian territories

Donor commitment (US dollars)	2003 (US$ millions)	2004 (US$ millions)	2005 (US$ millions)	2006 (US$ millions)	2007 (US$ millions)
Total committed by donors	200.32	296.278	242.075	457.573	340.193
CAP requested	293.7	305	301.452	394.883 (rev.)	454.6
CAP covered	175.8	173.9	195.7	273.5	263.4
CERF	NA	NA	NA	7.1	3.8
UNRWA EA (covered in parentheses)	202 (143)	190 (121)	185.8 (126.6)	177 (rev.) (140.6)	245 (141)

Source: From OCHA's Financial Tracking Service (FTS), updated May 2008, for the Appeals of 2007 (Appeals and commitments for 2008 not included): http://www.reliefweb.int/rw/fts.nsf/doc105?OpenForm&emid=ACOS-635PFR&yr=2007

Table 2: Contributions of Main Donors, 2003–2007

2003 (US$ millions)		2004 (US$ millions)		2005 (US$ millions)		2006 (US$ millions)		2007 (US$ millions)	
U.S.	62	UAE	90	ECHO	6.4	ECHO	86.8	ECHO	77.9
EC	45	U.S.	43	Japan	34.5	U.S.	78.8	U.S.	75.9
UN	22	EC	41	U.S.	30.8	Sweden	58.9	Norway	31
Norway	11.9	Japan	19	Saudi Arabia	20.8	Norway	33.3	Japan	18
		UK	13	Switzerland	15.7	Japan	29.4	Sweden	15
		Denmark	11.1	Canada	13.3	EC	21.5	Canada	14
				Sweden	10.7	Denmark	18.3	Spain	13
						Switzerland	16.2		
						Canada	12.3		
						France	11.1		

Note: Donation amounts are included only if donor contributed over US$10 million

level of coverage of the UN appeals, the proportion of the United Nations Relief and Works Agency (UNRWA) Emergency Appeals (EA) and its coverage.

In 2006, donors' humanitarian support peaked and all donors increased contributions significantly. In 2007, the total contribution was not as large, but was still higher than contributions prior to 2006. Furthermore, in 2007, TIM was already providing much of the aid to keep basic services functional and most likely captured the majority of donors' allocations for this purpose.

Regarding the GHD *principles* of flexibility and earmarking, a limited number of donor agencies seem to have adopted greater flexibility and less earmarking, according to participants of the HRI Survey. In some cases, it seems that some donors have consolidated longer-term funding, making it more reliable; this is the case for the UK when funding UNRWA and the ICRC, and Spain with Spanish NGOs. It should be noted that these types of funding arrangements are difficult to track as HA and are not normally accounted for as such.

UNRWA is one of the main service providers for Palestinians in the WB and Gaza, as it is responsible for the 1.5 million refugees in the occupied Palestinian territories. UNRWA has a regular budget provided by donors and launches a number of Emergency Appeals (EA) to cover emergency situations. UNRWA's EA are included within the CAP process, and reach a level of coverage similar to the global CAP. However, the figure in Table 1 does not reflect the total amount UNRWA would direct to cover emergency needs, as a significant proportion of the general budget is flexible enough to be diverted to emergency aid.

Table 2 shows that there have been significant shifts in the main donors over time. The U.S. and the European Commission (EC) – including a significant shift to the European Commission Humanitarian (Aid) Office (ECHO) from 2005 – have consistently been the main donors. Also worthy of mention is the fact that the Financial Tracking Service (FTS) captures almost exclusively OECD Development Assistance Committee (DAC) donors, with only minor contributions from Russia and the United Arab Emirates (UAE) in 2007, in contrast to significant contributions from the UAE and Saudi Arabia in previous CAPs. Table 2 shows main donors' contributions, from 2003 to 2007, to the occupied Palestinian territories.

The UN Consolidated Appeals Process (CAP)

The UN CAP has been established in the occupied Palestinian territories since 2003, in response to the alarm created by the aggravation of the situations affecting civilians since the start of the 2000 *intifada*. At that stage, humanitarian coordination capacity was still weak and the integration of projects in the CAP was perceived not to be responding to a real needs assessment.

All sectors have been targeted by HA, especially since 2006, because of increased redirection of development aid to HA channels. Those include agriculture, coordination, education, food aid, health, job creation, protection, and water and sanitation.

The CAP has become progressively more solid and has successfully integrated more actors. It should also be noted that the 2008 CAP includes a significantly higher number of agencies and NGOs than in the past. However, donors tend to maintain their own channels of aid flow, as the difference between total commitments and CAP coverage show. In some cases, such as the UK, bilateral funding arrangements with implementing partners overcome the project-oriented approach within the CAP.

In 2007, the occupied Palestinian territories was the third world crisis in terms of CAP total requirements (after Sudan, with a CAP requirement of US$1.22 billion, and the Democratic Republic of the Congo, with US$687 million) and per beneficiary (US$221, after the Democratic Republic of the Congo, with US$391 per beneficiary, and Chad, with US$311).[23]

After the peak of donations in 2006, when donors mobilised more HA and the CAP received more funds than ever before, both in absolute terms and in proportion to the requirements, the 2007 CAP requested even more funds than the previous year and managed to reach an amount of funding similar to 2006. The 2008 CAP is in the same area as the 2007 one (US$467 million), and requirements are justified by the precarious situation on the ground and the evident increase in dependency on HA. The confirmed donor trend for 2008 of cutting funds for HA is raising concern in some agencies: in addition to raising food prices, the UN World Food Programme is likely to experience serious difficulties in providing the same level of food aid in 2008 as it has previously, while any development mech-

anism that would decrease food insecurity is not likely to have an impact in the short term.

Implementing agencies suggested that adherence to GHD *principles* 3 and 9, which refer to donor support for livelihoods, has been especially wanting in the occupied Palestinian territories. They argued that donor policies are increasing dependency on humanitarian aid: approximately 80 percent of Gaza residents receive some type of food aid.[24]

The Central Emergency Response Fund (CERF)

The CERF has been used moderately in the occupied Palestinian territories. Since its creation in 2006, around US$11 million have been allocated to the territories, of which, during 2007, US$2.5 million were designated for rapid response and US$3.8 million for underfunded emergencies. The mechanism benefited UN agencies – namely UNRWA, the World Health Organization (WHO), the United Nations Children's Fund (UNICEF), and the United Nations Development Fund for Women (UNIFEM). The CERF evaluation (in process) should provide some elements of judgement for the need to mobilise this mechanism in a crisis with such levels of humanitarian funding in 2007.

The Humanitarian Emergency Response Fund (HERF)

The Humanitarian Emergency Response Fund (HERF) is a specific mechanism to address limited and urgent humanitarian needs. Created in the summer of 2007, HERF has specific limitations for the allocation of resources, with a maximum of US$200,000 that can be made available in 48 hours. Its purpose is to support NGOs in the rapid response to emergency situations. It is interesting that the fund has been allocated primarily to situations caused by natural disasters such as droughts, cold waves, and floods. It is still a young initiative and is not yet well known by partners in the field.

The HERF is funded by Sweden and Spain (providing US$1 million each) and administered by OCHA and donor representatives. Funds have not been completely allocated so far, but there is a will to replenish the fund once exhausted and to open it to other donors.

The very nature of the emergencies funded to date may add to the arguments on the difficulties in identifying real and clear-cut humanitarian needs. However, as the instrument becomes better understood, it is possible that new requests could widen the scope of intervention.

International Committee of the Red Cross (ICRC)

ICRC operations in the occupied Palestinian territories are among the largest in the world. In addition to the specific mandate for protection, the ICRC carries out relief activities in the territories mainly with cash for work projects, food aid, and water and sanitation interventions. The ICRC visits to detainees are an integral and principal part of its presence in the territories.

In 2007, the ICRC's Emergency Appeal for the occupied Palestinian territories was initially the second largest (71 million Swiss francs (CHF), or 45 million euros) after Sudan (CHF 73 million), but at the end of the year it was the third largest, overtaken by Iraq (CHF 91 million) and Sudan (CHF 105 million). For 2008, the initial appeals for these top three crises amounts to CHF 107 million for Iraq, CHF 106 million for Sudan, and CHF 68 million for the O&AT (Occupied and Autonomous Territories, in ICRC terminology).[25]

Donor coordination

Consistent with the high profile of donor involvement in the post-Oslo consolidation process of a Palestinian entity, a number of coordination mechanisms were put in place. The Ad Hoc Liaison Committee (AHLC) is the principal coordination mechanism on policy and political matters related to the development effort in the West Bank and Gaza Strip. The members of the AHLC are Canada, the European Union, Japan, Norway, Russia, Saudi Arabia, and the United States. Israel and the Palestinian Liberation Organization are associated members of the AHLC, as are Egypt, Jordan, Tunisia, and the United Nations.

The AHLC established the Local Aid Coordination Committee (LACC), which is comprised of the Palestinian Authority and all the donor agencies that contribute to the Palestinians with representation in the area. Approximately 30 donors are represented at the monthly meetings of the LACC. The co-chairs of the LACC are Norway, in its capacity as Chair of the AHLC; the Office of the United Nations Special Coordinator for the Middle East Peace Process (UNSCO),[26] and the World Bank.

The LACC agreed on the establishment of 12 sectoral sub-committees, known as Sector Working Groups. These working groups seek to direct donor assistance towards the needs and priorities identified by the PA, with input from the United Nations and the World Bank. Each working group consists of all donors interested in that particular sector, with one donor representative leading the group; representatives of relevant PA ministries; and the World Bank and/or the United Nations as Secretariat. The 12 working groups cover the following sectors: agriculture, education, employment creation, environment, health, infrastructure and housing, institution-building, police, private sector, public finance, tourism, and transport and telecommunications. The UN has been providing technical assistance for the Sector Working Groups linked to the expertise of a particular agency – WHO, Food and Agriculture Organization (FAO), UNICEF, the United Nations Educational, Scientific and Cultural Organization (UNESCO), the United Nations Population Fund (UNFPA), and so on.

The collapse of dialogue among the parties and of development efforts after 2000, with a shift to humanitarian and emergency responses, somehow has voided the meaning of the main coordination mechanisms. Nevertheless, the structure remains, making it difficult to create a more humanitarian-oriented alternative for coordination. OCHA's efforts on information sharing and dissemination are to be praised, but the fact that the deputy of UNSCO has been appointed as Humanitarian Coordinator further reinforces the mix among the AHLC, the LACC, and the humanitarian coordination. These structures are very much linked to the basic conditionality of aid regarding the support of the peace process and the model of society promoted by donors.

Although its performance has been inconsistent, the setup of Sector Working Groups still plays a role in the current situation. Unfortunately, since donors have decreased their commitments to development, the dynamics for coordination have weakened and the momentum to create alternative humanitarian ones has only partially succeeded. The cluster approach seems difficult to apply in this context, as it should overwrite the Sector Working Groups. The current setup does not grant leadership to the relevant UN agencies acting in support of the sectors, nor does it make them accountable.

The humanitarian community has pressured for ad hoc sector meetings to discuss the emergency situation that began in 2006 and to coordinate responses. The EU has established the Humanitarian Sector Group, which brings together EU Member States and ECHO on a weekly basis, and invites UN agencies or Red Cross/Red Crescent Societies in order to monitor the humanitarian situation. But humanitarian actors responding to the HRI Survey do not consider donor coordination optimal. Conditionality, political agendas, confused mandates, and unclear accountability are impairing humanitarian sector coordination.

The UN has not gained leadership and has probably not done enough to get away from the Sector Working Groups setup and their implicit conditionality. The consolidated Appeal process, however, has gained legitimacy, involving more actors and providing an accepted framework.

Overall, most respondents to the HRI Survey agreed that coordination is a complex issue in the territories, one that donors do not address properly. OCHA plays a role in the coordination of humanitarian partners and information sharing, but donors' involvement is not evident. The multiple coordination forums and the diverse political agendas seem to affect the actual coordination of humanitarian aid.

Conclusions and recommendations

The crisis in the occupied Palestinian territories has been defined as a political crisis with humanitarian consequences. The difficulties of defining what constitutes a humanitarian crisis in the territories provide an interesting framework for comparing GHD *principles* with practices on the ground.

The humanitarian system in the occupied Palestinian territories needs to clarify coordination roles and responsibilities. Interviewees perceive donor coordination as weak, probably as a result of the political determinants of donor's behaviour. Moreover, donor coordination in the humanitarian field is still influenced by general coordination mechanisms stemming from the Oslo peace process' arrangements with explicit conditionality. Sector accountability is far from being properly addressed.

Donors' humanitarian aid peaked during 2006 and 2007, enhancing the shift from development aid to relief and increasing the dependency of Palestinians on external short-term aid. Already 70 percent of the population in Gaza live in poverty and 80 percent receive food rations.

Furthermore, financial tracking systems need to be improved. All OECD-DAC donors are present in this conflict and many of them are accounted for through the OCHA FTS. However, donors who develop longer-term funding arrangements and reduce earmarking are difficult to follow in a system designed to capture short-term, project-oriented funding. In addition, a significant portion of relief aid reaches Gaza through different channels and is not being tracked. On the whole, it is

difficult to obtain reliable information on the complete picture of donors' funding flows.

The conditionality some donors apply for implementing relief programs has been widely contested. The HRI Survey has shown that donors can mobilise funds from different official sources, applying varying levels of conditionality and flexibility.

Donors actively promote evaluations, but do less to facilitate learning among humanitarian actors. HA in the occupied Palestinian territories offers an interesting case study for learning strategies and linking relief and development mechanisms. Moreover, it would be very interesting to promote a better understanding of donors' influence in shaping Palestinian society and creating elites.

Notes

1 The Humanitarian Response Index team, composed of Lucía Fernández, Stuart Reigeluth, and Ricardo Solé-Arqués, visited the occupied Palestinian territories in March 2008. The opinions expressed here are those of the author and do not necessarily reflect those of DARA.

2 The term *occupied Palestinian territories* (oPt) is used by the United Nations Office for the Coordination of Humanitarian Affairs (OCHA). The World Bank refers to the Palestinian Territories as *The West Bank and Gaza;* the International Committee of the Red Cross (ICRC) refers to them as *occupied and autonomous territories.*

3 Three hundred and ninety-two Palestinians were killed in conflict-related incidents, and 491 were killed by internal conflict: OCHA oPt protection of civilians summary data tables, February 2008.

4 *Hamas,* Arabic for "Islamic Resistance Movement," is classified by the U.S. and the European Union as a terrorist organization.

5 OCHA oPt, 2007, 2008; OCHA oPt, 2007a; ICRC 2006a; World Bank, 2006; World Bank, 2008.

6 WFP/FAO. 2007.

7 PCBS, 2007.

8 OCHA oPt 2007, 2008; OCHA oPt 2007a; WFP/FAO, 2007.

9 See OCHA oPt 2007a; OCHA oPt, 2008b; PRCS monthly and annual "violation reports"; Physicians for Human Rights Israel report; OCHA oPt, 2008c: ICRC, 2007; Dugard, 2008; Human Rights Watch, 2008; and B'Tselem, 2007.

10 ICRC, 2006a.

11 World Bank, 2008.

12 World Bank, 2007.

13 See: World Bank, 2006; 2008.

14 Brouwer, 2000.

15 According to estimates by the Palestinian Academic Society for the Study of International Affairs (PASSIA), total donor disbursements since the establishment of the PNA in 1994 until October 2005 amounted to roughly US$5 billion. This accounts for only part of donors' allocation to the crisis, as it is accepted that external contributions reach over 1 billion US dollars yearly since 2002. And much of the Arab world support is not accounted for.

16 Le More et al., 2005.

17 The more frequently mentioned is the "Certification regarding terrorist financing" US anti-terrorism certification (ATC), but other donors have introduced similar mechanisms.

18 ICRC, 2006b.

19 The legitimacy of this government is at least dubious as it cannot be ratified by the Legislative Council because the majority of the elected MoLC are detained in Israel.

20 Adding contributions to TIM and emergency and relief aid, the figure is likely to reach over US$1.2 billion for 2006. Many other contributions not accounted for and the support to Hamas in Gaza can take total external support to record figures.

21 The first mechanism (TIM) is a specific tool designed for the complex Palestinian context, while those related to CAP, CERF, HERF, and ICRC appeals are more focused on the general aim of developing more flexible and predictable dynamics to properly fund humanitarian crises and therefore are quite relevant to the GHD framework.

22 World Bank, 2004.

23 Source, OCHA oPt, 2008a.

24 OCHA, 2007b.

25 ICRC Appeals 2008, Key data, ICRC.

26 UNSCO was established in 1994 after the Oslo Accords, and acts as UN Secretary General Representative to the PA, and, since 2002, as Secretary General Special Envoy to the Middle East Quartet.

References

Brouwer, Imco. 2000. "US civil society assistance to the Arab world: The cases of Egypt and Palestine." European University Institute Working Paper RSC No. 2000/5. Florence.

B'Tselem. 2007. "Human Rights in the Occupied Palestinian Territories." Annual Report 2007.

Dugard, John. 2008. "Report of the Special Rapporteur on the situation of human rights in the Palestinian territories occupied since 1967." At: http://daccessdds.un.org/doc/UNDOC/GEN/G08/402/29/PDF/G0840229.pdf?OpenElement

Human Rights Watch. 2008. *World Report 2008.* "Israel/Occupied Palestinian Territories: Events of 2007". At: http://hrw.org/englishwr2k8/docs/2008/01/31/isrlpa17596.htm

International Committee of the Red Cross (ICRC). 2006a. Annual Report.

———. 2006b. Financial Report.

———. 2007. "Dignity denied in the Palestinian Territories." November. At: http://www.icrc.org/web/eng/siteeng0.nsf/htmlall/palestine-report-131207

Le More, Anne, Michael Keating, and Robert Lowe (eds.). 2005. *Aid, Diplomacy, and Facts on the Ground: The Case of Palestine.* London: Chatham House.

Office for the Coordination of Humanitarian Affairs – occupied Palestinian territory (OCHA oPt). 2007, 2008. CAP documents. At: www.ochaopt.org

———. 2007a. *Humanitarian Monitor,* Number 19. November. At: http://www.ochaopt.org/documents/Humanitarian_Monitor_Nov07.pdf

———. 2007b. Special Focus: Occupied Palestinian Territory. December. At: http://www.ochaopt.org/documents/Gaza_Special_Focus_December_2007.pdf

———. 2008a. Consolidated Appeal 2008 summary document. At: www.ochaopt.org

———. 2008b. Protection database. February.

———. 2008c. "Protection of civilians: Weekly briefing notes." February.

Palestinian Central Bureau of Statistics (PCBS). Poverty in the Palestinian Territory. 2007.

Palestinan Red Crescent Society (PRCS). Monthly and annual "violation reports." At: http://www.palestinercs.org/modules/news/index.php?storytopic=6

Physicians for Human Rights (PHR). Israel report. At: http://physiciansforhumanrights.org/

World Bank. 2004. Four years: Intifada, closures and Palestinian economic crisis, an assessment." October. Washington, DC: World Bank.

———. 2006. West Bank and Gaza: Country economic memorandum. September. Washington, DC: World Bank.

———. 2007. Economic Monitoring Report to the Ad Hoc Liaison Committee, no. 41039 v2, September. Washington, DC: World Bank.

———. 2008. Economic Developments and Prospects." March. Washington, DC: World Bank.

World Food Programme/Food and Agriculture Organization (WFP/FAO). 2007. Comprehensive Food Security and Vulnerability Assessment (CFSVA).

Peru

AT A GLANCE

Country data *(2006 figures, unless otherwise noted)*

- 2007 Human Development Index: ranked 87th of 177 countries
- Population: 27.59 million
- GNI per capita (Atlas method, current US$): US$2,980
- Population living on less than US$2 a day (1990–2005): 30.6 percent
- Life expectancy: 71 years
- Infant mortality rate: 21 per 1,000 live births
- Under-five infant mortality rate: 25 per 1,000
- Population undernourished (2002–2004): 12 percent
- Population with sustainable access to improved water source (2004): 83 percent
- Adult literacy rate (over 15 yrs of age): 88 percent
- Primary education completion rate: 100 percent
- Gender-related development index (2005): ranked 75th of 177 countries
- Official development assistance (ODA): US$468 million
- 2007 Corruption Perception Index: ranked 72nd out of 179 countries

Sources: Transparency International, 2007; UNDP, 2007a, and 2007b; World Bank, 2008.

The crisis

- Earthquake (7.0 on Richter scale) struck central coast on 15 August 2007, affecting 30,000 square kilometres; relatively minor in comparison with previous disasters;
- Initial estimates of only 35,214 families affected increased to 131,135 (or 655,674 people); 519 died; 1,291 injured;
- 139,521 homes damaged/destroyed; 1,278 schools damaged; 14 hospitals destroyed, 112 more severely damaged;
- Although affected region relatively small and wealthy, income disparity is high; earthquake particularly affected poorest and most vulnerable.

Sources: Instituto Nacional de Defensa Civil, 2007.

The humanitarian response

- UN Flash Appeal launched 28 August 2007 requested US$36.9 million;
- US$13.8 million (more than one-third of total) requested for food security; US$5.3 million for education; US$5 million for shelter and camp management;
- Appeal received only 50 percent of requested funds; CERF provided half of total;
- IFRC Appeal received more money than UN Appeal, excluding CERF;
- As of June 2008, total contributions came to US$50 million, including contributions to the Flash Appeal, the IFRC appeal and others; largest donors EC/ECHO (more than US$11.29 million, 22.5 percent); CERF (US$9.59 million, 19.1 percent); private (US$8.87 million, 17.7 percent); U.S. (US$3.16 million, 6.3 percent); Sweden (US$2.58 million, 5.1 percent);
- Among top 10 OECD/DAC donor countries: Italy, UK, Canada, Belgium, and Spain.

Sources: OCHA FTS.

Earthquake in Peru
Realities and Myths

RICCARDO POLASTRO, Head of Evaluation, DARA

© Sergio Urday/epa/Corbis

Introduction[1]

Although an estimated 80 percent of the population of Peru live in earthquake-prone areas and are exposed to high risks, the earthquake that struck the Ica Region in August 2007 was relatively minor in comparison with the terrible consequences of the great Ancash earthquake of 1970.[2] Nevertheless, it received a great deal of media attention, since there was little competition from other crises at the time. As a result, international donors were drawn to the crisis, at least in the initial phase of the emergency. While donors were quick to respond, they found that the Peruvian government was unable to effectively coordinate with international actors. These two factors, compounded by the absence of a clear contingency plan, a focus on the initial emergency phase,

and weak national institutions, constituted the principal complications faced in the humanitarian response. Thus, the Peru earthquake highlights some of the difficulties in implementing the Good Humanitarian Donorship (GHD) *Principles* which promote the strengthening of local capacity and a sustained response.

The crisis: Lack of disaster risk awareness

The earthquake which struck the provinces of Chincha, Ica, Nazca, and Pisco along the central coast of Peru on 15 August 2007 at 18:34 measured 7.0 on the Richter scale. It was followed by more than 500 aftershocks, 40 of which measured more than 4.0 on the Richter scale.

The disaster affected a vast geographical area of 30,000 square kilometres.

It became apparent later that the initial estimates by the Instituto Nacional de Defensa Civil (INDECI), the Peruvian National Institute for Civil Defence, proved to be lower than the actual damage sustained. Initially, INDECI estimated that only 35,214 families had been affected, but this figure increased to 131,135 families (655,674 people), of whom 519 died and 1,291 were injured, demonstrating the need for a sustained response. Moreover, 139,521 homes were damaged or destroyed, 1,278 schools were damaged, 14 hospitals were destroyed, and the structure of 112 more severely damaged.[3] Because the affected region is relatively small and wealthy, accounting for approximately 3 percent of GDP, there was a very low national and international NGO presence prior to the disaster. Nevertheless, according to the Gini Index, income disparity is high throughout the country, and the earthquake affected the poorest and most vulnerable, those without access to resources. Security problems emerged in the affected areas as a result of disruptions to the electricity supply and there were episodes of looting.

The town that bore the brunt of the earthquake was Pisco. According to INDECI, 80 percent of the city's buildings collapsed, as most were built with adobe bricks and straw matting. Tragically, 300 people who sought refuge in a cathedral were killed when it collapsed. Also hit by the earthquake was Chinca Alta, where 70 percent of the buildings collapsed or were damaged, and the hospital destroyed.

Despite Peru's significant history of natural disasters and the international community's previous investment in disaster preparedness, the impact of the earthquake was exacerbated by an overall lack of risk reduction measures. For example, buildings – despite their location in risk-prone areas – were made of low quality materials which did not withstand the seismic shock. In fact, a January 2008 study concluded that only 20 percent of urban Pisco is located on safe foundations, the other areas being deemed medium to high risk because of their high silt and sand content.[4] Overall, awareness of the risk of earthquakes is low in the affected communities and local authorities often failed to enforce either seismic building codes or land-use regulations.[5]

Following the earthquake, contested claims over land ownership – due to the lack of land titles – posed a major problem. In the majority of cases, there was no way to determine ownership of buildings, a situation which created disputes among the local population. The earthquake also created political shock waves. Central and local authorities, belonging to opposing political parties, blamed each other for failing to address the situation and, as a result were unable to communicate and work with each other effectively. Local institutions and local communities quickly became frustrated with the ineffectiveness of national institutions, especially of the *Fondo para la Reconstrucción del Sur* (FORSUR), the Fund for the Reconstruction of the South, accusing them of corruption.[6]

The donor response: ECHO takes the lead

Early media coverage was significant, with the result that donors contributed rapidly to the emergency response. In fact, Peru was fortunate that no other emergencies were competing for attention at the time. Had the Bangladesh cyclone occurred earlier, IFRC officials believe that it would have negatively affected the response and may have reduced funding.[7]

A UN Flash Appeal was launched on 28 August 2007, requesting US$36.9 million for urgent humanitarian needs and some early recovery activities over a six-month period. Priority sectors included food security (US$13.8 million, more than one-third of the funds requested), education (US$5.3 million) and shelter and camp management (US$5 million). The Appeal stressed that the humanitarian consequences of the disaster were far beyond initial estimates and that a significant proportion of the affected population was dependent on external aid and food insecure. Donors already funding UN agencies generally contributed to the Flash Appeal, except for those with multi-year partnership agreements such as the Nordic countries. Some donors, such as Finland and New Zealand, gave direct contributions to the World Food Programme (WFP) as part of the Appeal, reflecting their perception of the priorities and their favoured funding channels. Overall, the Appeal received only 50 percent of the requested funds, of which the UN Central Emergency Response Fund (CERF) provided half. CERF funds were requested 48 hours after the earthquake and were essential in order to activate the UN response. In part, the limited response to the Appeal reflected the poorly articulated and inadequately developed nature of the Appeal, the result of the excessive speed with which it was launched. However, significant levels of funding were raised outside the UN Appeal.

The Appeal launched by the IFRC received more money than the UN Appeal, excluding CERF. This may have been, in part, because the IFRC was already on the ground and is perceived as being more effective in humanitarian operations than UN agencies. In fact, other actors, such as the UN, Oxfam, and Action Contre la Faim (ACF) responded more slowly. Their ability to raise funds positioned the Red Cross family as the major actor in the humanitarian response. However, it is important to emphasise that 40 percent of IFRC contributions came from non-traditional sources, such as companies, foundations, and associations.[8] This reflects the growing trend towards corporate social responsibility.

As of June 2008, OCHA's Financial Tracking Service (FTS) reported total donor contributions at US$50 million, including contributions to the Flash Appeal, the IFRC appeal and other NGO appeals.[9] The EC/ECHO was the largest funding source with more than US$11.29 million (22.5 percent of the total), followed by CERF with US$9.59 million (19.1 percent); private donors, US$8.87 million (17.7 percent); the United States, US$3.16 million (6.3 percent); and Sweden, US$2.58 million (5.1 percent). Other OECD/DAC countries among the top 10 donors included Italy, the UK, Canada, Belgium, and Spain.

However, the EC/ECHO's position in the top three donors varied over time. Although it released funds within 24 hours of the disaster, the majority of its pledges were still uncommitted three months later. The agency also maintained a presence in the field to monitor the situation and, as a result, made a second allocation of €6 million. Many organisations interviewed felt that ECHO was not only a key strategic partner, but was predictable in its actions and consulted with them on priority sectors and areas of intervention.[10] Some implementing agencies also expressed the view that ECHO and its disaster-preparedness programme (DIPECHO) worked hand in hand and promoted relief programmes in line with GHD Principles 8 and 9. Furthermore, DIPECHO's Risk Reduction Indicators (RRI) were utilised to monitor the effectiveness of risk-reduction measures and to strengthen the capacity of affected local communities.

Some OECD/DAC donors provided in kind contributions; for example, France provided water-pumps, the U.S. shelter materials, and Spain non-food relief items. Others tightly earmarked their funds; for example, Spain funded artisan fishing recovery, thereby not following good practice as reflected in GHD Principle 5.

The implementation of the humanitarian response: Why did national mechanisms fail?

In the first two weeks of the emergency, 92 camps were established, housing some 33,000 people. Approximately 90 percent of the emergency response was concentrated in Pisco, although a large number of scattered rural communities were also badly hit. In general, the humanitarian assistance provided by national, regional, and international actors alleviated the immediate suffering of the affected population, and no epidemic outbreaks were reported. Nevertheless, it is important to disaggregate the local, central, and international elements of the response; while the initial response was swift, the transition to recovery was slow.

Response capacity

The national response capacity collapsed within 48 hours and initial national assessments were poor and inaccurate. On 16 August, the government declared a state of emergency in the Ica department and in Cañete province, and immediately deployed INDECI assessment teams. Within 48 hours of the earthquake, the government, unable to cope with the situation, called for international support. Why, in a disaster-prone country like Peru, despite the investment in disaster preparedness and the strong coping mechanisms of local communities, did the national emergency response fail? The reason is twofold: first, the absence of a clear national coordination mechanism and the weakness of national emergency structures led to a slow, uncoordinated, and ineffective response; second, national capacity to respond was hindered by the lack of a contingency plan and adequate preparation.[11] These shortcomings were compounded by the fact that some communities ignored community-based disaster risk reduction and preparedness measures and because disaster risk reduction was not an institutional priority.[12]

Three national Red Cross Societies, American, German and Spanish, supported the relief operation with both resources and in-country personnel, the later two agencies having staff on the ground prior to the earthquake. Within hours, the Red Cross fielded teams to assess the damage; later, UN personnel were sent to support the government's limited capacity to conduct needs assessments. However, assessments in remote areas were delayed due to difficult access, reducing the effectiveness and timeliness of the response. In fact, initially there was significant disparity among figures reported, leading to duplication of efforts in the first phase of the response in priority sectors and some geographical areas. Figures could only be corroborated several weeks after the disaster.

Confusion increased when the media reported food shortages and epidemics throughout the affected region. However, the government dispelled these disaster myths promptly by announcing that food prices remained normal and that crops had not been damaged.[13] Nevertheless, WFP reported that after the earthquake, 32 percent of the population were severely food insecure, as irrigation systems were disrupted and many had lost their livelihoods.

Although broadly in line with GHD Principle 6, donor needs assessments varied substantially in nature and scope. Sweden and the Netherlands relied on their partners' assessments, while others such as Canada, Belgium, and Italy carried them out, but not systematically. ECHO and the United States Agency for International Development and Office of Foreign Disaster Assistance (USAID/OFDA) deployed teams to the field to monitor needs, and then adapted their response accordingly.

The majority of international NGOs already present in Peru were focussed on long-term development programmes, but lacked specialised relief personnel or stand-by supplies. These were rapidly flown in and NGOs mushroomed around the disaster area. Nevertheless, some organisations lacked the logistical capacity to reach the scattered population and faced logistical bottlenecks.

Coordination mechanisms

Not only were national inter-institutional coordination mechanisms and strategic decision making excessively cumbersome, but political interference further reduced the speed and effectiveness of the response. Ineffective local emergency committees, hampered by poor leadership and funding, created problems in the field.[14] As mentioned earlier, central coordination structures lacked accurate information with which to plan, make decisions, and coordinate activities.[15] In fact, little had changed since the June 2001 earthquake, when Save the Children reported that the humanitarian response was hindered by coordination difficulties, poor community organisation, and the remoteness of affected areas.[16] In contrast, the Red Cross Movement response was well coordinated from the outset by the IFRC Regional Delegation for Latin America and actively supported by the Pan-America Disaster Response Unit in Panama.

Gradually, as in many disasters, coordination among other actors improved. Regular meetings co-chaired by INDECI and the United Nations Disaster Assessment and Coordination team (UNDAC) helped to coordinate humanitarian assistance and recovery programmes, and placed greater emphasis on longer-term planning in order to address the transition from emergency to recovery. INDECI established an inter-sector Emergency Operation Centre that facilitated decision making about the most appropriate use of available resources. When UNDAC's mission ended in September, OCHA was requested to take over coordination with governmental and local authorities and international donors.[17]

Due to the small scale of the disaster and government incapacity, the UN Country Team advised against the implementation of the cluster approach, even though other major humanitarian actors thought it would be useful.[18] However, 11 sectors and lead UN agencies were identified, based on agency capacity and needs. The government identified counterparts to co-chair sector meetings. Unfortunately, however, no single organisation had the final responsibility for a sector.

Regular coordination meetings were held within the humanitarian community. But some organisations considered these meetings unproductive, as not all information was shared and some that was exchanged was not based on common data sources. In the early stages after the earthquake, field coordination was considered poor and only active in Pisco. The effectiveness of coordination varied in each sector, according to the capacity of the national counterpart in the field and the involvement of local authorities. While the health sector was coordinated better than others, there were no coordination mechanisms for camp management.[19]

Donor coordination proved weak in identifying potential synergies and complementarities. Bilateral agendas prevailed over a coordinated approach to bridging the relief-development gap.

Recovery myths and limitations

The transition from relief to recovery and long-term development was a major flaw in the humanitarian response. The prevailing myth that an emergency ends in a question of days or weeks was again debunked in Peru. According to the Pan American and World Health Organizations, "the earthquake of Peru showed once again that even though the cameras and broadcasters are gone from a disaster, conditions are far from normal."[20] Two months after the disaster, thousands of people in remote areas still needed shelter and access to food, safe water, sanitation facilities, and health care, illustrating the need to connect relief, recovery, and development, as expressed in the GHD *Principles.*

One important factor hindering reconstruction was the lack of participation of the affected population in the recovery effort. For example, the government announced that affected families would be given priority in a cash-for-work programme for debris clearance and house reconstruction, through the *"Construyendo Perú"* initiative. Unfortunately, this proposal never became a reality. In fact, four months after the initial emergency relief operation, the transition into the next stage had hardly begun.

Yet another factor complicating recovery was the ineffectiveness of FORSUR, which had been established to manage the reconstruction efforts. Four months after the earthquake, it was slow to act, as its operational base was still located in distant Lima, and it had no implementation plan. The lack of progress created discontent and led to mass protests in November. According to the President of FORSUR, reconstruction was delayed because they had not yet received foreign pledges earmarked for reconstruction.[21] However, in a public opinion survey, 37 percent of people were convinced that the reason FORSUR had not made progress was corruption; 17 percent believed that political interference was the cause.[22] Ica Eusebio Valdez, President of the *Coordinadora Regional de Ciudadania,* said that FORSUR "is a phantom institution that has not carried out any concrete action." Some donors, such as Canada – already engaged in recovery and long-term development – did not trust FORSUR, and decided not to contribute funds. Instead, they worked through international partners such as the IFRC. However, it should be noted that the inefficiency of FORSUR was due, in part, to the strict control systems and cumbersome bureaucracy created to prevent corruption following the widespread fraud of the Fujimori government.[23]

Some donors, such as the Dutch, who expressed interest in funding reconstruction, turned their attention elsewhere when the Bangladesh cyclone struck and political and media attention shifted to other fronts – in contravention of GHD Principle 11. Nevertheless, some agencies, such as ECHO, USAID, and the Canadian International Development Agency (CIDA) funded international NGOs such as CARE and Caritas to build temporary shelters. In early September, the Japan International Cooperation Agency (JICA) dispatched a team to assess long-term reconstruction needs in the most heavily damaged areas.

The limited recovery efforts failed to address livelihoods. No comprehensive analysis or efforts to reduce the vulnerability of the affected population and increase their capacity were carried out. Very few donors focused on the livelihood components of the early-recovery programmes, such as emergency rehabilitation of farming activities. Support for the resumption of small scale agricultural activities, as carried out by the Belgian government and ECHO, represented an excellent bridge between relief and development.

Although the overall initial emergency response was effective, much work remains to be done in recovery and reconstruction, especially for the most vulnerable, such as families living in overcrowded camps or in inappropriate shelters, and with limited access to basic services. With this critical need in mind, donors should more actively and systematically support programmes in line with GHD Principle 7. It would also be vitally important to promote Principle 8, and strengthen the capacity of the government and communities to prevent, prepare for, mitigate, and respond to, future disasters. The weaknesses of Peruvian institutions were evident and must be attributed primarily to national political interference, rather than to limited donor involvement. Unfortunately, little has been accomplished to improve the situation in either of these areas.

Conclusion

The case of the 2007 Peru earthquake reflects a positive trend in private sector donations as part of a corporate social responsibility agenda. Non-traditional donors should be encouraged to contribute to disaster risk reduction in local communities. However, an important consideration which emerges from the above analysis is that assistance is not necessarily more efficient when it is the first to arrive, but when it best responds to real needs.

It is evident that because the Peruvian government was not sufficiently prepared to collect information and coordinate with international actors, they hindered the humanitarian response. Institutions established for the purpose of coordination cannot exist in name only, but must be operational, with clear roles and responsibilities, and with a strong presence in the field. Donors should strengthen and support the government's coordination capacity to prevent, prepare for, mitigate, and respond to, future disasters. One of the most important lessons from this disaster is the need to reinforce preparedness at a central level as well as in the provinces and municipalities, by making disaster risk reduction an institutional priority. Indeed, local capacity building continues to be a real need, as the local authorities of the 25 regions, 123 provinces, and 1,900 municipalities *all* require training in disaster preparedness.

Similarly, in order to guarantee long-term benefits, donors – in keeping with the Hyogo Framework for Action – should support capacity-building initiatives for community organisations, and strengthen community resilience and local-level risk reduction efforts, through risk assessment and awareness training. Efforts should be made to map hazard-prone areas and analyse disaster risk with local community representatives, as well as with state and non-state actors. Donors should fund efforts to train, retrain, and equip local community-based disaster management committees in disaster preparedness and early warning, in order to overcome failures of the public administration. Given the problems created by the lack of land titles, donors and implementing partners should work to identify existing land ownership patterns and advocate for the rights of the affected population and for proper legal registration.

Beyond supporting disaster risk reduction and support for the initial emergency phase, there is a clear need for donors to provide sustained funding into the mid-term and recovery phases. These measures would not only increase the effectiveness of their investment, but would help to bridge the gap between relief – often considered by media and donors as the "sexier," more attractive side of an emergency response – and development, which receives far less attention. Donors should therefore fund the integration of disaster risk reduction measures into recovery and longer-term development programmes, in keeping with the basic "build-back-better-and-safer" principle. In order to achieve maximum impact, recovery should also be participatory and engage local communities in training and decision making. Lastly, the overall recovery programme must be jointly assessed by the government, donors, local and international organisations, and affected communities, so that specific lessons can be learned, and transparency and accountability increased.

The importance of effective joint assessments and joint monitoring is also evident from the humanitarian response to the earthquake in Peru. Information must be shared in a transparent way among all actors in the response system. Similarly, the government of such a disaster-prone country, should, with the support of the international donor community, draw up a disaster management plan, which includes a clear contingency plan, and which defines the response coordination mechanisms and the roles and responsibilities of governmental and local actors. The international humanitarian community should shift from a more reactive response to a more cost-effective investment in preparedness.

Notes

1   The HRI team, composed of Aldara Collet, Valentina Ferrara, and Riccardo Polastro visited Peru in November 2007. The opinions expressed here are those of the author and do not necessarily reflect those of DARA.

2   The 1970 Ancash earthquake caused an estimated 48,000 to 66,000 deaths and affected 3.2 million people. For further details see Emergency Events Database (EM-DAT) at: http://www.emdat.be/Database/CountryProfile/countryprofile.php#top10lists

3   Instituto Nacional de Defensa Civil, 2007.

4   As reported by the International Federation of the Red Cross and Red Crescent Societies (IFRC), 2008, p. 3.

5   European Commission Humanitarian (Aid) Office (ECHO), 2007.

6   Ipsos Apoyo, 2007.

7   HRI field interview.

8   Including the ALAS Foundation, Alcatel Lucent Foundation, BNP Paribas, Exxon Mobile, Galaxy Latin America, Germanischer Lloyd Peru, Goodyear, KLM, Kraft Food, JT International Foundation, the Monsanto Fund, the OPEC Fund for International Development, Petrolife Petroleum Company, the SAFRA Edmond J. Philanthropic and the Telefónica Foundation.

9   OCHA, FTS.

10 HRI field interview.

11 Elhawary and Castillo, 2008.

12 ECHO, 2007.

13 OCHA, 2007a.

14 IFRC, 2007.

15 *The Economist,* 2007.

16 Clulow, 2001.

17 Initially, OCHA did not manage coordination of the response. During the HRI field visit a number of donors complained about OCHA's limited presence.

18 OCHA, 2007c.

10 OCHA, 2007b.

20 Pan American Health Organization, 2007.

21 This amount includes Sol/178 million from the Ministry of Economy and Finance and Sol/500 million from foreign donations (equivalent to US$60 and US$169 million, respectively, at the time of the mission).

22 Ipsos Apoyo, 2007. The survey was carried out on a sample population of 1,007 people between 18 and 70 years, in 16 representative cities of the country.

23 This explains why the government initially asked for in-kind rather than cash donations. The problem is so severe that most of the public budget goes unspent.

References

Clulow, M. 2001. *Peru, Alliance Earthquake Response.* Save the Children Fund. January. At: http://apps.odi.org.uk/erd/ReportDetail.aspx?reportID=3128

Elhawary, Samir and Gerardo Castillo. 2008. "The role of the affected state: A case study on the Peruvian earthquake response." HPG Working Paper. April. At: http://www.odi.org.uk/HPG/papers/wpaffectedstate-peru.pdf

European Commission Humanitarian (Aid) Office (ECHO). 2007. Emergency Humanitarian Aid Decision 23 02 01. Brussels. At: http://ec.europa.eu/echo/files/funding/decisions/2007/peru_02000_en.pdf

The Economist. 2007. "*Peru's Political Tremors.*" The Economist Intelligence Unit. At: 24/09/2007 http://www.economist.com/displayStory.cfm?story_id=9857040

Emergency Events Database (EM-DAT). At: http://www.emdat.be/Database/CountryProfile/countryprofile.php#top10lists

Instituto Nacional de Defensa Civil. 2007. "Informe de Emergencia No. 349." 13 November. At: www.indeci.gob.pe

International Federation of the Red Cross and Red Crescent. 2007. *Operations Update: Peru Earthquake No. 1.* 19 August. At: http://www.ifrc.org/docs/appeals/07/MDRPE003_01.pdf

International Federation of the Red Cross. 2008. *Operations Update: Peru Earthquake No. 6.* 6 February. At: http://www.ifrc.org/docs/appeals/07/MDRPE00306.pdf

Ipsos Apoyo. 2007. "Opinión Data: Resumen de encuestas a la opinión publica." Año 8(94). At: http://economia.unmsm.edu.pe/Servicios/Banco%20Estad%C3%ADstico/Datos/AOM_OpinionData_26.11.07.pdf

Office for the Coordination of Humanitarian Affairs (OCHA). Financial Tracking Service.

———. 2007a. *Earthquake OCHA Situation Report No. 8.* At: http://www.reliefweb.int/rw/rwb.nsf/db900sid/EKOI-76C2X8?OpenDocument

———. 2007b. *Earthquake OCHA Situation Report No. 11.* At: http://www.reliefweb.int/rw/RWB.NSF/db900SID/EKOI-76H3BH?OpenDocument

———. 2007c. *Peru Earthquake Flash Appeal 2007.* At: http://ochaonline.un.org/cap2005/webpage.asp?Page=1604

Pan American Health Organization. 2007. "Earthquake in Peru." In *Disasters: Preparedness and Mitigation in the Americas* 108. October. At: http://www.paho.org/English/dd/Ped/ped1007e.pdf

Sri Lanka

AT A GLANCE

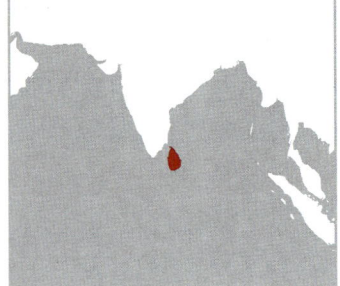

Country data *(2006 figures, unless otherwise noted)*

- 2007 Human Development Index: ranked 99th of 177 countries
- Population: 19.89 million
- GNI per capita (Atlas method, current US$): US$1,310
- Population living on less than US$2 a day (1990–2005): 41.6 percent
- Life expectancy: 75 years
- Infant mortality rate (2006): 11 per 1,000 live births
- Under-five infant mortality rate (2006): 13 per 1,000
- Population undernourished (2002–2004): 22 percent
- Population with sustainable access to improved water source (2004): 79 percent
- Adult literacy rate (over 15 yrs of age) (1995–2005): NA
- Primary education completion rate: 108 percent
- Gender-related development index (2005): ranked 88th of 177 countries
- Official development assistance (ODA): US$796 million
- 2007 Corruption Perception Index: ranked 94th out of 179 countries

Sources: Transparency International, 2007; UNDP, 2007a and 2007b; World Bank, 2008.

The crisis

- Conflict between Sri Lankan state and Liberation Tigers of Tamil Eelam (LTTE) lasted over 25 years, claiming over 70,000 lives, displacing hundreds of thousands;
- Violence increased following collapse of 2006 ceasefire; over 4,200 civilian causalities and assassinations in military confrontations and terrorist attacks;
- Number of IDPs increased from 66,203 to 208,717 by August 2006, rising to 308,612 end-March 2007, adding to .5 million people already uprooted by 2004 tsunami and past conflict;
- 104,678 IDPs returned to homes in Batticaloa in December 2007;
- Chronic under-development; Sri Lanka categorised as middle-income food-deficit country; 41.6 percent live below poverty line;
- Severe humanitarian crisis in north-east; child malnutrition levels high in conflict zones; 40 percent children underweight; 25 percent stunted; 23 percent wasted.

Sources: UNHCR, 2007; UNDP, 2008; and World Food Programme, 2008.

The humanitarian response

- Participants in 2003 Tokyo Conference on Reconstruction and Development of Sri Lanka pledged US$4.5 billion for four years; (the tsunami donors had pledged US$5.5 billion for Sri Lanka);
- Total 2007 humanitarian aid to Sri Lanka US$132.7 million;
- Largest donors were United States (US$35.2 million, 26.6 percent); EC/ECHO (US$18.1 million, 13.7 percent); Norway (US$12.8 million, 9.7 percent); CERF (US$11.8 million, 8.9 percent); and Australia (US$10.4, 7.9 percent); unspent from 2006 (US$5.4 million, 4.1 percent);
- 2007 CHAP increased from US$66 million to US$133 million, 74 percent funded;
- 25 humanitarian workers killed in 2006 and 22 in 2007, making Sri Lanka one of most dangerous places for aid workers in the world; UNICEF openly accused by government of helping the LTTE; other aid actors targets of suspicion, under parliamentary investigation.

Sources: Tsunami Evaluation Coalition, 2006; and OCHA Financial Tracking System, 2008a.

Sri Lanka

A Forgotten Complex Emergency – Back to War Again

RICCARDO POLASTRO, Head of Evaluation, DARA

© German Red Cross

Introduction[1]

The internal conflict between the Sri Lankan state and the Liberation Tigers of Tamil Eelam (LTTE) has lasted more than 25 years, claimed over 70,000 lives, and displaced hundreds of thousands of people. The conflict has often been defined as an ethnic struggle between the predominantly northern Tamil minority – who claim they have been denied their human rights and equitable participation in the country's governance – and the dominant Sinhalese majority, with the Muslim minority also drawn into the conflict. The result has been a complex emergency and grave humanitarian crisis, compounded by the renewed pursuit by both the government and LTTE of military solutions. Sri Lankan society has been increasingly polarised and radicalised along

ethno-political lines, and humanitarian actors are subject to suspicion and hostility. While violations of international humanitarian law and human rights are pervasive and committed by all sides in the conflict, access to the needy population is severely limited and exacerbated by one of the world's worst security situations for humanitarian actors. By 2008, the International Crisis Group wrote: "The humanitarian crisis is deepening, abuses of human rights by both sides are increasing, and those calling for peace are being silenced."[2]

Throughout its decades-long history, the conflict has varied in intensity and location, and, since the progressive collapse of the internationally-sponsored ceasefire in 2006, has seen an increase in violence. The government has retaken much of the east, the frontline of hostilities has shifted north towards LTTE-controlled areas, and terrorist attacks by the LTTE have increased.

The scarcity of media coverage of this deteriorating humanitarian situation may perhaps be explained by the protracted and fluid nature of the conflict. Since the crisis has relatively limited regional impact – India being the most engaged regional player – it is not considered "news." Due to its re-escalation, donors and media are tiring of the conflict, especially after the enthusiasm of the 2003 Tokyo Conference for Peace and Reconstruction. Disappointment has translated into donor reluctance to fund recovery activities and in some cases have scaled down assistance. The new phase of military confrontation has both displaced sections of the civilian population, increasing humanitarian needs, and also created the conditions for return by people who were previously displaced, particularly in the east. The humanitarian response to this situation provides an opportunity to analyse donor behaviour in light of the Good Humanitarian Donorship (GHD) *Principles* regarding impartiality, neutrality, and independence, protection of civilians, funding in proportion to needs, and linking relief to recovery and long-term development (Principles 2, 3, 6, and 9).

The conflict and its impact: International humanitarian law, human rights, and forced displacement

Prior to the Ceasefire Agreement (CFA) of February 2002, 65,000 people lost their lives; 1.7 million – one-fifth of the population – were internally displaced, and the economy severely damaged. The CFA facilitated the longest period of peace for the northeast since 1983 and access for the first time by relief agencies. Internally displaced persons (IDPs) and refugees began to return to their homes in LTTE-controlled areas after more than three decades.[3]

However, Norwegian-brokered peace talks stalled when monitors reported escalating ceasefire violations by both sides in mid-2006, peaking in intensity in July of that year.[4] As the situation deteriorated, the four co-chairs of the peace negotiations (the United States, the EU, Japan, and Norway) threatened to pull out of the talks and freeze all assistance other than humanitarian aid. Although the government and LTTE met in October of 2006, this only reinforced the perception that neither party was willing to talk meaningfully.[5] Since then, violence has become a persistent reality. In 2007, fighting escalated in the north and east, with the government claiming by mid-2007 to have control over the east, including several traditional LTTE strongholds.[6]

The government formally ended the ceasefire in January 2008, with both parties clearly determined to find a military solution. Implementing agencies reported growing extremism on both sides along ethnic, religious, and political lines.[7]

Since the ceasefire ended, more than 4,200 civilian causalities and assassinations have been reported, the consequence of increasing military confrontations and terrorist attacks, particularly LTTE suicide bombings. The level of insecurity among the civilian population is multiplied by several factors, including the emergence of new paramilitary groups on the government side, the increasing polarisation, politicisation, and militarisation of society, and grave human rights violations by all sides, for which no one is held accountable. When the UN recorded more disappearances in Sri Lanka last year than in any other country, the United States, Switzerland, and the EC, pressed to send in human rights monitors, a proposal which was rejected by the government.[8]

All parties to the conflict are accused of deliberately violating international humanitarian law by targeting civilians, and of indiscriminate bombardment, the use of human shields, attacks on hospitals and places of refuge, extra-judicial killings, abductions, disappearances, targeted assassinations, and persistent conflict-induced displacement.[9] The civilian population is trapped in the conflict, which compels them to flee; but they are prevented from escaping areas under direct attack. Large numbers of people are brutally uprooted, in most cases without any military imperative. Both the government and the LTTE have generally failed to protect civilians in conflict-torn areas and do not respond to the needs of the IDPs in their areas of control. According to the UN Guiding Principles on Internal Displacement, the government is primarily responsible for the protection and security of IDPs, while the LTTE is responsible for those in areas under its control. Indeed, the protection of basic human rights represents one of the fundamental challenges of the conflict. For example, IDP camps are infiltrated by armed men and people are abducted.[10] Furthermore, many are unable to return due to the fluid and insecure situation. In the words of one displaced person: "I still don't feel it's safe enough to return. The situation is still unpredictable. Only yesterday someone in the village was injured by a mine. My three girls are the most important thing for me, and I won't put them at risk in any way."[11]

The displaced are primarily from the Tamil and Muslim minorities, particularly in the east. The UN estimates that the number of IDPs soared from 66,203 to 208,717 between July and August 2006, rising again to 308,612 at the end of March 2007, following government incursions along the east coast. This new wave of displacement comes in the wake of the uprooting of some half a million people by the 2004 Indian Ocean tsunami and previous conflict. As a result, Asia has one of the highest population displacements both in absolute terms and as a percentage of the population (2.3 percent).[12] According to the Norwegian Refugee Council, in August 2007, the number reached approximately 460,000.[13] However, the government maintains that the forced displacement due to the conflict is not as significant as is claimed by the international community.[14] The UN High Commissioner for Refugees (UNHCR) estimates that the total number of IDPs fell to just under 188,000 by December 2007, mainly due to the number of returnees to the eastern district of Batticaloa following the reestablishment of government control in the area.[15] The majority of the displaced remain concentrated in the north, in areas under LTTE control.

More than 18,000 have fled by boat to India, while some 100,000 refugees live in more than 100 refugee camps in Tamil Nadu, India. Their health conditions are generally poor, with many women and children suffering from anaemia, skin disease, and malnutrition. There is also a large and active Tamil diaspora, primarily in Canada, the UK, and Australia.

Donor behaviour: Fatigue from ceaseless conflict

Participants in the 2003 Tokyo Conference on Reconstruction and Development of Sri Lanka pledged US$4.5 billion over a four year period. In contrast, during the tsunami donors pledged US$5.5 billion for Sri Lanka.[16]

Total contributions of humanitarian aid in 2007 to Sri Lanka amounted to more than US$132.7 million.[17] The largest donors were the United States with US$35.2 million (26.6 percent of total funding); EC/ECHO with US$18.1 million (13.7 percent); Norway with US$12.8 million (9.7 percent); the Central Emergency Response Fund (CERF) with US$11.8 million (8.9 percent); and Australia with US$10.4 (7.9 percent). A further US$5.4 million (4.1 percent) consisted of unspent funds carried over from the previous year, mainly from money committed to the tsunami response.

In response to the changing humanitarian situation, the UN Common Humanitarian Action Plan (CHAP) more than doubled in 2007, increasing from US$66 million to US$133 million. However, CHAP did not include all humanitarian assistance, because many organisations did not include operations already funded. For example, it represents only 40 percent of ECHO funds.

In 2007, the contribution via CERF to UN agencies was significant.[18] However, some donors interviewed consider that this new instrument is not being used effectively to promote early action to reduce loss of life and respond to time-critical needs, complaining that it has been used primarily to bridge the funding gap in CHAP.[19] The UN is absorbing most unearmarked funds, thus draining available resources for NGOs and the Red Cross Red Crescent Movement. Some donors consider that CERF is cumbersome and bureaucratic and that the UN machinery is not only more expensive, but reaches fewer beneficiaries, has a smaller impact, and is less flexible and accountable.[20]

Dialogue with the government is problematic, as it has become more nationalistic and less open to criticism from donors, in part because it is less dependent on traditional bilateral aid, and receives more support from regional allies such as China, India, and Pakistan. The President claimed that Sri Lanka is "no longer a poor country thriving on aid and subsidies of the world. Our per capita income has risen to US$1,625 now. We need not bow our head to anyone, but we are prepared to listen to the constructive criticism and prudent advice of others."[21] Donor engagement with the LTTE is practically impossible because of its violent tactics and its classification as a terrorist organisation by numerous countries, including the United States and the EU.

To date, funding for humanitarian causes in Sri Lanka has never been a major problem. The 2007 CHAP was 74 percent funded. Most donors present in the country actively support GHD Principles 10 and 14 and contribute to the UN and the ICRC, as well as to CHAP. In line with GHD Principle 5, CERF, ECHO, and USAID provided timely humanitarian funding. However, in the case of ECHO, some implementing partners pointed out that the administrative process in Brussels was long and the transfer of funds slow. As a result, the implementing agencies had to use their own funds, despite having to begin and complete the project according to the time line approved in the programme document.

Organisations interviewed during the field mission reported an important degree of donor engagement at a senior level on advocacy issues. For example, in the Consultative Committee on Humanitarian Affairs (CCHA) ambassadors raised issues related to international humanitarian law, human rights violations, taxation, and the denial of visas to international staff.[22] Implementing agencies repeatedly described the dialogue between humanitarian actors and donors as constructive, and donors generally felt that the partnership was an equal one.

Lack of a common donor approach

Despite the good working relationship between humanitarian actors and donors, many in the international community consider the main problem to be the lack of commonality in the approach used by various donors. On the one hand, Japan, the largest OECD/DAC provider of development assistance in Sri Lanka, takes a somewhat uncritical stance towards the government. The western donor community, on the other, prefers to use a rights-based approach and conditional aid. According to representatives interviewed, EU countries were more sensitive to and actively engaged in the humanitarian issues, while the United States seems more active around conflict issues.[23]

According to humanitarian actors interviewed, some donors are showing a lower level of engagement because of the collapse of the peace process and the apparently endless nature of the crisis. In addition, some donors fear that their funds could be used to fund armed groups, given the high levels of corruption and the culture of impunity. At a meeting with UN agencies in March 2008, some donors expressed their intention not to invest funds beyond humanitarian aid. In fact, some donors such as the UK, German and Spanish governments have cut their aid budgets in the last year and are withdrawing from the country. Others, notably Denmark, Sweden, and the Netherlands, plan to follow suit. In part, this trend shows that the country is no longer considered a priority, since the parties to the conflict have formally withdrawn from the peace process and because Sri Lanka, overall, has achieved the economic and human development indicators of a middle-income country. However, it is important to note that internal conditions vary considerably, and are much worse in the conflict-torn north and east.

Therefore, according to UN officials, obtaining money for recovery has become a major challenge due to donor fatigue, the volatile context, and the continu-ing conflict, especially in the north. Many organisations find themselves back at square one, dealing mainly with emergency needs rather than recovery and long-term development. Even though resettlement has taken place in some areas, recovery has not yet begun. According to a December 2007 report by UNHCR, 104,678 people returned to Batticaloa after the area came under government control. And because most programmes are short term, building local partner capacity is not a priority. At present, some donors see an underlying tension between GHD Principle 9 (*provide humanitarian assistance in ways that are supportive of recovery and long-term development*) and Principle 2 (*humanitarian action must not favour any side in an armed conflict*).

Therefore, in 2007, donors primarily supported emergency assistance and protection-related activities, such as food, shelter, water, and sanitation interventions aimed at meeting the increasing needs of the conflict-affected population. Only Japan, Australia, Canada, Denmark, the EC Uprooted Fund, Germany and Norway (through the UNDP transition programme), and the United States (through United Methodist Committee on Relief) are actively engaged in funding recovery in the government-controlled areas in the east.

To remain impartial and prevent the misuse of aid, 12 key donors and the UN adopted a set of Guiding Principles for Humanitarian and Development Assistance in May 2007. These included impartiality, non-discrimination, respect for human dignity, consultation and participation, and coordination to protect humanitarian space.[24] A number of these principles reflect the Red Cross Code of Conduct and are in line with many of the GHD *Principles* and objectives. The Guiding Principles are aimed at improving aid effectiveness and cooperation among government authorities, donors, and implementing agencies, safeguarding humanitarian space, and promoting respect for international humanitarian and human rights law.

However, the parties to the conflict have not abided by these principles. Multiple violations of security, access, impartiality, transparency and accountability, as well as respect for human dignity have been reported.

Implementation of the humanitarian response: Changing needs and shrinking humanitarian space

Sri Lanka suffers from widespread and chronic under-development and is categorised as a middle-income food-deficit country in which an average 41.6 percent of the population lives below the poverty line.[25] However, 25 years of conflict have had a major impact on economic and social development and have created – especially in the north and east – a severe humanitarian crisis. Under-five malnutrition levels are especially high in these areas, with 40 percent of children underweight, 25 percent stunted, and 23 percent wasted.[26]

Renewed conflict and increasing displacement

With regard to Sri Lanka, the humanitarian system has experienced a structural shift since 2005, with many assuming that the country was moving towards peace. When this turned out not to be the case, the staff and financial resources of most humanitarian agencies found themselves unable to cope with the needs created by renewed conflict.[27] Increased violence in late 2006 and a sharp increase in the numbers of displaced posed a serious challenge to the humanitarian community and prompted many organisations to reorient their activities and issue revised appeals. For example, the World Food Programme had to suspend its mother and child nutrition and school feeding programmes in order to meet the basic food needs of 50 percent more people.[28] Similarly, the ICRC shifted its focus from community-based health programmes to emergency activities, including the provision of medical supplies to hospitals.[29] Schooling for more than 250,000 children was disrupted, requiring emergency classes in temporary buildings. By May 2007, Jaffna and Batticaloa districts were considered "humanitarian emergencies;" Kilinochchi, Mullaitivu, Mannar, Vavuniya, and Trincomalee were assessed as "acute food and livelihood crises," and Ampara was classified as "chronically food-insecure."[30] Moreover, many unregistered IDPs, living outside the camps with host families, did not receive any support or government rations, especially in areas under LTTE control, or where the population was perceived as not supporting the government.

In general, in 2007, humanitarian actors were better prepared than in previous years. Learning from the previous months' sudden influx of IDPs, and in line with CHAP, they created a contingency plan for more than 500,000 persons. Therefore, as of early 2008, most organisations were better prepared to respond to new displacements.

The ICRC Head of Delegation expressed concern about "the impact the heightened violence is having on civilians," particularly in the north.[31] The continued deterioration of the situation made the need for life-saving and life-sustaining activities more acute. Since mid-2007,

despite strong coping mechanisms, the growing humanitarian concern is civilian access to basic food supplies and non-food relief items. Interviewees reported little freedom of movement for civilians – with an attendant impact on their livelihoods and employment opportunities – and increased difficulties accessing food and health care. The movement of goods was also seriously affected, resulting in shortages and price increases. Government fishing bans further aggravated the situation. There are reports of forced recruitment into guerrilla groups and armed factions.[32] Key survey informants revealed that in the northern Vanni district forced recruitment of civilians continues, with one to two people per family estimated to be coerced into joining the LTTE.[33]

The situation in the east was drastically different. With the collapse of the ceasefire and a successful government offensive since 2006, many IDPs were able to return to areas which had previously been under LTTE control. Upon returning, however, they faced acute difficulties. Many found their homes and basic infrastructure damaged or destroyed. They could not work, as tools and equipment had been looted, and they lacked the funds to replace them. Property restitution, ethnic prejudice, security threats, and landmines were only some of the problems returnees experienced, especially those who had been displaced several times. Security concerns, embargoes, and the closure of main transport routes threaten livelihoods in the long term and building materials are not easily available. Lastly, the capacity to protect returnees has fluctuated according to the political climate, and a number of human rights organisations have reported forced resettlement and questioned whether the IDPs are returning voluntarily.[34] Only UNHCR and ICRC managed to continue to guarantee basic protection. Nevertheless, as resettlement proceeds, ethnic tensions are on the rise, as the best land is being assigned to government supporters. Interviewees considered the situation potentially explosive.[35]

In government controlled areas, and other areas without active hostilities, the link between emergency relief, rehabilitation, and development is weak because most donors consider Sri Lanka to be an ongoing humanitarian, rather than a post-conflict, situation. Therefore, they fund relief activities primarily. Donors fear that engaging in recovery activities will result in reduced aid effectiveness and a rise in inequality, since the government, instead of providing aid impartially, neutrally, and in proportion to need, tends to favour its supporters. It is necessary to ensure that any aid to Sri Lanka is distributed equitably among those in need, so as not to exacerbate tensions among different ethnic groups. In March 2008, only Japan, the Netherlands, Norway, and Switzerland attended a UN-sponsored donor meeting on recovery efforts.

Restricted humanitarian access

While the humanitarian community faces increasing difficulties in Sri Lanka because of insecurity and reduced humanitarian space, the difference in approach between the local and the central government is significant. Local government authorities generally accept and recognise the value of humanitarian actions, but the central government does not always facilitate such activities.[36] For example, the government restricted access to the main supply routes by road and by sea, preventing essential humanitarian aid from reaching the affected population. As a result of this closure, the Jaffna peninsula is suffering severe shortages and increased prices for food and basic supplies. Humanitarian space also diminished progressively, with limited access to the areas of Jaffna and the Vanni region, and other areas under the LTTE control, leaving the civilian population isolated. Access and presence in the Vanni area is limited to only 12 international organisations, a significant reduction from the 300 that were operating in the LTTE-controlled area after the tsunami.[37]

Atmosphere of hostility and suspicion

Moreover, suspicion of humanitarian organisations created further barriers to an effective response. As Médecins Sans Frontières (MSF) points out, "this lack of respect for humanitarian aid comes at a time when areas near the front line of fighting have lost nearly all of their medical specialists and hospitals no longer have the human resources to treat the wounded."[38] Humanitarian organisations such as UNICEF were openly accused by government officials of helping the LTTE, and Save the Children Fund and World Vision are presently under parliamentary investigation. The polarised political atmosphere explains these events. Even John Holmes, the UN Under-Secretary General for Humanitarian Affairs, was subjected to criticism when Minister Jeyaraj publicly called him a terrorist, in August 2007, for saying that Sri Lanka had one of the world's worst safety records for humanitarian workers.[39]

In this hostile atmosphere, the work of disseminating the mandate of humanitarian organisations is even more important. A Tufts University report suggests that aid agencies may have failed to do so: "… aid agencies were identified as being ineffective in communicating

their mandates. This failure of communication enables local political interests to construct populist interpretations of humanitarianism. The negative local political construction of the humanitarian enterprise was shown to have hampered the delivery and effectiveness of assistance. It has also endangered the lives of aid workers."[40] This contributes to the grim picture for realising in practice the fundamental principles of humanitarian aid.

To make matters worse, the questionable effectiveness and transparency of the humanitarian response to the 2004 tsunami has tarnished the reputation of humanitarian action.[41] With regard to GHD Principles 5 and 6, it must be acknowledged that neither public nor private funds in Sri Lanka have always been allocated in proportion to need – evident when one compares the staggering amounts of loosely earmarked money allocated after the tsunami with funding for the renewed conflict in Sri Lanka. This discrepancy is due not only to severe constraints imposed in the field, but also to the fact that some donors, such as the United States, have refrained from funding humanitarian or other programmes in LTTE-controlled areas because the LTTE is considered a terrorist organisation.

In this charged atmosphere, humanitarian workers have been subject to violent attack. The killing of 25 humanitarian workers in 2006 and 22 in 2007 makes Sri Lanka one of the world's most dangerous places for humanitarian workers. And although the security situation has improved slightly, access and timeliness have continued to suffer. As observed during the HRI mission in February, there were numerous checkpoints in Colombo and throughout the country, reducing humanitarian access and increasing the time necessary to deliver aid. Tamil staff members are often stopped. Further constraints include the closure of Forward Defence Lines, the imposition of curfews, complications in obtaining visas and work permits for NGO workers, and the increasing taxation of relief items. The situation is further complicated by restrictions on the transport of relief items and the lack of fuel in some areas. The combination of these factors prevented humanitarian actors from responding predictably and effectively to basic needs and obtaining access, further shrinking the humanitarian space which had opened up after the Ceasefire Agreement and the tsunami.

Coordination

Led by the UN Humanitarian Coordinator, the Inter-Agency Standing Committee (IASC) Country Team in Sri Lanka acts as the main framework for humanitarian coordination, with OCHA serving as its secretariat. The IASC Country Team consists of 31 members from the UN, ICRC, and NGO community.[42] While the IASC works on sectoral coordination, the Consultative Committee on Humanitarian Affairs

(CCHA) focuses on advocacy. In fact, many coordination platforms exist in Sri Lanka, such as the Consortium of Humanitarian Agencies (CHA), a network of NGOs that coordinates with the government, the IASC and the CCHA. Although these mechanisms and bodies have made for better information exchange, they have not improved operational decision making, as most humanitarian organisations continue to operate independently. According to the national humanitarian NGO coordinating body, the only example of effective coordination is the Mine Action Steering Committee. However, local NGOs report that coordination has improved since the December 2004 tsunami, thanks to OCHA leadership, and that the UN and NGOs are working more closely than they did before.

The UN has not formally introduced the cluster approach in Sri Lanka, but has established effective sectoral coordination for food, logistics, nutrition, shelter, water-sanitation, and hygiene, providing a framework for a coordinated response.[43] However, OCHA's approach to coordination, following the shift to conflict-related activities after the tsunami, has been the subject of criticism. Furthermore, OCHA presently faces considerable difficulty, given the discomfort of the government with CHAP's focus on areas under LTTE control. The agency is also understaffed and there is a clear need for better coordination among the UN agencies.

In addition, the structure of the Sri Lankan government itself created problems for coordination. The central government has more than 80 ministries, some fragmented and covering the same sector, making it difficult for international organisations to know which ones they should coordinate with. For example, UNHCR, the lead agency for IDPs, has a multitude of government counterparts, complicating advocacy, cooperation, and coordination. A mixture of English, Indian, and Sri Lankan organisational and decision-making styles and a lack of a national comprehensive plan further complicate coordination.

Donor perceptions of the quality of coordination vary, some considering it chaotic, with the interests of larger donors prevailing over smaller donors' attempts to work in a more harmonised way. Other donors considered that donor coordination functioned well, citing the donor group chaired by the EC, which has a reduced number of key participants, facilitating management and information exchange.[44]

Conclusion

With large swathes of the country back at war, the prospects for an improved humanitarian situation look gloomier than ever. The number of violations of international humanitarian and human rights law has increased dramatically. There have been numerous security incidents involving humanitarian workers. Humanitarian access and space have been compromised, reducing the timeliness, coverage, and effectiveness of assistance, and the protection of civilians.

Promoting humanitarian and human rights law and realising in action the principles governing IDPs are two important aspects of the donor agenda. However, even though 11 OECD/DAC donors[45] supported the Guiding Principles for Humanitarian and Development Assistance – thus promoting the GHD and general principles of humanitarian action – the parties to the conflict have neither endorsed nor honoured these principles. Donors must promote humanitarian principles through better public education, by offering training for all national stakeholders, and by defining clear implementation mechanisms to put them into practice. Unfortunately, the government's view that those who do not support the government are supporting the LTTE makes the upholding of independence, neutrality, and impartiality, and preserving humanitarian space in Sri Lanka complex and challenging. Donors must continue to urge all parties to respect humanitarian space and improve access.

Response in proportion to need is fundamental to making the international community accountable to the local population and the general public. The supply-driven response following the tsunami helped to arouse the current suspicion towards humanitarian action in Sri Lanka. Donors must not permit this to recur. Funds should only be released when assistance can be absorbed and does not overlook local capacities.

While funding for relief operations is available, the major gap is in recovery. In line with the GHD *Principles,* donors should fund the recovery-based strategies of humanitarian organisations. This will go far to guaranteeing urgent humanitarian assistance as well as the medium- and long-term assistance so necessary for rebuilding conflict-stricken areas in the north and east, and therefore promoting the development of the entire country. Nevertheless, some donors are beginning to express concern that continuous humanitarian aid will encourage the parties in the conflict to direct their social welfare budgets towards the war effort and neglect their own responsibility to protect civilians.

Finally, donors must define common ground and action and jointly set common criteria for their involvement in and response to the crisis. This agreement is crucial in order to engage safely in reconstruction and avoid ethnic engineering. Donors must engage in long-term planning, focus on recovery and state-building, and foster democracy. To this end, OECD/DAC donors should enlist the support of other donors such as India, China, Pakistan, and Iran.

Notes

1   The HRI team, composed of Daniela Mamone, Hnin Nwe, and Riccardo Polastro visited Sri Lanka in February 2008. The opinions expressed here are those of the author and do not necessarily reflect those of DARA.

2   International Crisis Group, 2008.

3   Arbeitsgemeinschaft Entwicklungspolitischer Gutachter (AGEG [German Association of Development Consultants]) and the European Commission Humanitarian Office (ECHO), 2005.

4   See Sri Lankan Government, 2008.

5   International Crisis Group, 2006.

6   ICRC, 2008a.

7   HRI field interview.

8   Sengupta, 2008.

9   Human Rights Watch, 2007.

10   Amnesty International, 2007.

11   ICRC, 2008c.

12   Norwegian Refugee Council, 2007.

13   Norwegian Refugee Council, 2008. The highest internal displacement in Asia is in India with 600,000, followed by Bangladesh and Myanmar, each with 500,000.

14   It is difficult to determine the exact numbers of IDPs, due to the overlap between those displaced by the conflict before and after 2006 and those displaced by the 2004 tsunami.

15   UNHCR, 2007.

16   Tsunami Evaluation Coalition, 2006.

17   OCHA Financial Tracking System, 2008a.

18   Sri Lanka is the 8th recipient country of CERF funds. Between March 2006 and June 2008, Sri Lanka received a total of US$27.8 million, corresponding to 3.29 percent of the total funds disbursed by CERF for the same period.

19   CERF, 2007.

20   HRI field interview.

21   Mathes, 2008.

22   The CCHA is chaired by the Ministry of Disaster Management and Human Rights, attended by the Ministry of Defence, the Ministry of Foreign Affairs, and other line ministries, and has additional standing members such as embassies, UNHCR, the Resident Coordinator, and ICRC.

23   According to the former US Ambassador to Sri Lanka, "The main US strategic interest in Sri Lanka is in ensuring that a terrorist organisation does not obtain its goals through the use of terror."(Lunstead, 2007.)

24   Australia, Canada, the EC, Germany, Japan, Korea, the Netherlands, Norway, Sweden, Switzerland, the UK, and the United States.

25   UNDP, 2008.

26   World Food Programme, 2008.

27   UNHCR, 2006.

28   World Food Programme, 2007a.

29   ICRC, 2008a.

30   World Food Programme, 2007b.

31   ICRC, 2008b.

32   ICRC, 2008a.

33   HRI field interview.

34   Ibid.

35   Ibid.

36   HRI field interview.

37   The list of organisations includes ZOA (Netherlands), Forut (Norway-Sweden), Oxfam, Save the Children Fund, World Vision, the Danish Refugee Council, the Norwegian Refugee Council, ASB/Solidar, Médecins Sans Frontières, German Agro Action, UN agencies, and the International Committee of the Red Cross.

38   Médecins Sans Frontières, 2007.

39   Jayasekera, 2007.

40   Feinstein International Center, 2007.

41   The Tsunami Evaluation Coalition identified several weaknesses, including rare coordination or sharing of assessments; supply-driven, unsolicited, and inappropriate aid; and limited participation of the affected-population, all of which have combined to create negative perceptions on the part of the local population. See Telford et al., 2006.

42   For a full list see: OCHA. Humanitarian Portal – Sri Lanka.

43   OCHA, 2008b.

44   HRI field interview.

45   The 12th donor is the Republic of Korea, which is not on the OECD/DAC.

References

Arbeitsgemeinschaft entwicklungspolitischer Gutachter (AGEG) and the European Commission Humanitarian (Aid) Office (ECHO). 2005. *The Evaluation of ECHO's Actions in Sri Lanka and in the Tamil Refugee Camps in Tamil Nadu, India.* July. At: http://ec.europa.eu/echo/files/policies/evaluation/2005/sri_lanka.pdf

Amnesty International. 2007. "Sri Lanka: Armed Groups Infiltrating Refugee Camps." 14 March. At: http://www.amnesty.org/en/library/asset/ASA37/007/2007/en/dom-ASA370072007en.html

Central Emergency Response Fund. 2007. *Interim Review.* September. At: http://ochaonline.un.org/ToolsServices/EvaluationandStudies/ESSReports/tabid/1325/Default.aspx

Feinstein International Center. 2007. *Humanitarian Agenda 2015 Sri Lanka Country Study.* October. At: http://fic.tufts.edu/downloads/HA2015SriLankaCountryStudy.pdf

Human Rights Watch. 2007. "Return to War. Human Rights Under Siege." August. At: http://www.hrw.org/reports/2007/srilanka0807/srilanka0807webwcover.pdf

International Conference of the Red Cross and Red Crescent (ICRC). 2008a. *Annual Report 2007.* May. At: http://www.icrc.org/web/eng/siteeng0.nsf/htmlall/section_annual_report_2007?OpenDocument

———. 2008b. "Sri Lanka-ICRC Bulletin No.1/2008." 8 February. At: www.reliefweb.int/rw/rwb.nsf/db900sid/AMMF-7BMDEM?OpenDocument&rc=3&cc=lka

———. 2008c. "Civilians' plight: Testimonies of victims of Sri Lanka's 25-year conflict." At: http://www.icrc.org/web/eng/siteeng0.nsf/html/sri-lanka-feature-testimonies-050608

International Crisis Group (ICG). 2006. *Sri Lanka: The Failure of the Peace Process.* Asia Report 124. 28 November. At: http://www.crisisgroup.org/library/documents/asia/south_asia/sri_lanka/124_sri_lanka___the_failure_of_the_peace_process.pdf

———. 2008. *Sri Lanka's Return to War: Limiting the Damage.* Asia Report No. 146. 20 Feb. At: http://www.crisisgroup.org/library/documents/asia/south_asia/sri_lanka/146_sri_lanka_s_return_to_war___limiting_the_damage.pdf

Jayasekera, Sandun A. 2007. "Jeyaraj Accuses Holmes of Being a Terrorist." *Daily Mirror.* 16 August. At: http://www.dailymirror.lk/2007/08/16/front/1.asp

Lunstead, Jeffrey. 2007. *The United States' Role in Sri Lanka's Peace Process 2002–2006.* Colombo: The Asia Foundation.

Mathes, Rohan. 2008. "No Pause in Anti-LTTE Drive." *Daily News.* 3 March. At: http://www.dailynews.lk/2008/03/03/pol01.asp

Médecins Sans Frontières. 2007. "Top Ten Most Underreported Humanitarian Stories of 2007." 20 December. At: http://msf.org/msfinternational/invoke.cfm?objectid=F77A3EAE-15C5-F00A-2512CE940378E72C&component=toolkit.report&method=full_html

Norwegian Refugee Council. 2007. *Civilians in the Way of Conflict: Displaced People in Sri Lanka.* Internal Displacement Monitoring Centre. Norwegian Refugee Council. Geneva. 26 September. At: http://www.internal-displacement.org/8025708F004BE3B1/(httpInfoFiles)/882EB0DAEEA545A4C12573620026E7EB/$file/Sri_lanka_special_report_sep07.pdf

———. 2008. *Internal Displacement. Global Overview and Trends in 2007.* April. At: http://www.internal-displacement.org/8025708F004BE3B1/(httpInfoFiles)/BD8316FAB5984142C125742E0033180B/$file/IDMC_Internal_Displacement_Global_Overview_2007.pdf

Office for the Coordination of Humanitarian Affairs (OCHA). *Financial Tracking System.* 2008a. *Sri Lanka 2007.* At: http://ocha.unog.ch/fts/reports/daily/ocha_R24_E15220___08061707.pdf

———. 2008b. *Humanitarian Portal – Sri Lanka.* At: http://www.humanitarianinfo.org/sriLanka_hpsl/Sectors_Clusters.aspx

Sengupta, Somini. 2008. "Ethnic Divide Worsens as Sri Lanka Conflict Escalates." *The New York Times.* 8 March. At: http://www.nytimes.com/2008/03/08/world/asia/08lanka.html

Sri Lankan Government. 2008. "CFA Violations at a Glance." Secretariat for Coordinating the Peace Process. At: http://www.peaceinsrilanka.com/peace2005/Insidepage/AtaGlance/Ceasefire.asp

Telford, J, J. Cosgrave, and R. Houghton. 2006. *Joint Evaluation of the international response to the Indian Ocean tsunami: Synthesis Report.* London: Tsunami Evaluation Coalition.

Tsunami Evaluation Coalition. 2006. *Funding the Tsunami Response. Thematic Evaluation Report.* July. At: http://www.tsunami-evaluation.org/NR/rdonlyres/BBA2659F-967C-4CAB-A08F-BEF67606C83F/0/funding_final_report.pdf

United Nations Development Programme (UNDP). 2008. *Human Development Report 2007/2008. Fighting Climate Change: Human Solidarity in a Divided World.* At: http://hdr.undp.org/en/media/hdr_20072008_en_complete.pdf

United Nations High Commissioner for Refugees (UNHCR). 2006. *Global Report 2006.* At: http://www.unhcr.org/gr06/index.html

———. 2007. "IDPs and Returnees by District. 9 December." At: http://www.humanitarianinfo.org/sriLanka_hpsl/Files/Thematic%20Maps/Displacement%20Maps/IDP-Access%20Maps/LK01069_LK01069_COL_SL_Displacement_IDP-RET_PUB_V2_22FEB08.pdf

World Food Programme. 2007a. "WFP Ramps up Food Aid for Thousands Fleeing Conflict in Eastern Sri Lanka." 20 March. At: http://www.wfp.org/english/?ModuleID=137&Key=2410

———. 2007b. "Executive Brief: Sri Lanka Integrated Food Security and Humanitarian Phase Classification (IPC)." May. At: http://www.ipcinfo.org/attachments/Ex_Brief_IPC_Sri_Lanka_June_2007.pdf

———. 2008. "Budget Revision WFP Sri Lanka." At: http://www.wfp.org/operations/current_operations/BR/100671_0704.pdf

Sudan

AT A GLANCE

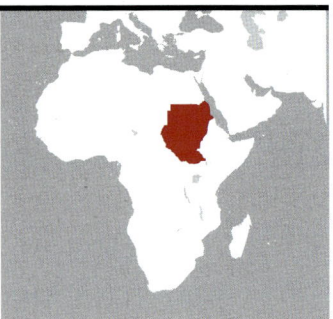

Country data *(2006 figures, unless otherwise noted)*

- 2007 Human Development Index: ranked 147th of 177 countries
- Population: 37.71 million
- GNI per capita (Atlas method, current US$): US$800
- Population living on less than US$2 a day (1990–2005): NA
- Life expectancy (in years): 58
- Infant mortality rate: 61 per 1,000 live births
- Under five infant mortality rate: 90 per 1,000
- Population undernourished (2002–2004): 26 percent
- Population with sustainable access to improved water source: 70 percent
- Adult literacy rate (over 15 yrs of age): NA
- Primary education completion rate: 47 percent
- Gender-related development index (2005): ranked 130th of 177 countries
- Official development assistance (ODA): US$2.058 billion
- 2007 Corruption Perception Index: ranked 172nd out of 179 countries

Sources: Transparency International (TI); 2007; UNDP, 2007a and 2007b; World Bank, 2008.

The crisis

- 5.8 million displaced in Darfur, Khartoum, and South Sudan;
- Since 2003, 90,000 killed and over 200,000 died from conflict-related causes;
- 4.2 million people in Darfur rely on humanitarian aid, over 2 million of whom are in IDP camps;
- Almost 250,000 displaced between January and August 2007, some for third or fourth time; more than 400 died in clashes; 300,000 displaced in 2007, many repeatedly;
- 1,3 million displaced people reported to have returned to their homes;
- August 2007 floods affected over 625,000; crops and basic infrastructure damaged; population exposed to disease, whooping cough, meningitis and diarrhoea;

Sources: International Organization for Migration; Amnesty International; AfricaFocus; IDMC; OHCHR.

The humanitarian response

- 2007 UN Work Plan for Sudan most extensive humanitarian operation in the world assisting 5.5 million people; despite overall increase in 2007 funding, only US$290 million secured, leading to shortfalls;
- UN and partners more than doubled recovery and development component from US$212 million in 2006 to US$563 million in 2007;
- Largest DAC donors unchanged from 2006: U.S., US$536.3 million; EC/ECHO, US$173.5 million plus US$27.2 million; UK, US$107.3 million; Netherlands, US$70.3 million; Canada US$58.2 million; almost US$30 million from CERF.

Sources: OCHA, UN and Partners.

Sudan
A Tragedy of Epic Proportions

JUDITH HERRERA, MD, MPH, International Consultant

© Michael Freeman/Corbis

Interlinking conflicts: Dynamics in 2007[1]

As in 2006, the 2007 humanitarian operation in Sudan was the most extensive in the world, coping with the aftermath of interrelated conflicts mainly in the west and south of the country. Circumstances have not improved. On the contrary, the humanitarian situation deteriorated dramatically, with violence, brutality, gross human rights violations, and mass civilian displacements increasing throughout the country. According to Amnesty International (AI), torture was widespread and systematic in some areas, including Darfur; human rights defenders and foreign aid organisations were harassed and freedom of expression curtailed.[2] In addition to man-made atrocities, floods in July and August intensified suffering for the already vulnerable population.

Humanitarian access shrank drastically due to insecurity, government restrictions, and an inability to act effectively and swiftly in the field.

During this period, a major political crisis took place in the south, due to the withdrawal of southerners from the unity government. Clashes continued between the Sudan People's Liberation Army (SPLA) and government supported militias, and among rival ethnic groups. In Darfur, destructive policies were pursued to create a chaotic environment. Civilians were under constant attack by Janjaweed militia, air attacks by the Government of Sudan (GoS) or armed groups. With guns easily available, fighting has continued within and among ethnic groups, and between clans,[3] resulting in more than 400 deaths by August 2007.[4]

The volatile mix of spillover from Darfur, conflict between the Sudanese Armed Forces (SAF) and the SPLA, and the breakdown of the Nuba Mountains agreement now create an increased risk of conflict in the central region of Kordofan. In the east, although a peace agreement was signed and the state of emergency lifted, there are reports of pockets of violence as a consequence of the continuing marginalisation of the region. In May and June 2007, more than 2,500 people fled South Darfur for refuge in the Central African Republic. In Chad, about 130,000 internally displaced people (IDPs) and many from the local population have not received food aid since December 2007.[5]

Throughout 2007, the GoS narrowed its position with respect to international intervention in the conflict. Despite the deteriorating humanitarian situation, Sudan received less attention from the international media than in previous years, and no longer seemed a priority for the international community. There was a complete failure by the international community to protect humanitarian space. The upcoming 2009 elections are already intensifying existing struggles for power and control of resources.

Humanitarian impact of the crisis: Greater need, less access

The humanitarian situation became even more catastrophic in 2007, with ongoing violence, obstruction of aid, the weakened state of displaced people, and the lack of a comprehensive humanitarian strategic plan. As a consequence of pervasive poverty and continuous conflict, Sudan ranks 147th out of 170 countries.[6] Key indicators demonstrate that a significant percentage of population is vulnerable to man-made and natural disasters. Optimistic estimates indicate that the under-five mortality rate is 90 per 1000 live births; 26 percent of the population is undernourished, and 30 percent do not have access to safe drinking water.[7]

Although life in South Sudan is more peaceful, social and economic marginalisation is still the rule. People struggle to find alternative ways to survive, as basic services such as health, education, access to safe water, infrastructure, and transportation are scarce or nonexistent. While a total of 600,000 people were expected to return to their homes, half in organised returns and the rest spontaneously, UN sources report actual numbers of spontaneous returnees during the year at 185,319.[8]

Food security remains one of the major humanitarian problems, with only 30 percent of the conflict-affected population considered food self-sufficient, leaving over 3 million people in need of assistance. The price of cereals increased fivefold in some areas and pre-harvest studies of Darfur suggest a hunger gap of 70 to 78 percent for many sectors. Despite the serious risk of local famine, the World Food Programme (WFP) is underfunded and pressuring NGOs to lower distribution amounts.[9]

Due to the refusal of the government's Humanitarian Aid Commission (HAC) to allow the gathering and dissemination of data, data are lacking concerning malnutrition. Nevertheless, figures from September 2007 indicate that Global Acute Malnutrition (GAM) passed the threshold of 15 percent in a number of camps in Darfur. Middle Upper Arm Circumference (MUAC) surveys recently conducted in April 2008 by the UN found one third of children under five to be acutely malnourished.[10]

As insecurity prevents distribution of food, water, and primary health care services, people will soon be at mortal risk of the usual rainy season diseases, such as cholera, dysentery, and malaria. There have already been more than 140 cases of whooping cough in west Darfur where medical personnel have difficulty reaching the affected population.

Systematic murder, rape, abduction, and displacement make the Darfur conflict one of the worst imaginable. It has been documented that since 2003, 90,000 people have been killed outright and over 200,000 have died from conflict-related causes.[11] As reported by Amnesty International (USA), the UN estimates that 4.2 million people in Darfur rely on humanitarian aid, over 2 million people of those in IDP camps.[12] Among the 4 million affected by the conflict, roughly 1.8 million are younger than 18, of whom some 1 million are in IDP camps.[13] According to UN figures, between January and August 2007, almost 250,000 fled their homes, some for the third or fourth time, and more than 400 died in clashes.[14] Overall, in 2007, some 300,000 were displaced, many of them repeatedly.[15] According to the UN Office for the Coordination of Humanitarian Aid (OCHA), 100,000 more were added early in 2008.

Of the more than 65 IDP camps in Sudan and 12 in Chad, most are already overcrowded, with 130,000 in the Gereida[16] and 90,000 in the Kalma camps, respectively. Chad has more than 240,000 Darfur refugees. The UN estimates 5.8 million displaced people in Darfur,

Khartoum, and South Sudan.[17] By mid-2007 1,325,535 displaced people were reported to have returned to their homes, especially people from South Sudan,[18] the same number benefiting from UNHCR protection and assistance.

Assault and robbery are daily occurrences, with rape and other violence a constant threat for women, most cases unreported, with the attackers acting with total impunity. During the second half of 2007, 57 rapes were documented by UN experts.[19]

Social life in the IDP camps, already complex because of the diversity, shows signs of unheard of degradation, with people begging in the markets or eating leftover garbage. Unemployed youth with few prospects for employment are recruited by or join armed groups, or become part of camp gangs. The UN documented 10 incidents of fighting between vigilante groups based on ethnic origin in only six days in October 2007.

The African Union Mission in Sudan (AMIS) failed to stop killings, displacement of civilians, or looting. No international treaty protects the rights of the displaced, and often the entity in charge of their protection is the same one which forced them to abandon their homes.

Returnees and forced resettlement

Since the onset of the crisis, local administrators have pressured displaced people to return to their homes but many have refused because of insecurity. The Memorandum of Understanding (MoU) signed between the IOM and the GoS in 2004 to ensure that returns are strictly voluntary has been violated on occasions.[20] In some camps, there has been actual repression; in others, economic persuasion.[21]

Unverified official data claim that thousands of people have returned to their home lands. Reports show otherwise.[22] According to UNHCR, land abandoned by the displaced from 2003 to 2005 has subsequently been occupied by Arab groups – in some cases by Chadian refugees – creating land tenure struggles.

Reports have emerged of agreements between local Arab or other armed groups with IDPs in some regions to create safe enclaves where they can work in agriculture. This has given farmers hope, but they must still live under control of the Arab or armed groups.

Natural disasters

Compounding the conflicts, floods in August 2007 affected over 625,000 people throughout Sudan, damaging large swathes of crops, destroying basic infrastructure, and exposing the population to disease – 140 cases of whooping cough in Darfur, 12,000 cases of meningitis and 8,300 of watery diarrhoea in South Sudan.[23]

The humanitarian response: More funds, less quality

The deteriorating humanitarian and security situation of 2006 continued in 2007. Although there were some positive signs when the South Sudan Government (GoSS) resumed activities in Khartoum, the situation remained unstable. While the obstacles faced by humanitarian actors in 2007 changed little, logistical challenges increased, as access by land was restricted. Funding shortfalls were reported, but the principal problem was widespread violence and insecurity, targeting even humanitarian workers.

As a result, access to victims in Darfur decreased significantly and the quality of services suffered. Nevertheless, humanitarian agencies managed to continue supporting the affected population, although with diminished scope and quality. As in 2006, activities covered the full range of humanitarian assistance, in the face of floods and disease. According to the United Nations High Commissioner for Human Rights (OHCHR), humanitarian agencies were able to provide food and livelihood assistance for a total of 4 million people throughout Sudan, and support over 180,000 displaced people during the North-South return process.[24]

Services included health, water, and sanitation, disaster preparedness, education, protection, and mine action. Various NGOs and UNICEF provided for high schools in all IDP camps serving 28 percent of school age children, 46 percent of whom are girls. Although coverage is still low – according to Save the Children about half (650,000) the children in Darfur do not receive *any* education – it is an improvement over the situation prior to the onset of the Darfur crisis. According to one *IRIN* report, 8 million square metres of road were demined in this period, but little has been done for communities directly.[25]

More than 13,000 humanitarian workers are deployed in Darfur alone, including staff of 13 UN agencies, the Red Cross and Red Crescent Movement, and around 80 international NGOs. All these humanitarian actors have made enormous efforts to meet the needs of the most vulnerable, but efficiency has been sacrificed substantially to security concerns. Some reports indicate that circumstances allow for access to only 40 percent of the affected population.

Very few organisations stay in the field, but instead fly in and out for a few hours at a time.[26] Land transportation being extremely dangerous, most dare not drive, as attacks on vehicles and theft are rife. The UN recently reported that 28 percent of beneficiaries and 29 percent of destinations can only be reached by air.[27]

From January to November 2007, 128 UN and NGO vehicles were hijacked and 74 convoys attacked, causing some agencies to withdraw completely. This situation has not changed in 2008.

Expatriates are disappearing from the field as a consequence of continuing attacks, with most organisations delegating responsibility for implementation to local employees who face fewer risks. The ICRC is one of very few organisations with expatriate personnel on the ground.[28]

Alarming signs of reduced access appeared with the increasing numbers of malnourished people and a rise in outbreaks of disease.[29] WFP reported the slowing of food delivery – due to the hijacking of 56 trucks, 36 of which are missing, along with 29 drivers – threatening timely assistance to more than 2 million people. WFP estimates the current shortfall in food in transit to Darfur at approximately 50 percent.[30] UNICEF reported that the March 2008 kidnapping of the state water corporation staff – along with all drilling equipment – threatened to deprive 180,000 of clean water this year. The loss could affect up to 400,000 people.[31]

According to one interviewee from an INGO, humanitarian workers actually contributed to the social chaos in the affected areas of Sudan, explaining that poor coordination, competition among NGOs for scarce human resources, and the inability of UN agencies and INGOs to come up with standard criteria in the course of field activities have created more problems than solutions, and led to even greater confusion among people in the IDP camps.

International donor response

Funding and coverage

In 2007, the UN work plan for Sudan constituted the most extensive humanitarian operation in the world in funding and coverage. Approximately 5.5 million people were assisted, at a total cost of some US$1.33 billion for humanitarian assistance, and US$560 million for recovery and development. By the end of 2007, the UN reported 82 percent receipt of all funds pledged or committed. The 2007 Appeal for Sudan represented 30 percent of the total call for US$3.9 billion to support assistance for 27 million people in 29 countries.[32]

Flexible funding mechanisms, such as the Common Humanitarian Fund (CHF) and the Central Emergency Response Fund (CERF) were thought to be successful tools in allocating funds for humanitarian efforts during this period. However, these funding mechanisms were less effective than expected, because they did not release funds in a timely manner, due to conflicts of interest NGOs faced in accessing and participating in decision-making processes and coordination.

The UN and its partners more than doubled the recovery development component from US$212 million in 2006 to US$563 million in 2007. This shift was particularly pronounced in the South Sudan programme, where development and recovery (US$356 million) exceeds humanitarian assistance (US$280 million). The United Nations and Partners announced that the work plan for 2008 would focus on governance, strengthening basic services, and capacity building for the government of Southern Sudan.[33] However, figures and statements from interviewees showed clearly that humanitarian assistance is still the priority in Sudan, mainly, but not only, because of Darfur. Most funds (80 percent) were given to the UN agencies, with around 19 percent going to INGOs, and the remainder to national NGOs. The same distribution pattern was followed for recovery and development funds.[34]

The real total of humanitarian assistance received for Sudan in 2007 increased by almost US$1.5 billion, including the Appeal and other donations, as well as Sudan's internal contribution of 3.8 percent of the total. At end-2007, 1.3 percent was registered in uncommitted pledges, with an additional US$18 million in response to the August floods. Of the 23 OECD/DAC members, 19 contributors were registered by OCHA's Financial Tracking Service (FTS), excluding Austria, Portugal, Luxembourg, and New Zealand, although the latter was mentioned in the survey.

The largest DAC donors remained unchanged from 2006, with the United States contributing US$536.3 million (36.7 percent of the total, smaller than 2006), EC/ECHO US$173.5 million plus US$27.2 million, respectively (13.8 percent), the UK US$107.3 million (7.3 percent), the Netherlands US$70.3 million (4.8 percent), and Canada US$58.2 million (4 percent). The carry-over from 2006 represented 2.4 percent of 2007 funding, with almost US$30 million coming from CERF and the majority of donations from the DAC donors except the EC and the United States.[35] Many of the organisations interviewed in Sudan during the survey in March mentioned that some 80 percent of their funds came mainly from the CHF and CERF, and the rest from bilateral support.

UN agencies received far more funding than NGOs or the National Red Cross and Red Crescent Societies, with each UN agency supported by an average of at least five donors. Local NGOs received the least bilateral funding from DAC donors. The distribution of funding among regions changed: the South received 38.3 percent from the CHF, and Darfur 26.2 percent.[36] The remaining regions received significantly less funding: Abyei (1.8 percent) and North Sudan (0.8 percent) received the least.

Regarding actual coverage, Darfur heads the list with 71 percent, followed by South Sudan (66 percent), and Abyei and Kordofan each with 64 percent. Khartoum received only 18 percent.[37] Actual coverage figures show that fund distribution was not based exclusively on needs, despite the intention of donors to follow this principle.

Most stakeholders and analysts are convinced that decisions are still politically based. For example, the funds allocated to the Cross-Sector Support for Return which received 11.5 percent of the CHF, when both North and South governments pressured the displaced to return for the elections.

The sector distribution list is headed by Health/Nutrition (19.3 percent), followed by Food (17.8 percent), and Water and Sanitation (15.7 percent). Least funded were Basic infrastructure and Settlement Development with only 1.2 percent.[38] The distribution of funds by sector gives a clear picture of how donors prioritised humanitarian activities, regardless of work plans, allowing them to demonstrate results faster, and increase their visibility. Nevertheless, as coverage was partial everywhere, it remains questionable if all needs were covered sufficiently and proportionately.

The UN reports that, despite the overall increase in funding in 2007, only US$290 million was secured for the work plan. This led to shortfalls.[39] The trend in 2008 seems to continue in the same direction, as funding provided at the beginning of the year covers only 36 percent of the amount needed for humanitarian operations, particularly in transport, essential for the security of humanitarian efforts.

In March 2008, Poverty News Blog issued a press alert in which 14 international NGOs, among them Oxfam and Care, warned that vital assistance to millions of people across Sudan would be jeopardised without a renewed commitment to provide long-term funding for humanitarian flights.[40] UN Humanitarian Air Services warned that flights could close within weeks due to the shortfall.[41] According to this source, donors pledged to maintain the service during April but, as of this writing (June 2008), nothing further had been confirmed. WFP also expressed concerns about the real risk of not meeting their goals due to the combination of funding shortfalls, the rainy season, and security concerns.

Donor performance in light of the Good Humanitarian Donorship (GHD)

Principles

The programmed humanitarian priorities for 2007 were in line with the GHD *Principles* and clearly advocated protection of and humanitarian assistance to all in need (especially the most vulnerable), strengthening of community coping mechanisms, promotion of self reliance, and enhancement of humanitarian access to affected populations. To achieve recovery and development, the work plan and programmed priorities aimed to enhance local capacity governance and sustainability – significant undertakings, given the context in Sudan. Partial progress having been achieved in 2007, they remain priorities for 2008.

With respect to the donor commitments to provide funding based on needs assessments (Principles 2 and 6), the 2007 work plan proposed that the UN and partners would assess all regions in Sudan and place equal emphasis on humanitarian and development requirements. However, information from the field confirmed that decisions were based not only on needs, but on factors of visibility and politics regarding which regions to work in. Some local NGO interviewees described cases in which donors pushed a particular NGO to work in a certain region, even when they had neither presence in the region nor experience in the specific field. Other interviewees expressed the view that there were overlapping needs assessments, and no sharing of information. Some INGOs stated that communities were tired of people coming to assess needs, making empty promises, and not following up with action.

With regard to Principles 5, 7, 8, 9, and 13, linking relief and development and flexible funding, most stakeholders recognised that some progress has been made. The work plans of the UN and partners focused more on early recovery. Many UN agencies and NGOs are currently working in this sector, especially in South

Sudan. However, most of the interviewees expressed the acute need for more flexible funding and an increase in long-term arrangements which will permit them to actually achieve the planned objectives. But some indicated their perception that the majority of donors are not prepared to invest in what they call "software," meaning the time-consuming work of partnering with communities and beneficiaries to increase awareness and active participation. INGO interviewees reported that most donors are not yet ready to fund this component, because, in their view, it does not yield measurable results.

In accordance with Principles 10 and 14 (working with humanitarian partners), the 2007 work plan placed greater emphasis on state-level planning, giving priority to consultation with government and partners. It has been reported that collaboration with and inclusion of the Sudanese counterparts increased in 2007, and that the UN and partners were better able to deliver basic services and address emergencies and to transfer knowledge and capacity to others. According to the UN 2008 Humanitarian Appeal, 2007 saw greater collaboration between governments and UN/Partners, in such areas as joint assessments, response, and policy development. The outcomes include a successful response to the flooding, disease outbreaks, progress in demining, and the signature of the Joint Communiqué for Darfur to facilitate humanitarian activities and administrative procedures.

However, not all stakeholders share this perception. According to some local NGO representatives, these statements represent wishful thinking. In practice, they say, local counterparts are dealing with problems in the field, with very few resources and little or no support.[42] There were cases describing wasteful use of resources and a disrespectful attitude on the part of UN personnel.

On the other hand, some funding mechanisms were put in place to promote better coordination between UN and NGOs. Despite high funding for Darfur and the shift in the work plan focus, the CHF was widely supported and was expected to facilitate a flexible response to humanitarian needs. However, some INGO interviewees expressed dissatisfaction concerning the discretionary and ineffective way these funds were managed. According to some INGOs,[43] the system works poorly because of administrative regulations, restrictions, and inefficiency within the UN Secretariat. Another reported reason for failure was the General Assembly members' suspicion concerning the internal political dynamics of the INGOs. Yet other sources mentioned secrecy in the allocation process and the risk of losing

political neutrality by association with the UN in the humanitarian and political arenas.

UN sources highlight the benefits of greater structure and more power for the Humanitarian Coordinator. UN agencies expressed discontent with the overwhelming amount of time spent in planning, having less direct access to donors to make a case when needed, and violations of the allocation process.

Political involvement and commitment

Judging by funds received, Sudan is attracting the attention of the international community, even though media coverage has decreased significantly. In 2007, the Security Council passed four resolutions (1755, 1769, 1779, and 1784), concerning peacekeeping forces and the full implementation of the Comprehensive Peace Agreement (CPA). However, some analysts and experts in African studies[44] contend that there are reasons why Sudan – and Darfur in particular – are receiving so much attention from the international community. Professor Mamdani[45] stated that other conflicts in Africa which involve extreme humanitarian atrocities – viz. Somalia – receive even less attention than Darfur, and are sometimes not even addressed.

According to other analysts,[46] Darfur's strategic geo-political location has political and economical implications for powerful countries, and thus for the War on Terror and the oil industry. They state further that the role of the international community has been weak and paradoxical. Although DAC donors committed troops for the African (peacekeeping) Mission in Sudan (AMIS) to improve security and protect civilians and humanitarian workers, the soldiers were not paid by the European Commission for seven months. Canada assigned civilian helicopter pilots to the mission, but their refusal to go to dangerous locations jeopardized the operation.[47]

Under these circumstances, it is understandable why this mission failed and had to be replaced by the UN hybrid force (UNAMID) – still not fully deployed. The international community has been weak in responding to the repeated GoS defiance of Security Council resolutions. This weakness calls into question the extent to which donors are committed to GHD Principle 16, calling for the implementation of international guidelines and respect for humanitarian law.

Moreover, the international community's fragmented understanding of the conflict in Sudan has contributed to their inability to deal with the real causes of the conflict and to find lasting solutions for one of the most severe humanitarian crises the world has yet faced. For this reason, some analysts believe that international guarantors and the UN remain disengaged from implementation of the CPA, not only because of the overwhelming situation in Darfur, but also because there is no consensus on the way forward in the political arena.[48]

Conclusion

The situation in Sudan does not show signs of quick resolution. As elections loom, violence and fighting may increase. Despite progress in CPA implementation and with UNAMID barely begun, many yet unsolved issues could trigger resumed hostilities between North and South. Civilians and humanitarian actors are increasingly targeted in a lawless land, which shows no respect for basic human rights and dignity.

Delivery of the 2008 programme is linked to CPA benchmarks, mainly resolution of the boundary demarcation process, the census, and other election preparations. But fulfilment of the CPA depends on humanitarian access, which, in turn, is at the mercy of both the rainy season and the political and security environment in sensitive areas. Under these circumstances, the international community's commitment to Sudan must be not only robust but more effective, as results so far show that, despite ample funding, lasting solutions to the conflicts have not been achieved.

Alleviating the suffering of the civilian population is paramount. The international community should begin by obtaining unrestricted access to the victims and a firm respect for humanitarian space by all belligerents. Political and military means must be used to achieve this objective as quickly and efficiently as possible, as called for in the GHD *Principles,* in particular, the respect of the international humanitarian law and human rights.

Effective delivery of humanitarian assistance calls for donors to evaluate whether the funding pool is implemented properly, whether funds are being released in a timely manner, and whether the various stakeholders are actually working together and supporting each other in responding to the desperate needs. Donors must become more flexible, support long-term investments with longer-term funding and make administrative procedures more accessible and simpler for all stakeholders. Greater effort must be made to allocate funds according to need, irrespective of political considerations.

Humanitarian agencies should also be willing to revise their own performance and make necessary adjustments to improve coordination and services, using well defined and common criteria. Beyond plans and statements, INGOs should ensure that local actors are able to take over before leaving the country.

If peace is to come to Sudan, the underlying causes of the conflicts must be addressed with clear and unified strategies. The international community must reinforce its commitment to the affected population by funding humanitarian, recovery, and development needs sufficiently. At the same time, the international community must clarify its political approach, and exert pressure on all parties of the conflict to end hostilities by fully engaging in negotiations for a win-win outcome. This includes critically revising their political and economic interests, which tend to fuel the conflagration instead of solving it. Strict observance of all GHD *Principles* is essential to these goals.

Notes

1   The HRI team, composed of Philippe Benassi, Judith Herrera, and Rosario Palacio visited the Sudan in March 2008. The opinions expressed here are those of the author and do not necessarily reflect those of DARA.

2   AI (USA), 2007a.

3   AI (USA), 2007b.

4   Ibid.

5   AI, 2008c.

6   United Nations Development Programme, 2007–2008.

7   Ibid.

8   IOM, 2008, p. 3.

9   Reeves, 2008.

10 Ibid.

11 AI (USA), 2008.

12 AI (USA), 2007b.

13 AI (Canada), 2008.

14 Ibid.

15 AI (USA), 2007a.

16 International Committee of the Red Cross (ICRC), 2008b.

17 AfricaFocus, 2008.

18 IDMC, 2007.

19 AI, 2008a, p. 10.

20 United Nations Mission in Sudan, 2007, p. 3.

21 AI, 2008a, p. 21.

22 AI, 2008a, p. 20.

23 OHCHR, 2008, p. 34.

24 Ibid.

25 IRIN, 2008b.

26 Briefing with Patrick Vial, Head of Delegation, ICRC Sudan, 25 March, 2008.

27 Reeves, 2008.

28 ICRC, 2008a.

29 UNICEF, 2008a.

30 World Food Programme. 2008.

31 UNICEF, 2008b.

32 OCHA, 2007.

33 United Nations and Partners, 2007b.

34 OCHA, Financial Tracking Service (FTS).

35 Ibid.

36 United Nations and Partners, 2007a and 2007b.

37 OCHA (FTS), 2008a.

38 OCHA (FTS), 2008b and United Nations, 2007.

39 UN and Partners. 2007b.

40 Poverty News Blog, 2008.

41 Reeves, 2008.

42 Professor Mahmoud Mamdani, Director of the Institute of African Studies at Columbia University, mentioned that during his visit to the region during the Darfur-Darfur dialogue, the NGOs complained that they were dismissed by INGOs, including UN agencies.

43 Porter, 2007.

44 Mahmood Mamdani, from an address during Barcelona Conference, April 2008.

45 Ibid.

46 AI, 2008b; ICG, 2008; IRIN, 2008a.

47 Amnesty International, 2007.

48 ICG, 2008.

References

AfricaFocus Bulletin. 2008. "Africa: Internal Displacement Update." 20 April. At: http://www.africafocus.org/docs08/disp0804.php

Amnesty International (USA). 2007a. *2007 Annual Report for Sudan.* At: http://www.amnestyusa.org/annualreport.php?id=ar&yr= 2007&c=SDN

———. 2007b. "Darfur: 'When Will They Protect Us?'" 14 September. At: http://www.amnestyusa.org/document.php?id=ENGAFR540432007 &lang=e

———. 2008. "Guns, Fear and Hopelessness Create Volatile Mix in Camps Sheltering One Million Displaced Darfuri Children." 21 January. At: http://www.amnestyusa.org/document.php?lang= e&id=ENGUSA20080121003

Amnesty International. 2007. "Obstruction and Delay: Peacekeepers needed in Darfur now." 22 October. At: http://www.amnesty.org/ en/library/asset/AFR54/006/2007/en/dom-AFR540062007en.html

———. 2008a. "Displaced in Darfur, a generation of anger." 1 January. At: http://www.amnestyusa.org/pdf/idp_report.pdf

———. 2008b. "Anger rises as insecurity worsens for Darfur's displaced children." 22 January 2008. At: www.amnesty.org/en/for-media/ press-releases/sudan-anger-insecurity-worsen-darfurs-displaced-children-20080122

———. 2008c. "Sudan: Civilians killed and displaced in Darfur clashes." 11 February. At: http://www.amnestyusa.org/document.php?lang= e&id=ENGUSA20080211001

Amnesty International Canada. 2008. "Sudan/Darfur: Childhood Under Attack." 15 April. At: http://www.amnesty.ca/take_action/actions/ sudan_children_attacked.php

International Committee of the Red Cross (ICRC) 2008a. "Darfur: Meeting basic needs and providing vital health care." 1 January. At: http://www.icrc.org/web/eng/siteeng0.nsf/htmlall/sudan-photos-280108?OpenDocument&style=Custo_Final.5&View=defaultBody6

———. 2008b. "Sudan: ICRC prolongs support for 130,000 displaced in South Darfur." 19 May. At: http://www.icrc.org/web/eng/ siteeng0.nsf/htmlall/sudan-news-190508?opendocument

International Crisis Group. 2008. "Sudan's comprehensive peace agreement: Beyond the crisis." Africa Report No.50. March. At: www.crisisgroup.org/home/index.cfm?id=1145&l=4 –

Internal Displacement Monitoring Centre. 2007. "6 million estimated IDPs in Sudan (November 2007)." At: http://www.internal-displacement. org/8025708F004CE90B/(httpEnvelopes)/CA38A0F0F269546F8025 70B8005AAFAD?OpenDocument#sources

International Organization of Migration (IOM). 2008 . *IOM Sudan Newsletter.* March. At: www.reliefweb.int/rw/RWFiles2008.nsf/ FilesByRWDocUnidFilename/ASAZ-7EEHSW-full_report.pdf/ $File/full_report.pdf

IRIN, Humanitarian News and Analysis. 2008a. "SUDAN: Rising tension in Abyei as clashes displace hundreds." March. At: www.irinnews.org/ report.aspx?ReportId=77419

———. 2008b."SUDAN: Landmines continue to plague the south." 29 June. At: http://www.irinnews.org/Report.aspx?ReportId=71211

Office for the Coordination of Humanitarian Affairs (OCHA). Financial Tracking Service (FTS).

———. 2007. *Humanitarian Appeal 2007.* At: http://ochadms.unog.ch/ quickplace/cap/main.nsf/h_Index/CAP_2007_Humanitarian_Appeal/ $FILE/CAP_2007_Humanitarian_Appeal_SCREEN.pdf?Open Element

———. (FTS) 2008a. Consolidated Appeal: Sudan Work Plan 2007 (Humanitarian Action component) List of Appeal Projects (grouped by region). At: http://ocha.unog.ch/fts/reports/daily/ocha_R33_ A743___08062707.pdf

———. (FTS) 2008b. Consolidated Appeal: Sudan Work Plan 2008 (Humanitarian/Early Recovery Component) Table D: Requirements, Commitments/Contributions and Pledges per Sector. At: http://ocha.unog.ch/fts/reports/daily/ocha_R3sum_A799___ 08062711.pdf

Porter, Toby. 2007. "The frustration of CERF." Humanitarian Practice Network. 9 October. At: http://www.globalpolicy.org/socecon/ develop/oda/cerf/2007/1009toby.htm

Poverty News Blog. 2008. "Aid agencies warn more than 2 million people risk being cut off from assistance without more funding for vital Sudan aid flights." 31 March. At: http://povertynewsblog.blogspot. com/2008_03_01_archive.html

Reeves, Eric. 2008. "Humanitarian conditions in Darfur, two months before the rainy season." *Sudan Tribune.* 5 April. At: www.sudan tribune.com/spip.php?article26651

UNICEF. 2008a. "Statement by the Office of Resident and Humanitarian Coordinator for Sudan on attacks against humanitarian actors." 26 March. At: www.unicef.org/media/media_43385.html

———. 2008b. "UNICEF relieved at release of state water corporation drivers in Darfur, but repeats call for end to all attacks." 28 March. At: http://www.unicef.org/infobycountry/media_43404.html

United Nations. 2007.Central Emergency Response Fund. 2008. "Sudan – Facts and Figures." At: http://ochaonline.un.org/ Default.aspx?tabid=1726

United Nations and Partners. 2007a. *Common Humanitarian Fund: 2007 Allocations.* At: http://www.unsudanig.org/workplan/chf/2007/ index.html

———. 2007b. *2008 Work Plan for Sudan.* 6 December. At: www.unsudanig.org/workplan/2007/docs/WP07_Document.pdf

United Nations Development Programme. 2007–2008. *Human Development Index 2007–2008.* At: http://hdrstats.undp.org/ countries/data_sheets/cty_ds_SDN.html

United Nations High Commissioner for Human Rights (OHCHR). 2008. *Humanitarian Appeal 2008.* At: http://www.ohchr.org/Documents/ Countries/CAP2008.pdf

United Nations Mission in Sudan. Office of the Spokesperson. 2007 UNMIS News Bulletin. 30 October. At: http://www.unmis.org/ english/2007Docs/PIO-UNMISbulletin-oct30.pdf

World Food Programme. 2007. "Sudan Health Highlights." Week 34. At: www.unsudanig.org/docs/EHA%20WEEK%2034%20Highlights.pdf

———. 2008. "Hijacking cut WFP food supplies for Darfur as funding shortfall threatens humanitarian air service." 10 March. At: http://www.wfp.org/english/?ModuleID=137&Key=2790

HRI 2008 Field Mission Teams

AFGHANISTAN ....Marta Marañón, Farhad Antezar
(Groupe URD), Annette Courteix
(Groupe URD) and Lucía Fernández

BANGLADESH ....Philip Tamminga, Valentina Ferrara
and Daniela Ruegenberg

CENTRAL AFRICAN REPUBLIC ....Silvia Hidalgo, Carlos Oliver and
Soledad Posada

CHAD ....Ricardo Solé Arques, Ana Romero
and Kim Wuyts

COLOMBIA ....Fernando Espada, Marybeth
Redheffer and Nacho Wilhelmi

DEMOCRATIC REPUBLIC OF THE CONGO.............Gilles Gasser, Aldara Collet,
Carlos Oliver, Soledad Posada
and Kim Wuyts

NICARAGUA ....Gilles Gasser, Aldara Collet and
Ana Romero

OCCUPIED PALESTINIAN TERRITORIES................Ricardo-Solé Arques, Lucía
Fernández and Stuart Reigeluth

PERU ....Riccardo Polastro, Aldara Collet
and Valentina Ferrara

SRI LANKA...Riccardo Polastro, Daniela Mamone
and Hnin Nwe Win

SUDAN ....Judith Herrera, Philippe Benassi
and Rosario Palacio

4

PART FOUR

Donor Profiles

Introduction

The donor profiles in this section provide some salient features of donor humanitarian assistance. For each donor, a short summary describing the key actors involved in the delivery of its humanitarian aid programme, the policies that guide them, and how they have incorporated the GHD and their interaction with other humanitarian partners is provided.

A spider web chart (HRI scores by Pillar) shows each donor's scores for each of the five Pillars of the Humanitarian Response Index (HRI) 2008, relative to the DAC average. In a table (HRI results), selected best and worst results for a donor in this year's HRI are listed under the corresponding Pillars.

Next, key figures of a donor's humanitarian aid for 2006 and 2007 are presented in a table (Overview of humanitarian aid), including estimates for total humanitarian aid, made up of bilateral humanitarian aid reported to the OECD, and estimates of multilateral aid. Bilateral humanitarian aid for 2006 and 2007 is defined by the OECD as "bilateral transactions … undertaken by a donor country directly with a developing country" and includes all flows, regardless of the channel, for which the "donor effectively controls the disposal of the funds by specifying the recipient or other aspects of the disbursement (e.g., purpose),"[1] that is, earmarked. The data used by OECD contain a number of drawbacks. First, the 2007 figures are still preliminary. Second, due to differences in national data classification and treatment, it is unclear whether all countries reporting their bilateral humanitarian aid have adopted the same treatment of the delivery of humanitarian aid by armed forces, land mine clearance—which should be counted separately as code DAC 15250—and, in the case of EU countries, their treatment of contributions to ECHO. Third, the OECD data do not have a separate category for multilateral humanitarian aid within the multilateral official development assistance category. For this reason, it was necessary to estimate multilateral humanitarian aid based on data supplied by the main multilateral

humanitarian organisations. Core funding to UNHCR, UNICEF, WFP, UNRWA, UN/OCHA, ICRC, IFRC, and CERF was used to approximate multilateral humanitarian aid. Multi-bilateral aid to these organisations that is earmarked to a specific country is included in the bilateral humanitarian aid category. We used 2007 figures for all core funding, except to ICRC and UNRWA, which were approximated by using 2006 data.

On the second page of each donor profile, the bilateral and multilateral aid categories of the overview table are shown as charts, with their respective components.

The next table (Funding per emergency) lists the top-ten emergencies that received the donor's funding in 2007, based on OCHA FTS data. It shows the amounts in US dollars and the percentage of funding to each emergency as a proportion of a donor's total 2007 funding reported in the FTS. The second pie chart (Regional distribution of funding) shows the same data split across regions and the final bar chart (Sectoral distribution of funding) shows it split across CAP sectors, relative to the sum total of CAP sectoral budgets in 2007.

---

1 See OECD Development Co-operation Directorate (2007), at: http://www.odamoz.org.mz/extra/DAC-CRSManual.pdf

Australia

Australia is the 9th most generous humanitarian donor among the OECD/DAC group, relative to its size. Its bilateral humanitarian aid amounted to US$201 million in 2007. AusAID, the Australian Agency for International Development, manages the coordination and communication of humanitarian action within its wider overseas aid program. AusAID is an administratively autonomous agency within the Foreign Affairs and Trade portfolio. Its Humanitarian Action Policy (January 2005) is strongly based on the GHD Principles, and guides Australia's response to emerging humanitarian needs. It is framed within the broader context of conflict prevention, peace-building, and post-conflict recovery programmes, and development assistance, as set out in its 2001 Strategy on *Peace, Conflict and Development Policy*. Australia's humanitarian action remains primarily focused on the Asia-Pacific region. Australia has established regional emergency response standby mechanisms together with key donors in the Pacific, empowering prevention and preparedness, and capacity-building for reducing vulnerability to natural disasters. AusAID's delivery channel depends on consideration of the most effective and efficient response. If government systems are failing, or operating outside the Asia-Pacific region, Australia's assistance is channelled mainly to community organisations, NGOs or other civil society organisations. Australia supports humanitarian partnerships with leading multilateral and international organisations, including the WFP, OCHA, and the ICRC.

Source: DAC Peer Review for Australia (OECD, 2005), at: http://www.ausaid.gov.au

HRI 2008 scores by pillar

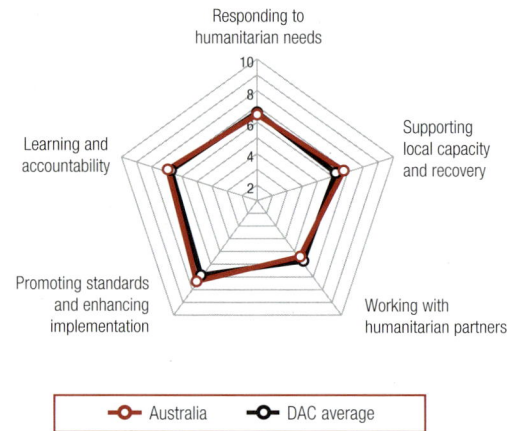

HRI 2008 results

HIGHEST SCORES	SCORE	RANK
Responding to humanitarian needs		
Funding needs assessments	7.81	1
Timely funding	7.65	1
Working with humanitarian partners		
Promoting ICRC	8.57	1
Promoting standards and enhancing implementation		
Supporting needs of internally displaced persons	7.93	1
Facilitating safe humanitarian access	6.95	1

LOWEST SCORES	SCORE	RANK
Responding to humanitarian needs		
Funding to crisis countries with historical ties and geographical proximity	1.99	21
Working with humanitarian partners		
Funding to NGOs	1.94	19
Unearmarked funding	3.56	18
Promoting standards and enhancing implementation		
Donor engagement in protection and assistance to civilians	7.50	17
Respecting or promoting human rights	8.16	15

Overview of humanitarian aid	Australia			Share of total DAC (%)	
	2006	2007[4]		2006	2007[4]
Total humanitarian aid (estimated), of which:	238.7	227.1		2.9	2.5
Bilateral[1]	191.2	201.1		2.8	3.2
Multilateral[2] (estimated*), of which:	47.5	26.0		3.0	1.6
Central Emergency Response Fund**	7.6	8.8		2.6	2.3
Funding to other pooled mechanisms[3]***	0.0	0.0		0.0	0.0
Official development assistance	2,123	2,471		2.0	2.4
				DAC average	
Total humanitarian aid per capita (USD)[5]	11	11		22	23
Total humanitarian aid per / official development assistance	13.3	10.7		12.2	11.3
Overseas development assistance / gross national income	0.30	0.30		0.46	0.44

Notes: All data are given in current USD m unless otherwise indicated.

1 Based on OECD/DAC definition of bilateral humanitarian aid, which is provided directly by a donor country to a recipient country and includes non-core earmarked contributions to multilateral humanitarian organisations known as multi-bilateral aid.

2 Core unearmarked humanitarian flows to UNHCR, UNICEF, WFP, UNRWA, UN/OCHA, ICRC and IFRC. 2007 core funding to UNRWA and ICRC proxied by 2006 data.

3 For 2006, these were IFRC's Disaster Relief Emergency Fund (DREF), Sudan Common Humanitarian Fund (CHF), Democratic Republic of Congo (DRC) Pooled Fund, and Emergency Response Funds (ERF) for DRC, Indonesia, Somalia, Republic of Congo, and Ethiopia. For 2007, these were DREF, CHF, DRC Pooled Fund, and ERFs for Central African Republic, DRC, Ethiopia, Indonesia, and Iraq.

4 All 2007 OECD/DAC data are provisional.

5 Where 2007 population data not available, 2006 data used.

Sources: All data from OECD-DAC except: (*) UNHCR, UNICEF, WFP, UNRWA, UN/OCHA, ICRC and IFRC; (**) OCHA; (***) OCHA, IFRC; US Federal Reserve.

Main channels of humanitarian aid, 2007

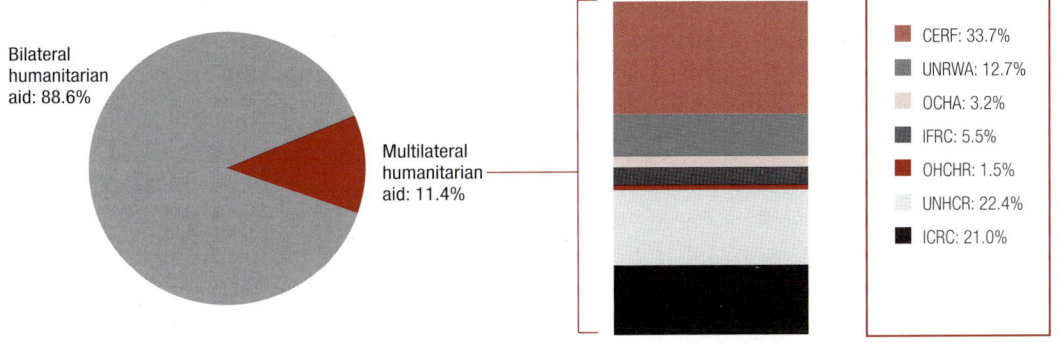

Bilateral humanitarian aid: 88.6%

Multilateral humanitarian aid: 11.4%

- CERF: 33.7%
- UNRWA: 12.7%
- OCHA: 3.2%
- IFRC: 5.5%
- OHCHR: 1.5%
- UNHCR: 22.4%
- ICRC: 21.0%

Notes: see notes (1), (2) and (4) in Overview of humanitarian aid table.
Sources: Bilateral humanitarian aid: OECD-DAC. Estimated multilateral humanitarian aid: UNHCR, UNICEF, WFP, UNRWA, UN/OCHA, ICRC and IFRC.

Funding per emergency, 2007

Crisis	(USD m)	(% of total)
Sudan	17.6	17.5
Sri Lanka	10.5	10.4
Iraq (incl. Iraqi refugees in neighbouring countries)	9.4	9.4
occupied Palestinian territories	9.3	9.3
Indonesia	9.0	8.9
Timor-Leste	8.4	8.3
Zimbabwe	5.7	5.7
Lebanon	3.8	3.7
Korea, DPR	3.3	3.2
Somalia	2.8	2.8
Total top 10 emergencies	**79.7**	**79.2**
Total	**100.6**	**100.0**

Notes: Funding to these emergencies includes all flows inside and outside an appeal that had been reported to OCHA/FTS and attributed to the emergency at the time of the database download on 8th May 2008.
Source: OCHA/FTS.

Regional distribution of funding, 2007

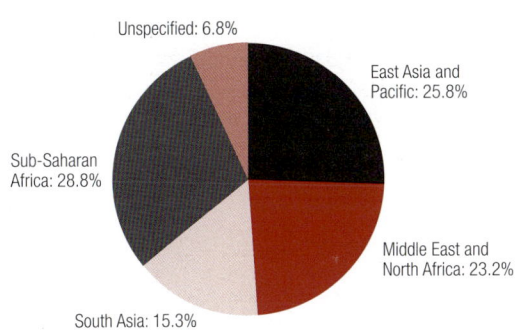

Unspecified: 6.8%
East Asia and Pacific: 25.8%
Sub-Saharan Africa: 28.8%
Middle East and North Africa: 23.2%
South Asia: 15.3%

Notes: Funding to these regions includes all flows inside and outside an appeal that had been reported to OCHA/FTS and attributed to a region at the time of the database download on 8th May 2008. Non-attributed flows are shown as 'unspecified'.
Source: OCHA/FTS.

Sectoral distribution of funding to UN Appeals, 2007 (%)

- Country funding
- UN appeal budget

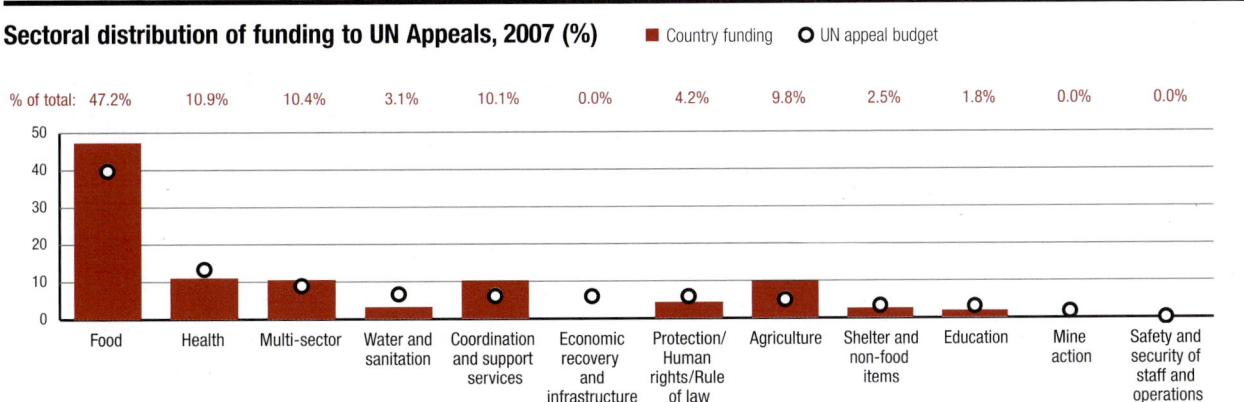

% of total:	47.2%	10.9%	10.4%	3.1%	10.1%	0.0%	4.2%	9.8%	2.5%	1.8%	0.0%	0.0%

Food / Health / Multi-sector / Water and sanitation / Coordination and support services / Economic recovery and infrastructure / Protection/ Human rights/Rule of law / Agriculture / Shelter and non-food items / Education / Mine action / Safety and security of staff and operations

Notes: Funding to these sectors include only flows inside an appeal that had been reported to OCHA/FTS and attributed to a sector at the time of the database download on 30th June 2008. Distribution of budget based on all 2007 UN appeals.
Source: OCHA/FTS.

Austria

Austria is the 21st most generous humanitarian donor among the OECD/DAC group, relative to its size. Its bilateral humanitarian aid amounted to US$5 million in 2007. The Austrian Development Cooperation and Cooperation with Eastern Europe (ADC) at the Federal Ministry for European and International Affairs sets Austria's humanitarian policy strategy and programmes. The Austrian Ministry of the Interior is in charge of coordinating international crisis response. The Austrian Development Agency (ADA) is the operational arm of ADC, responsible for the implementation of all bilateral programmes and projects in partner countries and administering the corresponding budget. Its document, *Internationale humanitäre Hilfe Leitlinie der Österreichischen Entwicklungs- und Ostzusammenarbeit* (June 2007) outlines Austrian humanitarian policy and is based on the European Consensus on Humanitarian Aid, international humanitarian conventions, and the basic principles of GHD.

Source: DAC Peer Review for Austria (OECD, 2004), at: http://www.ada.gv.at/

HRI 2008 scores by pillar

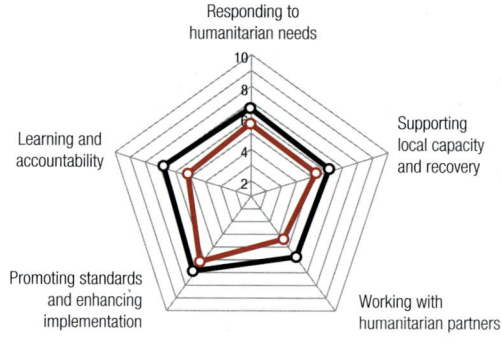

Austria — DAC average

HRI 2008 results

HIGHEST SCORES	SCORE	RANK
Responding to humanitarian needs		
Funding to crisis countries with historical ties and geographical proximity	9.97	2
Sectoral distribution of funding through UN appeals	10.00	1
Distribution of funding relative to ECHO's Crisis and Vulnerability Indices	10.00	1
Supporting local capacity and recovery		
Strengthening local capacity for response and mitigation	6.70	5
Working with humanitarian partners		
Helping governments and local communities achieve better coordination	6.57	8

LOWEST SCORES	SCORE	RANK
Responding to humanitarian needs		
Reallocation of funds from other crises	4.81	22
Timely funding to complex emergencies with UN appeals	1.43	22
Supporting local capacity and recovery		
Aligned to long-term development aims	6.11	23
Working with humanitarian partners		
Flexible funding	6.02	23
Promoting standards and enhancing implementation		
Donor engagement in protection and assistance to civilians	7.09	22

Overview of humanitarian aid	Austria			Share of total DAC (%)	
	2006	2007[4]		2006	2007[4]
Total humanitarian aid (estimated), of which:	19.5	7.8		0.2	0.1
Bilateral[1]	16.9	4.5		0.3	0.1
Multilateral[2] (estimated*), of which:	2.6	3.2		0.2	0.2
Central Emergency Response Fund**	0.0	0.4		0.0	0.1
Funding to other pooled mechanisms[3]***	0.0	0.0		0.0	0.0
Official development assistance	1,498	1,798		1.4	1.7

				DAC average	
Total humanitarian aid per capita (USD)[5]	2	1		22	23
Total humanitarian aid per / official development assistance	1.8	0.6		12.2	11.3
Overseas development assistance / gross national income	0.47	0.49		0.46	0.44

Notes: All data are given in current USD m unless otherwise indicated.

(1) Based on OECD/DAC definition of bilateral humanitarian aid, which is provided directly by a donor country to a recipient country and includes non-core earmarked contributions to multilateral humanitarian organisations known as multi-bilateral aid.

(2) Core unearmarked humanitarian flows to UNHCR, UNICEF, WFP, UNRWA, UN/OCHA, ICRC and IFRC. Does not include contributions through EC. 2007 core funding to UNRWA and ICRC proxied by 2006 data.

(3) For 2006, these were IFRC's Disaster Relief Emergency Fund (DREF), Sudan Common Humanitarian Fund (CHF), Democratic Republic of Congo (DRC) Pooled Fund, and Emergency Response Funds (ERF) for DRC, Indonesia, Somalia, Republic of Congo, and Ethiopia. For 2007, these were DREF, CHF, DRC Pooled Fund, and ERFs for Central African Republic, DRC, Ethiopia, Indonesia, and Iraq.

(4) All 2007 OECD/DAC data are provisional.

(5) Where 2007 population data not available, 2006 data used.

Sources: All data from OECD-DAC except: (*) UNHCR, UNICEF, WFP, UNRWA, UN/OCHA, ICRC and IFRC; (**) OCHA; (***) OCHA, IFRC; US Federal Reserve.

Main channels of humanitarian aid, 2007

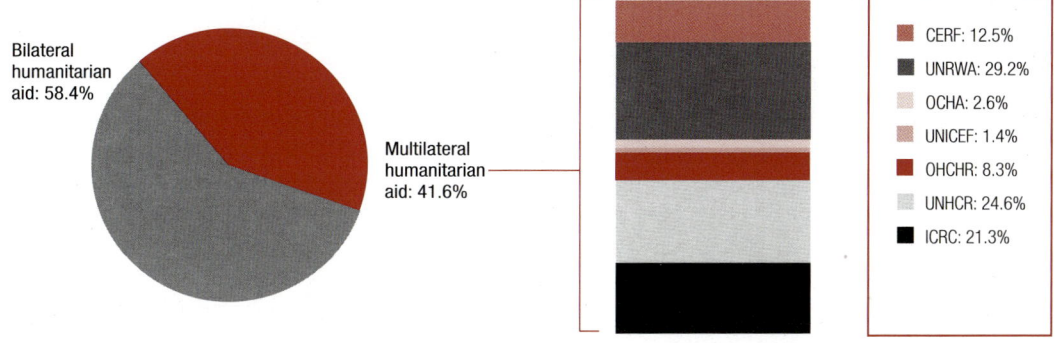

Bilateral humanitarian aid: 58.4%

Multilateral humanitarian aid: 41.6%

- CERF: 12.5%
- UNRWA: 29.2%
- OCHA: 2.6%
- UNICEF: 1.4%
- OHCHR: 8.3%
- UNHCR: 24.6%
- ICRC: 21.3%

Notes: see notes (1), (2) and (4) in Overview of humanitarian aid table.
Sources: Bilateral humanitarian aid: OECD-DAC. Estimated multilateral humanitarian aid: UNHCR, UNICEF, WFP, UNRWA, UN/OCHA, ICRC and IFRC.

Funding per emergency, 2007

Crisis	(USD m)	(% of total)
occupied Palestinian territories	2.0	26.1
Uganda	1.4	18.2
Sudan	0.5	7.1
Mozambique - floods - February	0.4	5.3
Madagascar - floods / cyclones - January - April	0.4	4.7
Cote d'Ivoire	0.3	3.9
Lebanon	0.3	3.7
Somalia	0.3	3.5
Zimbabwe	0.2	2.6
Nepal	0.2	2.3
Total top 10 emergencies	**5.8**	**77.4**
Total	**7.5**	**100.0**

Notes: Funding to these emergencies includes all flows inside and outside an appeal that had been reported to OCHA/FTS and attributed to the emergency at the time of the database download on 8th May 2008.
Source: OCHA/FTS.

Regional distribution of funding, 2007

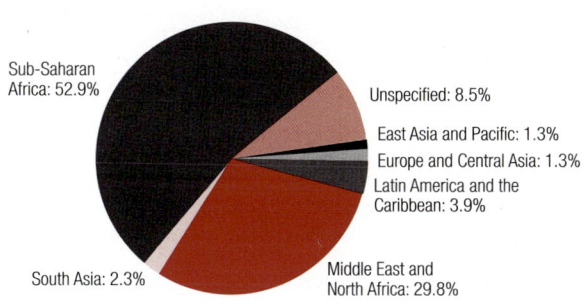

Sub-Saharan Africa: 52.9%
Unspecified: 8.5%
East Asia and Pacific: 1.3%
Europe and Central Asia: 1.3%
Latin America and the Caribbean: 3.9%
Middle East and North Africa: 29.8%
South Asia: 2.3%

Notes: Funding to these regions includes all flows inside and outside an appeal that had been reported to OCHA/FTS and attributed to a region at the time of the database download on 8th May 2008. Non-attributed flows are shown as 'unspecified'.
Source: OCHA/FTS.

Sectoral distribution of funding to UN Appeals, 2007 (%)

■ Country funding   ○ UN appeal budget

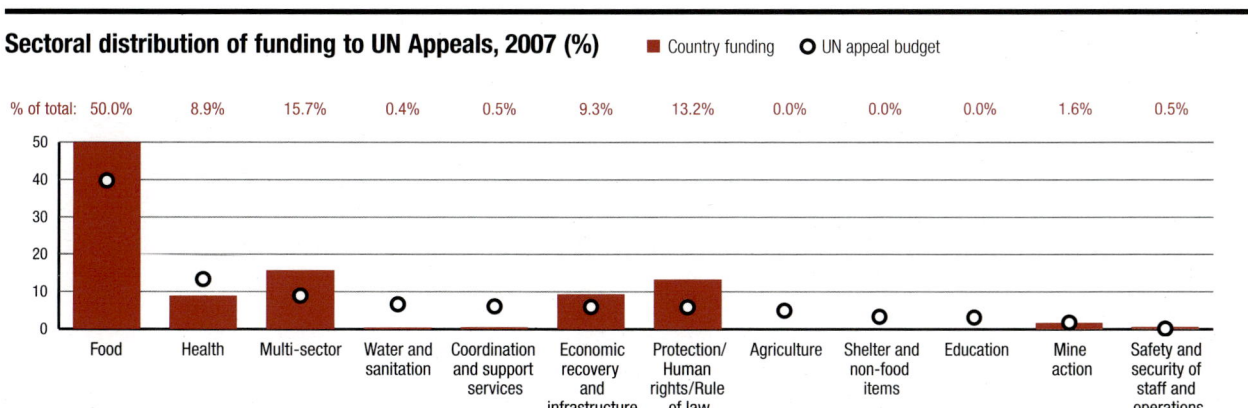

% of total: 50.0% | 8.9% | 15.7% | 0.4% | 0.5% | 9.3% | 13.2% | 0.0% | 0.0% | 0.0% | 1.6% | 0.5%

Food, Health, Multi-sector, Water and sanitation, Coordination and support services, Economic recovery and infrastructure, Protection/Human rights/Rule of law, Agriculture, Shelter and non-food items, Education, Mine action, Safety and security of staff and operations

Notes: Funding to these sectors include only flows inside an appeal that had been reported to OCHA/FTS and attributed to a sector at the time of the database download on 30th June 2008. Distribution of budget based on all 2007 UN appeals.
Source: OCHA/FTS.

Belgium

Belgium is the 14th most generous humanitarian donor among the OECD/DAC group, relative to its size. Its bilateral humanitarian aid amounted to US$76 million in 2007. Both the Ministry for Foreign Affairs and the Ministry for Development Cooperation are responsible for Belgian humanitarian aid, which is administrated by the Department for Special Programmes, focusing on emergency aid, rehabilitation and food aid, prevention and rehabilitation activities, and the Department for Multilateral and European Programmes, both within the Directorate-General for Development Cooperation (DGDC). There are other special programmes relating to humanitarian assistance, in particular the Belgian Survival Fund which exclusively finances programmes in Africa aimed at ensuring the survival of people threatened by hunger, undernourishment, poverty, and exclusion in countries faced with food shortage.

Source: DAC Peer Review for Belgium (OECD, 2005), at: http://www.dgcd.be/

HRI 2008 scores by pillar

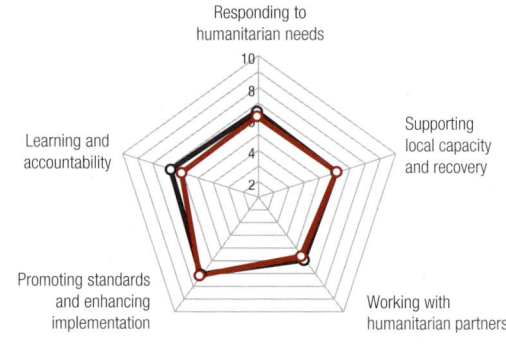

HRI 2008 results

HIGHEST SCORES	SCORE	RANK
Responding to humanitarian needs		
Funding to forgotten emergencies and those with low media coverage	10.00	1
Distribution of funding relative to ECHO's Crisis and Vulnerability Indices	9.60	3
Supporting local capacity and recovery		
Involvement of beneficiaries in monitoring and evaluation	7.47	2
Working with humanitarian partners		
Consistent support for implementation of humanitarian action	8.21	1
Promoting standards and enhancing implementation		
Affirming primary role of civilian organizations	9.37	1

LOWEST SCORES	SCORE	RANK
Responding to humanitarian needs		
Timely funding	5.82	22
Commitment to on-going crises	5.92	21
Timely funding to complex emergencies with UN appeals	4.04	20
Supporting local capacity and recovery		
Strengthening local capacity for response and mitigation	6.23	19
Learning and accountability		
Number of evaluations	1.43	20

Overview of humanitarian aid

	Belgium 2006	Belgium 2007[4]	Share of total DAC (%) 2006	Share of total DAC (%) 2007[4]
Total humanitarian aid (estimated), of which:	99.9	88.9	1.2	1.0
Bilateral[1]	86.4	76.5	1.3	1.2
Multilateral[2] (estimated*), of which:	13.5	12.4	0.9	0.8
Central Emergency Response Fund**	2.7	3.0	0.9	0.8
Funding to other pooled mechanisms[3]***	1.9	5.1	0.7	0.6
Official development assistance	1,978	1,953	1.9	1.9

			DAC average	DAC average
Total humanitarian aid per capita (USD)[5]	9	8	22	23
Total humanitarian aid per / official development assistance	7.4	7.1	12.2	11.3
Overseas development assistance / gross national income	0.50	0.43	0.46	0.44

Notes: All data are given in current USD m unless otherwise indicated.

(1) Based on OECD/DAC definition of bilateral humanitarian aid, which is provided directly by a donor country to a recipient country and includes non-core earmarked contributions to multilateral humanitarian organisations known as multi-bilateral aid.

(2) Core unearmarked humanitarian flows to UNHCR, UNICEF, WFP, UNRWA, UN/OCHA, ICRC and IFRC. Does not include contributions through EC. 2007 core funding to UNRWA and ICRC proxied by 2006 data.

(3) For 2006, these were IFRC's Disaster Relief Emergency Fund (DREF), Sudan Common Humanitarian Fund (CHF), Democratic Republic of Congo (DRC) Pooled Fund, and Emergency Response Funds (ERF) for DRC, Indonesia, Somalia, Republic of Congo, and Ethiopia. For 2007, these were DREF, CHF, DRC Pooled Fund, and ERFs for Central African Republic, DRC, Ethiopia, Indonesia, and Iraq.

(4) All 2007 OECD/DAC data are provisional.

(5) Where 2007 population data not available, 2006 data used.

Sources: All data from OECD-DAC except: (*) UNHCR, UNICEF, WFP, UNRWA, UN/OCHA, ICRC and IFRC; (**) OCHA; (***) OCHA, IFRC; US Federal Reserve.

Main channels of humanitarian aid, 2007

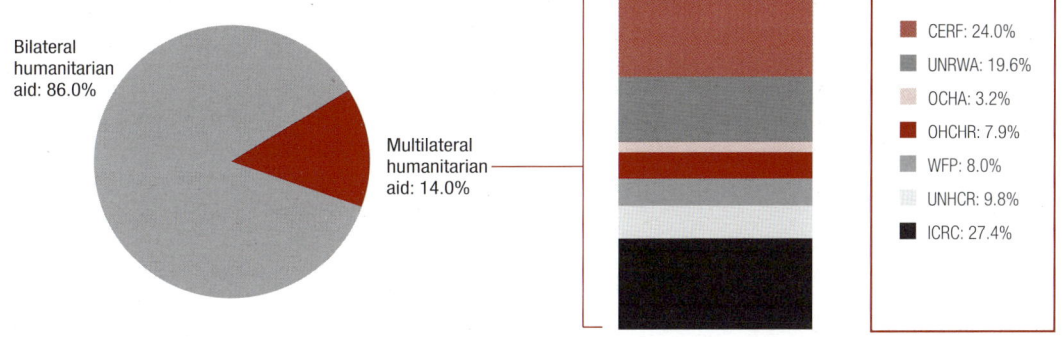

Bilateral humanitarian aid: 86.0%

Multilateral humanitarian aid: 14.0%

- CERF: 24.0%
- UNRWA: 19.6%
- OCHA: 3.2%
- OHCHR: 7.9%
- WFP: 8.0%
- UNHCR: 9.8%
- ICRC: 27.4%

Notes: see notes (1), (2) and (4) in Overview of humanitarian aid table.
Sources: Bilateral humanitarian aid: OECD-DAC. Estimated multilateral humanitarian aid: UNHCR, UNICEF, WFP, UNRWA, UN/OCHA, ICRC and IFRC.

Funding per emergency, 2007

Crisis	(USD m)	(% of total)
Democratic Republic of Congo	19.9	25.6
Burundi	8.1	10.4
occupied Palestinian territories	5.4	7.0
Sudan	4.9	6.2
Lebanon	2.8	3.6
Somalia	2.7	3.4
Uganda	2.6	3.3
Afghanistan	2.4	3.1
Bangladesh - Cyclone Sidr - November	2.4	3.1
Iraq (incl. Iraqi refugees in neighbouring countries)	2.3	3.0
Total top 10 emergencies	**53.4**	**68.8**
Total	**77.6**	**100.0**

Notes: Funding to these emergencies includes all flows inside and outside an appeal that
had been reported to OCHA/FTS and attributed to the emergency at the time of the database download on 8th May 2008.
Source: OCHA/FTS.

Regional distribution of funding, 2007

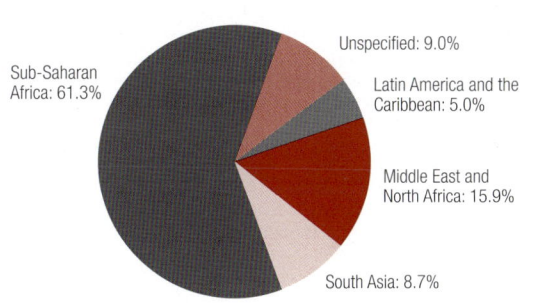

Unspecified: 9.0%

Sub-Saharan Africa: 61.3%

Latin America and the Caribbean: 5.0%

Middle East and North Africa: 15.9%

South Asia: 8.7%

Notes: Funding to these regions includes all flows inside and outside an
appeal that had been reported to OCHA/FTS and attributed to a region at
the time of the database download on 8th May 2008. Non-attributed flows
are shown as 'unspecified'.
Source: OCHA/FTS.

Sectoral distribution of funding to UN Appeals, 2007 (%)

■ Country funding   ○ UN appeal budget

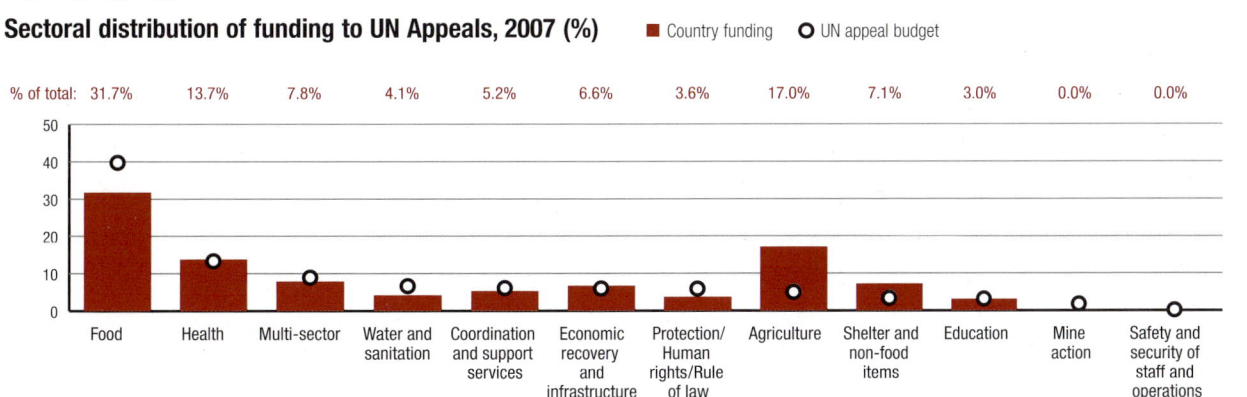

% of total:	31.7%	13.7%	7.8%	4.1%	5.2%	6.6%	3.6%	17.0%	7.1%	3.0%	0.0%	0.0%

Food, Health, Multi-sector, Water and sanitation, Coordination and support services, Economic recovery and infrastructure, Protection/Human rights/Rule of law, Agriculture, Shelter and non-food items, Education, Mine action, Safety and security of staff and operations

Notes: Funding to these sectors include only flows inside an appeal that had been reported to OCHA/FTS and attributed to a sector at the time of the database download on
30th June 2008. Distribution of budget based on all 2007 UN appeals.
Source: OCHA/FTS.

Canada

Canada is the 11th most generous humanitarian donor among the OECD/DAC group, relative to its size. Its bilateral humanitarian aid amounted to US$274 million in 2007. Canada's Department of Foreign Affairs and International Trade (DFAIT) is responsible for the policy formulation of its humanitarian aid, while the Canadian International Development Agency (CIDA), within the Ministry of International Cooperation, is responsible for implementation. Humanitarian action is funded from CIDA's budget for international assistance. Canada is currently preparing a policy document which formalises its approach to humanitarian action. CIDA has established a "crisis pool" that allows it to fund major, unforeseen crises, without adversely affecting ongoing funding. For 2007–2008, the crisis pool was on the order of US$300 million and rolls over funds from year to year. Canadian humanitarian funds may be used for early recovery activities, while the crisis pool allows funding lasting up to two years for recovery activities. The Department of National Defence has a crisis cell with its Rapid Disaster Assessment and Response Team. Canada's humanitarian aid policy is broadly aligned with the GHD Principles and has also formulated a GHD Domestic Implementation Plan.

Sources: DAC Peer Review for Canada (OECD, 2007); GHD Domestic Implementation Plan for Canada; and CIDA, at: http://www.acdi-cida.gc.ca

HRI 2008 scores by pillar

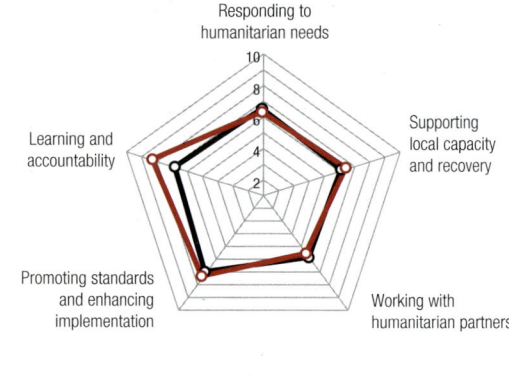

HRI 2008 results

HIGHEST SCORES	SCORE	RANK
Responding to humanitarian needs		
Commitment to on-going crises	7.57	4
Distribution of funding relative to ECHO's Crisis and Vulnerability Indices	9.42	4
Promoting standards and enhancing implementation		
Implementing human rights law	7.48	5
Learning and accountability		
Participation in main accountability initiatives	7.57	3
Number of evaluations	10.00	1

LOWEST SCORES	SCORE	RANK
Responding to humanitarian needs		
Funding needs assessments	6.04	17
Sectoral distribution of funding through UN appeals	5.23	17
Working with humanitarian partners		
Supporting contingency planning and strengthening response capacity	4.50	19
Consistent support for implementation of humanitarian action	6.88	17
Learning and accountability		
Commitment to accountability in humanitarian action	8.15	15

Overview of humanitarian aid

Overview of humanitarian aid	Canada		Share of total DAC (%)	
	2006	2007[4]	2006	2007[4]
Total humanitarian aid (estimated), of which:	316.8	361.8	3.8	3.9
Bilateral[1]	230.9	273.9	3.4	4.4
Multilateral[2] (estimated*), of which:	85.8	87.9	5.5	5.5
Central Emergency Response Fund**	21.9	35.1	7.6	9.3
Funding to other pooled mechanisms[3]***	3.1	6.7	1.1	0.8
Official development assistance	3,684	3,922	3.5	3.8
			DAC average	
Total humanitarian aid per capita (USD)[5]	10	11	22	23
Total humanitarian aid per / official development assistance	12.5	11.8	12.2	11.3
Overseas development assistance / gross national income	0.29	0.28	0.46	0.44

Notes: All data are given in current USD m unless otherwise indicated.

1 Based on OECD/DAC definition of bilateral humanitarian aid, which is provided directly by a donor country to a recipient country and includes non-core earmarked contributions to multilateral humanitarian organisations known as multi-bilateral aid.

2 Core unearmarked humanitarian flows to UNHCR, UNICEF, WFP, UNRWA, UN/OCHA, ICRC and IFRC. 2007 core funding to UNRWA and ICRC proxied by 2006 data.

3 For 2006, these were IFRC's Disaster Relief Emergency Fund (DREF), Sudan Common Humanitarian Fund (CHF), Democratic Republic of Congo (DRC) Pooled Fund, and Emergency Response Funds (ERF) for DRC, Indonesia, Somalia, Republic of Congo, and Ethiopia. For 2007, these were DREF, CHF, DRC Pooled Fund, and ERFs for Central African Republic, DRC, Ethiopia, Indonesia, and Iraq.

4 All 2007 OECD/DAC data are provisional.

5 Where 2007 population data not available, 2006 data used.

Sources: All data from OECD-DAC except: (*) UNHCR, UNICEF, WFP, UNRWA, UN/OCHA, ICRC and IFRC; (**) OCHA; (***) OCHA, IFRC; US Federal Reserve.

Main channels of humanitarian aid, 2007

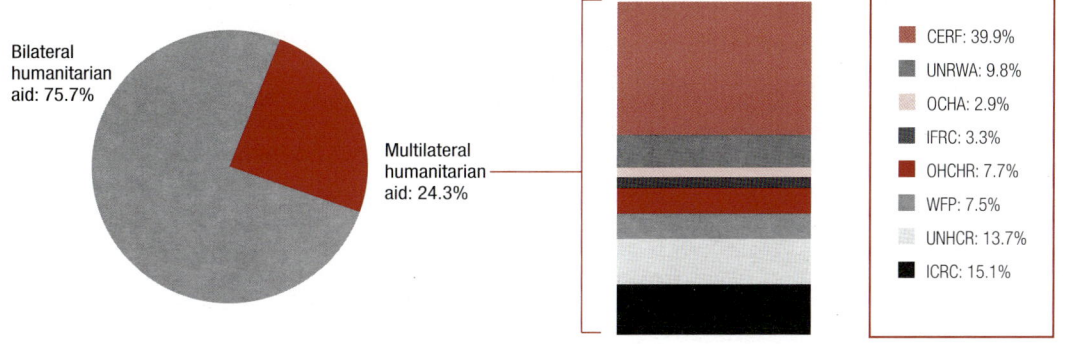

Bilateral humanitarian aid: 75.7%

Multilateral humanitarian aid: 24.3%

- CERF: 39.9%
- UNRWA: 9.8%
- OCHA: 2.9%
- IFRC: 3.3%
- OHCHR: 7.7%
- WFP: 7.5%
- UNHCR: 13.7%
- ICRC: 15.1%

Notes: see notes (1), (2) and (4) in Overview of humanitarian aid table.
Sources: Bilateral humanitarian aid: OECD-DAC. Estimated multilateral humanitarian aid: UNHCR, UNICEF, WFP, UNRWA, UN/OCHA, ICRC and IFRC.

Funding per emergency, 2007

Crisis	(USD m)	(% of total)
Sudan	58.3	21.3
Afghanistan	18.4	6.7
occupied Palestinian territories	14.3	5.2
Haiti	10.3	3.8
Somalia	9.2	3.4
Democratic Republic of Congo	8.3	3.0
Uganda	8.0	2.9
Chad	7.1	2.6
Great Lakes Region	6.8	2.5
Zimbabwe	5.9	2.1
Total top 10 emergencies	**146.6**	**53.6**
Total	**273.5**	**100.0**

Notes: Funding to these emergencies includes all flows inside and outside an appeal that had been reported to OCHA/FTS and attributed to the emergency at the time of the database download on 8th May 2008.
Source: OCHA/FTS.

Regional distribution of funding, 2007

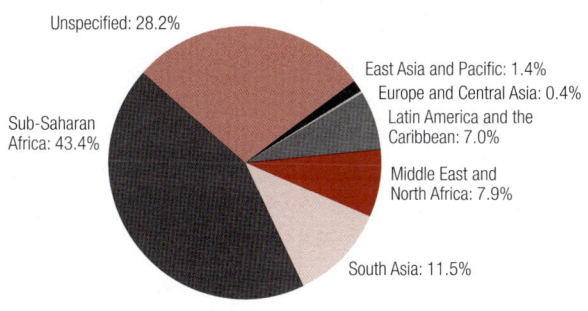

Unspecified: 28.2%

East Asia and Pacific: 1.4%
Europe and Central Asia: 0.4%
Latin America and the Caribbean: 7.0%

Sub-Saharan Africa: 43.4%

Middle East and North Africa: 7.9%

South Asia: 11.5%

Notes: Funding to these regions includes all flows inside and outside an appeal that had been reported to OCHA/FTS and attributed to a region at the time of the database download on 8th May 2008. Non-attributed flows are shown as 'unspecified'.
Source: OCHA/FTS.

Sectoral distribution of funding to UN Appeals, 2007 (%)

■ Country funding   ○ UN appeal budget

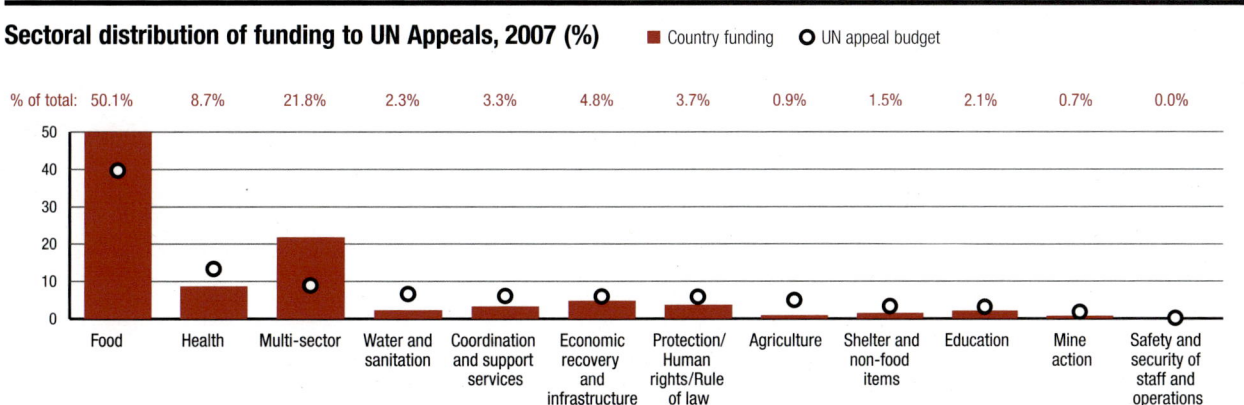

% of total: 50.1% 8.7% 21.8% 2.3% 3.3% 4.8% 3.7% 0.9% 1.5% 2.1% 0.7% 0.0%

Food | Health | Multi-sector | Water and sanitation | Coordination and support services | Economic recovery and infrastructure | Protection/ Human rights/Rule of law | Agriculture | Shelter and non-food items | Education | Mine action | Safety and security of staff and operations

Notes: Funding to these sectors include only flows inside an appeal that had been reported to OCHA/FTS and attributed to a sector at the time of the database download on 30th June 2008. Distribution of budget based on all 2007 UN appeals.
Source: OCHA/FTS.

Denmark

Denmark is the 6th most generous humanitarian donor among the OECD/DAC group, relative to its size. Its bilateral humanitarian aid amounted to US$140 million in 2007. The Danish International Development Agency (DANIDA) within the Ministry of Foreign Affairs and the Ministry of Defence both play a role in humanitarian action. Denmark has been strongly engaged in promoting the GHD initiative. Its strategy is contained in its 2002 *Strategic Priorities in Danish Humanitarian Assistance,* which predates the GHD initiative. Its humanitarian interventions in the context of violent conflicts are concentrated on select countries or regions. It contains a strong rights perspective, is oriented toward protecting vulnerable groups and IDPs, and integrating relief and development, including an emphasis on building local and regional capacity and crisis prevention. The general budget line for humanitarian assistance may be used for early recovery activities. Denmark has formulated a GHD Domestic Implementation Plan. Its Humanitarian Contact Group (HCG), which brings together Danish public and private organisations, is the central body for planning and coordinating humanitarian assistance. As part of international emergency preparedness efforts, it also works through its International Humanitarian Service, which funds emergency response mechanisms for Danish NGOs. Denmark has multi-year framework agreements with major humanitarian organisations.

Sources: GHD Domestic Implementation Plan for Denmark; DAC Peer Review for Denmark (OECD, 2007), at: http://www.um.dk/

HRI 2008 scores by pillar

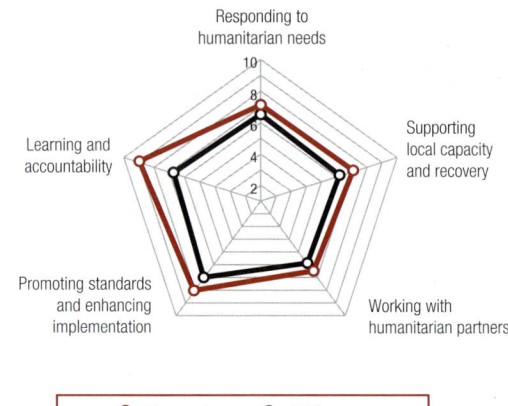

HRI 2008 results

HIGHEST SCORES	SCORE	RANK
Responding to humanitarian needs		
Impartiality	8.98	1
Supporting local capacity and recovery		
Funding to international disaster risk mitigation mechanisms	10.00	1
Working with humanitarian partners		
Supporting contingency planning and strengthening response capacity	6.13	1
Learning and accountability		
Participation in main accountability initiatives	10.00	1
Supporting learning and accountability initiatives	8.11	1

LOWEST SCORES	SCORE	RANK
Responding to humanitarian needs		
Distribution of funding relative to ECHO's Crisis and Vulnerability Indices	6.52	22
Funding to forgotten emergencies and those with low media coverage	1.88	21
Supporting local capacity and recovery		
Funding to strengthen local capacity	2.54	15
Strengthening preparedness	6.72	17
Promoting standards and enhancing implementation		
Supporting needs of internally displaced persons	6.84	16

Overview of humanitarian aid	Denmark		Share of total DAC (%)	
	2006	2007[4]	2006	2007[4]
Total humanitarian aid (estimated), of which:	218.4	211.9	2.6	2.3
Bilateral[1]	151.0	151.8	2.2	2.4
Multilateral[2] (estimated*), of which:	67.4	60.1	4.3	3.7
Central Emergency Response Fund**	8.4	9.2	2.9	2.4
Funding to other pooled mechanisms[3]***	0.2	0.8	0.1	0.1
Official development assistance	2,236.1	2,563.0	2.1	2.5
			DAC average	
Total humanitarian aid per capita (USD)[5]	40	39	22	23
Total humanitarian aid per / official development assistance	14.9	12.8	12.2	11.3
Overseas development assistance / gross national income	0.8	0.8	0.5	0.4

Notes: All data are given in current USD m unless otherwise indicated.
(1) Based on OECD/DAC definition of bilateral humanitarian aid, which is provided directly by a donor country to a recipient country and includes non-core earmarked contributions to multilateral humanitarian organisations known as multi-bilateral aid.
(2) Core unearmarked humanitarian flows to UNHCR, UNICEF, WFP, UNRWA, UN/OCHA, ICRC and IFRC. Does not include contributions through EC.
(3) For 2006, these were IFRC's Disaster Relief Emergency Fund (DREF), Sudan Common Humanitarian Fund (CHF), Democratic Republic of Congo (DRC) Pooled Fund, and Emergency Response Funds (ERF) for DRC, Indonesia, Somalia, Republic of Congo, and Ethiopia. For 2007, these were DREF, CHF, DRC Pooled Fund, and ERFs for Central African Republic, DRC, Ethiopia, Indonesia, and Iraq.
(4) All 2007 OECD/DAC data are provisional.
(5) Where 2007 population data not available, these were proxied by 2006 data.
Sources: All data for 2006 from OECD-DAC except: (*) UNHCR, UNICEF, WFP, UNRWA, UN/OCHA, ICRC and IFRC; (**) OCHA; (***) OCHA, IFRC; US Federal Reserve. Bilateral data for 2007 from Ministry of Foreign Affairs of Denmark, and Multilateral data from Ministry of Foreign Affairs of Denmark, and IFRC.

Main channels of humanitarian aid, 2007

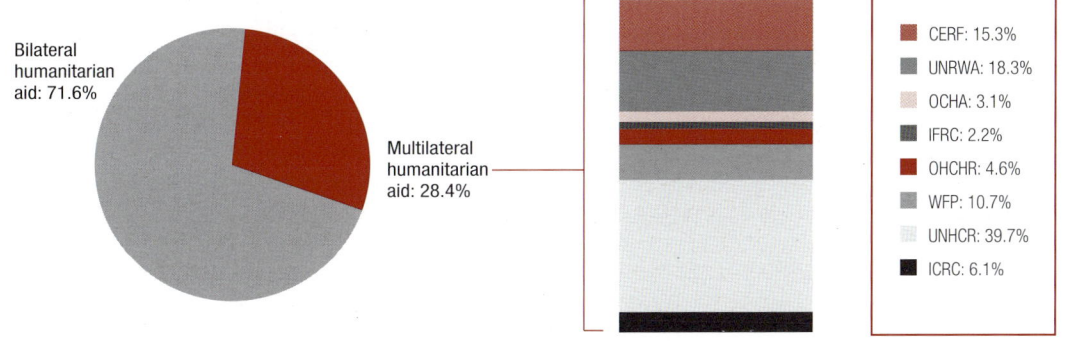

Bilateral humanitarian aid: 71.6%

Multilateral humanitarian aid: 28.4%

- ■ CERF: 15.3%
- ■ UNRWA: 18.3%
- ■ OCHA: 3.1%
- ■ IFRC: 2.2%
- ■ OHCHR: 4.6%
- ■ WFP: 10.7%
- □ UNHCR: 39.7%
- ■ ICRC: 6.1%

Notes: see (1) and (2) in Overview of humanitarian aid table.
Sources: Bilateral humanitarian aid: MInistry of Foreign Affairs of Denmark. Estimated multilateral humanitarian aid: Ministry of Foreign Affairs, and IFRC.

Funding per country, 2007

Crisis	(USD m)	(% of total)
Iraq (incl. Iraqi refugees in neighbouring countries)	26.5	20.1
Sudan	22.0	16.7
Somalia	8.8	6.7
Uganda	5.5	4.2
Bangladesh - Cyclone Sidr - November	4.9	3.7
Democratic Republic of Congo	3.8	2.9
Chad	2.8	2.1
Burundi	2.7	2.0
Sri Lanka	2.6	2.0
Liberia	2.6	2.0
Total top 10 countries	**82.2**	**62.3**
Total	**131.8**	**100.0**

Notes: This table is adjusted to the information kindly provided by Danish government,
reflecting funding by country rather than emergency.
Source: Ministry of Foreign Affairs of Denmark, and IFRC.

Regional distribution of funding, 2007

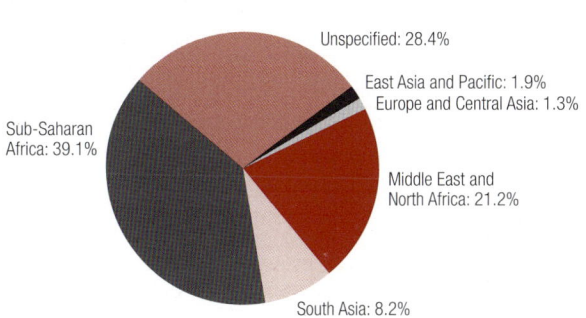

Unspecified: 28.4%

East Asia and Pacific: 1.9%
Europe and Central Asia: 1.3%

Sub-Saharan Africa: 39.1%

Middle East and North Africa: 21.2%

South Asia: 8.2%

Notes: Multilateral flows are shown as 'unspecified'.
Source: Ministry of Foreign Affairs of Denmark.

Sectoral distribution of funding to UN Appeals, 2007 (%)

■ Country funding   ○ UN appeal budget

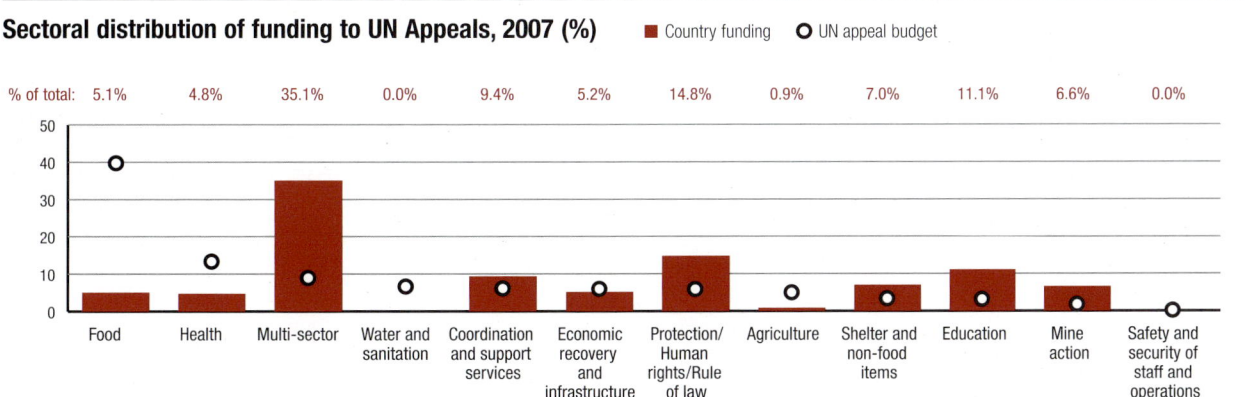

% of total:	5.1%	4.8%	35.1%	0.0%	9.4%	5.2%	14.8%	0.9%	7.0%	11.1%	6.6%	0.0%

Food | Health | Multi-sector | Water and sanitation | Coordination and support services | Economic recovery and infrastructure | Protection/ Human rights/Rule of law | Agriculture | Shelter and non-food items | Education | Mine action | Safety and security of staff and operations

Notes: Funding to these sectors include only flows inside an appeal that had been reported to OCHA/FTS and attributed to a sector at the time of the database download on
30th June 2008. Distribution of budget based on all 2007 UN appeals.
Source: OCHA/FTS.

European Commission

The EC's bilateral humanitarian aid amounted to US$1.33 billion in 2007. The European Commission's relief assistance is provided through its Humanitarian Aid Department (ECHO). This aid is complementary to the humanitarian assistance of individual European Union (EU) countries and makes up roughly half of total EU humanitarian funding. It is funded by the contributions of EU Member States. ECHO's mandate is defined in Council Regulation (EC No. 1257/96), which embraces the basic principles of humanitarian aid. The new *European Consensus on Humanitarian Aid* guides the implementation of humanitarian aid and sets out ECHO's comparative advantage and added value vis-à-vis the bilateral policies of Member States. ECHO has a large field presence, including 43 field offices, and bases financing decisions on its own needs assessments, which determine how it earmarks aid. Its fast-track primary emergency decision allows it to provide up to €3 million almost immediately to respond to sudden crises. ECHO's DRR strategy rests on three factors: strengthening the resilience of vulnerable communities (through DIPECHO), integrating disaster preparedness in humanitarian relief action, and advocacy for integrating DRR into development cooperation. As a very large donor, the EC has traditionally relied less on multilateral organisations and does not to contribute to pooled funding. ECHO operates under a legal obligation to evaluate the activities it funds.

Sources: ECHO; DAC Peer Review for the EC (OECD, 2007).

HRI 2008 scores by pillar

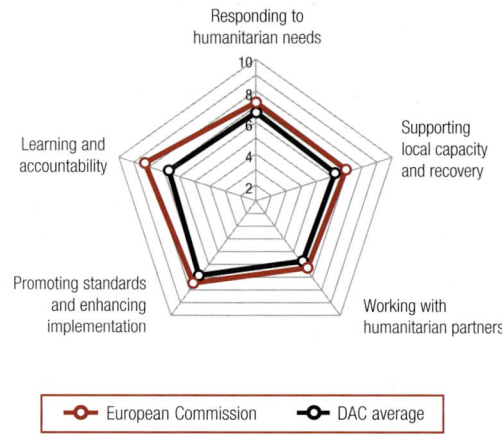

—○— European Commission   —●— DAC average

HRI 2008 results

HIGHEST SCORES	SCORE	RANK
Responding to humanitarian needs		
Commitment to on-going crises	7.64	2
Donor capacity for informed decision-making	7.63	1
Supporting local capacity and recovery		
Involvement of beneficiaries in design and implementation	8.03	1
Learning and accountability		
Encouraging regular evaluations	8.29	2
Number of evaluations	9.67	2

LOWEST SCORES	SCORE	RANK
Responding to humanitarian needs		
Funding to crisis countries with historical ties and geographical proximity	5.96	20
Reallocation of funds from other crises	5.25	18
Supporting local capacity and recovery		
Ensuring rapid recovery of sustainable livelihoods	6.74	18
Working with humanitarian partners		
Reducing earmarking	5.51	23
Unearmarked funding	1.43	23

Overview of humanitarian aid	EC		Share of total DAC (%)	
	2006	2007[4]	2006	2007[4]
Total humanitarian aid (estimated), of which:	1,287.2	1,433.1	15.5	15.5
Bilateral[1]	1,155.8	1,328.4	17.1	21.1
Multilateral[2] (estimated*), of which:	131.4	104.7	8.4	6.5
Central Emergency Response Fund**	0.0	0.0	0.0	0.0
Funding to other pooled mechanisms[3]***	0.0	0.0	0.0	0.0
Official development assistance	10,245	11,771	9.8	11.4
			DAC average	
Total humanitarian aid per capita (USD)[5]	n/a	n/a	22	23
Total humanitarian aid per / official development assistance	13.6	12.9	12.2	11.3
Overseas development assistance / gross national income	n/a	n/a	0.46	0.44

Notes: All data are given in current USD m unless otherwise indicated.

1 Based on OECD/DAC definition of bilateral humanitarian aid, which is provided directly by a donor country to a recipient country and includes non-core earmarked contributions to multilateral humanitarian organisations known as multi-bilateral aid.

2 Core unearmarked humanitarian flows to UNHCR, UNICEF, WFP, UNRWA, UN/OCHA, ICRC and IFRC. 2007 core funding to UNRWA and ICRC proxied by 2006 data.

3 For 2006, these were IFRC's Disaster Relief Emergency Fund (DREF), Sudan Common Humanitarian Fund (CHF), Democratic Republic of Congo (DRC) Pooled Fund, and Emergency Response Funds (ERF) for DRC, Indonesia, Somalia, Republic of Congo, and Ethiopia. For 2007, these were DREF, CHF, DRC Pooled Fund, and ERFs for Central African Republic, DRC, Ethiopia, Indonesia, and Iraq.

4 All 2007 OECD/DAC data are provisional.

5 Where 2007 population data not available, 2006 data used.

Sources: All data from OECD-DAC except: (*) UNHCR, UNICEF, WFP, UNRWA, UN/OCHA, ICRC and IFRC; (**) OCHA; (***) OCHA, IFRC; US Federal Reserve.

Main channels of humanitarian aid, 2007

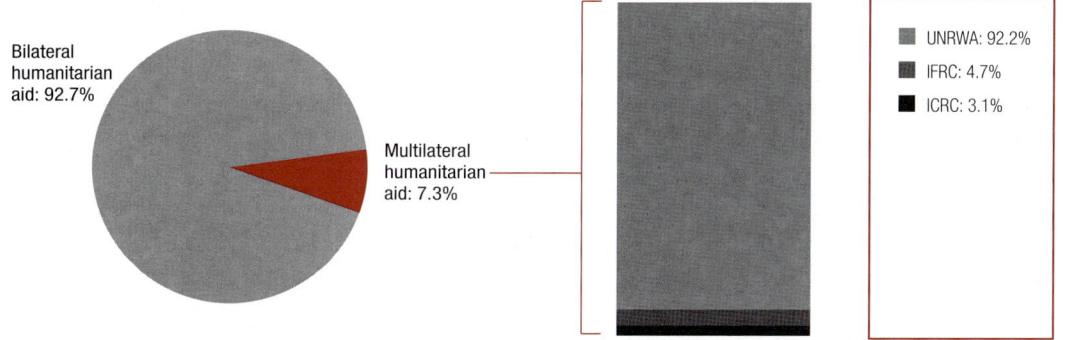

Bilateral humanitarian aid: 92.7%

Multilateral humanitarian aid: 7.3%

- UNRWA: 92.2%
- IFRC: 4.7%
- ICRC: 3.1%

Notes: see notes (1), (2) and (4) in Overview of humanitarian aid table.
Sources: Bilateral humanitarian aid: OECD-DAC. Estimated multilateral humanitarian aid: UNHCR, UNICEF, WFP, UNRWA, UN/OCHA, ICRC and IFRC.

Funding per emergency, 2007

Crisis	(USD m)	(% of total)
Sudan	203.3	19.0
occupied Palestinian territories	82.6	7.7
Democratic Republic of Congo	69.7	6.5
Chad	39.8	3.7
Uganda	35.9	3.3
Afghanistan	35.6	3.3
North Caucasus	34.2	3.2
Burundi	33.0	3.1
Zimbabwe	30.3	2.8
Somalia	27.0	2.5
Total top 10 emergencies	**591.5**	**55.2**
Total	**1071.9**	**100.0**

Notes: Funding to these emergencies includes all flows inside and outside an appeal that had been reported to OCHA/FTS and attributed to the emergency at the time of the database download on 8th May 2008.
Source: OCHA/FTS.

Regional distribution of funding, 2007

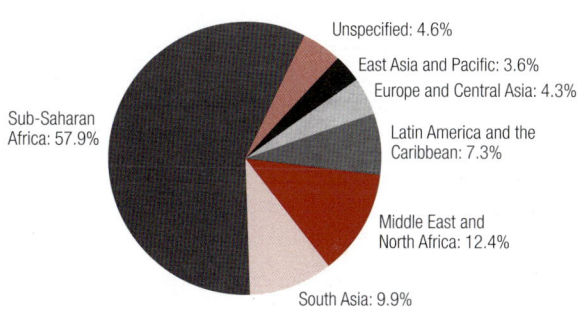

Unspecified: 4.6%
East Asia and Pacific: 3.6%
Europe and Central Asia: 4.3%
Sub-Saharan Africa: 57.9%
Latin America and the Caribbean: 7.3%
Middle East and North Africa: 12.4%
South Asia: 9.9%

Notes: Funding to these regions includes all flows inside and outside an appeal that had been reported to OCHA/FTS and attributed to a region at the time of the database download on 8th May 2008. Non-attributed flows are shown as 'unspecified'.
Source: OCHA/FTS.

Sectoral distribution of funding to UN Appeals, 2007 (%)

■ Country funding ○ UN appeal budget

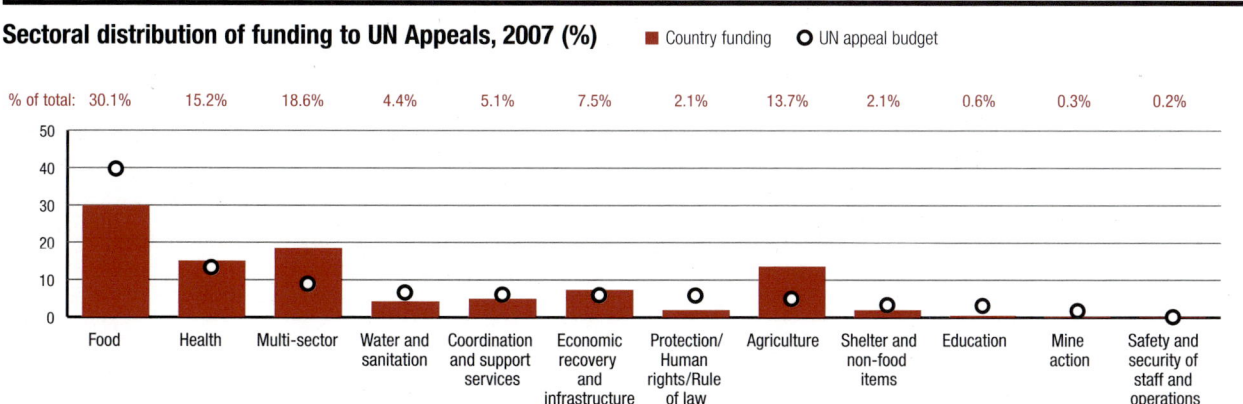

% of total: 30.1% 15.2% 18.6% 4.4% 5.1% 7.5% 2.1% 13.7% 2.1% 0.6% 0.3% 0.2%

Food | Health | Multi-sector | Water and sanitation | Coordination and support services | Economic recovery and infrastructure | Protection/ Human rights/Rule of law | Agriculture | Shelter and non-food items | Education | Mine action | Safety and security of staff and operations

Notes: Funding to these sectors include only flows inside an appeal that had been reported to OCHA/FTS and attributed to a sector at the time of the database download on 30th June 2008. Distribution of budget based on all 2007 UN appeals.
Source: OCHA/FTS.

The Humanitarian Response Index 2008

Finland

Finland is the 8th most generous humanitarian donor among the OECD/DAC group, relative to its size. Its bilateral humanitarian aid amounted to US$100 million in 2007. The Unit for Humanitarian Assistance within the Ministry for Foreign Affairs is in charge of Finnish humanitarian assistance. A new policy framework *Humanitarian Assistance Guidelines* (2007) defines Finland's humanitarian action and constitutes its plan for implementing the GHD Principles. Except for sudden-onset disasters in industrialised countries, humanitarian assistance is financed through a budget alloca-tion from the development cooperation budget. The strategy states that humanitarian assistance should be concentrated on the poorest developing countries and on ODA-recipient countries. The great majority of its humanitarian aid is directed at long-term crises, based on UN CAPs, or the Red Cross Red Crescent appeals. Finland does not perform its own needs assessments. It primarily channels its aid through multilateral organisations, especially the UN, as well as through a few experienced Finnish NGOs.

Sources: DAC Peer Review of Finland (OECD, 2003); Ministry of Foreign Affairs, at:
http://formin.finland.fi/

HRI 2008 scores by pillar

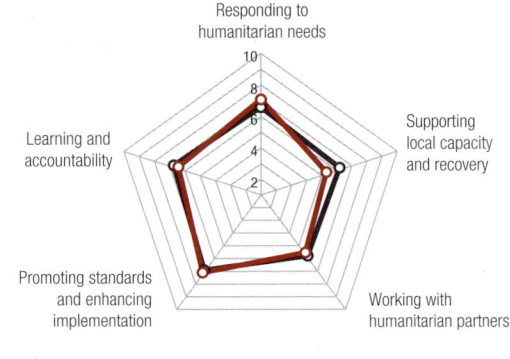

- Finland
- DAC average

HRI 2008 results

HIGHEST SCORES	SCORE	RANK
Responding to humanitarian needs		
Timely funding to onset disasters and IFRC emergency appeals	8.47	4
Saving lives and maintaining dignity	8.93	2
Supporting local capacity and recovery		
Strengthening preparedness	7.22	5
Promoting standards and enhancing implementation		
Respecting or promoting international humanitarian law	8.65	2
Learning and accountability		
Commitment to accountability in humanitarian action	8.71	1

LOWEST SCORES	SCORE	RANK
Responding to humanitarian needs		
Timely funding	6.14	21
Supporting local capacity and recovery		
Strengthening local capacity for response and mitigation	5.24	23
Strengthening resilience to cope with crises	5.63	23
Ensuring rapid recovery of sustainable livelihoods	5.56	23
Working with humanitarian partners		
Consistent support for implementation of humanitarian action	6.30	21

Overview of humanitarian aid

	Finland 2006	Finland 2007[4]	Share of total DAC (%) 2006	Share of total DAC (%) 2007[4]
Total humanitarian aid (estimated), of which:	96.9	130.7	1.2	1.4
Bilateral[1]	70.4	99.6	1.0	1.6
Multilateral[2] (estimated*), of which:	26.5	31.0	1.7	1.9
Central Emergency Response Fund**	5.2	6.7	1.8	1.8
Funding to other pooled mechanisms[3]***	0.0	0.0	0.0	0.0
Official development assistance	834	973	0.8	0.9
			DAC average	
Total humanitarian aid per capita (USD)[5]	18	25	22	23
Total humanitarian aid per / official development assistance	21.3	23.0	12.2	11.3
Overseas development assistance / gross national income	0.40	0.40	0.46	0.44

Notes: All data are given in current USD m unless otherwise indicated.

(1) Based on OECD/DAC definition of bilateral humanitarian aid, which is provided directly by a donor country to a recipient country and includes non-core earmarked contributions to multilateral humanitarian organisations known as multi-bilateral aid.

(2) Core unearmarked humanitarian flows to UNHCR, UNICEF, WFP, UNRWA, UN/OCHA, ICRC and IFRC. Does not include contributions through EC. 2007 core funding to UNRWA and ICRC proxied by 2006 data.

(3) For 2006, these were IFRC's Disaster Relief Emergency Fund (DREF), Sudan Common Humanitarian Fund (CHF), Democratic Republic of Congo (DRC) Pooled Fund, and Emergency Response Funds (ERF) for DRC, Indonesia, Somalia, Republic of Congo, and Ethiopia. For 2007, these were DREF, CHF, DRC Pooled Fund, and ERFs for Central African Republic, DRC, Ethiopia, Indonesia, and Iraq.

(4) All 2007 OECD/DAC data are provisional.

(5) Where 2007 population data not available, 2006 data used.

Sources: All data from OECD-DAC except: (*) UNHCR, UNICEF, WFP, UNRWA, UN/OCHA, ICRC and IFRC; (**) OCHA; (***) OCHA, IFRC; US Federal Reserve.

Main channels of humanitarian aid, 2007

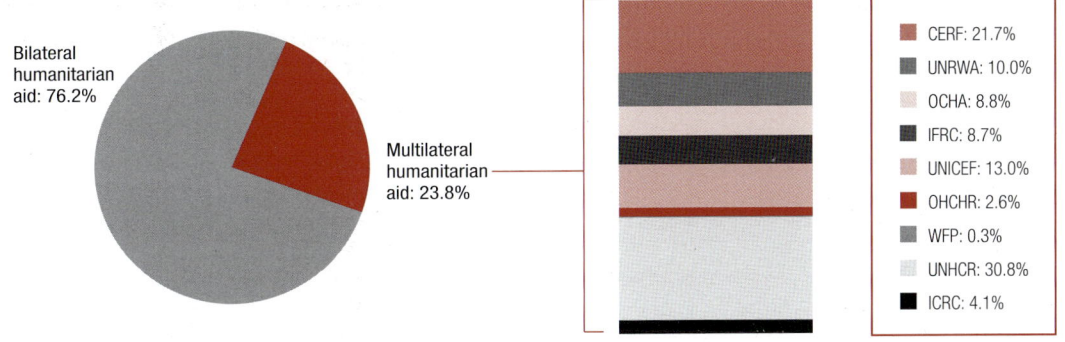

Bilateral humanitarian aid: 76.2%

Multilateral humanitarian aid: 23.8%

- CERF: 21.7%
- UNRWA: 10.0%
- OCHA: 8.8%
- IFRC: 8.7%
- UNICEF: 13.0%
- OHCHR: 2.6%
- WFP: 0.3%
- UNHCR: 30.8%
- ICRC: 4.1%

Notes: see notes (1), (2) and (4) in Overview of humanitarian aid table.
Sources: Bilateral humanitarian aid: OECD-DAC. Estimated multilateral humanitarian aid: UNHCR, UNICEF, WFP, UNRWA, UN/OCHA, ICRC and IFRC.

Funding per emergency, 2007

Crisis	(USD m)	(% of total)
Sudan	8.9	8.4
Chad	7.0	6.6
Democratic Republic of Congo	6.4	6.1
Somalia	5.0	4.7
Uganda	4.1	3.9
occupied Palestinian territories	4.0	3.7
Afghanistan	3.0	2.9
Central African Republic	2.6	2.4
Pakistan - floods / cyclone - July	2.0	1.9
Burundi	1.6	1.5
Total top 10 emergencies	**44.6**	**42.2**
Total	**105.8**	**100.0**

Notes: Funding to these emergencies includes all flows inside and outside an appeal that had been reported to OCHA/FTS and attributed to the emergency at the time of the database download on 8th May 2008.
Couroo: OCHА/VFTS.

Regional distribution of funding, 2007

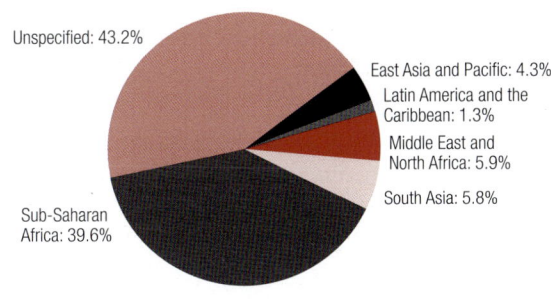

Unspecified: 43.2%

East Asia and Pacific: 4.3%

Latin America and the Caribbean: 1.3%

Middle East and North Africa: 5.9%

South Asia: 5.8%

Sub-Saharan Africa: 39.6%

Notes: Funding to these regions includes all flows inside and outside an appeal that had been reported to OCHA/FTS and attributed to a region at the time of the database download on 8th May 2008. Non-attributed flows are shown as 'unspecified'.
Source: OCHA/FTS.

Sectoral distribution of funding to UN Appeals, 2007 (%)

■ Country funding   ○ UN appeal budget

% of total: 30.2% 15.0% 35.6% 1.1% 4.2% 0.0% 8.9% 2.4% 1.6% 0.3% 0.7% 0.0%

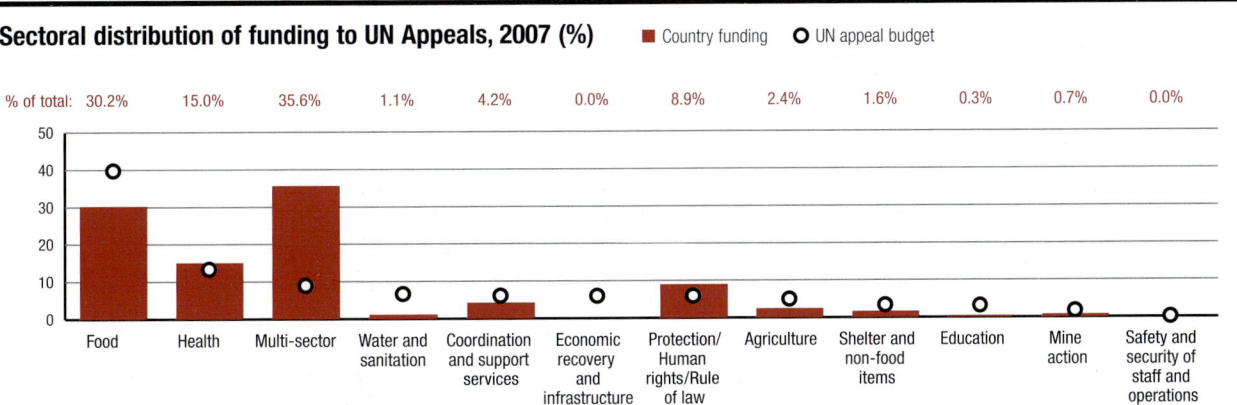

Food · Health · Multi-sector · Water and sanitation · Coordination and support services · Economic recovery and infrastructure · Protection/ Human rights/Rule of law · Agriculture · Shelter and non-food items · Education · Mine action · Safety and security of staff and operations

Notes: Funding to these sectors include only flows inside an appeal that had been reported to OCHA/FTS and attributed to a sector at the time of the database download on 30th June 2008. Distribution of budget based on all 2007 UN appeals.
Source: OCHA/FTS.

France

France is the 19th most generous humanitarian donor among the OECD/DAC group, relative to its size. Its bilateral humanitarian aid amounted to US$57 million in 2007, less than 1 percent of its ODA. The Ministry of Foreign Affairs is in charge of humanitarian action through the Délégation à l'Action Humanitaire (DAH), which coordinates humanitarian action and the UN Division, which is in charge of multilateral aid. The Ministry of Development Cooperation plays a role in rehabilitation, governance and mine clearance. France does not have a formal policy for its humanitarian action, but is currently developing a GHD implementation plan and relies on the *European Consensus on Humanitarian Aid* and the GHD *Principles* to underpin its decisions. Funding for humanitarian action is available via three separate funding allocations within a budget line: one for bilateral assistance, including to NGOs and for military assets, a second for core contributions to UN humanitarian agencies and CERF, and the third for food aid. France has access to other funding envelopes for humanitarian action, primarily for DRR activities. France performs bilateral humanitarian needs assessments in coordination with their local embassies. In addition to needs, the decision to fund a crisis is also influenced by historical and linguistic ties and the political context.

Sources: OECD Peer Review (2008); Ministry of Foreign Affairs, at: http://www.diplomatie.gouv.fr/

HRI 2008 scores by pillar

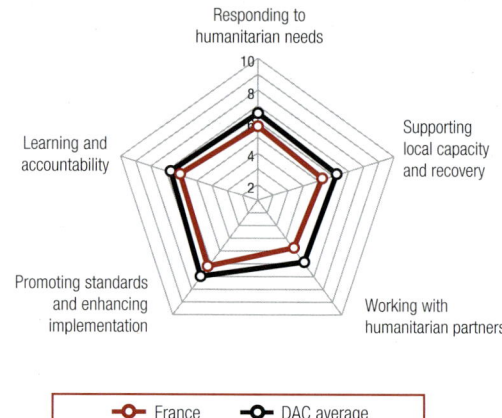

—○— France   —○— DAC average

HRI 2008 results

HIGHEST SCORES	SCORE	RANK
Responding to humanitarian needs		
Distribution of funding relative to ECHO's Crisis and Vulnerability Indices	8.45	10
Sectoral distribution of funding through UN appeals	7.22	10
Funding to forgotten emergencies and those with low media coverage	10.00	1
Working with humanitarian partners		
Unearmarked funding	7.39	9
Promoting standards and enhancing implementation		
Implementing human rights law	6.79	8

LOWEST SCORES	SCORE	RANK
Responding to humanitarian needs		
Saving lives and maintaining dignity	7.33	23
Supporting local capacity and recovery		
Involvement of beneficiaries in design and implementation	6.02	23
Working with humanitarian partners		
Helping governments and local communities achieve better coordination	4.98	23
Promoting standards and enhancing implementation		
Respecting or promoting human rights	6.80	23
Learning and accountability		
Commitment to accountability in humanitarian action	7.17	23

Overview of humanitarian aid

Overview of humanitarian aid	France		Share of total DAC (%)	
	2006	2007[4]	2006	2007[4]
Total humanitarian aid (estimated), of which:	81.7	94.3	1.0	1.0
Bilateral[1]	47.9	56.9	0.7	0.9
Multilateral[2] (estimated*), of which:	33.8	37.4	2.2	2.3
Central Emergency Response Fund**	1.3	1.3	0.4	0.3
Funding to other pooled mechanisms[3]***	0.0	0.0	0.0	0.0
Official development assistance	10,601	9,940	10.2	9.6

			DAC average	
Total humanitarian aid per capita (USD)[5]	1	1	22	23
Total humanitarian aid per / official development assistance	1.0	1.5	12.2	11.3
Overseas development assistance / gross national income	0.47	0.39	0.46	0.44

Notes: All data are given in current USD m unless otherwise indicated.

(1) Based on OECD/DAC definition of bilateral humanitarian aid, which is provided directly by a donor country to a recipient country and includes non-core earmarked contributions to multilateral humanitarian organisations known as multi-bilateral aid.

(2) Core unearmarked humanitarian flows to UNHCR, UNICEF, WFP, UNRWA, UN/OCHA, ICRC and IFRC. Does not include contributions through EC. 2007 core funding to UNRWA and ICRC proxied by 2006 data.

(3) For 2006, these were IFRC's Disaster Relief Emergency Fund (DREF), Sudan Common Humanitarian Fund (CHF), Democratic Republic of Congo (DRC) Pooled Fund, and Emergency Response Funds (ERF) for DRC, Indonesia, Somalia, Republic of Congo, and Ethiopia. For 2007, these were DREF, CHF, DRC Pooled Fund, and ERFs for Central African Republic, DRC, Ethiopia, Indonesia, and Iraq.

(4) All 2007 OECD/DAC data are provisional.

(5) Where 2007 population data not available, 2006 data used.

Sources: All data from OECD-DAC except: (*) UNHCR, UNICEF, WFP, UNRWA, UN/OCHA, ICRC and IFRC; (**) OCHA; (***) OCHA, IFRC; US Federal Reserve.

Main channels of humanitarian aid, 2007

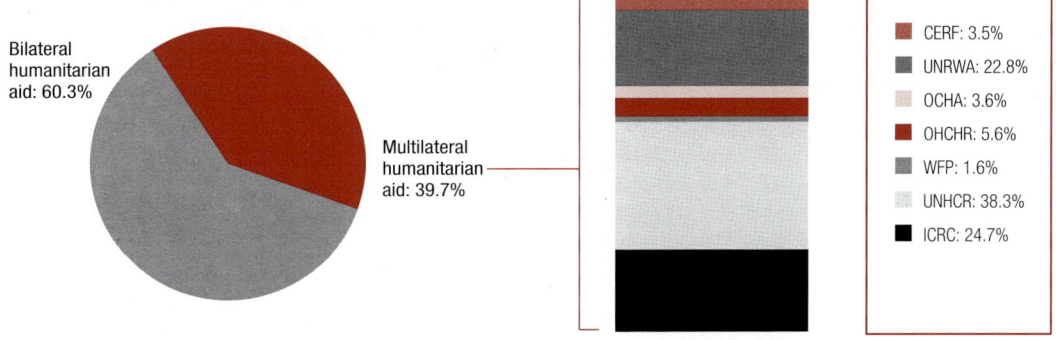

Bilateral humanitarian aid: 60.3%

Multilateral humanitarian aid: 39.7%

- CERF: 3.5%
- UNRWA: 22.8%
- OCHA: 3.6%
- OHCHR: 5.6%
- WFP: 1.6%
- UNHCR: 38.3%
- ICRC: 24.7%

Notes: see notes (1), (2) and (4) in Overview of humanitarian aid table.
Sources: Bilateral humanitarian aid: OECD-DAC. Estimated multilateral humanitarian aid: UNHCR, UNICEF, WFP, UNRWA, UN/OCHA, ICRC and IFRC.

Funding per emergency, 2007

Crisis	(USD m)	(% of total)
Democratic Republic of Congo	7.8	8.0
Chad	6.7	6.9
occupied Palestinian territories	5.1	5.3
Sudan	4.4	4.6
Central African Republic	4.3	4.4
Somalia	2.8	2.9
Uganda	1.9	2.0
Burundi	1.8	1.8
Iraq (incl. Iraqi refugees in neighbouring countries)	1.4	1.4
Bangladesh - floods - August	1.3	1.4
Total top 10 emergencies	**37.5**	**38.7**
Total	**97.0**	**100.0**

Notes: Funding to these emergencies includes all flows inside and outside an appeal that
had been reported to OCHA/FTS and attributed to the emergency at the time of the database download on 8th May 2008.
Source: OCHA/FTS.

Regional distribution of funding, 2007

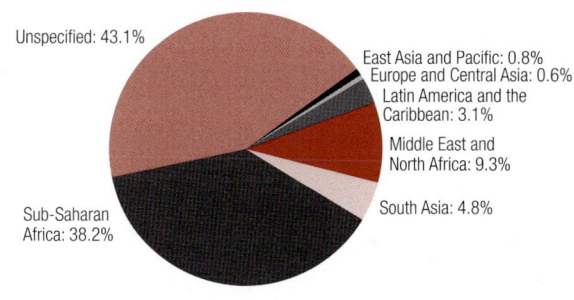

Unspecified: 43.1%

East Asia and Pacific: 0.8%
Europe and Central Asia: 0.6%
Latin America and the Caribbean: 3.1%

Middle East and North Africa: 9.3%

South Asia: 4.8%

Sub-Saharan Africa: 38.2%

Notes: Funding to these regions includes all flows inside and outside an
appeal that had been reported to OCHA/FTS and attributed to a region at
the time of the database download on 8th May 2008. Non-attributed flows
are shown as 'unspecified'.
Source: OCHA/FTS.

Sectoral distribution of funding to UN Appeals, 2007 (%)

■ Country funding   ○ UN appeal budget

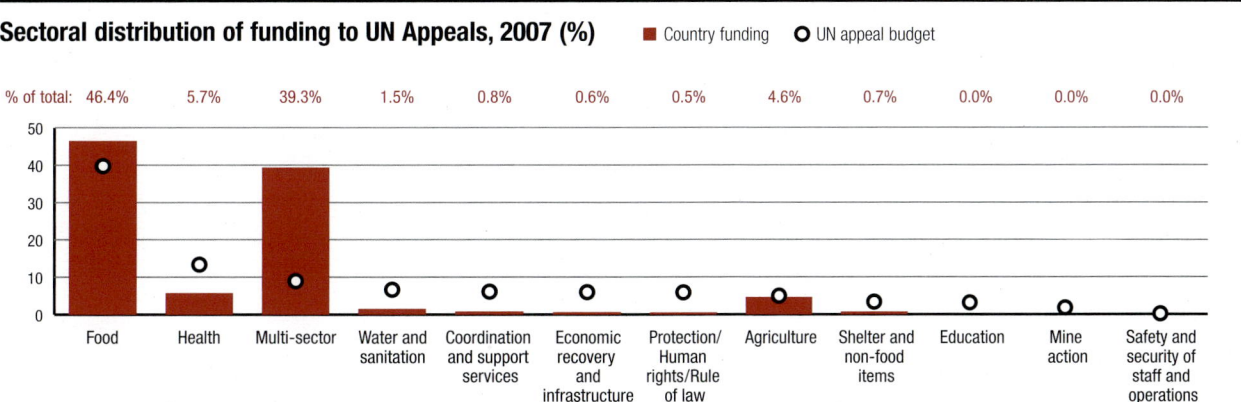

% of total:	46.4%	5.7%	39.3%	1.5%	0.8%	0.6%	0.5%	4.6%	0.7%	0.0%	0.0%	0.0%

Food | Health | Multi-sector | Water and sanitation | Coordination and support services | Economic recovery and infrastructure | Protection/ Human rights/Rule of law | Agriculture | Shelter and non-food items | Education | Mine action | Safety and security of staff and operations

Notes: Funding to these sectors include only flows inside an appeal that had been reported to OCHA/FTS and attributed to a sector at the time of the database download on
30th June 2008. Distribution of budget based on all 2007 UN appeals.
Source: OCHA/FTS.

Germany

Germany is the 16th most generous humanitarian donor among the OECD/DAC group, relative to its size. Its bilateral humanitarian aid amounted to US$284 million in 2007. Germany has a comprehensive humanitarian action policy contained in its humanitarian report to parliament prepared by its Federal Foreign Office (FFO). Responsibility for humanitarian action is split between the FFO, responsible for humanitarian response, and its Federal Ministry for Economic Cooperation and Development (BMZ), which provides transitional assistance and food aid, and over-sees the integration of relief and development activities. The guiding principles for its humanitarian aid are laid down in its 1993 Twelve Basic Rules of Humanitarian Assistance Abroad, subscribed to by all members of the multi-stakeholder Humanitarian Aid Coordination Centre (HACC). German budget legislation largely restricts support of humanitarian aid organisations to earmarked project financing only, with a few exceptions destined for various UN relief agencies. Germany has a designated budget line for DRR, through which it disburses between 5 and 10 per-cent of its budget. National and international NGOs receive a large share of German aid. The BMZ can offer three-year funding programmes that are renewed annually.

Sources: DAC Peer Review for Germany (OECD, 2006); Federal Foreign Office, at: http://www.auswaertiges-amt.de

HRI 2008 scores by pillar

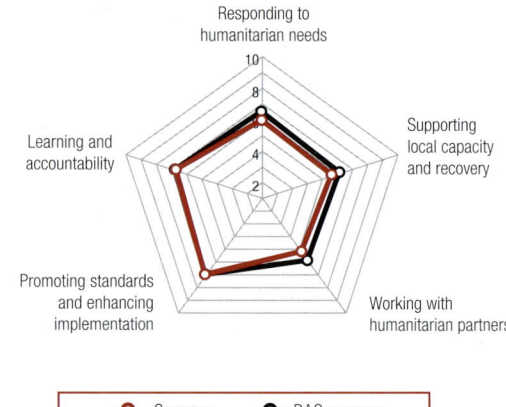

Germany — DAC average

HRI 2008 results

HIGHEST SCORES	SCORE	RANK
Responding to humanitarian needs		
Independence	8.29	4
Impartiality	8.83	2
Neutrality	8.69	1
Working with humanitarian partners		
Predictable funding	8.04	5
Funding to NGOs	10.00	1

LOWEST SCORES	SCORE	RANK
Supporting local capacity and recovery		
Aligned to long-term development aims	6.56	21
Strengthening government capacity for response and mitigation	5.52	20
Working with humanitarian partners		
Helping governments and local communities achieve better coordination	5.59	20
Unearmarked funding	2.68	20
Learning and accountability		
Encouraging regular evaluations	6.83	21

Overview of humanitarian aid	Germany		Share of total DAC (%)	
	2006	2007[4]	2006	2007[4]
Total humanitarian aid (estimated), of which:	374.7	302.4	4.5	3.3
Bilateral[1]	357.4	283.9	5.3	4.5
Multilateral[2] (estimated*), of which:	17.3	18.5	1.1	1.2
Central Emergency Response **Fund	0.0	6.3	0.0	1.7
Funding to other pooled mechanisms[3]***	0.0	0.0	0.0	0.0
Official development assistance	10,435	12,267	10.0	11.8
			DAC average	
Total humanitarian aid per capita (USD)[5]	5	4	22	23
Total humanitarian aid per / official development assistance	5.3	3.7	12.2	11.3
Overseas development assistance / gross national income	0.36	0.37	0.46	0.44

Notes: All data are given in current USD m unless otherwise indicated.

(1) Based on OECD/DAC definition of bilateral humanitarian aid, which is provided directly by a donor country to a recipient country and includes non-core earmarked contributions to multilateral humanitarian organisations known as multi-bilateral aid.

(2) Core unearmarked humanitarian flows to UNHCR, UNICEF, WFP, UNRWA, UN/OCHA, ICRC and IFRC. Does not include contributions through EC. 2007 core funding to UNRWA and ICRC proxied by 2006 data.

(3) For 2006, these were IFRC's Disaster Relief Emergency Fund (DREF), Sudan Common Humanitarian Fund (CHF), Democratic Republic of Congo (DRC) Pooled Fund, and Emergency Response Funds (ERF) for DRC, Indonesia, Somalia, Republic of Congo, and Ethiopia. For 2007, these were DREF, CHF, DRC Pooled Fund, and ERFs for Central African Republic, DRC, Ethiopia, Indonesia, and Iraq.

(4) All 2007 OECD/DAC data are provisional.

(5) Where 2007 population data not available, 2006 data used.

Sources: All data from OECD-DAC except: (*) UNHCR, UNICEF, WFP, UNRWA, UN/OCHA, ICRC and IFRC; (**) OCHA; (***) OCHA, IFRC; US Federal Reserve.

Main channels of humanitarian aid, 2007

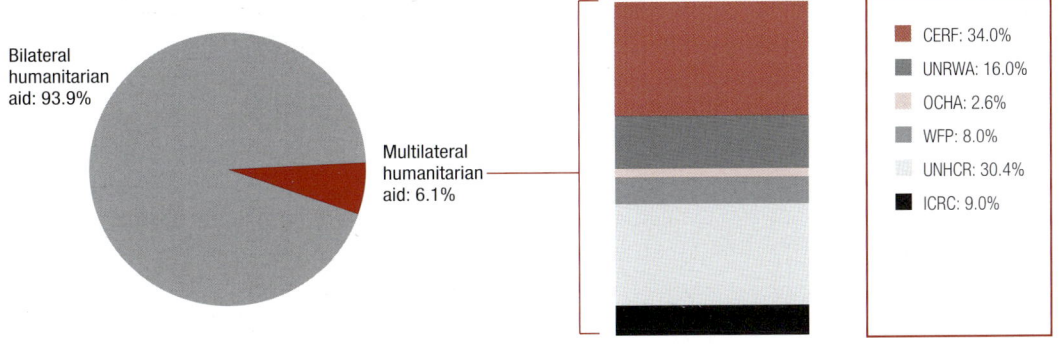

Bilateral humanitarian aid: 93.9%

Multilateral humanitarian aid: 6.1%

- CERF: 34.0%
- UNRWA: 16.0%
- OCHA: 2.6%
- WFP: 8.0%
- UNHCR: 30.4%
- ICRC: 9.0%

Notes: see notes (1), (2) and (4) in Overview of humanitarian aid table.
Sources: Bilateral humanitarian aid: OECD-DAC. Estimated multilateral humanitarian aid: UNHCR, UNICEF, WFP, UNRWA, UN/OCHA, ICRC and IFRC.

Funding per emergency, 2007

Crisis	(USD m)	(% of total)
Afghanistan	32.2	13.9
Sudan	23.3	10.1
Somalia	12.7	5.5
Democratic Republic of Congo	12.2	5.2
Chad	9.3	4.0
Uganda	6.8	2.9
Iraq (incl. Iraqi refugees in neighbouring countries)	6.5	2.8
Zimbabwe	5.9	2.6
occupied Palestinian territories	5.2	2.3
Burundi	5.2	2.2
Total top 10 emergencies	**119.3**	**51.4**
Total	**232.0**	**100.0**

Notes: Funding to these emergencies includes all flows inside and outside an appeal that had been reported to OCHA/FTS and attributed to the emergency at the time of the database download on 8th May 2008.
Source: OCHA/FTS.

Regional distribution of funding, 2007

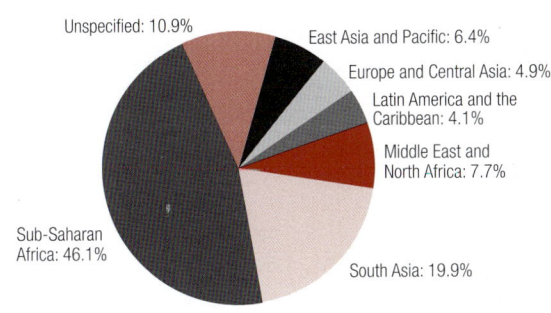

Unspecified: 10.9%
East Asia and Pacific: 6.4%
Europe and Central Asia: 4.9%
Latin America and the Caribbean: 4.1%
Middle East and North Africa: 7.7%
South Asia: 19.9%
Sub-Saharan Africa: 46.1%

Notes: Funding to these regions includes all flows inside and outside an appeal that had been reported to OCHA/FTS and attributed to a region at the time of the database download on 8th May 2008. Non-attributed flows are shown as 'unspecified'.
Source: OCHA/FTS.

Sectoral distribution of funding to UN Appeals, 2007 (%)

- Country funding
- UN appeal budget

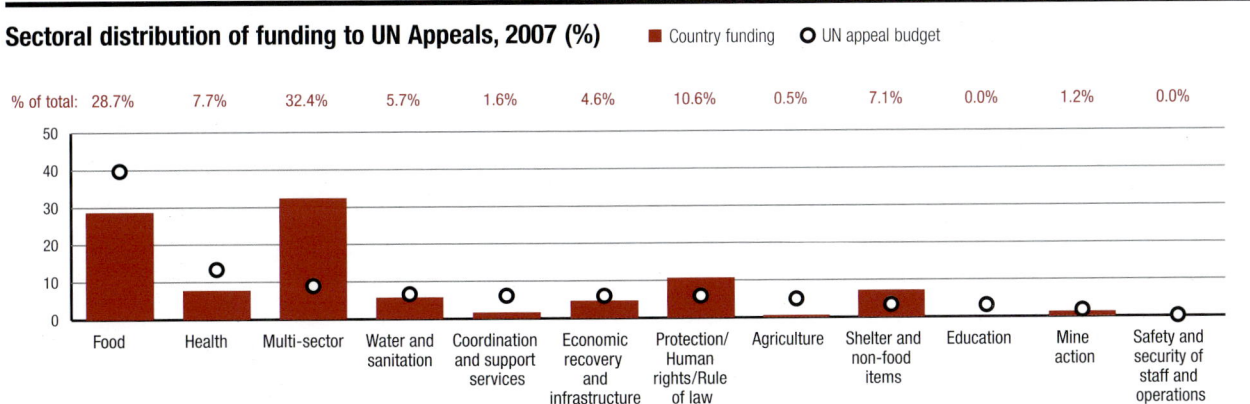

	Food	Health	Multi-sector	Water and sanitation	Coordination and support services	Economic recovery and infrastructure	Protection/ Human rights/Rule of law	Agriculture	Shelter and non-food items	Education	Mine action	Safety and security of staff and operations
% of total:	28.7%	7.7%	32.4%	5.7%	1.6%	4.6%	10.6%	0.5%	7.1%	0.0%	1.2%	0.0%

Notes: Funding to these sectors include only flows inside an appeal that had been reported to OCHA/FTS and attributed to a sector at the time of the database download on 30th June 2008. Distribution of budget based on all 2007 UN appeals.
Source: OCHA/FTS.

Greece

Greece is the 17th most generous humanitarian donor among the OECD/DAC group, relative to its size. Its bilateral humanitarian aid amounted to US$13 million in 2007. The Foreign Ministry's International Development Cooperation Department (Hellenic Aid) is responsible for monitoring, coordinating, supervising and promoting humanitarian assistance. Humanitarian aid is channelled in two categories: emergency humanitarian and food programmes (which can be more protracted and address multi-year crises) and emergency distress relief activities, such as the provision of in-kind gifts, mobilisation of Greek civil society and provision of support, personnel, and other resources from other ministries, particularly Defence and the Ministries of Health and Civil Protection. Policies and principles underpinning Greek humanitarian assistance are set out within the five-year programme approved by the Inter-Ministerial Committee. Annual planning is based on this framework, with Hellenic Aid requesting proposals for its humanitarian programme, identifying countries and sectoral priorities which should guide implementing organisations. Greece does not carry out formal needs assessments, relying on large NGOs for this purpose and, if relevant, on the Greek diaspora of a particular country. By law, Hellenic Aid can only finance Greek or international NGOs and requires NGOs to have a local partner in affected countries. Its contributions to multilateral organisations are typically earmarked.

Sources: Hellenic Aid; DAC Peer Review for Greece (OECD, 2006).

HRI 2008 scores by pillar

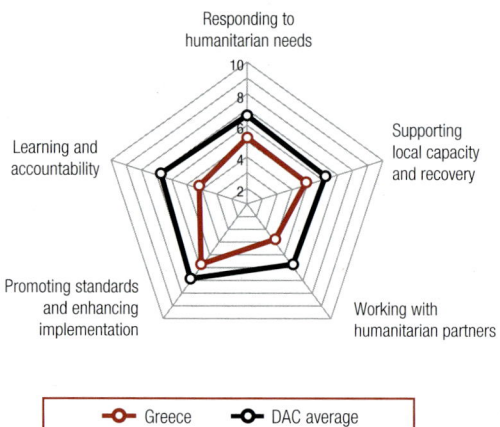

Greece — DAC average

HRI 2008 results

HIGHEST SCORES	SCORE	RANK
Responding to humanitarian needs		
Timely funding to complex emergencies with UN appeals	6.92	10
Funding to crisis countries with historical ties and geographical proximity	9.87	6

LOWEST SCORES	SCORE	RANK
Responding to humanitarian needs		
Impartiality	7.45	23
Supporting local capacity and recovery		
Involvement of beneficiaries in monitoring and evaluation	5.64	23
Working with humanitarian partners		
Predictable funding	5.65	23
Promoting standards and enhancing implementation		
Facilitating safe humanitarian access	4.29	23
Learning and accountability		
Supporting learning and accountability initiatives	4.51	23

Overview of humanitarian aid	Greece		Share of total DAC (%)	
	2006	2007[4]	2006	2007[4]
Total humanitarian aid (estimated), of which:	21.6	14.9	0.3	0.2
Bilateral[1]	19.2	12.7	0.3	0.2
Multilateral[2] (estimated*), of which:	2.4	2.3	0.2	0.1
Central Emergency Response Fund**	0.1	0.0	0.0	0.0
Funding to other pooled mechanisms[3]***	0.0	0.0	0.0	0.0
Official development assistance	424	501	0.4	0.5

			DAC average	
Total humanitarian aid per capita (USD)[5]	2	1	22	23
Total humanitarian aid per / official development assistance	11.4	6.0	12.2	11.3
Overseas development assistance / gross national income	0.17	0.16	0.46	0.44

Notes: All data are given in current USD m unless otherwise indicated.
(1) Based on OECD/DAC definition of bilateral humanitarian aid, which is provided directly by a donor country to a recipient country and includes non-core earmarked contributions to multilateral humanitarian organisations known as multi-bilateral aid.
(2) Core unearmarked humanitarian flows to UNHCR, UNICEF, WFP, UNRWA, UN/OCHA, ICRC and IFRC. Does not include contributions through EC. 2007 core funding to UNRWA and ICRC proxied by 2006 data.
(3) For 2006, these were IFRC's Disaster Relief Emergency Fund (DREF), Sudan Common Humanitarian Fund (CHF), Democratic Republic of Congo (DRC) Pooled Fund, and Emergency Response Funds (ERF) for DRC, Indonesia, Somalia, Republic of Congo, and Ethiopia. For 2007, these were DREF, CHF, DRC Pooled Fund, and ERFs for Central African Republic, DRC, Ethiopia, Indonesia, and Iraq.
(4) All 2007 OECD/DAC data are provisional.
(5) Where 2007 population data not available, 2006 data used.
Sources: All data from OECD-DAC except: (*) UNHCR, UNICEF, WFP, UNRWA, UN/OCHA, ICRC and IFRC; (**) OCHA; (***) OCHA, IFRC; US Federal Reserve.

Main channels of humanitarian aid, 2007

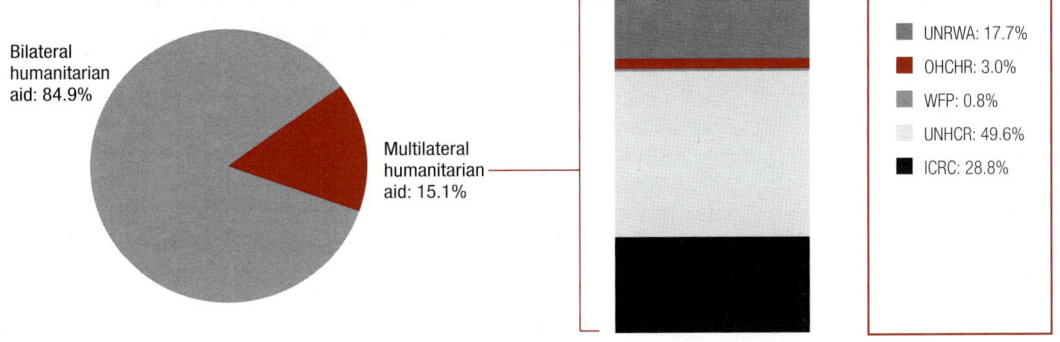

Bilateral humanitarian aid: 84.9%

Multilateral humanitarian aid: 15.1%

- UNRWA: 17.7%
- OHCHR: 3.0%
- WFP: 0.8%
- UNHCR: 49.6%
- ICRC: 28.8%

Notes: see notes (1), (2) and (4) in Overview of humanitarian aid table.
Sources: Bilateral humanitarian aid: OECD-DAC. Estimated multilateral humanitarian aid: UNHCR, UNICEF, WFP, UNRWA, UN/OCHA, ICRC and IFRC.

Funding per emergency, 2007

Crisis	(USD m)	(% of total)
Lebanon - Refugee Camp Crisis - May	0.7	12.6
Iraq (incl. Iraqi refugees in neighbouring countries)	0.7	11.6
Sudan	0.6	9.9
occupied Palestinian territories	0.4	7.3
West Africa	0.4	7.3
Bangladesh - Cyclone Sidr - November	0.3	5.3
Viet Nam - floods - August	0.3	5.3
Lebanon	0.3	5.1
Central America - Hurricane Felix - September	0.2	3.9
Ethiopia	0.2	3.8
Total top 10 emergencies	**4.0**	**72.1**
Total	**5.6**	**100.0**

Notes: Funding to these emergencies includes all flows inside and outside an appeal that had been reported to OCHA/FTS and attributed to the emergency at the time of the database download on 8th May 2008.
Source: OCHA/FTS.

Regional distribution of funding, 2007

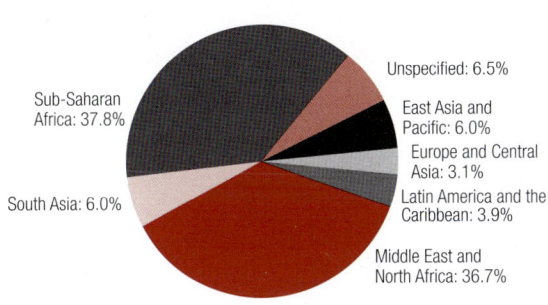

Sub-Saharan Africa: 37.8%

South Asia: 6.0%

Unspecified: 6.5%

East Asia and Pacific: 6.0%

Europe and Central Asia: 3.1%

Latin America and the Caribbean: 3.9%

Middle East and North Africa: 36.7%

Notes: Funding to these regions includes all flows inside and outside an appeal that had been reported to OCHA/FTS and attributed to a region at the time of the database download on 8th May 2008. Non-attributed flows are shown as 'unspecified'.
Source: OCHA/FTS.

Sectoral distribution of funding to UN Appeals, 2007 (%)

■ Country funding ○ UN appeal budget

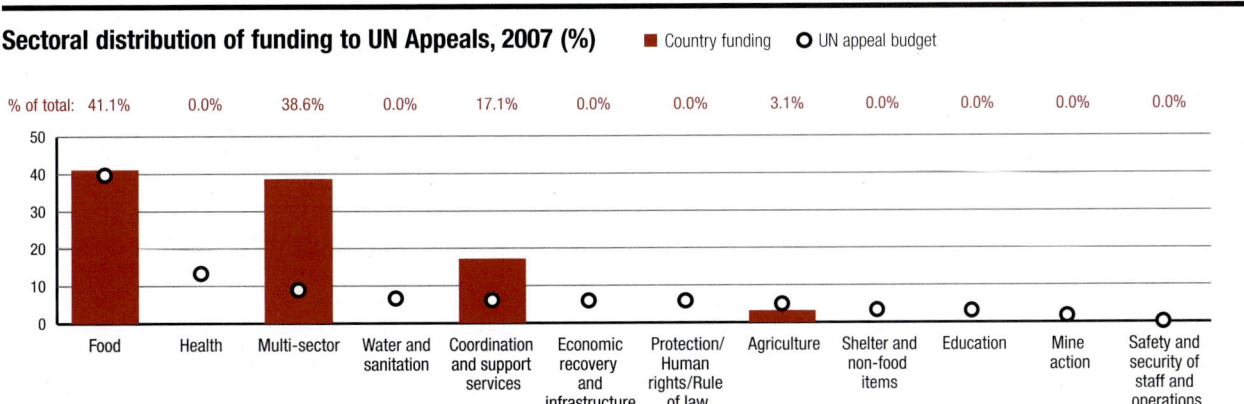

% of total: 41.1% 0.0% 38.6% 0.0% 17.1% 0.0% 0.0% 3.1% 0.0% 0.0% 0.0% 0.0%

Food | Health | Multi-sector | Water and sanitation | Coordination and support services | Economic recovery and infrastructure | Protection/ Human rights/Rule of law | Agriculture | Shelter and non-food items | Education | Mine action | Safety and security of staff and operations

Notes: Funding to these sectors include only flows inside an appeal that had been reported to OCHA/FTS and attributed to a sector at the time of the database download on 30th June 2008. Distribution of budget based on all 2007 UN appeals.
Source: OCHA/FTS.

Ireland

Ireland is the 4th most generous humanitarian donor among the OECD/DAC group, relative to its size. Its bilateral humanitarian aid amounted to US$129 million in 2007. Irish Aid, the official development cooperation programme managed by the Department of Foreign Affairs has primary responsibility for the government's overall international humanitarian response. Although Ireland has not crafted a stand-alone Humanitarian Policy document, their policy is contained in the 2005 *White Paper on Irish Aid,* which is closely aligned with the GHD initiative. Ireland also has a GHD Domestic Implementation Plan and budget lines which allow it to pursue a twin-track approach of emergency and recovery assistance. Its Emergency Preparedness and Post-Emergency Recovery Fund (EPPR) aims to return post-emergency societies to their livelihoods, supporting capacity-building for emergency preparedness. Irish Aid has ongoing multi-year funding relationships with several key humanitarian agencies. Ireland has boosted its own operational capabilities through its Rapid Response Initiative (RRI), which includes measures to enhance the emergency response capacities of international humanitarian response agencies.

Sources: GHD Domestic Implementation Plan for Ireland; Irish Aid, at: http://www.irishaid.gov.ie

HRI 2008 scores by pillar

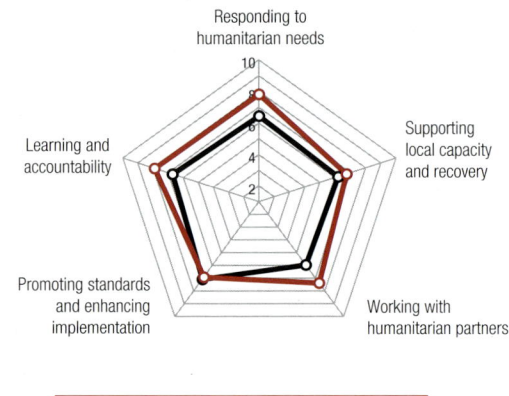

Ireland — DAC average

HRI 2008 results

HIGHEST SCORES	SCORE	RANK
Responding to humanitarian needs		
Commitment to on-going crises	8.33	1
Generosity of humanitarian assistance	8.43	4
Supporting local capacity and recovery		
Funding to strengthen local capacity	10.00	1
Working with humanitarian partners		
Funding to CERF and other quick disbursement mechanisms	10.00	1
Funding UN coordination mechanisms and common services	10.00	1
Learning and accountability		
Participation in main accountability initiatives	10.00	1

LOWEST SCORES	SCORE	RANK
Supporting local capacity and recovery		
Ensuring rapid recovery of sustainable livelihoods	6.60	20
Strengthening government capacity for response and mitigation	5.07	23
Working with humanitarian partners		
Reducing earmarking	5.87	20
Helping governments and local communities achieve better coordination	5.37	21
Promoting standards and enhancing implementation		
Donor engagement in protection and assistance to civilians	7.20	20

Overview of humanitarian aid

	Ireland		Share of total DAC (%)	
	2006	2007[4]	2006	2007[4]
Total humanitarian aid (estimated), of which:	141.0	198.4	1.7	2.2
Bilateral[1]	87.2	129.2	1.3	2.1
Multilateral[2] (estimated*), of which:	53.8	69.2	3.5	4.3
Central Emergency Response Fund**	12.6	26.3	4.4	6.9
Funding to other pooled mechanisms[3]***	3.8	29.2	1.3	3.6
Official development assistance	1,022	1,190	1.0	1.1
			DAC average	
Total humanitarian aid per capita (USD)[5]	33	47	22	23
Total humanitarian aid per / official development assistance	22.3	24.1	12.2	11.3
Overseas development assistance / gross national income	0.54	0.54	0.46	0.44

Notes: All data are given in current USD m unless otherwise indicated.

(1) Based on OECD/DAC definition of bilateral humanitarian aid, which is provided directly by a donor country to a recipient country and includes non-core earmarked contributions to multilateral humanitarian organisations known as multi-bilateral aid.

(2) Core unearmarked humanitarian flows to UNHCR, UNICEF, WFP, UNRWA, UN/OCHA, ICRC and IFRC. Does not include contributions through EC. 2007 core funding to UNRWA and ICRC proxied by 2006 data.

(3) For 2006, these were IFRC's Disaster Relief Emergency Fund (DREF), Sudan Common Humanitarian Fund (CHF), Democratic Republic of Congo (DRC) Pooled Fund, and Emergency Response Funds (ERF) for DRC, Indonesia, Somalia, Republic of Congo, and Ethiopia. For 2007, these were DREF, CHF, DRC Pooled Fund, and ERFs for Central African Republic, DRC, Ethiopia, Indonesia, and Iraq.

(4) All 2007 OECD/DAC data are provisional.

(5) Where 2007 population data not available, 2006 data used.

Sources: All data from OECD-DAC except: (*) UNHCR, UNICEF, WFP, UNRWA, UN/OCHA, ICRC and IFRC; (**) OCHA; (***) OCHA, IFRC; US Federal Reserve.

Main channels of humanitarian aid, 2007

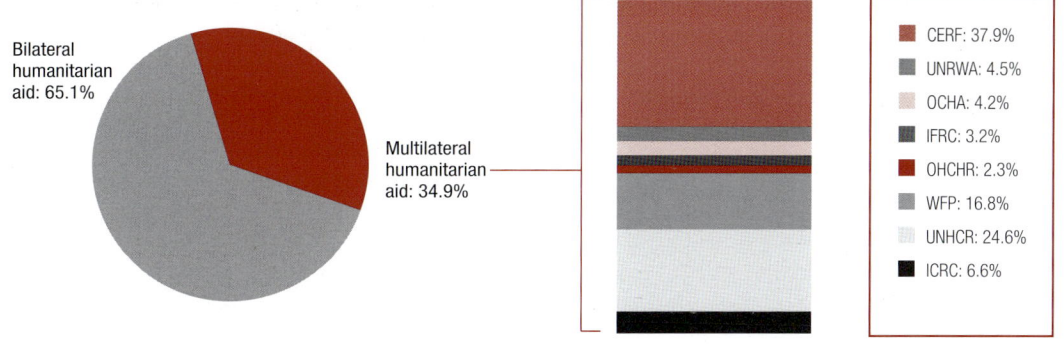

Bilateral humanitarian aid: 65.1%

Multilateral humanitarian aid: 34.9%

- CERF: 37.9%
- UNRWA: 4.5%
- OCHA: 4.2%
- IFRC: 3.2%
- OHCHR: 2.3%
- WFP: 16.8%
- UNHCR: 24.6%
- ICRC: 6.6%

Notes: see notes (1), (2) and (4) in Overview of humanitarian aid table.
Sources: Bilateral humanitarian aid: OECD-DAC. Estimated multilateral humanitarian aid: UNHCR, UNICEF, WFP, UNRWA, UN/OCHA, ICRC and IFRC.

Funding per emergency, 2007

Crisis	(USD m)	(% of total)
Sudan	17.9	9.4
Liberia	11.9	6.2
Democratic Republic of Congo	10.1	5.3
Somalia	9.9	5.2
Chad	8.7	4.5
Iraq (incl. Iraqi refugees in neighbouring countries)	7.6	4.0
Sierra Leone	6.6	3.5
Malawi	5.7	3.0
Zimbabwe	5.7	3.0
Central African Republic	5.5	2.9
Total top 10 emergencies	**89.4**	**46.9**
Total	**190.6**	**100.0**

Notes: Funding to these emergencies includes all flows inside and outside an appeal that had been reported to OCHA/FTS and attributed to the emergency at the time of the database download on 8th May 2008.
Source: OCHA/FTS.

Regional distribution of funding, 2007

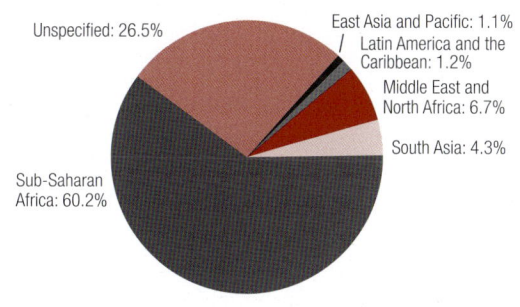

Unspecified: 26.5%

East Asia and Pacific: 1.1%
Latin America and the Caribbean: 1.2%
Middle East and North Africa: 6.7%
South Asia: 4.3%

Sub-Saharan Africa: 60.2%

Notes: Funding to these regions includes all flows inside and outside an appeal that had been reported to OCHA/FTS and attributed to a region at the time of the database download on 8th May 2008. Non-attributed flows are shown as 'unspecified'.
Source: OCHA/FTS.

Sectoral distribution of funding to UN Appeals, 2007 (%)

■ Country funding ○ UN appeal budget

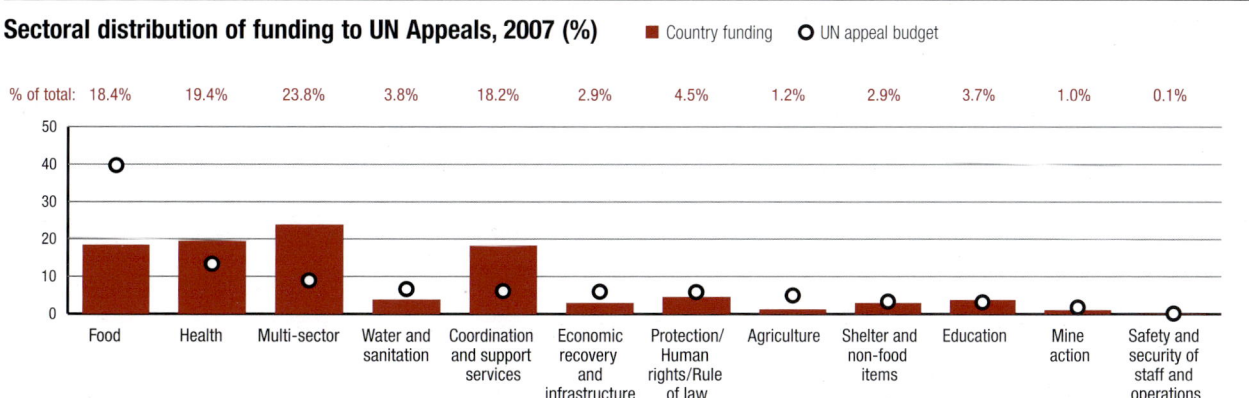

| % of total: | 18.4% | 19.4% | 23.8% | 3.8% | 18.2% | 2.9% | 4.5% | 1.2% | 2.9% | 3.7% | 1.0% | 0.1% |

Food | Health | Multi-sector | Water and sanitation | Coordination and support services | Economic recovery and infrastructure | Protection/ Human rights/Rule of law | Agriculture | Shelter and non-food items | Education | Mine action | Safety and security of staff and operations

Notes: Funding to these sectors include only flows inside an appeal that had been reported to OCHA/FTS and attributed to a sector at the time of the database download on 30th June 2008. Distribution of budget based on all 2007 UN appeals.
Source: OCHA/FTS.

Italy

Italy is the 18th most generous humanitarian donor among the OECD/DAC group, relative to its size. Its bilateral humanitarian aid amounted to US$78 million in 2007. Humanitarian assistance is conducted by the Ministry of Foreign Affairs (DGCS). In order to maintain full flexibility to adapt different responses to different crises, the DGCS does not have a defined strategy for humanitarian aid, but is generally guided by the EC Code of Conduct and the EC Consensus of Humanitarian Aid. Italy does not have a crisis cell on permanent call or standby and does not actively participate in needs assessments, relying to a very large extent on UN sources for this purpose. However, funding to crises appears to be less guided by needs, as DGCS endeavours to specialise on a small number of interventions where it can make a difference. Consequently, it targets those countries in which it has prior experience. Legally, the DGCS may fund any organisations, but in practice, it prefers Italian NGOs. It does not have multi-year funding arrangements in place, but may informally commit to extended programmes.

Source: Ministry of Foreign Affairs.

HRI 2008 scores by pillar

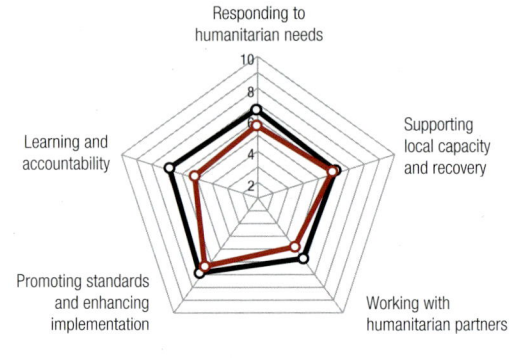

HRI 2008 results

HIGHEST SCORES	SCORE	RANK
Responding to humanitarian needs		
Timely funding to onset disasters and IFRC emergency appeals	8.51	3
Funding to crisis countries with historical ties and geographical proximity	9.86	7
Supporting local capacity and recovery		
Strengthening local capacity for response and mitigation	6.68	7
Strengthening government capacity for response and mitigation	6.73	3
Working with humanitarian partners		
Helping governments and local communities achieve better coordination	6.72	5

LOWEST SCORES	SCORE	RANK
Responding to humanitarian needs		
Reallocation of funds from other crises	5.06	21
Timely funding to complex emergencies with UN appeals	1.57	21
Supporting local capacity and recovery		
Funding to strengthen local capacity	1.43	23
Working with humanitarian partners		
Predictable funding	6.79	21
Learning and accountability		
Supporting learning and accountability initiatives	5.87	21

Overview of humanitarian aid

	Italy			Share of total DAC (%)	
	2006	2007[4]		2006	2007[4]
Total humanitarian aid (estimated), of which:	88.5	91.0		1.1	1.0
Bilateral[1]	74.0	78.4		1.1	1.2
Multilateral[2] (estimated*), of which:	14.5	12.6		0.9	0.8
Central Emergency Response Fund**	0.0	2.7		0.0	0.7
Funding to other pooled mechanisms[3]***	0.0	0.0		0.0	0.0
Official development assistance	3,641	3,929		3.5	3.8
				DAC average	
Total humanitarian aid per capita (USD)[5]	2	2		22	23
Total humanitarian aid per / official development assistance	4.4	7.4		12.2	11.3
Overseas development assistance / gross national income	0.20	0.19		0.46	0.44

Notes: All data are given in current USD m unless otherwise indicated.

(1) Based on OECD/DAC definition of bilateral humanitarian aid, which is provided directly by a donor country to a recipient country and includes non-core earmarked contributions to multilateral humanitarian organisations known as multi-bilateral aid.

(2) Core unearmarked humanitarian flows to UNHCR, UNICEF, WFP, UNRWA, UN/OCHA, ICRC and IFRC. Does not include contributions through EC. 2007 core funding to UNRWA and ICRC proxied by 2006 data.

(3) For 2006, these were IFRC's Disaster Relief Emergency Fund (DREF), Sudan Common Humanitarian Fund (CHF), Democratic Republic of Congo (DRC) Pooled Fund, and Emergency Response Funds (ERF) for DRC, Indonesia, Somalia, Republic of Congo, and Ethiopia. For 2007, these were DREF, CHF, DRC Pooled Fund, and ERFs for Central African Republic, DRC, Ethiopia, Indonesia, and Iraq.

(4) All 2007 OECD/DAC data are provisional.

(5) Where 2007 population data not available, 2006 data used.

Sources: All data from OECD-DAC except: (*) UNHCR, UNICEF, WFP, UNRWA, UN/OCHA, ICRC and IFRC; (**) OCHA; (***) OCHA, IFRC; US Federal Reserve.

Main channels of humanitarian aid, 2007

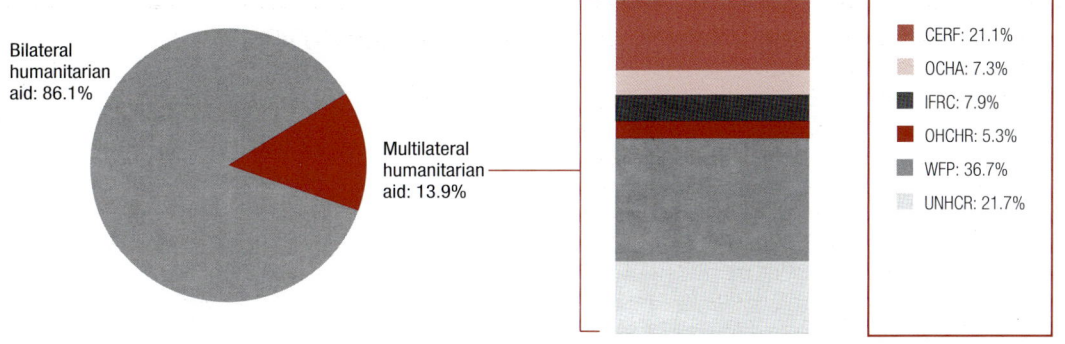

Bilateral humanitarian aid: 86.1%

Multilateral humanitarian aid: 13.9%

- CERF: 21.1%
- OCHA: 7.3%
- IFRC: 7.9%
- OHCHR: 5.3%
- WFP: 36.7%
- UNHCR: 21.7%

Notes: see notes (1), (2) and (4) in Overview of humanitarian aid table.
Sources: Bilateral humanitarian aid: OECD-DAC. Estimated multilateral humanitarian aid: UNHCR, UNICEF, WFP, UNRWA, UN/OCHA, ICRC and IFRC.

Funding per emergency, 2007

Crisis	(USD m)	(% of total)
Lebanon	12.8	11.4
Sudan	12.6	11.2
Somalia	7.8	7.0
Afghanistan	7.8	6.9
occupied Palestinian territories	7.7	6.9
Iraq (incl. Iraqi refugees in neighbouring countries)	5.5	4.9
Bangladesh - Cyclone Sidr - November	4.5	4.0
Korea, DPR	3.1	2.8
Uganda	2.5	2.2
Mauritania	2.3	2.0
Total top 10 emergencies	66.6	59.3
Total	112.3	100.0

Notes: Funding to these emergencies includes all flows inside and outside an appeal that had been reported to OCHA/FTS and attributed to the emergency at the time of the database download on 8th May 2008.
Source: OCHA/FTS.

Regional distribution of funding, 2007

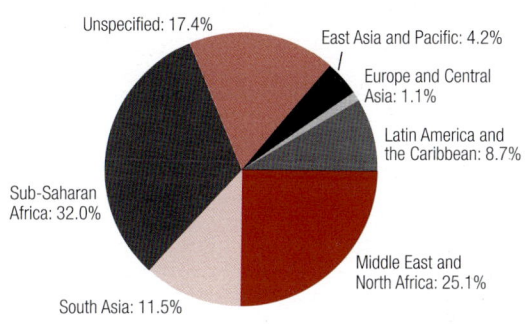

Unspecified: 17.4%
East Asia and Pacific: 4.2%
Europe and Central Asia: 1.1%
Latin America and the Caribbean: 8.7%
Middle East and North Africa: 25.1%
South Asia: 11.5%
Sub-Saharan Africa: 32.0%

Notes: Funding to these regions includes all flows inside and outside an appeal that had been reported to OCHA/FTS and attributed to a region at the time of the database download on 8th May 2008. Non-attributed flows are shown as 'unspecified'.
Source: OCHA/FTS.

Sectoral distribution of funding to UN Appeals, 2007 (%)

■ Country funding ○ UN appeal budget

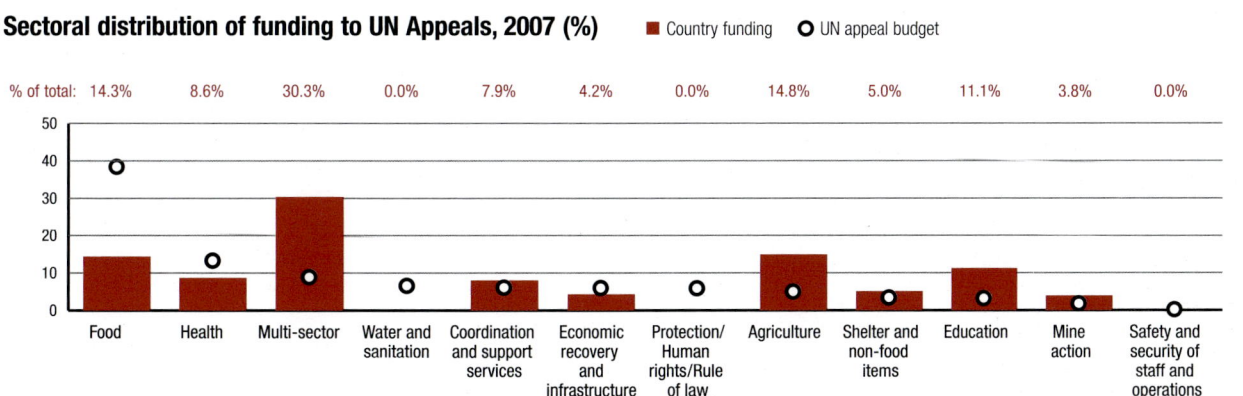

% of total: 14.3% 8.6% 30.3% 0.0% 7.9% 4.2% 0.0% 14.8% 5.0% 11.1% 3.8% 0.0%

Food, Health, Multi-sector, Water and sanitation, Coordination and support services, Economic recovery and infrastructure, Protection/Human rights/Rule of law, Agriculture, Shelter and non-food items, Education, Mine action, Safety and security of staff and operations

Notes: Funding to these sectors include only flows inside an appeal that had been reported to OCHA/FTS and attributed to a sector at the time of the database download on 30th June 2008. Distribution of budget based on all 2007 UN appeals.
Source: OCHA/FTS.

Japan

Japan is the 20th most generous humanitarian donor among the OECD/DAC group, relative to its size. Its bilateral humanitarian aid amounted to US$98 million in 2007. The main actors in humanitarian conflict-related assistance are the Ministry of Foreign Affairs and the Japan International Cooperation Agency (JICA). The latter is in charge of grant aid and technical assistance and falls under the portfolio of the MFA. Japan's humanitarian assistance is underpinned by the 1987 Law Concerning the Dispatch of Japan Disaster Relief Teams (JDR Law), which provides a comprehensive basis for international disaster relief but restricts its scope to natural disasters and man-made disasters other than those arising from conflict. In the early 1990s, the Japanese government enacted another law, in connection with UN Peacekeeping Operations, which expanded its international humanitarian relief operations. Since 2000, policies have shifted to emphasis the importance of integrating relief and development, which has now become a priority area. Most humanitarian assistance is channelled through UN agencies, although Japan has recently begun to increase its support for NGOs and to diversify its areas of assistance. JDR teams that are sent out to major disaster areas around the globe specialise on SAR operations and provide medical care or undertake rehabilitation work.

Sources: DAC Peer Review for Japan (OECD, 2004); Overseas Development Institute.

HRI 2008 scores by pillar

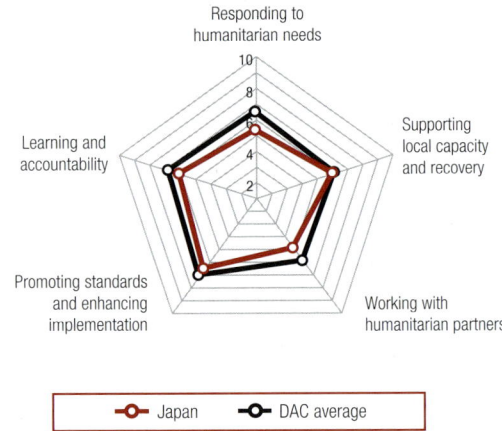

Japan ———— DAC average

HRI 2008 results

HIGHEST SCORES	SCORE	RANK
Responding to humanitarian needs		
Distribution of funding relative to ECHO's Crisis and Vulnerability Indices	9.37	5
Supporting local capacity and recovery		
Strengthening preparedness	7.31	3
Working with humanitarian partners		
Supporting UN leadership and coordination role	8.18	5
Promoting standards and enhancing implementation		
Affirming primary role of civilian organizations	9.10	2
Supporting needs of internally displaced persons	7.86	2

LOWEST SCORES	SCORE	RANK
Responding to humanitarian needs		
Funding to crisis countries with historical ties and geographical proximity	1.43	22
Funding to forgotten emergencies and those with low media coverage	1.43	22
Working with humanitarian partners		
Funding to NGOs	1.44	22
Unearmarked funding	1.73	22
Promoting standards and enhancing implementation		
Implementing refugee law	1.68	21

Overview of humanitarian aid

	Japan		Share of total DAC (%)	
	2006	2007[4]	2006	2007[4]
Total humanitarian aid (estimated), of which:	232.7	114.2	2.8	1.2
Bilateral[1]	182.8	98.1	2.7	1.6
Multilateral[2] (estimated*), of which:	49.9	16.1	3.2	1.0
Central Emergency Response Fund**	7.5	0.0	2.6	0.0
Funding to other pooled mechanisms[3]***	0.0	0.0	0.0	0.0
Official development assistance	11,187	7,691	10.7	7.4

			DAC average	
Total humanitarian aid per capita (USD)[5]	2	1	22	23
Total humanitarian aid per / official development assistance	3.2	2.0	12.2	11.3
Overseas development assistance / gross national income	0.25	0.17	0.46	0.44

Notes: All data are given in current USD m unless otherwise indicated.

1　Based on OECD/DAC definition of bilateral humanitarian aid, which is provided directly by a donor country to a recipient country and includes non-core earmarked contributions to multilateral humanitarian organisations known as multi-bilateral aid.

2　Core unearmarked humanitarian flows to UNHCR, UNICEF, WFP, UNRWA, UN/OCHA, ICRC and IFRC. 2007 core funding to UNRWA and ICRC proxied by 2006 data.

3　For 2006, these were IFRC's Disaster Relief Emergency Fund (DREF), Sudan Common Humanitarian Fund (CHF), Democratic Republic of Congo (DRC) Pooled Fund, and Emergency Response Funds (ERF) for DRC, Indonesia, Somalia, Republic of Congo, and Ethiopia. For 2007, these were DREF, CHF, DRC Pooled Fund, and ERFs for Central African Republic, DRC, Ethiopia, Indonesia, and Iraq.

4　All 2007 OECD/DAC data are provisional.

5　Where 2007 population data not available, 2006 data used.

Sources: All data from OECD-DAC except: (*) UNHCR, UNICEF, WFP, UNRWA, UN/OCHA, ICRC and IFRC; (**) OCHA; (***) OCHA, IFRC; US Federal Reserve.

Main channels of humanitarian aid, 2007

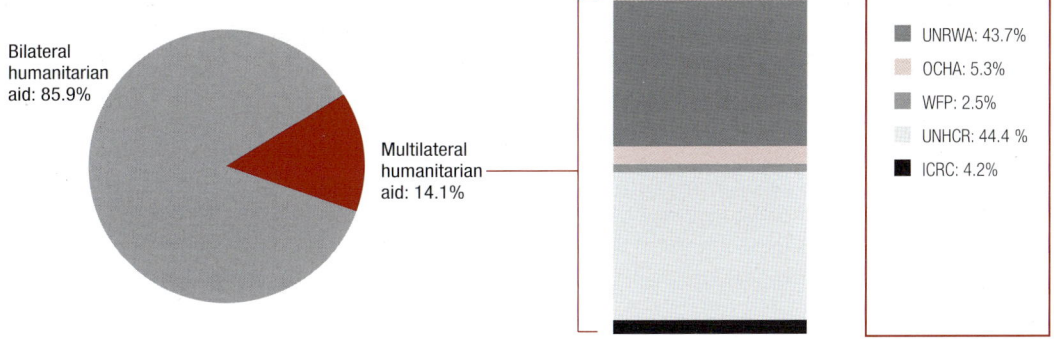

Bilateral humanitarian aid: 85.9%

Multilateral humanitarian aid: 14.1%

- UNRWA: 43.7%
- OCHA: 5.3%
- WFP: 2.5%
- UNHCR: 44.4 %
- ICRC: 4.2%

Notes: see notes (1), (2) and (4) in Overview of humanitarian aid table.
Sources: Bilateral humanitarian aid: OECD-DAC. Estimated multilateral humanitarian aid: UNHCR, UNICEF, WFP, UNRWA, UN/OCHA, ICRC and IFRC.

Funding per emergency, 2007

Crisis	(USD m)	(% of total)
Sudan	44.6	20.4
Iraq (incl. Iraqi refugees in neighbouring countries)	39.6	18.1
occupied Palestinian territories	18.4	8.4
West Africa	16.2	7.4
Burundi	11.1	5.1
Chad	7.8	3.6
Uganda	7.3	3.4
Nepal	7.1	3.2
Somalia	6.3	2.9
Zimbabwe	6.1	2.8
Total top 10 emergencies	**164.4**	**75.4**
Total	**218.1**	**100.0**

Notes: Funding to these emergencies includes all flows inside and outside an appeal that had been reported to OCHA/FTS and attributed to the emergency at the time of the database download on 8th May 2008.
Source: OCHA/FTS.

Regional distribution of funding, 2007

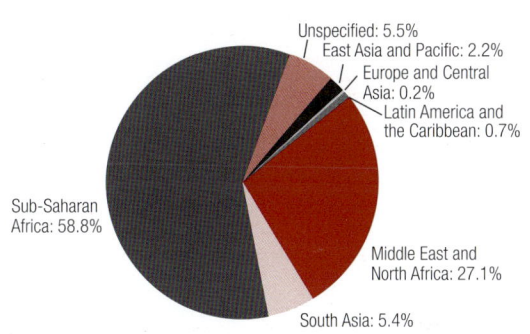

Unspecified: 5.5%
East Asia and Pacific: 2.2%
Europe and Central Asia: 0.2%
Latin America and the Caribbean: 0.7%
Sub-Saharan Africa: 58.8%
Middle East and North Africa: 27.1%
South Asia: 5.4%

Notes: Funding to these regions includes all flows inside and outside an appeal that had been reported to OCHA/FTS and attributed to a region at the time of the database download on 8th May 2008. Non-attributed flows are shown as 'unspecified'.
Source: OCHA/FTS.

Sectoral distribution of funding to UN Appeals, 2007 (%)

■ Country funding ○ UN appeal budget

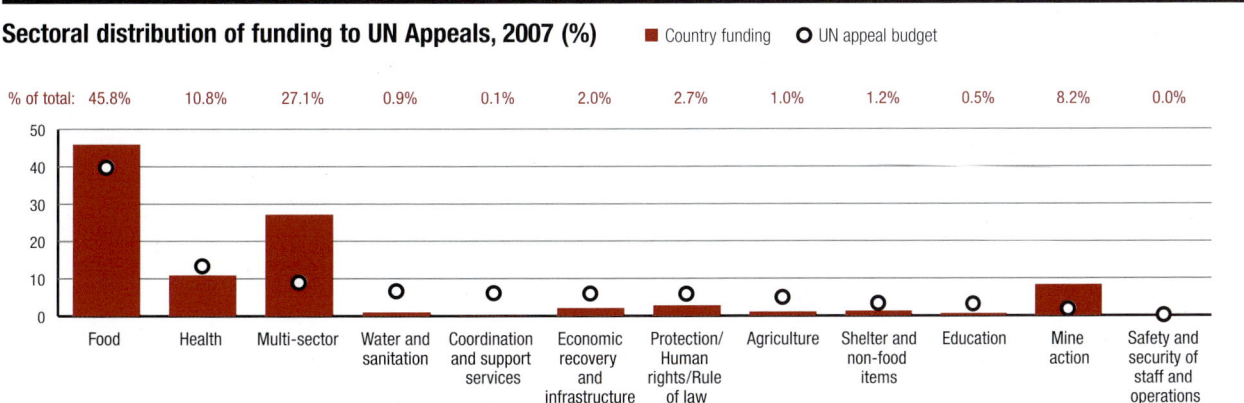

% of total: 45.8% 10.8% 27.1% 0.9% 0.1% 2.0% 2.7% 1.0% 1.2% 0.5% 8.2% 0.0%

Food | Health | Multi-sector | Water and sanitation | Coordination and support services | Economic recovery and infrastructure | Protection/ Human rights/Rule of law | Agriculture | Shelter and non-food items | Education | Mine action | Safety and security of staff and operations

Notes: Funding to these sectors include only flows inside an appeal that had been reported to OCHA/FTS and attributed to a sector at the time of the database download on 30th June 2008. Distribution of budget based on all 2007 UN appeals.
Source: OCHA/FTS.

Luxembourg

Luxembourg is the 2nd most generous humanitarian donor among the OECD/DAC group, relative to its size. Its bilateral humanitarian aid amounted to US$34 million in 2007. Luxembourg's humanitarian aid is managed by the Development Cooperation Directorate (DCD) within its Ministry of Foreign Affairs and guided by a General Humanitarian Strategy. Its current policy is informed by both the GHD initiative and the *European Consensus on Humanitarian Aid*. Luxembourg is currently in the process of formulating a detailed policy document for its humanitarian action, slated for completion in 2008. Luxembourg has broadened the scope of its humanitarian action by setting funding targets for prevention action (minimum 5 percent), and early recovery assistance (up to 20 percent). It has multi-year funding agreements with the ICRC, UNHCR, and WFP, and annual partnership agreements with four national humanitarian NGOs. A large portion of its budget is channelled through the multilateral route, consistent with its status as a small donor. It is also a significant contributor to CERF. DCD maintains an ongoing dialogue with its NGO partners, helping to increase the predictability of funding. It has a crisis cell on permanent call.

Sources: Ministry of Foreign Affairs; DAC Peer Review for Luxembourg (OECD, 2008).

HRI 2008 scores by pillar

HRI 2008 results

HIGHEST SCORES	SCORE	RANK
Responding to humanitarian needs		
Generosity of humanitarian assistance	10.00	1
Supporting local capacity and recovery		
Funding to international disaster risk mitigation mechanisms	10.00	1
Working with humanitarian partners		
Funding to CERF and other quick disbursement mechanisms	10.00	1
Funding UN Consolidated Inter-Agency Appeals	10.00	1
Funding IFRC and ICRC Appeals	10.00	1

LOWEST SCORES	SCORE	RANK
Responding to humanitarian needs		
Timely funding to onset disasters and IFRC emergency appeals	1.62	20
Sectoral distribution of funding through UN appeals	4.60	20
Supporting local capacity and recovery		
Strengthening local capacity for response and mitigation	5.82	20
Promoting standards and enhancing implementation		
Respecting or promoting human rights	7.93	19
Learning and accountability		
Participation in main accountability initiatives	1.43	21

Overview of humanitarian aid	Luxembourg		Share of total DAC (%)	
	2006	2007[4]	2006	2007[4]
Total humanitarian aid (estimated), of which:	47.3	46.3	0.6	0.5
Bilateral[1]	37.2	33.5	0.6	0.5
Multilateral[2] (estimated*), of which:	10.1	12.8	0.6	0.8
Central Emergency Response Fund**	4.0	5.6	1.4	1.5
Funding to other pooled mechanisms[3]***	0.0	0.3	0.0	0.0
Official development assistance	291	365	0.3	0.4
			DAC average	
Total humanitarian aid per capita (USD)[5]	100	96	22	23
Total humanitarian aid per / official development assistance	23.1	18.3	12.2	11.3
Overseas development assistance / gross national income	0.84	0.90	0.46	0.44

Notes: All data are given in current USD m unless otherwise indicated.

(1) Based on OECD/DAC definition of bilateral humanitarian aid, which is provided directly by a donor country to a recipient country and includes non-core earmarked contributions to multilateral humanitarian organisations known as multi-bilateral aid.

(2) Core unearmarked humanitarian flows to UNHCR, UNICEF, WFP, UNRWA, UN/OCHA, ICRC and IFRC. Does not include contributions through EC. 2007 core funding to UNRWA and ICRC proxied by 2006 data.

(3) For 2006, these were IFRC's Disaster Relief Emergency Fund (DREF), Sudan Common Humanitarian Fund (CHF), Democratic Republic of Congo (DRC) Pooled Fund, and Emergency Response Funds (ERF) for DRC, Indonesia, Somalia, Republic of Congo, and Ethiopia. For 2007, these were DREF, CHF, DRC Pooled Fund, and ERFs for Central African Republic, DRC, Ethiopia, Indonesia, and Iraq.

(4) All 2007 OECD/DAC data are provisional.

(5) Where 2007 population data not available, 2006 data used.

Sources: All data from OECD-DAC except: (*) UNHCR, UNICEF, WFP, UNRWA, UN/OCHA, ICRC and IFRC; (**) OCHA; (***) OCHA, IFRC; US Federal Reserve.

Main channels of humanitarian aid, 2007

Bilateral humanitarian aid: 72.3%

Multilateral humanitarian aid: 27.7%

- CERF: 43.8%
- UNRWA: 16.2%
- OCHA: 4.6%
- IFRC: 0.4%
- OHCHR: 1.0%
- UNHCR: 13.3%
- ICRC: 20.7%

Notes: see notes (1), (2) and (4) in Overview of humanitarian aid table.
Sources: Bilateral humanitarian aid: OECD-DAC. Estimated multilateral humanitarian aid: UNHCR, UNICEF, WFP, UNRWA, UN/OCHA, ICRC and IFRC.

Funding per emergency, 2007

Crisis	(USD m)	(% of total)
Sudan	2.7	10.3
Iraq (incl. Iraqi refugees in neighbouring countries)	1.6	6.2
West Africa	1.5	5.9
Burundi	1.3	5.1
Great Lakes Region	1.3	4.9
Somalia	1.2	4.8
Uganda	1.1	4.3
West Africa - regional floods - September	1.0	3.9
Sri Lanka	0.8	3.1
Democratic Republic of Congo	0.7	2.8
Total top 10 emergencies	**13.2**	**51.2**
Total	**25.8**	**100.0**

Notes: Funding to these emergencies includes all flows inside and outside an appeal that had been reported to OCHA/FTS and attributed to the emergency at the time of the database download on 8th May 2008.
Source: OCHA/FTS.

Regional distribution of funding, 2007

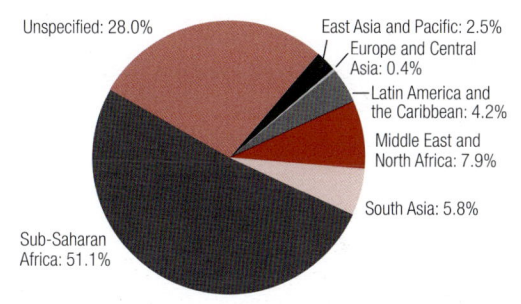

Unspecified: 28.0%
East Asia and Pacific: 2.5%
Europe and Central Asia: 0.4%
Latin America and the Caribbean: 4.2%
Middle East and North Africa: 7.9%
South Asia: 5.8%
Sub-Saharan Africa: 51.1%

Notes: Funding to these regions includes all flows inside and outside an appeal that had been reported to OCHA/FTS and attributed to a region at the time of the database download on 8th May 2008. Non-attributed flows are shown as 'unspecified'.
Source: OCHA/FTS.

Sectoral distribution of funding to UN Appeals, 2007 (%)

■ Country funding   ○ UN appeal budget

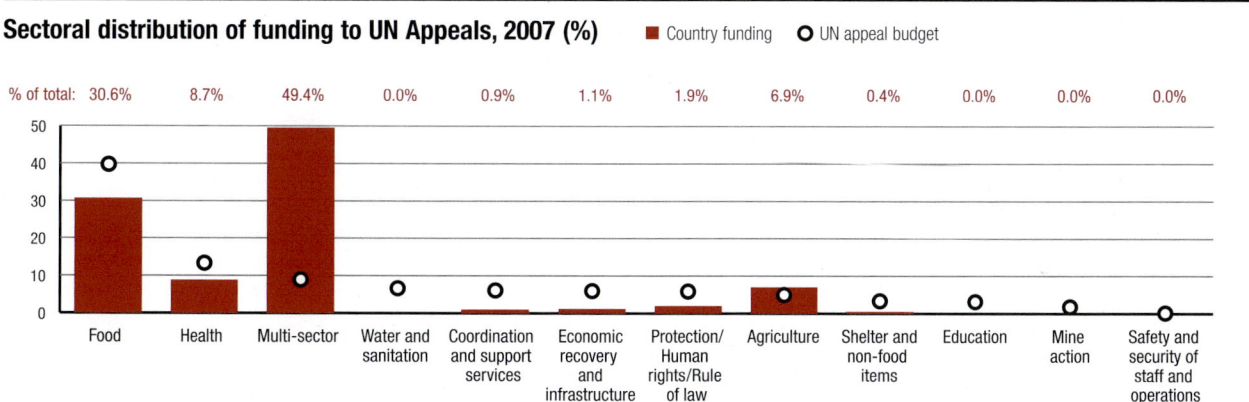

% of total:	30.6%	8.7%	49.4%	0.0%	0.9%	1.1%	1.9%	6.9%	0.4%	0.0%	0.0%	0.0%

Food | Health | Multi-sector | Water and sanitation | Coordination and support services | Economic recovery and infrastructure | Protection/ Human rights/Rule of law | Agriculture | Shelter and non-food items | Education | Mine action | Safety and security of staff and operations

Notes: Funding to these sectors include only flows inside an appeal that had been reported to OCHA/FTS and attributed to a sector at the time of the database download on 30th June 2008. Distribution of budget based on all 2007 UN appeals.
Source: OCHA/FTS.

Netherlands

The Netherlands is the 5th most generous humanitarian donor among the OECD/DAC group, relative to its size. Its bilateral humanitarian aid amounted to US$338 million in 2007. The Humanitarian Aid Division of the Ministry of Foreign Affairs is in charge of the humanitarian portfolio, accountable to the Ministers of Foreign Affairs and of Development Cooperation. In its strategy document, the Grant Policy Framework for Humanitarian Aid 2008, it distinguishes protracted from acute crises, limiting its interventions in the former to specific countries and specific sectors. The Netherlands has a GHD Domestic Implementation Plan and was instrumental in the formulation of the GHD Principles. In line with demand, the humanitarian aid budget typically receives substantial top-ups during the year, and is used mainly for complex emergencies. The Netherlands pursues an integrated approach to humanitarian intervention that encompasses transitional elements. A Stability Fund finances operational conflict prevention or peace-building, mainly in Dutch partner countries. The Netherlands rarely provides bilateral humanitarian aid directly to governments, choosing to work through multilateral channels or NGOs. It allows multi-year funding for up to two years in the case of protracted crises, and limited reallocations across budget lines.

Sources: DAC Peer Review of the Netherlands (OECD, 2006); GHD Domestic Implementation Plan for the Netherlands; Ministry of Foreign Affairs, at: http://www.minbuza.nl

HRI 2008 scores by pillar

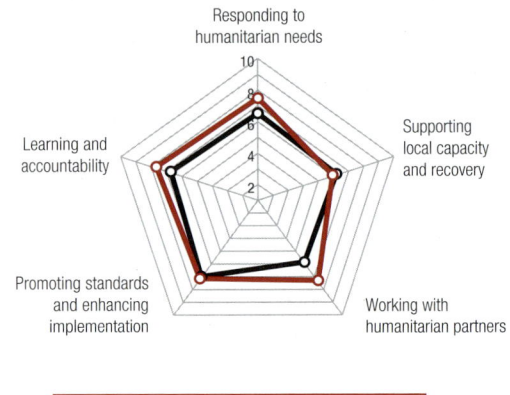

— Netherlands   — DAC average

HRI 2008 results

HIGHEST SCORES	SCORE	RANK
Responding to humanitarian needs		
Generosity of humanitarian assistance	6.89	5
Working with humanitarian partners		
Promoting NGOs and the Red Cross Movement	8.35	4
Predictable funding	8.13	3
Unearmarked funding	10.00	1
Funding to CERF and other quick disbursement mechanisms	10.00	1
Promoting standards and enhancing implementation		
Implementing refugee law	6.95	4

LOWEST SCORES	SCORE	RANK
Responding to humanitarian needs		
Neutrality	8.06	16
Supporting local capacity and recovery		
Funding to strengthen local capacity	2.14	18
Strengthening resilience to cope with crises	6.59	17
Funding to international disaster risk mitigation mechanisms	1.72	17
Promoting standards and enhancing implementation		
Implementing international humanitarian law	5.58	18

Overview of humanitarian aid	Netherlands		Share of total DAC (%)	
	2006	2007[4]	2006	2007[4]
Total humanitarian aid (estimated), of which:	631.4	552.9	7.6	6.0
Bilateral[1]	396.8	338.2	5.9	5.4
Multilateral[2] (estimated*), of which:	234.6	214.8	15.1	13.4
Central Emergency Response Fund**	51.9	53.4	18.0	14.1
Funding to other pooled mechanisms[3]***	71.3	135.9	25.4	16.8
Official development assistance	5,452	6,215	5.2	6.0
			DAC average	
Total humanitarian aid per capita (USD)[5]	39	34	22	23
Total humanitarian aid per / official development assistance	14.7	11.8	12.2	11.3
Overseas development assistance / gross national income	0.81	0.81	0.46	0.44

Notes: All data are given in current USD m unless otherwise indicated.

(1) Based on OECD/DAC definition of bilateral humanitarian aid, which is provided directly by a donor country to a recipient country and includes non-core earmarked contributions to multilateral humanitarian organisations known as multi-bilateral aid.

(2) Core unearmarked humanitarian flows to UNHCR, UNICEF, WFP, UNRWA, UN/OCHA, ICRC and IFRC. Does not include contributions through EC. 2007 core funding to UNRWA and ICRC proxied by 2006 data.

(3) For 2006, these were IFRC's Disaster Relief Emergency Fund (DREF), Sudan Common Humanitarian Fund (CHF), Democratic Republic of Congo (DRC) Pooled Fund, and Emergency Response Funds (ERF) for DRC, Indonesia, Somalia, Republic of Congo, and Ethiopia. For 2007, these were DREF, CHF, DRC Pooled Fund, and ERFs for Central African Republic, DRC, Ethiopia, Indonesia, and Iraq.

(4) All 2007 OECD/DAC data are provisional.

(5) Where 2007 population data not available, 2006 data used.

Sources: All data from OECD-DAC except: (*) UNHCR, UNICEF, WFP, UNRWA, UN/OCHA, ICRC and IFRC; (**) OCHA; (***) OCHA, IFRC; US Federal Reserve.

Main channels of humanitarian aid, 2007

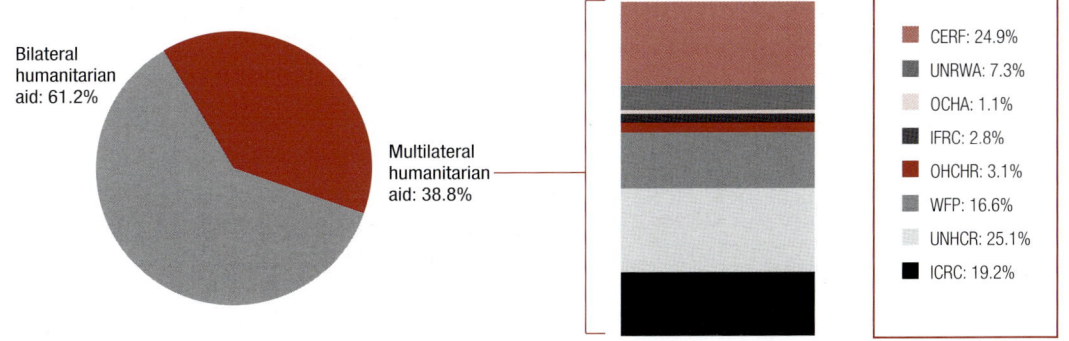

Bilateral humanitarian aid: 61.2%

Multilateral humanitarian aid: 38.8%

- CERF: 24.9%
- UNRWA: 7.3%
- OCHA: 1.1%
- IFRC: 2.8%
- OHCHR: 3.1%
- WFP: 16.6%
- UNHCR: 25.1%
- ICRC: 19.2%

Notes: see notes (1), (2) and (4) in Overview of humanitarian aid table.
Sources: Bilateral humanitarian aid: OECD-DAC. Estimated multilateral humanitarian aid: UNHCR, UNICEF, WFP, UNRWA, UN/OCHA, ICRC and IFRC.

Funding per emergency, 2007

Crisis	(USD m)	(% of total)
Sudan	70.4	17.4
Democratic Republic of Congo	38.0	9.4
Afghanistan	19.2	4.7
Somalia	17.7	4.4
Iraq (incl. Iraqi refugees in neighbouring countries)	12.5	3.1
Pakistan	9.3	2.3
North Caucasus	9.1	2.2
Uganda	9.0	2.2
Bangladesh - Cyclone Sidr - November	7.9	1.9
Chad	7.9	1.9
Total top 10 emergencies	**201.0**	**49.7**
Total	**404.7**	**100.0**

Notes: Funding to these emergencies includes all flows inside and outside an appeal that had been reported to OCHA/FTS and attributed to the emergency at the time of the database download on 8th May 2008.
Source: OCHA/FTS.

Regional distribution of funding, 2007

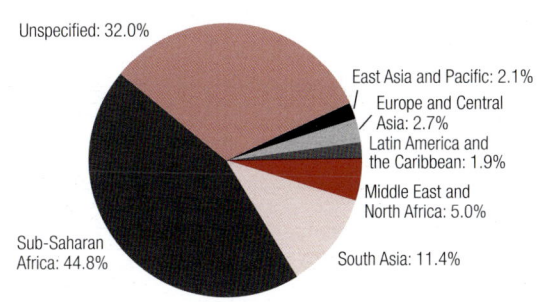

Unspecified: 32.0%

East Asia and Pacific: 2.1%
Europe and Central Asia: 2.7%
Latin America and the Caribbean: 1.9%
Middle East and North Africa: 5.0%
South Asia: 11.4%
Sub-Saharan Africa: 44.8%

Notes: Funding to these regions includes all flows inside and outside an appeal that had been reported to OCHA/FTS and attributed to a region at the time of the database download on 8th May 2008. Non-attributed flows are shown as 'unspecified'.
Source: OCHA/FTS.

Sectoral distribution of funding to UN Appeals, 2007 (%)

■ Country funding   ○ UN appeal budget

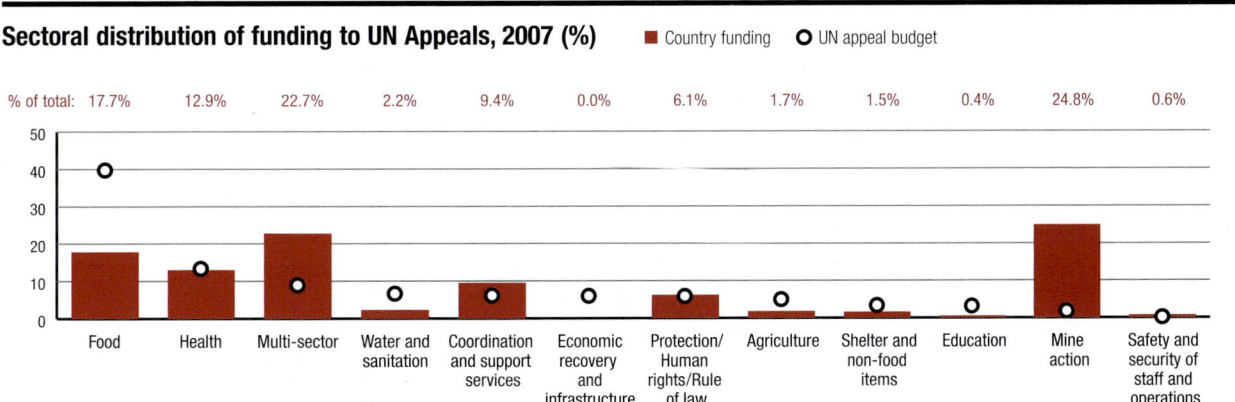

% of total: 17.7% 12.9% 22.7% 2.2% 9.4% 0.0% 6.1% 1.7% 1.5% 0.4% 24.8% 0.6%

Food | Health | Multi-sector | Water and sanitation | Coordination and support services | Economic recovery and infrastructure | Protection/ Human rights/Rule of law | Agriculture | Shelter and non-food items | Education | Mine action | Safety and security of staff and operations

Notes: Funding to these sectors include only flows inside an appeal that had been reported to OCHA/FTS and attributed to a sector at the time of the database download on 30th June 2008. Distribution of budget based on all 2007 UN appeals.
Source: OCHA/FTS.

New Zealand

New Zealand is the 12th most generous humanitarian donor among the OECD/DAC group, relative to its size. Its bilateral humanitarian aid amounted to US$22 million in 2007. The Ministry of Foreign Affairs and Trade is responsible for humanitarian assistance, administered by NZAID. Due to NZAID's semi-autonomy, its mandate extends beyond aid management and implementation, providing contestable policy advice, meaning that its views may differ from those of the MFA. The independent International Development Advisory Committee (IDAC) established in early 2004 also plays a role in defining broader policy issues, including by undertaking public consultation and contracting research. The MFA meets regularly with representatives from Council for International Development (CID), the umbrella organisation for New Zealand NGOs. Within NZAID's humanitarian programme, the NGO funding window for emergency and disaster relief has been established to channel support via New Zealand NGOs to their partners in disaster and emergency situations. A number of NGO activities, including those of civil society organisations in partner countries, can be funded directly under NZAID bilateral and regional programmes. NZAID has formal four-year strategic relationship agreements with four major NGOs, which include core funding, covering up to 95 percent of organisations' budgets.

Source: DAC Peer Review for New Zealand (OECD, 2005).

HRI 2008 scores by pillar

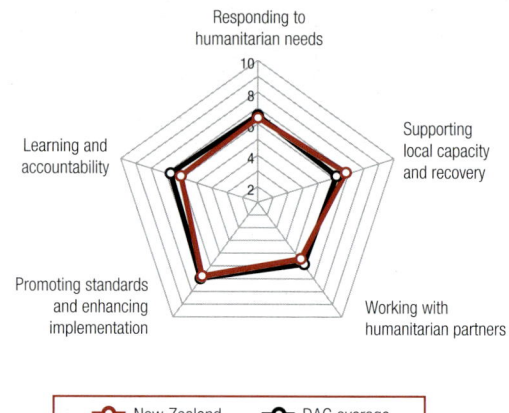

New Zealand   DAC average

HRI 2008 results

HIGHEST SCORES	SCORE	RANK
Supporting local capacity and recovery		
Funding to strengthen local capacity	10.00	1
Ensuring rapid recovery of sustainable livelihoods	7.83	1
Working with humanitarian partners		
Helping governments and local communities achieve better coordination	7.25	1
Reducing earmarking	7.76	1
Flexible funding	8.08	1

LOWEST SCORES	SCORE	RANK
Responding to humanitarian needs		
Funding in proportion to need	6.86	19
Commitment to on-going crises	6.61	19
Supporting local capacity and recovery		
Involvement of beneficiaries in monitoring and evaluation	5.99	21
Funding to international disaster risk mitigation mechanisms	1.43	19
Working with humanitarian partners		
Funding to NGOs	1.48	21

Overview of humanitarian aid

	New Zealand 2006	New Zealand 2007[4]	Share of total DAC (%) 2006	Share of total DAC (%) 2007[4]
Total humanitarian aid (estimated), of which:	27.2	29.3	0.3	0.3
Bilateral[1]	21.5	22.0	0.3	0.3
Multilateral[2] (estimated*), of which:	5.7	7.4	0.4	0.5
Central Emergency Response Fund**	0.0	0.8	0.0	0.2
Funding to other pooled mechanisms[3]***	0.0	0.0	0.0	0.0
Official development assistance	259	315	0.2	0.3

	New Zealand 2006	New Zealand 2007[4]	DAC average 2006	DAC average 2007[4]
Total humanitarian aid per capita (USD)[5]	7	7	22	23
Total humanitarian aid per / official development assistance	13.4	12.0	12.2	11.3
Overseas development assistance / gross national income	0.27	0.27	0.46	0.44

Notes: All data are given in current USD m unless otherwise indicated.

1 Based on OECD/DAC definition of bilateral humanitarian aid, which is provided directly by a donor country to a recipient country and includes non-core earmarked contributions to multilateral humanitarian organisations known as multi-bilateral aid.

2 Core unearmarked humanitarian flows to UNHCR, UNICEF, WFP, UNRWA, UN/OCHA, ICRC and IFRC. 2007 core funding to UNRWA and ICRC proxied by 2006 data.

3 For 2006, these were IFRC's Disaster Relief Emergency Fund (DREF), Sudan Common Humanitarian Fund (CHF), Democratic Republic of Congo (DRC) Pooled Fund, and Emergency Response Funds (ERF) for DRC, Indonesia, Somalia, Republic of Congo, and Ethiopia. For 2007, these were DREF, CHF, DRC Pooled Fund, and ERFs for Central African Republic, DRC, Ethiopia, Indonesia, and Iraq.

4 All 2007 OECD/DAC data are provisional.

5 Where 2007 population data not available, 2006 data used.

Sources: All data from OECD-DAC except: (*) UNHCR, UNICEF, WFP, UNRWA, UN/OCHA, ICRC and IFRC; (**) OCHA; (***) OCHA, IFRC; US Federal Reserve.

Main channels of humanitarian aid, 2007

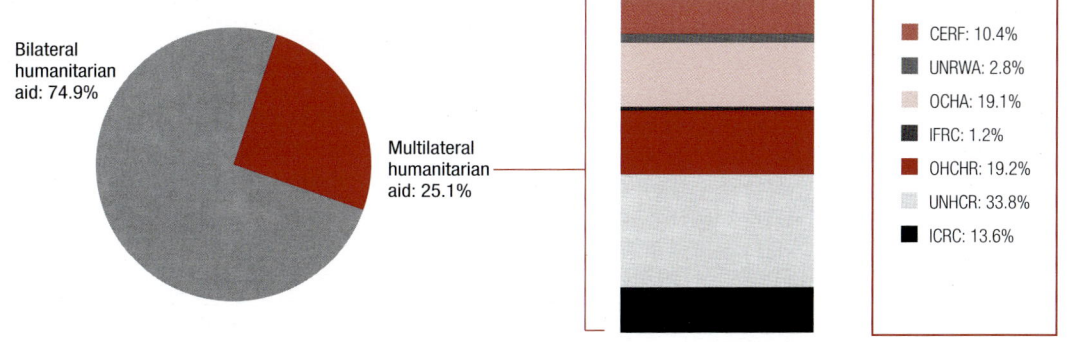

Bilateral humanitarian aid: 74.9%

Multilateral humanitarian aid: 25.1%

- CERF: 10.4%
- UNRWA: 2.8%
- OCHA: 19.1%
- IFRC: 1.2%
- OHCHR: 19.2%
- UNHCR: 33.8%
- ICRC: 13.6%

Notes: see notes (1), (2) and (4) in Overview of humanitarian aid table.
Sources: Bilateral humanitarian aid: OECD-DAC. Estimated multilateral humanitarian aid: UNHCR, UNICEF, WFP, UNRWA, UN/OCHA, ICRC and IFRC.

Funding per emergency, 2007

Crisis	(USD m)	(% of total)
Iraq (incl. Iraqi refugees in neighbouring countries)	1.3	13.5
occupied Palestinian territories	1.1	11.6
Nepal	0.9	9.5
Somalia	0.8	7.8
Timor-Leste	0.7	7.4
Viet Nam	0.5	5.4
Sri Lanka	0.4	4.0
Bangladesh - cyclone Sidr - November	0.4	4.0
Korea DPR - floods - August	0.4	3.9
Peru - Earthquake - August	0.4	3.6
Total top 10 emergencies	**6.9**	**70.7**
Total	**9.7**	**100.0**

Notes: Funding to these emergencies includes all flows inside and outside an appeal that had been reported to OCHA/FTS and attributed to the emergency at the time of the database download on 8th May 2008.
Source: OCHA/FTS.

Regional distribution of funding, 2007

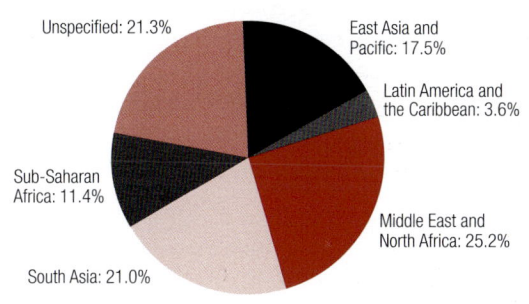

Unspecified: 21.3%
East Asia and Pacific: 17.5%
Latin America and the Caribbean: 3.6%
Middle East and North Africa: 25.2%
Sub-Saharan Africa: 11.4%
South Asia: 21.0%

Notes: Funding to these regions includes all flows inside and outside an appeal that had been reported to OCHA/FTS and attributed to a region at the time of the database download on 8th May 2008. Non-attributed flows are shown as 'unspecified'.
Source: OCHA/FTS.

Sectoral distribution of funding to UN Appeals, 2007 (%)

■ Country funding O UN appeal budget

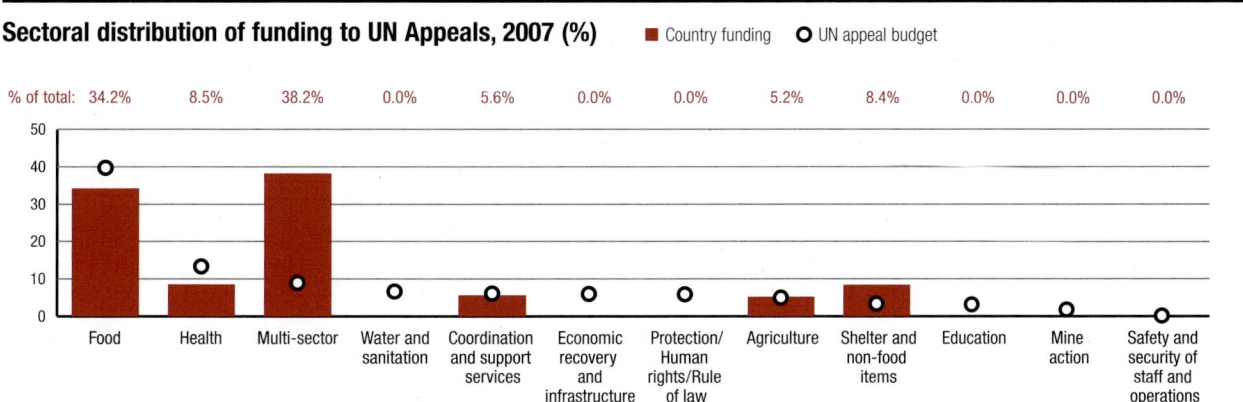

% of total: 34.2% | 8.5% | 38.2% | 0.0% | 5.6% | 0.0% | 0.0% | 5.2% | 8.4% | 0.0% | 0.0% | 0.0%

Food, Health, Multi-sector, Water and sanitation, Coordination and support services, Economic recovery and infrastructure, Protection/Human rights/Rule of law, Agriculture, Shelter and non-food items, Education, Mine action, Safety and security of staff and operations

Notes: Funding to these sectors include only flows inside an appeal that had been reported to OCHA/FTS and attributed to a sector at the time of the database download on 30th June 2008. Distribution of budget based on all 2007 UN appeals.
Source: OCHA/FTS.

Norway

Norway is the most generous humanitarian donor among the OECD/DAC group, relative to its size. Its bilateral humanitarian aid amounted to US$324 million in 2007. The Ministry of Foreign Affairs is responsible for humanitarian action, splitting the portfolio among three agencies: the Department for Global Affairs, for emergency response; the Regional Department in charge of transitional assistance; and the International Development Policy Department overseeing peace-building activities. Its policy is contained in its annual budget submission to Parliament, however a new humanitarian strategy is expected to be ready by September 2008. Norway has a long tradition of involvement in conflict resolution and emphasises an integrated approach to security, humanitarian, and development aid. Its approach to disaster prevention is summarised in a 2007 White Paper. Norway concurrently provides humanitarian assistance, assistance for peace and reconciliation, transitional assistance, and long-term development assistance, all funded through different budget lines. Norway provides multi-year funding arrangements for longer-term programmes and channels a large share of its budget to pooled funding mechanisms. Their national and international NGO partners are actively encouraged to involve beneficiaries in the projects. Through the Norwegian Emergency Preparedness System, Norway has a strong emergency response capacity, offering personnel, services and relief products.

Sources: Ministry of Foreign Affairs; DAC Peer Review for Norway (OECD, 2005).

HRI 2008 scores by pillar

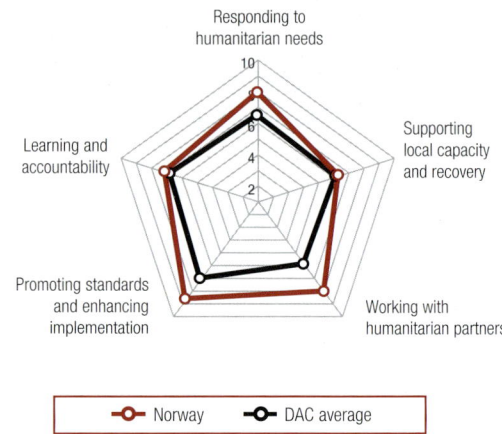

Norway   DAC average

HRI 2008 results

HIGHEST SCORES	SCORE	RANK
Responding to humanitarian needs		
Generosity of humanitarian assistance	10.00	1
Working with humanitarian partners		
Funding UN coordination mechanisms and common services	10.00	1
Supporting UN leadership and coordination role	8.50	1
Promoting standards and enhancing implementation		
Implementing international humanitarian law	10.00	1
Implementing refugee law	10.00	1

LOWEST SCORES	SCORE	RANK
Responding to humanitarian needs		
Commitment to on-going crises	5.83	22
Timely funding to onset disasters and IFRC emergency appeals	1.54	21
Distribution of funding relative to ECHO's Crisis and Vulnerability Indices	7.01	19
Supporting local capacity and recovery		
Strengthening local capacity for response and mitigation	6.25	18
Funding to strengthen local capacity	2.29	17

Overview of humanitarian aid	Norway		Share of total DAC (%)	
	2006	2007[4]	2006	2007[4]
Total humanitarian aid (estimated), of which:	413.1	471.3	5.0	5.1
Bilateral[1]	309.1	324.2	4.6	5.2
Multilateral[2] (estimated*), of which:	104.0	147.1	6.7	9.2
Central Emergency Response Fund**	30.0	55.1	10.4	14.6
Funding to other pooled mechanisms[3]***	17.1	74.4	6.1	9.2
Official development assistance	2,954	3,727	2.8	3.6
			DAC average	
Total humanitarian aid per capita (USD)[5]	89	100	22	23
Total humanitarian aid per / official development assistance	18.8	16.5	12.2	11.3
Overseas development assistance / gross national income	0.89	0.95	0.46	0.44

Notes: All data are given in current USD m unless otherwise indicated.

(1) Based on OECD/DAC definition of bilateral humanitarian aid, which is provided directly by a donor country to a recipient country and includes non-core earmarked contributions to multilateral humanitarian organisations known as multi-bilateral aid.

(2) Core unearmarked humanitarian flows to UNHCR, UNICEF, WFP, UNRWA, UN/OCHA, ICRC and IFRC. Does not include contributions through EC. 2007 core funding to UNRWA and ICRC proxied by 2006 data.

(3) For 2006, these were IFRC's Disaster Relief Emergency Fund (DREF), Sudan Common Humanitarian Fund (CHF), Democratic Republic of Congo (DRC) Pooled Fund, and Emergency Response Funds (ERF) for DRC, Indonesia, Somalia, Republic of Congo, and Ethiopia. For 2007, these were DREF, CHF, DRC Pooled Fund, and ERFs for Central African Republic, DRC, Ethiopia, Indonesia, and Iraq.

(4) All 2007 OECD/DAC data are provisional.

(5) Where 2007 population data not available, 2006 data used.

Sources: All data from OECD-DAC except: (*) UNHCR, UNICEF, WFP, UNRWA, UN/OCHA, ICRC and IFRC; (**) OCHA; (***) OCHA, IFRC; US Federal Reserve.

Main channels of humanitarian aid, 2007

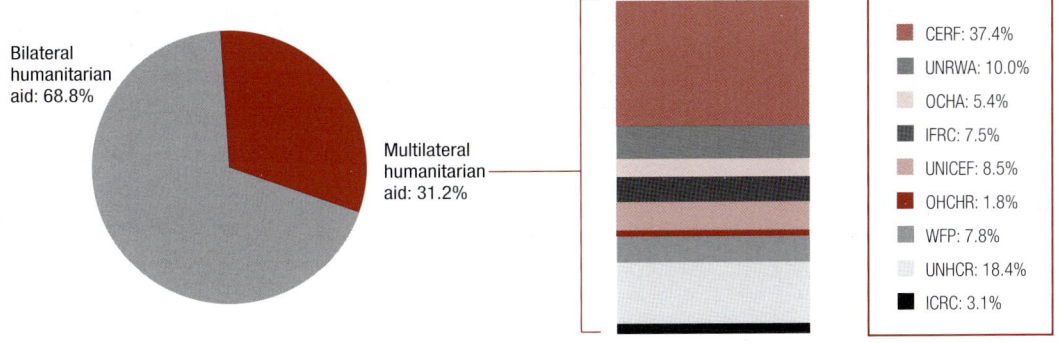

Bilateral humanitarian aid: 68.8%

Multilateral humanitarian aid: 31.2%

- CERF: 37.4%
- UNRWA: 10.0%
- OCHA: 5.4%
- IFRC: 7.5%
- UNICEF: 8.5%
- OHCHR: 1.8%
- WFP: 7.8%
- UNHCR: 18.4%
- ICRC: 3.1%

Notes: see notes (1), (2) and (4) in Overview of humanitarian aid table.
Sources: Bilateral humanitarian aid: OECD-DAC. Estimated multilateral humanitarian aid: UNHCR, UNICEF, WFP, UNRWA, UN/OCHA, ICRC and IFRC.

Funding per emergency, 2007

Crisis	(USD m)	(% of total)
Sudan	40.6	9.3
Somalia	32.0	7.3
occupied Palestinian territories	31.2	7.1
Afghanistan	25.6	5.8
Uganda	21.6	4.9
Democratic Republic of Congo	17.7	4.0
Iraq (incl. Iraqi refugees in neighbouring countries)	16.7	3.8
Sri Lanka	12.8	2.9
Lebanon	9.6	2.2
Colombia	7.6	1.7
Total top 10 emergencies	**215.4**	**49.2**
Total	**438.2**	**100.0**

Notes: Funding to these emergencies includes all flows inside and outside an appeal that had been reported to OCHA/FTS and attributed to the emergency at the time of the database download on 8th May 2008.
Source: OCHA/FTS.

Regional distribution of funding, 2007

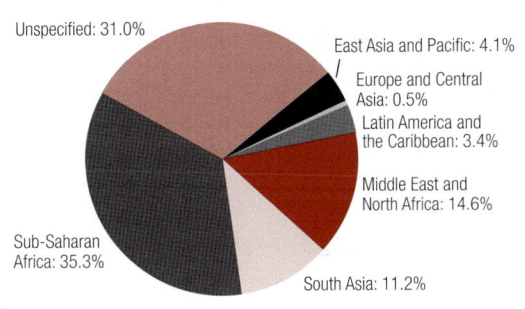

Unspecified: 31.0%

East Asia and Pacific: 4.1%

Europe and Central Asia: 0.5%

Latin America and the Caribbean: 3.4%

Middle East and North Africa: 14.6%

Sub-Saharan Africa: 35.3%

South Asia: 11.2%

Notes: Funding to these regions includes all flows inside and outside an appeal that had been reported to OCHA/FTS and attributed to a region at the time of the database download on 8th May 2008. Non-attributed flows are shown as 'unspecified'.
Source: OCHA/FTS.

Sectoral distribution of funding to UN Appeals, 2007 (%)

■ Country funding   ○ UN appeal budget

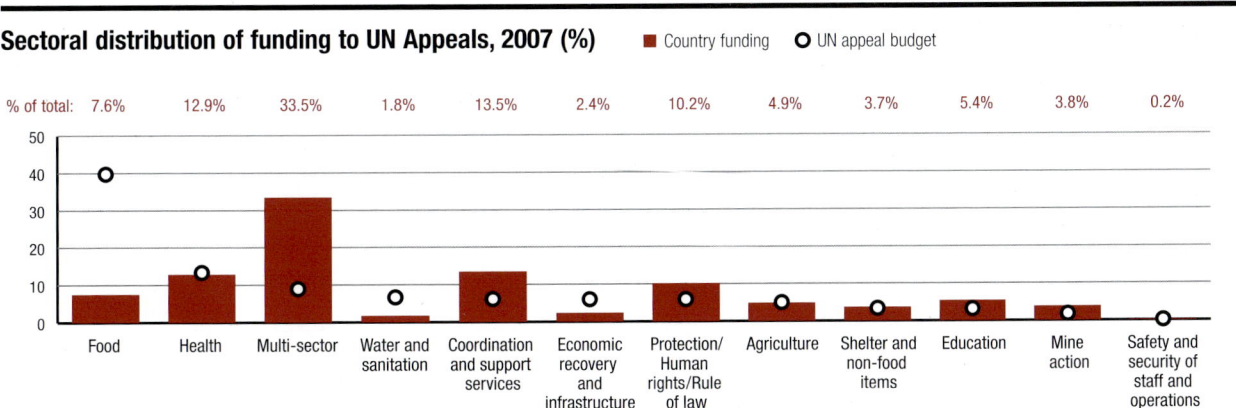

% of total:	7.6%	12.9%	33.5%	1.8%	13.5%	2.4%	10.2%	4.9%	3.7%	5.4%	3.8%	0.2%

Food · Health · Multi-sector · Water and sanitation · Coordination and support services · Economic recovery and infrastructure · Protection/Human rights/Rule of law · Agriculture · Shelter and non-food items · Education · Mine action · Safety and security of staff and operations

Notes: Funding to these sectors include only flows inside an appeal that had been reported to OCHA/FTS and attributed to a sector at the time of the database download on 30th June 2008. Distribution of budget based on all 2007 UN appeals.
Source: OCHA/FTS.

Portugal

Portugal is the least generous humanitarian donor among the OECD/DAC group, relative to its size. Its bilateral humanitarian aid amounted to US$0.4 million in 2007. Part of the Ministry of Foreign Affairs, a small unit within the Portuguese Institute for Development Support (IPAD) coordinates humanitarian aid, and is also responsible for relations with NGOs. Portugal does not have an overall strategy for its humanitarian aid. It provides its assistance chiefly in-kind or via civil society organisations. In the case of emergencies in specific countries, Portuguese humanitarian flows are channelled via international NGOs and multilateral organisations, but there is no overall preference for working with the UN. Portugal's humanitarian aid is chiefly provided in-kind or via civil society organisations.

Source: DAC Peer Review for Portugal (OECD, 2006).

HRI 2008 scores by pillar

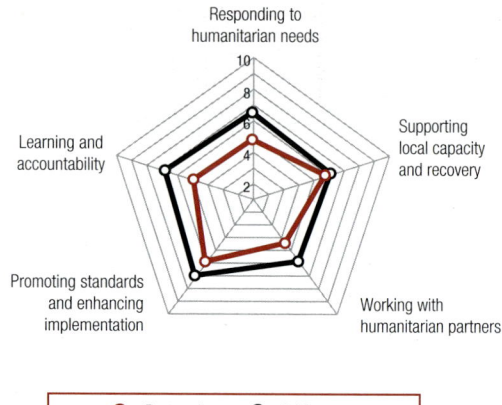

HRI 2008 results

HIGHEST SCORES	SCORE	RANK
Supporting local capacity and recovery		
Involvement of beneficiaries in design and implementation	7.76	2
Involvement of beneficiaries in monitoring and evaluation	7.39	4
Working with humanitarian partners		
Unearmarked funding	10.00	1
Promoting standards and enhancing implementation		
Facilitating safe humanitarian access	6.32	4

LOWEST SCORES	SCORE	RANK
Responding to humanitarian needs		
Distribution of funding relative to ECHO's Crisis and Vulnerability Indices	1.43	23
Reallocation of funds from other crises	3.66	23
Generosity of humanitarian assistance	1.43	22
Supporting local capacity and recovery		
Strengthening preparedness	4.76	23
Working with humanitarian partners		
Funding to NGOs	1.43	23
Promoting standards and enhancing implementation		
Affirming primary role of civilian organizations	6.27	23

Overview of humanitarian aid	Portugal		Share of total DAC (%)	
	2006	2007[4]	2006	2007[4]
Total humanitarian aid (estimated), of which:	9.6	2.9	0.1	0.0
Bilateral[1]	7.0	0.4	0.1	0.0
Multilateral[2] (estimated*), of which:	2.6	2.4	0.2	0.2
Central Emergency Response Fund**	0.3	0.3	0.1	0.1
Funding to other pooled mechanisms[3]***	0.0	0.0	0.0	0.0
Official development assistance	396	403	0.4	0.4
			DAC average	
Total humanitarian aid per capita (USD)[5]	1	0	22	23
Total humanitarian aid per / official development assistance	4.5	1.4	12.2	11.3
Overseas development assistance / gross national income	0.21	0.19	0.46	0.44

Notes: All data are given in current USD m unless otherwise indicated.
(1) Based on OECD/DAC definition of bilateral humanitarian aid, which is provided directly by a donor country to a recipient country and includes non-core earmarked contributions to multilateral humanitarian organisations known as multi-bilateral aid.
(2) Core unearmarked humanitarian flows to UNHCR, UNICEF, WFP, UNRWA, UN/OCHA, ICRC and IFRC. Does not include contributions through EC. 2007 core funding to UNRWA and ICRC proxied by 2006 data.
(3) For 2006, these were IFRC's Disaster Relief Emergency Fund (DREF), Sudan Common Humanitarian Fund (CHF), Democratic Republic of Congo (DRC) Pooled Fund, and Emergency Response Funds (ERF) for DRC, Indonesia, Somalia, Republic of Congo, and Ethiopia. For 2007, these were DREF, CHF, DRC Pooled Fund, and ERFs for Central African Republic, DRC, Ethiopia, Indonesia, and Iraq.
(4) All 2007 OECD/DAC data are provisional.
(5) Where 2007 population data not available, 2006 data used.
Sources: All data from OECD-DAC except: (*) UNHCR, UNICEF, WFP, UNRWA, UN/OCHA, ICRC and IFRC; (**) OCHA; (***) OCHA, IFRC; US Federal Reserve.

Main channels of humanitarian aid, 2007

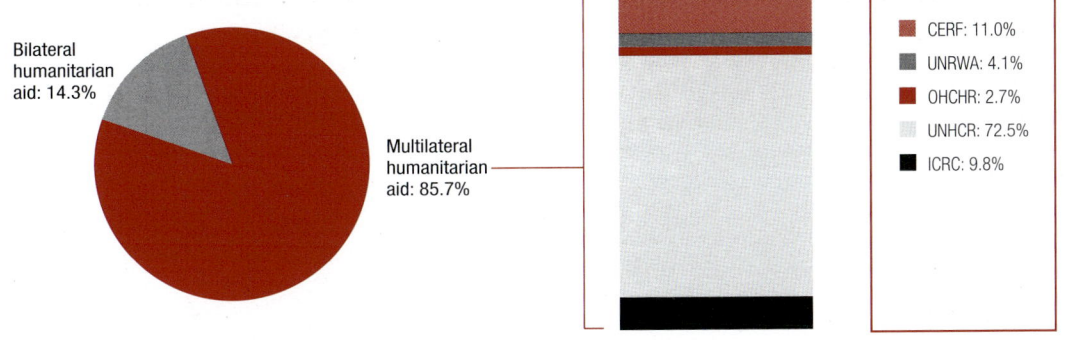

Bilateral humanitarian aid: 14.3%

Multilateral humanitarian aid: 85.7%

CERF: 11.0%
UNRWA: 4.1%
OHCHR: 2.7%
UNHCR: 72.5%
ICRC: 9.8%

Notes: see notes (1), (2) and (4) in Overview of humanitarian aid table.
Sources: Bilateral humanitarian aid: OECD-DAC. Estimated multilateral humanitarian aid: UNHCR, UNICEF, WFP, UNRWA, UN/OCHA, ICRC and IFRC.

Funding per emergency, 2007

Crisis	(USD m)	(% of total)
Mozambique	0.1	24.9
Total	**0.4**	**100.0**

Notes: Funding to these emergencies includes all flows inside and outside an appeal that had been reported to OCHA/FTS and attributed to the emergency at the time of the database download on 8th May 2008.
Source: OCHA/FTS.

Regional distribution of funding, 2007

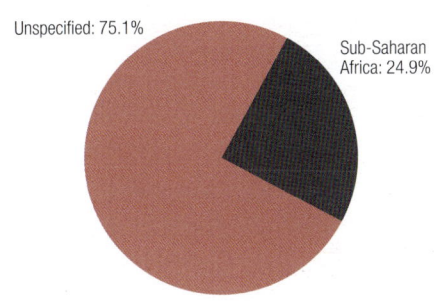

Unspecified: 75.1%

Sub-Saharan Africa: 24.9%

Notes: Funding to these regions includes all flows inside and outside an appeal that had been reported to OCHA/FTS and attributed to a region at the time of the database download on 8th May 2008. Non-attributed flows are shown as 'unspecified'.
Source: OCHA/FTS.

Sectoral distribution of funding to UN Appeals, 2007 (%)   ■ Country funding   ○ UN appeal budget

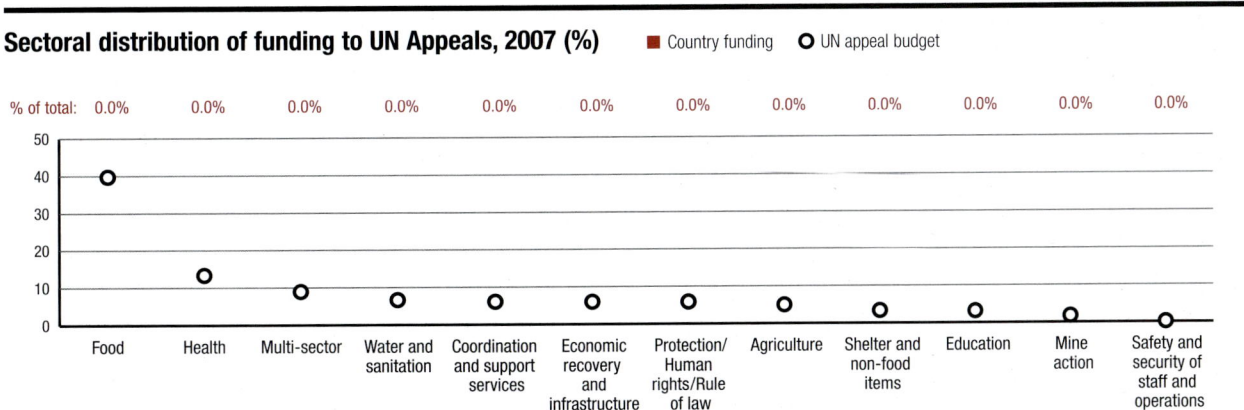

% of total: 0.0%   0.0%   0.0%   0.0%   0.0%   0.0%   0.0%   0.0%   0.0%   0.0%   0.0%   0.0%

Food | Health | Multi-sector | Water and sanitation | Coordination and support services | Economic recovery and infrastructure | Protection/ Human rights/Rule of law | Agriculture | Shelter and non-food items | Education | Mine action | Safety and security of staff and operations

Notes: Funding to these sectors include only flows inside an appeal that had been reported to OCHA/FTS and attributed to a sector at the time of the database download on 30th June 2008. Distribution of budget based on all 2007 UN appeals.
Source: OCHA/FTS.

Spain

Spain is the 15th most generous humanitarian donor among the OECD/DAC group, relative to its size. Its bilateral humanitarian aid amounted to US$167 million in 2007. The Spanish International Aid Agency (AECI) of the Ministry of Foreign Affairs and Cooperation is responsible for the coordination of humanitarian assistance. Its *Cooperation Master Plan for 2005–2008* acknowledges the limits of the definition of humanitarian action contained in Article 12 of the International Development Cooperation Act, which creates a legal framework for action. Spain's recent *Humanitarian Action Strategy Paper* provides another important reference point, detailing the concepts and criteria for action. Spain earmarks 5 percent of its humanitarian budget for preparedness. Spain has multi-year funding arrangements with two Spanish humanitarian NGOs.

Sources: OECD Peer Review (2007); Ministry of Foreign Affairs and Cooperation, http://www.aeci.es

HRI 2008 scores by pillar

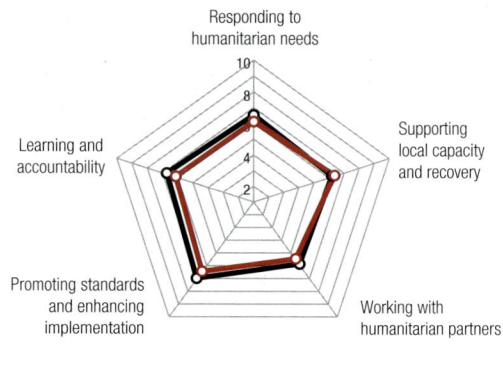

Spain — DAC average

HRI 2008 results

HIGHEST SCORES	SCORE	RANK
Responding to humanitarian needs		
Timely funding to onset disasters and IFRC emergency appeals	10.00	1
Supporting local capacity and recovery		
Strengthening local capacity for response and mitigation	6.91	3
Strengthening resilience to cope with crises	7.47	2
Working with humanitarian partners		
Longer-term funding arrangements	6.05	3
Promoting standards and enhancing implementation		
Affirming primary role of civilian organizations	8.91	4

LOWEST SCORES	SCORE	RANK
Responding to humanitarian needs		
Neutrality	7.70	20
Working with humanitarian partners		
Supporting effective coordination efforts	6.40	20
Promoting standards and enhancing implementation		
Facilitating safe humanitarian access	5.01	20
Implementing international humanitarian law	3.47	20
Learning and accountability		
Commitment to accountability in humanitarian action	8.02	20

Overview of humanitarian aid

	Spain 2006	Spain 2007[4]	Share of total DAC (%) 2006	Share of total DAC (%) 2007[4]
Total humanitarian aid (estimated), of which:	189.6	231.3	2.3	2.5
Bilateral[1]	137.4	166.8	2.0	2.7
Multilateral[2] (estimated*), of which:	52.2	64.5	3.3	4.0
Central Emergency Response Fund**	10.0	20.7	3.5	5.5
Funding to other pooled mechanisms[3]***	0.0	18.8	0.0	2.3
Official development assistance	3,814	5,744	3.7	5.5

			DAC average	
Total humanitarian aid per capita (USD)[5]	4	5	22	23
Total humanitarian aid per / official development assistance	9.1	8.6	12.2	11.3
Overseas development assistance / gross national income	0.32	0.41	0.46	0.44

Notes: All data are given in current USD m unless otherwise indicated.

(1) Based on OECD/DAC definition of bilateral humanitarian aid, which is provided directly by a donor country to a recipient country and includes non-core earmarked contributions to multilateral humanitarian organisations known as multi-bilateral aid.

(2) Core unearmarked humanitarian flows to UNHCR, UNICEF, WFP, UNRWA, UN/OCHA, ICRC and IFRC. Does not include contributions through EC. 2007 core funding to UNRWA and ICRC proxied by 2006 data.

(3) For 2006, these were IFRC's Disaster Relief Emergency Fund (DREF), Sudan Common Humanitarian Fund (CHF), Democratic Republic of Congo (DRC) Pooled Fund, and Emergency Response Funds (ERF) for DRC, Indonesia, Somalia, Republic of Congo, and Ethiopia. For 2007, these were DREF, CHF, DRC Pooled Fund, and ERFs for Central African Republic, DRC, Ethiopia, Indonesia, and Iraq.

(4) All 2007 OECD/DAC data are provisional.

(5) Where 2007 population data not available, 2006 data used.

Sources: All data from OECD-DAC except: (*) UNHCR, UNICEF, WFP, UNRWA, UN/OCHA, ICRC and IFRC; (**) OCHA; (***) OCHA, IFRC; US Federal Reserve.

Main channels of humanitarian aid, 2007

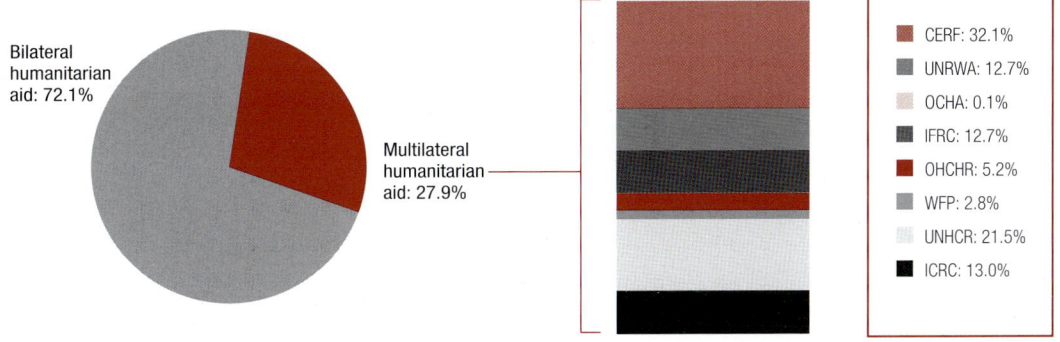

Bilateral humanitarian aid: 72.1%

Multilateral humanitarian aid: 27.9%

- CERF: 32.1%
- UNRWA: 12.7%
- OCHA: 0.1%
- IFRC: 12.7%
- OHCHR: 5.2%
- WFP: 2.8%
- UNHCR: 21.5%
- ICRC: 13.0%

Notes: see notes (1), (2) and (4) in Overview of humanitarian aid table.
Sources: Bilateral humanitarian aid: OECD-DAC. Estimated multilateral humanitarian aid: UNHCR, UNICEF, WFP, UNRWA, UN/OCHA, ICRC and IFRC.

Funding per emergency, 2007

Crisis	(USD m)	(% of total)
occupied Palestinian territories	14.2	15.9
Sudan	11.8	13.1
Democratic Republic of Congo	5.5	6.1
West Africa	4.6	5.2
Chad	3.3	3.7
Uganda	2.8	3.1
Haiti	2.0	2.2
Timor-Leste	1.9	2.2
Somalia	1.7	1.9
Kenya	1.7	1.9
Total top 10 emergencies	**49.5**	**55.3**
Total	**89.6**	**100.0**

Notes: Funding to these emergencies includes all flows inside and outside an appeal that had been reported to OCHA/FTS and attributed to the emergency at the time of the database download on 8th May 2008.
Source: OCHA/FTS.

Regional distribution of funding, 2007

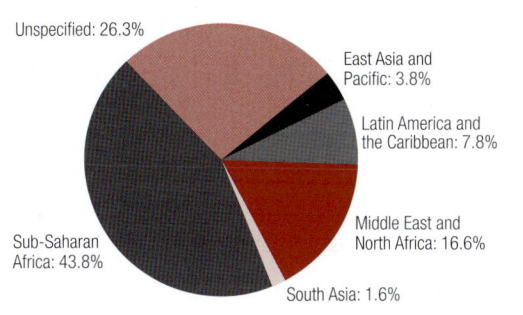

Unspecified: 26.3%

East Asia and Pacific: 3.8%

Latin America and the Caribbean: 7.8%

Middle East and North Africa: 16.6%

South Asia: 1.6%

Sub-Saharan Africa: 43.8%

Notes: Funding to these regions includes all flows inside and outside an appeal that had been reported to OCHA/FTS and attributed to a region at the time of the database download on 8th May 2008. Non-attributed flows are shown as 'unspecified'.
Source: OCHA/FTS.

Sectoral distribution of funding to UN Appeals, 2007 (%)

■ Country funding ○ UN appeal budget

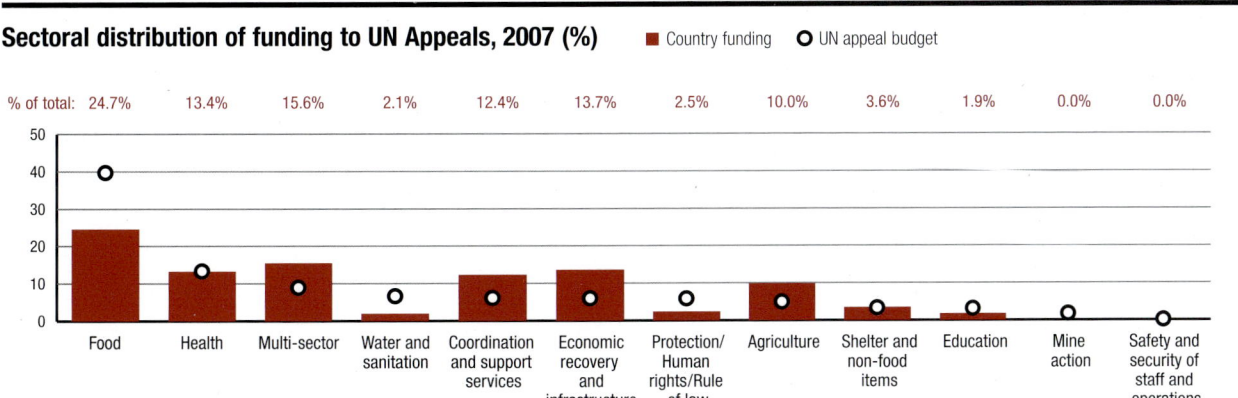

% of total: 24.7% 13.4% 15.6% 2.1% 12.4% 13.7% 2.5% 10.0% 3.6% 1.9% 0.0% 0.0%

Food | Health | Multi-sector | Water and sanitation | Coordination and support services | Economic recovery and infrastructure | Protection/ Human rights/Rule of law | Agriculture | Shelter and non-food items | Education | Mine action | Safety and security of staff and operations

Notes: Funding to these sectors include only flows inside an appeal that had been reported to OCHA/FTS and attributed to a sector at the time of the database download on 30th June 2008. Distribution of budget based on all 2007 UN appeals.
Source: OCHA/FTS.

Sweden

Sweden is the 3rd most generous humanitarian donor among the OECD/DAC group, relative to its size. Its bilateral humanitarian aid amounted to US$297 million in 2007. Swedish humanitarian aid management is shared between the Ministry of Foreign Affairs, responsible for policy and coordination, and the Swedish International Development Cooperation Agency (SIDA), overseeing implementation. Sweden has recently overhauled and streamlined its strategy for international development cooperation, which covers humanitarian assistance. Notwithstanding this development, the government's 2004 Humanitarian Aid Policy and its Guidelines, which fully embraces good practice and emphasises rights, continue to apply. Sweden has been a key promoter of the GHD initiative and has a GHD Domestic Implementation Plan. Since 2005, transition funding is primarily covered by the development cooperation budget and only occasionally through the humanitarian budget. Sweden provides substantial support to multilateral organisations and pooled funding mechanisms. Multi-year funding arrangements running up to three years are offered. SIDA directs its support primarily to Swedish NGOs but may also fund foreign NGOs. Partners must have long experience in the humanitarian sector, have adopted established international codes of conduct, and are encouraged to participate in UN-led coordination efforts. Some Swedish NGOs also have access to rapid-response funds for contingencies.

Sources: Ministry of Foreign Affairs, SIDA; DAC Peer Review for Sweden (OECD, 2005); GHD Domestic Implementation Plan for Sweden.

HRI 2008 scores by pillar

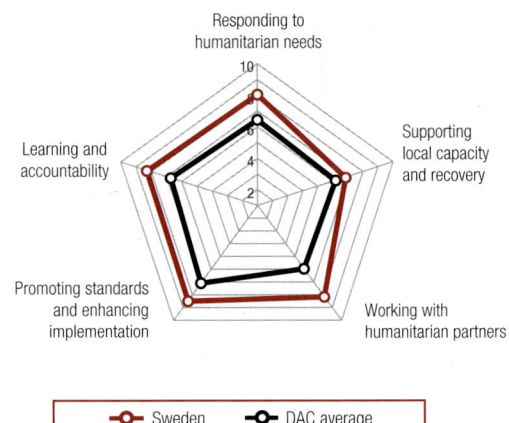

—O— Sweden   —O— DAC average

HRI 2008 results

HIGHEST SCORES	SCORE	RANK
Responding to humanitarian needs		
Funding to crisis countries with historical ties and geographical proximity	10.00	1
Generosity of humanitarian assistance	9.26	3
Supporting local capacity and recovery		
Involvement of beneficiaries in monitoring and evaluation	7.59	1
Working with humanitarian partners		
Funding UN Consolidated Inter-Agency Appeals	10.00	1
Funding IFRC and ICRC Appeals	10.00	1
Promoting standards and enhancing implementation		
Implementing international humanitarian law	10.00	1

LOWEST SCORES	SCORE	RANK
Responding to humanitarian needs		
Sectoral distribution of funding through UN appeals	1.69	21
Distribution of funding relative to ECHO's Crisis and Vulnerability Indices	6.95	20
Supporting local capacity and recovery		
Funding to strengthen local capacity	3.05	11

Overview of humanitarian aid	Sweden			Share of total DAC (%)	
	2006	2007[4]		2006	2007[4]
Total humanitarian aid (estimated), of which:	469.7	491.0		5.7	5.3
Bilateral[1]	295.0	296.6		4.4	4.7
Multilateral[2] (estimated*), of which:	174.7	194.4		11.2	12.1
Central Emergency Response Fund**	41.1	51.1		14.3	13.5
Funding to other pooled mechanisms[3]***	28.0	106.8		10.0	13.2
Official development assistance	3,955	4,334		3.8	4.2

				DAC average	
Total humanitarian aid per capita (USD)[5]	52	54		22	23
Total humanitarian aid per / official development assistance	16.5	16.6		12.2	11.3
Overseas development assistance / gross national income	1.02	0.93		0.46	0.44

Notes: All data are given in current USD m unless otherwise indicated.
(1) Based on OECD/DAC definition of bilateral humanitarian aid, which is provided directly by a donor country to a recipient country and includes non-core earmarked contributions to multilateral humanitarian organisations known as multi-bilateral aid.
(2) Core unearmarked humanitarian flows to UNHCR, UNICEF, WFP, UNRWA, UN/OCHA, ICRC and IFRC. Does not include contributions through EC. 2007 core funding to UNRWA and ICRC proxied by 2006 data.
(3) For 2006, these were IFRC's Disaster Relief Emergency Fund (DREF), Sudan Common Humanitarian Fund (CHF), Democratic Republic of Congo (DRC) Pooled Fund, and Emergency Response Funds (ERF) for DRC, Indonesia, Somalia, Republic of Congo, and Ethiopia. For 2007, these were DREF, CHF, DRC Pooled Fund, and ERFs for Central African Republic, DRC, Ethiopia, Indonesia, and Iraq.
(4) All 2007 OECD/DAC data are provisional.
(5) Where 2007 population data not available, 2006 data used.
Sources: All data from OECD-DAC except: (*) UNHCR, UNICEF, WFP, UNRWA, UN/OCHA, ICRC and IFRC; (**) OCHA; (***) OCHA, IFRC; US Federal Reserve.

Main channels of humanitarian aid, 2007

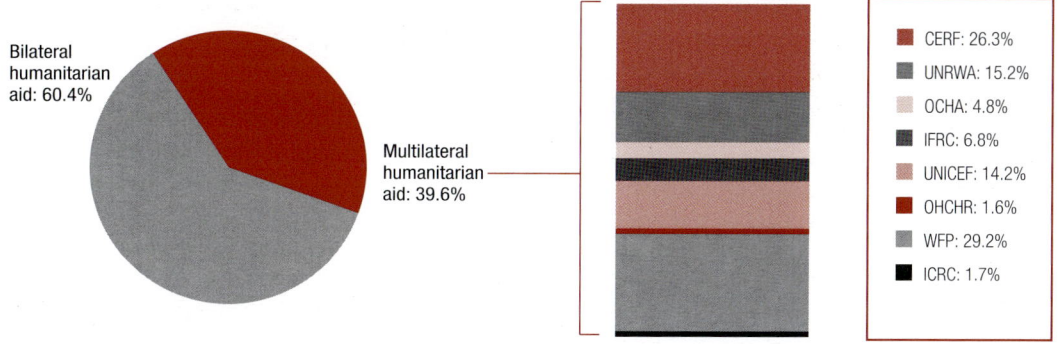

Bilateral humanitarian aid: 60.4%

Multilateral humanitarian aid: 39.6%

- CERF: 26.3%
- UNRWA: 15.2%
- OCHA: 4.8%
- IFRC: 6.8%
- UNICEF: 14.2%
- OHCHR: 1.6%
- WFP: 29.2%
- ICRC: 1.7%

Notes: see notes (1), (2) and (4) in Overview of humanitarian aid table.
Sources: Bilateral humanitarian aid: OECD-DAC. Estimated multilateral humanitarian aid: UNHCR, UNICEF, WFP, UNRWA, UN/OCHA, ICRC and IFRC.

Funding per emergency, 2007

Crisis	(USD m)	(% of total)
Sudan	30.4	8.3
Democratic Republic of Congo	22.4	6.1
West Africa	19.5	5.3
occupied Palestinian territories	15.5	4.2
Somalia	14.5	4.0
Uganda	11.0	3.0
Iraq (incl. Iraqi refugees in neighbouring countries)	9.0	2.4
Chad	7.1	1.9
Central African Republic	6.8	1.8
Zimbabwe	6.7	1.8
Total top 10 emergencies	**142.9**	**39.0**
Total	**366.9**	**100.0**

Notes: Funding to these emergencies includes all flows inside and outside an appeal that had been reported to OCHA/FTS and attributed to the emergency at the time of the database download on 8th May 2008.
Source: OCHA/FTS.

Regional distribution of funding, 2007

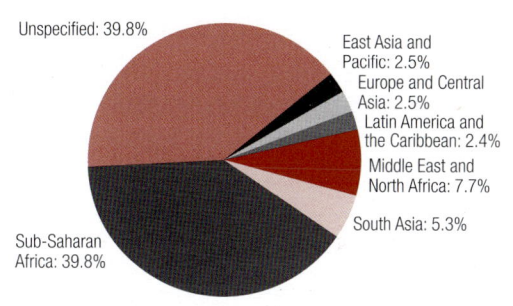

Unspecified: 39.8%

East Asia and Pacific: 2.5%
Europe and Central Asia: 2.5%
Latin America and the Caribbean: 2.4%
Middle East and North Africa: 7.7%
South Asia: 5.3%

Sub-Saharan Africa: 39.8%

Notes: Funding to these regions includes all flows inside and outside an appeal that had been reported to OCHA/FTS and attributed to a region at the time of the database download on 8th May 2008. Non-attributed flows are shown as 'unspecified'.
Source: OCHA/FTS.

Sectoral distribution of funding to UN Appeals, 2007 (%)

■ Country funding   ○ UN appeal budget

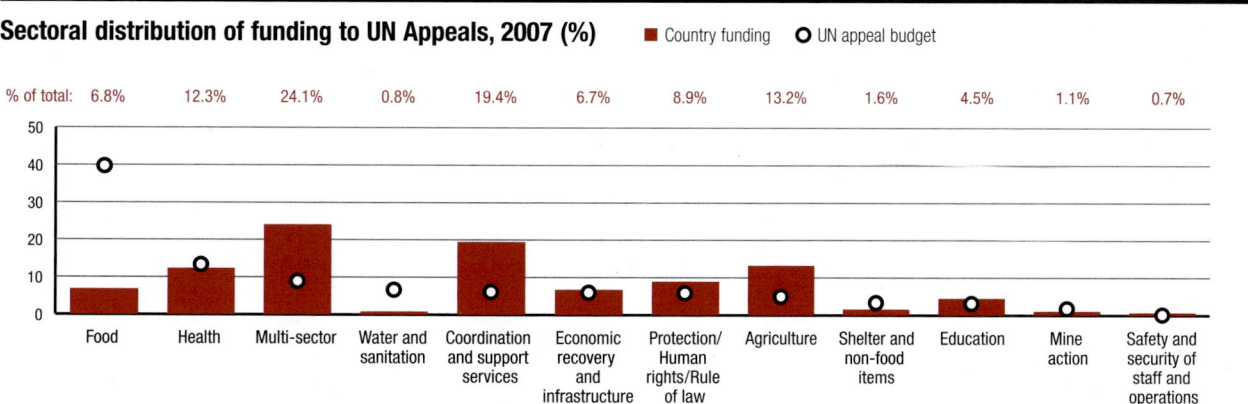

% of total:	6.8%	12.3%	24.1%	0.8%	19.4%	6.7%	8.9%	13.2%	1.6%	4.5%	1.1%	0.7%

Food | Health | Multi-sector | Water and sanitation | Coordination and support services | Economic recovery and infrastructure | Protection/ Human rights/Rule of law | Agriculture | Shelter and non-food items | Education | Mine action | Safety and security of staff and operations

Notes: Funding to these sectors include only flows inside an appeal that had been reported to OCHA/FTS and attributed to a sector at the time of the database download on 30th June 2008. Distribution of budget based on all 2007 UN appeals.
Source: OCHA/FTS.

Switzerland

Switzerland is the 7th most generous humanitarian donor among the OECD/DAC group, relative to its size. Its bilateral humanitarian aid amounted to US$165 million in 2007. The overall responsibility for Swiss humanitarian action rests with the Swiss Agency for Development and Cooperation (SDC), within the Ministry of Foreign Affairs. Switzerland's Humanitarian Action Strategy rests on a legal mandate, which provides both a clear distinction between the objectives of humanitarian aid and development cooperation, and a corresponding budget structure. SDC is both a donor and an implementing agency, managing the delivery of approximately one-sixth of the annual humanitarian aid budget. The budget line for DRR made up some 7 percent of the overall humanitarian aid budget in 2007. Switzerland hosts many of the large multi-lateral humanitarian organisations and provides them with strong financial backing. The humanitarian budget is channelled in roughly equal measure to bilateral pro-grammes or Swiss NGOs, to the Red Cross Movement and to the UN. Switzerland is currently awaiting Parliamentary approval for allocating a humanitarian budget line with a duration of least four years. Currently, DRR, early recovery, and reconstruction programmes can receive funding for up to three years. Switzerland also has multi-year funding agreements in place with the ICRC and WFP. It has a rapid response team (RRT) and a Swiss Rescue Team.

Source: Swiss Agency for Development and Cooperation; DAC Peer Review for Switzerland (OECD, 2005).

HRI 2008 scores by pillar

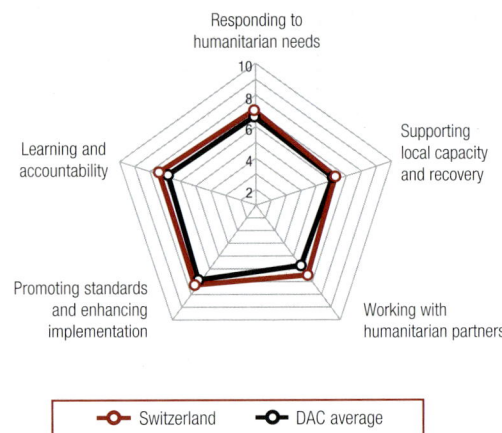

HRI 2008 results

HIGHEST SCORES	SCORE	RANK
Responding to humanitarian needs		
Saving lives and maintaining dignity	9.07	1
Supporting local capacity and recovery		
Strengthening resilience to cope with crises	7.62	1
Working with humanitarian partners		
Funding IFRC and ICRC Appeals	10.00	1
Promoting standards and enhancing implementation		
Respecting or promoting human rights	8.74	1
Respecting or promoting international humanitarian law	8.90	1

LOWEST SCORES	SCORE	RANK
Responding to humanitarian needs		
Sectoral distribution of funding through UN appeals	1.43	22
Distribution of funding relative to ECHO's Crisis and Vulnerability Indices	6.87	21
Timely funding to complex emergencies with UN appeals	5.54	18
Promoting standards and enhancing implementation		
Implementing human rights law	5.34	15
Learning and accountability		
Encouraging regular evaluations	7.63	14

Overview of humanitarian aid	Switzerland		Share of total DAC (%)	
	2006	2007[4]	2006	2007[4]
Total humanitarian aid (estimated), of which:	257.2	248.2	3.1	2.7
Bilateral[1]	175.4	165.3	2.6	2.6
Multilateral[2] (estimated*), of which:	81.8	83.0	5.3	5.2
Central Emergency Response Fund**	3.9	8.2	1.4	2.2
Funding to other pooled mechanisms[3]***	0.2	0.0	0.1	0.0
Official development assistance	1,646	1,680	1.6	1.6
			DAC average	
Total humanitarian aid per capita (USD)[5]	34	33	22	23
Total humanitarian aid per / official development assistance	20.5	19.6	12.2	11.3
Overseas development assistance / gross national income	0.39	0.37	0.46	0.44

Notes: All data are given in current USD m unless otherwise indicated.

1   Based on OECD/DAC definition of bilateral humanitarian aid, which is provided directly by a donor country to a recipient country and includes non-core earmarked contributions to multilateral humanitarian organisations known as multi-bilateral aid.

2   Core unearmarked humanitarian flows to UNHCR, UNICEF, WFP, UNRWA, UN/OCHA, ICRC and IFRC. 2007 core funding to UNRWA and ICRC proxied by 2006 data.

3   For 2006, these were IFRC's Disaster Relief Emergency Fund (DREF), Sudan Common Humanitarian Fund (CHF), Democratic Republic of Congo (DRC) Pooled Fund, and Emergency Response Funds (ERF) for DRC, Indonesia, Somalia, Republic of Congo, and Ethiopia. For 2007, these were DREF, CHF, DRC Pooled Fund, and ERFs for Central African Republic, DRC, Ethiopia, Indonesia, and Iraq.

4   All 2007 OECD/DAC data are provisional.

5   Where 2007 population data not available, 2006 data used.

Sources: All data from OECD-DAC except: (*) UNHCR, UNICEF, WFP, UNRWA, UN/OCHA, ICRC and IFRC; (**) OCHA; (***) OCHA, IFRC; US Federal Reserve.

Main channels of humanitarian aid, 2007

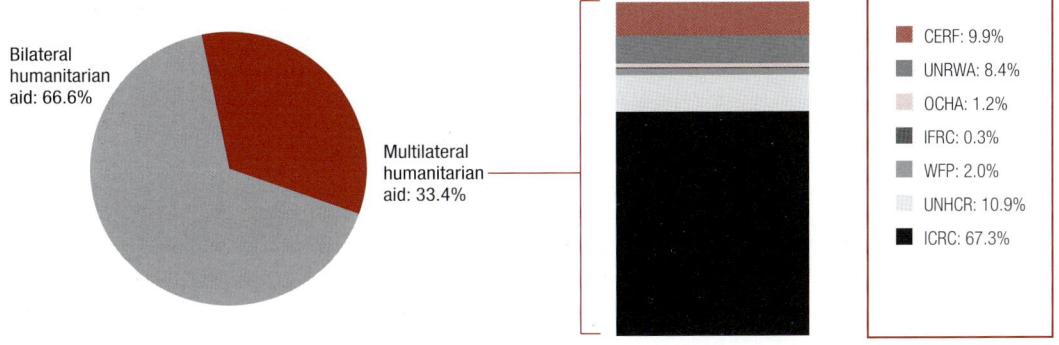

Bilateral humanitarian aid: 66.6%

Multilateral humanitarian aid: 33.4%

CERF: 9.9%
UNRWA: 8.4%
OCHA: 1.2%
IFRC: 0.3%
WFP: 2.0%
UNHCR: 10.9%
ICRC: 67.3%

Notes: see notes (1), (2) and (4) in Overview of humanitarian aid table.
Sources: Bilateral humanitarian aid: OECD-DAC. Estimated multilateral humanitarian aid: UNHCR, UNICEF, WFP, UNRWA, UN/OCHA, ICRC and IFRC.

Funding per emergency, 2007

Crisis	(USD m)	(% of total)
occupied Palestinian territories	7.0	3.2
Liberia	6.2	2.9
Sudan	5.9	2.7
West Africa	5.5	2.5
Sri Lanka	3.7	1.7
Chad	3.7	1.7
Democratic Republic of Congo	3.5	1.6
Iraq (incl. Iraqi refugees in neighbouring countries)	3.4	1.6
Zimbabwe	3.4	1.6
North Caucasus	3.3	1.5
Total top 10 emergencies	**45.7**	**21.0**
Total	**217.5**	**100.0**

Notes: Funding to these emergencies includes all flows inside and outside an appeal that had been reported to OCHA/FTS and attributed to the emergency at the time of the database download on 8th May 2008.
Source: OCHA/FTS.

Regional distribution of funding, 2007

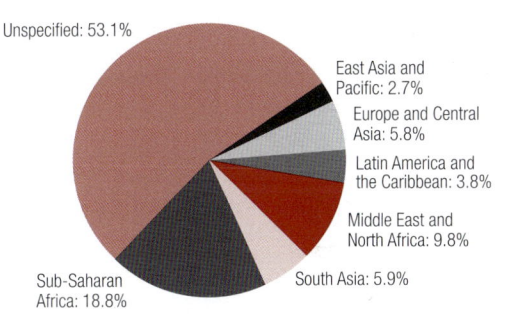

Unspecified: 53.1%

East Asia and Pacific: 2.7%
Europe and Central Asia: 5.8%
Latin America and the Caribbean: 3.8%
Middle East and North Africa: 9.8%
South Asia: 5.9%
Sub-Saharan Africa: 18.8%

Notes: Funding to these regions includes all flows inside and outside an appeal that had been reported to OCHA/FTS and attributed to a region at the time of the database download on 8th May 2008. Non-attributed flows are shown as 'unspecified'.
Source: OCHA/FTS.

Sectoral distribution of funding to UN Appeals, 2007 (%)

■ Country funding   ○ UN appeal budget

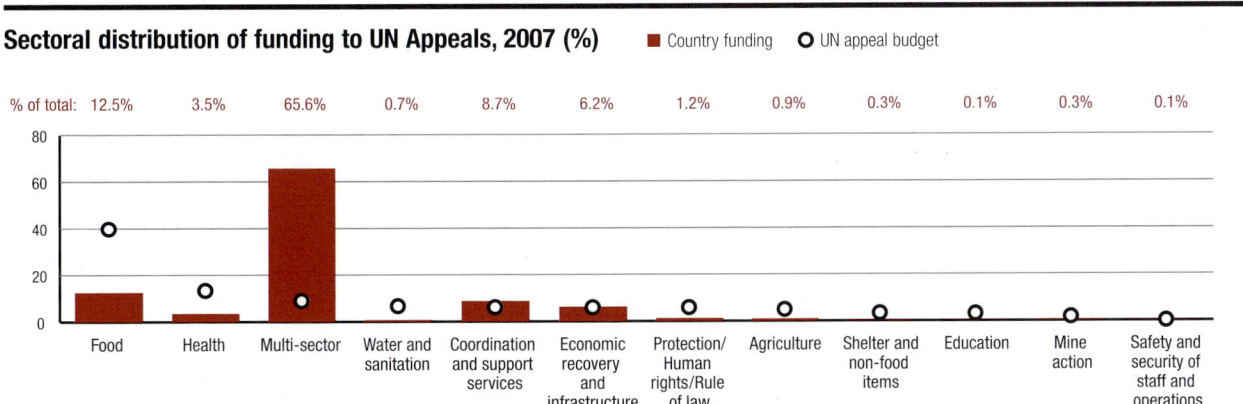

% of total: 12.5%   3.5%   65.6%   0.7%   8.7%   6.2%   1.2%   0.9%   0.3%   0.1%   0.3%   0.1%

Food | Health | Multi-sector | Water and sanitation | Coordination and support services | Economic recovery and infrastructure | Protection/ Human rights/Rule of law | Agriculture | Shelter and non-food items | Education | Mine action | Safety and security of staff and operations

Notes: Funding to these sectors include only flows inside an appeal that had been reported to OCHA/FTS and attributed to a sector at the time of the database download on 30th June 2008. Distribution of budget based on all 2007 UN appeals.
Source: OCHA/FTS.

United Kingdom

The UK is the 10th most generous humanitarian donor among the OECD/DAC group, relative to its size. Its bilateral humanitarian aid amounted to US$521 million in 2007. The Department for International Development (DFID) is in charge of humanitarian assistance, guided by its 2004 Humanitarian Policy. In protracted emergencies, DFID runs humanitarian programmes from its country office to ensure maximum policy coherence between humanitarian aid and development cooperation. The UK has been a key supporter of the GHD and promoted their formal endorsement by the OECD/DAC, which led to the inclusion of humanitarian aid within the DAC Peer Reviews. It has formulated a GHD Domestic Implementation Plan and is a strong advocate for humanitarian reform. DFID has a policy on Disaster Risk Reduction, published in March 2006, and commits to use 10 percent of its humanitarian budget to finance DRR in specific situations. In 2006, it launched a new Conflict and Humanitarian Fund, through which NGOs have access to more regular DFID funding. It relies on partnership agreements with its humanitarian partners and supports multi-year funding of up to four years. Adherence to the IASC guidelines and principles of humanitarian action is a prerequisite for receiving DFID funds, assessed through evaluations.

Sources: Department for International Development; DAC Peer Review for UK (OECD, 2006); GHD Domestic Implementation Plan for the UK.

HRI 2008 scores by pillar

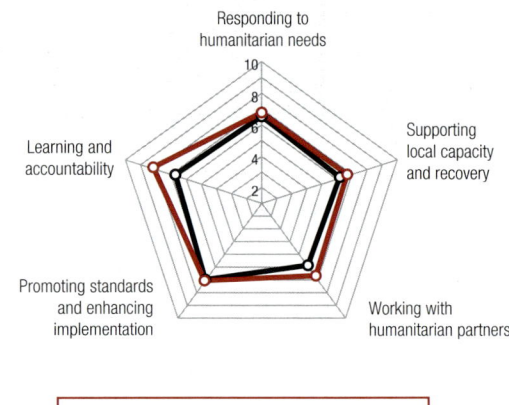

United Kingdom   DAC average

HRI 2008 results

HIGHEST SCORES	SCORE	RANK
Responding to humanitarian needs		
Sectoral distribution of funding through UN appeals	10.00	1
Supporting local capacity and recovery		
Involvement of beneficiaries in monitoring and evaluation	7.41	3
Working with humanitarian partners		
Funding to CERF and other quick disbursement mechanisms	10.00	1
Funding to NGOs	10.00	1
Learning and accountability		
Encouraging regular evaluations	8.52	1

LOWEST SCORES	SCORE	RANK
Responding to humanitarian needs		
Saving lives and maintaining dignity	8.20	18
Impartiality	8.21	18
Distribution of funding relative to ECHO's Crisis and Vulnerability Indices	7.69	17
Working with humanitarian partners		
Supporting contingency planning and strengthening response capacity	5.06	13
Promoting standards and enhancing implementation		
Implementing human rights law	6.09	14

Overview of humanitarian aid

	United Kingdom 2006	United Kingdom 2007[4]	Share of total DAC (%) 2006	Share of total DAC (%) 2007[4]
Total humanitarian aid (estimated), of which:	1,035.5	737.2	12.5	8.0
Bilateral[1]	834.6	521.1	12.4	8.3
Multilateral[2] (estimated*), of which:	200.9	216.1	12.9	13.5
Central Emergency Response Fund**	69.9	83.7	24.3	22.1
Funding to other pooled mechanisms[3]***	154.7	431.8	55.2	53.3
Official development assistance	12,459	9,921	11.9	9.6

			DAC average	DAC average
Total humanitarian aid per capita (USD)[5]	17	12	22	23
Total humanitarian aid per / official development assistance	11.9	14.2	12.2	11.3
Overseas development assistance / gross national income	0.51	0.36	0.46	0.44

Notes: All data are given in current USD m unless otherwise indicated.

(1) Based on OECD/DAC definition of bilateral humanitarian aid, which is provided directly by a donor country to a recipient country and includes non-core earmarked contributions to multilateral humanitarian organisations known as multi-bilateral aid.

(2) Core unearmarked humanitarian flows to UNHCR, UNICEF, WFP, UNRWA, UN/OCHA, ICRC and IFRC. Does not include contributions through EC. 2007 core funding to UNRWA and ICRC proxied by 2006 data.

(3) For 2006, these were IFRC's Disaster Relief Emergency Fund (DREF), Sudan Common Humanitarian Fund (CHF), Democratic Republic of Congo (DRC) Pooled Fund, and Emergency Response Funds (ERF) for DRC, Indonesia, Somalia, Republic of Congo, and Ethiopia. For 2007, these were DREF, CHF, DRC Pooled Fund, and ERFs for Central African Republic, DRC, Ethiopia, Indonesia, and Iraq.

(4) All 2007 OECD/DAC data are provisional.

(5) Where 2007 population data not available, 2006 data used.

Sources: All data from OECD-DAC except: (*) UNHCR, UNICEF, WFP, UNRWA, UN/OCHA, ICRC and IFRC; (**) OCHA; (***) OCHA, IFRC; US Federal Reserve.

Main channels of humanitarian aid, 2007

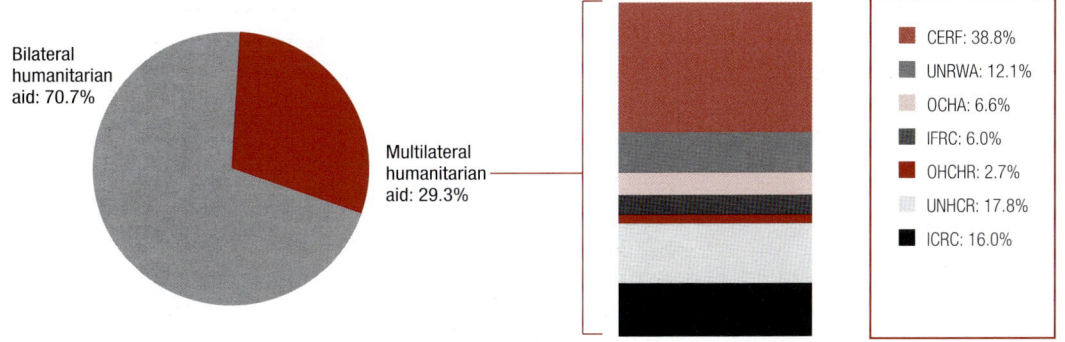

Bilateral humanitarian aid: 70.7%

Multilateral humanitarian aid: 29.3%

- CERF: 38.8%
- UNRWA: 12.1%
- OCHA: 6.6%
- IFRC: 6.0%
- OHCHR: 2.7%
- UNHCR: 17.8%
- ICRC: 16.0%

Notes: see notes (1), (2) and (4) in Overview of humanitarian aid table.
Sources: Bilateral humanitarian aid: OECD-DAC. Estimated multilateral humanitarian aid: UNHCR, UNICEF, WFP, UNRWA, UN/OCHA, ICRC and IFRC.

Funding per emergency, 2007

Crisis	(USD m)	(% of total)
Sudan	107.4	23.6
Democratic Republic of Congo	62.5	13.7
Zimbabwe	36.7	8.1
Uganda	34.8	7.6
Iraq (incl. Iraqi refugees in neighbouring countries)	19.4	4.3
Somalia	16.2	3.6
Chad	10.6	2.3
Ethiopia	7.6	1.7
Pakistan	5.9	1.3
Pakistan - floods / cyclone - July	4.8	1.1
Total top 10 emergencies	**306.0**	**67.2**
Total	**455.1**	**100.0**

Notes: Funding to these emergencies includes all flows inside and outside an appeal that had been reported to OCHA/FTS and attributed to the emergency at the time of the database download on 8th May 2008.
Source: OCHA/FTS.

Regional distribution of funding, 2007

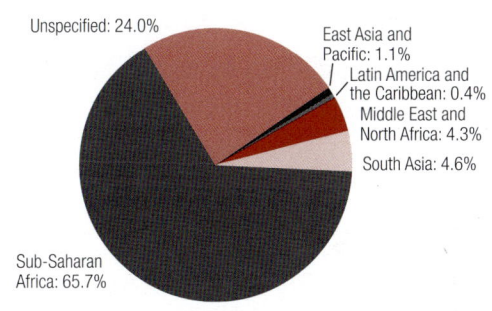

Unspecified: 24.0%

East Asia and Pacific: 1.1%
Latin America and the Caribbean: 0.4%
Middle East and North Africa: 4.3%
South Asia: 4.6%

Sub-Saharan Africa: 65.7%

Notes: Funding to these regions includes all flows inside and outside an appeal that had been reported to OCHA/FTS and attributed to a region at the time of the database download on 8th May 2008. Non-attributed flows are shown as 'unspecified'.
Source: OCHA/FTS.

Sectoral distribution of funding to UN Appeals, 2007 (%)

■ Country funding ○ UN appeal budget

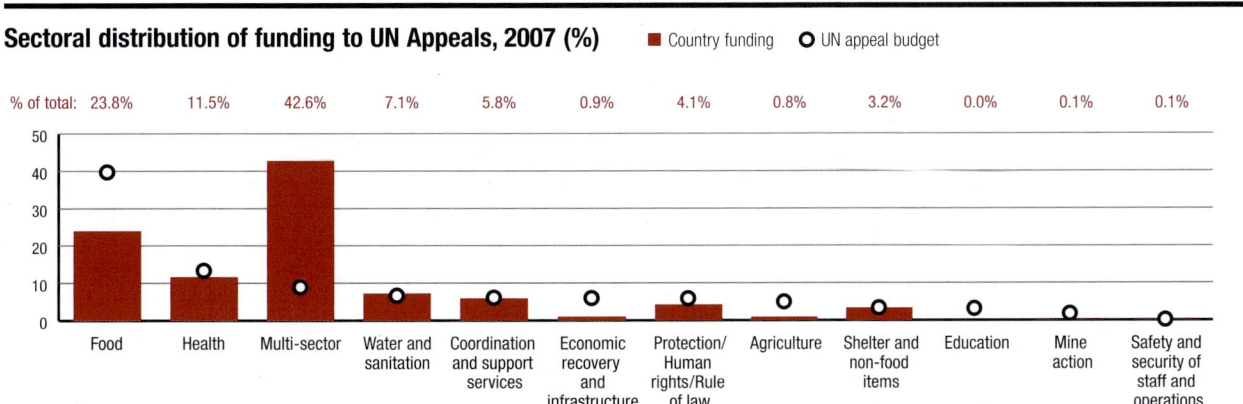

| % of total: | 23.8% | 11.5% | 42.6% | 7.1% | 5.8% | 0.9% | 4.1% | 0.8% | 3.2% | 0.0% | 0.1% | 0.1% |

Food | Health | Multi-sector | Water and sanitation | Coordination and support services | Economic recovery and infrastructure | Protection/ Human rights/Rule of law | Agriculture | Shelter and non-food items | Education | Mine action | Safety and security of staff and operations

Notes: Funding to these sectors include only flows inside an appeal that had been reported to OCHA/FTS and attributed to a sector at the time of the database download on 30th June 2008. Distribution of budget based on all 2007 UN appeals.
Source: OCHA/FTS.

United States

The United States is the 13th most generous humanitarian donor among the OECD/DAC group, relative to its size. Its bilateral humanitarian aid amounted to US$2.96 billion in 2007. The US humanitarian work is divided among three main actors: the USAID Office for Foreign Disaster Assistance (OFDA), its Food for Peace Program (FFP), and the State Department's Bureau of Population, Refugees, and Migration (PRM). The latter focuses on providing protection and assistance for refugees and victims of conflict. Food for Peace, accounting for almost half of the total humanitarian budget, is in charge of emergency food aid. Finally, OFDA, with the smallest budget, coordinates international disaster assistance, channels most of its funding through NGOs. Due to the complex institutional structures that govern its massive humanitarian aid budget of over US$3 billion, there is no single policy strategy. However, the Foreign Assistance Framework (2006) spells out a new orientation for humanitarian assistance, including a stronger emphasis on integrating relief and development. A GHD implementation plan is currently in preparation.

Source: PRM; FFP; OFDA; DAC Peer Review for US (OECD, 2006).

HRI 2008 scores by pillar

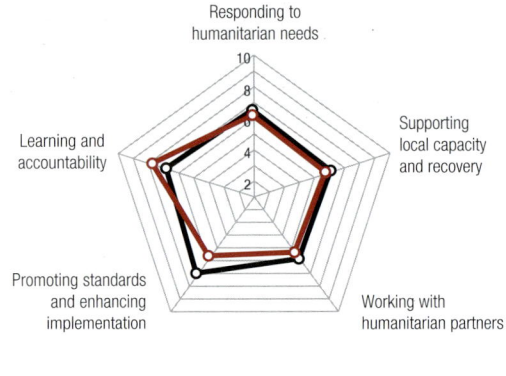

United States — DAC average

HRI 2008 results

HIGHEST SCORES	SCORE	RANK
Responding to humanitarian needs		
Timely funding	7.46	4
Donor capacity for informed decision-making	7.29	2
Sectoral distribution of funding through UN appeals	10.00	1
Working with humanitarian partners		
Supporting contingency planning and strengthening response capacity	5.44	6
Promoting standards and enhancing implementation		
Donor engagement in protection and assistance to civilians	8.04	6

LOWEST SCORES	SCORE	RANK
Responding to humanitarian needs		
Independence	7.00	22
Neutrality	7.66	21
Working with humanitarian partners		
Unearmarked funding	2.03	21
Promoting standards and enhancing implementation		
Implementing international humanitarian law	1.43	22
Implementing human rights law	1.43	22

Overview of humanitarian aid

	United States			Share of total DAC (%)	
	2006	2007[4]		2006	2007[4]
Total humanitarian aid (estimated), of which:	3,167.0	3,144.9		38.1	34.1
Bilateral[1]	3,021.6	2,959.8		44.8	47.1
Multilateral[2] (estimated*), of which:	145.4	185.1		9.3	11.5
Central Emergency Response Fund**	10.0	0.0		3.5	0.0
Funding to other pooled mechanisms[3]***	0.1	0.2		0.0	0.0
Official development assistance	23,532	21,753		22.5	21.0
				DAC average	
Total humanitarian aid per capita (USD)[5]	11	10		22	23
Total humanitarian aid per / official development assistance	15.0	16.6		12.2	11.3
Overseas development assistance / gross national income	0.18	0.16		0.46	0.44

Notes: All data are given in current USD m unless otherwise indicated.

1 Based on OECD/DAC definition of bilateral humanitarian aid, which is provided directly by a donor country to a recipient country and includes non-core earmarked contributions to multilateral humanitarian organisations known as multi-bilateral aid.

2 Core unearmarked humanitarian flows to UNHCR, UNICEF, WFP, UNRWA, UN/OCHA, ICRC and IFRC. 2007 core funding to UNRWA and ICRC proxied by 2006 data.

3 For 2006, these were IFRC's Disaster Relief Emergency Fund (DREF), Sudan Common Humanitarian Fund (CHF), Democratic Republic of Congo (DRC) Pooled Fund, and Emergency Response Funds (ERF) for DRC, Indonesia, Somalia, Republic of Congo, and Ethiopia. For 2007, these were DREF, CHF, DRC Pooled Fund, and ERFs for Central African Republic, DRC, Ethiopia, Indonesia, and Iraq.

4 All 2007 OECD/DAC data are provisional.

5 Where 2007 population data not available, 2006 data used.

Sources: All data from OECD-DAC except: (*) UNHCR, UNICEF, WFP, UNRWA, UN/OCHA, ICRC and IFRC; (**) OCHA; (***) OCHA, IFRC; US Federal Reserve.

Main channels of humanitarian aid, 2007

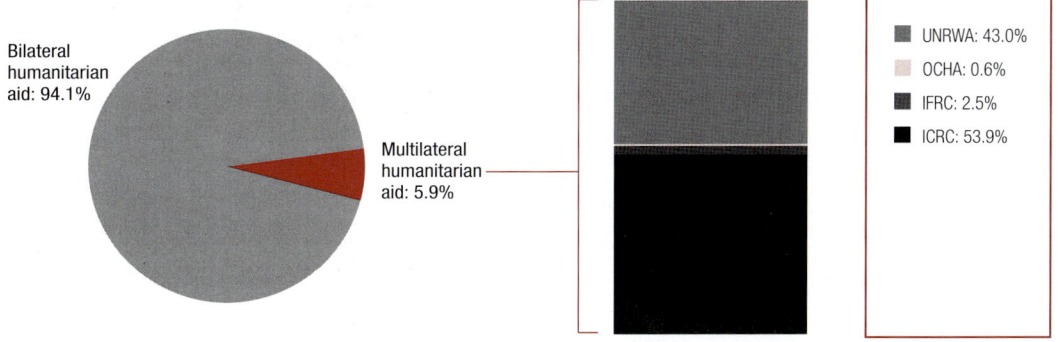

Bilateral humanitarian aid: 94.1%

Multilateral humanitarian aid: 5.9%

- UNRWA: 43.0%
- OCHA: 0.6%
- IFRC: 2.5%
- ICRC: 53.9%

Notes: see notes (1), (2) and (4) in Overview of humanitarian aid table.
Sources: Bilateral humanitarian aid: OECD-DAC. Estimated multilateral humanitarian aid: UNHCR, UNICEF, WFP, UNRWA, UN/OCHA, ICRC and IFRC.

Funding per emergency, 2007

Crisis	(USD m)	(% of total)
Sudan	536.3	27.3
Ethiopia	294.7	15.0
Zimbabwe	170.2	8.7
Chad	133.5	6.8
Somalia	120.1	6.1
Democratic Republic of Congo	115.0	5.8
Iraq (incl. Iraqi refugees in neighbouring countries)	114.3	5.8
Uganda	87.4	4.4
occupied Palestinian territories	76.0	3.9
Sri Lanka	35.2	1.8
Total top 10 emergencies	**1682.6**	**85.5**
Total	**1966.9**	**100.0**

Notes: Funding to these emergencies includes all flows inside and outside an appeal that had been reported to OCHA/FTS and attributed to the emergency at the time of the database download on 8th May 2008.
Source: OCHA/FTS.

Regional distribution of funding, 2007

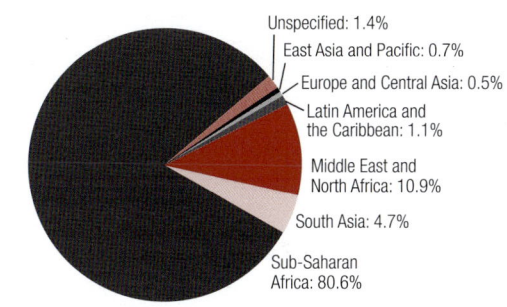

Unspecified: 1.4%
East Asia and Pacific: 0.7%
Europe and Central Asia: 0.5%
Latin America and the Caribbean: 1.1%
Middle East and North Africa: 10.9%
South Asia: 4.7%
Sub-Saharan Africa: 80.6%

Notes: Funding to these regions includes all flows inside and outside an appeal that had been reported to OCHA/FTS and attributed to a region at the time of the database download on 8th May 2008. Non-attributed flows are shown as 'unspecified'.
Source: OCHA/FTS.

Sectoral distribution of funding to UN Appeals, 2007 (%)

- Country funding
- UN appeal budget

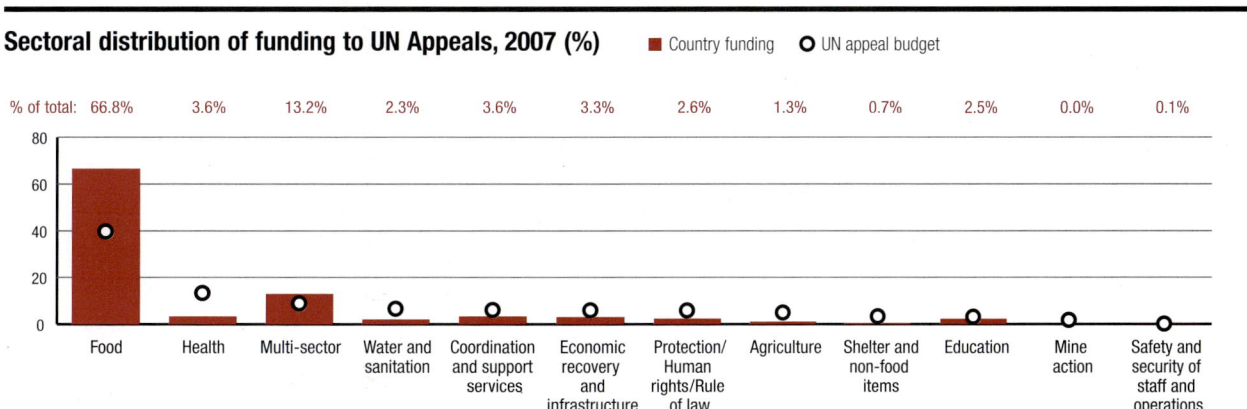

% of total: 66.8% 3.6% 13.2% 2.3% 3.6% 3.3% 2.6% 1.3% 0.7% 2.5% 0.0% 0.1%

Food, Health, Multi-sector, Water and sanitation, Coordination and support services, Economic recovery and infrastructure, Protection/Human rights/Rule of law, Agriculture, Shelter and non-food items, Education, Mine action, Safety and security of staff and operations

Notes: Funding to these sectors include only flows inside an appeal that had been reported to OCHA/FTS and attributed to a sector at the time of the database download on 30th June 2008. Distribution of budget based on all 2007 UN appeals.
Source: OCHA/FTS.

Acronyms

AA...................Federal Foreign Office (Germany)

ACBAR...........Agency Coordinating Body for Afghan Relief

ACF.................Action Contre la Faim

ADA................Austrian Development Agency

ADB................Asian Development Bank

ADC................Austrian Development Cooperation

AECI...............Spanish Agency for International Cooperation

AETF..............Afghanistan Emergency Trust Fund

AGEG............Arbeitsgemeinschaft Entwicklungspolitischer Gutachter (German Association of Development Consultants)

AHLC.............Ad Hoc Liaison Committee

ALNAP..........Active Learning Network for Accountability and Performance in Humanitarian Action

AMIS..............African Union Mission in Sudan

ANDS..............Afghanistan National Development Strategy

AU...................African Union

AUC...............Autodefensas Unidas de Colombia

BMZ................Bundesministerium für wirtschaftliche Zusammenarbeit und Entwicklung (Federal Ministry for Economic Cooperation and Development, Germany)

BPHS..............Basic Package of Health (Care) Services

CAF...............Country Assistance Framework (Congo)

CAFOD...........Catholic Agency for Overseas Development

CAP...............Consolidated Appeals Process

CAP...............Coordinated Aid Programme (Central African Republic)

CAR...............Central African Republic

CARE.............Christian Action Research and Education

CCA...............Comité de Crises Alimentaire (Committee for Food Crises)

CCHA.............Consultative Committee on Humanitarian Affairs

CEMAC..........Economic and Monetary Community of the Central African States

CERF.............Central Emergency Response Fund (United Nations)

CFA................Ceasefire Agreement (Sri Lanka)

CHA...............Consortium of Humanitarian Agencies

CHAP.............Common Humanitarian Action Plan

CHF...............Common Humanitarian Fund

CIC.................Center on International Cooperation

CID.................Council for International Development (New Zealand)

CIDA..............Canadian International Development Agency

CIH.................Centre d'information humanitaire (Humanitarian Information Centre)

CIMIC.............Civilian-Military Coordination (NATO)

CINEP.............Centro de Investigación y Educación Popular

CIP.................Centre for International Policy

CODHES........Council for Human Rights and Displacement (Colombia)

COMPAS........Centre on Migration Policy and Society

COOPI...........Cooperazione Internazionale

CPA................Comprehensive Peace Agreement (Sudan)

CPI.................Corruption Perception Index (Transparency International)

CPIA..............Provincial Inter-Agency Committees (Congo)

CRS...............Catholic Relief Services

CSO...............civil society organisation

DAC...............Development Assistance Committee (OECD)

DAH...............*Délégation à l'Action Humanitaire* (France)

DANIDA..........Danish International Development Agency

DARA.............Development Assistance Research Associates

DART.............Disaster Assistance Relief Teams

DCD...............Development Cooperation Directorate (Ireland)

DCHA.............(Bureau for) Democracy, Conflict and Humanitarian Assistance (United States)

DCI.................Development Cooperation Ireland

DDR...............Disarmament, Demobilisation and Reintegration

DER...............Disasters and Emergency Response (Bangladesh)

DEV...............Directorate-General for Development (European Community)

DFAIT	Department of Foreign Affairs and International Trade (Canada)
DFID	Department for International Development (UK)
DGCS	General Direction of Development Cooperation (Italy)
DGDC	Directorate-General for Development Cooperation (Belgium)
DI	Development Initiatives
DIPECHO	Disaster Preparedness ECHO
DMB	Disaster Management Bureau (Bangladesh)
DMV/HH	Humanitarian Aid Division (Netherlands)
DPA	Darfur Peace Agreement
DRC	Democratic Republic of Congo
DREF	(International Federation) Disaster Relief Emergency Fund
EA	Emergency Appeals
EC	European Commission
ECHO	European Commission Humanitarian (Aid) Office
EES	European Evaluation Society
ELN	Ejercito de Liberación Nacional (Colombia)
EMOP	Emergency Mode Operation Plan
EPC	European Policy Centre
EPPR	Emergency Preparedness and Post-Emergency Recovery Fund (Ireland)
EPPR	Emergency, Prevention, Preparedness, and Response
ERDF	European Regional Development Fund (EU)
ERF	Emergency Response Fund
ESF	European Social Fund (EU)
ESPA	Eastern Sudan Peace Agreement
ESSP	Emergency Support Services Project
EUFOR	European Union Force
EuropeAid	EuropeAid Co-operation Office (European Community)
EWS	Early Warning System
FARC	Fuerzas Armadas Revolucionarias de Colombia
FAO	Food and Agriculture Organization (United Nations)
FCA	Forgotten Crisis Assessment
FED	Fond européen pour le développement (Congo)
FEWSNET	Famine Early Warning System Network
FFO	Federal Foreign Office (Germany)
FORSUR	Fondo para la Reconstrucción del Sur (Peru)
FRIDE	Fundación para las Relaciones Internacionales y el Diálogo Exterior
FTS	Financial Tracking Service (OCHA)
GAM	Global Acute Malnutrition
GHA	Global Humanitarian Assistance

GHD	Good Humanitarian Donorship
GIEWS	Global Information and Early Warning System
GoS	Government of Sudan
GoSS	Government of South Sudan
GTZ	Deutsche Gesellschaft für Technishe Zusammenarbeit
HA	humanitarian assistance or humanitarian aid
HACC	Humanitarian Aid Coordination Centre (Germany)
HAP	Humanitarian Action Plan
HAP	Humanitarian Assistance Programme
HAPI	Humanitarian Accountability Partnership International
HAU	Humanitarian Affairs Unit (Afghanistain)
HCG	Humanitarian Coordination Group
HDC	Humanitarian Contact Group (Denmark)
HDPT	Humanitarian and Development Partnership Team
HDR	Human Development Report (UNDP)
HERF	Humanitarian Emergency Response Fund
HFA	Hyogo Framework for Action
HPG	Humanitarian Policy Group (ODI, UK)
HPN	Humanitarian Practice Network
IANDS	Interim Afghanistan National Development Strategy
IAR	International Atrocities Regime
IASC	Inter-Agency Standing Committee (UN)
ICF	Interim Cooperation Framework ICGInternational Crisis Group
ICG	International Crisis Group
ICRC	International Committee of the Red Cross
ICVA	International Council of Voluntary Agencies
IDAC	International Development Advisory Committee (New Zealand)
IDEAS	International Development Evaluation Association
IDF	Israeli Defense Force (Israel)
IDMC	Internal Displacement Monitoring Centre
IDP	Internally Displaced Person
IERP	Integrated Emergency Response Program
IFI	International Financial Institutions
IFRC	International Federation of Red Cross and Red Crescent (Societies)
IHL	International humanitarian law
IMC	International Medical Corps
IMF	International Monetary Fund
INDECI	Instituto Nacional de Defensa Civil (Peru)
INGO	International nongovernmental organisation
INSARAG	International Search and Rescue Advisory Group

IOM ....International Organization for Migration

IPAD...............Portuguese Institute for Development Support

IPC.................Integrated Food Security and Humanitarian Phase Classification

IRC.................International Rescue Committee

IRIN................Humanitarian News and Analysis (OCHA)

ISAF...............International Security Assistance Force (Afghanistan)

ISDR ....International Secretariat for Disaster Reduction (United Nations)

ISDR ....International Strategy for Disaster Reduction

JCMB..............Joint Coordination and Monitoring Board (Afghanistan)

JEM ....Justice and Equality Movement (Sudan)

JDR(L) ....Japan Disaster Relief (Law)

JICA................Japan International Cooperation Agency

LACC ....Local Aid Coordination Committee

LCD ....Local Consultative Group (Bangladesh)

LOD ....long-term debt

LP ....Listening Poject

LRA ....Lord's Resistance Army (Sudan)

LRC ....Lebanese Red Cross

LRRD..............linking relief, rehabilitation, and development

LTTE ....Liberation Tigers of Tamil Eelam

MAS...............Muerte a Secuestradores (Colombia)

MCDA ....Military and Civil Defence Assets

MDG ....Millennium Development Goals

MFA ....Ministry of Foreign Affairs

MIF.................Multinational Interim Force

MINURCAT .....United Nations Mission in the Central African Republic

MOD ....Ministry of Defence

MONUC ....United Nations Mission in the Democratic Republic of Congo

MOU ....Memorandum of Understanding

MSF ....Médecins Sans Frontières

MSU ....Mediation Support Unit

MUAC ....Middle Upper Arm Circumference (measurement)

NAF ....Needs Analysis Framework

NAFM ....Needs Assessment Framework Matrix

NCCI ....NGO Coordination Committee in Iraq

NGO...............non-governmental organisation

NORAD...........Norwegian Agency for Development Cooperation

NSP ....National Solidarity Programme (Afghanistan)

NZAid ....New Zealand Agency for International Development

OCHA ....Office for the Coordination of Humanitarian Affairs (United Nations)

ODA ....Official Development Assistance

ODI ....Overseas Development Institute

OECD/DAC .....Organisation for Economic Co-operation and Development-Development Assistance Committee

OFDA ....Office of Foreign Disaster Assistance (United States)

OHCHR...........Office of the High Commissioner for Human Rights (United Nations)

oPt ....occupied Palestinian territories

OTI.................Office of Transition Initiatives (United States, USAID)

PAHO..............Pan-American Health Organization

PF ....Pooled Fund

PLO ....Palestine Liberation Organization

PMC...............Project management cycle

PA ....Palestinian Authority

PRM...............(Bureau of) Population, Refugees, and Migration (United States)

PRSP ....Poverty Reduction Strategy Paper

PRT................Provincial Reconstruction Team

PU ....Première Urgence

QIP.................quick impact projects

RELEX ....Directorate-General for External Relations (European Community)

RCO...............(UN) Resident Coordinator's Office

RRI.................Risk Reduction Indicators

RRI.................Rapid Response Initiative

RRM...............rapid reaction mechanism

RRT ....Rapid Response Team

SAF................Sudanese Armed Forces

SCHR.............Steering Committee for Humanitarian Response

SDC ....Swiss Agency for Development and Cooperation

SCF................Save the Children Fund

SIDA ....Swedish Development Cooperation Agency

SMART ....Standardized Monitoring and Assessment of Relief and Transitions (United States)

SMS ....short message service

SPHERE ....Humanitarian Charter and Minimum Standards in Disaster Response

SPLA ....Sudan People's Liberation Army

SPLM..............Sudan People's Liberation Movement (Sudan)

SWOT ....Strengths, Weaknesses, Opportunities and Threats

TEC................Tsunami Evaluation Coalition

TIM...............Temporary International Mechanism

UFDR..............Union of Democratic Forces for Unity (Central African Republic)

UNAIDS..........Joint United Nations Programme on HIV/AIDS

UNAMA..........United Nations Mission in Afghanistan

UNDAC...........United Nations Disaster Assessment and Coordination

UNDP..............United Nations Development Programme

UNESCO........United Nations Educational, Scientific and Cultural Organization

UNFPA...........United Nations Population Fund

UNHCR..........Office of the United Nations High Commissioner for Refugees

UNICEF..........United Nations Children's Fund

UNIFEM..........United Nations Development Fund for Women

UNIFIL...........United Nations Interim Force in Lebanon

UNAMIR.........UN Assistance Mission for Rwanda

UNMIS...........United Nations Mission in Sudan

UNRWA..........United Nations Relief and Works Agency

UNSCO..........United Nations Special Coordinator for the Middle East Peace Process

URD...............Urgence, Réhabilitation, Développement

USAID...........United States Agency for International Development

WASH...........water, sanitation and hygiene

WB................West Bank

WFP...............World Food Programme

WHO..............World Health Organization

Appendix

Questionnaire on Good Practice in Humanitarian Donorship[1]

Following are the questions asked during each field visit to the relevant agencies actively working with donors, which had given them funding for that particular crisis. The target survey group included national and international NGOs, UN agencies, funds, and programmes, as well as other international organisations active in the field and involved in humanitarian action. A fuller discussion of the survey and underlying methodological issues is presented in Chapter 1 of the *Index*.

Objectives of humanitarian action

1.01 In your view are the donor's objectives for humanitarian action consistent with saving lives, alleviating suffering, and maintaining human dignity?

Not at all	1 2 3 4 5 6 7	Completely and fully

1.02 In your view are the donor's objectives for humanitarian action consistent with preventing, or strengthening preparedness for, emergencies?

Not at all	1 2 3 4 5 6 7	Completely and fully

2.01 Are the donor's humanitarian actions impartial, meaning implemented solely on the basis of need, without discrimination between or within affected populations?

Not at all	1 2 3 4 5 6 7	Completely and fully

2.02 Are the donor's humanitarian actions neutral, meaning not favouring any side in an armed conflict or dispute?

Not at all	1 2 3 4 5 6 7	Completely and fully

2.03 Are the donor's humanitarian actions independent of political or economic objectives?

Not at all	1 2 3 4 5 6 7	Completely and fully

2.04 Are the donor's humanitarian actions independent of military objectives?

Not at all	1 2 3 4 5 6 7	Completely and fully

General principles

3.01 How actively is the donor engaged in protection and assistance to civilians?

Not at all	1 2 3 4 5 6 7	Completely and fully

4.01 In the crisis, does the donor respect and promote the protection of human rights?

Not at all	1 2 3 4 5 6 7	Completely and fully

4.02 In the crisis, does the donor respect and promote international humanitarian law and refugee law?

Not at all	1 2 3 4 5 6 7	Completely and fully

5.01 To allow you to respond immediately to the most pressing humanitarian needs, the donor permits you to reallocate funds from another crisis.

Not at all	1 2 3 4 5 6 7	Completely and fully

5.02 Does the donor fund your needs assessment in order to allow you better respond to humanitarian needs?

Not at all	1 2 3 4 5 6 7	Completely and fully

5.04 To allow you to respond immediately to the most pressing humanitarian needs, the donor provides funding in a timely manner.

Not at all   1 2 3 4 5 6 7   Completely and fully

6.01 The donor's humanitarian funding is allocated on the basis of needs assessments and in proportion to need.

Not at all   1 2 3 4 5 6 7   Completely and fully

6.02 Does the donor have the requisite humanitarian expertise or has the donor deployed emergency teams in the country/region that enable informed decision-making?

Not at all   1 2 3 4 5 6 7   Completely and fully

7.01 In the design and implementation of the humanitarian response, has the donor requested that you consult with the beneficiaries and ensure their active involvement?

Not at all   1 2 3 4 5 6 7   Completely and fully

7.02 In the monitoring and evaluation of the humanitarian response, has the donor requested that you consult with the beneficiaries and ensure their active involvement?

Not at all   1 2 3 4 5 6 7   Completely and fully

8.01 If appropriate to the crisis context, the donor has strengthened (through your projects or otherwise) the capacity of the Government to prevent, prepare for, mitigate, and respond to humanitarian crises.

Not at all   1 2 3 4 5 6 7   Completely and fully

8.02 The donor has strengthened the capacity of local communities to prevent, prepare for, mitigate, and respond to humanitarian crises.

Not at all   1 2 3 4 5 6 7   Completely and fully

8.03 The donor has supported programs that increase or strengthen resilience, meaning building the capacity to cope with crises.

Not at all   1 2 3 4 5 6 7   Completely and fully

8.04 The donor has ensured that governments and local communities are better able to coordinate effectively with humanitarian partners.

Not at all   1 2 3 4 5 6 7   Completely and fully

8.05 More generally, the donor supports and facilitates coordination efforts of the humanitarian system.

Not at all   1 2 3 4 5 6 7   Completely and fully

9.01 Has the donor provided humanitarian assistance in ways that are supportive of recovery and/or long-term development?

Not at all   1 2 3 4 5 6 7   Completely and fully

9.02 Has the donor provided humanitarian assistance to ensure the rapid recovery of sustainable livelihoods?

Not at all   1 2 3 4 5 6 7   Completely and fully

10.01 In implementing humanitarian action, the donor supports and promotes the vital role of non-governmental organizations and the Red Cross and Red Crescent Movement.

Not at all   1 2 3 4 5 6 7   Completely and fully

10.02 In implementing humanitarian action, the donor supports and promotes the central role of the United Nations in providing leadership and coordination of international humanitarian action.

Not at all   1 2 3 4 5 6 7   Completely and fully

10.03 In implementing humanitarian action, the donor supports and promotes the special role of the International Committee of the Red Cross.

Not at all   1 2 3 4 5 6 7   Completely and fully

Good practices in donor financing, management, and accountability

(a) Funding

11.01 Donor support for your humanitarian action in an ongoing crisis has been affected by the needs of new crises elsewhere.

Not at all   1 2 3 4 5 6 7   Completely and fully

12.01 Funding from the donor has been provided to you predictably, in a reliable manner.

Not at all   1 2 3 4 5 6 7   Completely and fully

13.01 Has the donor reduced earmarking, or enhanced its flexibility? [Earmarking: when a donor requires its funds to be used for specific, predefined items. Eg. detailed budget line allocations]

Not at all   1 2 3 4 5 6 7   Completely and fully

13.02 Does the donor provide the necessary flexibility in the use of funds to help you adapt your program to changing needs?

Not at all   1 2 3 4 5 6 7   Completely and fully

13.03 Has the donor introduced longer-term funding arrangements that allow you to improve program assistance (in relevant areas)?

Not at all   1 2 3 4 5 6 7   Completely and fully

(b) Promoting standards and enhancing implementation

15.01 The donor requests your adherence to good practice and your commitment to promoting accountability, efficiency and effectiveness in implementing humanitarian action.

Not at all   1 2 3 4 5 6 7   Completely and fully

16.01 Does the donor address the specific needs of internally displaced persons and promote the use of related international guidelines?

Not at all   1 2 3 4 5 6 7   Completely and fully

17.01 Has the donor supported your implementation of humanitarian action throughout the whole crisis?

Not at all   1 2 3 4 5 6 7   Completely and fully

17.02 The donor has helped to facilitate safe humanitarian access.

Not at all   1 2 3 4 5 6 7   Completely and fully

18.01 The donor has supported mechanisms for your organization's contingency planning.

Not at all   1 2 3 4 5 6 7   Completely and fully

18.02 Such support has included funds to strengthen your capacity for response.

Not at all   1 2 3 4 5 6 7   Completely and fully

19.01 Does the donor affirm the primary position of civilian (as opposed to military) organizations in implementing humanitarian action?

Not at all   1 2 3 4 5 6 7   Completely and fully

(c) Learning and accountability

21.01 Does the donor support learning and accountability initiatives?

Not at all   1 2 3 4 5 6 7   Completely and fully

22.01 The donor encourages regular evaluations.

Not at all   1 2 3 4 5 6 7   Completely and fully

Finally, in this emergency, were there donors whose funding you rejected? (Specify the donor and the reason for rejecting the funding, e.g., donor's political agenda, lack of flexibility, etc.)

_____

_____

_____

Note

1 The questionnaire reproduced in this Appendix does not include the original instructions and other supporting explanations, which need not be reproduced here.

Glossary

1. **Accountability:** Accountability is the means by which individuals and organisations report to a recognised authority, or authorities, and are held responsible for their actions. (Edwards & Hulme, 1995).

   See: http://www.odi.org.uk/alnap/pdfs/QualityProforma05.pdf

2. **Armed conflict:** An international armed conflict means fighting between the armed forces of at least two states. It should be noted that wars of national liberation have been classified as international armed conflicts.

   According to IHL, a non-international armed conflict means fighting on the territory of a state between the regular armed forces and identifiable armed groups, or between armed groups fighting one another. To be considered a non-international armed conflict, fighting must reach a certain level of intensity and extend over a certain period of time.

   See: http://www.icrc.org/web/eng/siteeng0.nsf/htmlall/5kzf5n?opendocument

3. **Beneficiaries:** Individual, groups, or organisations who have been designated as the intended recipients of humanitarian assistance or protection in an aid intervention.

   The term "beneficiary" is concerned with the contractual relationship between the aid agency and the persons whom the agency has undertaken to assist. The term has come under scrutiny as in some cultures or contexts it may be interpreted negatively. Alternative suggestions are: people affected by disaster; the affected population; recipients of aid; claimants; clients.

   See: http://www.oxfam.org.uk/resources/downloads/HAP/HAP_book.pdf

4. **Capacity:** A combination of all the strengths and resources available within a community, society, or organization that can reduce the level of risk, or the effects of a disaster. Capacity may include physical, institutional, social, or economic means as well as skilled personal or collective attributes, such as leadership and management. Capacity may also be described as *capability.*

   See: http://www.adrc.or.jp/publications/terminology/top.htm

5. **Central Emergency Response Fund (CERF):** A stand-by fund established by the United Nations to enable more timely and reliable humanitarian assistance to those affected by natural disasters and armed conflicts.

   The CERF is a tool for pre-positioning funding for humanitarian action. The CERF was established to upgrade the current Central Emergency Revolving Fund by including a grant element based on voluntary contributions by governments and private sectors such as corporations, individuals, and NGOs.

   See: http://ochaonline.un.org/cerf/WhatIstheCERF/tabid/1706/Default.aspx

6. **Civil-military coordination:** The essential dialogue and interaction between civilian and military actors in humanitarian emergencies that is necessary to protect and promote humanitarian principles, avoid competition, minimize inconsistency, and, when appropriate, pursue common goals. Basic strategies range from coexistence to cooperation. Coordination is a shared responsibility facilitated by liaison and common training.

   See: www.humanitarianinfo.org/iasc/_tools/download.asp?docID=88&type=prod

7. **Civil society:** Conglomerate of individuals and groups active in society, including:

   a. NGOs (nongovernmental organisations) which bring people together in a common cause, such as environmental, human rights, charitable, educational and training organisations, consumer associations, etc.;

   b. CBOs (community-based organisations), i.e., grassroots organisations which pursue member-oriented objectives), such as youth organisations, family associations, and all organisations through which citizens participate in local and municipal life;

   c. the so-called labour-market players (i.e., trade unions and employer federations, also called the social partners);

   d. organisations representing social and economic players, which are not social partners in the strict sense of the term, such as religious communities.

   See: http://ec.europa.eu/civil_society/coneccs/question.cfm?CL=en

8. **Civilians and civilian population:** A civilian is any person who is not a member of the armed forces of a party to the conflict, including militias and resistance movements with have a leader responsible for subordinates, which have with a clear, recognizable sign, carry arms openly and follow the laws and customs of war. Parties to the conflict also include armed forces that profess allegiance to an authority not recognized by the Detaining Power and those who take up arms to resist invading forces, without having had time to form themselves into regular armed units, provided they carry arms openly and respect the laws and customs of war.

The civilian population comprises all persons who are civilians. The presence within the civilian population of individuals who do not come within the definition of civilians does not deprive the population of its civilian character.

See: http://www.icrc.org/ihl.nsf/WebART/470-750064?OpenDocument

9. **Cluster approach:** Introduced in December 2005, the cluster approach identifies predictable leadership for areas of response and is designed around the concept of "partnership" between UN agencies, NGOs, international organisations, and the International Red Cross and Red Crescent Movement (except the International Committee of the Red Cross). Eleven clusters were created: agriculture, camp coordination/management, early recovery, education, emergency shelter, emergency telecommunications, health, logistics, nutrition, protection, and water sanitation and hygiene.

Cluster leads are responsible for ensuring that response capacity is in place and that assessment, planning, and response activities are carried out in collaboration with partners and in accordance with agreed standards and guidelines.

See: www.humanitarianreform.org

10. **Code of Conduct for the International Red Cross and Red Crescent Movement and NGOs in Disaster Response:** Developed and agreed upon by eight of the world's largest disaster response agencies in 1994, it represents a huge leap forward in setting standards for disaster response. The International Federation uses it to monitor its own standards of relief delivery and to encourage other agencies to set similar standards. It has been signed by 447 NGOs.

The Code of Conduct is the expression of a common operational approach for providing help to those in need, based on strongly cherished principles and International Humanitarian Law.

See: http://www.ifrc.org/publicat/conduct/ and http://www.icrc.org/web/eng/siteeng0.nsf/html/64ZAHH

11. **Common Humanitarian Action Plan (CHAP):** A strategic plan for humanitarian response in a given country or region. It provides:

a. A common analysis of the context in which humanitarian takes place

b. An assessment of needs;

c. Best, worst, and most likely scenarios;

d. Identification of roles and responsibilities, i.e., who does what and where;

e. A clear statement of longer-term objectives and goals; and

f. A framework for monitoring the strategy and revising it if necessary.

The CHAP is the foundation for developing a Consolidated Appeal, and is as such part of the Coordinated Appeals Process (CAP).

See: http://ochaonline.un.org/cap2005/webpage.asp?MenuID=7888&Page=1241

12. **Common Humanitarian Funds (CHFs):** A new humanitarian financing instrument being piloted in Sudan (since 2005) and the Democratic Republic of Congo (since 2006). It provides a mechanism allowing donors to put money into a central fund to support humanitarian action in a particular country. The UN Humanitarian Coordinator can then draw on this fund to underwrite strategic priorities quickly and easily. Rather than making bilateral decisions in support of agencies within the CAP, funding decisions are deferred to the Humanitarian Coordinator and his team, using the CHAP as a central strategic tool. A total of seven donors have participated in the funds in DRC and Sudan.

See: http://www.humanitarianreform.org/humanitarianreform/Default.aspx?tabid=204

13. **Complex emergency:** A humanitarian crisis in a country, region or society where there is total or considerable breakdown of authority, resulting from internal or external conflict, which requires an international response that goes beyond the mandate or capacity of any single agency and/or the ongoing United Nations country program.

Such "complex emergencies" are typically characterized by: extensive violence and loss of life; massive displacements of people; widespread damage to societies and economies; the need for large-scale, multi-faceted humanitarian assistance; the hindrance or prevention of humanitarian assistance by political and military constraints; significant security risks for humanitarian relief workers in some areas.

See: www.humanitarianinfo.org/iasc/_tools/download.asp?docID=88&type=prod

14. **Consolidated Appeal:** A reference document on the humanitarian strategy, programme and funding requirements in response to a major or complex emergency.

See: www.reliefweb.int/cap

15. **Consolidated Appeal Process (CAP)/ UN Consolidated Inter-Agency Appeals Process:** An inclusive and coordinated programming cycle through which national, regional, and international relief systems mobilize to respond to selected major or complex emergencies that require a system-wide response to humanitarian crisis. A common humanitarian strategy is elaborated through the CAP along with an action plan to implement this strategy. Projects included in the CAP support the humanitarian strategy. CAP serves to promote a coordinated strategy and a common fundraising platform, and advocate for humanitarian principles.

Its cycle includes: strategic planning leading to a Common Humanitarian Action Plan (CHAP); resource mobilisation (leading to a Consolidated Appeal or a Flash Appeal); coordinated programme implementation; joint monitoring and evaluation; revision, if necessary; and reporting on results.

See: www.reliefweb.int/cap

16. **Contingency Planning:** Contingency planning is a management tool used to analyze the impact of potential crises and ensure that adequate and appropriate arrangements are made in advance to respond in a timely, effective and appropriate way to the needs of the affected population(s). Contingency planning is a tool to anticipate and solve problems that typically arise during humanitarian response.

See: http://www.humanitarianreform.org/humanitarianreform/Portals/1/cluster%20approach%20page/IA%20CP%20Guidelines%20Publication_%20Final%20version%20Dec%202007.pdf

17. **Coordination:** The systematic use of policy instruments to deliver humanitarian assistance in a cohesive and effective manner. Such instruments include strategic planning, gathering data and managing information, mobilising resources and ensuring accountability, orchestrating a functional division of labour, negotiating and maintaining a serviceable framework with host political authorities, and providing leadership. See Minear, L., Chelliah., U, Crisp, J., Mackinlay, J. and Weiss, T. (1992) UN Coordination of the International Humanitarian Response to the Gulf Crisis 1990–1992 (Thomas J. Watson Institute for International Studies: Providence, Rhode Island) Occasional Paper 13).

See: http://ochaonline.un.org/Coordination/tabid/1085/Default.aspx

18. **Coping capacity:** The means by which people or organizations use available resources and abilities to face adverse consequences that could lead to a disaster. In general, this involves managing resources, both in normal times, as well as during crises or adverse conditions. The strengthening of coping capacities usually builds resilience to withstand the effects of natural and human-induced hazards.

See: http://www.unisdr.org/eng/library/lib-terminology-eng%20home.htm

19. **Crisis (humanitarian):** Any situation in which there is an exceptional and widespread threat to human life, health, or subsistence. Such crises tend to occur in situations of vulnerability, in which a number of pre-existing factors (poverty, inequality, lack of access to basic services) are further exacerbated by a natural disaster or armed conflict which vastly increases their destructive effects.

See: http://www.escolapau.org/img/programas/alerta/alerta/alerta07006i.pdf

20. **Development:** Human development is a process of enlarging people's choices. In principle, these choices can be infinite and change over time. But at all levels of development, the three essential ones are for people to lead a long and healthy life, to acquire knowledge and to have access to resources needed for a decent standard of living. If these essential choices are not available, many other opportunities remain inaccessible.

But human development does not end there. Additional choices, highly valued by many people, range from political, economic and social freedom to opportunities for being creative and productive, and enjoying personal self-respect and guaranteed human rights"

See: http://www.undp.kz/script_site.html?id=214

21. **Disaster:** A serious disruption of the functioning of a community or a society causing widespread human, material, economic or environmental losses which exceed the ability of the affected community or society to cope using its own resources.

It is a function of the risk process, that is, a combination of hazards, conditions of vulnerability, and insufficient capacity or measures to reduce the potential negative consequences of risk. Disasters can include natural disasters like earthquakes and floods, as well as man-made disasters, which can be sudden or long-term.

See: http://www.unisdr.org/eng/library/lib-terminology-eng%20home.htm and http://www.ifrc.org/what/disasters/Types/index.asp

22. **Disaster preparedness:** Activities and measures taken in advance to ensure effective response to the impact of hazards, including the issuance of timely and effective early warnings, and the temporary evacuation of people and property from threatened locations.

See: http://www.unisdr.org/eng/library/lib-terminology-eng%20home.htm

23. **Disaster risk management:** The systematic process of using administrative decisions, organization, operational skills, and capacities to implement policies, strategies and the coping capability of the society and community to lessen the impact of natural hazards and related environmental and technological disasters. This comprises different activities, such as structural and non-structural measures to avoid (prevention) or limit (mitigation and preparedness) the adverse effects of hazards.

See: http://www.unisdr.org/eng/library/lib-terminology-eng%20home.htm

24. **Disaster risk reduction (disaster reduction):** The conceptual framework of elements which minimize vulnerability and disaster risk throughout a society to avoid (prevent) or limit (mitigate and be prepared for) the adverse impacts of hazards, within the broad context of sustainable development.

See: http://www.unisdr.org/eng/library/lib-terminology-eng%20home.htm

25. **Early warning:** The provision of timely and effective information, through identified institutions, that allows individuals exposed to a hazard to take action to avoid or reduce their risk and prepare for effective response. (same source as above)

See: http://www.unisdr.org/eng/library/lib-terminology-eng%20home.htm

26. **Early warning systems:** include a chain of concerns, namely: understanding and mapping the hazard; monitoring and forecasting impending events; processing and disseminating understandable warnings to political authorities and the population, and undertaking appropriate and timely actions in response to the warnings.

See: http://www.unisdr.org/eng/library/lib-terminology-eng%20home.htm

27. **Earmarking:** Earmarking is a device by which a bilateral donor agency specifies the geographic or sectoral areas in which a multilateral agency or NGO may spend its contribution. There are different degrees of earmarking: by agency, by country, by sector, or by project.

See: http://ocha.unog.ch/fts/exception-docs/FTSDocuments/The_Quality_of_Money-Donor_Behavior_in_Humanitarian_Financing.pdf

28. **Effectiveness:** Effectiveness measures the extent to which an activity achieves its purpose, or whether this can be expected to happen on the basis of the outputs. Implicit within the criteria of effectiveness is timeliness.

See: http://www.odi.org.uk/alnap/pdfs/QualityProforma05.pdf

29. **Efficiency:** Efficiency measures the qualitative and quantitative outputs achieved as a result of inputs. This generally requires comparing alternative approaches to achieving an output, to see whether the most efficient approach has been used.

See: http://www.odi.org.uk/alnap/pdfs/QualityProforma05.pdf

30. **Emergency:** An emergency is a "crisis" which calls for immediate humanitarian response.

See: http://ocha.unog.ch/fts/exception-docs/AboutFTS/Definitions-Glossary.doc

31. **Emergency Response Fund (ERF):** In some countries Emergency Response Funds are used as a mechanism for NGOs and UN agencies to cover unforeseen humanitarian needs, and have been used since 1997. An ERF is often established and administered by the Humanitarian Coordinator's (HC) office with an advisory board made of up of UN Agencies and in some cases NGOs (for example in Somalia and Ethiopia).

See: http://www.humanitarianreform.org/humanitarianreform/Default.aspx?tabid=72

32. **Evaluation of Humanitarian Action (EHA):** A systematic and impartial examination of humanitarian action intended to draw lessons to improve policy and practice and enhance accountability. EHA is:

   a. Commissioned by or in cooperation with the organisation(s) whose performance is being evaluated;

   b. Undertaken either by a team of non-employees (external) or by a mixed team of non-employees (external) and employees (internal) from the commissioning organisation and/or the organisation being evaluated;

   c. An assessment of policy and/or practice against recognised criteria (e.g., the DAC criteria);

   d. A description of findings, conclusions, and recommendations.

See: http://www.alnap.org/themes/evaluation.htm

33. **Famine:** A catastrophic food shortage affecting large numbers of people due to climatic, environmental, and socio-economic causes. The cause of the famine may produce great migrations to less affected areas.

See: http://www.ifrc.org/what/disasters/Types/drought/

34. **Financial Tracking Service (FTS):** A global, real-time database which records all reported international humanitarian aid, including that for NGOs and the Red Cross/Red Crescent Movement, bilateral aid, in-kind aid, and private donations. FTS focuses particularly on Consolidated and Flash Appeals, both because they cover the major humanitarian crises, and because their funding requirements are well defined. This allows FTS to indicate to what extent populations in crisis receive humanitarian aid in proportion to needs. FTS is managed by the UN Office for Coordination of Humanitarian Affairs (OCHA). All FTS data are provided by donors or recipient organizations.

See: http://ocha.unog.ch/fts2/

35. **Flash Appeal (UN):** The Flash Appeal is a tool for structuring a coordinated humanitarian response for the first three to six months of an emergency. The UN Humanitarian Coordinator triggers it in consultation with all stakeholders. The Flash Appeal is issued within one week of an emergency. It provides a concise overview of urgent life-saving needs and may include recovery projects that can be implemented within the time frame of the Appeal.

See: http://ochaonline.un.org/cap2005/webpage.asp?MenuID=9196&Page=1483

36. **Fragile states:** States which fail to provide basic services to poor people because they are unwilling or unable to do so. Such states are unable or unwilling to harness domestic and international resources effectively for poverty reduction.

See: http://www.oecd.org/dataoecd/30/62/34041714.pdf and http://stats.oecd.org/glossary/detail.asp?ID=7235

37. **Food security:** Food security exists when all people, at all times, have physical and economic access to sufficient, safe and nutritious food to meet their dietary needs in order to lead an active and healthy life.

See: http://www.rlc.fao.org/en/prioridades/seguridad/

38. **Good Humanitarian Donorship (GHD):** In 2003 a number of donor governments created the Good Humanitarian Donorship (GHD) initiative to work towards achieving efficient and principled humanitarian assistance. 24 donor bodies have now signed up to these principles. The GHD initiative provides a forum for donors to discuss good practice in Humanitarian Financing and other shared concerns. By defining principles and standards it provides both a framework to guide official humanitarian aid and a mechanism for encouraging greater donor accountability.

See: http://www.goodhumanitariandonorship.org/

39. **Good practices:** successful approaches adopted by other organisations or individuals and shared within the sector.

See: http://www.oxfam.org.uk/resources/downloads/HAP/HAP_book.pdf

40. **Humanitarian access:** Where protection is not available from national authorities or controlling non-state actors, vulnerable populations have a right to receive international protection and assistance from an impartial humanitarian relief operation. Such action is subject to the consent of the state or parties concerned and does not prescribe coercive measures in the event of refusal, however unwarranted.

See: www.ochaonline.un.org

41. **Humanitarian action:** Humanitarian action includes the protection of civilians and those no longer taking part in hostilities, and the provision of food, water and sanitation, shelter, health services, and other items of assistance, undertaken for the benefit of affected people and to facilitate the return to normal lives and livelihoods.

Humanitarian action should be guided by the humanitarian principles of *humanity,* meaning the centrality of saving human lives and alleviating suffering wherever it is found; *impartiality,* meaning the implementation of actions solely on the basis of need, without discrimination between or within affected populations; *neutrality,* meaning that humanitarian action must not favour any side in an armed conflict or other dispute where such action is carried out; and *independence,* meaning the autonomy of humanitarian objectives from the political, economic, military, or other objectives that any actor may hold with regard to areas where humanitarian action is being implemented. GHD Principles 1, 2, 3.

See: www.goodhumanitariandonorship.org

42. **Humanitarian aid:** Humanitarian aid is assistance designed to save lives, alleviate suffering and maintain and protect human dignity during, and in the aftermath of, emergencies. To be classified as humanitarian, aid should be consistent with the humanitarian principles of humanity, impartiality, neutrality and independence.

See: http://www.globalhumanitarianassistance.org/pdfdownloads/GHA%202007.pdf

43. **Human dignity:** respect for each and every human being, in a spirit of solidarity, irrespective of their origins, beliefs, religions, status or gender.

See: http://www.ifrc.org/what/values/dignity.asp

44. **Human rights:** Human rights are rights inherent to all human beings, whatever their nationality, place of residence, sex, national or ethnic origin, colour, religion, language, or any other status. Are all equally entitled to human rights without discrimination. These rights are all interrelated, interdependent and indivisible.

Universal human rights are often expressed and guaranteed by law, in the forms of treaties, customary international law, general principles and other sources of international law. International human rights law lays down obligations of governments to act in certain ways or to refrain from certain acts, in order to promote and protect human rights and fundamental freedoms of individuals or groups.

See: http://www.ohchr.org/EN/Issues/Pages/WhatareHuman Rights.aspx

45. **Humanitarian reform:** Humanitarian reform aims to dramatically enhance humanitarian response capacity, predictability, accountability, and partnership. It represents an ambitious effort by the international humanitarian community to reach more beneficiaries with more comprehensive, needs-based relief and protection, in a more effective and timely manner.

The reform has four main objectives:

a. Sufficient humanitarian response capacity and enhanced leadership, accountability, and predictability in "gap" sectors/areas of response, ensuring trained staff, adequate commonly-accessible stockpiles, surge capacity, agreed standards and guidelines;

b. Adequate, timely, and flexible humanitarian financing, including through the Central Emergency Response Fund;

c. Improved humanitarian coordination and leadership, a more effective Humanitarian Coordinator (HC) system, more strategic leadership, and coordination at the sectoral and intersectoral level;

d. More effective partnerships between UN and non-UN humanitarian actors.

See: http://www.humanitarianreform.org/humanitarianreform/ Default.aspx?tabid=109

46. **Humanitarian space:** The area in which humanitarian actors operate on the ground to access those in need of assistance without compromising the safety of aid workers. To maintain humanitarian access, humanitarian space must be respected.

See: www.ochaonline.un.org

47. **Humanitarian system:** The formal humanitarian system has a range of operators. It is currently managed mainly by the UN and the Red Cross/Red Crescent movement. It also relies on a growing number of more or less independent NGO agencies which use both private and government money. All these implementers receive firm policy instructions from the humanitarian departments of their donor governments, although much of this policy is worked out in a continuous policy dialogue between donors and providers. UN agencies are often "subcontractors" of the system while nongovernmental and Red Cross/Crescent organisations operate independently or as semi-independent subcontractors.

See: http://www.odi.org.uk/ALNAP/publications/RHA2005/rha05_ Ch1.pdf

48. **Humanity:** Humanity is one of the seven fundamental principles of the International Red Cross Red Crescent Movement. The other principles are impartiality, neutrality, independence, voluntary service, unity and universality.

Born initially out of the desire to bring assistance without discrimination to the wounded on the battlefield, this principle seeks in its national and international application to prevent and alleviate human suffering wherever it may be found. Its purpose is to protect life and health and to ensure respect for the human being. It promotes mutual understanding, friendship, cooperation, and lasting peace amongst all peoples.

See: http://www.ifrc.org/what/values/principles/humanity.asp

49. **Hyogo Framework for Action:** The Hyogo Framework for Action is the result of negotiations during the World Conference on Disaster Reduction in January 2005. It recognizes the interrelated nature of disaster reduction, poverty eradication, and sustainable development and agrees to promote a culture of disaster prevention and resilience through risk assessments, early warning systems, etc. The five priorities for action are:

i. Ensure that disaster risk reduction is a national and a local priority with a strong institutional basis for implementation

ii. Identify, assess and monitor disaster risks and enhance early warning

iii. Use knowledge, innovation and education to build a culture of safety and resilience at all levels

iv. Reduce the underlying risk factors

v. Strengthen disaster preparedness for effective response at all levels

See: http://www.unisdr.org/wcdr/intergover/official-doc/L-docs/Hyogo-framework-for-action-english.pdf

50. **Impartiality (non-legal):** Impartiality is one of the seven fundamental principles of the International Red Cross Red Crescent Movement. It states that no discrimination should be made as to nationality, race, religious beliefs, class or political opinions. It endeavours to relieve the suffering of individuals, being guided solely by their needs, and to give priority to the most urgent cases of distress.

See: http://www.ifrc.org/what/values/principles/index.asp

51. **Independence:** Independence is one of the seven fundamental principles of the International Red Cross Red Crescent Movement. It states that humanitarian assistance and humanitarian actors, while auxiliaries in the humanitarian services of their governments and subject to the laws of their respective countries, must always be autonomous, so that the assistance may be given in accordance with the principles of impartiality and neutrality.

See: www.ifrc.org

52. **Internally Displaced Persons (IDPs):** Persons or groups of persons who have been forced or obliged to leave their homes or habitual residence as a result of, or in order to avoid, the effects of armed conflict, situations of generalized violence, violations of human rights, or natural or man-made disasters, and who have not crossed an internationally recognized state border. A series of 30 non-binding "Guiding Principles on Internal Displacement" based on refugee law, human rights law, and international humanitarian law articulate standards for protection, assistance, and solutions for such internally displaced persons.

See: www.ochaonline.un.org

53. **International Committee of the Red Cross and Red Crescent Mandate:** The ICRC has a legal mandate from the international community. That mandate has two sources:

- the 1949 Geneva Conventions, which task the ICRC with visiting prisoners, organizing relief operations, reuniting separated families and similar humanitarian activities during armed conflicts;

- the Statutes of the International Red Cross and Red Crescent Movement, which encourage it to undertake similar work in situations of internal violence, where the Geneva Conventions do not apply.

See: http://www.icrc.org/Web/Eng/siteeng0.nsf/htmlall/section_mandate?OpenDocument

54. **International Humanitarian Law (IHL):** 1) International humanitarian law is a set of rules which seek, for humanitarian reasons, to limit the effects of armed conflict. It protects persons who are not or are no longer participating in the hostilities and restricts the means and methods of warfare. International humanitarian law is also known as the law of war or the law of armed conflict.

See: http://www.icrc.org/web/eng/siteeng0.nsf/htmlall/section_ihl_in_brief

55. **International Refugee Law:** The body of customary international law and international instruments that establishes standards for refugee protection. The cornerstone of refugee law is the 1951 Convention and its 1967 Protocol relating to the Status of Refugees.

See: http://www.unhcr.org/cgi-bin/texis/vtx/refworld/rwmain?docid=42ce7d444&page=search

56. **Livelihoods:** Those capabilities, assets (both material and social resources), and activities required for a means of living. A livelihood is sustainable when it can cope with and recover from stresses and shocks, maintain or enhance its capabilities and assets, and provide net benefits to other livelihoods locally and more widely, both in the present and in the future, while not undermining the natural resource base.

See: http://www.fao.org/sd/pe4_en.htm

57. **Local capacity:** participation in the programme should reinforce people's sense of dignity and hope in times of crisis, and people should be encouraged to participate in programmes in different ways. Programmes should be designed to build upon local capacity and to avoid undermining people's own coping strategies.

See: http://www.sphereproject.org/component/option,com_docman/task,doc_view/gid,12/Itemid,26/lang,English/

58. **Malnutrition:** A major health problem, especially in developing countries. A clean water supply, sanitation, and hygiene, given their direct impact on the incidence of infectious disease, especially diarrhoea, are important for preventing malnutrition. Both malnutrition and inadequate water supply and sanitation are linked to poverty. The impact of repeated or persistent diarrhoea on nutrition-related poverty and the effect of malnutrition on susceptibility to infectious diarrhoea are reinforcing elements of the same vicious circle, especially among children in developing countries.

See: http://www.who.int/water_sanitation_health/diseases/malnutrition/en/

59. **Millennium Development Goals (MDG):** The eight Millennium Development Goals range from halving extreme poverty to halting the spread of HIV/AIDS and providing universal primary education – all by the target date of 2015 – form a blueprint agreed to by all the world's countries and leading development institutions. They have galvanized unprecedented efforts to meet the needs of the world's poorest people.

The eight MDGs are:

Goal 1 .....Eradicate extreme poverty and hunger
Goal 2 .....Achieve universal primary education
Goal 3 .....Promote gender equality and empower women
Goal 4 .....Reduce child mortality
Goal 5 .....Improve maternal health
Goal 6 .....Combat HIV/AIDS, malaria, and other diseases
Goal 7 .....Ensure environmental sustainability
Goal 8 .....Develop a Global Partnership for Development

See: http://www.un.org/millenniumgoals/

60. **Needs:** There are two sets of needs to be met in any disaster, conflict or emergency: immediate life support and longer-term rehabilitation. Although the degree and importance of these basic needs may vary in magnitude and priority from one disaster to another, they are often the same:

- Search and rescue
- Sufficient shelter (including "mobile shelter," clothing)
- Adequate food
- Safe and adequate water supply and disposal
- Health and social care
- Protection from violence and harassment

See: http://www.reliefweb.int/ocha_ol/programs/response/mcdunet/0guidad.html

61. **Needs Assessment Framework (NAF):** Joint needs assessments, with a view to improving the overall prioritisation of response.

See: http://ochaonline.un.org/cap2005/GetBin.asp?DocID=1540

62. **Neutrality:** Neutrality is one of the seven fundamental principles of the International Red Cross Red Crescent Movement. It states that in order to continue to enjoy the confidence of all, humanitarian actors may not take sides in hostilities or engage at any time in controversies of a political, racial, religious, or ideological nature.

See: www.ifrc.org

63. **Official Development Assistance (ODA):** Official financing flows are administered with the objective of promoting the economic development and welfare of developing countries. ODA is concessional in character—that is, below market rate—with a grant element of at least 25 percent of the total (using a fixed 10 percent rate of discount). By convention, ODA flows consist of contributions by donor government agencies to developing countries (bilateral ODA), and also to multilateral institutions. ODA receipts comprise disbursements by bilateral donors and multilateral institutions. Lending by export credit agencies for the sole purpose of export promotion is excluded.

See: http://stats.oecd.org/glossary/detail.asp?ID=6043

64. **Organisation for Economic Co-operation and Development-Development Assistance Committee (OECD-DAC):** is the principal body through which the OECD deals with issues related to cooperation with developing countries.

See: http://www.oecd.org/department/0,2688,en_2649_33721_1_1_1_1_1,00.html

65. **Paris Declaration on Aid Effectiveness:** The Paris Declaration, endorsed on 2 March 2005, is an international agreement to which over one hundred ministers, heads of agencies and other senior officials subscribed and committed their countries and organisations to continue to increase efforts in harmonisation, alignment and managing aid for results with a set of monitorable actions and indicators.

See: http://www.oecd.org/document/18/0,3343,en_2649_3236398_35401554_1_1_1_1,00.html

66. **Participation:** processes of information sharing, consultation, decision-making, implementation, and resource control with, of, and by, beneficiaries of humanitarian action. These different facets of participation are often taken to represent increasing gradations of beneficiary involvement in projects, as follows:

- Information sharing: minimally informing affected populations about measures and decisions affecting them;

- Consultation: some level of consultation with beneficiaries within programme guidelines;

- Decision-making: direct involvement of affected populations in decisions made during the project cycle;

- Implementation: engagement in the practical activities related to implementation of the given project;

- Resource control: control over project resources assumed by the beneficiary population; all the major decisions over these resources and over any new initiatives are made by them. (INTRAC 2001)

See: http://www.rsc.ox.ac.uk/PDFs/Childrens%20Participation%20Synthesis%20Feb%202004.pdf

67. **Pooled Funding:** The objective of Pool Funding a multi-donor initiative is to support the timely allocation and disbursement of donor resources to the most critical humanitarian needs under the overall management of the Humanitarian Coordinator.

   Pooled funds are similar to ERFs, often established to ensure flexibility and adequate funding using needs based approach aiming for flexible, timely, predictable and adequate funding for areas within the agreed Humanitarian Action Plan.

   See: http://www.humanitarianreform.org/humanitarianreform/Default.aspx?tabid=72

68. **Preparedness:** Activities designed to minimize loss of life and damage, to organise the temporary removal of people and property from a threatened location and facilitate timely and effective rescue, relief and rehabilitation.

   See: http://www.reliefweb.int/rw/lib.nsf/db900sid/LGEL-5EQNZV/$file/dha-glossary-1992.pdf?openelement

69. **Prevention:** Activities to provide outright avoidance of the adverse impact of hazards and means to minimize related environmental, technological and biological disasters.

   Depending on social and technical feasibility and cost/benefit considerations, investing in preventive measures is justified in areas frequently affected by disasters. In the context of public awareness and education, related to disaster risk reduction changing attitudes and behaviour contribute to promoting a "culture of prevention".

   See: http://www.unisdr.org/eng/library/lib-terminology-eng%20home.htm

70. **Proportionality:** Allocate humanitarian funding in proportion to needs and on the basis of needs assessments

   See: http://www.goodhumanitariandonorship.org/

71. **Protection:** A concept that encompasses all activities aimed at obtaining full respect for the rights of the individual in accordance with the letter and spirit of human rights, refugee and international humanitarian law. Protection involves creating an environment conducive to respect for human beings, preventing and/or alleviating the immediate effects of a specific pattern of abuse, and restoring dignified conditions of life through reparation, restitution and rehabilitation.

   See: http://www.unhcr.org/cgi-bin/texis/vtx/refworld/rwmain?docid=42ce7d444&page=search

72. **Quality and accountability initiatives:** During the past decade the humanitarian community has initiated a number of inter-agency initiatives to improve accountability, quality and performance in humanitarian action. Four of the most widely known initiatives are the Active Learning Network for Accountability and Performance in Humanitarian Action (ALNAP) , Humanitarian Accountability Partnership International (HAP-I), People In Aid, and the Sphere Project.

   All initiatives share a common goal which is to improve accountability, quality and performance in humanitarian action.

   See: http://www.hapinternational.org/pool/files/q-&-a-on-q-&-a.pdf

73. **Recovery (early):** Recovery focuses on restoring the capacity of national institutions and communities after a crisis. Early recovery is that which begins in a humanitarian relief setting immediately following a natural disaster or armed conflict. Guided by development principles, the early recovery phase aims to generate self-sustaining, nationally-owned processes to stabilize human security and address underlying risks that contributed to the crisis.

   See: http://www.undp.org/cpr/we_do/_recovery.shtml

74. **Resident Coordinator or Humanitarian Coordinator:** The Resident Coordinator is the head of the UN Country Team. In a complex emergency, the RC or another competent UN official may be designated as the Humanitarian Coordinator (HC). In large-scale complex emergencies, a separate HC is often appointed.

   See: http://www.reliefweb.int/rw/lib.nsf/db900sid/KKEE-6DMRTJ/$file/glossary.pdf?openelement

75. **Resilience:** The capacity of a system, community or society potentially exposed to hazards to adapt, by resisting or changing in order to reach and maintain an acceptable level of functioning and structure. This is determined by the degree to which the social system is capable of organizing itself to increase its capacity for learning from past disasters for better future protection and to improve risk reduction measures.

   See: http://www.unisdr.org/eng/library/lib-terminology-eng%20home.htm

76. **Sustainable Livelihoods:** See "Livelihoods"

77. **Timeliness:** providing information and analysis in time to inform key decisions about response

   See: http://www.odi.org.uk/HPG/papers/hpgbrief13.pdf

About the Authors

MARY B. ANDERSON

Mary B. Anderson is Executive Director of CDA Collaborative Learning Projects, a small non-profit organisation, based in Cambridge, Massachusetts (USA). She has written widely on issues of humanitarian and development assistance and peace-building and conflict resolution efforts. Her books include: *Rising from the Ashes: Development Strategies in Times of Disaster* (with Peter Woodrow, Lynne Rienner), *Do No Harm: How Aid Can Support Peace—Or War,* (Lynne Rienner Publishers); *Options for Aid in Conflict: Lessons from Field Experience* (LCPP Project, CDA); *Confronting War: Critical Lessons for Peace Practitioners* (with Lara Olson, Reflecting on Peace Practice Project, CDA) and numerous articles.

JOHN COSGRAVE

John Cosgrave is an independent Irish consultant with more than 30 years of experience in over 55 countries in humanitarian action and development programmes. He has worked as an independent consultant in the humanitarian sector since 1997, having spent most of his previous professional life managing NGO projects and programmes in the aftermath of natural disasters and complex political emergencies. His work for NGOs, governments, and the United Nations is focused on humanitarian action, evaluation, training, and operations. He combines broad experience with theoretical concepts to produce a coherent world-view of humanitarian action which he communicates through writing and training. Trained initially as a problem-solver (in civil, military, mechanical, and agricultural engineering), and later as a manager and social scientist, he holds two Master's degrees, and is currently studying for a third. He is based near Cork in Ireland where he lives with his wife and four children.

FERNANDO ESPADA

Fernando Espada is an independent communications consultant. During the elaboration of the Humanitarian Response Index 2008 he was Communications Director of DARA. Prior to that, he was Managing Editor of the Spanish edition of *Foreign Policy Magazine,* published by the Fundación para las Relaciones Internacionales y el Diálogo Exterior (FRIDE), by agreement with the Carnegie Endowment for International Peace. From 2002 to 2006, he was Deputy Director of FRIDE. He is co-author, with Silvia Hidalgo, of the 2006 FRIDE policy paper "Towards a New Spanish Cooperation Policy."

LUCÍA FERNÁNDEZ

Lucía Fernández is Coordinator at DARA, where she has worked since 2005. She has participated in evaluations of humanitarian action and development interventions for various stakeholders in North Africa, South America, and South East Asia. After the 2004 tsunami, she participated in the Funding Study of the Tsunami Evaluation Coalition, acquiring insight into official donor policies of humanitarian funding. She participated in HRI missions in 2007 and 2008. Before coming to DARA, Lucía worked at Grupo DEX evaluating projects co-funded by the European Social Fund and the European Regional Development Fund of the European Union. She has dealt with the politics of humanitarian issues while working for CARE International and the Delegation of the European Commission to the United Nations in New York. She holds a BA in Journalism from Universidad Complutense (Madrid), and an MA in International Affairs from Columbia University (New York), where she specialised in development.

GILLES GASSER

Gilles Gasser is a journalist and independent consultant, specialising in humanitarian aid issues and communication. He was head of mission of the NGO Équilibre in Bosnia and Herzegovina from 1993 to 1996 and later worked as an expert from 1997 to 2000 in the humanitarian offices of the European Commission in Sarajevo, Tirana, and Pristina. He has undertaken studies for the Tsunami Evaluation Coalition, "Conversations on Democracy" for the Club of Madrid, and various projects with Fundación para las Relaciones Internacionales y el Diálogo Exterior (FRIDE). As a journalist he has travelled to Belfast, New Caledonia, Israel, the Palestinian Territories, El Salvador, Guatemala, Brazil, and the Dominican Republic.

FRANÇOIS GRÜNEWALD

An engineer in agriculture science and rural economy, François Grünewald spent 28 years working on development, emergency, and post disaster rehabilitation projects in Africa, Asia (Cambodia, Laos, Thailand), Central Europe, Middle East and Central/Latin America, as well as at agency headquarters, with NGOs, the UN, and the International Committee of the Red Cross. In 1997, he became chairman of Groupe URD (Urgence-Réhabilitation-Développement), carrying out several research and evaluation projects for the European Union, the UN and various NGOs. He served as team leader for the evaluation of the UN response to the Bar el Ghazal famine in 1998, of the Post-Mitch inter-NGO evaluation process, of the DFID/UNICEF evaluation of the Darfur response, of the French response to the tsunami, and of the Inter-Agency Standing Committee's evaluation of the international response to the crisis in the Horn of Africa. In 2008, he was team leader of the ECHO strategic planning mission in Chad. He has contributed to several books and articles on complex emergencies and the management of social and natural disasters.

JUDITH HERRERA

Judith Herrera is an international consultant in public health, strategic planning, and participatory and community based approaches. She is trained as a medical doctor, and has more than 20 years of experience in marginalised and conflict areas, mainly in Latin America and Africa. Dr. Herrera served for seven years as Program Coordinator, Trainer and Evaluator for the International Committee of the Red Cross, and has worked in Darfur. She was a consultant for Red Cross National Societies, and is currently on leave from the ICRC, collaborating with Public Health Consultants, based in the Netherlands. Dr. Herrera conducts research in the fields of epidemiology and anthropology. Close to grassroots and beneficiaries, she promotes the implementation of participatory, community-based approaches, and trains health staff in different parts of the world. She is a lecturer in the MA programme on International Cooperation in Barcelona, and holds degrees in Public Health and Community Development from the University of Mexico and El Colegio de la Frontera Sur (Mexico).

SILVIA HIDALGO

Silvia Hidalgo has over 15 years of experience in the field of humanitarian aid and development. She has been Director of DARA since 2003. As an evaluator she has worked for both donor governments and the Red Cross, and assessed the performance of multi-stakeholder country strategies, UN agencies, and NGOs. She was instrumental in initiating and developing the Humanitarian Response Index, and is a member of the Board of the Fundación para las Relaciones Internacionales y el Diálogo Exterior (FRIDE), and full member of ALNAP. She holds a BA in Economics and Political Science and an MA in International Relations from the University of Pennsylvania.

TOBY LANZER

Between June 2006 and July 2008, Toby Lanzer worked for the United Nations as Resident and Humanitarian Coordinator in the Central African Republic, heading UN agency relief, recovery, and development work in the country. Beginning with UNDP in Angola in 1992, his career with the United Nations has included heading the UN's humanitarian coordination offices in Georgia (1996–1998) and Moscow at the height of the crisis in Chechnya (1999–2003). Before taking up his post in Bangui, Central African Republic, he worked in Geneva, leading the UN's global work on emergency appeals. He received his Bachelor's degree from the University of New Hampshire in 1987, and went on to complete a Master's degree in International Affairs at Columbia University in 1992. In 1995–1996 he specialised in forced migration and international relations at Oxford.

MARTA MARAÑÓN

Marta Marañón has been the Deputy Director of DARA since 2003. Ms. Marañón is an evaluation expert committed to improving the quality of aid and the empowerment of the local populations in partner countries. She has experience in evaluation in the fields of international development, humanitarian action, capacity building and organisational performance, and has carried out work in complex situations, conducting evaluations or studies in Afghanistan, Algeria, Brazil, Colombia, Kenya, Mauritania, Mexico, Morocco, Niger, and Uzbekistan. She holds a BA in Geography and three MAs, in Landscape and Land Use Management, Cultural Management, and Evaluation of Public Policies and Programmes. Her thematic areas of expertise include environmental sustainability, sustainable livelihoods, community and rural development, disaster risk reduction and educational systems. Founder member of Foundation Educación Activa, she is also a member of the Royal Geographic Society, UK.

LARRY MINEAR

Dr. Minear has worked for more than 30 years in operational, research and advocacy on humanitarian and development policy issues. Following an initial posting in the Sudan in 1972–73, he worked from 1974–1991 in Washington, D.C. as an NGO advocate for improved US humanitarian and development policies. In 1991, he co-founded the Humanitarianism and War Project, directing it until his retirement in mid-2006. His writings include *The Humanitarian Enterprise: Dilemmas and Discoveries* (2000), *The Charity of Nations: Humanitarian Action in a Calculating World* (2004, with Ian Smillie), and *The U.S. Citizen-Soldier and the Global War on Terror: The National Guard Experience* (2007). The publications of the Humanitarianism and War Project from 1991–2006 include a score of country case studies, thematic reviews, and books, and are available at hwproject.tufts.edu. Since 2006, the work has been carried forward by the Feinstein International Center at Tufts University and is available at fic.tufts.edu.

RICCARDO POLASTRO

Riccardo Polastro heads the evaluation department of DARA. He has 15 years of experience in the humanitarian and development sectors and has worked in more than 40 countries for the Red Cross Movement, the UN, NGOs, and donors. He lectures in several universities at the MA level on development-related topics. His 2007 publications include: *Angola: Conflict and Humanitarian Implications* (*FRIDE,* Spain); "The Pakistan Earthquake: Testing Reform of the Humanitarian System," (*Humanitarian Response Index,* Palgrave Macmillan, UK); and in 2008, "Development Relief: Linking Relief, Rehabilitation and Development" (*Public Policy Perspectives,* vol.1 n.1, Brazil); "The Indian Ocean Tsunami: Regulation and Coordination of Humanitarian Aid Actors" (ICEI, Spain). He is a member of the European Evaluation Society, International Development Evaluation Association, Hautes Études en Sciences Sociales of Paris, and the Active Learning Network for Accountability and Performance in Humanitarian Action. He is a PhD candidate in Peace and Security and holds an Advanced Studies Diploma, an MA in International Relations, and Maîtrise from the École des Hautes Études en Sciences Sociales, Paris.

DAVID ROODMAN

David Roodman is a Research Fellow at the Center for Global Development in Washington, D.C., an independent think tank dedicated to changing policies of rich-country governments to benefit poor countries. He has been architect and manager of the Commitment to Development Index since the inception of the project in 2002. The Index is widely recognised as the most comprehensive measure of rich-country policies towards the developing world. He is a member of the HRI Peer Review Committee, and regularly advises other index projects. His current interests include microfinance and the econometrics of foreign aid effectiveness. He is the author of The Natural Wealth of Nations: Harnessing the Market for the Environment. Roodman majored in theoretical mathematics at Harvard College, graduating in 1990.

RICARDO SOLÉ-ARQUÉS

Dr. Solé-Arqués is a specialist in internal medicine and public health, and serves as an international consultant on public health and humanitarian aid. He has been involved in complex emergencies since the early 1990s, serving as an ECHO expert in Bosnia, Kosovo, Angola, and Colombia. He was WHO coordinator for the office of the West bank and Gaza in 2003 and for the ECHO regional health sector, responsible for the Regional Support Office in Amman in 2006, covering Central Asia, the Middle East, and North Africa's humanitarian operations. He has carried out extensive consultancy and evaluation work in the Middle East, Africa, and Central and South America for a number of international organisations, including Médecins Sans Frontières, Médecins du Monde, the World Health Organization, the European Commission Humanitarian (Aid) Office, and the European Commission. With DARA, he collaborated on the Tsunami Evaluation Coalition, in the evaluation of projects in the Amazon basin in Brazil, and as team leader of the HRI survey in Haiti in 2007. He participates in the Peer Review Committee.

PHILIP TAMMINGA

Philip Tamminga is the Humanitarian Response Index Project Manager. He has over twenty years of practical and research experience in international development and humanitarian assistance issues. He specialises in governance and accountability issues, policy and strategy development, programme design, management and evaluation, and communications. He is the former Head of Planning, Monitoring, Evaluation and Reporting for the International Federation of Red Cross and Red Crescent, and played a key role in shaping the strategic policy framework for the Federation. Prior to his involvement with the International Federation, he was Head of Delegation for the Canadian Red Cross in Nicaragua and Honduras, managing Hurricane Mitch recovery, housing reconstruction, and community health programmes in those countries, as well as carrying out extensive research on community development programmes in Latin America. He holds a BA in Latin American Studies and an MA in Communications and International Development from Simon Fraser University, and continues to do research and teach in the fields of development and humanitarian assistance.